5

Entrepreneurial Finance

Philip J. Adelman
Professor, DeVry University

Alan M. Marks, MBA
Retired Professor, DeVry University
Certified Financial Planner, CFP®

Prentice Hall
Upper Saddle River, New Jersey
Columbus, Ohio

Library of Congress Cataloging-in-Publication Data

Adelman, Philip J.
    Entrepreneurial finance / Philip J. Adelman, Alan M. Marks.—5th ed.
        p. cm.
    Includes index.
    ISBN-13: 978-0-13-502529-1
    ISBN-10: 0-13-502529-X
    1. Small business—Finance.   I. Marks, Alan M.   II. Title.
HG4027.7.A338 2010
658.15'92—dc21

                                            2008040042

Editor in Chief: Vernon Anthony
Acquisitions Editor: Gary Bauer
Editorial Assistant: Megan Heintz
Production Coordination: Renata Butera
Project Manager: Renata Butera
Senior Operations Supervisor: Joanne Riker
Art Director: Jayne Conte
Cover Designer: Bruce Kenselaar
Cover photo: © Chris Collins / CORBIS All Rights Reserved
Director of Marketing: David Gesell
Marketing Manager: Leigh Ann Sims
Marketing Assistant: Les Roberts
Copyeditor: Mercedes L. Heston

This book was set in Bembo by Aptara®, Inc., and was printed and bound by Hamilton Printing. The cover was printed by Lehigh Phoenix.

Pearson Education Ltd., London   Pearson Education Australia Pty. Limited
Pearson Education Singapore Pte. Ltd.   Pearson Education North Asia Ltd. , Hong Kong
Pearson Education Canada, Inc.   Pearson Educación de Mexico, S.A. de C.V.
Pearson Education—Japan   Pearson Education Malaysia Pte. Ltd.

Prentice Hall
is an imprint of

www.pearsonhighered.com

10 9 8 7 6 5 4 3 2 1
ISBN-13: 978-0-13-502529-1
ISBN-10:   0-13-502529-X

To my wife, Hannah B. Adelman,
for her support and continued belief in my abilities;
and to my children, Eddie, Danny, and Tova, for being my cheerleaders.

Philip J. Adelman

To my loving and supportive family—my wife, Cheryl, and my children, Jamie and Jared Marks,
who gave me the encouragement to realize that my goal is achievable.

Alan M. Marks

To DeVry University, who gave us the
opportunity to use our creative talents to teach.

Contents

Chapter 10 Capital Budgeting 299

Chapter 11 Personal Finance 333

Appendix A Working with Spreadsheets and Calculators 381

Appendix B Time-Value-of-Money Tables 393

Appendix C Answers to Even-Numbered Exercises and Problems 401

Glossary 425
Index 439

Preface

Welcome to our fifth edition. The authors realize that the applicability of the basic business concepts of this text will benefit more individuals than just the initially targeted small-business owner.

NEW TO THE FIFTH EDITION

In this edition, we include short case studies of small businesses at the end of each chapter. Chapter 2 has updated material on the Small Business Administration (SBA), with a discussion of new programs that have been developed to assist veterans and severely disabled veterans including loans and grants. We also added updated sources of financing, the requirements for obtaining federal contracts, and the need for businesses to develop succession plans. Chapter 4 has updated financial ratios that include averaging information from two balance sheets when data for the ratio is taken from both the income statement and balance sheet (statement of financial position). Chapter 8 introduces fixed interest loans to include both fixed principal commercial loans and bridge loans. Chapter 9 includes a discussion of adjustable rate mortgages (ARMs) and illustrates the problem with an upside-down mortgage when real estate values decline. Chapter 11 is updated to show changes in retirement programs and now includes a discussion of Medicare insurance and an explanation of the new Medicare Prescription Drug Plan and income replacement insurance policies.

We have written this textbook for the more than 99 percent of business owners and managers in the United States who manage sole proprietorships, partnerships, limited liability companies, or small non-public corporations. We are targeting those individuals and students who wish to learn more about the financial aspects of business entrepreneurship. We make complex theory easy to understand and discuss vital issues with a direct and clear delivery of material. We apply many of the techniques that are found in traditional corporate finance texts to businesses at an understandable level.

Most people who want to start a business come from all types of occupations (e.g., blue collar, trade, professional, technical, engineering). Their formal education may be in something other than business. This book is written primarily as a textbook for the education institution that caters to the concerns of individuals wishing to enhance their abilities in those areas of business that lead to successful entrepreneurship. This text can also be used by universities, community colleges, and technical colleges offering programs in finance and entrepreneurship. Of the more than 28 million businesses in the United States, approximately 72 percent are sole proprietorships, 8 percent are partnerships, 7 percent are C corporations, and 12 percent are Subchapter S corporations; less than 1 percent are publicly traded corporations. However, almost all financial textbooks are written for the large corporation and do not address the needs of more than 99 percent of all business. In addition, the majority of these business establishments have fewer than 20 employees.[1] For these businesses, the owner is pretty much the chief financial officer, the chief executive officer, and the chief operating officer. Such a business owner needs a working knowledge of finance, because he or she has no staff support on a full-time basis to assist in planning.

Our textbook differs from the typical financial textbook. Traditional financial texts are written for college juniors, seniors, or graduate students with the assumption that the student has had several courses in accounting and that this student will be working for a major corporation. This is not usually the case. Our textbook provides the critical financial information required for the majority of students and entrepreneurs entering the business world today. The resources used in writing a business plan often omit many of the financial aspects that the owner may need to determine the financial health of an existing or future business. Because many students may come from a non-business background rather than having a prior formal business education, we begin our text by outlining the basic economic factors affecting finance. We then discuss the advantages and disadvantages of various forms of business ownership. The text provides examples of financial statements for each type of business ownership. We devote more time than most financial texts discussing working capital and inventory management, because even though the sales may increase, a new business may fail because of poor working capital and inventory management techniques.

Most business managers have been trained to judge the profitability of a project in terms of payback and break-even analysis. We have taken corporate capital budgeting techniques and adapted them by showing the weighted average cost of capital as it exists for most business owners. We also demonstrate the importance of the time value of money as a tool in both business planning and personal financial planning, and we simplify the use of this tool. We provide the reader with specific examples in which each of the six time-value-of-money formulas is actually used by individuals and businesses.

---

[1]Internal Revenue Service, *Statistics of Income Bulletin, Historical Table, Spring 2005.* U.S. Securities and Exchange Commission filings. Retrieved January 5, 2007, from http://www.irs.gov/newsroom/article/0,,id=140248,00.html

All individuals, regardless of whether they work for the traditional publicly traded corporation, must make decisions about their retirement plans. Traditional financial textbooks do not cover personal financial planning. Because of this, we devote all of Chapter 11 to this vital topic, which includes an in-depth discussion of risk management as well as those investment vehicles that enable the entrepreneur to plan for personal financial goals. We believe that it is imperative for business managers not only to run their business successfully on a day-to-day basis, but to have those skills that enable them to plan for their personal and family's future as well.

Thanks to Timothy Ackley and Joyce Barden at DeVry University, Phoenix, Arizona for their expert assistance and advice. Special thanks to the reviewers of this text: Kris G. Gulick, University of Northern Iowa; David K. Hensley, University of Iowa; Daniela Quast, Montgomery College; Joseph C. Stokes, Isenberg School of Management, University of Massachusetts at Amherst; and Daniel Yates, University of Findlay.

Philip J. Adelman
Alan M. Marks

CHAPTER 1

Financial and Economic Concepts

Learning Objectives

When you have completed this chapter, you should be able to:

- Understand the basic concept and importance of finance as it relates to individuals and business.
- Understand the basic economic concepts of finance.
- Distinguish between marginal revenue and marginal cost.
- Distinguish between economic capital and financial capital.
- Determine the opportunity cost of making decisions.
- Identify the relationships among savings, income, expenditures, and taxes.
- Identify those factors that affect interest rates.
- Understand the relationships between supply and demand for money and prevailing market interest rates.
- Describe the role of the Federal Reserve and the tools used to achieve the goals of economic growth, price stability, and full employment.
- Understand the relationship between risk and return on investment.
- Compare systematic risk to unsystematic risk and discuss their impact on business.

This book is written to give the individual who has no formal education in finance a brief overview of finance from both personal and business perspectives. The book is primarily for people who want to start their own business, or those who want to analyze companies and investments but who do not have the time to pursue a formal course of study in a traditional business college setting. This book can be used as a supplementary text in any college business course, as well as in a traditional college finance course. In the United States, approximately 33 percent of all businesses close within the first four years.[1] Usually, this is not because the businesses offer poor products or services, but because of poor financial management or a lack of adequate financial capital.

 BASIC FINANCIAL CONCEPTS

Finance is essentially any transaction in which money or a money-like instrument is exchanged for other money or another money-like instrument. An individual who finances a car typically has a specific amount of money set aside for a down payment. That individual must obtain the balance of the sale price to purchase the car. He or she can finance the car by signing a *promissory note* (a loan agreement) for the cash needed to pay the car dealer. The financial part of purchasing the car involves the money used for the down payment and the signing of a promissory note. The actual sale of the car is an exchange process that can be associated with marketing: The seller exchanges the car for the buyer's money; however, the car has been financed by the exchange of a promissory note for money. It is important to note that in any financial transaction there are suppliers and users of funds. In purchasing a car, the down payment is funds supplied by the buyer of the car, whereas the funds for the promissory note are supplied by the lender. The buyer is the user of the lender's funds.

For the business manager who wants to build a new plant, methods of financing may include using cash generated from current sales, borrowing funds from financial institutions such as banks or insurance companies, borrowing funds from select individuals, selling stocks, or using personal savings. Bonds, which are discussed in Chapter 11, are not really a viable source of financial capital for the majority of businesses. Bonds are normally available only to large corporations. Therefore, business entrepreneurs rely predominantly on lending institutions or their own funds to satisfy their needs for additional financial capital.

Businesses acquire capital assets through the use of financial capital. A plant, facility, or factory is a *fixed,* or *capital,* asset, and include buildings, machinery, and equipment. Capital assets are used by businesses to increase revenue or sales. Financial assets such as stocks, bonds, or savings may also be used to increase revenue, because they can be used to acquire capital assets.

For most individuals and businesses, financial transactions are undertaken for the purpose of exchanging a sum of money today for the expectation of obtaining more money in the future. We buy stock at today's price because we believe that the stock will increase in value or that the corporation will generate a profit

---

[1]Headd, B. (2002) Redefining Business Success, U.S. Small Business Administration. Retrieved April 9, 2008, from http://www.sba.gov/advo/stats/bh_sbe03.pdf.

and provide us with cash or stock dividends in the future. A *dividend* is an after-tax payment that may be made by a corporation to a stockholder. However, dividend payments are not guaranteed. We can sell the stock after it *appreciates* (goes up in value), or not sell and possibly receive dividends. Similarly, we invest money in a business today because we expect greater returns for our money in the future. We can stay with the business and pay ourselves from our profits, or wait for the business to appreciate and sell it to another business owner.

IMPORTANCE OF FINANCE

Any individual who starts or manages a business must have a basic understanding of finance, a fact is especially true in today's volatile market. *Prime interest rates* (the rate of interest that banks charge their best business customers) have been as low as 1.5 percent (December 1934) and as high as 21.5 percent (December 1980).[2] If we expect to obtain greater returns from our investments in the future, we must understand finance, its relationship to interest rates, and how to obtain proper financing. Without this understanding, our individual and business efforts may fail. However, before we can develop more of an understanding of finance, we must begin by understanding the basic economic concepts that relate to finance.

ECONOMIC CONCEPTS OF FINANCE

The United States operates on the basic principle that within the confines of the marketplace, all individuals can achieve their own objectives in a free-enterprise system. Such a system is known as a *market economy*. A market economy such as ours consists of several markets. A **market** is any organized effort through which buyers and sellers freely exchange goods and services. Some of these markets in our economy include real estate markets, in which property is exchanged; retail markets, in which final goods and services are exchanged; the Internet, in which information is exchanged; and the commodity market, in which *basic commodities* (raw materials such as agricultural products, precious metals, and oil) are exchanged. The *financial marketplace* is the market that deals with finance. The three primary participants in this financial marketplace are individual households, businesses, and government. In our free-enterprise financial-market system, the primary savers of funds are households. They are the suppliers of funds to other individuals, businesses, and government, who are the users of funds.

---

[2]Federal Reserve Bank of St. Louis, Historical Prime Rate Table, available at http://research.stlouisfed.org/fed2/data/PRIM.txt.

SCARCE RESOURCES

The central theme of economics is one of scarcity. Items are scarce because normal people want more than they currently have. Humans have unlimited desires for goods and services. We live in a world of scarce resources, so we are willing to pay a positive price to obtain goods and services. For the individual, financial means and time are limited resources. Because individuals have limited financial means, they must make choices about which resources they want to obtain and in what time period they want to obtain them. The four types of scarce resources of typical concern in both business and economics are natural resources, human resources, capital resources, and entrepreneurial resources.

Natural Resources

Natural resources consist of natural products such as minerals, land, and wildlife. They exist in nature and have not been modified by human activity. In economic terms, we consider the payment made for natural resources to be rent. Natural resources are referred to in some economic textbooks as **land**.

Human Resources

Human resources are the mental and physical talents of people. Human resources are also referred to by economists as **labor**. The economic payment for human labor is wages. There are, of course, different levels of wages. Wages are paid by business owners and are based on the marginal revenue product of the human resource and the availability of the human resource. We have heard many arguments about the value of professional athletes and their high salaries, but the fact remains that based on marginal revenue product, these people are paid a fair salary.

Before continuing our discussion of this area, we must define some terms. The word **marginal**, as we use it here, is related to the addition of one more unit of measurement. It is an incremental change. **Marginal revenue product** is the additional revenue we obtain by selling one more unit of product to create an incremental increase in revenue. **Marginal physical product** is the additional product that results from hiring one more unit of labor. **Marginal cost** is the incremental cost of hiring that one more unit of labor or the incremental cost of producing one more unit of output.

For example, say that you own a professional basketball team. Your team is average, and for the past two years you have averaged 16,000 ticket sales per game for an arena that seats 20,000 people. However, you have noticed that when the Phoenix Suns come to town, you sell all 20,000 seats. You determine that the additional seats are sold because Phoenix has a superstar who people are willing to pay to see. Therefore, you seek to hire a superstar. For your own team, you want an athlete of the caliber of Shaquille O'Neal. How much would you be willing to pay this basketball player?

You estimate that if you hired a superstar, who would then become your marginal physical product, you would sell out the arena. The average price of a ticket is $50. You could sell 4,000 more tickets for each game and bring in extra revenue of $200,000 ($50 a seat times 4,000 seats) for each home game. Because there are 41 home games, you would make an additional $8.2 million in ticket sales. The $8.2 million in ticket sales is your marginal revenue product. This figure does not include additional television revenue or sales of food, beverages, or team sports memorabilia. Based on the marginal revenue product of a superstar, you would be willing to pay a marginal cost of up to $8.2 million to hire this basketball player. If you owned this team and could get a player like Shaquille O'Neal for $7 million a year, would you hire him? Of course you would, because you would clear a profit of $1.2 million (8.2 million revenue − $7 million salary).

These athletes are obviously a scarce resource. If you advertise in the paper, how many people with the talents of a superstar will apply for the job? Conversely, if you own a pizza parlor and advertise for a delivery driver, how many people with the mental and physical talent to deliver pizza will apply for the job? You will probably have several applicants, because there are hundreds of people in your community who have pizza-delivery skills. What is the marginal revenue product of pizza delivery? If your average pizza sells for $14 and the average driver can deliver 4 pizzas an hour, then the marginal revenue product is $56 per hour. Therefore, the absolute maximum amount you would be willing to pay a driver is $56 per hour; however, considering both marginal revenue product and the availability of pizza delivery people, you may be able to hire a new driver for a minimum wage of $5.85 per hour. On May 25, 2007, the Fair Labor Standards Act (FLSA) was amended to increase the federal minimum wage in three steps: to $5.85 per hour effective July 24, 2007; to $6.55 per hour effective July 24, 2008; and to $7.25 per hour effective July 24, 2009.[3]

Capital Resources

Capital resources are separated into two categories: economic capital and financial capital. **Economic capital** consists of those items that people manufacture by combining natural and human resources. Examples include buildings and equipment of business and government enterprises, such as roads and bridges. The economic payment for capital, which includes both economic and financial capital, is interest. It is absolutely essential that we distinguish between economic capital and financial capital. Economic capital is interchangeable with the terms **physical capital** and **fixed assets**—those capital resources that are used to make more items. **Financial capital** is a dollar-value claim on economic capital and, therefore, it may include several types of assets, such as cash,

---

[3]U.S. Department of Labor, Employment Law Guide. Retrieved December 5, 2007, from http://www.dol.gov/compliance/guide/minwage.htm.

accounts receivable, stocks, and bonds. When a provider of funds holds financial capital, the provider has a dollar-value legal claim on economic capital. For example, if you borrowed money from a bank to finance a new delivery truck for your business, the bank supplied you with financial capital. The title to your vehicle is actually in the name of the bank. The promissory note that you signed with the bank is the dollar-value claim that the bank has on your fixed asset (vehicle). A *promissory note* is an accounts payable that has in it a written promise to pay a sum of money by one party, the maker or payer, to the payee. The payer pays interest to the payee at an interest rate for a specific amount of time (e.g., 90 days). The *maturity value* of the note is the principal plus interest that is paid to the payee.

Entrepreneurial Resources

Entrepreneurial resources are the individuals who assume risk and begin business enterprises. The entrepreneur combines land, labor, and capital resources to produce a good or service that we value more than the sum of the individual parts. Without the entrepreneur, resources would not normally be combined, except as needed for *subsistence,* or just enough to sustain life. The economic payment made to the entrepreneur is *profit.* The entrepreneur seeks to make as much profit as possible. Therefore, when entrepreneurs form businesses, they try to make profits that exceed the wages paid to labor. The owner of a professional sports team—the entrepreneur—normally makes more than any player on that team. The owner of the pizza shop should make more in profit than any employee makes in wages.

OPPORTUNITY COSTS

In any market transaction, both the buyer and the seller usually believe that they obtained the best use of their scarce resources. The economic basis for this belief revolves around the concept of **opportunity costs**, which is the highest value surrendered when a decision to invest funds is made. *Opportunity cost* is a quantifiable term. For example, an individual who has $20,000 may decide to invest in stocks or bonds, place the money in savings, buy a new car, or place a down payment on a house. The individual investor determines what annual return can be expected from these choices and constructs a table based on expected financial return. Table 1–1 lists the investment opportunities mentioned here and the expected annual gain or loss from each alternative. The investor naturally takes other factors into consideration, such as the risk associated with investing in the stock market or the pleasure received from driving a new car.

In looking at Table 1–1, we see that the car actually *depreciates* (loses economic value) over time, whereas all other assets increase in value. Nevertheless, the investor decides to buy the car. As mentioned, factors other than pure

TABLE 1–1 Expected Financial Returns of Investment Opportunity

Investment Opportunity	Expected Annual Return (%)
Purchase stock	11
Purchase home	9
Purchase bonds	6
Place money in bank savings account	2
Purchase new car	−15

finance, such as a requirement for transportation or the enjoyment that can be obtained from driving a car, go into the decision. When the decision is made to purchase the car, the purchaser spends $20,000. He loses the opportunity to purchase the 11-percent yielding stock for $20,000. This percentage is the return that the investor can expect to realize if he invested in stock, and it is also the highest value surrendered when the car is purchased, because he bought the car instead of the stock. If we had decided to purchase stock, then the opportunity cost would have been the return from the purchase of a home, or 9 percent. The return from the home purchase would have been the highest value surrendered when we chose stock. Once again, choosing to purchase an asset is the actual decision. The highest value that we surrender in purchasing the stock is the return from the home, so its return of 9 percent is the opportunity cost of the decision. In other words, we surrender the opportunity to purchase a home, which would appreciate in value at 9 percent, if we chose to invest in stocks at an 11-percent return. Any purchase decision from the choices in Table 1–1 other than stock results in an opportunity cost of 11 percent.

One economic concept of finance central to any market transaction is that every party to the transaction has the expectation of gain from the transaction. In the case of the car purchase, the buyer obviously valued the car more than the $20,000. To the buyer, surrendering the $20,000 to buy the car resulted in a greater benefit than would have been obtained by picking some other item. Otherwise, the car would not have been purchased. The car dealer, however, valued the $20,000 more than the car. Otherwise, the dealer would not have sold the car. This win–win situation is central to all free-enterprise market transactions. Both the buyer and the seller believe that they gain from a transaction.

SAVINGS, INCOME, EXPENDITURES, AND TAXES

Let us look at how the $20,000 was made available to purchase the car in the previous example. Most people generate savings to make large market transactions. Savings can only be achieved if all expenditures are less than total income. Therefore, it is essential to determine exactly where savings originate. We begin with the concept of gross income.

Gross income for the individual is all the money received from all sources during a year, including wages, tips, interest earned on savings and bonds, income from rental property, and profits to entrepreneurs. Gross income is subject to taxation by our government. One reason for taxation is that there are items that we consume or have available to us that we do not want to pay for directly. Examples include public education, good roads, safe drinking water, and police and fire protection. The money that we use to finance these public goods comes from taxes and government user fees. **Taxes** are payments to a government for goods and services provided by the government. For most of us, the government collects taxes on our wages before we are paid for our labor. If you have income from sources other than wages, the federal government requires that you pay estimated taxes, normally on a quarterly basis, to lessen what may be a great financial burden when annual income taxes are due.

There are three basic forms of taxes that a government can, and does, collect: progressive taxes, regressive taxes, and proportional taxes. **Progressive taxes** take a larger percentage of income as that income increases. With each step up in income, a greater percentage of taxes is due. For example, if Tom Childress makes $20,000 in wages a year and pays $3,000 in taxes, and Jane Smith earns $60,000 and pays $16,800 in taxes, then Tom pays 15 percent of his income in taxes, whereas Jane pays 28 percent. The actual tax rates are established by legislation at the federal, state, and local levels. The percentage is a proportion and is calculated by taking the amount paid, dividing it by the gross income received, and multiplying the answer by 100. The formula for tax percentage is as follows:

$$\text{Tax percentage} = \frac{\text{Tax payment in dollars}}{\text{Income in dollars}} \times 100$$

For Tom Childress,

$$\text{Tax percentage} = \frac{\$3,000}{\$20,000} \times 100 = 15\%$$

For Jane Smith,

$$\text{Tax percentage} = \frac{\$16,800}{\$60,000} \times 100 = 28\%$$

Regressive taxes take a higher percentage of your income as your income decreases. Sales taxes are a typical example of regressive taxes. Lower-income individuals must use a higher percentage of their income to purchase goods and services. For example, a person making $800 per month will probably have to spend all of his income to survive. If we have a 5 percent sales tax, this individual will pay $40 per month in sales taxes on his $800 income. If, however, another individual makes $5,000 a month, she may spend only $4,000 and save the remaining $1,000 each month. Therefore, she pays a 5 percent sales tax on $4,000, or $200 per month in sales tax. However, the $200 is only 4 percent of her $5,000 income. Thus, the wealthier individual pays 4 percent of income in sales taxes, whereas the lower-income individual pays 5 percent. Consequently, the tax is regressive. Because many politicians realize the hardship that regressive taxes may place on lower-income individuals, there are several cities and states that exempt food and medicine from sales taxes.

Regarding **proportional taxes**, the percentage paid stays the same regardless of income. For many of us, Social Security and Medicare taxes are proportional. As income increases by $1.00, 7.65 percent of that dollar, or $0.0765, is paid in Social Security and Medicare taxes. It is important to note that the employee in an employee–employer relationship pays 7.65 percent tax, which consists of 6.2 percent for Social Security and 1.45 percent for Medicare; the employer also pays 7.65 percent, which adds up to 15.30 percent tax. The self-employed entrepreneur pays the full 15.30 percent. The only true proportional tax in the United States currently is the Medicare tax, which is 1.45 percent of wages, with no upper limit. Social Security has a tax rate of 6.2 percent, but it was capped at an income level of $97,500 for 2007 and $102,000 for 2008.[4] Therefore, Social Security is proportional for wages up to $97,500, but it becomes a regressive tax for people earning more than $102,000 in 2008. For example, we previously discussed an athlete making $7 million per year. His Medicare tax of 1.45 percent is proportional, and he pays 1.45 percent of $7 million, or $101,500, in Medicare taxes. His Social Security tax for 2008 was $6,324.00 ($102,000 times 6.2 percent). The percentage of his salary that he pays in Social Security taxes is only 0.0009, or 9 basis points. Note that a *basis point* is one one-hundredth of 1 percent (0.0001). The person making $102,000 or less pays 6.2 percent of salary in Social Security; therefore, Social Security taxes are proportional to them, but regressive to the athlete.

Flat-Tax Proposals

A flat-tax proposal goes something like this: There is no tax paid on the first $30,000 of income for a family of four; then there is a 17 percent flat tax on all income that exceeds $30,000. Given the previous description, would implementation of this proposal mean a progressive, regressive, or proportional tax? The answer is not obvious, but the proposal is for a progressive income tax, which is illustrated by Table 1–2.

When evaluating Table 1–2, we notice that there are no taxes paid on our $30,000 income; therefore, the percentage of income paid in taxes is 0 percent.

---

[4]Social Security Administration located on the Internet at http://www.ssa.gov.

TABLE 1–2 Flat Tax Proposal

Gross Income ($)	Taxes Paid ($)	Percentage of Income Paid in Taxes%
30,000	—	0.00
40,000	1,700	4.25
50,000	3,400	6.80
60,000	5,100	8.50
70,000	6,800	9.71
80,000	8,500	10.63
90,000	10,200	11.33
100,000	11,900	11.90
110,000	13,600	12.36
120,000	15,300	12.75
130,000	17,000	13.08
140,000	18,700	13.36

However, we pay an additional $1,700 in taxes on each $10,000 earned above $30,000. Thus, the family earning $70,000 pays $6,800 in taxes, or 17 percent of the $40,000 that was earned above the $30,000 exemption. Notice that this equates to a 9.71 percent income tax on the family income of $70,000. Also, we see that as income increases from $30,000 to $140,000, the tax rate continues to increase as a percentage of income. Therefore, the flat-tax proposal is actually a progressive income tax proposal.

The preceding methods may be used by government to collect its income to provide the goods and services previously mentioned. In any event, when we subtract taxes from gross income, we are left with **disposable income**—that which one has after paying federal, state, and perhaps local taxes. **Discretionary income** is disposable income minus fixed expenses such as rent, utilities, and insurance. Discretionary income can be either consumed (spent) or saved. In economic terms, consumption is the same as spending.

Many households generate incomes that exceed their required expenditures. Households can save this excess income or invest it however they choose with businesses, financial institutions, or brokerage institutions and can become suppliers of funds to the financial marketplace. In the financial marketplace, the buyers or users of funds are those people and institutions (government and business) requiring money, which they obtain through loans. A *loan* is a principal amount of money that is exchanged for a promise to repay this principal amount plus interest. The interest charged can be said to be the annual rent for the principal amount of money. The amount of rent paid in dollars and cents is determined by the interest rate in effect at the time of the loan. There are many factors that affect these interest rates, but five are of primary concern: the supply of money saved, the demand for borrowed funds, the Federal Reserve policy, inflation, and risk. These factors are discussed in the following sections.

SUPPLY OF MONEY SAVED

The **supply of money saved** is primarily the total money that is placed in demand deposit (checking) accounts, savings accounts, and money market mutual funds. Money market mutual funds can be purchased separately, but they may be held as cash in brokerage accounts. The **law of supply** states that as the payment for, or the *price,* of an item increases, the quantity of the item supplied to the market will increase, ceteris paribus. *Ceteris paribus* is a Latin phrase that means "all else remains the same." In economic terms, the law of supply relates to the price paid and the quantity of a resource that is provided at that price. In finance, the concept of the law of supply can be demonstrated by comparing the amount of money saved with interest rate amounts paid for the money. A simple illustration of this can be given with a supply table that depicts the incomes and expenses of several families. Table 1–3 provides the income and expenses of seven individual households or small businesses. As we see in Chapter 2, most small businesses (more than 92%) are organized as sole proprietorships, partnerships, or Sub-chapter S corporations. Profits earned by these businesses are transferred to the individual owner's personal tax forms. Subsequently, taxes paid by these businesses are actually paid by the individual household on his or her income tax form.

Table 1–3 shows several factors of gross income and discretionary income:

1. We have a progressive tax system. As income increases, the amount of income paid in federal taxes also increases as a percentage of income. The Jones family, earning $30,000, pays 17.43 percent of its annual income in federal taxes; however, the Charles family earns $150,000 and pays 28.33 percent of its annual income in federal taxes.
2. Fixed expenses decrease as a percentage of income, as income increases. For the Jones family, fixed expenses consume 65.58 percent of annual income ($19,673 ÷ $30,000); but the Charles family spends only 33.08 percent of its income on fixed expenses ($49,620 ÷ $150,000).

TABLE 1–3 Income and Expenses of Variable Households

Household Name	Gross Income ($)	Income, Social Security, and Medicare Taxes ($)	Federal Taxes Paid as a Percentage of Gross Income	Disposable Income ($)	Fixed Expenses ($)	Discretionary Income ($)
Jones	30,000	5,228	17.43%	24,773	19,673	5,100
Roberts	50,000	9,758	19.52%	40,243	32,683	7,560
Smith	70,000	16,502	23.57%	53,499	40,179	13,320
Brown	90,000	23,432	26.04%	66,569	41,369	25,200
Meeks	110,000	29,912	27.19%	80,088	41,208	38,880
Adams	130,000	36,202	27.85%	93,798	46,998	46,800
Charles	150,000	42,492	28.33%	107,508	49,620	57,888

Department of the Treasury, Internal Revenue Service, Publication 15 (Rev. January 2008).

3. Discretionary income increases as wealth increases. Therefore, the Jones family has 17 percent ($5,100 ÷ $30,000) of its income to save or spend as it wishes, but the Charles family has 38.59 percent ($57,888 ÷ $150,000) of its annual income to save or spend as it wishes.

Thus, as wealth increases, the amount of discretionary income increases. Because discretionary income can be either consumed or saved, we expect that the supply of money saved increases as the price paid for money (interest rate) increases. **Supply tables** are generated by determining how much of a product or service people or businesses are willing and able to provide to the market at various prices. Because money is a scarce resource, we can generate a supply table by determining how much money people place in their savings as interest rates increase. We ask several individuals with different amounts of discretionary income what percentage of their money they save at different and varying interest rates.

Table 1–4 shows how much money families are willing to save as interest rates increase. Note that some people save money at a 4 percent interest rate, whereas others do not invest in savings until interest rates reach 6 or 8 percent. As interest rates approach 20 percent, virtually every family puts some of its discretionary income into savings. Notice that there is a definite limit to the amount of money that can be supplied regardless of the interest rate. People are limited in their amount of discretionary income. Even though everyone would like to save more money, financial situations dictate that every household has a limit to the amount of money that can be saved, because money is scarce.

TABLE 1–4 Supply Table: Money Saved for Seven Sample Families

Annual Interest Rate (%)	Annual Savings ($000)							
	Jones	Roberts	Smith	Brown	Meeks	Adams	Charles	Total
0	$ —	$ —	$ —	$ —	$ —	$ —	$ —	$ —
2	—	—	—	—	—	—	—	—
4	—	—	—	500	780	1,940	5,790	9,010
6	—	—	670	1,250	1,940	2,720	7,530	14,110
8	100	200	930	1,760	2,020	3,890	12,000	20,900
10	200	500	1,500	3,000	3,500	7,000	16,000	31,700
12	250	750	2,500	5,000	6,000	10,000	20,000	44,500
14	300	1,000	3,250	9,000	12,000	15,000	25,000	65,550
16	400	1,200	4,500	12,000	18,000	23,000	31,000	90,100
18	500	1,500	6,000	15,000	25,000	28,000	38,000	114,000
20	500	1,700	8,000	18,000	30,000	32,000	40,000	130,200
22	500	1,700	8,000	18,000	30,000	33,000	41,000	132,200
24	500	1,700	8,000	18,000	30,000	33,000	41,200	132,400

For example, the Jones family has a gross income of $30,000. After paying taxes, rent, utilities, and other contractual obligations, it is left with a discretionary income of only $5,100. This money is all the family has left to pay for items such as food, entertainment, clothing, and savings. For a family in this situation, virtually all the discretionary income is consumed just to survive. Therefore, regardless of how high interest rates on savings rise, this family can never afford to save more than $500 a year.

Conversely, the Charles family, with a gross income of $150,000, is left with discretionary income of $57,888. Therefore, this family can afford to save much more as a percentage of its total income. The Charles family can save 71 percent of its discretionary income ($41,200 ÷ $57,888) and still have $16,688 per year ($57,888 − $41,200) for food, clothing, and entertainment. This gives the Charles family almost $1,400 per month for spending, even after it saves 71 percent of its discretionary income.

The total supply of money available in the marketplace can be shown visually with a **supply curve** (Figure 1–1). The curve is generated from the supply table (Table 1–4) by horizontally summing the total money saved by the seven families at varying interest rates. At an interest rate of 10 percent, we can calculate $31,700 in total savings for all these families. At an interest rate of 20 percent, we calculate $130,200 in savings. Of course, if we obtained this figure

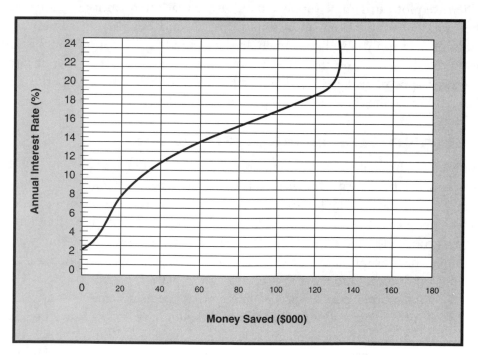

FIGURE 1–1
Supply of money.

for all families in the United States, then we would have a supply curve that represented the total supply of money saved.

For the United States, there are four measures of the money supply: M1, M2, M3, and L. Of primary interest to us is M1, which consists mostly of money in circulation and money in checking accounts (demand deposits); and M2, which includes M1 plus money in passbook savings accounts, retail money-market accounts (accounts that use short-term securities), and small time deposits (certificates of deposit, or CDs, in amounts of less than $100,000). For our purposes, when we discuss the money supply and personal savings, we are referring to M2. If we could survey the entire population and add across the supply table to obtain the total amount of money that could be saved by the population at varying interest rates, we could calculate the amount of money in savings accounts and money-market funds for the United States, or M2 minus M1. The problem is that the figures for the United States are difficult to comprehend because the numbers are so large. For example, for February 2008, M1 was $1,367.7 billion; M2 was $7,602.2 billion; and the savings accounts in commercial and thrift institutions totaled $6,234.5 billion, giving the United States more than $6.2 trillion in savings.[5] The numbers are so large that the government typically rounds to the closest $100 million. In other words, the figures are fairly accurate, give or take $100 million.

Because of the size of these numbers, we will stay with our micro-examples. When we plot our sample supply curve, we see that the quantity of money supplied for the sample population slopes upward and is based on summing the results of the supply table horizontally. In the example given for our sample families (Table 1–4), we find that there is no money in savings at an interest rate of 2 percent; approximately $31,700 in savings at an interest rate of 10 percent; and $130,200 in savings at a rate of 20 percent.

DEMAND FOR BORROWED FUNDS

Another factor that determines interest rates is the demand for money. The **demand for borrowed funds** is all the money that is demanded in our economy at a given price. The **law of demand** states that as the price of an item decreases, people will demand a larger quantity of that item, ceteris paribus (all else remains the same). Therefore, as interest rates go down, borrowing increases. It becomes cheaper for us to borrow more money so that we can purchase additional capital assets (Table 1–5).

In our example, Ann Smith determines that she wants a new home and can afford monthly payments of $500. If she did not have to pay any interest to finance the home and could obtain a 30-year mortgage (360 monthly payments times $500 per month), she could afford to purchase a $180,000 home. However,

---

[5]*Money Stock Measures*, Federal Reserve Statistical Release H.6, April 3, 2008.

TABLE 1–5 Ann Smith's Demand for Money

Interest Rate (%)	Amount Financed ($)	Interest Paid ($)
0	$180,000	$ —
1	155,454	24,546
2	135,274	44,726
3	118,595	61,405
4	104,731	75,269
5	93,141	86,859
6	83,396	96,604
7	75,154	104,846
8	68,142	111,858
9	62,141	117,859
10	56,975	123,025
11	52,503	127,497
12	48,609	131,391
13	45,200	134,800
14	42,199	137,801
15	39,543	140,457
16	37,181	142,819
17	35,071	144,929
18	33,177	146,823
19	31,468	148,532
20	29,922	150,078
21	28,516	151,484
22	27,233	152,767
23	26,059	153,941
24	24,980	155,020

if she had to pay 10 percent interest and wanted to maintain a $500 monthly payment, she would have less money available for financing. She could only afford to buy a house worth $56,975, because the total interest on the mortgage would be $123,025. The total amount financed plus the total interest paid must be $180,000 (360 monthly payment times $500 per payment). Details about calculation of these numbers are covered in Chapter 9. What holds true for the individual in general holds true for the economy. We see that the dollar amount demanded for housing increases as interest rates go down. In addition, more families in the economy can afford to purchase homes at lower interest rates. This relationship between the cost of financing, or *market interest rates,* and the demand for items of high-dollar value holds true for governments and businesses, as well as for individuals.

A **demand table** (Table 1–5) is generated by determining how much individuals are willing to borrow at varying interest rates. We used the home purchase as an example, but in reality, the quantity demanded for big-ticket items and, literally, thousands of other items increases as the cost of borrowing decreases. The **demand curve** (Figure 1–2) is nothing more than the horizontal summation of a demand table, or in this case, plotting Ann Smith's demand for borrowed funds at varying interest rates.

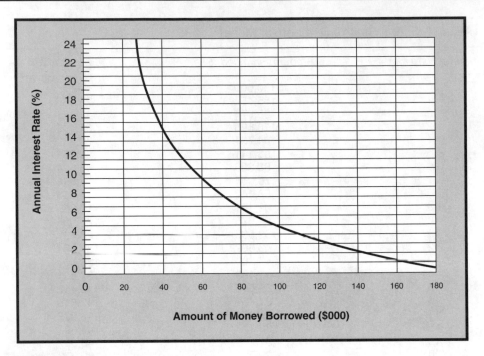

FIGURE 1–2
Demand for money.

We cannot look at supply and demand separately. To determine the actual market interest rate, we must integrate both the supply curve and the demand curve. **Supply** and **demand** are obtained by combining the two curves. The interest rate at which the supply curve and the demand curve intersect is known as the *equilibrium point,* and theoretically, at that interest rate, the financial market will be cleared. In other words, the quantity of money supplied to the market is exactly equal to the quantity of money demanded in the market. *Equilibrium,* therefore, is the point at which the quantity supplied and the quantity demanded are equal. If the market is in equilibrium, then the market price is the equilibrium price. If we compare Table 1–4 with Table 1–5, or look at Figure 1–3, we note that Ann Smith can borrow approximately $45,000 at an interest rate between 12 and 13 percent. If she wants to borrow more than this amount, she must pay a higher rate, because the households are not willing to save more than $45,000 unless interest rates are higher.

Households borrow funds to invest in businesses if interest rates are within some range that makes the investment seem profitable. If market interest rates are above that range, households prefer to save their money rather than invest in a business or some other capital asset. At 18 percent, households save more and borrow less. As this procedure continues, the quantity of money saved increases. When the supply of money saved exceeds the demand for money, there is a surplus of money in the marketplace. Institutions pay less for savings and interest rates begin to fall. Therefore, as more and more people

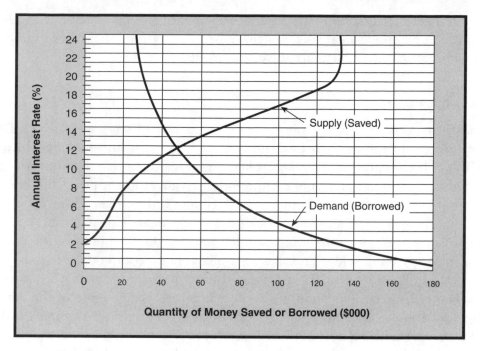

FIGURE 1–3
Supply and demand curves for money.

save, and borrow less, lending institutions find themselves with money that they cannot loan out. They do not want to attract any more savings, and interest rates begin to fall as lending institutions cut the price they are willing to pay to attract savers.

FEDERAL RESERVE POLICY

Supply of and demand for money are the critical factors affecting interest rates, all other things being equal. In a totally free-market system, those factors alone dominate the interest rates paid for money. We currently do not have a totally free-market for money; thus, other factors must be included, such as the Federal Reserve.

The **Federal Reserve** is the central bank of the United States. It is often referred to as *the Fed,* and is responsible for controlling the monetary policy of the United States. **Monetary policy** is governmental action to change the supply of money to expand or contract economic activity. The U.S. government has some broad general goals, and the Fed is responsible for trying to achieve and maintain these goals. The three basic goals are economic growth, price stability, and full employment. We must have growth in our economy because every year, more people enter the nation's workforce and the economy must create jobs for these people. We must have price stability if consumers are to maintain their confidence in the economic system. We must have full employment to ensure that Americans who want to work can find work.

Unfortunately, some of these goals are diametrically opposed to one another and the government must seek to strike a balance between them. For example, we will not have price stability if we have inflation.

INFLATION

Inflation occurs when the average price of goods and services increases. The measure of inflation that is most often used is the **consumer price index (CPI),** which represents a market basket of goods and services that the average American consumer purchases each month. The government prices this basket of goods and services each month and determines if the basket has increased in price (inflation) or decreased in price (deflation). As individual consumers, we cannot determine if we have inflation because we do not purchase the entire basket every month, and we normally get mixed signals from our purchases. For example, if gasoline increases in price and food decreases in price, then we do not know if we have inflation. It is only when the average price of the entire basket of goods and services increases that inflation exists for the economy. If the CPI changes and the inflation rate increases by 7 percent between January of one year and January of the next year, then a basket of goods and services that cost $100 in January of the first year will cost $107 the next January.

Based on our previous discussion of supply and demand, we can see that what is occurring in the marketplace when we have inflation is that the demand for the items in the basket is exceeding the supply of goods in the basket. This is the result of too many dollars chasing too few goods. Therefore, consumers are bidding up the price of the basket of goods and services. We have too many dollars chasing too few goods. The Fed has goals for inflation. If these goals are exceeded, the Fed intervenes by making adjustments in the money supply to dampen demand. If the supply of money available in the marketplace is reduced, then interest rates go up and consumers are not able to purchase as many goods and services as before. When this happens, the demand for items in the basket decreases and prices begin to fall. The Federal Reserve has three primary tools that it uses to control the money supply: open market operations, bank reserve requirements, and the discount rate.

Open market operations consist of the Fed purchasing or selling U.S. securities. Because security obligations (Treasury bills, notes, and bonds) of the United States are considered to be the safest possible investment, there is always a demand for these instruments. Open market operations are the most significant tool of the Fed, and this tool is in constant use. The Fed can determine exactly how much the money supply is being expanded or contracted by its open market operations. To increase the money supply, the Fed purchases government securities and pays for them with cash. This provides the economy with more money to lend. Subsequently, the money supply is increased, and the net effect is that banks have more money to lend and quite often the Federal Funds

Rate decreases. The Fed Funds Rate allows a bank to borrow needed funds from another bank that has a surplus in its account with the Fed. The interest rate that the first bank pays to the second bank in return for borrowing the funds is negotiated between the two banks, and the weighted average of this rate is the *effective federal funds rate*. When the Fed wants to decrease the money supply, it sells securities. These securities are paid for with cash by households and institutions. The money supply is decreased because the Fed takes this currency out of circulation.

The Fed also establishes a **reserve requirement** for banks in the United States. These reserves are the percentage of deposits placed in banks that must be maintained to conduct daily operations and that cannot be used for lending purposes. These reserves may be kept on deposit with the Fed or can be maintained in each bank's vault. The banking institution must hold the amount of this reserve requirement in reserves. For example, if the reserve requirement is 10 percent and a bank has $100 million on deposit, then the bank can only loan out $90 million because it must keep $10 million in reserves. If the Fed increased the reserve requirement to 15 percent, then the bank could only loan $85 million. Obviously, a small change in reserve requirements drastically affects the money supply. Changes to the reserve–requirement ratio are seldom used.

The **discount rate** is the rate of interest that the Fed charges banks to borrow money from the Fed. Banks can borrow money from the Fed when they want to make loans but find that they do not have sufficient reserves. This makes the Fed the lender of last resort for the banking industry. Although the Fed does not control market interest rates directly, it does have an effect on them. Because banks earn their profits on loans, there must be a difference between what the banks pay for money and what they charge for money that is borrowed by households, governments, and businesses. The discount rate charged by the Fed to its member banks is normally the nation's lowest lending rate. Occasionally, the Federal Funds rate, the interest rate that banks charge each other for overnight loans, is the lowest interest rate, as can be seen in Table 1–6.

If the Fed believes that there is too much borrowing in the marketplace, it may tighten credit by increasing the discount rate. When interest rates increase, it becomes more difficult for us to borrow as the payments on our loans increase. This situation dampens the demand for money and cools off the economy. However, too much cooling may lead the nation into a recession, yet cutting the discount rate may lead to inflation.

RISK

We discussed four of the five major variables that affect market interest rates—supply of money, demand for money, Federal Reserve monetary policy, and inflation. The fifth factor is risk.

TABLE 1–6 Money Rates, as of April 7, 2008

Type of Rate	Definition	Rate (%)
Discount	The charge on loans to depository institutions by the New York Federal Reserve Bank	2.50
Federal Funds	The rate banks charge each other for overnight loans in minimum amounts of $1 million	2.23
T-bill, 3 months	The rate on government treasury bills sold at a discount of face value in units of $10,000	1.33
Prime	The interest rate that banks charge their most creditworthy customers	5.25

Source: Federal Reserve Statistical Release H.15—April 7, 2008.

Risk involves the probability that the actual return on an investment will be different from the desired return. When we talk about risk taking in business or finance, we are discussing an individual's tolerance for investments. These investments may or may not return what is desired. In general, younger people tend to be risk takers and older people tend to be more risk averse. For example, the purchase of a U.S. bond or Treasury bill is considered to be a risk-free investment. The probability that the government will not pay interest and principal on the bond is negligible. Conversely, investing in a new business is more risky. As noted earlier, approximately 33 percent of all new businesses in the United States fail in the first four years. If we were to invest in a new business, we would, therefore, demand a higher probable return on our investment than if we invested in government securities. It would not be wise to take more risk and not expect a higher return. If we expected the business investment to provide us with the same return as a government bond, we would purchase the bond and eliminate the risk factor.

Risk can be divided into two categories: systematic risk and unsystematic risk. **Systematic risk** is associated with economic, political, and sociological changes that affect all participants on an equal basis. For example: The September 11, 2001, terrorist attack on the World Trade Center and the Pentagon resulted in a great deal of change. Economically, people became afraid to fly, and demand for air travel decreased so drastically that most major airlines laid off substantial numbers of employees. By January 2002, airfares were at their lowest level in 12 years as airlines tried to lure travelers back to flying. In addition, unemployment rose to 5.4 percent in October 2001, the largest one-month increase in a generation. Politically, Congress passed legislation to increase homeland security and alleviate risk. The overall Defense Department budget was increased by $48 billion. The war in Afghanistan cost $1.8 billion per month, and an additional $10 billion was allocated to the war on terrorism.[6] Sociologically, people became uncertain about their future and were willing to accept many changes in security clearances when

---

[6]Newsday.com online reports, January 22, 2002, November 3, 2001, and February 5, 2002.

attending sporting events, concerts, and other public gatherings. People began converting stocks to cash in anticipation of an uncertain future. All of these examples are factors of systematic risk because the effect was national.

Unsystematic risk is unique to an individual, firm, or industry. In business, unsystematic risk is often based on management capabilities, competition within the industry, vendor reliability, and variables that relate to microeconomics. With the current failure of Bear Stearns and the continued reporting of decreased home values and foreclosures, the perceived value of American financial stability has changed in the mind of the investment community. For the six months between October 1, 2007, through March 31, 2008, the Dow Jones Industrial Average fell by more than 1,800 points, from 14,087 to 12,263. Oil prices were also a problem, rising from $25 per barrel to more than $110 between January 2000 and April 2008.[7]

The total risk of a business is based on a series of variables and incorporates both systematic and unsystematic risk. When a person starts a business, lenders consider unsystematic factors such as the type of business and the uncertainty that exists with respect to the firm's earnings and future profitability. Additional items include the experience and financial and capital assets of the owner, business location, and several other factors that relate directly to the business. The lenders consider all risk factors and determine if they will grant the loan. If unsystematic risk is perceived to be too high, the loan is denied. If unsystematic risk is within the range specified as acceptable in the guidelines of the lender, the loan is granted. The interest rate charged for this loan represents a combination of the systematic and unsystematic risk factors. If the prime lending rate is 4.5 percent and the unsystematic risk factor is considered to be 3 percent, then the financial institution will grant the loan at an interest rate of 7.5 percent or more, but never less than 7.5 percent. In effect, the borrower is paying a risk premium of 3 percent to get the loan.

As noted in Table 1–6, the *prime lending rate* is that rate charged by banks to their best customers. As risk increases, so does the interest rate. Banks may charge less than prime to a customer who they perceive will repay the loan with no problems. Banks may charge prime plus 3 or 4 percent to a company they consider to be risky.

In addition, the amount of the down payment on capital purchases such as land, buildings, and machinery may vary based on risk assessment by the bank. For example, a veteran may be entitled to a Veterans Administration (VA) loan with no down payment. If the veteran defaults on the loan, the loan is guaranteed by the government of the United States. If another person with the same income tries to obtain a conventional home loan from a bank, the bank may require a down payment of 10 to 20 percent of the home value, because the bank

---

[7]OilNergy, NYMEX Light Sweet Crude Oil Price. Retrieved April 11, 2008, from http://www.oilnergy.com.

perceives unsystematic risk as being higher for the second individual. This loan is guaranteed only by the income of the individual. The base lending rate for business loans is normally the prime rate in existence at the time of the loan request.

Businesses often face the risk of interest rate fluctuations. This risk can have an impact on a business if the business has a variable-rate loan. In periods of low interest rates, businesses tend to borrow more because capital can be obtained at a lower cost. In periods of rising interest rates, capital becomes expensive to obtain and maintain. For example, one of the authors had a $150,000 business loan that was granted by a bank at prime plus 2 percent. When the prime rate rose by 2 percent during one year, the payments on this loan increased by $246 per month. As interest rates move up, businesses are forced to pay a higher price for money they have previously borrowed, which eats away at their profitability.

Another problem that the businessperson might face is that home mortgage rates for 2006 through 2008 were very low. Many people obtained mortgages with either interest-only loans or variable rate loans (Adjustable Rate Mortgages, or ARMs), which are loans made that have fluctuating interest rates. Because of their initial low rates, borrowers start off with lower monthly payments than fixed rate mortgage borrowers pay. ARMs are normally tied to the some specific Government Security index or the Prime Lending Rate. As an entrepreneur with an adjustable rate mortgage, your business could be harmed severely if rates go up because you have incurred an additional cost. Can the entrepreneur cover these costs? Interest-only loans do not reduce the principal. When interest rates increase, many of these people may be unable to make their loan payments because the rate charged for the loan has increased. For example, if you have a $200,000 interest-only mortgage financed at 5.35 percent, the monthly interest payment is $891.67. If the lending rate increases by 2 percent to 7.35, the monthly interest payment rises to $1,225. This is an increase of $333.33. What you are essentially doing is renting money, and as the rates go up, the rent becomes more expensive. You can verify these numbers by using the link to the Excel amortization table, located on the Internet at www.prenhall.com/adelman.

The management of risk is dealt with extensively in Chapter 11. If we are to succeed in business, we must reduce our risk to acceptable limits; otherwise, bankruptcy may be the result. Therefore, to succeed, the business owner must develop plans to minimize risk and place the business in a competitive and profitable position.

CONCLUSION

In this chapter, we introduced basic financial concepts. We discussed the importance of finance and its relationship to those economic concepts involving the scarcity of resources, opportunity costs, savings, income, expenditures, and taxes. Because the business owner or manager usually makes decisions concerning the acquisition of financial capital, interest rates are fully discussed with respect to supply and demand, Federal Reserve policy, inflation, and risk.

It is essential that we have a basic knowledge of these factors before we attempt to set goals, establish ownership of a business, and write a business plan prior to starting our own business. These topics are covered in Chapter 2.

REVIEW AND DISCUSSION QUESTIONS

1. What is finance?
2. What is a market?
   a. Name five types of markets in which you participate.
   b. What markets trade economic resources?
3. Compare marginal revenue, marginal cost, and marginal revenue product.
4. Distinguish between economic and financial capital.
5. Discuss the value of the entrepreneur. What distinguishes the entrepreneur from the labor resource? Why are entrepreneurs unique?
6. What is opportunity cost?
7. What makes up gross income?
8. Compare progressive, regressive, and proportional taxes. Give at least one example of each type of tax.
9. What is the law of supply?
10. What is a supply table? How do you obtain a supply curve from a supply table?
11. What is the law of demand?
12. Explain the concept of a surplus of money versus a shortage of money.
13. What is the Federal Reserve? What are the Fed's three tools for controlling the money supply?
14. What is risk? What is the difference between systematic and unsystematic risk?

EXERCISES AND PROBLEMS

1. Carry Yoki's Lounge consists of the following: Carry, the owner, believed that people would come to hear a band play on Friday, Saturday, and Sunday evenings. During the remainder of the week, she believed her customers would watch sporting events on several television sets located throughout the lounge. Carry employed two bartenders, three servers, two assistant servers, two cooks, one dishwasher, and a cleanup person. She had a bar, 15 bar stools, 4 tables, 40 chairs, 4 television sets, and a satellite dish. She had an oven, stove, grill, refrigerator, sinks, dishes, and glassware. Carry started this business with $50,000 of her own money, and she borrowed $150,000

from the bank. From this description, list each of the scarce resources that are used in Carry Yoki's Lounge.

2. Joe Fixit has an appliance-repair business. He has more business than he can handle and wants to hire another repair person. Joe estimates that three appliances can be repaired each hour by a qualified person. Joe bills out labor at $45 per hour, but he stipulates that the minimum charge for appliance-repair estimates is $30 plus parts. What is the marginal revenue product of a qualified repair person? What is the maximum hourly wage that he would pay an employee?

3. Sam Smith is currently employed as a mechanical engineer and is paid $65,000 per year plus benefits that are equal to 30 percent of his salary. Sam wants to begin a consulting firm and decides to leave his current job. After his first year in business, Sam's accountant informs him that he has made $45,000 with his consulting business. Sam also notices that he paid $6,000 for a health insurance policy, which was his total benefit during his first year. What was Sam's opportunity cost?

4. Sara Lee just graduated from college with a degree in accounting. She had five job offers: Bean Counters CPA, $35,000; Assets R Us, $27,000; The Debit Store, $30,000; J & J's CPAs, $33,000; and The Double Entry Shop, $40,000. What was her opportunity cost if she accepted the job with The Double Entry Shop?

5. Sam Club earned $50,000 and paid taxes of $10,000. Samantha Heart earned $60,000 and paid taxes of $12,000. If these taxes were paid to the same government agency, is the tax on income progressive, regressive, or proportional? How did you reach this conclusion?

6. You read an article in this morning's paper that states that inflation is accelerating and will reach 6 percent this year. If the Fed believes this statement and has set a goal of 3 percent inflation, what will it likely do at the next meeting of the Federal Open Market Committee?

7. A friend came into your office and said that his bank was out to kill local business. You asked him what he meant by this remark, and he said that he read an article that said his bank had just loaned $10 million to a major automobile manufacturer at a rate of 4 percent, which is less than prime. But your friend just borrowed $50,000 from the same bank, which charged him prime plus 3 percent, or 7.5 percent. Your friend has been in business for two years, and last year he had a loss of $2,000. How can you explain this difference in interest rates to your friend?

RECOMMENDED TEAM ASSIGNMENT

1. Using online research, determine what tools the Federal Reserve Bank used in the past year to affect the economy of the United States in order to reach the Fed's goals.

2. Using two teams, provide an argument which agrees (Pro) with the Fed action and an argument which opposes (Con) the Fed action.

CASE STUDY: MACY'S HOUSEWARES, INCORPORATED

Philip Pomerantz was raised in Poughkeepsie, New York, and as long as he can remember he always wanted to run his own business. He started his first business venture as a paperboy with a morning, afternoon, and Sunday route at the age of 12. He learned about customer service and placed the papers between the screen door and the front door. When people in the neighborhood heard about his excellent service, he received more and more orders. He soon built the route into a business with more than 150 customers and soon had two other kids helping him deliver the papers. This was in the 1930s, during the Depression, and Phil often made more in a month than his customers. On graduating high school, he went to the University of Wisconsin and majored in Labor Economics. He graduated during World War II, and went to work in Buffalo, New York, for War Industries, with various factories making materials for the Armed Forces. While working in Buffalo, he met his wife, Kayla, and got married in 1943. Phil continued to want his own business and while working in War Industries, he decided to get some practical experience in retailing. He got a part time job with W. T. Grant, one of the largest chain stores in the United States, in the hardware department. He soon exceeded the sales of all clerks in the store and asked his boss to take him off of hourly wages and place him on a commission. His boss explained that W. T. Grant only paid hourly wages and fired him.

After being fired, Phil started looking around for hardware stores to purchase and got a pamphlet from the state of New York entitled, "How to Start Your Own Business." The state pamphlet stressed the fact that one was better off buying an existing business that had established customers than to try and begin a business from scratch. With his degree in labor economics and his experience in retailing, he looked at several stores that were for sale. He soon determined that they were all in declining areas and the books confirmed that annual revenue in these stores was decreasing rather than increasing.

Phil had several uncles who were successful entrepreneurs and were also looking for a business that he might purchase. They notified him that Macy's Housewares in Hudson, New York, was for sale. The first time he looked at the store he was really taken aback when he saw pots and pans hanging from the ceiling. However, when he looked at their books, he found that sales were steady and the margin of profit was good. The business was a typical country store that sold housewares (pots, pans, dishes, small appliances, etc.) and farm supplies, which included seeds in bulk and fertilizer.

The business was evaluated on location, inventory, 5 years of sales, and average mark up. Phil offered to purchase the business for the purchase price of the existing inventory. The owner, Frank Macy, accepted this bid and agreed to stay with the business for one month. Mr. Macy also owned the building and Phil negotiated a lease for the premises. After ten years, Phil bought the building. Coming from a big city, there were several items that were for sale in this rural community that he had never seen. For example, most of the farms used outhouses and didn't have indoor plumbing, so on cold nights they actually used an indoor chamberpot (commode) which was kept in the bedroom, under the bed.

In the 1940s, it took a long time to evaluate inventory, because every item was marked with a code that let the owner know how much had been paid for the item. They also had fair-trade laws that required that all national brands be fair-traded, meaning that the manufacturer set the retail price based on a 40 percent mark up. This included large manufacturing firms like Corning, Revereware, and Rubbermaid. There were no discount stores and the only thing that separated one business from another was customer service, as all retailers had to sell fair-traded items at the same price. Items like seeds, which were not covered by fair-trade laws, provided the largest profit margins. A pound of garden seeds like radishes could be purchased by Macy's for $1.00. Phil could sell a quarter of an ounce of seeds for 15 cents, because most people with a small backyard garden didn't need more than that. Kayla and Phil worked this store together for more than 30 years. Both of their children were raised in the store and worked there until they went away to college.

When Phil bought the store, he and his wife determined that they really couldn't afford to purchase items in large quantities because they didn't have the cash and definitely didn't have storage space. They determined that the product distributors could actually be the warehouse. The distributor's salespeople called on Macy's Housewares on a monthly basis, but because he sold items from many manufacturers, he had at least one salesperson call on him every week. With a good inventory system and ordering essentially replacement items for those that had been sold, Phil was able to turn his inventory nine times a year, as opposed to the industry average of three times.

Phil and Kayla actually had no savings and no bank credit when they bought Macy's. Financing the store was done by having his uncles who were businessmen with established credit sign the note for the bank. Phil soon learned that banks can be used to make money, as all of his vendors sent invoices that included "2/10 net 30." When cash was short, he would go to the bank and borrow money against his credit line at 5 percent and take the cash discounts, which saved him more than 31 percent on the money. During the Christmas season, he learned that if you paid the vendors in cash for deliveries, they would often provide discounts in excess of 2 percent.

What's in a name? Macy's Housewares original owner was Frank Macy, who was a cousin of R. H. Macy. Knowing this, Phil immediately incorporated the business and registered his trademark to protect the name and assets. He would often call vendors and state that he was Macy's primary buyer and arrange to obtain shipments at the same price given to R. H. Macy.

As time went by, the fair-trade laws were rescinded and the distributors were put out of business. A small retailer then had to purchase directly from the manufacturer. The manufacturers required purchases in much larger lot sizes, and discounters, who were open on Sunday, began advertising product prices that were often less than Macy's purchase price. Phil could not compete against these discounters and decided to upgrade his merchandise lines and provide better lines than the discounters. He knew that wealthier people had a tendency to shop quality rather than price, and Phil began carrying lines like Noritake China. He attended trade shows and arranged to pay for one complete service of several patterns of china, which he displayed in the store. He sold complete sets and individual pieces and backordered all sales because he carried no stock. One of his advantages was that he could order individual pieces to replace items that were broken by the user. Larger department stores typically didn't provide this level of customer service.

During their 30 years in business, Phil and Kayla set aside enough for their future. When he turned 65 they decided to sell their business and retire. There was one serious problem. Although the mark-up on items was 40 percent, the actual net profit margin was about 10 percent. Phil wanted to sell the business during the early 1980s when banks were paying depositors 15 percent interest on their savings accounts. The Pomerantzes, therefore, could find no buyers for their business as people could just deposit money in a savings account and earn more than if they invested in a business like Macy's. As a result, they decided to liquidate their inventory and closed the business. Phil hired a liquidating company and managed to sell most of his inventory at a price that was equal to or greater than what he had paid for it. They purchased the building for $12,000 in the early 1970s and sold it in 1986 for $30,000. The entire business district where Macy's Housewares was located in Hudson, New York, is now an upscale art colony, and the entire retail district is no longer in existence. On retiring, Phil and Kayla moved to Arizona, where they reside today.

QUESTIONS

1. What effect did changes in government regulations have on the way Macy's had to conduct its business?
2. What effect did the economy and current interest rates have on the ability of Macy's to sell their business?

CHAPTER 2

Financial Management and Planning

Learning Objectives

When you have completed this chapter, you should be able to:

♦ Describe the five basic functions of a manager and how they relate to a business.
♦ Distinguish between strategic plans and functional plans.
♦ Understand the three factors that must be addressed when establishing goals.
♦ Describe the financial goals of a for-profit organization.
♦ Trace the three-step process to take when using control.
♦ Compare and contrast the basic forms of business ownership (sole proprietor, partnership, and corporation).
♦ Distinguish between limited and unlimited liability.
♦ Compare and contrast general partnership, limited partnership, and a limited liability company.
♦ Understand the role that the franchise plays when establishing a business.
♦ Understand the basic components of a SWOT analysis.
♦ Know what basic factors are required to complete a business plan.
♦ Understand the basic sources of financing for a business.
♦ Know how important it is to have a business succession plan.

To achieve a financial objective, a businessperson must be both a manager and a leader. Although there are no universally accepted definitions of **management**, for our purposes here, we can essentially define it as the process of working with or through others to achieve an individual or business goal by efficiently and effectively using resources.

MANAGEMENT FUNCTIONS

A manager performs five basic functions: planning, organizing, staffing, directing, and controlling operations. These functions are discussed in the following sections.

PLANNING

Planning is a systematic process that takes us from some current state to some future desired state. Planning involves establishing goals and developing processes and methods for achieving those goals. There are several types of planning with which we should be concerned as business owners and managers.

Strategic planning is the development of long-term plans for our business. Strategic planning involves establishing overall company priorities. In addition, the strategic planner allocates resources and takes the steps necessary to meet the strategic goals. The strategic plan answers the following question: Where do we want our business to be at some future date? It is important to note that strategic plans have a time horizon that usually exceeds 1 year. Strategic plans most often have time horizons of 5 years or more. Some industries require strategic plans that cover 15 years.

Functional plans for business are driven by the strategic plan. They are related to specific functional areas such as accounting, marketing, or human resources. If you currently own a pizza-parlor restaurant and would like to open 10 additional restaurants in your community within 5 years, your goal can be accomplished by using a strategic plan. Each of these restaurants, however, must hire personnel; as a result, you must have a personnel plan. This functional plan supports the strategic plan. Each restaurant also requires equipment; as a result, you must have a capital budgeting plan. Each restaurant requires a marketing strategy, so you must also have to have a marketing plan. Each restaurant must provide products and services to customers in a specific manner to guarantee consistency of quality with respect to the product; as a result, you must have an operational plan. All of the preceding are functional plans that support the strategic plan of your business.

Another functional plan involves **financial planning**, which consists of gathering all a firm's monetary requirements for the support of each functional plan. The company, therefore, must convert these functional plans into an overall budget for the firm. This budget then drives the financial and financing requirements. The reason so many businesses fail is because of a lack of adequate financial planning. Nobody begins a business with a plan for failure, but too many businesses have been started with a failure to plan.

Goal setting is a precursor to establishing a plan. A goal is a measurable objective that can be reached in a specified time frame. All goals must have three characteristics: (1) They must be measurable (10 restaurants); (2) they must be achievable (Is it feasible to open the 10 restaurants?); and (3) they must have a time frame connected to them (e.g., within 5 years). In many texts, the terms *goals* and *objectives* are interchangeable; however, there is a difference. *Goals* are normally considered to be long term; o*bjectives* are intermediate goals that measure progress toward the overall long-term goal.

Continuing with the previous example, you might set an objective of having two more restaurants operating next year and an additional two in the following year. By opening two restaurants each year over the next 5 years, you will achieve all intermediate goals (objectives) and accomplish the strategic goal of opening 10 restaurants in 5 years.

There are three basic financial goals required by a for-profit organization: maximize the wealth of the business owners (investors) over the life of the business, meet interest payments on debt, and grow.

These goals require that our company have one overall goal: to make money now and to make more money in the future.[1] If a satisfactory return on investment is not reached by the individual owner, that owner may become discouraged and look to invest elsewhere. A business that is not making a profit may cease to exist. In addition, if interest payments on debt are not made, banks or other creditors may force the enterprise into bankruptcy. For the individual business owner, bankruptcy can make it difficult, if not impossible, to obtain future credit. Finally, a business enterprise must grow. If it does not grow, it probably will not be competitive in the marketplace and will cease to exist.

To avoid these problems, the manager must develop business plans based on definite and obtainable goals. Once definite goals have been established, then plans should be written that allow accomplishment of each goal. The beginning of financial planning requires basic knowledge of financial analysis, financial forecasting, and the development of budgets (which are plans converted to financial terms). These items are covered in detail in subsequent chapters (e.g., financial analysis is covered in Chapters 3 and 4; forecasting is covered in Chapter 6; different types of budgets, such as pro forma financial statements, are covered in Chapter 6; and capital budgeting is covered in Chapter 10).

ORGANIZING

The second function of the manager is **organizing**. Once a plan has been written, the owners (managers) must develop an organization that allows them to carry out the plan. For most start-up companies, structure is fairly simple, with one or two employees and virtually no departments. As the business grows, however, definite structures and departments must be established. If you are the single owner of a restaurant, you can probably interview and hire every employee. If you reach your goal of having 10 restaurants, you need someone to recruit for

---

[1]Eliahu Goldratt, *The Haystack Syndrome: Sifting Information Out of the Data Ocean* (Croton-on-Hudson, NY: North River Press, 1990).

you. You must decide whether you will give (or *delegate*) the responsibility for hiring to each store manager or to a central personnel office. With small businesses, you are not subject to many government rules and regulations. As a business grows, you need more experts to assist you. Organizing a business is related to planning. A functional plan should answer the following questions:

◆ Who will do it?
◆ What skills do they need?
◆ What is the time frame that we have set in which to have it accomplished?
◆ Where will it be accomplished?
◆ How do we get it accomplished?

Answers to these questions allow us to define our organization. For example, you may want to interview applicants and hire a manager for each of your 10 stores. You may also permit these managers to hire their own employees; alternatively, you could have your central personnel department screen and test all applicants and then send only those people who are qualified to your stores to be interviewed by the individual managers you have previously selected.

Within the context of financial management, a business's organization involves monitoring financial plans and determining how to obtain the funds required to carry out these plans. In a business, financial organization may be carried out entirely by the owner or manager. As the business grows, a definite organizational structure must be developed to obtain and monitor funds.

STAFFING

The **staffing** function requires that the manager obtain the most capable personnel to implement the business plans. Each functional plan involves people. As a result, the overall planning process must also deal with specific jobs. For each specific job, we must determine the job requirements. *Job requirements* are what the job requires with respect to education, training, and basic skills. A job description also should be developed for each position. It depicts the duties that must be performed by the employee who is hired.

DIRECTING

The fourth function of an owner or manager is leading or directing. **Directing** is providing proper guidance and direction to others who work to accomplish the organization's mission. The entrepreneur is the person who leads and directs the business. Employees try to emulate employers and managers whom they respect. As owners of an organization, we must be honest if we expect our employees to be honest. We must be truthful if we expect them to be truthful. We should guide by the Golden Rule: Treat our employees as we would want to be treated if we were in their situation. Good employers and managers have long-term, loyal employees. Employers and managers who cannot effectively lead experience high employee turnover.

Directing in the financial arena is carried out through the budgeting process. Through the budgeting process, financial assets are disbursed to specific areas and functions of the business. To carry out efficient operations, managers must direct the flow of financial assets properly.

CONTROLLING

Controlling, next to planning, is the most difficult process to undertake. Controlling is essentially a three-step process that involves establishing a standard of measurement, measuring actual performance against the standard, and taking corrective action when actual performance varies from the established standard. Financial control begins with setting standards to follow. It compares actual expenditures and income with projected standards, and it determines problem areas. Next, controlling takes corrective action by developing and implementing solutions to problems. Financial control also requires owners to protect the financial assets of the company by developing sound internal auditing (monitoring) and control procedures. This feat cannot be accomplished reasonably without the development of adequate strategic and functional financial plans.

Let's look at the following example: We have a loan that is due on the tenth of each month. If the loan is not paid on time, we are assessed a late fee of $100. We establish a standard that requires all loan payments are sent 5 days prior to the due date. Last month, we received a notice of late payment and were assessed the $100 late fee. We must now take corrective action. First, we must find out what happened. Let's say that the accounts payable clerk issued the check on time, and the check was mailed on the fifth of the month, but was not received by the bank until the twelfth. Corrective action now requires us to either increase the lead time or find another method of getting the payment to the lender on time. The corrective action might be to make the payment via a direct funds transfer from our checking account to the lender. This would eliminate the possibility of a mail delay as well as avoid any future late fees and possibly a poor credit rating.

BUSINESS ORGANIZATIONS AND OWNERSHIP

One of the first decisions that must be made when planning a business is what form of ownership it will entail. The four forms of business ownership are *sole proprietorship, partnership, corporation,* and *limited liability company.* A *franchise,* although not a specific business form, is also discussed. Within the context of the partnership form of business, there are general and limited partnerships. There are also several forms of corporate ownership. The two primary types of corporations are *public* and *private.* The limited liability company is a hybrid, having

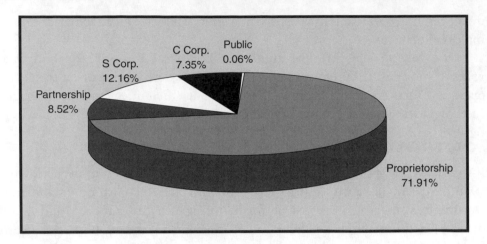

FIGURE 2–1
United States business forms by percentage.
(Source: Internal Revenue Service, *SOI Bulletin,* Historical Table, Fall 2007. Excel ver. 4. 2005. Securities and Exchange Commission Filings.)

some of the characteristics of both the partnership and the corporation. Which form is appropriate depends on the situation of the owner. If you are just starting a business as a single entity, it may be appropriate to begin as a sole proprietor; if you desire to own only a portion of a business, a form of corporate ownership or limited partnership may be in order.

As we continue, it will become apparent that the decision to use a specific form of business ownership is contingent on several factors, including liability, tax advantages, financial support, the owner's desires, and the type and location of the business. It is important to note that tax advantages are subject to change as our government changes tax laws. One should always consult a tax professional to determine the current status of these laws. In 2002, more than 26 million business organizations filed tax returns in the United States.[2] The breakdown of these is shown in Figure 2–1.

SOLE PROPRIETORSHIP

The business form most widely used today is the **sole proprietorship**, which is operated by an individual for profit. Personal incentive and satisfaction contribute to the sole proprietor's ability to make a business work.

Advantages of a Sole Proprietorship

The sole proprietorship has several advantages over the other forms of business ownership. There are no formal, federal, legal requirements with which to comply

---

[2]Internal Revenue Service, *SOI Bulletin, Historical Table,* Summer 2005. Excel ver. 4, August 2005, Securities and Exchange Commission filings.

to establish the sole proprietorship. Local governments (city, county, or state) may require a license for tax purposes, but the fees are normally quite small and the forms are usually easy to fill out. Title to the property of the business is in the owner's name. The sole proprietor conducts the business alone or within a tight family structure. The business requires no formal organizational structure. For this reason, all that is needed to start a business (with the exception of local licenses) is an idea and the desire to conduct business in a reputable and legal fashion.

From an accounting standpoint, sole-proprietorship business tax procedures can be relatively simple, because all income from the business is reported on the owner's individual tax return. The sole proprietor can determine the type of and contribution to a retirement plan, and can take maximum advantage of tax laws pertaining to sheltering income. The owner is usually the manager of the business and has total control over how managerial authority is exercised on a daily basis. The freedom to take action allows the owner to make decisions and take action without delay. The owner can choose to change products, services, or business locations. The owner can determine goals or sell the business without consulting anyone else. Often this total freedom is the optimum path and provides the most satisfaction to the individual owner.

Disadvantages of a Sole Proprietorship

The sole proprietorship also has several disadvantages. The *capital structure* (the combination of debt and equity financing) of the business is limited because the owner depends on individual resources to operate the business. Financing the business is totally dependent on the wealth and credit standing of the owner. As a sole proprietor, one may find it difficult to borrow from outside resources. Having a detailed financial plan and the ability to fill out a loan package are necessities if the business owner desires to raise additional capital.

The sole proprietor also has unlimited liability. All property of the business is in the owner's name. The owner is responsible for all debts of the business and is legally liable for any problems that the business may have. For example, if someone is injured in the sole proprietor's store, the owner can be sued personally. If the owner is found guilty and a large judgment is rendered to the injured party, the proprietor may have to dip into personal assets (e.g., house, car, furniture) to pay the judgment.

In addition, the life of the business is limited to the life of the owner. If the business owner dies, the business legally ceases to exist. If the proprietor leaves the business to a spouse or child, this person must relicense the business in his or her name. Transfer of ownership takes time, and overall disruptions in business continuity may occur. Thus, the death or poor health of the owner tends to dissolve the proprietorship.

Two additional disadvantages may plague a sole proprietor. First, a business owner may lack the managerial skills necessary to operate a business. Second, the inability of a star employee to obtain ownership (or at least a vested interest) in the business may give that employee the incentive to look elsewhere for employment.

PARTNERSHIP

A **partnership** is an association of two or more persons who carry out a business as co-owners for a profit. There are essentially two types of partnerships: the *general partnership* and the *limited partnership*. All partnerships, in the authors' opinion, should be formed with a formal partnership agreement that specifies the legal arrangements and business responsibilities of each partner. Because of the complexities associated with partnerships, it is strongly recommended that any partnership agreement be written in consultation with an attorney.

The **general partnership** has an important advantage over the proprietorship. Because there is more than one owner, there is more expertise; the partners have more combined knowledge than the sole proprietor. Often partnerships are formed because of these differences in expertise. One partner may be an excellent technician who lacks salesmanship. The other may be an excellent salesperson who has no technical ability. Obviously, if such a situation exists, the firm is better off using the expertise of both partners. The partners may have an equal voice in management, or may be limited by the partnership agreement.

The general partnership also has several disadvantages that are similar to those of the proprietorship. Each partner is personally liable for the acts of the partnership. Financing of the business is limited by the assets and credit ratings of the individual partners. Ownership is difficult to transfer, and profits are taxed to the individual partners on their personal tax returns. The partnership has a limited life and is legally terminated when one partner dies, unless the partnership agreement is very specific with regard to a transfer of ownership. For example, you may have an excellent relationship with your partner, but do not get along with your partner's spouse. If your partner dies, you may find yourself with a new partner (partner's spouse) with whom you may disagree or who is totally incompetent, unless there is a specific buy–sell provision in the partnership agreement.

The *buy–sell agreement* prevents a partner from selling a partnership interest to an outsider without the consent of the other partners. It establishes the purchase price of each partner's interest in the business should a partner have a triggering event. A triggering event can be bankruptcy, death, disability, divorce, retirement, or termination of employment. If a partner dies, the buy–sell agreement prevents one of the heirs from selling their interest in the partnership to an outsider. The agreement is usually backed by life insurance with the remaining partners as beneficiaries so that they have the funds to purchase the deceased partner's share of the business. The buy–sell agreement may also include non-compete clauses. Essentially, the buy–sell agreement preserves the continuity of ownership and ensures that everyone is treated fairly.

The **limited partnership** involves one or more general partners and normally several limited partners. The most widely used form of limited partnership occurs with real estate development and holdings. In such a partnership, the general partner is in charge of day-to-day operations and is personally liable for the partnership. The limited partners are basically investors, and their liability is limited to the amount of their investment in the partnership. They are not involved with the daily operations. The limited partners are prohibited by law from making or taking part in any day-to-day management decisions. For example, John Adams finds a large apartment complex for sale for $1 million. John is a real estate management expert who believes that the purchase would provide a good profit if the apartment complex were handled properly. John has $50,000 to invest in this venture. He locates 19 other people who are willing to invest $50,000 each in this apartment complex. John now has the $1 million to purchase the complex. He would become the general partner, and the other 19 investors would be the limited partners.

Now assume that the apartment complex has a major fire in which several tenants are severely injured, and the tenants sue the partnership. The tenants receive a judgment of $3 million. John is personally liable as the general partner. The other 19 partners have a limited liability of $50,000 each. This amount reflects the magnitude of their individual investments. Other than in the general areas of limited and unlimited liability, the limited partnership has the same advantages and disadvantages of the general partnership. To avoid the unlimited-liability problem that John faced in the partnership outlined here, he could have formed his organization as a limited liability partnership or corporation.

In a **limited liability partnership (LLP)**, all of the partners have limited liability and can participate in the day-to-day management of the company. The limited liability partnership is not legal in all of the states and you must check with your own state to determine if one can be formed. For example, in California and New York, the LLP is limited to professionals like physicians, lawyers, and accountants.[3] The LLP is not as desirable as the limited liability company (LLC), which is discussed in detail later in this chapter. The LLC can be formed in a state that protects the owner's business interest against the claims of his or her personal creditors. In other words, you can't lose your LLC because you have a very large personal Visa or MasterCard bill. This is not possible with the LLP because no state affords this protection. For this reason, we do not recommend the LLP.

A variation of the limited partnership is the **master limited partnership**. Ownership interests are sold as ownership percentages that trade as shares on a stock exchange like the shares of a corporation. However, unlike a corporation that can raise new capital by issuing additional shares and diluting earnings, a master limited partnership cannot. It cannot sell more than 100 percent interest

---

[3]Thomas Clearing House. http://www.toolkit.cch.com/text/p12_4265.asp.

in the partnership. The day-to-day operations of a master limited partnership are controlled by the master limited partner, who has at least 50 percent or more of the ownership interest in the partnership. An advantage of the master limited partnership is that it has more liquidity than a limited partnership, because owners can sell their shares on the stock exchange.

CORPORATION

The **corporation** is a legal entity according to U.S. law, so it may accomplish the same tasks as an individual. It may buy and sell assets, enter into legal contracts, hire and fire employees, and so forth. Corporations are incorporated in any 1 of the 50 states or one of the territories of the United States and are chartered by the state or territory for tax purposes. All corporations are C corporations unless 100 percent of the stockholders vote to select Subchapter S corporation status. C corporations are taxed as corporations; corporate income tax is paid by the corporation on its profit, before any profit is distributed to the shareholder. S corporations have special tax status. The corporation does not pay income tax on its profit. The shareholders receive their proportionate share of the S corporation's profit and report this as income on their individual income tax statements. It is imperative to consult an attorney and a tax professional when forming a corporation because the laws pertaining to forming the corporation varies by state, and the corporation is subject to state law and federal rules and regulations.

Ownership of a corporation is based on shares of stock, or percentage of ownership. The number of shares owned by an individual divided by the total shares outstanding (sold) determines the percentage of ownership held by that individual. There are essentially two types of corporations: the public corporation and the private, or closely held, corporation.

A **public corporation** is one whose stock is traded on the open market. Public corporations represent fewer than 1 percent of all business organizations in the United States (fewer than 30,000 of more than 25 million) (Figure 2-1).[4] These corporations are governed by the Securities and Exchange Commission (SEC) and must meet several federal reporting requirements. All public corporations must send an annual report to each stockholder and file an annual Form 10-K report (basically a set of financial statements) with the SEC. Both forms are available to the public. Annual reports can be obtained easily by calling a corporation and requesting a copy. Form 10-K reports also can be obtained by calling the corporation, may be found at any large public library or university library, or on the Internet through the Electronic Data Gathering and Retrieval System (EDGAR).[5] All public corporations must file electronically. Corporate

---

[4]U.S. Securities and Exchange Commission, *1998 Annual Report to Congress,* available at http://www.sec.gov.

[5]U.S. SEC, *New Fee Payment Instructions*, Effective Feb. 4, available at http://www.sec.gov.

advantages and disadvantages are usually the opposite of the individual and partnership advantages and disadvantages.

Advantages of a Corporation

Advantages for the corporation are numerous. From a financial standpoint, the corporation has tremendous advantages over the sole proprietorship or partnership. The corporation has almost unlimited access to financial capital because it may raise capital by selling stock (acquiring new owners), by borrowing from banks (as does the sole proprietor), or by borrowing from the public through issuing bonds. A corporate bond, like a government bond, is borrowed money. The corporation must pay interest on the face value of the bond for the duration of the bond's life. On the maturity date of the bond, the corporation must redeem the bond at face value. Stocks and bonds are more thoroughly discussed in Chapter 11. A corporation has unlimited life, as long as it is financially stable and is not forced into a liquidating bankruptcy. Ownership in a corporation is passed from one owner to another through the sale of the corporation's stock, by gift, or by inheritance.

The owners of the corporation have limited liability because ownership is limited to the number of shares of stock held by an individual. The corporation has unlimited liability because it can be sued for unlimited amounts, until it becomes bankrupt. The individual owner of a corporation, in a court action, is liable only for his or her investment in the corporation. For example, say you buy $1,000 in stock in XYZ Corp. This corporation is sued for developing and selling a product that results in the death of several customers. In a court action, the corporation loses a $100 million lawsuit that forces XYZ Corp. into bankruptcy. Your only liability is the $1,000 investment. Thus, the corporation has unlimited liability, but you, as the individual owner, have limited liability. You can never lose more than your $1,000 investment even if the corporation ceases to exist. When we hear that a corporation has *limited liability,* that means the corporate owner actually has limited liability.

Disadvantages of a Corporation

The corporation also has many disadvantages. There are formal federal and state legal requirements that must be met, including an annual audit by an independent, impartial, outside auditor, of which the corporation bears the cost. Other requirements include the filing of numerous forms and compliance with several laws that apply only to corporations, including the Form 10-K requirements discussed earlier.

Another disadvantage is that business ownership is widely held. Stockholders elect a board of directors at an annual meeting, and the board selects the key managers of the corporation. Owners, therefore, are separated from the business and have little or no control over how the business is run on a daily basis. The owner usually has little say in business products, location, or goal setting.

From a financial point of view, the biggest disadvantage of the corporation is double taxation. The corporation pays federal tax on its profits; then the corporation may distribute a share of its profits back to the owner as a dividend. You, as a stockholder, must declare the dividend as ordinary income and pay personal income tax at your current tax rate. For example, in 2006, a corporation was subject to a maximum tax rate of 35 percent of net profit in excess of $18.33 million. The maximum tax rate for an individual is also 35 percent. Assume that you owned 1,000 shares in a corporation that was subject to the maximum corporate tax rate of 35 percent. The corporation had to pay 35 percent in federal taxes on each dollar of profit. The corporation then sent you a dividend of $5 per share. You then had an additional $5,000 in income (1,000 shares times $5 dividend per share). If your personal tax rate was 35 percent, then you paid 35 percent in tax on each dollar of dividend income. What is the total tax paid on each dollar earned by the corporation and paid to you in the form of a dividend? It is not 35 percent + 35 percent, or 70 percent; the total tax rate on each of these corporate dollars earned was in fact 57.75 percent. For each dollar that the corporation had in operating profit, 35 cents was paid in taxes (35 percent). This left 65 cents for every dollar earned to be paid as a dividend. You then received this 65-cent net profit in the form of dividends. You then paid 35 percent of the 65 cents paid to you in dividends, or you paid 22.75 cents in taxes on the dividend distribution. Thus, the total amount of taxes paid on the original dollar of corporate earnings was 35 cents by the corporation and 22.75 cents by you, for a total tax of 57.75 cents, which is also 57.75 percent.

Can you be in a corporation and avoid the double taxation rate? You can put your money into a private corporation that has received Subchapter S status from the Internal Revenue Service (IRS). As explained earlier, S corporation profit is distributed to the stockholder as ordinary income, and the stockholder pays income tax on this profit at his or her normal tax rate.

Other Corporations

A **private corporation** is one that has been formed under state law but does not sell its stock to the public. Federal law allows individuals to form small corporations. An example of a private corporation is the *professional corporation,* which can have a single owner. We typically find physicians, accountants, and other professionals in this type of corporation. A professional corporation has the designation "P.C." after the title of the corporation, such as in an individual's name (e.g., Sidney Jones, M.D., P.C.). Like large corporations, private corporations have the advantages of limited liability. They have the disadvantages of limited management expertise and limited ability to raise cash, like the proprietorship or partnership. They are also subject to double taxation, like the public corporation.

The **Subchapter S corporation** is privately held and has filed for and been granted Subchapter S status by the IRS. The Subchapter S corporation must have more than 1 but not more than 100 shareholders.[6] States authorize these corporations in different forms, and again, we advise consulting an attorney and an accountant to determine which form is best for you.

The Subchapter S corporation is, for the most part, the best of both worlds. It has the advantages of the sole proprietorship or partnership. The form of the business and the business products are determined by a small group of owners. Stock (ownership) can be transferred easily. There is no double taxation; profits flow through to the individual. Federal reporting is minimal, because the corporation must simply file for a federal tax number and permission to function in accordance with one of the IRS codes governing this type of corporation. Once this permission is granted, reporting of corporate profits or losses is included on the owner's personal tax forms.

Liability is limited to the owner's investment in the corporation. Unfortunately, because the stock is not traded publicly, the Subchapter S corporation is limited in its access to capital. For this reason, some businesses, although they begin as private or Subchapter S corporations, change their status to that of a public corporation by expanding their ownership base and publicly trading stock as they expand and require more capital.

Although the owner of a corporation cannot normally be sued as an individual, in several recent cases managers and owners have been sued when they have been shown to have done something blatantly illegal. A famous case involved the president of an Illinois corporation who knowingly failed to provide his worker with proper safety protection, and the worker was killed on the job. The company had been in violation of Occupational Safety and Health Administration (OSHA) guidelines for a long period, and there was substantial evidence that the owner knew what the requirements were but chose to ignore them. The owner was charged with and convicted of murder.

LIMITED LIABILITY COMPANY

A **limited liability company (LLC)** is a hybrid business entity having features of both a partnership and a corporation. It is taxed as a partnership and its members enjoy limited liability like corporate shareholders. Like a partnership, an LLC establishes an agreement that defines the functions, responsibilities, and financial and tax provisions of the members. Furthermore, like a corporation, it is a legal entity. It can open up a bank account and get a tax identification number. A few types of businesses generally cannot be LLCs, such as banks and insurance

[6]Internal Revenue Service, Instructions for Form 2553 (Revised December 2007). *Election by a Small Business Corporation.*

TABLE 2–1 Comparison of C Corporation and LLC[a]

	C Corporation	LLC
Similarities		
Legal entity	X	X
State filing	X	X
Personal assets are protected from creditors	X	X
Few ownership restrictions	X	X
Can have foreign owners	X	X
Differences		
Owned by stockholders	X	
Owned by members or managers		X
Hold annual meetings	X	
Keep written minutes of meetings	X	
Annual audits and filing with SEC	X	
Taxable entity	X	
Pass through tax entity		X
Flexibility and simplicity		X
Must use IRS corporate tax forms	X	
Can choose to file as a sole proprietorship, partnership, or corporation[b]		X

[a] http://www.score.org/leg_5.

[b] For LLCs, the exact method of filing should be checked by going to the following reference: Internal Revenue Service, "Frequently Asked Questions Related to LLCs" available at http://www.irs.gov/faqs/index.html.

companies. Check your state's requirements and the federal tax regulations for further information. There are special rules for foreign LLCs.

In addition, the LLC may have either a written or an oral agreement among the members, but we strongly recommend a written agreement. The advantages of an LLC include limited liability of members, income flow and losses to individual-member tax returns, and active management by all members of the LLC without the risk of liability associated with a limited partnership. Foreign investors may have ownership in the LLC, as well as corporations, trusts, and estates. A disadvantage is that the LLC cannot be used by professionals such as physicians and attorneys. The LLC is appropriate for both start-up and mature businesses. It is recognized in all 50 states and the District of Columbia. Table 2–1 compares the similarities and differences of a C corporation and a limited liability company.

When you begin a business, the type of ownership is one of your primary considerations. We advise forming an LLC any time there may be substantial personal liability for you, the owner. One cannot normally begin as a public corporation because there is no demand for the stock of a company unless it develops a revolutionary new product or until it develops a track record of profitability. Therefore, the remainder of this text concentrates on the financial requirements for a sole proprietorship, partnership, LLC, or private corporation. Public corporations are discussed briefly and only when necessary.

FRANCHISE

Although franchises are not a form of business ownership, it is a good idea to understand their basic structure. A **franchise** is a business in which the buyer, who is the *franchisee,* purchases the right to sell the goods or services of the seller, who is the *franchiser.* Franchisers provide four advantages: name recognition; standardized policies and procedures for product and service delivery; marketing skill in the form of strategy and advertising; and training of employees, managers, and franchisees. The franchisee, in exchange for these services, signs a franchise agreement that obligates the franchisee to conduct business in a manner prescribed by the franchiser. The franchisee normally agrees to provide the franchiser with a percentage of gross sales on a monthly basis. Franchisers essentially own a percentage of your cash flow. One of the disadvantages of the franchise is that you are not truly your own boss. You must comply with the contractual obligations agreed to in the franchise agreement. However, there are several reasons for entering into a franchise agreement: You have a proven product, a guaranteed sales area, good training, and, in many cases, a guaranteed profit margin. You must understand that some franchises do fail. Some franchisers are better than others. If you are considering this type of business, check out the franchise thoroughly. Talk to franchisees who were not recommended by the franchiser. Find out how many hours are actually involved, what profit margins really exist, and the actual amount of your financial obligation. If you are then satisfied, consider going into the franchise. Although more than 33 percent of all new businesses fail in the first 4 years, the franchise failure rate is less than 10 percent.

NON-PROFIT ORGANIZATIONS

Non-profit organizations are run as a business but view profit and money as taking a backseat to its main objective of supporting both the public and private sectors. These organizations seem to be altruistic and benefit society. Non-profits are usually found in the following areas: the environment, the arts, charities, religion, and research. In addition, these organizations may also be referred to as *not-for-profit organizations.* They are funded by donations and staffed by volunteers and employees. The difference between a non-profit and a for-profit corporation is that the for-profit organization issues stock and may pay dividends. The non-profit does not issue stock or pay dividends. However, like for-profit corporations, nonprofits may still have employees and can compensate their directors within reasonable bounds. Non-profit organizations can apply for tax-exempt status, which allows them to be exempt from income taxes. Also, individuals who are donors can deduct the amount contributed to the tax-exempt non-profit organization and pay less taxes. For specific guidelines on establishing a non-profit organization, you should check IRS Publication 557, *Tax Exempt Status for Your Organization.* Beginning in 2008, certain small tax-exempt organizations can now file by using a new e-postcard. Note that if an organization doesn't file, they lose their tax-exempt status.[7]

 ## STARTING A BUSINESS

Obviously, when we start a new business, one of the first decisions involves legal formation. The business does not exist until the owners establish it. The business cannot exist until the owners choose the legal form under which the business is to operate.

For most new businesses, the owner must determine how much money is required to begin the business. If the owner does not have the financial capital to begin the business with personal equity, then some financing must be obtained from outside parties. The owner then needs a valid loan proposal; but we, the owners, cannot get a loan proposal together unless we have a basic understanding of business forms (Chapter 3), forecasting procedures (Chapters 5 and 6), and business and personal finance (Chapter 11).

The remainder of this chapter pertains to the requirements for starting your own business. Most management texts include a recommendation to perform a *SWOT analysis*. The acronym **SWOT** stands for **strengths, weaknesses, opportunities**, and **threats**. *Strengths* and *weaknesses* pertain to the internal workings of a company. *Opportunities* and *threats* pertain to those external factors outside of the company's control that the company must take into consideration.

Strengths are the core competencies of your business. They are those factors that make your business succeed because you perform in these areas better than your competitors. Your strengths might be in management, products, operations, marketing, or finance. You must analyze your business and determine those areas where you are proficient. **Weaknesses** are those areas where your company definitely needs improvement. You might have a lack of personnel training, antiquated equipment, inexperienced workers, or a lack of financing. Remember that strengths for one business might be a weakness for another within the same industry.

Before you seriously consider venturing into a business, we strongly recommend that you and any of the prospective principals or partners in this business contemplate your individual strengths and weaknesses. Make a list and include under *Strengths* those items that you really enjoy doing. Include your areas of expertise. Under *Weaknesses,* include items that you really dislike and items in which you lack expertise, as well as the things that you prefer not to do or things that go against your grain. For example, say that you are a plumber and you take much satisfaction in knowing that when you place fixtures in a new

---

[7]Internal Revenue Service, IRS Publication 557, *Tax Exempt Status for Your Organization.* (Rev. March 2005).

house, the owners will be satisfied. Every fixture will work as advertised. List this quality as a Strength. You can make good money doing this job on your own. You would really like to start your own plumbing company, but you do not have any idea of where to begin. List not having a plan for investing your money as a Weakness. Wanting to start your own business and not knowing where to begin also is a Weakness. We hope that this book will help you in your weak areas and teach you how, as you build your business, to take advantage of your strengths and overcome those weaknesses.

When you start a business, you plan to be involved for several years. If you detest a certain job function, then you had better include hiring someone to perform this function as part of your business plan. The reason we recommend listing those things that you really like to do is that you may be doing them for a long time. Most successful businesspeople are those who really enjoy doing whatever it is that makes their business a success.

Understand that when you own or manage a business, you are *they*. For example, say you own a business that is open on a 24-hour basis, and you have just worked the day shift from 7 A.M. to 4 P.M. If you are only an employee, you go home. If it is your business and an employee who is supposed to work from 4 P.M. to midnight calls in sick, you are the one who fills in. It is your "baby store," and it just got sick. You are the doctor and the nursemaid. If you want your business to succeed, you must constantly nurture it and pay attention to every important detail. The rewards are astronomically high, and your efforts will pay off in the future.

Opportunities are factors that exist *in* the business environment. If utilized, Opportunities help the business grow and prosper. For example, you are the plumber previously described, and as you continue your assessment, you realize that your community is growing at a rate of 5 percent a year. A 5-percent growth rate means new construction and more housing. Each new living complex requires plumbing fixtures, which is an opportunity for your new business to grow. Opportunities, then, also are factors that exist outside your business, but that if recognized and taken advantage of, help your business grow.

Threats are factors that exist in the environment that may impede the growth of your business, directly or indirectly. As a plumber, you know there is competition from other plumbers in your area. Each competitor is a potential Threat to your ability to land a contract. In addition, you may have new government regulations that impose different requirements on the attachment of plumbing fixtures—what was legal last week may not be legal this week. Understand that opportunities and threats are not the same for every business, and when factors in the environment change, the requirements for your business must also change. For example, consider the convenience store industry. Many years ago, convenience stores were the only places open 24 hours a day. If you needed a container of milk for your child at 2 A.M., the only place to buy this was at a Circle K, a 7-Eleven, or some other convenience store. With the introduction of bar coding and the expansion of supermarkets, these stores found it profitable to remain open 24 hours a day. If there was a convenience store located on the same block as a supermarket, however, a new threat developed for the convenience store: The milk sold by the supermarket was at a lower price and was just as convenient to buy as that in the convenience store. Several of these stores have disappeared as a result of new competition brought about by changes in technology.

Another threat to the convenience store industry is the gas station. Years ago, gas stations were open only until 6 P.M. Now, the oil companies have entered the convenience store market and pose yet another threat to this industry. As a business owner, you must continuously monitor such changes in your environment and adjust your business plans accordingly. If you look at the convenience store industry in large cities, you will see that convenience stores with gas pumps are now located at major intersections. The convenience store in the middle of the block has all but disappeared.

If you have finished a SWOT analysis and still want to begin a business, it is time to write a *business plan*. Your business plan will result in requirements for financing, as the plan is converted into a budget. Although we do not explain here how to write an actual business plan, we do outline the requirements for a loan proposal, as presented by the Small Business Administration (SBA). The SBA's home page provides documentation on the Internet that includes all elements of a business plan.[8] The SBA also includes sample business plans, an online business planning workshop and detailed step-by-step instructions for writing business plans, and provides information on several excellent texts that discuss writing a business plan. Our purpose in this text is to illustrate how to develop and interpret the financial data required for the business plan.

DEVELOPMENT OF A BUSINESS PLAN

The Service Core of Retired Executives' (SCORE's) requirements for writing a business plan include the following general areas.

EXECUTIVE SUMMARY

The SBA, SCORE, and the authors recommend that an executive summary be attached to the beginning of the business plan. However, the executive summary should be written last because it recaps your overall business plan and convinces the reader to review your plan completely. The **executive summary** is the part of the business plan that investors review before they determine whether they want to read further. Your objective is to convince venture-capital investors or

---

[8]Detailed business plan outlines can be found on the SBA home page on the Internet at http://www.sba.gov.

other lenders to study your plan further. In approximately two pages or less, the executive summary should contain the following: your business strategy for success; a brief description of the market and what makes your business unique in that market; a brief description of the product or service; a brief description of the management team's qualifications that will add to the success of the business; a summary of annual revenue and expense projections, including net income (most lenders require 3-year projections); an estimate of how much money you need; and a statement of how you will use it. Once again, the executive summary is the initial introduction to the business plan that captures the reader's attention and entices the reader to learn more about the company.

GENERAL COMPANY DESCRIPTION

In the general company description, you begin by stating what business you will actually be in and what you will accomplish. The reader is going to look for a mission statement and specific goals and objectives. A **mission statement** is a brief statement explaining the purpose of the company and its guiding principles. The mission statement is not specific, but general in nature. For example: "The Walt Disney Company is committed to producing unparalleled entertainment experiences for the whole family based on its rich legacy of quality creative content and exceptional storytelling."[9] Wendy's mission statement is "to deliver superior quality products and services for our customers and communities through leadership, innovation and partnerships."[10]

Company goals should describe where you want your business to be at some future date. What is its destination? **Company objectives** are the milestones or progress markers used to see if we are on track in reaching our goal.

The *business philosophy* is what is important to you in your business. You should include a brief statement of who you will market your products to. A more thorough explanation should be stated in the marketing plan. Also include statements about your industry and where your niche is in the industry. This area should include your strengths and core competencies, factors that lead to success.

Identify the form of business ownership that you have selected for your business (sole proprietorship, partnership, corporation, or limited liability company). Explain your reasons for selecting your ownership structure. Include the advantages and the logical justification of your decision.

Products and Services

Provide a thorough description of the products and services that you intend to market.

---

[9]Walt Disney Company, *2004 Annual Report*. Retrieved from http://corporate.disney.go.com/investors/annual_reports/2004/introduction/company_overview/overview.html.

[10]Wendy's International Inc. http://www.wendys-invest.com/main/plan.php.

Marketing Plan

The **marketing plan** is that part of the business plan that describes how your business will move your products or services from the producer to the consumer. The marketing plan includes the identification of the why and how of market research as well as who you are targeting. In addition, a *marketing mix*—a marketing strategy consisting of the product, price, promotion, and place—should be created. The marketing plan should also contain a *positioning statement,* which defines what position your product or service occupies in the mind of the consumer.

Market research must be accomplished to make sure that you are on track and gathering information from two sources of data: primary and secondary. *Primary research* is gathering your own data firsthand; examples include focus groups, checking internal company records, interviews, mailings, and questionnaires. *Secondary research* uses existing information that is not part of your own company's records; it uses public information via libraries, the Internet, or industry publications. This allows you to gather information about your products and how your competitor's products and services differ from yours.

Identify your target market in terms of who are your customers. Use demographic information such as age, gender, income, race, educational level, residence, and home ownership. Your marketing mix should consist of

- **Product.** What decisions will you make with regard to branding, packaging, and labeling?
- **Promotion.** What is your message, and how will you convey this message? Design a promotional mix that includes advertising, sales promotion, personal selling, and public relations.
- **Price.** What factors affect your pricing decision? What is your pricing strategy? Example: Will you price below the competition?
- **Place.** What channels of distribution (place) will be used to reach your market? How will you position your product or service in the mind of the consumer?
- What macro- and microeconomic variables may have an effect on your product or service?

One of the items quite often overlooked in a small business marketing plan is government contracts as a source of revenue and a place to market your company. Too few small businesses realize the importance of obtaining government contracts. We discuss the federal government's contracting programs, especially those for small business. It is important to understand that virtually all state, county, and municipal governments as well as the federal government issue contracts. Many of these governments and their agencies cooperate with the SBA and provide specific assistance programs for small business. The federal government guidelines for awarding contracts are covered in the Federal Acquisition

Regulation (FAR), specifically Part 19, Small Business Programs.[11] The SBA counsels and assists small businesses and contracting personnel to insure that a fair proportion of contracts awarded for supplies and services are placed with small businesses (19.201 a).

Set-asides are federal government programs that identify specific business groups who are underrepresented in obtaining contracts. Businesses owned by members of these groups are given preference when contracts are awarded. There are specific set-aside provisions for the following types of small businesses:

♦ Historically Underutilized Business Zone (HUBZone) is an urban or rural area that has been determined to be underutilized and needs development. The SBA helps promote economic development by providing contract preferences to small businesses that are established in these areas and employ individuals who live in these areas.

♦ In addition, there are set-aside programs for specific classes of small businesses that include businesses owned by women, veterans, and disabled veterans. The SBA has personnel who are trained in helping these groups obtain necessary financing and contracting support. For veterans and disabled veterans, the SBA uses the Patriot Express Program, which assists these groups in expediting their requests.

In order to qualify for government contract consideration, your business must register and create a business profile with the Central Contractor Registration at www.ccr.gov. The Central Contractor Registration (CCR) is the primary registrant database for the U.S. Federal Government. The website provides Internet links and specific guidance for registration. Prior to registration, a small business must meet the following four requirements:

1. Have a Data Universal Numbering System (DUNS) Number provided by Dun and Bradstreet (D&B). You can request a DUNS number online at no charge. Obtaining a DUNS number for your business takes approximately 24 hours.

2. Have a Tax Identification Number (TIN) and Taxpayer Name. This information is obtained from the IRS.

3. Have statistical information, which includes receipts, number of employees, and locations of your business. Complete requirements are found on the CCR home page.

4. Have Electronic Funds Transfer (EFT) information, which requires your bank routing number and account numbers, for payment of invoices.[12]

---

[11]General Services Administration; Department of Defense; National Aeronautics and Space Administration. (March 2005) *Federal Acquisition Regulation*, Volume I—Parts 1 to 51.

[12]Central Contract Registration, *Small Business, Start New Registration*. Retrieved January 16, 2008 from http://www.ccr.gov/start.aspx.

Operational Plan

The *operational plan* describes how your business will actually deliver your product or service. It should include the location, processes, equipment, and people that will be used to provide the products or services to your customer. Classify your business by the amount of customer contact (high contact or low contact). *High contact* is working directly with the customer, such as getting a haircut or massage. *Low contact* is repairing something for a customer, such as a computer. How is value added to your product? What is the process used from input to transformation to output and subsequent delivery of the product or service? How is your facility laid out? What worker training is required? The link to the operational plan template is contained on the accompanying website (www. prenhall.com/adelman). It provides the details that must be included in the operational plan: production, location, legal environment (licensing, bonding, permits), personnel, inventory, suppliers, credit policies, and management of accounts receivable and payable. Much of this requires specific financial knowledge, which is covered in Chapters 3 through 10.

Management and Organization

Describe who will manage the business on a day-to-day basis. What are the qualifications of the management team and the distinctive competencies of the managers? If your business includes more than 10 people, you must have an organizational chart. Include position descriptions of key employees. Who are your professional advisors? Do you have an insurance agent, banker, attorney, accountant, board of directors, or advisory board?

Personal Financial Statements

You must include the personal financial statements for each owner or major stockholder, which shows assets, liabilities, and net worth. These items are covered in detail in Chapter 3.

Start-Up Expenses and Capital

All the expenses required for starting a business take considerable research, which we cover in detail in Chapter 6. You must determine all start-up costs associated with beginning a business, including construction, rent, equipment, personnel, utilities, licenses, deposits, advertising, inventory, and a myriad of other expenses that are unique to each business enterprise. There is a link to an Excel template for start-up expenses on the accompanying website and on the SCORE home page. After conducting all of your research, SCORE recommends adding a 20 percent contingency expense to these figures, because things always occur that were not planned for.

Financial Plan

The financial plan consists of a 12-month projection, a 4-year profit projection, break-even analysis, income statements, balance sheets, and cash-flow projections. These items are so important to the success of a business that we devote several sections and chapters to them. Financial statements (personal financial, income, balance sheets, and cash flow) are covered in Chapter 3; analysis of financial statements in Chapter 4; break-even analysis in Chapter 5; and projections, forecasting, and pro forma statements in Chapter 6. There are also links to templates for these statements contained on the accompanying website and on the SCORE home page.

Appendices

To complete your business plan, you must attach supporting documentation. These may include brochures, advertising materials, business cards, industry studies, maps and photos of location, detailed lists of equipment owned or to be purchased, copies of leases or contracts, letters of support from suppliers and future customers, market research studies, and a list of assets available as collateral for a loan. You basically want to include all materials that are required to support the assumptions made in the business plan.

The previous information is a synopsis of information contained in the SCORE "Business Plan for a Startup Business." SCORE also has a template for a "Business Plan for an Established Business." Links for these templates are contained on the Prentice Hall website for this textbook. They can also be found on the SCORE home page at http://www.score.org in the Business Toolbox, Template Gallery.

The IRS also has a checklist for starting a business. The checklist is found on the IRS home page at http://www.irs.gov. At this website, simply type in the keyword *checklist* in keyword search terms at the upper right side of the page. The checklist requires that a business complete five items:

- ◆ Apply for an Employer Identification Number (EIN).
- ◆ Select a business structure.
- ◆ Choose a tax year.
- ◆ Choose your accounting method.
- ◆ Complete the required forms if you have employees.
- ◆ Pay your business taxes.[13]

BUSINESS OWNERSHIP SUCCESSION PLANS

A specific item that is not covered in a typical business plan is the *succession plan*. Because many small businesses are family owned, it is extremely important for

---

[13]Internal Revenue Service, United States Department of the Treasury, Checklist for Starting a Business. Retrieved January 18, 2008 from http://www.irs.gov/businesses/small/article/0,,id=98810,00.html.

the entrepreneur to determine who will take over the business if the entrepreneur is unable to function because of accident, severe illness, or death. As previously pointed out in the discussion concerning partnerships, a buy–sell agreement is activated if a triggering event occurs. It is important to understand that this agreement is used as a way of transferring family and business ownership across generations. The buy–sell agreement is one aspect of succession planning. Gaining acceptance from all owners and involved family members is a requirement of establishing a successful succession plan. In addition to general partnerships, such transfers may also occur in sole proprietorships, C-corporations, S-corporations and LLCs. However, it is imperative that the sole proprietor have a business succession plan in place, because the assets of the family are usually the assets of the business. The buy–sell agreement is a tangible item that is overt, whereas the overall business succession plan is intangible and covert. The reason for this is that there is a multitude of non-financial factors that should be recognized by the entrepreneur:

- The owner's and spouse's goals should be on the same page with respect to continuing or discontinuing the business on the owner's death.
- Does the entrepreneur want his or her heirs to receive ownership rights directly, or in a trust?
- Should ownership be held by family members only, or should it be allowed to pass to non-family members?
- An entrepreneur should gather as much data as possible from his or her spouse and children and use this feedback when formulating a buy–sell agreement or a specific succession plan with an attorney and other advisors.

FINANCING A BUSINESS OR RAISING CAPITAL

An integral part of your business plan includes a section on how you plan to obtain financing or raise capital. There are *suppliers* of funds and *users* of funds. Bankers and investors are suppliers of funds. There is a very important difference between bankers and investors. *Bankers* and other lenders increase your debt. Loans of any type fall under debt financing. *Investors* provide you with equity financing for your business in exchange for partial ownership. The investor is the supplier of funds, and you (the entrepreneur) are the user of funds.

Bankers differ from investors in several ways, and a business plan must address these differences. Bankers are normally not investors, but are lenders (suppliers of funds). Bankers are looking for assurance of interest payments and repayment of the principal amount of the loan. They insist on the inclusion of the following items in your proposal:

- The amount of the loan
- How the funds will be used
- What the loan will accomplish and how it will make the business stronger

♦ How many years it will take to repay the loan
♦ What collateral you are offering for the loan

Investors are partial owners of the business and are looking for company growth and an increase in company equity so they can increase their return on equity. For the investor, the business plan should include

♦ The amount of the investment
♦ The short-term proportion of the investment
♦ The long-term proportion of the investment
♦ The percentage of the business that the investor will actually own
♦ The involvement of the investors in managing and overseeing the company
♦ The number of years it will take to recover the investment
♦ The *profit potential* (return on equity) of the business
♦ The proposed exit strategy for the investor (e.g., purchase agreement, initial public offering)

Any lender or investor is going to want to know what your financial commitment is to the business. Are you using savings, loans from family members, second mortgages, or credit? There are several sources of funds for start-up or expanding companies. Some of them are **personal assets**, which include an individual's savings, credit cards, and home-equity loans.

A business normally goes through several stages from its initial stage to maturity.

♦ **Seed/Start-Up Stage:** The initial stage. In this beginning stage the company has a concept and is normally less than 18 months old.
♦ **Early Stage:** Company is less than 3 years old and the product or service is commercially available.
♦ **Expansion Stage:** Company is older than 3 years and has high revenue growth but may or may not show a profit. Even if it shows a profit, it may not generate a sufficient amount of cash flow to stay afloat.
♦ **Later Stage:** Product or service is widely available. The company generates revenue and probably has a positive cash flow.[14]

SOURCES OF FINANCING

There are several sources of financing for business:

Personal assets include the individual's savings, investments (stocks and bonds), credit cards, and home-equity loans.

Equity financing includes company-retained earnings and using the fixed assets of a company (buildings, equipment, and inventory) as collateral to obtain loans.

---

[14]Susan Preston. Federal Document Clearing House Congressional Testimony, *Congressional Quarterly, Inc.*, April 13, 2005.

Small Business Administration, which has two major programs: 7(a) for general business purposes and 504 for the purchase of buildings or major equipment. The SBA does not actually lend the money, but is a guarantor for small business loans.

The SBA's 504 Loan Program is primarily for major machinery or building construction or expansion, and is designed primarily to enable small businesses to create and retain jobs. A typical 504 project requires only a 10 percent down payment from the borrower. Applications are normally made through the state's Certified Development Corporation.

The 7(a) Guarantee Loan Program is the SBA's primary multipurpose small business loan program. The SBA provides the lender with a guarantee for reimbursement for a percentage of the loan amount. The maximum amount of the guarantee is $2,000,000. Interest rates may be fixed or variable and are pegged to the prime lending rate, with prime plus 2.25 percent as the minimum and prime plus 4.75 percent as the maximum. This depends on the loan amount and the maturity period of the loan. The SBA requires that the borrower complete the following prior to applying for an SBA guaranteed loan:

1. Create your business plan and or a loan proposal.
2. Learn how to approach a lender by attending a free SCORE loan clinic or meet with a Small Business Development Center counselor or visit a Women's Business Center.
3. Make an appointment with an SBA 7(a) lender.

There are several other SBA programs, many of which target specific groups.

♦ Micro-loan Technical Assistance Grants expand and enhance organizations that provide small businesses with technical assistance.
♦ SBA Micro-loan program provides funding to non-profit intermediaries who make micro-loans in amounts ranging from $100 to $35,000. These are primarily for businesses that are profitable, but need some assistance and would not normally qualify for traditional loans.
♦ Patriot Express Pilot Loan Initiative: The United States has had thousands of service-related injuries and family displacements since 9/11. We have actually been involved in this military action for a period that exceeds World War II. Realizing this, the SBA began a loan initiative specifically geared toward

> assisting veterans and members of the military community wanting to establish or expand small businesses. Eligible military community members include: Veterans, Service-disabled veterans, active-duty service members eligible for the military's Transition Assistance Program, Reservists and National Guard members, Current spouses of any of the above, the widowed spouse of a service member or veteran who died during service or of a

service-connected disability. The SBA and its resource partners are focusing additional efforts on counseling and training to augment this loan initiative.[15]

♦ **The U.S. Chamber of Commerce** is another source of financing and general information for small business. On a local basis, there are chambers of commerce located within most cities, and many of these organizations are concerned with the success of small businesses.

Angel Investors provide the seed money for the start-up and early stages of company growth. They are usually wealthy individuals who are committed to seeing businesses succeed in their local communities. They provide their own money ranging from $25,000 to $250,000. They usually take an active position and provide mentoring and experience to the company. Angels are looking for a positive return on investment, but are also aware that they could lose their entire investment.[16]

Venture capitalists normally provide financing at the expansion and later stages of business development. They tend to invest in companies with proven track records that require financing to expand enough to become profitable and eventually a public company. The venture capital firms typically invest several million dollars with the full expectation of a significant return on their investment.

There are several sources of capital and the SBA (http://www.sba.gov) is an excellent source for initial queries with regard to loans and equity financing. We recommend that you shop for money and financing. Ask other business owners where they obtained their financing. How satisfied were they? What are the local sources of capital? Does your state have agencies that are devoted to assisting business? Do you have angels in your community?

Grants

Grants are moneys provided to business and other entities that don't have to be repaid as long as the grantee performs the services for which the grant was approved. There are many groups and organizations eligible to apply for government grants. The total annual dollar value of government grants exceeds $400 billion. Included in this program are small businesses as defined by the SBA. The most common size standards for small businesses are as follows:

♦ 500 employees for most manufacturing and mining industries
♦ 100 employees for all wholesale trade industries
♦ $6 million for most retail and service industries
♦ $28.5 million for most general- and heavy-construction industries

---

[15] *SBA Patriot Express, Your Key to Business Success*. Retrieved December 21, 2007, from http://www.sba.gov/patriotexpress/index.html.

[16] Susan, Preston. Federal Document Clearing House Congressional Testimony, *Congressional Quarterly, Inc.*, April 13, 2005.

♦ $12 million for all special trade contractors

♦ $0.75 million for most agricultural industries

Note that about one fourth of industries have a size standard that is different from these levels. They vary from $0.75 million to $28.5 million for size standards based on average annual revenues, and from 100 to 1,500 employees for size standards based on number of employees.[17]

CONCLUSION

In this chapter, we discussed the functions of management and how they relate to business. Special emphasis was placed on the requirement for the entrepreneur to set specific business goals and its importance to business planning. We distinguished between limited and unlimited liability and compared and contrasted the various legal business forms. The advantages and disadvantages of each business form were discussed. We then provided an outline of the development of a business plan. We also discussed the importance of writing a business succession plan and provided in-depth coverage of financing a business.

Note how much of the plan contains requirements for financial forms that must be submitted to obtain a business loan or equity financing. The methods used to generate these forms and a deeper understanding of their meanings are covered in later chapters. In Chapter 3, we begin by defining the forms; in Chapter 4, we analyze the forms; and in Chapter 6, we generate pro forma financial statements.

Filling out forms is one thing; making sure that they are correct and will be accepted by a lending institution or investor is another. We hope to facilitate the latter with this textbook.

REVIEW AND DISCUSSION QUESTIONS

1. What is planning? Compare strategic planning with functional planning.
2. What role does goal setting play in the planning process?
3. Develop a list of at least 10 products that exist today that did not exist 10 years ago.
4. What are the five functions of a manager?
5. What are the three steps of controlling?
6. List and briefly explain three forms of business ownership.
7. What is meant by *unlimited liability*?
8. How does a limited partnership differ from a general partnership?

---

[17]Grants.gov: *Who Is Eligible for a Grant?* Retrieved December 21, 2007, from http://grants.gov/aboutgrants/eligibility.jsp.

9. What advantages does a corporation have over a sole proprietorship? What are the disadvantages of a corporation?

10. What distinct advantage does a private or Subchapter S–corporation have over the public corporation?

11. What are the pitfalls of franchising?

12. List and describe the components of a SWOT analysis.

13. List the major components of a business plan. What components are of primary concern to you, and why?

14. What is the significance of a business succession plan?

15. What role does the buy–sell agreement occupy in a business succession plan?

16. Discuss the federal government's contracting programs.

EXERCISES AND PROBLEMS

1. Carol Jones wants her business to increase sales by 50 percent over the next 5 years. To do this, she must hire three more people. She wants to determine how to evaluate these people, so she lists their job specifications and develops job descriptions. She also lists where these employees would work and what training they would require. What management functions is Carol performing, and how do they apply to this scenario?

2. Jerry is a personnel manager for a large retail department store. He just received a memo stating that the company will build three new stores in Phoenix over the next 5 years, with one store opening in 24 months, one opening in 36 months, and one opening in 60 months. The memo that Jerry received relates to what type of business plan? If Jerry is directed to develop a personnel plan for Phoenix, what type of planning will Jerry be doing?

3. Joe Doe just started a business. He wants the business income to flow directly to his own personal tax return, but he wants to make sure that he has limited liability. What form(s) of business ownership would you recommend for Joe?

4. You buy 1,000 shares of ABC Co. at $6 per share. The company is sued for millions of dollars, and ABC Co. is forced into bankruptcy. The newspaper stated that the cost of this suit would amount to $12 per share of stock. What is the maximum amount of money you can lose with this investment? Why?

5. Sam Jones, Mary Adams, and Larry Brown have been talking about starting their own business for several years. Sam is an electronic repairman, Mary is a partner in a large law firm, and Larry is an excellent salesperson. Sam and Larry will work in the business on an equal basis. It costs $100,000 to start this business. Sam has no money, Mary has $60,000, and Larry has $40,000. If they form a partnership, how would you recommend that they organize?

6. Barry McGuire wants to purchase a dry-cleaning establishment. Barry has heard of the SWOT analysis and wants to use this methodology to determine whether he should purchase the business. He found the following information: The dry cleaner is located in a busy shopping center and currently does all the cleaning on the premises. It has three commercial

accounts that make up 20 percent of its business. The population in the local area is growing by approximately 6 percent per year. Located across the street in another shopping center is a price-cutting dry cleaner that advertises heavily in the local area. With the exception of this shopping center and the property across the street, all property in this area is zoned residential. Most of the residents in this area are professional people who wear suits to work. The shop has an assumable lease, and the lease has a fixed rental fee for the next 5 years. Barry has had 5 years of experience in the dry-cleaning business and would run the shop full time. Based on this information, perform a SWOT analysis.

7. Joe Latte wants to open up a coffee and gelato shop. He figures with the popularity of coffee shops and Italian ice cream shops that a combination business will be a clear winner. Write a two-page paper describing the following elements of a business plan: description of the business, factors affecting location, and product or service to be offered.

8. Joe Latte completed a business plan and determines that it will take $120,000 to open the coffee and gelato shop. He has $30,000 of his own money and will have to obtain $90,000 in loans or grants. How should Joe go about getting financing? What is the probability that he can obtain a grant to start a combination coffee and Italian ice cream shop?

SUGGESTED GROUP PROJECT

1. Determine a business for the group to start. Do a SWOT analysis on the business and the team members.
2. Each team member selects two factors that help make up a business plan and explains these factors to their other teammates. Teams determine what is covered and how it relates to the rest of the plan's factors

CASE STUDY: INTRODUCTION TO ENTREPRENEURSHIP

© 2008 Phillip J. Adelman and Alan M. Marks

Arthur Martin was raised in New York City during the 1950s. Art's very first job was working in his grandfather's candy store and coffee shop. He was 9 years old when he began working part-time during his summer break from school. While at the store, he learned the American Monetary System and how to ring up a sale for cash and give change. He could not put it into words, but he knew that some customers owed his grandfather money, and somehow his grandfather kept a record of this. He knew this because when certain individuals said, "Put it on my tab," they meant, "I have no money now but I will pay you later when I get paid." He also learned inventory control as well as customer service. With respect to inventory, he observed that some items were more important than others. Art's grandfather made sure that the store had a safety stock of top-selling cigarettes as well as a safety stock of coffee. One of Art's responsibilities was to make sure that the cigarette display behind the counter was always filled to the top of the display. Also, Art had to make sure the bottled beverages were cold by always keeping the refrigerator well stocked. Art's grandfather sold the business when Art was 11.

When Art was 12, he worked for a butcher store as a delivery boy. He remembers going from one apartment building to another on his bicycle with the meat delivery bag in his basket. He got paid $3 per day, and even more money from the tips he received from the people he delivered to than the butcher was paying him. Between deliveries, Art sat in the butcher shop while waiting for a delivery and watched what took place. He learned that an important part of business was to make the customer feel that he or she was special—or at least get them to perceive that they were special. Art's use of observation at the job site was a valuable experience. He noticed that the customer was always right.

When Art was 14, he applied for working papers that would allow him to work a 40-hour workweek at minimum wage during his summer break. Art got a job at S.E. Nichols in the Greenwich Village section of New York City as a stockboy. S.E. Nichols was a 5&10 chain store that had 11 stores scattered around the New York City Metropolitan Area. Their competitors were W.T. Grant, J.C. Penny, F.W. Woolworth, and Kresges, which later became K-Mart. At that time the minimum wage was $1.00 per hour. Art started working in the stockroom and was subsequently asked to work upstairs on the floor. All managers in the company started in the stockroom. It was the stockroom where retailing began. As the shipments came in, it was the stock clerk's job to match the inventory against the invoice. As a stock clerk, you could create a system where you could learn what was carried by the store, its cost price, and how much of the item you had in stock at the time. If you were asked to work on the floor, it meant that you were on your way to management. It was here on the floor that Art supervised 21 counters and the individuals associated with each counter. Each counter represented a separate department; for example, there was the cosmetic counter, the housewares counter, and the stationery counter.

Art was given a great deal of responsibility and the authority to make decisions. He purchased glassware that the consumer bought and in so doing he taught himself how to forecast. By using experience and a little intuition, Art became excellent in forecasting. He continued to work at the 5&10 for 4 years. He worked all day Saturday and two evenings a week during his senior year in high school. When Art was about to graduate high school, Management approached him and asked him if he would consider starting out as an assistant manager and eventually moving up the corporate ladder. He knew retailing very well, but he also knew that he did not want to miss out on a college education.

QUESTIONS

1. What were the management functions that Art used in his grandfather's store and at S.E. Nichols? How were these functions carried out by the business?
2. Based on the duties that Art performed in his grandfather's store and at S.E. Nichols, should Art be paid minimum wage? If your answer is yes, why? If your answer is no, why not?
3. Art's grandfather asks you to advise him on what form of business ownership he should create. Select a form of ownership for Art's grandfather and list and explain its advantages and disadvantages.

BUSINESS PLAN OUTLINE

Use the following outline as a guide.

Elements of a Business Plan

1. Cover sheet
2. Statement of purpose
3. Table of contents
    I. The Business
        A. Description of business
        B. Marketing
        C. Competition
        D. Operating procedures
        E. Personnel
        F. Business insurance
        G. Financial data
    II. Financial Data
        A. Loan applications
        B. Capital equipment and supply list
        C. Balance sheet
        D. Break-even analysis
        E. Pro Forma Income Projections (Profit and Loss Statements)
            ◆ Three-year summary
            ◆ Detail by month, first year
            ◆ Detail by quarters, second and third years
            ◆ Assumptions on which projections were based
        F. Pro Forma Cash Flow
            ◆ Three-year summary
            ◆ Detail by month, first year
            ◆ Detail by quarters, second and third years
            ◆ Assumptions on which projections were based
    III. Supporting Documents
        A. Tax returns of principals for the past 3 years
        B. Personal financial statement (all banks have these forms)
        C. In the case of a franchised business, a copy of the franchise contract and all supporting documents provided by the franchisor
        D. Copy of proposed lease or purchase agreement for building space
        E. Copy of licenses and other legal documents
        F. Copy of resumes of all principals
        G. Copies of letters of intent from suppliers, and so on.

CHAPTER 3

Financial Statements

Learning Objectives

When you have completed this chapter, you should be able to:

- ♦ Understand how financial statements are used by businesses.
- ♦ Understand the differences and similarities between a personal cash flow statement and a business income statement.
- ♦ Distinguish between fixed and variable expenses.
- ♦ Understand the changes in income statements that exist with different forms of business.
- ♦ Understand the differences and similarities that exist between a personal statement of financial position and a business balance sheet.
- ♦ Analyze the components of the basic accounting equation.
- ♦ Distinguish between assets and liabilities.
- ♦ Understand the relationship between fixed assets and depreciation.
- ♦ Understand the significance of the statement of cash flows.
- ♦ Given the basic data for a company, construct a financial statement.
- ♦ Understand the problems that may exist with financial statements.

Every business, regardless of its legal business form, has the same basic financial statements. These statements are used by the business for the internal control of finance, as well as by external parties who want to invest in the business or who will provide the business with financial capital for start-up or for continuing operations. These external parties are current or potential creditors (e.g., banks, vendors, landlords) and investors (e.g., angels, venture capitalists, future partners, stockholders, owners). Creditors and investors use these statements to determine the basic health of the business. Data from these statements are used to evaluate a company's track record, present status, and future financial direction.

In this chapter, we discuss financial statements for individuals, sole proprietorships, partnerships, and corporations. When these forms are identical, we note it in the text; however, when there is a difference in the forms, we will note each variation with a separate form.

For the *public corporation* (a corporation whose stock is publicly traded), the SEC requires that financial statements be audited by an independent certified public accountant (CPA) in accordance with accounting principles established by the Financial Accounting Standards Board (FASB). Although audits are not required for (private) businesses, we recommend that you use an accountant to help you set up the books and provide you with a compilation or review of the business's financial statements. Hiring an accountant is money well spent, because it allows the entrepreneur to concentrate on managing the business, rather than on spending many hours reinventing a wheel that is already round. In addition, most accountants can save you added expense in the long run by recognizing and solving problems that arise in the normal course of your business.

Most of us as business owners will not have a full-time accountant—and we do not necessarily need one; however, we definitely need some type of accounting information system that performs the accounting function. There are several excellent computerized accounting packages on the market for businesses. Once a system is established, your accountant may spend very little time evaluating your books, except at year-end, when they must be closed out and taxes must be paid. The amount of time the accountant spends on your books depends on the complexity of the business and external user requirements (e.g., lending institution requirements). Lending institutions may require monthly, quarterly, or annual statements.

Most of us are familiar with personal financial statements if we have ever applied for credit, purchased a home, or applied for a bank loan. We begin by looking at a typical bank application form. When any customer applies for a business loan, most banks require a **financial statement (personal form)**. This statement is a single form that actually is composed of two segments—the statement of financial position and the personal cash flow statement—and is shown in Table 3–1. We cover all the information required for this form by looking separately at the component forms, and then we compare what we see with the typical statements required in business.

We begin by looking at the individual's **cash flow statement** and discussing its business equivalent, the **income statement**. We next evaluate an individual's **statement of financial position** and expand our discussion to show how this form equates in business to the **balance sheet**, or a company's statement of financial position.

TABLE 3–1 Financial Statement, Personal Form

FINANCIAL STATEMENT Personal Form

First Any Kind of Bank:		Office:	
Name:		Social Security No:	
Address:		Business Phone:	
City, State, Zip:		Home Phone:	
Spouse Name:		Social Security No:	
Assets:	In Dollars	Liabilities:	In Dollars
Cash in This Bank: Checking		Loans Payable This Bank:	
Savings:		Loans Payable Other Financial Institutions: (Schedule 6)	
Cash In Other Financial Institutions:		Accounts Payable Other Firms & Individuals: (Schedule 6)	
		Credit Cards:	
Marketable Stocks and Bonds: (Schedule 1)		Income & Other Taxes Payable:	
Accounts Receivable: (Schedule 2)		Real Estate Taxes:	
Total Current Assets		Total Current Liabilities:	
Notes or Mortgages Receivable: (Schedule 3)		Other Real Estate Indebtedness: (Schedule 5)	
Cash Surrender Value Life Insurance: (Schedule 4)		Life Insurance Loans: (Schedule 4)	
Vehicles (Year & Make):		Other Long-Term Debts: (Describe)	
Real Estate: (Schedule 5)			
Other Personal Property:		Total Liabilities:	
Total Assets:		Total Assets-Total Liabilities = Net Worth	
Annual Income:		Annual Fixed Expenses:	
Gross Salary:		Real Estate Payments: (Schedule 3)	
Spouse's Gross Salary:		Rent:	
Bonuses & Commissions:		Income Taxes:	
Income from Securities: (Schedule 1)		Property Taxes:	
Rental or Lease Income: (Schedule 3)		Alimony, Child Support:	
Mortgages or Contract Income: (Schedule 3)		Insurance Premiums:	
Other Income (Describe):		Other (Describe):	
Total Gross Income:		Total Annual Expenses:	
Less-Total Expenses:			
Net Cash Income:			

PERSONAL CASH FLOW STATEMENT

Table 3–2 shows a personal cash flow (income) statement, which evaluates all earnings, or *inflows,* and expenses, or *outflows.* Our inflows are basically all annual income before taxes. Included in income are wages and salaries, interest income on investments, dividend income on stock investments, and capital gains on the sale of assets that have appreciated. Outflows are expenses, which are typically of two types: First are those over which we have some control, such as food, clothing, and automobile expenses and are called **variable expenses** because the amount that we spend each month or year typically varies. For example, automobile expenses include gas, oil, and maintenance. We usually do not spend the same amount per month on automobile expenses. The second type of expenses are those over which we have little or no control, such as mortgage payments, automobile loan or lease payments, property taxes, insurance, income taxes, and loan payments, and are called **fixed expenses**, which are often contractual in nature.

TABLE 3–2 Jones Family, Personal Income Statement

The Tom Jones Family
Personal Income Statement
(Cash Flow Statement)
January 1, 2008 to December 31, 2008

INCOME			
Salaries		$60,000	
Interest Income		740	
TOTAL INCOME			$60,740
FIXED EXPENSES			
Mortgage Payment	$9,600		
Automobile Payment	5,040		
Property Taxes	1,235		
Insurance	4,500		
Income Taxes	5,032		
Savings and Investment	1,200		
Personal Loan Payment	900		
TOTAL FIXED EXPENSES		$27,507	
VARIABLE EXPENSES			
Food	$5,485		
Transportation	2,500		
Utilities	1,800		
Clothes and Personal	2,700		
Recreation and Vacation	2,780		
TOTAL VARIABLE EXPENSES		$15,265	
TOTAL EXPENSES			$42,772
(Cash Balance at the end of the year)			$17,968

After paying all variable and fixed expenses, we arrive at *net cash income,* which is our personal bottom line. Creditors look at this figure to determine if we can afford to increase our fixed expenses in the form of a loan, or if we can afford to increase our variable expenses in the form of a credit card. You may consider yourself in financial trouble if you already have a low or negative net cash income.

In looking at Table 3–2, we note that the Tom Jones family has net cash income of $17,968 at the end of 2008. This figure is sufficient for a bank to grant additional credit in the form of a credit card or for the family to qualify for a fixed loan. For example, if Tom wanted to purchase a new car with monthly payments of $450, many banks would grant him this loan. If he purchased the new car, his annual loan obligation would be $5,400. Table 3–2 shows he has net cash income of $17,968, which is more than enough to cover the new car loan obligation of $5,400. It would not be unusual for the bank to grant additional credit to Tom Jones: Let's be honest: You or I would also grant this loan.

INCOME STATEMENT
CHART OF ACCOUNTS

In accounting, the *general ledger,* also known as the *nominal ledger,* is a collection of all of the firm's accounts and uses double-entry bookkeeping to track these accounts, which are all activities of a business. The general ledger uses a chart of accounts that lists every transaction of the business. When you first organize a business, your accountant or the accounting software that you purchased for the business breaks all entries into a chart of accounts, and each account is accompanied by a reference number. For most small business the chart of accounts lists four numbers for each item; for example: Asset accounts use 1,000 to 1,999; Liability accounts 2,000 to 2,999, and so on. Financial statements consolidate the chart of account entries. We provide a case study at the end of this chapter that shows financial statements using the chart of accounts. However, within the textbook, because this is a financial text and not an accounting text, we use consolidated business forms.

Let us now look at an income statement for a business and see how this equates to the cash flow statement for Tom Jones. The **income statement** is like a motion picture: It shows what has happened during the accounting period with regard to the revenues (income) and expenditures (expenses) of the business. The normal accounting period is 1 year; however, companies typically generate an income statement on a monthly basis to determine how the company is doing, and to compare a specific month to the same month in previous years and to past months during the current year.

For external reporting, corporations typically generate quarterly income statements. They often issue quarterly reports to stockholders and other creditors and investors. For forecasting and internal auditing, however, they use monthly income statements to compare results with those from the same month in previous years. In addition, if you apply for a business loan through a Small Business Administration (SBA) resource, they require a monthly pro forma income statement for the first year of a company's operation and quarterly for the next 2 years. A **pro forma** financial statement is developed to project the future condition of a business based on a forecast. It projects future income and expenses as determined by a forecast of future operations.

The income statement for a business can be equated with the personal cash flow statement or personal income statement (Table 3–2). When we compare this personal income statement with a company's income statement (Table 3–3), we see several similarities.

A business income statement can be divided into three sections. The first section shows gross revenues (sales) minus returns and allowances, which equals net sales; net sales minus cost of goods sold equals gross profit. The second section shows gross profit minus operating expenses, which equals operating income (net income before interest and taxes). The third section shows operating income minus interest, which equals earnings before taxes minus taxes (if the business is a corporation), which equals net income (profit).

TABLE 3–3 Income Statement for a Sole Proprietorship, Partnership, Limited Liability Company, or Subchapter S-Corporation

The Tom Jones Company
Income Statement
January 1, 2008, through December 31, 2008

Gross Sales	$350,642		
Less: Returns and Allowances	2,366		
Net Sales		$348,276	
Cost of Goods Sold		124,276	
Gross Profit			$224,000
Operating Expenses			
Salaries Expense	$95,000		
Rent Expense	24,000		
Property Taxes Expense	2,500		
Depreciation Expense	6,000		
Utilities Expense	10,250		
Advertising Expense	9,250		
Insurance Expense	3,000		
Total Operating Expenses		150,000	
Operating Income			$74,000
Other Expenses			
Interest Expense		10,000	
Net Income*			$64,000

*This line on an Income Statement for a Corporation appears as Net Income before Income Taxes; see Table 3–3a.

Let's define the preceding terms more carefully. **Revenues** are all sales of products and services for the company. Next we consider **returns and allowances**. Regardless of how perfect we wish to make our products, there will always be some customers who are not satisfied or some products that were sold but are defective. In such cases, we usually provide a refund of purchase price or grant some allowance (increased warranty, partial credit on next purchase, etc.) to the customer. Another type of allowance comes into play when the company is a manufacturer and the customer is a retailer. The retailer may be given allowances in the form of a trade discount or a series of discounts for services that are performed by the retailer for the manufacturer. For example, if you manufacture bicycles, you could give your retailer a trade discount for assembling and displaying your product in a highly marketable fashion. In addition, you might offer a trade discount for retail promotion or advertising. Some retailers who buy your bicycles for resale might take advantage of one or more of your discounts. Because you do not know in advance how much these amounts are, you keep track of it during the accounting period. **Net sales** are the revenue you have after you have accounted for any sales returns and allowances and any sales discounts.

Cost of goods sold (COGS) is the amount it costs us to obtain the items that we sell. COGS typically include the costs of materials, direct labor, and overhead allocated specifically to the product. For the retail store, these are the total costs, to the store, of its merchandise (including freight and cost of merchandise). For the manufacturing firm, there are manufacturing labor costs, measurable machine costs, costs of raw materials and fabricated parts, and the allocation of factory overhead. COGS represents most of the variable costs of manufacturing firms. **Variable costs** are driven directly by the volume of product flow. The **gross profit** of a company is determined by subtracting COGS from net sales. An item is usually variable and is part of COGS if

The company allocates a percentage of the sales dollar to the item in question (e.g., factory overhead that is based on a percentage of direct labor or material cost)

The company can measure the cost that is used by the item in question accurately (raw material or component parts)

The cost occurs before the item is ready for sale

Operating expenses are usually the **fixed costs** of a business. Salaries for executives and administrative personnel, rental expenses, insurance, and advertising expenses are usually fixed and known in advance. When we say *fixed costs,* however, we do not necessarily mean that they do not vary; we mean that these are the expenses of a business that are not directly related to revenues or cost of goods sold. For example, the utility bills may vary considerably during the year, but they are still placed under the category of operating expenses. If you live in the northern United States, you know that your heating bill is much higher for January than it is for July, but this is still considered to be a fixed cost and is placed under operating expenses because it is not directly related to COGS. If an item cannot be allocated or measured based on sales dollars, it is usually an operating expense.

Operating income appears on the income statement as the result of subtracting the sum of our operating expenses from gross profit. Operating income can also be thought of as earnings from operations before interest and taxes are paid.

Interest expense is the interest accrued during the accounting period on money borrowed by our company. Once this interest expense is subtracted from operating income, we obtain earnings before taxes.

Earnings before taxes (net income before taxes) is the income we have before we pay income taxes to the governments that collect such taxes on the profits of businesses. This amount is the bottom line for the sole proprietorship, partnership, limited liability company (LLC), or Subchapter S corporation, because the profit of such a company is considered to be personal income and is reported on the individual's income tax statement. As discussed in Chapter 2, however, the corporation is subject to double taxation, and Table 3–3a shows the continuation of the income statement for a corporation.

Provision for income taxes (less income taxes) is based on the fact that corporate incomes are subject to a corporate income tax owed to the federal, state, and possibly municipal governments, all of which may charge income taxes on corporate earnings.

Net income is the profit after provision for income taxes and interest expenses for the corporation, and the profit after interest expense for the sole proprietorship, partnership, LLC, or Subchapter S corporation. (Table 3–3 and Table 3–3a show this difference.) For the corporation, this figure is net profit, after paying all expenses, including interest and taxes (shown in Table 3–3a as $53,000). For the sole proprietorship, partnership, LLC, or Subchapter S corporation, this item appears on the income statement immediately after interest expense (shown in Table 3–3 as $64,000) because income taxes for these businesses are paid by the individual owners rather than by the business.

Table 3–3a Income Statement, Corporation

The Tom Jones Company
Income Statement
January 1, 2008, through December 31, 2008

Net Income before Income Taxes*	$64,000
Less: Provision for Income Taxes	11,000
Net Income	$53,000
Net earnings per share of common stock:	$ 0.53
(100,000 shares outstanding)	

*This is the Net Income line on Table 3–3 for a sole proprietorship, partnership, subchapter S corporation or limited liability company. Taxes calculated from IRS Publication 542 (Rev February 2006), Tax Rate Table, page 17.

In this textbook, we use *C corporation* and *corporation* as one and the same. Subchapter S corporations are referred to as *Subchapter S corporations.* Remember that an income statement does not reflect cash flow. Sales for many businesses are recognized when the sale is made. However, sales may not all be paid for in cash; some may be on credit. Therefore, the income statement may show a sale as revenue, when in fact we may not collect the money for several months if the customer has charged this sale on a revolving credit line. In addition, expenses are recognized when we incur them, not when we pay them. This is the *accrual method of accounting.*

Say, for example, that your business pays its employees on the first and the fifteenth of each month. When you close out the books at the end of the month, you show all wages and salaries that are owed to your employees from the sixteenth to the last day of the month, but the checks will not be written or paid for until the beginning of the next month. In addition, taxes may be owed and other expenses may have been incurred but not yet actually paid for by your firm.

Earnings per share are how much a corporation has earned for each share of common stock outstanding. To obtain this figure, the corporation takes its net income and divides it by the total number of shares of common stock outstanding. For example, as shown in Table 3–3a, the Tom Jones Company had net income of $53,000 and 100,000 shares of common stock outstanding; its earnings per share were 53 cents. We obtain the number of shares outstanding from the balance sheet, which we discuss shortly.

Corporations are allowed to distribute their profit in the form of dividends to stockholders or to retain their earnings for future investment. *Retained earnings* provide the firm with an internal source of financing that can be used to purchase capital equipment and to acquire or merge with other companies. An advantage of using retained earnings for financing future operations is that the owners provide the capital so the company does not need external financing in the form of debt.

STATEMENT OF FINANCIAL POSITION

The **statement of financial position** (a personal balance sheet) indicates all items that are owned (assets) by the individual (or family) and all items that are owed (liabilities) by the individual (or family) at a specific point in time. Therefore, the statement of financial position is written with an *as of* date (the specific day for which it is valid); see Table 3–4 for the Tom Jones family statement of financial position. This statement is typically part of a bank loan application, and it is also computed by financial planners to assist an individual with planning a financial strategy.

TABLE 3–4 Statement of Financial Position (Balance Sheet)

**The Tom Jones Family
Statement of Financial Position
As of December 31, 2008**

Assets			
Cash and Cash Equivalents			
Cash and Checking Account	$ 1,900		
Savings Account	4,000		
Total Cash and Cash Equivalents		$ 5,900	
Invested Assets			
Stocks and Bonds	38,000		
Life Insurance Cash Value	5,500		
Total Invested Assets		$ 43,500	
Use Assets			
Residence	310,000		
Automobiles	45,000		
Furniture, clothing, jewelry, etc.	52,000		
Total Use Assets		$407,000	
Total Assets			$456,400
Liabilities and Net Worth			
Liabilities			
Homeowners Insurance Payable	975		
Credit Card Payable	4,500		
Automobile Note Payable	22,400		
Home Mortgage Payable	138,000		
Total Liabilities			$165,875
Net Worth			290,525
Total Liabilities and Net Worth			$456,400

As we did for the income statement, we now discuss each item on the statement of financial position to ensure our thorough understanding of this financial statement as business managers or owners. An **asset** is any item that is used or owned by the individual, business, or corporation. Assets usually are listed on these statements in order of **liquidity** (a measure of how fast an asset can be converted into cash). In other words, cash is the most liquid of assets, then savings accounts, certificates of deposit (because of the penalty for turning them into cash before the due date), and then stocks and bonds. The preceding items are **current assets**, because they usually can be converted into cash during the accounting year. Land, buildings, furniture, and clothing are **fixed assets**, because they usually are not used up during the accounting year. They are the least liquid of assets. It may be difficult to dispose of these items and obtain cash.

Looking at Table 3–4, we note that the current assets for Tom Jones and his family consist of cash and cash equivalents in the amount of $5,900 and invested assets of $43,500. The fixed assets (also called *use assets*) on the statement of financial position amount to $407,000. The total assets of the Tom Jones family are worth $456,400, but this does not necessarily reflect the wealth of the family, because many use assets are not usually owned free and clear, so the family may owe something on these items. To determine the family's real worth, we must determine how much is owed (what the family's total liabilities are).

Liabilities are that part of assets that is owed to others. These items are primarily financed by debt. Tom Jones owes $975 on his homeowner's insurance, has a credit card balance of $4,500, and owes $22,400 on his automobiles, which were listed as $45,000 for two cars. He also has a mortgage on his home of $138,000, even though the home is worth $310,000. Therefore, the total liabilities for the Tom Jones family are $165,875. When we subtract total liabilities from total assets, we arrive at the net worth of the family, which is $290,525.

Note that the statement of financial position formula is always

Assets = Liabilities + Net worth

It can also be written as

Assets − Liabilities = Net worth

Note that the net worth figure represents how much cash the family could obtain if it disposed of all its assets at the value listed on the statement of financial position. This statement of financial position is equivalent to the balance sheet of a business, which we turn to next.

BALANCE SHEET

The **balance sheet** (or, in accounting texts, the *statement of financial position*) for the business (Table 3–5) lists all assets and liabilities. It is like a snapshot taken at an instant in time. There are some minor differences in definitions between the individual statement of financial position and the business balance sheet, and we discuss them as we go through Table 3–5.

The balance sheet formula is often referred to as the *basic accounting equation,* and is similar to the equation for the statement of financial position:

Total assets = Total liabilities + Owner's equity

Assets in the business are like assets for the individual; they are everything that the business has a right to use or own. Current assets usually can be converted into cash during the accounting year, and they are not covered by federal depreciation schedules. Like the individual's current assets, those of the business include cash, savings, and marketable securities. In addition, the business has accounts receivable and inventory listed as current assets. **Accounts receivable**

TABLE 3–5 Balance Sheet (Statement of Financial Position), Sole Proprietorship

The Tom Jones Company
Balance Sheet
As of December 31, 2008

Assets			
Current Assets			
Checking Account		$ 2,000	
Certificates of Deposit		50,000	
Accounts Receivable		40,000	
Inventory		35,000	
Total Current Assets			$127,000
Fixed Assets			
Land		$ 50,000	
Buildings	$250,000		
Less: Accumulated Depreciation	50,000	200,000	
Equipment	$ 50,000		
Less: Accumulated Depreciation	6,000	44,000	
Total Fixed Assets			$294,000
Total Assets			$421,000
Liabilities and Owner's Equity			
Current Liabilities			
Accounts Payable–Trade		$ 16,500	
Notes Payable–Bank		5,000	
Taxes Payable		3,000	
Total Current Liabilities			$ 24,500
Long-Term Liabilities			
Building Mortgage Payable		$180,000	
Equipment Loan Payable		30,000	
Total Long-Term Liabilities			$210,000
Total Liabilities			$234,500
Owner's Equity			$186,500
Total Liabilities and Owner's Equity			$421,000

are the credit sales for which money has not been collected. **Inventory** items are those the business has in stock but has not yet sold.

Fixed assets have an expected life in excess of 1 year and are usually depreciated in accordance with tax laws. All fixed assets for a business are carried on the books at purchase price, less depreciation. These are valued differently than the fixed assets of an individual, because when we generate a statement of financial position (personal balance sheet) we usually use current market value for our fixed assets, but the business balance sheet is prohibited from doing this by *generally accepted accounting principles (GAAP)*.

Depreciation is the wearing out of a business asset during its useful life. The government recognizes that some assets last for more than 1 year and that these items usually wear out as they are used. Therefore, the government establishes depreciation schedules, and for tax purposes, businesses are obligated to depreciate assets according to methods or schedules provided by the government.

The depreciation schedule for an asset is determined primarily by tax law, and the business usually has no choice in determining the life of an asset. The business may have a choice in determining the actual method of depreciation to use for an asset. To determine this specific schedule, an owner must contact an accountant, because the laws change on a regular basis. For example, if we constructed a building in 1986 and opened the building in 1986, the building had to be depreciated according to an *accelerated cost recovery system (ACRS)* schedule over a period of 18 years. If, however, the building was not completed until 1987, then the business had to use a straight-line depreciation schedule under the *modified accelerated cost recovery system (MACRS)* for 31.5 years. The business has no choice in this matter. If the building was opened for use on December 31, 1986, it is depreciated on one schedule; if it opened on January 1, 1987, it is depreciated on another schedule.

Many businesses, however, maintain two depreciation schedules, one for tax reporting purposes and one that is realistic for the business in question. Further examples are provided in Chapter 10, when we discuss capital budgeting.

Several categories of fixed assets are listed on the balance sheet. **Land** is a fixed asset that does not wear out with normal use, so it is always carried on the books at the price that the company paid for it. Although land may appreciate or depreciate in value, we do not know in advance what will happen, so no adjustments are made on the balance sheet until land is actually sold.

Buildings are carried on the books at the price paid, and accumulated depreciation is shown as a deduction on the balance sheet. In other words, every year, the total depreciation shown on the income statement (Table 3–3) is transferred to the balance sheet at the end of the year. For example, the Tom Jones Company has buildings worth $250,000 listed on the balance sheet (Table 3–5), with accumulated depreciation of $50,000 as of December 31, 2008. The December 31, 2007, balance sheet shows the same value for the building ($250,000), but the accumulated depreciation is listed as $44,000. The $6,000 depreciation expense listed on the income statement (Table 3–3) at the end of 2008 is transferred to the December 31, 2008, balance sheet as an addition to the previous year's accumulated depreciation (e.g., $44,000 + $6,000 = $50,000 accumulated depreciation). Therefore, depreciated fixed assets are carried on the books at the price paid, but every year accumulated depreciation increases, and thus lower the value of the asset on the balance sheet.

Equipment includes all items such as machinery, fixtures, and automobiles. It may be necessary to break these assets down by specific type because of depreciation schedules in use at the time of purchase. When any fixed asset is sold or disposed of, both its cost and accumulated depreciation are removed from the balance sheet.

Total assets are the sum of current and fixed assets. For the Tom Jones Company, total assets are $421,000 ($294,000 in fixed assets and $127,000 in current assets). **Liabilities** for the firm are what is owed by the firm to others (creditors). Liabilities, like assets, are divided into two categories, current and long term. **Current liabilities** are those obligations that the firm expects to pay off during the current accounting year. Those items that are included in current liabilities are accounts payable, notes payable, and taxes payable. **Accounts payable** are the debts that are owed to vendors. Any present goods or services that were delivered to the firm but that were not paid for as of the date of the balance sheet are listed as accounts payable. **Notes payable** are promises to pay a creditor or lender the amount owed plus interest for a specified period of time, usually 1 year or less. They can be owed to a lending institution, an individual, or a group of persons. **Taxes payable** are the accrued taxes that are owed but not actually paid as of the date of the balance sheet. Examples include city and state sales taxes that were collected during December, but that are not actually paid to the state until January of the following year. This also includes taxes taken out of employee pay, but not yet actually paid to the government, such as income taxes and taxes for the *Federal Insurance Contribution Act (FICA),* which includes Social Security and Medicare. Most of us combine FICA and Medicare and call it Social Security, but for the business owner, these are calculated separately (6.20 percent Social Security + 1.45 percent Medicare = 7.65 percent).

Note: The business must match the employee's 6.20 percent contribution to Social Security and the 1.45 percent contribution to Medicare. Therefore, the business actually pays taxes of 12.4 percent Social Security up to an annual limit and 2.9 percent in Medicare for a total FICA tax of 15.30 percent. Medicare payments for both employer and employee are not subject to an annual limit.

Total current liabilities are nothing more than the sum of all current liabilities for a company, as depicted on the balance sheet. For the Tom Jones Company, total current liabilities as of midnight, December 31, 2008, were $24,500.

Long-term debt is the amount the company owes but does not expect to pay during the current accounting year. Examples include mortgages on buildings, loans on equipment, and possibly bonds. For the Tom Jones Company, long-term liabilities were $210,000—$180,000 in building mortgage payable and $30,000 in equipment loan payable. (Bonds were discussed briefly in Chapter 2 under corporate financing and are discussed more fully in Chapter 11 on personal finance.) Note that the portion of long-term debt that we expect to pay during the current accounting period is shown under current liabilities. For example, if our company had $1,000,000 in bonds and was expecting to retire $100,000 this year, then we show current maturities of long-term debt under current liabilities of $100,000 and bonds under long-term debt of $900,000.

Total liabilities are the sum of current liabilities and long-term debt. The Tom Jones Company has total liabilities of $234,500.

Owner's equity is the net worth of a company. It is the same as the net worth of the individual Tom Jones, as shown on the statement of financial position (personal balance sheet). Using our balance sheet formula (Total assets = Total liabilities + Owner's equity), the owner's equity must be $186,500, because the total assets ($421,000) must always equal the sum of total liabilities ($234,500) plus owner's equity ($186,500).

Note: By applying simple algebra, there are three forms to the accounting equation:

Total assets = Total liabilities + Owner's equity

or

Owner's equity = Total assets − Total liabilities

or

Total liabilities = Total assets − Owner's equity

In other words, the balance sheet must always balance. We discuss cases of negative owner's equity in Chapter 5 when we discuss bankruptcy.

How the owner's equity is shown on the balance sheet is determined by the form of business ownership. We show three different owner's equity tables to illustrate the differences in the bottom portion of the balance sheet. For all businesses, regardless of type of ownership, assets and liabilities are treated the same; however, the owner's equity portion of the balance sheet is depicted differently for each type of ownership.

SOLE PROPRIETORSHIP

For the sole proprietor, the owner's equity is simply the business assets minus the business liabilities. This remainder is the amount that the owner could obtain for the business if it were sold at its current book value, as shown in Table 3–5. **Book value** is the value of an asset on the company's books after depreciation has been determined. It is probably an unrealistic figure in regard to the actual value of the business because it is based on historical value rather than fair market value. Land and buildings usually appreciate in value over time, whereas equipment and machinery depreciate in value.

PARTNERSHIP

For the partnership, the owner's equity is shown according to the partnership agreement, as shown in Table 3–6. The actual money invested in the firm has nothing to do with this figure, because it represents what the business could be sold for (at book value) and how much would remain after paying off all liabilities.

TABLE 3–6 Balance Sheet, Partnership

Tom Jones and Partners

Partners' Equity		
Tom Jones	$18,650	
Larry Smith	83,925	
Kathy Moore	83,925	
Total Partner's Equity		$186,500
Total Liabilities and Partners' Equity		$421,000

The method of dividing owner's equity and profits is always determined by the partnership agreement. For example, say that Tom Jones had a great idea for a business, but he had little money. He contacted two friends, Larry Smith and Kathy Moore, and convinced them to invest in his business. Tom had to raise $100,000 to start the business and obtain the bank loans to finance the purchase of the land, the building, and equipment. He had $10,000, and Larry and Kathy each agreed to put up $45,000. Now he had the $100,000. The partnership agreement that was drawn up stated that each partner would receive profits in accordance with his or her original investment, and that Tom would be the working partner and would receive a salary of $35,000 per year. Tom's salary is listed as part of the $95,000 salaries expense on the income statement (Table 3–3). The $64,000 net income (Table 3–3), or profit, that was made in 2008, will be split, with 10 percent going to Tom, 45 percent to Larry, and 45 percent to Kathy. So Tom receives $6,400 (10 percent of the $64,000 net income) from the profit plus his $35,000 salary, or a total of $41,400. Larry and Kathy receive $28,800 each (45 percent of the $64,000 net income for each partner). Because this business is a partnership, these incomes are reported on each partner's income tax forms, with each partner paying taxes based on his or her individual income. The partnership files an IRS form 1065, U.S. Return of Partnership Income, and each partner receives and IRS schedule K-1 (form 1065-B), which lists the individual partner's tax liability.

The partners' equity portion of the business is the same as the proprietor's equity (Table 3–5) $186,500 (Table 3–6), and is divided in accordance with the partnership agreement (10 percent for Tom and 45 percent each for Larry and Kathy). As Table 3–6 indicates, Tom has $18,650 in equity ($186,500 × 10 percent), and Larry and Kathy each have $83,925 ($186,500 × 45 percent). The total equity for the partners is $186,500 ($18,650 + $83,925 + $83,925). The equity portion is not the same as the corporation's balance sheet (Table 3–7) because the corporation pays income tax of $11,000, which reduces stockholder's equity from $186,500 to $175,500.

TABLE 3–7 Balance Sheet (Statement of Financial Position), Corporation

The Tom Jones Corporation
Balance Sheet
As of December 31, 2008

Assets		
Current Assets		
Checking Account	$ 2,000	
Certificates of Deposit	50,000	
Accounts Receivable	40,000	
Inventory	35,000	
Total Current Assets		$127,000
Fixed Assets		
Land	$ 50,000	
Buildings	$250,000	
Less: Accumulated Depreciation	50,000	200,000
Equipment	$ 50,000	
Less: Accumulated Depreciation	6,000	44,000
Total Fixed Assets		$294,000
Total Assets		$421,000
Liabilities and Stockholder's Equity		
Current Liabilities		
Accounts Payable–Trade	$ 16,500	
Notes Payable–Bank	5,000	
Taxes Payable	14,000	
Total Current Liabilities		$ 35,500
Long-Term Liabilities		
Building Mortgage Payable	$180,000	
Equipment Loan Payable	30,000	
Total Long-Term Liabilities		$210,000
Total Liabilities		$245,500
Stockholders' Equity		
Preferred Stock, $5 par (10,000 Shares)	$ 50,000	
Common Stock, $0.10 par (100,000 Shares)	10,000	
Paid-in Capital in Excess of Par–Common	50,000	
Total Paid-in Capital	$110,000	
Retained Earnings	65,500	
Total Stockholders' Equity		$175,500
Total Liabilities and Stockholder's Equity		$421,000

PUBLIC CORPORATIONS

Table 3–7 shows the owner's equity portion of the balance sheet for a corporation. As explained in Chapter 2, corporations can raise funds by selling bonds (long-term debt) or by selling stock. Let's assume that the Tom Jones Company, whose balance sheet for 2007 is shown in Table 3–7a, decides to go public during 2008. The Tom Jones Corporation sold 10,000 shares of preferred stock

TABLE 3–7a Balance Sheet (Statement of Financial Position), Corporation

The Tom Jones Company
Balance Sheet
As of December 31, 2007

Assets			
Current Assets			
Checking Account		$ 3,000	
Certificates of Deposit		—	
Accounts Receivable		23,000	
Inventory		18,000	
Total Current Assets			$ 44,000
Fixes Assets			
Land		$ 50,000	
Buildings	$100,000		
Less: Accumulated Depreciation	45,000	55,000	
Equipment	$ 50,000		
Less: Accumulated Depreciation	5,000	45,000	
Total Fixed Assets			$150,000
Total Assets			$194,000
Liabilities and Owner's Equity			
Current Liabilities			
Accounts Payable–Trade		$ 8,000	
Notes Payable–Bank		3,500	
Taxes Payable			
Total Current Liabilities			$ 11,500
Long-Term Liabilities			
Building Mortgage Payable		$135,000	
Equipment Loan Payable		35,000	
Total Long-Term Liabilities			$170,000
Total Liabilities			$181,500
Owner's Equity		$ 12,500	12,500
Total Liabilities and Owner's Equity			$194,000

(Table 3–7) at $5 per share, which equals $50,000. It also sold 100,000 shares of common stock at 60 cents a share. Of the 60 cents per share (Table 3–7), 10 cents is the par value and 50 cents is the paid-in capital in excess of par. These were the 100,000 shares that were used to determine earnings per share of common stock on the income statement (Table 3–3a). The figure for paid-in capital in excess of par is what the Tom Jones Corporation actually obtained, above par value, for its stock offer. In other words, the corporation sold 100,000 shares of common stock and raised capital of $60,000. Because the par value is 10 cents, the 100,000 shares show up on the balance sheet as common stock at par $10,000; and the capital in excess of par ($50,000) indicates that the corporation raised $60,000 with its common stock offer. *Accumulated retained earnings* is money that is not distributed to stockholders but is retained by the corporation for future investment.

OWNER'S EQUITY

How owner's equity is depicted on the balance sheet depends on the form of company ownership. In all cases, however, the balance sheet formula must be maintained.

For a sole proprietorship,

Assets = Liabilities + Owner's equity

For a partnership,

Assets = Liabilities + Partners' equity

For a corporation,

Assets = Liabilities + Stockholders' equity

 # STATEMENT OF CASH FLOWS

The income statement and balance sheet do not actually show cash flow during the accounting period if the business is using an accrual system of accounting, because revenue is recognized when earned and not received, whereas expenses are recognized when incurred and not paid. To determine what has happened to our *working capital account* (the amount of cash available) between the beginning and the end of the current year, we must show how the company's cash has flowed into and out of the business during the year. Table 3–8 shows the statement of cash flows for the Tom Jones Corporation.

The statement of cash flows (Table 3–8) is based on the comparison of two consecutive balance sheets (Table 3–7 balance sheet as of December 31, 2008, and Table 3–7a balance sheet as of December 31, 2007) and the current income statement (Table 3–3 and Table 3–3a, January 1 through December 31, 2008).

The first section of the statement of cash flows (Table 3–8) identifies all operating sources and uses of cash and is referred to as **cash flow from operating activities**, which is the difference between all the cash received by the business and all the cash paid out by the business in conducting its day-to-day operations. The first line of the statement of cash flows is net income as obtained from the income statement (Table 3–3a), which is $53,000. The remainder of the cash flow from operating activities is adjustments made to reconcile net income to net cash. The process is to list the differences in balance sheet figures from the prior year (Table 3–7a) to the current year (Table 3–7). The first thing that we add back is depreciation expense, which is listed on the income statement as an operating expense, but it is not an actual expenditure, so it must be added back. Note that the total annual accumulated depreciation $6,000 on the income statement (Table 3–3) includes $5,000 for building depreciation and

---

TABLE 3–8 Statement of Cash Flows

The Tom Jones Corporation
Statement of Cash Flows
For the Year Ended December 31, 2008
Increase (Decrease) in Cash and Cash Equivalents
(Amounts in thousands)

Cash flows from operating activities		
Net Income		$ 53,000
Adjustments to reconcile net income to net cash provided by operating activies		
Depreciation Expense	6,000	
Increase in Accounts Receivable	(17,000)	
Increase in Inventory	(17,000)	
Increase in Accounts Payable	8,500	
Increase in Notes Payable	1,500	
Increase in Taxes Payable	14,000	(4,000)
Net Cash provided by Operating Activities		$ 49,000
Cash flows from investing activities:		
Acquisition of plant assets	(150,000)	
Net cash outflow from investing activities		(150,000)
Cash flows from financing activities:		
Proceeds from issuance of preferred stock	50,000	
Proceeds from issuance of common stock	60,000	
Proceeds from Mortgage Payable	45,000	
Payment of long-term debt	(5,000)	
Net cash inflow from financing activities		$150,000
Net increase in cash		$ 49,000
Cash balance, December 31, 2007		3,000
Cash balance, December 31, 2008		$ 52,000

$1,000 for equipment depreciation, and is the same on both the income statement and the difference in depreciation on the balance sheets. Building accumulated depreciation increases by $5,000 from $45,000 (Table 3–7a) to $50,000 (Table 3–7) and equipment accumulated depreciation increases by $1,000 from $5,000 (Table 3–7a) to $6,000 (Table 3–7). The lines on the cash flow from operations are taken directly from the differences in the current asset and current liability portions of the balance sheets, not counting cash or cash equivalents. We begin with accounts receivable and notice that they increased by $17,000 between 2008 and 2007 ($40,000 in Table 3–7 and $23,000 in Table 3–7a). An increase in accounts receivable represents the amount of money that we did not collect. So this is actually a cash outflow. An increase in inventory indicates that we have purchased inventory that was not sold, which is a cash outflow. However, an increase in accounts payable means that we have $8,500 more cash because we did not pay our vendors for material received ($16,500 in Table 3–7 minus $8,000 in Table 3–7a). The same thing holds true for notes payable and taxes payable, because it is money that we have not yet paid but we still owe. After adjustments to net income, we had a net outflow of $4,000. Thus, net income of $53,000 minus the net outflow of $4,000 results in net cash provided by operating activities of $49,000. We had less available funds than our net income figure indicated.

The next section of the statement of cash flow **cash flows from investing activities**, which is the net difference between the acquisition of plant and equipment (fixed assets) on the two balance sheets. We increased buildings by $150,000 ($100,000 to $250,000), which is an outflow.

Our final section is **cash flow from financing activities**, which is the net difference between the increase in owner's equity as a result of the issuance of stock to raise cash and the increase in debt as a result of the issuance of bonds or other long-term debt instruments. Our sample company went public and issued both preferred stock in the amount of $50,000 and common stock in the amount of $60,000 for a total infusion of cash of $110,000. We also increased our long-term liabilities by $45,000 ($135,000 to $180,000) when we increased our mortgage payable. This is an inflow of cash because the lender provided the money. The company also reduced its long-term debt by $5,000 by reducing the equipment loan payable, so the net cash inflow from financing activities is $150,000 ($110,000 stock + $45,000 mortgage − $5,000 equipment loan).

The final step in generating a statement of cash flows is to sum the total of cash flow provided by operating activities, investment activities, and financing activities. This adds up to $49,000. We add this total of $49,000 to the ending cash balance on the 2007 balance sheet of $3,000 to arrive at a cash balance of $52,000. This is reflected on the 2008 balance sheet as cash of $2,000 and a certificate of deposit of $50,000. So whatever number we get as a net increase or decrease in cash, we add to the previous year's balance sheet and arrive at the cash balance for the current year's balance sheet.

The authors believe that understanding cash flow is vital if you are going to start a business. It is imperative that one be able to differentiate between *cash flow* and *free cash flow. Cash flow* from operations or operating cash can be found on the statement of cash flows under net cash provided by operating activities. As noted previously, we begin with net income and add back depreciation. In addition, we include the identification of the sources and uses of cash and make adjustments in order to reconcile net income to cash from operations.

Free cash flow is found by adding depreciating paper expense and amortization to net income to give us cash flow from operations. Once completed, we subtract estimated capital expenditures and arrive at free cash flow. *Capital expenditures* are monies spent to acquire or upgrade physical assets such as property, industrial buildings, and equipment. A modification of capital expenditures might be to make an additional adjustment for changes in working capital that is also subtracted from operating cash flow. For our sample company, if we take the $53,000 net income and add back the depreciation expense of $6,000, we obtain cash flow from operations of $59,000. We then subtract the $150,000 in capital expenditures to arrive at a negative free cash flow of $91,000. This indicates that the company needs additional financing which was obtained by issuing stock.

As shown, the income statement and balance sheet do not reflect the actual cash flow accurately during the accounting year. If owners and other interested parties are to determine the company's effectiveness, we must also have a statement of cash flows.

PROBLEMS WITH FINANCIAL STATEMENTS

We must remember that financial statements are written by people, and they are governed by tax and other laws. Therefore, when evaluating financial statements, we must be cautious. It is important to note that in some cases, fixed assets are carried on the balance sheet in an amount that does not necessarily reflect their true value, because even though depreciation is shown, the item is always placed there at the value paid (*book value*).

For example, one of the authors of this text has an LLC that holds his non-owner occupied residential real estate. In October 2003, he purchased a condo for $253,000 (book value). Real estate values in the Scottsdale area have been appreciating significantly. If he had sold the condo in October 2005, he could have received $500,000 (market value) on his $253,000 investment. The condo increased in value by an average of 40.58 percent per year for 2 years. The average profit of 40.58 percent was calculated using the formula for Internal Rate of Return which is discussed thoroughly in Chapter 8. In addition, the book value is actually $236,936 because the condo has an accumulated depreciation of $16,063 ($253,000 purchase price − $16,063 accumulated depreciation = $236,936 book value). Therefore, if the property were sold, the owner would have to declare a profit of $263,064, which is the difference between the market value of $500,000 and the book value of $236,936. Note that not all real estate transactions result in an increase in market value. An example of a significant loss in a real estate transaction was the Scottsdale Galleria, which was valued at $125 million (initial book value) when it opened its doors in May 1991. By 1993, "Mitsubishi Bank Ltd. claimed the Galleria management defaulted on $94.2 million in loans and owed about $2.1 million in interest payments." It was sold at auction in September 1993 for $20 million (market value).[1] These are two extreme examples of the difference between book value and market value of assets. What are a firm's assets really worth? The current market value is always the actual value that an asset commands in the marketplace if sold today.

---

[1]Michele McDonald, "Lone Bidder Purchases Mall for $20 Million," *The Mesa Tribune*, September 30, 1993, p. B1.

Another example might be a 35-year-old fully depreciated rental property across the street from Disney World. The book value is $0, because the property is fully depreciated. However, the market value of the property may well exceed $1 million dollars because of its proximity to Disney World.

Book value may not show the actual value of a business. Different businesses use different methods of accounting. Some businesses use the *cash method* of accounting, whereas some businesses use the *accrual method,* in which sales are recognized as completed when the transaction is made, even though the customer may still owe a considerable amount, which is carried on the seller's books as accounts receivable. Can the accounts receivable actually be collected at their face value in the future? Yes, if the customer is a good credit risk. Sometimes it may be necessary to sell accounts receivable for a fraction of their worth. At times, balance sheets also show large inventories that are obsolete or cannot be sold. In this case the inventories may be sold at a considerable loss or disposed of completely. For example, consider the thousands of stores that carry pet foods. The FDA issued a recall notice in February 2008 because of the deaths of several cats and dogs. The cause was determined to be the result of a tainted Chinese supply of a pet food additive.[2] These companies may have shown millions of dollars worth of pet foods on their books, but these items could not be given away because the government prohibited their sale.

We are all familiar with the embarrassing and spectacular bankruptcies of Enron, MCI (post-bankruptcy version of WorldCom), and WorldCom in which companies altered their books and misstated earnings by several billion dollars. As a result of these fraudulent statements, several of the senior officers were sentenced and are now in prison. The most notable example is Bernard Ebbers, CEO of WorldCom. Ebbers was sentenced to 25 years in prison on July 13, 2005.[3] These misstatements of earnings and other fraudulent schemes led Congress to pass the Sarbanes–Oxley Act, the main objective of which is to protect investors by improving accuracy and reliability of corporate disclosures in accordance with securities law. The act significantly tightened the reins on how information is reported. It also banned corporations from making loans to corporate executives. WorldCom gave Ebbers $400 million dollars in low-interest loans so he wouldn't have to sell his WorldCom stock and depress its value in the marketplace.[4]

Many of us consider the statement of cash flows as the most meaningful of the financial statements. When evaluating the cash position of a company, pay particular attention to *Cash flows from operating activities.* Is the company

---

[2] U.S. Food and Drug Administration (FDA). Retrieved April 8, 2008, from http://www.fda.gov/oc/opacom/hottopics/petfood.html

[3] Ann Thompson, "Ebbers Sentenced to 25 Years in Prison," retrieved January 5, 2008, from http://www.msnbc.msn.com/id/8474930.

[4] Kathleen Pender, "Corporate Reins Now Too Tight," *San Francisco Chronicle*, August 9, 2005, p. D1.

receiving the majority of its cash flows from operating activities rather than the sale of stock or the accumulation of additional debt? This single factor is extremely important in evaluating the overall health of a company that has been in business for several years.

 # CONCLUSION

In this chapter, we introduced personal and business financial statements and discussed their similarities and differences. We compared financial statements for different forms of business ownership, and showed the relationships among income statement, balance sheet, and cash flow statement. We also pointed out some of the problems that may exist with financial statements. We discussed the relationship between fixed assets and depreciation, and their impact on both book value and fair market value.

When reading any financial statement, be cautious, find out some background on the company, and determine for yourself how accurate the statement is.

REVIEW AND DISCUSSION QUESTIONS

1. How are financial statements used by business?
2. Compare variable and fixed expenses.
3. Describe the basic format of an income statement, listing all its sections.
4. What is the primary difference between the income statement of a sole proprietorship or partnership and the income statement of a corporation?
5. What is a *personal statement of financial position*?
6. What is the difference between the time periods listed on an income statement and on a balance sheet?
7. What is the importance of liquidity?
8. List the categories that are on the balance sheet for a business.
9. What is the accounting equation for the balance sheet?
10. What is the difference between a *current asset* and a *fixed asset*?
11. Compare owner's equity in a sole proprietorship, partners' equity in a partnership, and stockholders' equity in a corporation.
12. What is the purpose of the statement of cash flows?
13. List the components of the statement of cash flows.
14. Why are fixed assets carried on the balance sheet at a price that may not reflect the true value of the assets?
15. Compare free cash flow to net increase in cash on the statement of cash flows. Using the Internet, find one company with a positive free cash flow and one in the same industry but with a negative free cash flow. Which of these companies do you consider to be the better investment? Why?

EXERCISES AND PROBLEMS

1. Given the personal cash flow statement in Table 3–2, use your own data to determine your disposable income at the end of the current year. Please include income from all sources, fixed expenses, and variable expenses.

2. Given the statement of financial position in Table 3–4, use your own data to determine your net worth. Make sure that student loans are included in liabilities, if applicable.

3. The Happy Auto Shop has the following annual information: gross sales, $700,000; net sales, $696,000; and gross profit, $448,000. What are the shop's returns and allowances and cost of goods sold?

4. Construct a personal income statement for the Humperdinck family using the following information: salaries, $42,000; mortgage payment, $7,980; food, $2,400; interest income, $150; transportation, $1,200; dividend income, $190; automobile payment, $3,060; clothes and personal, $2,000; student loan payment, $1,700; property taxes, $1,100; utilities, $3,000; insurance, $2,100; income taxes, $9,700; and recreation and vacation, $2,000. What is the family's disposable income?

5. Construct a statement of financial position (balance sheet) for the Humperdinck family using the following information: cash, $50; checking account, $2,500; student loan balance, $6,000; stocks and bonds, $2,600; savings account, $5,850; residence, $110,000; automobile, $12,000; savings account, $5,800; automobile loan balance, $12,000; 401(k) retirement account, $15,000; furniture, clothing, jewelry, $8,000; credit card balance, $4,000; and mortgage loan balance, $99,000.

6. Construct an income statement using the following information: net sales, $500,000; salaries, $100,000; rent, $24,000; COGS, $250,000; utilities, $25,000; payroll taxes, $25,000; insurance, $12,000; and interest expense, $5,450. Make sure that you include gross profit, operating expenses, and net profit.

7. George's Pizzeria has the following information as of December 31, 2008: cash, $2,000; pizza ovens, $25,000; furniture, $12,500; accounts payable, $3,500; notes payable, $12,500; accumulated depreciation, $10,000; wages payable, $1,500; taxes payable, $2,500; and equipment loan, $18,000. Construct a balance sheet for George. Do you think he has a problem with his current balance sheet? If so, what is it?

8. State the stockholders' equity of the Alphabet Corporation if it has a current net profit of $1,500,000, beginning-of-the-period retained earnings of $3,675,000, 1 million shares of common stock issued at a par value of $1 per share, and paid-in capital in excess of par of $12.50 per share.

9. State your current cash balance if you have the following information: total cash receipts of $624,000; a cash balance at the end of last year of $60,000; total cash payments of $540,000; cash outflow from investing activities of $100,000; and cash inflows from financial activities of $172,000.

RECOMMENDED TEAM ASSIGNMENTS

1. Compare and contrast the financial statements of at least two companies within the same industry.
2. As a team, chose a well-known corporation and obtain its financial statements. Isolate the fixed and variable expenses on the income statement and determine how these items affect the balance sheet.
3. Using the same company as in question 2, reconcile the income statement to the statement of cash flows.

CASE STUDY: DPSYSTEMS, LLC

© 2008 Philip J. Adelman and Alan M. Marks

David Sobelman was born and raised in Glendale, Arizona, where he attended Glendale public schools. After high school, he enrolled in the Computer Information Systems degree program at DeVry University. In 1997, he graduated with a Bachelor of Science Degree in Computer Information Systems. DeVry offers two areas that try to provide students with real-world experience. One is the Senior Project course, in which students develop projects for companies in the area where their campuses are located; the other is an intern program with industry, where students work part-time while attending classes.

David's senior project included writing a client/server application in PowerBuilder for a photography company. The application was so useful that the company continued to use it (with some modifications) for more than 10 years since its initial development. David did part-time work as a consultant for the photographer to update and modify the application. While a student at DeVry, he was also an intern with Salt River Project (SRP), a primary supplier of electricity and water in Phoenix. On graduation, he was hired full-time by SRP as a programmer, working on their customer information systems. After 1 year, David quit SRP and went to work at Integrated Information Systems (IIS) which was a start-up company that was quickly expanding. He was the 60th employee of IIS. After a year, David determined that he was not happy with the IIS expansion and reorganization plans and began looking for another opportunity. He found a job with Choice Hotels International. Subsequently to David leaving IIS, the company expanded very rapidly, went public, and declared bankruptcy within 3 years.

He currently works with Choice Hotels at their Western Headquarters in Phoenix, where he is involved in developing Choice Hotels' web-based property management system (PMS). As of this publication, their PMS is the most widely used system in the industry, and the only hotel company to successfully develop and deploy such a system used by more than 1,500 hotels.

Ever since graduating from college, David had an idea to develop a computer-based side business and chose to incorporate DPS, as they were his initials. His primary intention was to create a business that contained a continuous revenue stream. Through the years he has worked with family and friends on a part-time basis, helping with their computer upgrades, fixing computers, installing software, and the like. In 2001, David was elected to the board of his home owner's association (HOA). One of his goals when he was elected was to put together a website for the community that would provide information about the association to the homeowners. There was a short time between quitting IIS and going to work for Choice when David taught himself Hypertext Markup Language (HTML) and how to work with and build web pages. Within a year, David created a very dynamic user-friendly web page for his HOA.

When a community is going to be developed by a builder, they typically hire a management company to manage the day-to-day business of the HOA. The management company often bills the developer to create an HOA website. Having a website in place enhances the viability of the development and makes it easier for the developer transition to a property-owner HOA. Once 75 percent of the homes within the community are sold, the homeowners elect a board of directors and can then keep the current management association or hire a new one. The management company handles all homeowner notifications, inspects the properties, pays invoices, and manages the day-to-day operations of the association. The property management company that manages several hundred associations in the Phoenix area in addition to the one in which David lives was very satisfied with the quality and functionality of the website David put together. They were impressed by what the web page offered to the homeowners and how it helped open the communications link between homeowners, the Board of Directors, and the management company.

The Information Technology (IT) department of the management company was primarily involved in computer hardware and had no real interest in writing software or building websites. As a member of his own HOA board of directors, David met and became familiar with the inner workings of the management company. He developed a proposal and asked the company if they would like him to develop similar websites for each of their HOAs. The management company doesn't actually pay for the website maintenance because the sites are actually paid for by each individual HOA. David is notified by the management company when any information must be added or removed from an individual HOA website. David's company charges each HOA a nominal monthly charge to host and update each HOA website. He manages his company out of his home, and almost all correspondence with the management company is handled via email.

This part-time job provides David with an additional gross income in excess of $64,000 and a net income including salary and profit in excess of $44,000 per year. See the DPSystems income statement (Table 3–9) and balance sheet (Table 3–10) for 2007. David is an example of an outstanding young entrepreneur.

QUESTIONS

1. Develop a financial income statement and balance sheet by combining the chart of account items on the DPSystems income statement and balance sheet in Tables 3–9 and 3–10.
2. List the chart of account numbers and major categories used in DPSystems' accounting system.
3. How would a hotel chain use a property management system to incorporate items from individual hotels into their corporate financial statements?

TABLE 3–9 DPSystems Income Statement

**DPSystems Income Statement
January 1 through
December 31, 2007 Cash Basis**

	Jan–Dec 07
Ordinary Income/Expense Income	
4200 · Services	
4210 · Domain Registrations	2,580.00
4220 · Domain Hosting	11,130.00
4230 · Website Maintenance	44,090.00
Total 4200 · Services	57,800.00
4500 · Labor	6,450.00
Total Income	64,250.00
Expense	
5080 · Office Supplies	
5082 · Printer Supplies	394.18
5080 · Office Supplies—Other	158.77
Total 5080 · Office Supplies	552.95
5110 · Computer Accessories	560.36
5120 · Postage and Delivery	78.15
5130 · PDA Accessories	108.70
5260 · Utilities	
5261 · Internet	540.00
5262 · Wireless Phone	3,501.33
Total 5260 · Utilities	4,041.33
5330 · Promotions	1,390.60
5390 · Travel & Entertainment	
5391 · Entertainment	1,492.30
5392 · Meals	1,014.17
5393 · Travel	1,129.07
5394 · Gas	395.99
Total 5390 · Travel & Entertainment	4,031.53
5580 · Donations	1,881.96
5640 · Professional Fees	
5642 · Accounting	954.00
5643 · Cleaning Services	1,528.00
Total 5640 · Professional Fees	2,482.00
5700 · Software	
5701 · Desktop Software	107.56
5702 · PDA Software	99.35
Total 5700 · Software	206.91
5710 · Hardware	108.09
5720 · Bank Service Charges	78.90
5760 · Bad Debt	244.00
5800 · Dues and Subscriptions	142.45
6050 · Contract Services	80.00
6110 · Automobile Expense	34.88
6130 · Cash Discounts	3.00
6180 · Insurance	256.00
6260 · Printing and Reproduction	13.01
6300 · Repairs	
6340 · Automobile Repairs	553.98
Total 6300 · Repairs	553.98
6500 · Payroll—David Sobelman	15,000.00
6510 · Payroll Taxes	1,147.50
6700 · Domain Registrations	1,691.80
6710 · Domain Hosting	550.20
Total Expense	35,238.30
Net Ordinary Income	29,011.70
Other Income/Expense	
Other Income	
8100 · Interest Income	19.69
Total Other Income	19.69
Net Other Income	19.69
Net Income	29,031.39

TABLE 3–10 DPSystems Balance Sheet

DPSystems Balance Sheet
As of December 31, 2007
Cash Basis

	Dec 31, 07
ASSETS	
Current Assets	
Checking/Savings	
1030 · Money Market	7,242.93
1031 · Checking	4,695.29
1033 · Barter	1,416.99
Total Checking/Savings	13,355.21
Accounts Receivable	
1035 · Accounts Receivable	−50.00
Total Accounts Receivable	−50.00
Other Current Assets	
1040 · Undeposited Funds	410.00
Total Other Current Assets	410.00
Total Current Assets	13,715.21
Fixed Assets	
1400 · Depreciation Allowance	−19,865.97
1500 · Computers	
1505 · Hardware Parts	1,105.61
1500 · Computers—Other	3,135.87
Total 1500 · Computers	4,241.48
1520 · Furniture	12,522.43
1550 · Monitors	1,498.40
1560 · Printers	930.98
1570 · PDA	810.00
1590 · Misc Assets	3,902.62
Total Fixed Assets	4,039.94
Other Assets	
1700 · Organization Expense	620.00
1705 · Accumulated Amortization	−310.00
Total Other Assets	310.00
TOTAL ASSETS	18,065.15
LIABILITIES & EQUITY	
Liabilities	
Current Liabilities	
Credit Cards	
2200 · American Express	1,391.26
Total Credit Cards	1,391.26
Other Current Liabilities	
2350 · Payroll Withholdings	
2354 · State W/H Payable	600.00
Total 2350 · Payroll Withholdings	600.00
Total Other Current Liabilities	600.00
Total Current Liabilities	1,991.26
Total Liabilities	1,991.26
Equity	
3100 · Retained Earnings	21,624.39
3200 · David's Equity	
3210 · David's Equity Investments	2,993.46
3230 · David's Equity Draws	−37,455.73
3200 · David's Equity—Other	−119.62
Total 3200 · David's Equity	−34,581.89
Net Income	29,031.39
Total Equity	16,073.89
TOTAL LIABILITIES & EQUITY	18,065.15

CHAPTER 4

Analysis of Financial Statements

Learning Objectives

When you have completed this chapter, you should be able to:

♦ Understand the purpose of financial statement analysis.
♦ Perform a vertical analysis of a company's financial statements by
  Comparing those accounts on the income statement as a percentage of net sales and comparing those accounts on the balance sheet as a percentage of total assets for a period of two or more accounting cycles.
  Determining those areas within the company that require additional monitoring and control.
♦ Perform a horizontal analysis of a company's financial statements by
  Comparing the percentage change of components on a company's income statement and balance sheet for a period of 2 or more years.
  Determining those areas within the company that require additional monitoring and control.
♦ Perform ratio analysis of a company and compare those ratios with other companies within the same industry using industry averages.
♦ Analyze the relationships among the several categories of ratios in determining the health of a business.
♦ Distinguish among liquidity, activity, leverage, profitability, and market ratios.
♦ Know how to obtain financial statements and financial information from various sources.

Understanding financial statements provides little knowledge unless you can use the financial statements to determine potential profitability—either for your own firm or for a potential investment. As an entrepreneur, you will find that there is often no difference, in the eyes of a potential lender, between the financial statements of your firm and your own financial statements. As explained in Chapter 3, the personal statement of financial position is in most cases an offshoot of the business's balance sheet. For example, most of the sole proprietor's assets are invested in the business. If the proprietor wishes to obtain a loan, then it is imperative that his or her financial statements provide the lender with a picture of profitability, or potential profitability, that is at least as good as that of other firms in the same type of industry.

For example, if Linda Brown wants to open and operate a soft-serve yogurt shop, she will be required to furnish her lender with a statement of financial position, which in essence can be equated to a company's balance sheet. Linda must demonstrate sufficient net worth to secure a loan from her creditors. A lending institution often uses measurable criteria established for businesses of a similar nature to determine if Linda qualifies for the loan. Lenders are concerned primarily with the financial health of potential borrowers. Financial statement analysis is used by lenders predominately to determine how healthy an existing or potential business is.

Potential creditors use this analysis to determine if they will lend money to our firm (through loans, mortgages, bonds, the issuance of credit cards, or the extension of lines of credit). Financial statement analysis is also used externally by potential investors to determine if they will invest in our firm (through the purchase of stock or entry into partnerships).

Another purpose of financial statement analysis is to generate information that can be used by the business itself. Internally, as managers of a company, we use financial statement analysis to monitor and control specific items on the financial statements and to compare our business with those of our competitors in the same industry. If operating expenses are increasing and revenue is decreasing, for example, monitoring the data allows us to take corrective action. We know that we must develop a course of action that decreases expenses, increases revenue, or produces a combination effect of both cutting expenses and increasing revenue. If action is not taken, the net profit of the company declines. For Linda, if the cost of goods sold for soft-serve yogurt in 2007 was 30 percent of sales and in 2008 the cost of goods is 35 percent of sales, then she will probably find that she is losing money, or that at least her shop is not as profitable in 2008 as it was in 2007, unless she can determine some method of cutting operating expenses.

Several methods are available for us to use in comparing our business with those of our competitors. If other firms are publicly owned, we can obtain their financial reports by contacting the firm and asking for an annual report. We can go to the library and look at their annual reports or SEC Form 10-K. We also may make use of published financial data in sources such as *The Value Line Investment Survey,* or obtain the same or additional information from sources on the Internet. One such resource is the Security and Exchange Commission's (SEC) Electronic Data Gathering and Retrieval System (EDGAR), also mentioned in Chapter 2 (on the Internet at http://www.sec.gov/). Additional information is available in industry reports and data published by trade journals on specific industries.

There are essentially three methods of analyzing financial statements: vertical analysis, horizontal analysis, and ratio analysis. All calculations in this chapter are rounded to two decimal places because most items are reported as either a fraction or a percentage of dollar items. The authors believe that when using dollars, decimal places beyond two do not add significantly to the results.

 ## VERTICAL ANALYSIS

Vertical analysis is the process of using a single variable on a financial statement as a constant and determining how all other variables relate as a percentage of the single variable. The vertical analysis of the income statement is used to determine, specifically, how much of a company's net sales is being consumed by each individual entry on the income statement. For example, if sales are $100,000 and the cost of goods sold is $70,000, then 70 percent of net sales was consumed by the cost of goods sold. On the income statement, when conducting a vertical analysis, we always use net sales as 100 percent; therefore, each item on the income statement is divided by net sales to determine what percentage of net sales is being consumed by the item. The following formula is used in vertical analysis of an income statement:

$$\text{Percentage of net sales} = \frac{\text{Income statement item in \$}}{\text{Net sales in \$}} \times 100$$

Table 4–1 contains a vertical analysis of a hypothetical firm, Markadel Retail Store. Note that cost of goods sold for 2007 was 34.27 percent of net sales. If the industry average for this type of firm was 28 percent, then we could conclude that costs were excessive, and this might be a reason for lower gross profits.

Vertical analysis also can help in pricing products because a pattern of relationships exists between net sales, percentage of overhead, and profitability. Businesses generally, by way of a vertical analysis over time, can determine these relationships. For example, the Markadel Retail Store has computed total operating expenses of 46.48 percent of net sales (25.38 + 11.92 + 9.18) and operating income of 19.25 percent of net sales (Table 4–1). Therefore, Markadel, having used vertical analysis, can determine its average markup requirements as a percentage of sales.

TABLE 4–1 Sample Income Statement Data

Markadel Retail Store
Income Statement Data
From January 1 through December 31, 2007 and 2008

Account	Year 2007	Year 2008	Vertical Analysis 2007 (%)	Horizontal Analysis 2008–2007 (%)
Gross sales	$300,580	$315,487	101.73	4.96
Less returns	5,124	9,253	1.73	80.58
Net sales	295,456	306,234	100.00	3.65
Cost of goods sold	101,250	120,002	34.27	18.52
Gross profit	194,206	186,232	65.73	(4.11)
Operating expenses				
Administration	74,983	76,450	25.38	1.96
Advertising	35,214	37,250	11.92	5.78
Overhead	27,120	28,300	9.18	4.35
Operating income	56,889	44,232	19.25	(22.25)
Interest	7,000	6,250	2.37	(10.71)
Earnings before taxes	49,889	37,982	16.89	(23.87)
Taxes	7,483	5,697	2.53	(23.87)
Net income	$ 42,406	$ 32,285	14.35	(23.87)

Vertical analysis of the balance sheet is always carried out by using total assets as a constant, or 100 percent, and dividing every figure on the balance sheet by total assets. This tells us how much of our total assets is claimed by owners, and how much is obligated to creditors. The following formula is used in vertical analysis of a balance sheet:

$$\text{Percentage of total assets} = \frac{\text{Balance sheet item in \$}}{\text{Total assets in \$}} \times 100$$

Looking at Table 4–2, for 2007, we see that Markadel has current assets of $65,830, which is 30.77 percent of total assets. On initial analysis, this appears to be an extremely liquid firm; however, a further look indicates that only 7.24 percent of current assets are liquid enough (cash is 4.77 percent and notes receivable are 1.40 percent) to meet a creditor's claim. Accounts receivable (7.16 percent) and inventory (16.37 percent) amount to 23.53 percent of total assets. Thus, vertical analysis indicates that the firm may have to take drastic steps to either expedite accounts receivable or decrease inventory (possibly with a sale) in order to meet its obligations. Looking at current liabilities, we note that they are only 27.70 percent of total assets, but because cash and notes receivable are only 6.17 percent of total assets, this firm has a serious problem in its ability to meet short-term debt.

TABLE 4–2 Sample Balance Sheet Data

Markadel Retail Store
Balance Sheet Data
As of December 31, 2007 and 2008

Category	Year 2007	Year 2008	Vertical Analysis 2007 (%)	Horizontal Analysis 2007–2008 (%)
Current assets				
Cash	$ 10,210	$ 8,175	4.77	(19.93)
Notes receivable	3,000	5,000	1.40	66.67
Accounts receivable	15,320	18,025	7.16	17.66
Inventory	35,020	50,515	16.37	44.25
Prepaid insurance	1,000	1,500	0.47	50.00
Prepaid legal	1,280	1,602	0.60	25.16
Total current assets	65,830	84,817	30.77	28.84
Fixed assets				
Land	25,000	25,000	11.69	0.00
Buildings	135,000	135,000	63.10	0.00
Accumulated depreciation	(47,000)	(50,000)	21.97	6.38
Equipment	58,250	58,250	27.23	0.00
Accumulated depreciation	(23,150)	(28,150)	10.82	21.60
Total fixed assets	148,100	140,100	69.23	(5.40)
Total assets	$213,930	$224,917	100.00	5.14
Current liabilities				
Accounts payable	34,250	40,003	16.01	16.80
Notes payable	25,000	33,035	11.69	32.14
Total current liabilities	59,250	73,038	27.70	23.27
Long-term debt				
Mortgage payable	65,000	63,000	30.38	(3.08)
Bank loan payable	10,000	15,000	4.67	50.00
Total long-term debt	75,000	78,000	35.06	4.00
Total liabilities	134,250	151,038	62.75	12.51
Owner's equity	79,680	73,879	37.25	(7.28)
Total liabilities and owner's equity	$213,930	$224,917	100.00	5.14

HORIZONTAL ANALYSIS

Horizontal analysis is a determination of the percentage increase or decrease in an account from a base time period to successive time periods. The basic formula for horizontal analysis of any statement is

$$\text{Percentage change} = \frac{\text{New time period amount} - \text{Old time period amount}}{\text{Old time period amount}} \times 100$$

The formula shows us whether the change is positive or negative. If we use the income statement data (Table 4–1) and choose net profit for our horizontal analysis, we get the following:

$$\text{Percentage change} = \frac{\$32,285 - \$42,406}{\$42,406} \times 100 = -23.87\%$$

Note that net profit declined by 23.87 percent between 2007 and 2008, even though gross sales increased by 4.96 percent. This indicates that we must attempt to determine which areas of the business contributed to the declining profit. We note that returns increased by 80.58 percent and COGS increased by 18.52 percent, thereby contributing to a decline in gross profit of 4.11 percent. This indicates that the firm requires either a change in pricing policy, so that sales prices reflect increases in COGS, or a thorough evaluation of COGS to determine if the firm can do something to reduce costs. The firm must also look at returns to determine if the quality of merchandise is deteriorating.

Note: There is no relationship between percentages and actual dollar figures with horizontal analysis. The horizontal analysis percentage merely shows how rapidly a given line item on the income statement or balance sheet has changed during the period of analysis.

For example, using Table 4–1, the increase in returns and allowances of 80.58 percent represents only $4,129 ($9,253 − $5,124), whereas the increase in gross sales of 4.96 percent represents $14,907 ($315,487 − $300,580). Horizontal analysis is most useful for determining those areas that must be closely monitored.

A horizontal analysis of the balance sheet data (Table 4–2) indicates that the cash position is deteriorating, whereas accounts receivable is increasing by 17.66 percent and inventory is increasing by 44.25 percent. We therefore expect to find that total liabilities are increasing because of the firm's inability to generate cash and that the equity position is deteriorating. This is, in fact, true: Total liabilities increased by 12.51 percent and owner's equity declined by 7.28 percent. The balance sheet itself does not provide us directly with owner's equity. To obtain this, we must always apply the accounting equation:

Assets = Liabilities + Owner's equity

In 2007, owner's equity was $79,680; in 2008, it was $73,879. Using the percentage change formula, we find that owner's equity declined by 7.28 percent, or, after rounding, by 7 percent. If the firm attempted to attract new investors or obtain additional borrowing, it might find it difficult with the deteriorating profit and equity position noted on both the income statement and the balance sheet. As managers, we use the analysis internally to determine the need for a course of action for our firm. As creditors or investors, we use the analysis to determine if we want to either lend or invest money in this firm.

RATIO ANALYSIS

Vertical and horizontal analyses are primarily methods of analyzing a single firm. Although we could use vertical and horizontal analyses to compare two firms in the same industry, it is easier to use ratio analysis for this comparison. Normally, when we want to determine how our firm is doing in relationship to other firms in our own industry, we use **ratio analysis**, which is used to determine the health of a business, especially as that business compares with other firms in the same industry or similar industries. A *ratio* is nothing more than a relationship between two variables, expressed as a fraction. Therefore, a single ratio, by and of itself, is meaningless. It is only through comparison, using industry averages as a barometer, that we can determine the well-being of our business. This comparison allows us to determine whether our company is healthy or in need of repair.

There are several categories of ratios, each of which is used to measure the health of an organization in specific areas. If we use the human body as an example, we can say that if a person is suffering from a heart problem, he or she would not go to a gynecologist. In a business context, if there is a human resource problem, it can't be solved by going to a banker. Each ratio discussed in the following sections is of particular interest to specialists within the business community. Note, however, that if the total body is not in balance, then several apparently non-related health problems may occur. Likewise, although a business in disarray may look healthy in some areas, the overall picture is one that lacks stability. There are several categories of ratios that are important. Like the human body, if the business is to survive and prosper, then all those categories of ratios must operate in a healthy fashion.

TYPES OF BUSINESS RATIOS

There are several categories of business ratios, including liquidity, activity, leverage (debt), profitability, and market ratios. Each category addresses a particular area of a company's financial health. A profitable company usually has all areas working in harmony. We begin by discussing these categories of ratios.

LIQUIDITY RATIOS

Liquidity ratios determine how much of a firm's current assets are available to meet short-term creditors' claims and are of primary interest to potential investors and creditors, banks, and other lending institutions. The specific ratios that fall into this category are the current ratio and the *quick,* or *acid test, ratio.*

Current Ratio

The **current ratio** is calculated by dividing total current assets by total current liabilities. For example, using Table 4–2, we find that current assets for 2008 were $84,817 and current liabilities were $73,038.

$$\text{Current ratio} = \frac{\text{Current assets}}{\text{Current liabilities}} = \frac{\$84,817}{\$73,038} = 1.16$$

This indicates that for every dollar of short-term creditors' claims, the company had $1.16 to pay for these current obligations. If we divide 1 by 1.16, we see that the company would have had to dispose of approximately 86 percent of its current assets to meet its current obligations. The general rule for most industries is that the current ratio should be 2 or higher. However, one must also look at the industry average, because some industries are very capital intensive and have tremendous capital tied up in plant and equipment (e.g., utility firms, heavy-manufacturing firms), whereas others are highly labor intensive and have little tied up in plant and equipment (e.g., law firms, computer software development firms).

Quick (Acid Test) Ratio

The **acid test** or **quick ratio** is calculated by dividing the sum of total current assets minus inventory and minus prepaids by total current liabilities. The **acid test ratio** is given by the following:

$$\text{Quick ratio} = \frac{\text{Current assets} - \text{Inventory} - \text{Prepaids}}{\text{Current liabilities}}$$

$$\text{Quick ratio} = \frac{\$84,817 - \$50,515 - \$1,500 - \$1,602}{\$73,038}$$

$$\text{Quick ratio} = \frac{\$31,200}{\$73,038} = 0.43$$

We calculated the quick ratio using 2008 data from Table 4–2. Notice that we used current assets minus inventory, minus prepaid insurance, and minus prepaid legal. The reason that prepaid expenses are subtracted from current assets is that these are items that are owned and have been paid for by the company. Because they have been paid for, the company no longer has this cash to pay short-term creditors.

Therefore, for every dollar in creditors' claims, the company had only 43 cents to satisfy them using cash on hand. This ratio also does not include the sale of the company's inventory. It measures the ability of the firm to meet its short-term obligations without liquidating its inventory, which is extremely important in certain industries, especially for those firms with high seasonal sales (e.g., toy stores, garden equipment companies, pool supply firms) or are in industries that have rapid changes in product lines (e.g., personal computer dealers). If inventory must be eliminated during low-demand periods, the loss to the firm could be excessive. For example, if a pool supply store must generate cash during the off-season (January), then the sales prices for its products may have to be so low that the company is forced to sell at below its own cost of goods. Notice that in such a case, the firm actually loses money on every sale. Therefore, companies having a high current ratio may have so much inventory that they are giving an unclear picture of their ability to meet creditors' claims. Such a company may have so much tied up in inventory that it is actually overinvesting its own excess funds in inventory. An acid test reveals this problem. The general rule for most industries is that the quick ratio (acid test) must be 1 or higher, which allows the company to pay all of its short-term creditors with cash on hand.

ACTIVITY RATIOS

Activity ratios indicate how efficiently a business is using its assets. Assets are meaningless if they cannot be turned into cash in a timely manner to generate the revenue that the firm requires to meet its obligations. Activity ratios compare items on the income statement to items on the balance sheet. Because the income statement covers the entire year's flow of funds and the balance sheet covers only an instant in time, we use the average of the balance sheet items in calculating our ratios. For example, retail firms like Wal-Mart, Target, and Starbucks begin selling in the current year using the assets that existed on the balance sheet at the end of the previous year. During the year they build new stores, which changes assets and liabilities on the balance sheet. At the end of the current year the company is generating sales with the assets that were added during the entire year, so we use the average of the assets from the two balance sheets to compare an income statement item to a balance sheet item. The following ratios are included in this category.

Inventory Turnover Ratio

The **inventory turnover ratio** (or, simply, *inventory turnover*) indicates how efficiently a firm is moving its inventory. It basically states how many times per year the firm moves its average inventory. There are two formulas that may be used to calculate inventory turnover: One is net sales divided by average inventory at retail, and the other is COGS divided by average inventory at cost. Because both COGS and average inventory at cost can be obtained from figures readily available on the income statement and balance sheet of the company, we usually use the second formula, shown here, for our sample firm:

$$\text{Inventory turnover} = \frac{\text{COGS}}{\text{Average inventory}}$$

The average inventory is obtained by adding beginning and ending inventory for the year in question and dividing by 2.

$$\text{Average inventory} = \frac{\text{Beginning inventory} + \text{Ending inventory}}{2}$$

Beginning inventory for one year is typically the ending inventory for the previous year. It stands to reason that if we close our books on December 31, 2007, the beginning inventory for 2008 would be the same value as that listed for inventory on the balance sheet for 2007. Therefore, for the Markadel Retail Store, average inventory is ($35,020 + $50,515) ÷ 2 = $42,767.50. Cost of goods sold for 2008 was $120,002. The inventory turnover for Markadel was $120,002 ÷ $42,767.50 = 2.81. This means that Markadel turned its inventory over approximately 2.81 times in 2008.

To determine how long the average item is in stock, we would divide 365 (number of days in a year) by inventory turnover. Thus, Markadel carries its average inventory for 365 ÷ 2.81, or approximately 130 days. Depending on cash flow, the company may need financing to carry its inventory for this period of time.

Accounts Receivable Turnover Ratio

The **accounts receivable turnover ratio** allows us to determine how fast our company is turning its net credit sales into cash. The formula for this ratio is

$$\text{Accounts receivable turnover} = \frac{\text{Net credit sales}}{\text{Average net accounts receivable}}$$

In 2008, if we assume that all net sales for Markadel were credit sales, then we can use $306,234 for net credit sales. Accounts receivable were $18,025 in 2008 and $15,320 in 2007. We compute average net accounts receivables to be $16,672.50. Accounts receivable turnover would be $306,234 ÷ $16,672.50 = 18.37.

Accounts receivable turnover is most often used to determine the average collection period for a company. This formula is as follows:

$$\text{Average collection period} = \frac{\text{365 days per year}}{\text{Accounts receivable turnover}}$$

This means that Markadel turned its net credit sales into cash approximately 18 times a year in 2008, or it waited an average of 19.87 days (365 ÷ 18.37 = 19.87), or almost 20 days, to collect a credit sale. Nothing is inherently good or bad about the outcome of this ratio. It reflects on how well the company's actual collections compare with its credit policy. If Markadel has terms of 30 days, then its credit policy is probably too tight because it is collecting much faster than its terms indicate. We discuss this in more detail in Chapter 7, when we determine credit policies.

Fixed Asset Turnover Ratio

The **fixed asset turnover ratio** indicates how efficiently fixed assets are being used to generate revenue for a firm. The formula is

$$\text{Fixed asset turnover} = \frac{\text{Net sales}}{\text{Average fixed assets}}$$

To obtain the figures for fixed asset turnover, we refer to both the income statement (Table 4–1) and the balance sheet (Table 4–2) for the company. For Markadel, average fixed assets were $144,100, which is $148,100 fixed assets in 2008 + $140,100 fixed assets in 2007 ÷ 2. For Markadel in 2008, fixed asset turnover was ($306,234 net sales in 2008 ÷ $144,100) = 2.125. If we are running our business properly and have not invested in new equipment, we usually have a goal of improving this ratio on an annual basis, because the ratio should increase as a result of the depreciation aspect of fixed assets. We subtract depreciation on an annual basis, so the book value of fixed assets declines each year. Even if sales remain constant, we should see a larger ratio, which may be deceiving. When we purchase large quantities of fixed assets, however, we expect this ratio to decline because our fixed asset book value increases by the purchase price of the new fixed assets.

Total Asset Turnover Ratio

The **total asset turnover ratio** indicates how efficiently our firm uses its total assets to generate revenue for the firm. The formula used to calculate total asset turnover is

$$\text{Total asset turnover} = \frac{\text{Net sales}}{\text{Average total assets}}$$

This ratio, like the fixed asset turnover ratio, requires that we use both the income statement and the balance sheet to obtain the proper numbers. For Markadel, average total assets were $219,423.50, which is $224,917 total assets in 2008 + $213,930 total assets in 2007 ÷ 2. For Markadel in 2008, total asset turnover was ($306,234 ÷ $219,423,50) = 1.40. When a company increases its assets and is using the new assets more efficiently, it should see an increase in the total asset turnover ratio as these increased assets generate higher sales growth.

LEVERAGE RATIOS

Leverage (debt) ratios indicate what percentage of the business's assets is financed with creditors' dollars. In other words, it indicates what percentage of the business's assets actually belongs to the owners and what percentage is subject to creditors' claims.

Note: A *company's* debt *is its* total liabilities. Current debt *is* current liabilities, long-term debt *is* long-term liabilities, *and* total debt *is* total liabilities. Debt *and* liabilities *are synonymous terms with respect to analyzing financial statements.*

Debt-to-Equity Ratio

The **debt-to-equity ratio** indicates what percentage of the owner's equity is debt, or for every dollar of equity, how many dollars of debt the firm owes. The formula for the debt-to-equity ratio is

$$\text{Debt-to-quity ratio} = \frac{\text{Total liabilities}}{\text{Owner's equity}}$$

or

$$\text{Debt-to-equity ratio} = \frac{\text{Total liabilities}}{\text{Total assets} - \text{Total liabilities}}$$

All information for the debt-to-equity ratio is obtained from the balance sheet (Table 4–2). For Markadel in 2008, the debt-to-equity ratio was ($151,038 ÷ $73,879) = 2.04. Therefore, debt was slightly more than two times the value of the ownership of the firm. This indicates that the company is highly debt capitalized, which might be a result of the company being new (when a lender may loan up to 80 percent of the total assets of the firm) or the company being highly capital intensive. This situation is similar to that of the purchase of a new home, in which the owner pays $40,000 down on a $200,000 home. The mortgage on this home is $160,000. If the home is the individual's only asset, he or she has a debt-to-equity ratio of [($160,000 ÷ ($200,000 − $160,000)] = 4. This indicates that for every dollar in assets that the individual actually owns, he or she has $4 in debt. The ratio is neither good nor bad in itself, but it should be compared with that of other individuals, comparable firms within the industry, or industry averages. The reason for this comparison is that debt must be paid for by you or your firm. Debt payments include both principal and interest. If you have a considerably higher ratio than your competitors, then you will have much lower profit margins in a competitive industry. In a highly competitive industry, we are not free to set prices to cover debt. For example, McDonald's, Wendy's, and Burger King all have 99-cent specials. One of these firms could not decide to increase its price to $2 just because it had more debt.

Returning to our debt-to-equity calculation for Markadel, we notice that the debt-to-equity ratio for 2007 was [$134,250 ÷ ($213,930 − $134,250)] = ($134,250 ÷ $79,680) = 1.68. Once again, this indicates that $1.00 of owner's equity is supporting approximately $1.68 of creditors' claims. Therefore, Markadel increased its debt-to-equity ratio between 2007 and 2008. Because assets increased between 2007 and 2008, we can conclude that the purchase of these assets was financed with more debt than equity.

Debt-to-Total-Assets Ratio

The **debt-to-total-assets ratio** indicates what percentage of a business's assets is owned by creditors. The formula for the debt-to-total assets ratio is

$$\text{Debt-to-total-assets ratio} = \frac{\text{Total liabilities}}{\text{Total assets}}$$

The information for the debt-to-total-assets ratio is obtained from the balance sheet (Table 4-2). For Markadel in 2008, this ratio was ($151,038 ÷ $224,917) = 0.67. Therefore, approximately 67 cents of every dollar in assets used by the business was subject to creditors' claims. In 2007, the debt-to-total-assets ratio was ($134,250 ÷ $213,930) = 0.63. The ratio increased by 4 percent between 2007 and 2008, so in 2008, this company owed approximately 4 cents more to creditors on every dollar of assets owned or assets that they had the right to use.

Times-Interest-Earned Ratio

The times-interest-earned ratio shows the relationship between operating income and the amount of interest in dollars the company has to pay to its creditors on an annual basis. The formula for this ratio is

$$\text{Times-interest-earned ratio} = \frac{\text{Operating income}}{\text{Interest Expense}}$$

$$= \frac{\text{Net income} + \text{Interest Expense} + \text{Tax Expense}}{\text{Interest Expense}}$$

The figures for calculating this ratio are obtained from the income statement (Table 4–1). For Markadel in 2008, this ratio was ($44,232 ÷ $6,250) = 7.08. Notice that you may see this formula written as shown in both examples. If you use the full formula, then the ratio is ($32,285 + $6,250 + $5,697) ÷ $6,250 = 7.08. Therefore, Markadel's operating profit could decline by 7 times and the firm would still be able to meet its annual interest obligation. If operating income declined from $44,232 to $37,982, then the ratio would decrease by 1, to 6.08. If it declined by another $6,250, the ratio would again decline by 1, to 5.08. As mentioned, operating income could decline by 7 times this $6,250 figure and Markadel would still be able to pay interest on its debt. Again, this ratio by itself does not convey much information. What we should do is compare Markadel's ratio with the industry average to determine if the firm is better off than the average firm in the industry. We also can use a comparison of annual figures to determine if Markadel's ability to pay interest on debt is increasing or decreasing.

PROFITABILITY RATIOS

Profitability ratios are used by potential investors and creditors to determine how much of an investment is returned from either earnings on revenues or appreciation of assets. They are also used internally by managers to gauge how well their firms are performing in fiscal and calendar years. If a firm experiences sound current asset management as reflected in liquidity ratios, favorable leverage as determined by leverage ratios, and a substantial degree of turnover as reflected in activity ratios, then the profitability ratios should also be positive and improving. Both internal managers and outside investors compare the ratios of our company with those of our competitors or with industry averages.

Gross Profit Margin Ratio

The **gross profit margin ratio** is used to determine how much gross profit is generated by each dollar in net sales. To calculate gross profit margin, we use the following formula:

$$\text{Gross profit margin ratio} = \frac{\text{Gross profit}}{\text{Net sales}}$$

The data for this ratio are obtained from the income statement (Table 4–1). For Markadel in 2007, this ratio was ($194,206 ÷ $295,456) = 0.66, and in 2008 it was ($186,232 ÷ $306,234) = 0.61. Therefore, Markadel was less profitable in 2008 than it was in 2007. An analysis indicates that although sales increased, the percentage increase in COGS exceeded the percentage increase in sales, resulting in a lower gross profit margin. Looking at the horizontal analysis of sales and COGS for 2007 and 2008, we see that net sales increased by 3.65 percent, whereas COGS increased by 18.52 percent. This situation could very well lead Markadel into bankruptcy if its managers cannot determine how to control COGS in the future. In some situations the firm may have little or no control due to a natural disaster. For example, in August 2005, the Gulf Coast of the United States experienced Hurricane Katrina. This natural disaster had a tremendous effect on the total economies of Mississippi, Alabama, and Louisiana, with the most notable being in New Orleans. Hundreds of businesses ceased to exist as a result of the hurricane and the subsequent loss of life and infrastructure. In southeastern and east-central Mississippi, the main agricultural activity is raising chickens. Millions of chickens were lost in the storm, and surviving chickens died because air conditioning units were shut down because of power outages.[1] It follows, then, that the cost of chicken throughout the United States would increase as the result of a shortage of this very important food stock.

Operating Profit Margin Ratio

The **operating profit margin ratio** is used to determine how much each dollar of sales generates in operating income.

---

[1]Ken Flynn, "Storm Won't Help Area Cotton Prices," September 9, 2005. Retrieved January 5, 2008, from http://www.elpasotimes.com.

Note: Operating income, operating earnings, *and* operating profit *are all synonymous and may be used interchangeably. Income and earnings may be positive if the firm earned a profit or negative if the firm experienced a loss.*

The following formula uses operating income, which is actually a company's earnings before interest and taxes (EBIT):

$$\text{Operating profit margin ratio} = \frac{\text{Operating income}}{\text{Net sales}}$$

We continue to use Table 4–1 to obtain our data. For Markadel in 2007, the operating profit margin was ($56,889 ÷ $295,456) = 0.19, and in 2008 it was ($44,232 ÷ $306,234) = 0.14. Therefore, we see that Markadel earned about 19 percent, or 19 cents, on each dollar of sales in 2007, but in 2008, the store earned only 14 percent, or 14 cents on the dollar. This decrease was not the result of a decrease in sales, but the result of increases in both COGS and some operating expenses.

Net Profit Margin Ratio

The **net profit margin ratio** tells us how much a firm earned on each dollar in sales after paying all obligations, including interest and taxes. The formula for this ratio is

$$\text{Net profit margin ratio} = \frac{\text{Net profit}}{\text{Net sales}}$$

Looking at our income statement data in Table 4–1, we see that Markadel's net profit margin in 2007 was 14.35 percent ($42,406 ÷ $295,456), and in 2008 it was 10.54 percent ($32,285 ÷ $306,234). Overall, there was a decline in net profit of more than 23 percent between 2007 and 2008, even though net sales actually increased by 3.65 percent. This situation indicates that Markadel's managers have not been attentive to those details that contribute to a satisfactory bottom line.

Note: *All the preceding profitability ratios for 2007 were already calculated because of our vertical analysis of Markadel's income statement.*

Operating Return on Assets Ratio

The **operating return on assets ratio**, or *operating return on investment,* allows us to determine how much we are actually earning on each dollar in assets before paying interest and taxes. The formula for operating return on assets is

$$\text{Operating return on assets ratio} = \frac{\text{Operating income}}{\text{Average total assets}}$$

The calculation of this ratio requires us to use both the income statement (Table 4–1) and the balance sheet (Table 4–2). For Markadel in 2008, average total assets were obtained by adding total assets for 2007 and 2008 and dividing by 2. Therefore, 213,930 + 224,917 ÷ 2 = $219,423.50. Operating return on assets was found by dividing operating income $44,232 by average total assets 219,423.50 = 0.20. Thus, for every dollar in assets committed in 2008, 20 cents was generated in operating income.

Net Return on Assets Ratio

The **net return on assets (ROA) ratio** is also referred to as *net return on investment (ROI)* and tells us how much a firm earns on each dollar in assets after paying both interest and taxes. This ratio is useful when deciding if the firm is a good investment compared with other alternatives. The formula for net return on assets is

$$\text{Net return on assets ratio} = \frac{\text{Net income}}{\text{Average total assets}}$$

We must again use both the income statement and the balance sheet. For Markadel in 2008, this ratio was ($32,285 ÷ $219,423.50) = 0.15.

Return on Equity Ratio

The **return on equity (ROE) ratio** tells the stockholder or individual owner what each dollar of his or her investment is generating in net income. The formula for return on equity is

$$\text{Return on equity ratio} = \frac{\text{Net income}}{\text{Average owners equity}}$$

When we look at the income statement and balance sheet for Markadel, we find that in 2008 it was ($32,285 ÷ $76,779.50) = 0.42. When discussing ROE, we must note that there is constant pressure on corporate CEOs to increase annual earnings because the denominator of the equation normally increases as a result of the increase in retained earnings. If earnings remain stagnant, then ROE decreases, because a portion of earnings are normally added to owner's equity in the form of retained earnings. Therefore, with stagnant earnings the numerator remains constant and the denominator increases in value, so ROE declines. Debt can also distort a company's ROE. The more debt a company has, the higher the calculation of ROE, because the accounting equation shows decreased owner's equity when debt is increased. Thus, without any debt financing, a company's ROE and ROA are equal to each other as assets are financed totally by owner's equity capacity. We really must be careful in our evaluation of companies similar to this, because it is often advantageous for managers to increase debt financing and exhibit an increased return on equity.

Another method that companies use to reduce equity and increase ROE is through the buyback or retirement of shares of stock.

MARKET RATIOS

Market ratios are used to compare firms within the same industry. They are primarily used by investors to determine if they should invest capital in a company in exchange for ownership.

Earnings per Share Ratio

The **earnings per share ratio** is nothing more than the net profit or net income of the firm, less preferred dividends (if the company has preferred stock), divided by the weighted average number of shares of common stock outstanding (issued). The formula for calculating earnings per share ratio is

$$\text{Earnings per share ratio} = \frac{\text{Net income} - \text{Preferred dividends}}{\text{Weighted average number of common shares outstanding}}$$

If the firm is publicly held and has issued preferred stock, then preferred stock dividends are subtracted from net earnings prior to calculating earnings per share. The preferred stockholders are quasi-owners of a corporation (they do not normally have a vote), but they receive a specific dividend income. Therefore, the earnings per share ratio is typically more meaningful to the common, rather than the preferred, stockholder. Let us say that a corporation had net income after taxes in 2008 of $1,500,000. It also had 10,000 shares of preferred $100 stock that paid 7 percent, so the preferred stock dividend was $70,000 (10,000 shares times $100 value per share times 0.07). The balance sheet shows 90,000 shares of common stock outstanding in 2007 and 110,000 shares of common stock outstanding in 2008. Hence the weighted average outstanding shares were 100,000 shares; therefore, the earnings per share were

$$\text{Earning per share} = \frac{\$1,500,000 - \$70,000}{100,000} = \frac{\$1,430,000}{100,000} = \$14.30$$

This indicates that common stockholders were earning $14.30 for each share of stock they owned.

Price Earnings Ratio

The **price earnings ratio** is a magnification of earnings per share in terms of market price of stock per share. The price earnings ratio formula is

$$\text{Price earnings ratio} = \frac{\text{Market price of stock per share}}{\text{Earnings per share}}$$

For example, if the earnings per share are $14.30 and today's business section of the newspaper lists the corporate stock as selling for $143, then the price earnings ratio is ($143 ÷ $14.30) = 10. In other words, the stock is selling approximately at 10 times its earnings. If investors believe that the earnings per share will increase in the future, then the market price will eventually increase. If, however, the company receives adverse publicity (e.g., the WorldCom fiasco of 2002,; litigation against the tobacco companies by the state attorneys general), then the public may perceive that the price earnings ratio will decrease in the future, and the price of the stock will drop. A company has a price earnings ratio only if it earned a profit (has a positive net income on its income statement) during the previous reporting quarter; if the company had a loss, then there can be no price earnings ratio. Note that a decrease in earnings gives you a price earnings ratio, but it is higher than in the previous quarter, provided that the price of the stock remains the same. Often we hear that a company had a loss during the current quarter, when in fact the reporter means that earnings per share decreased. This loss is not a true loss, because the income statement still shows a positive net income.

The **price earnings to growth ratio (PEG ratio)** compares the **price to earnings (P/E) ratio** of a company to its earnings per share (EPS) growth rate over the next few years. It is a good indicator of determining the company's potential value of a share of stock. The P/E ratio of any company that is priced fairly equals its growth rate and its PEG is 1. In our previous example, we calculated the P/E ration as being 10 (stock price $143 ÷ $14.30 earnings per share). If the company is growing at 10 percent each year and it has a P/E ratio of 10, its PEG is equal to 10 ÷ 10, or 1. The value of each share of stock is priced correctly because the market pays a price 10 times earnings per share if it knows that the business in question will have a 10 percent growth rate. A PEG lower than 1 means that the stock is undervalued; a PEG higher than 1 indicates that the stock is overvalued. However, PEGs between 1 and 2 are considered to be in normal range. In addition, it should be ascertained that projected earnings per share represent future growth of earnings and do not pertain to the previous year's earnings.

$$\text{PEG ratio} = \frac{\text{Price Earnings Ratio}}{\text{Annual Expected Growth Rate in \%}}$$

$$= \frac{\frac{\text{Market Price of Stock per share}}{\text{Earnings Per Share}}}{\text{Annual Expected Growth Rate in \%}} = \frac{\frac{\$143}{\$14.30}}{10}$$

$$= 1$$

In the example, the company stock price of $143 is fair. However, if the growth rate were only 7 percent, the the PEG ratio would be 1.42 (10 ÷ 7 = 1.42), and the stock is considered to be overpriced. It the growth rate were 13 percent, then the PEG ratio would be 0.76 (10 ÷ 13 = 0.76), and the stock is considered to be undervalued. The authors consider the PEG ratio to be a better measure of stock value because it takes the company growth rate into consideration.

Operating Cash Flow per Share Ratio

The **operating cash flow per share ratio** compares the operating cash flow on the statement of cash flows to the average number of shares of common stock outstanding. As a result of the numerous financial scandals like Enron and WorldCom, we conclude that operating cash flow is a better measure of financial health than net income. Cash is much harder to manipulate under *generally accepted accounting principles (GAAP)* than is net income. The formula for operating cash flow per share is

$$\text{Operating cash flow per share ratio} = \frac{\text{Operating cash flow}}{\text{Average common shares of stock outstanding}}$$

The ratio uses information from both the statement of cash flows and the balance sheet. Using the statement of cash flow for the Moderately Large Corporation (MLC), December 31, 2008 (Table 4–3), the cash provided by operating activities was $149,000. Using the balance sheet for the MLC, the outstanding shares were 3,500,000 + 3,500,000 ÷ 2, which equals 3,500,000 (Table 4–4). When we plug these numbers into our formula, we obtain

$$\text{Operating cash flow per share} = \frac{\text{Operating cash flow}}{\text{Average common shares of stock outstanding}}$$

$$= \frac{\$149,000}{3,500,000} = \$0.04257 \text{ or 4 cents per share}$$

This indicates that the MLC generates $0.04 in positive cash flow for each share of stock outstanding. Many analysts now believe that operating cash flow is a much better predictor of a firm's stability and financial health than earnings per share, because it is actual cash that pays the bills and not accounts receivable. On the income statement cash and credit sales may not be separated, so a company may have a large portion of its sales from credit, which increases revenue and appears as accounts receivable on the balance sheet. If these credit sales are not collected, then earnings per share may overstate actual profitability of the firm significantly. In fraudulent cases like Enron and WorldCom, misstating accounts receivable was how these companies showed tremendous profits without actually having the money.

Free Cash Flow per Share

Free cash flow gives businesses the opportunity to set aside moneys from operating activities and use them to generate growth. This growth allows a business to finance projects on their own without help from external sources. It

TABLE 4–3 Moderately Large Corporation Consolidated Statement of Cash Flows

Consolidated Statement of Cash Flows
(in thousands)

Fiscal Year Ended	Dec. 31, 2008
OPERATING ACTIVITIES:	
Net earnings	$ 983
Adjustments to reconcile net earnings to net cash provided by operating activities:	
Depreciation	150
Accounts receivable	(132)
Inventories	(1,008)
Pepaid expenses and other current assets	(31)
Deferred income taxes	(4)
Accounts payable	187
Accrued compensation and related costs	6
Accrued taxes	(9)
Current portion of long term debt	7
Net cash provided by operating activities	149
INVESTING ACTIVITIES:	
Net additions to property, plant and equipment	(1,000)
Other assets	(7)
Net cash used by investing activities	(1,007)
FINANCING ACTIVITIES:	
Proceeds from issuance of long-term debt	800
Net cash used by financing activities	800
Net increase/(decrease) in cash and cash equivalents	(58)
CASH AND CASH EQUIVALENTS:	
Beginning of period	1,427
End of the period	$1,369

indicates that the business has done well in managing its free cash flow. The formula is

Free cash flow = Cash flow from operations − capital expenditures

A *capital expenditure* is money spent to acquire or upgrade physical assets that include equipment, property or industrial buildings. It does not include other business investment such as the purchase or sale of securities, repayments of debt, or proceeds from issuing stock.

Using the consolidated statement of cash flows for the MLC data for December 31, 2008, we plug these numbers into the formula as follows:

Free cash flow = $149,000 − 1,007,000 = ($858,000)

$$\text{Free cash flow per share} = \frac{\text{Free cash flow}}{\text{Average common shares outstanding}}$$

$$= \frac{(\$858,000)}{3,500,000} = (\$0.245) \text{ or a negative 25 cents per share}$$

TABLE 4–4 Moderately Large Corporation Consolidated Balance Sheet

Moderately Large Corporation Consolidated Balance Sheet
(in thousands except share data)

Fiscal Year Ended	Dec. 31, 2008	Dec. 31, 2007
ASSETS		
Current assets		
Cash and cash equivalents	$1,369	$1,427
Accounts receivable, net	1,008	876
Inventories	1,489	481
Prepaid expenses and other current assets	157	126
Deferred income taxes, net	44	40
Total current assets	4,066	2,950
Property, plant and equipment, net	3,137	2,287
Other assets	168	161
TOTAL ASSETS	$7,371	$5,398
LIABILITIES AND SHAREHOLDERS' EQUITY		
Current liabilities		
Accounts payable	$ 429	$ 242
Accrued compensation and related costs	104	98
Accrued taxes	132	141
Current portion of long-term debt	89	82
Total current liabilities	754	563
Long-term debt	2,630	1,830
Total liabilities	3,384	2,392
Shareholders' equity		
Common stock ($0.1 par value)—authorized,		
4,000,000 shares; issued and outstanding, 3,500,000	350	350
Paid-in capital in excess of par	2,415	2,415
Retained earnings	1,222	241
Total shareholders' equity	3,987	3,006
TOTAL LIABILITIES AND SHAREHOLDERS' EQUITY	$7,371	$5,398

Companies that have a large amount of free cash flow send a message that they can fend for themselves. They are able to pay off debt and buy back stock. Cash flow is very important if business owners want to survive. Two strong reasons why businesses fail are directly related to cash flow. One reason for failure is that they expand too rapidly and may have cash flow problems; another is that a business may be undercapitalized and not have enough cash flow to sustain themselves in a business crisis.

SOURCES OF COMPARATIVE RATIOS

Several public sources of comparative ratios are readily available to the investor or business owner. It is essential that these ratios be obtained to determine how well the individual firm is doing when compared with other firms in the same

or similar industries. Most of these source publications are available at local public libraries, college or university libraries, or on the Internet. Some of the
sources are as follows:

- ♦ **Industry Norms and Key Business Ratios.** New York: Dun &
  Bradstreet Credit Services.
- ♦ **Dun's Review.** New York: Dun & Bradstreet.
- ♦ **Quarterly Financial Report for Manufacturing, Mining, and Trade
  Corporations.** Washington, D.C.: Federal Trade Commission.
- ♦ **Statement Studies.** Philadelphia: Robert Morris Associates.
- ♦ **The Value Line Investment Survey.** New York: Value Line Publi-
  cations, Inc.

Other sources include the financial statements of other companies (if firms
are publicly held, then the annual reports and Form 10-K reports are available
from the corporation), trade journals, and business and industry publications.
Because both the sources and firm sizes vary, it may be necessary for the entrepreneur to use a combination of vertical, horizontal, and ratio analyses to obtain
a complete and clear picture of an industry.

 CONCLUSION

No single method of analysis gives a complete picture of our firm; therefore, we
presented the three most widely used and easily understood methods in this
chapter.

1. *Vertical analysis* is extremely useful as a monitoring tool to the business
owner, because most businesses complete monthly financial statements to be
used internally. Software programs can be set up to calculate a vertical analysis
automatically for the owners or managers of the business. Vertical analysis is a
rapid method of catching fluctuations in income statement or balance sheet
items. It uses pivotal accounts as a measure of how good the financial health
of the company is with regard to these accounts.

2. *Horizontal analysis* is useful as a control tool to compare actual annual
fluctuations with established company goals. It also can be performed on a
monthly or quarterly basis, if the owner believes that circumstances call for
tighter control. This type of analysis is also used to determine if short-term
objectives are being accomplished from period to period.

3. *Ratio analysis* is a means of identifying trends in a firm's liquidity, leverage, activity, profitability, and marketability. It is also used to determine if your
firm compares favorably with other firms in the same industry. Ratio analysis
makes you, as an owner or manager, more aware of the sore spots in your firm
that may be in need of repair.

As an entrepreneur, you must use financial analysis as a means of monitoring both your own and your competitors' performance. In addition, it allows you to establish standards and goals for your own firm for control purposes. If financial analysis is used properly, it allows the owner to identify variances in performance and to determine a course of corrective action in a timely manner.

REVIEW AND DISCUSSION QUESTIONS

1. What is the purpose of financial statement analysis?
2. Give an example of how financial statements can be used internally by the managers of a company.
3. List and briefly describe the three types of financial statement analysis.
4. If a company had sales of $2,587,643 in 1998 and sales of $3,213,456 in 2003, by what percentage did sales change during this time period? If the company had a goal of increasing sales by 25 percent over a 5-year period, did it meet its objectives?
5. If the company in question 4 sets a goal of increasing sales by 28 percent during the next 5 years, what should be the sales goal for 2008?
6. List and briefly describe the five categories of business ratios.
7. If a company computes its current ratio to be 3.56, what does this mean in terms of the company's current assets and current liabilities?
8. Why might a company have a high current ratio but a low quick ratio (acid test ratio)?
9. If a company has beginning inventory of $30,000 and ending inventory of $55,000, compute its average inventory. If the COGS is $140,000, compute its inventory turnover and determine how many days the average item is in stock.
10. A company computes its accounts receivable turnover to be 20. Based on this information, find the average collection period. If the company has a credit collection period of 30 days, explain the relationship between the *credit collection period* and the *average collection period*.
11. If a company finds that its fixed asset turnover (net sales/fixed assets) has fallen to less than 1, what does this indicate?
12. If a company has $181,000 in total liabilities and $225,000 in total assets, what percentage of total assets is being financed with the use of other people's money?
13. Distinguish between *gross profit margin, operating profit margin,* and *net profit margin* and provide the formula for each ratio.
14. Why is the *operating return on assets ratio* also referred to as the *operating return on investment*?
15. If a company's stock is currently selling for $12 per share and its price earnings ratio is 6, what are its earnings per share? What does this figure mean?

EXERCISES AND PROBLEMS

1. Samantha Knight is applying for a small-business loan. She provides the bank with the following information: cash in checking accounts, $5,000; cash in savings, $10,350; home market value, $145,500; first mortgage on house, $25,000; home equity loan limit, $70,000; home equity loan, $10,000; automobile market value, $19,000; automobile loan outstanding, $15,000; credit card debt, $1,500.
    a. Calculate the debt-to-asset ratio.
    b. Calculate the debt-to-equity ratio.
    c. What percentage of Samantha's assets are owned by others?
2. You receive the following partial balance sheet (Table 4–5) for 2008 and 2007 for a company that you are considering making an investment in. Perform a vertical analysis for each year on these accounts. Compare the two years, and describe those changes that were beneficial or detrimental to this company in one sentence.
3. You were not totally satisfied with the vertical analysis, so you now want to run a horizontal analysis of this company. Complete Table 4–6. Perform

TABLE 4–5 Balance Sheet, Sample Company

Category	2007	Vertical Analysis 2007	2008	Vertical Analysis 2008
Current assets	$ 7,000,000	_____	$ 9,000,000	_____
Total fixed assets	8,000,000	_____	6,000,000	_____
Total assets	15,000,000		15,000,000	
Current liabilities	$ 3,000,000	_____	$ 1,000,000	_____
Long term debt	4,000,000	_____	4,000,000	_____
Owner's equity	8,000,000		10,000,000	_____
Total liabilities & owner's equity	$15,000,000	_____	$15,000,000	_____

TABLE 4–6 Sample Balance Sheet

	2007	2008	Horizontal Analysis
Current assets	$ 7,000,000	$ 9,000,000	_____
Total fixed assets	8,000,000	6,000,000	_____
Total assets	15,000,000	15,000,000	_____
Current liabilities	$ 3,000,000	$ 1,000,000	_____
Long term debt	4,000,000	4,000,000	_____
Owner's equity	8,000,000	10,000,000	_____
Total liabilities & owner's equity	$15,000,000	$15,000,000	_____

a horizontal analysis on these accounts. Compare the changes in accounts, and describe the changes that were beneficial or detrimental to this company in one sentence.

4. Last month, you were vacationing in Phoenix and noticed that there were several Starbucks Coffee locations. You do not have any coffee locations in your city, except for a few local cafes. You also have a large college in your town and believe that, if Starbucks Coffee opened a location, they would be very successful. If you went to your public library, what sources would you use to find out more information about this company? If you are on the Internet, how can you obtain additional information on this company?

5. Given the balance sheet for the Moderately Large Corporation (Table 4–4), answer the following:
   a. For each year, calculate the following ratios: current, quick, debt-to-asset, and debt-to-equity.
   b. In a written explanation, state what each ratio means.
   c. Compare the ratios for the 2-year period and determine if the MLC is sufficiently liquid.
   d. How well is the MLC managing its debt?

6. Perform a horizontal analysis of the the MLC balance sheet (Table 4–4).
   a. Compare assets, liabilities, and owner's equity from one year to the next.
   b. Is the corporation better off in 2008 or in 2007?

7. Perform a vertical analysis of the MLC balance sheet (Table 4–4) for December 31, 2007.

8. Given the income statement for the MLC (Table 4–7) and balance sheet (Table 4–4), answer the following:
   a. Calculate the following ratios for 2007: operating profit margin, net profit margin, operating return on assets, net return on assets, and return on equity.
   b. In a written explanation, describe what each ratio means.
   c. In a brief paragraph, describe the overall profitability of the MLC.

9. Perform a horizontal analysis for the MLC income statement (Table 4–7) for 2006 and 2007. Write an explanation of this analysis.

10. Using both the balance sheet (Table 4–4) and the income statement (Table 4–7) for the MLC, answer the following:
   a. Calculate the following ratios for 2007: inventory turnover, fixed asset turnover, and total asset turnover.
   b. In a written explanation, describe what each ratio means.
   c. In a brief paragraph, describe how well you believe the MLC is managing its assets.

11. Given the profit loss (income statement) and balance sheet for Sam's Sandwich Delivery (Table 4–8), answer the following:
   a. Calculate the current and quick ratios.
   b. Using the inventory figure on the balance sheet as average inventory, calculate the inventory turnover ratio.
   c. Calculate the debt-to-equity ratio, debt-to-total-asset ratio, and operating profit margin ratio.
   d. Perform a vertical analysis of the income statement.

TABLE 4–7 Moderately Large Corporation Consolidated Statement of Earnings

Consolidated Statement of Earnings
(in thousands, except earning per share)

Fiscal Year Ended	Dec. 31, 2008	Dec. 31, 2007	Dec. 31, 2006
Net revenues			
Cash Sales	$2,888	$2,751	$2,456
Credit Sales	6,046	5,258	4,572
Total Net Revenues	8,935	8,009	7,028
Cost of Sales	5,361	4,405	3,725
Gross Profit	3,574	3,604	3,303
Salaries	1,258	1,183	1,112
Insurance	155	116	93
Depreciation	150	135	122
General and administrative expenses	489	479	361
Subtotal operating expenses	2,052	1,913	1,687
Operating income	1,522	1,691	1,616
Interest expense	10	11	11
Earnings before income taxes	1,512	1,680	1,605
Income taxes	529	588	562
Net Earnings	$ 983	$1,092	$1,043
Per Common Share			
Net Earnings Basic	$ 0.28	$ 0.31	$ 0.30
Net Earnings Diluted	$ 0.25	$ 0.27	$ 0.26
Weighted average shares outstanding:			
Basic	3,500	3,500	3,500
Diluted	4,000	4,000	4,000

    e. Perform a vertical analysis of the balance sheet.

    f. Based on your analysis, would you consider investing in Sam's Sandwich Delivery?

12. Go to your local library or on the Internet and look up the industry averages for the following groups of ratios: liquidity, activity, debt utilization, and profitability.

    a. Compare these ratios to the Starbucks ratios.

    b. After your analysis of Starbucks in the previous exercise, would you still recommend that Starbucks establish a location in your town?

13. The Handy Dandy Corporation has an income statement that indicates that operating income is $2,375,486 and net profit is $1,375,486. In 2006, the corporation had 1 million shares of common stock outstanding; in 2007, they had 3 million shares of common stock outstanding. What is this corporation's approximate earnings per share?

14. The Namleda Corporation has an income statement that indicates that operating income is $2,375,486 and pays interest of $100,000 and taxes of $900,000. The corporation currently has an average of 3 million shares of common stock outstanding and 1 million shares of preferred stock, which

TABLE 4–8 Financial Statements for Sam's Sandwich Delivery

Profit/Loss (Income Statement) for Six Months Ending 06–30–2008

Revenues			
Retail Sales	$68,283		
Wholesale Sales	104,417		
Total Revenues		$172,700	
Cost of Sales	52,067		
Gross Profit		$120,633	
Total Operating Expenses	111,117		
Operating Profit		$ 9,516	
Other Income/Expenses			
Interest Income	41		
Interest Expense	(651)		
Depreciation-Store Equipment	(292)		
Total Other Income/Expenses		(902)	
Net Profit			$ 8,614

BALANCE SHEET AS OF 06–30–2006

Assets			
Current Assets			
Change Fund		$ 569	
Cash in Bank-Checking		8,612	
Cash in Bank-Savings		9,622	
Accounts Receivable		6,843	
Inventories		2,607	
Total Current Assets			$28,253
Fixed Assets			
Furniture and Fixtures	4,296		
Less: Accum Depreciation	4,110	186	
Equipment	68,293		
Less: Accum Depreciation	67,725	568	
Transportation Equipment	31,168		
Less: Accum Depreciation	11,571	19,597	
Total Fixed Assets			$20,351
Total Assets			$48,604
Current Liabilities			
Accounts Payable Trade		6,208	
Accrued Payroll Taxes		3,464	
Accrued Sales Taxes		987	
Total Current Liabilities			$10,659
Long-Term Liabilities			
Auto Loans Payable		18,626	
Total Long-Term Liabilities			$18,626
Total Liabilities			$29,285
Stockholder's Equity			
Common Stock	83,081		
Retained Earnings	(72,376)		
Net Profit/Loss	8,614		
Total Equity			19,319
Total Liabilities and Equity			$48,604

pays a dividend of $1.00 per share. What is the corporation's approximate earnings per share?

RECOMMENDED TEAM ASSIGNMENT

1. Find the best publically traded company that is a competitor in the industry where you would like to start a business.
   a. Do a complete ratio analysis of this corporation. Based on the numbers, explain what the future looks like for this company.
   b. If you are to compete in this industry and maintain the same profit margin as your competitor, what must you hold your cost of goods sold to as a percentage of sales?
   c. What must you hold your operating expenses to as a percentage of sales?
   d. What return on equity ratio should you look for?
2. Evaluate the cash flow statement of the company in question 1. Explain why the numbers on the cash flow statement are more feasible than the numbers on the income statement for a potential investor.

CASE STUDY: MOSBACHER INSURANCE AGENCY[2]

©2007 Philip J. Adelman and Alan M. Marks

BACKGROUND

Gerson Mosbacher is a first-generation American whose parents came to the United States from Germany. The family only spoke German in the house, and the children were educated in the public school system of Chicago. Gerson graduated from the University of Illinois in 1967 with a degree in finance. He didn't really know what he wanted to do with the degree, and decided that he would party for the rest of his life and went to Florida with an engineering buddy. After being in Florida for a few months, his mother informed him that he received a draft notice. Knowing that he did not want to be a private in the army, he decided to volunteer for infantry Officer's Candidate School (OCS) at Fort Benning, Georgia. He had a roommate with previous military experience who mentored him to the eventual position of honor council chairman for the base. In this position, he learned about the importance of having connections and volunteering for the right assignments. Gerson, by this time, was engaged to be married, but his fiancée, Judy, informed him that if he went to Vietnam, she would wait for him, but did not want to get married. The Army was looking for people who were bilingual to move into intelligence, and Gerson, 2 weeks before graduation, filled out the forms to let the army know that he was fluent in German. Gerson graduated OCS, and 158 lieutenants out of his class were sent to Vietnam, but Gerson was transferred to Germany

---

[2]This case study was developed by the authors using personal interviews with Gerson Mosbacher during October 2007.

in Military Intelligence. Before he left for Germany, Gerson and Judy were married. Gerson still had no idea what he wanted to do once he left the service, but he knew that now, he actually had to make some kind of living as he was a family man.

During his tour in Germany, Gerson was approached by an American Continental Life Insurance agent to buy an insurance policy. The agent and Gerson hit it off, and by the end of the evening, Gerson was asked to try selling life insurance while in the military to see if he liked it.

GAINING EXPERIENCE

Gerson trained to obtain both an insurance license and the NASD security license because American Continental also sold securities. He completed these courses through correspondence courses and took the certifying exams in Paris. He started selling life insurance to other military people while still in the service, but realized that he didn't really like to sell insurance. However, because of his business background he saw the opportunity to recruit and train others to sell insurance for him. Before he left the Army, he already had 20 people under him who were selling insurance.

In 1969, Gerson left the service, but his wife Judy had a good job working for the U.S. Army Engineering Command in Frankfurt and they decided to remain in Germany after discharge. Gerson continued to expand his insurance agency and within 1 year, he had more than 100 people working for him in 12 countries, including people who were stationed at most military bases in NATO. He even went to the Middle East and sold insurance to American oil company employees.

Headquarters for the American Continental overseas operation was in Frankfurt. When Judy became pregnant in 1972, the Mosbachers decided to leave Germany and move back to the United States. They knew that they didn't want a cold-weather climate, and when they visited the Phoenix area, they decided to stay. For the first 5 years, Gerson flew back and forth to Europe to run his insurance agency. His operation was so large that a new boss at American Continental decided to cut his override commission from 10 percent to 0.05 percent, which effectively made it unprofitable to work for American Continental Insurance. Gerson left the company and, on his final flight back to Phoenix from Germany, had a seatmate who was working on some insurance forms. He asked the gentleman what he was doing, and was informed that the man was the District Manager for State Farm Insurance in Phoenix. They continued talking on the way back to Phoenix and Thomas Knobbe, the State Farm district manager, offered Gerson a job as a State Farm Agent starting at $600 a month. Gerson decided that this was not sufficient and subsequently went to work in Phoenix for Dean Witter as a commodities broker. He was not very good at this, and really didn't like it. After 2 years, he left Dean Witter and called Tom Knobbe to see if he could still come to work for State Farm as an Agent.

MOSBACHER INSURANCE COMPANY

In November 1976, Thomas Knobbe, the District manager for State Farm, allowed Gerson to became an agent, a job which by this time paid all of $700 a month. Tom allowed two new agents to work in his office rent-free while they were establishing their agencies. State Farm gave Gerson a rate book and asked him to develop a list of 2,000 potential clients. His boss said that because of the beauty of renewals, if Gerson worked hard and "kept his nose clean," he could probably make up to $50,000 a year with his own agency.

Entrepreneurship at work

Because Gerson knew that he didn't like to cold-call people and try to sell them insurance, he decided to use his own method. The Mosbachers joined everything—the local synagogue, the Toastmasters, the local Chamber of Commerce, and the like. He passed cards out to everyone he knew and asked people to call him when their policies were up for renewal. He also hired a phone solicitor to cold-call people and ask them if they would like a quote on their auto insurance policy. When the solicitor got a positive answer, Gerson would contact the person. At this point, he really didn't have a lot of clients.

He asked himself, where do people have to go when they move to Phoenix and don't have insurance? His answer was the Department of Motor Vehicles. Gerson set up a stool in the parking lot of the Maricopa County DMV along with a small tool kit and a pile of business cards. When people with out-of-state plates drove up, he would offer to take off their plates and replace them with Arizona plates when they came out. Gerson accepted no payment for his service, but instead handed them a business card and asked them to call when they decided to renew their policy so he could give them a quote on Arizona insurance, because they still had out-of-state insurance. Being a businessman, Gerson approached people based on the net worth of their automobiles—the car had to be relatively new and in good condition.

Although the Mosbachers had some savings, it quickly ran out during the 2 years as a commodities broker, and it took time to establish an insurance agency with no real customer base. Realizing they needed additional income, Judy got a job and worked at Boswell Hospital as a personnel assistant for 5 years until Mosbacher Insurance actually earned enough money for her to quit. She also worked in the agency helping Gerson.

Before long, Gerson learned that you can't judge a book by its cover. One day a man drove into the DMV with an old beat-up station wagon. He was having trouble getting his plates off as the bolts had rusted. He asked Gerson for some assistance, and he reluctantly helped the man. When the man came back with his Arizona plates, he asked Gerson for help in putting them on and offered to pay Gerson. He, of course, refused. The man then asked for his business card. A week later, the man called and asked for an auto insurance and homeowner's quote. The man happened to have just finished his residency in neurology, and eventually became the head neurosurgeon at one of the most prestigious hospitals in metropolitan Phoenix. He is still a client of Mosbacher Insurance.

In another situation, a gentleman who looked like a poor farmer came into the office. He was dressed in dirty jeans and work boots and drove an old car. He also owned and managed one of the largest mutual funds in the United States; he too is still a client of Mosbacher Insurance.

Another situation developed for Gerson because of his affiliations with the military and American Continental. Several of the people that he knew in the military moved to Phoenix and sold life insurance. If they didn't also sell health, auto, or homeowners insurance, they referred their clients to Gerson, and he became one of State Farm's largest health insurance writers as a new agent (those with fewer than 2 years in the business) in the United States.

The result

Within 3 years, Mosbacher Insurance Agency, Inc., was well established. Remember when Gerson's boss said that if he worked real hard, he could make $50,000 a year?

TABLE 4–9 Income Statement for Mosbacher Insurance Agency

Mosbacher Insurance Agency
Abbreviated Average Income Statement
January 1 to December 31

Category	Amount		
Revenue			$650,000
Operating Expenses			
Salary/Commission	150,000		
Phone, Computer, Utilities	10,000		
Postage	10,000		
Marketing, Printing & Advertising	25,000		
Insurance	20,000		
Rent	15,000		
Misc	20,000		
Total Operating Expenses		$250,000	
Operating Income			$400,000
Taxes		$ 75,000	
Net Income After Taxes			$325,000

Note: Expenses obtained via memo from Gerson Mosbacher, December 20, 2007.

Initially, Gerson worked for $700 a month gross, working 7 days a week, 12 to 15 hours a day—because he spent 8 hours a day at the DMV and then interviewed potential clients on evenings and weekends. Thirty-two years later, Mosbacher Insurance has gross income in excess of $65,000 a month (Table 4–9) with five full-time employees. Gerson learned early that if you pay people well, take care of them, and pay them more than they get anywhere else, they will stay with you. Most of Gerson's employees have been with him for more than 15 years.

One of the strategic advantages of the insurance business is renewals. If they are satisfied with their service, most people simply renew their policies and pay their premiums year after year. The agent who sells the policy gets a percentage of every premium dollar. Gerson, like most entrepreneurs, provides us with a formula for success—find out what you love to do, gain experience, work hard, and be willing to spend 60 to 80 hours a week building your business.

QUESTIONS

1. Using Table 4–9, peform a vertical analysis of the Mosbacher Insurance Agency.
   a. Using the Internet, obtain the income statement for the insurance company where you insure your automobile (casualty insurance company) and perform a vertical analysis of this company.
   b. Compare and contrast the two companies.
2. How did Gerson Mosbacher overcome the barriers to entrance into the market place?

CHAPTER 5

Profit, Profitability, and Break-Even Analysis

Learning Objectives

When you have completed this chapter, you should be able to:

♦ Understand the difference between *efficiency* and *effectiveness*.
♦ Distinguish between *profit* and *profitability*.
♦ Compare accounting and entrepreneurial profit.
♦ Understand the relationship of profit margin and asset turnover to the earning power of a company.
♦ Given the variable costs, revenue, and fixed costs of a business, determine the break-even point and contribution margin.
♦ Construct and analyze a break-even chart when given the variable costs, revenue, and fixed costs of a business.
♦ Understand the use of leverage and its relationship to profitability and loss.
♦ Compare and contrast the degree of operating, financial, and combined leverage and their effect on the profitability of a corporation.
♦ Distinguish between Chapter 11, Chapter 13, and Chapter 7 bankruptcies.

In Chapter 4, we gained an understanding of financial statements and their analysis. In this chapter, we begin exploring the methods that are necessary for planning our financial strategy. Prior to developing this strategy, it is necessary to define some key financial concepts that potential lenders (banks) or investors often discuss with the entrepreneur. Typical questions include the following:

1. What profit do you expect to obtain?
2. How profitable will your firm be in the future?

3. How profitable is your firm now?
4. What is your break-even point?

Before these questions can be answered adequately, we must understand the basic concepts behind them. Although a question pertaining to efficiency and effectiveness may not be asked directly, having a clear understanding of these terms helps when talking with a lender/investor. In this chapter, we review the concepts of efficiency and effectiveness and relate them to profit and profitability.

EFFICIENCY AND EFFECTIVENESS

Efficiency is obtaining the highest possible return with the minimum use of resources. **Effectiveness** is accomplishing a specific task or reaching a goal. For example, assume you are in the automobile repair business and employ two mechanics. Both mechanics are asked to complete a specific job (e.g., changing an alternator in a 2000 Chevrolet). One mechanic completes the job in 1.5 hours, and the other mechanic completes the job in 2.3 hours. Both mechanics were effective, because they both completed the job and accomplished the task. The first mechanic was more efficient, however, because that mechanic used less time. In this example, *mechanic-hours-worked* (the resource used) is the measure of efficiency for automobile repairs.

In financial planning the same principle applies. Assume that two people, James and Joan, want to make an investment and eventually earn $1,000 during 1 year. Both would be effective if they accomplished this task. If James decides to earn the $1,000 by keeping money in a savings account that returns 5 percent per year, then he must invest $20,000 ($20,000 × 0.05 = $1,000) to earn his $1,000. If Joan purchases a 1-year certificate of deposit (CD) that returns 10 percent, then she must purchase a $10,000 CD ($10,000 × 0.10 = $1,000) to earn her $1,000. James and Joan were both effective because they both attained their goal, which was the target return of $1,000; however, Joan was more efficient because she used less money to achieve the same goal. We find that effectiveness and efficiency are usually related to manufacturing and personal accomplishments (e.g., constructing a building, making a product, writing a book). Businesses must strive to achieve both efficiency and effectiveness consistently. Today, however, the greatest emphasis in the business community appears to be a constant quest to improve profit and profitability.

Businesses use both profit and profitability in the financial marketplace as measures of efficiency and effectiveness. The terms *profit* and *profitability*, like *efficiency* and *effectiveness*, are regarded as two separate concepts.

PROFIT

Profit is an absolute number earned on an investment. Other terms that indicate a profit include *net earnings* for a company, *interest* for savers, and *coupons* for bond-holders. There are two basic types of profit: accounting profit and entrepreneurial profit. For a business's financial statements, we use **accounting profit**, which is typically shown at the bottom of an income statement. This profit is basically what a business has left from its revenues after paying all expenses, including cost of goods, administrative expenses, overhead, interest, and taxes.

Entrepreneurial profit differs from accounting profit because it is based on the economic concept of opportunity costs (defined in Chapter 1). An entrepreneurial profit is the amount earned above and beyond what the entrepreneur would have earned if that person had chosen to invest time and money in some other enterprise. For example, assume that Sam Jones, an electrical engineer, quit his job with a major firm to open a business that manufactures a small electrical component. The job that Sam quit paid $50,000 per year. After his first year in business, Sam's income statement indicated that his firm had made a profit of $30,000. Thus, Sam had an accounting profit of $30,000, but an entrepreneurial loss of $20,000.

The opportunity cost surrendered to go into business on his own was $50,000 because Sam gave up a $50,000 job to go into a business that earned $30,000. His earnings of $30,000 resulted in an entrepreneurial loss of $20,000. At the end of the second year, Sam's business showed a profit of $90,000. Because Sam could have earned $50,000 in his old job (opportunity cost surrendered), he then had an entrepreneurial profit of $40,000. It is important for us to understand this concept because the small business owner hopes to make an entrepreneurial profit in addition to an accounting profit. Profit is directly related to the concepts of efficiency and effectiveness. The owner establishes a *profit goal* (measure of effectiveness) and attempts to reach this goal in the most *efficient* manner (the manner making the best use of resources).

PROFITABILITY

Profitability can be measured in a business by using a ratio obtained by dividing net profit by total assets. *Profitability,* therefore, is our return on investment and is related more to the concept of efficiency than that of effectiveness. For the business owner, profitability is how efficiently the business assets are being used in generating profit. To illustrate, assume that Mary Jones owns two businesses: a computer software sales company and a computer consulting firm. She invested $100,000 in the sales company, did not change her total asset investment during the accounting year, and received a profit of $2,000; she invested $10,000 in the consulting firm, did not change her total asset investment during the accounting year, and received a profit of $1,500. Because Mary did not change her total asset investment during the accounting year, her average total assets equals her initial investment. Therefore, Mary made a higher profit, or dollar amount, off the sales company. However, the consulting firm had greater profitability. With $10,000 in assets committed, the consulting firm generated a profit of $1,500, as opposed to $2,000 of profit generated on $100,000 in assets committed by the sales company.

We determine profitability by using the net return on assets ratio. As mentioned in Chapter 4, this ratio is sometimes referred to as simply *return on investment (ROI)*.

$$\text{ROI} = \frac{\text{Net profit (income)}}{\text{Average total assets}}$$

For the sales company,

$$\text{ROI} = \frac{\$2,000}{\$100,000} = 0.02 = 2\%$$

For the consulting firm,

$$\text{ROI} = \frac{\$1,500}{\$10,000} = 0.15 = 15\%$$

Therefore, Mary's investment in the consulting firm was much more profitable than her investment in the sales company. Profitability is one method of determining the efficiency of an owner's investment when compared with another investment; another method of determining if a business is using its assets efficiently is to compute its earning power.

EARNING POWER

The **earning power** of a company can be defined as the product of two factors: (1) the company's ability to generate income on the amount of revenue it receives, which is also known as *net profit margin;* and (2) its ability to maximize sales revenue from proper asset employment, also known as *total asset turnover.* Therefore, earning power is equal to net profit margin times total asset turnover. To calculate the earning power of a company, the following formulas are used:

$$\text{Net profit margin} = \frac{\text{Net profit (income)}}{\text{Net sales}}$$

and

$$\text{Total asset turnover} = \frac{\text{Net sales}}{\text{Average total assets}}$$

Therefore,

$$\text{Earning power} = \text{Net profit margin} \times \text{Total asset turnover}$$

$$= \frac{\text{Net profit (income)}}{\text{Net sales}} \times \frac{\text{Net sales}}{\text{Average total assets}}$$

Because sales cancel in the preceding formula,

$$\text{Earning power} = \frac{\text{Net profit (income)}}{\text{Average total assets}}$$

Companies that have a low inventory turnover (as discussed in Chapter 4) must compensate for low asset use by maintaining a high net profit margin, achieved by having a selling price that far exceeds the cost of the good. The markup must be greater in those companies that are not able to efficiently turn over their assets as readily as other companies. One example is a company that sells specialized heavy machinery. These companies do not do a high-volume business, and so must compensate for decreased turnover by having higher margins. Supermarkets, however, have very high inventory turnover ratios, and can therefore operate on low profit margins and still generate earning power.

When discussing the assets of a company, we must consider the debt and equity supporting them. For most businesses, the ownership of assets is divided into two portions. Recall that the basic accounting formula is Total assets = Total liabilities + Owner's equity, or Total assets − Total liabilities = Owner's equity. Hence the higher the liabilities, the lower the owner's equity. The liability portion of this formula indicates how much of a company is being financed by other people's money. Using other people's money is incurring debt.

Before we take on debt, it is essential to determine if our business is able to support the debt and provide us with a profit. One method of determining profit in advance of making an investment is through break-even analysis.

BREAK-EVEN ANALYSIS

Break-even analysis is a process of determining how many units of production must be sold or how much revenue must be obtained before we begin to earn a profit. The decision of whether to use units sold or revenues obtained in calculating the break-even point is based on several factors, one of which involves the firm's ability to determine its sales units. For a retail firm that deals in hundreds or perhaps thousands of individual items, the break-even point in terms of sales dollars is easier to compute than the break-even point in sales units. For the manufacturing firm that produces discrete units, however, the break-even point in units of production may be more appropriate.

In any event, we must identify several variables prior to determining the break-even point: fixed costs, variable costs, and sales, either in total dollar amounts or in price per unit.

BREAK-EVEN QUANTITY

Determining the break-even point using the **break-even quantity (BEQ)** method is achieved with the following formula:

$$BEQ = \frac{FC}{P - VC}$$

where

FC = fixed costs
P = price charged per unit
VC = variable cost per unit

Fixed costs (as discussed) are the costs of running a business that are not tied to the amount of production or sales. They are usually found on the income statement of a business as operating expenses. In other words, fixed costs are incurred even if there are no sales or revenues. For example, when you sign a lease, payments are due to the property owner every month and typically do not change, even though sales may increase or decrease. Usually, fixed costs include but are not limited to rent, utilities, insurance, executive salaries, clerical salaries, and servicing of debt.

Price is what the company charges for the product or service. In manufacturing, wholesale, or retail industries, it is the actual price received for the product. In service industries (for legal, accounting, consulting, plumbing, and electrical services), we often measure price in terms of hourly charges.

Variable costs are all costs associated with producing or procuring a product or service that is sold by a firm and are directly related to sales. For a manufacturing firm, variable costs include costs of raw materials, possibly production labor, and often costs of running production machinery (utility costs), because these items are not used unless a product is being manufactured. For a wholesale or retail firm, variable costs (cost of goods sold on the income statement) are those paid by the firm for the items that are sold, including freight, insurance of items in transit, and the price of merchandise.

Consider this example: Carl Einfeld manufactures toy trucks. He wants to know how many trucks he must sell to make a profit. He used his cost data to

TABLE 5-1 Cost Data for Carl's Toy Trucks

Cost Category	Payment Basis	Cost ($)
Rent	Monthly	2,000.00
Salaries	Monthly	5,000.00
Employee benefits	Annually	7,000.00
Insurance	Quarterly	1,500.00
Property taxes	Annually	3,000.00
Wood	Per truck	1.25
Paint and finishing	Per truck	0.25
Labor	Per truck	2.50
Packing and shipping	Per truck	2.00

generate Table 5–1. For break-even analysis, Carl must go through the following process:

1. He must first determine the values of the variables in our break-even formula (i.e., fixed costs, variable costs, and price).
2. Next, Carl must determine the time period used for break-even analysis. Let's assume that Carl wants to determine the break-even point on an annual basis. When examining Table 5–1, we note that fixed-cost items are paid in different time frames (rent and salaries are paid monthly, employee benefits and property taxes are paid annually, and insurance is paid quarterly).
3. Carl now must convert all fixed costs to the break-even time period. In our example, Carl is using annual break-even quantity. He could just as easily have determined the break-even point on a quarterly, monthly, or even daily basis. Note that to convert items that are paid weekly to a monthly basis, the following procedure should be used: Multiply the weekly figure by 52 (weeks per year) and divide the answer by 12 (months per year). This gives an accurate monthly charge.
4. Carl must use the break-even formula to determine the quantity of units that must be produced during the time period. This provides Carl with the number of trucks that he must produce each year in order to break even.

The fixed costs from Table 5–1 are rent, salaries, employee benefits, insurance, and property taxes. To determine total fixed costs, we annualize all figures, as follows:

$$
\begin{aligned}
FC &= (\text{Rent} \times 12) + (\text{Salaries} \times 12) + \text{Employee benefits} \\
&\quad + (\text{Insurance} \times 4) + \text{Property taxes} \\
&\quad (\$2,000 \times 12) + (\$5,000 \times 12) + \$7,000 + (\$1,500 \times 4) \\
&\quad + \$3,000 \\
&= \$24,000 + \$60,000 + \$7,000 + \$6,000 + \$3,000 \\
&= \$100,000/\text{year}
\end{aligned}
$$

Carl sells each toy truck for $10.

$$P = \$10/\text{truck}$$

The variable costs are added, as follows:

$$VC = \text{Wood} + \text{Paint and finishing} + \text{Labor} + \text{Packing and shipping}$$
$$= \$1.25 + \$0.25 + \$2.50 + \$2.00$$
$$= \$6.00/\text{truck}$$

Substituting these values into the BEQ formula, we have

$$BEQ = \frac{FC}{P - VC}$$
$$= \frac{\$100,000/\text{year}}{\$10/\text{truck} - \$6/\text{truck}} = \frac{\$100,000/\text{year}}{\$4/\text{truck}}$$
$$= 25,000 \text{ trucks/year}$$

Notice that we kept all units constant throughout our calculations; therefore, we finished with a break-even quantity of 25,000 trucks per year. If we had not converted fixed costs to annual costs, our calculations would have been incorrect. This point cannot be overemphasized: If units are not constant and used consistently in calculations, then your answers will be vague and confusing. If we had not converted all fixed costs to annual costs, then we would have

$$FC = \$2,000 + \$5,000 + \$7,000 + \$1,500 + \$3,000 = \$18,500$$

Placing this into our formula, we would have calculated our break-even quantity as follows:

$$BEQ = \frac{FC}{P - VC}$$
$$= \frac{\$18,500}{\$10/\text{truck} - \$6/\text{truck}} = 4,625 \text{ trucks}$$

If Carl sets up his assembly line to manufacture 4,625 trucks per year rather than 25,000, he will lose several thousand dollars.

Several other items can be obtained from the basic break-even formula, including contribution margin and revenue. In the BEQ equation, $P - VC$ is the **contribution margin**, or the amount of profit made by a company on each unit that is sold above and beyond the break-even quantity. It is also the amount the company loses for each unit of production by which it falls short of the break-even point. The contribution margin formula provides us with the profit made on each unit of production once the break-even point has been passed. In the case of Carl's toy trucks, Carl loses $4 on every truck sold below the break-even quantity, and makes a profit of $4 on every truck that is sold above it.

Note that the contribution margin includes all operating expenses (fixed costs) and profit for each unit produced. When the fixed costs are covered at the break-even point, the contribution margin consists of $4 profit per unit, which goes directly to increase operating income. This is easy to illustrate mathematically. Carl's break-even quantity is 25,000 units. The contribution margin of $4 times 25,000 units should represent his total fixed costs of $100,000. If Carl produces 35,000 units, which are 10,000 units above the break-even point, he makes a $40,000 profit (10,000 units $\times$ $4 contribution margin).

Revenue for any business is simply the sales price times the quantity sold ($R = P \times Q$). Therefore, Carl's revenue at the break-even point is $250,000 ($10/truck $\times$ 25,000 trucks/year).

With a slight modification, the BEQ formula can be used to determine the sales needed (in units) to make a specific profit and is calculated as follows:

$$\text{Total quantity} = \frac{FC + \text{Desired profit}}{P - VC}$$

Let us assume that Carl wants to make a profit of $30,000 on his toy truck line. He uses the BEQ formula, but adds the profit of $30,000 to the fixed costs. He then has the following:

$$\text{Total quantity} = \frac{\$100,000/\text{year} + \$30,000/\text{year}}{\$10/\text{truck} - \$6/\text{truck}}$$
$$= 32,500 \text{ trucks/year}$$

Therefore, Carl must manufacture 32,500 trucks per year in order to realize a $30,000 profit.

If the total quantity figure does not come out to an even number, we usually round up, because we cannot produce or sell less than one complete unit. If, in the previous example, we had a sales price of $9 per truck and a variable cost of $6, we then have a quantity of $130,000/($9 - $6) = 43,333.33 trucks, and so we round up to 43,334 trucks, because we cannot sell 33 percent of a truck. Also, note that our profit is less than $30,000 if we sell 43,333 trucks.

Consider the fact that most manufacturing firms such as Toyota or General Motors spend several hundred million dollars to build a manufacturing plant that produces a particular line of automobiles. They must know how many units they will produce each day. They must order all parts for assembly so that they arrive at the assembly lines within a specified time frame. If Toyota makes 60 Camrys per hour at its Tennessee plant and has two 8-hour shifts, it makes 960 Camrys per day. It needs 5 tires for each car, or 4,800 tires per day. Quantity break-even points are extremely important, because there are thousands of parts that must be ordered for an assembly line each day. However, if we have a store such as a Safeway grocery store, then total volume of sales in dollars is of utmost importance. We do not need to know how many cases of soda pop are sold at a particular store each day, but we must know what total dollar sales are required in order to break even, pay all bills, and make a profit on our investment in the store. For this type of firm (a retail store or service organization), we compute the break-even point in dollars rather than in units.

BREAK-EVEN DOLLARS

The variables and formula used to compute **break-even dollars (BE$)**, or revenue required for the break-even point, are basically the same as those used for BEQ, except that we express the contribution margin as a percentage of sales, or as a percentage of price, rather than as a dollar amount. Using Carl's toy truck company, the price is $10 for each truck and the variable costs of producing a truck are $6. Therefore, VC as a percentage of price is VC/P, or $6/$10, which yields 0.60 (60 percent of each sales dollar is consumed by variable costs of production). Thus, the contribution margin is 40 percent of each sales dollar. Our contribution margin formula for this calculation is Contribution margin = $1 - VC$ (expressed as a percentage of the sales dollar). (As previously discussed, a retail sales company may list COGS as a dollar figure without being able to determine the cost of each unit with regard to COGS. Such a company uses vertical analysis on its income statement data to determine COGS as a percentage of sales dollars.) We can now compute BE$ for Carl's toy truck company, as follows:

$$\text{BE\$} = \frac{FC}{1 - \left(\dfrac{VC}{P}\right)} = \frac{\$100{,}000/\text{year}}{1 - \left(\dfrac{\$6}{\$10}\right)} = \frac{\$100{,}000/\text{year}}{1 - 0.60}$$

$$= \frac{\$100{,}000/\text{year}}{0.40} = \$250{,}000$$

Note that as the variable costs as a percentage of sales increase, the contribution margin decreases and the break-even amount in dollars or units sold increases. This means that if sales remain stable as variable costs increase, the break-even amount changes. For example, if lumber costs increase so that Carl has to pay $1.75 for wood per truck, then VC increases by 50 cents per unit to $6.50. The contribution margin now decreases to 0.35 from 0.40. To break even, the company must now generate revenues of $285,714, rather than the $250,000 that we previously calculated. As noted, with a slight modification, the break-even formulas can determine the sales required in order to make a specific profit. Assume that Carl wants to make a profit of $50,000 next year. Variable costs remain at 60 percent of sales, and fixed costs are $100,000 per year. The formula for break-even dollars with profit is

$$\text{BE\$} = \frac{FC + \text{Desired profit}}{1 - \left(\dfrac{VC}{P}\right)} = \frac{\$100,000 + \$50,000}{1 - 0.60}$$

$$= \frac{\$150,000}{0.40} = \$375,000$$

Therefore, if Carl wants to make a profit of $50,000, then he must generate total toy truck revenue of $375,000.

BREAK-EVEN CHARTS

Plotting a **break-even chart**, or graph, can be done quite easily. Using Carl's toy truck company, we set up the vertical axis as dollar units and the horizontal axis as sales in units. We then plot a horizontal line indicating fixed costs of $100,000 (Figure 5–1). Next we plot the total revenue line from the intersection of the horizontal and vertical axes. This is rather easily accomplished, because if there are no sales, then revenue is zero. We choose a couple of points for

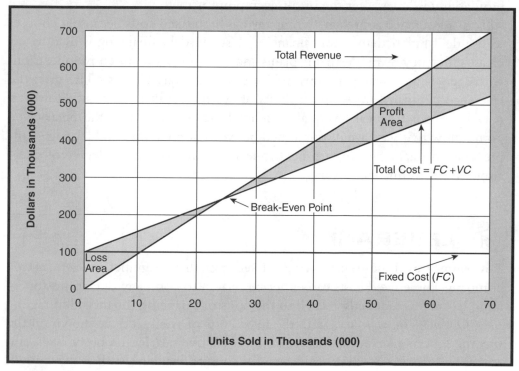

FIGURE 5–1
Break-Even Chart for Carl's Toy Trucks

the revenue line based on sales of even units (e.g., 50,000 units and $500,000 in sales, because the price is $10 per unit and Revenue = Sales × Units Sold). Then we plot our total cost line by plotting variable costs beginning from the intersection of the vertical axis and the fixed-cost line. Break-even charts are easy to analyze and allow the businessperson to see company profit or loss based on various sales volumes.

In analyzing a break-even chart, note that all points to the right of the break-even point indicate the profit for the firm. The profit for any number of units or amount of revenue is obtained by taking the difference between the total revenue line and the total cost line. We can choose any quantity to the right of the break-even point, move vertically, and determine the profit. For example, we can determine that if Carl sells 50,000 units, he should earn a profit of $100,000. Also, note that any sales quantity to the left of the break-even point results in a loss, because for these quantities, the total cost line lies above the total revenue line.

Companies may use two different strategies using various combinations of fixed and variable costs. These strategies use both conservative and a leveraged approach. In a conservative approach, a company has low fixed costs mainly because they choose to use equity, rather than debt financing. They may have high variable costs if they are labor intensive. This allows the company to break even sooner. However, because of their high variable costs, the company's contribution margin is lower than a competing firm that is less labor intensive. Thus, profitability is lower after the break-even point is met.

In a leveraged approach, a company has high fixed costs because it chooses to use debt rather than equity financing. Usually, debt financing is used to increase efficiency by modernizing plants and replacing labor-intensive operations with capital-intensive operations and lowering unit variable costs. This gives the leveraged company greater profitability above the break-even point. However, it takes longer to break even, and higher losses occur below the break-even point. Now that we have distinguished between conservative and leveraged approaches to financing, we turn next to leverage in terms of its degree of operating as well as financial leverage.

LEVERAGE

Leverage uses those items having a fixed cost that magnifies the return to a company. These fixed costs can either be related to company operations (operating leverage) or directly related to the costs of financing (financial leverage).

Operating leverage deals with the fixed costs of assets, and are shown on the income statement as leases, depreciation, executive salaries, property taxes, and so on. *Financial leverage* deals with the fixed costs of financing, such as the amount of interest a company pays on debt. It is important to note that operating leverage deals with the top part of the balance sheet, which includes the assets of a company, whereas financial leverage deals with the bottom part of the balance sheet, which includes the liabilities of a company. Next, we illustrate how we measure operating and financial leverage.

OPERATING LEVERAGE

Operating leverage is stated as the percentage change in operating income that occurs as a result of the percentage change in sales. The *degree of operating leverage (DOL)* for the MLC Chapter 4 can be expressed using the following formula:

$$DOL = \frac{\text{Percentage change in operating income}}{\text{Percentage change in sales}}$$

$$DOL = \frac{\left(\dfrac{\$1,691 - \$1,616}{\$1,616}\right) \times 100}{\left(\dfrac{\$8,009 - \$7,028}{\$7,038}\right) \times 100} = \frac{4.64}{13.96} = 0.33$$

For these calculations, we used numbers from MLC 2007 and 2006 income statements (Table 4–7). The DOL formula allows for the computation of DOL, which can be interpreted as a multiplier of the effect that a change in sales has on operating income. Thus, for every 1 percent change in sales, MLC experiences a 0.33 percent change in operating income, as calculated in the formula. For MLC, every increase or decrease in sales results in a corresponding increase or decrease in operating income by a multiple of 0.33. Thus, leverage acts like a double-edge sword.

We now compare the same information for VMware, a software company that provides virtualization solutions to customer desktops, using their income statements for 2007 and 2006 (Table 5–2) and find that the DOL for VMware is 1.08.

$$DOL = \frac{\text{Percentage change in operating income}}{\text{Percentage change in sales}}$$

$$DOL = \frac{\left(\dfrac{\$235,341 - \$120,639}{\$120,639}\right) \times 100}{\left(\dfrac{\$1,325,811 - \$703,904}{\$703,904}\right) \times 100} = \frac{95.08}{88.35} = 1.08$$

The higher the DOL, the greater the change in operating income resulting from an increase or decrease in sales. For example, if a corporation's DOL is 3, then for every 1 percent change in sales, operating income changes by 3 percent; so, an increase in sales of 10 percent increases operating income by 30 percent. Remember, however, that a decrease in sales of 10 percent decreases operating income by 30 percent.

TABLE 5–2 Abreviated Income Statement VMware

(All figures in thousands of dollars, except earnings per share [EPS])

	31–Dec–07	31–Dec–06
Total revenue	1,325,811	703,904
Operating expenses	1,090,470	583,265
Operating income	235,341	120,639
Other income and (expenses)		
Investment income	22,942	2,497
Interest expense	(17,757)	293
Other expenses, net	(48)	(882)
Total other income and (expenses)	5,137	1,908
Income before income taxes	240,478	122,547
Income tax expense	22,341	36,832
Income before cumulative effect of a change in accounting principle	$ 218,137	$ 85,715
Cumulative effect of a change in accounting principle, net of tax of $108		$ 175
Net income	$ 218,137	$ 85,890
Basic earnings per share	$ 0.62	$ 0.26
Diluted earnings per share	$ 0.61	0.26

Source: Securities and Exchange Commision 10k report

FINANCIAL LEVERAGE

Financing a company with other people's money is known as using **financial leverage**. The higher the amount of liabilities, the greater your financial leverage and the lower the amount of equity you have invested in the company. Any net income generated by the company ultimately gives you a greater return on equity if you use very little of your own money and more of other people's money.

For the business owner, financial leverage is the proportion of the company that is financed by debt. Leverage is a universal tool. It is a small force that can move a much larger force. In business terms, a small amount of owner's equity is supporting a large amount of assets. Any change in income magnifies the return on equity either positively or negatively. Most of us are familiar with a school see-saw, on which a small child's force can move a much larger child. As the small child moves further from the center of the seesaw, the fulcrum of the seesaw acts like a lever, and the larger child is supported by the smaller child. The larger child is said to be leveraged. The fulcrum, or *pivot point,* of the seesaw can be compared with the fixed costs of financing. The fixed costs of financing are the interest expenses paid on the amount of debt incurred. A small amount of equity uses this fulcrum to support the assets of a company (the larger child). A firm is said to be in heavy financial leverage if its fixed costs of financing are high.

You use financial leverage when, rather than using your own capital or equity, you use debt to finance your business. In highly leveraged businesses, owners use very little of their own resources (money) and instead use someone else's capital. This is referred to as *debt financing,* as opposed to *equity financing.*

The resulting profits give the business owner a greater return on equity because one's own financial capital is not tied to the business, and, therefore, can be used in some other capacity. As the business owner pays off the debt and continues to earn a profit, the returns can be extremely high.

Servicing the debt (paying interest on the loan) does not always have a positive ending. In a recession or economic downturn, leverage can work the other way. As you service the debt and profits decrease, it may be necessary to raise your prices to make a profit. If you are in a highly competitive business, an increase in price may result in decreased sales. In addition, if you are in a highly leveraged company and are competing with another firm that uses equity financing, you may find that the other company can charge a lower price and be more profitable because your margin must include the cost of servicing the debt. If you cannot raise prices, you must cut expenses, which also may negatively affect sales, service, and quality. Another thing to consider when using leverage is that business loans are often tied to prime lending rates; thus, interest payments on debt vary based on fluctuations in the prime rate of interest.

The **degree of financial leverage (DFL)** is stated as the percentage change in earnings per share that occurs as a result of the percentage change in operating income. Financial leverage can be expressed using the following formula:

$$DFL = \frac{\text{Percentage change in earnings per share}}{\text{Percentage change in operating income}}$$

$$DFL = \frac{\left(\dfrac{\$0.31 - \$0.30}{\$0.30}\right) \times 100}{\left(\dfrac{\$1,691 - \$1,616}{\$1,616}\right) \times 100} = \frac{3.33}{4.64} = 0.72$$

In this calculation, numbers from the MLC 2007 and 2006 income statement (Table 4–7) were used. The formula allows for the computation of DFL, which can be interpreted as a multiplier of the effect that a change in operating income has on earning per share. MLC has a DFL equal to 0.72. Thus, for every 1 percent change in operating income, MLCs experiences a 0.72 percent change in earnings per share.

Next, we calculate the DFL for VMWare, a firm that is more highly leveraged than MLC using Table 5–2, and we then compare it to the MLC.

$$DFL = \frac{\left(\dfrac{\$061 - \$0.26}{\$0.26}\right) \times 100}{\left(\dfrac{\$235,341 - \$120,639}{\$120,639}\right) \times 100} = \frac{134.62}{95.08} = 1.42$$

A DFL of 1.42 means that VMware should experience an increase or decrease in earnings per share of $1.42 for every 1 percent change in operating income. All other things being equal, a company with debt has a higher DFL than one with no debt. However, when one looks at companies in different industries as we have done here, one must temper the results, because they may not agree with the theory.

The **degree of combined leverage (DCL)** is stated as the percentage change in sales that has a multiplier effect on the change in earnings per share. DCL is calculated as DOL times DFL, and the formula is

$$DCL = DOL \times DFL = \left(\frac{\text{Percentage change in operating income}}{\text{Percentage change in sales}}\right)$$

$$\times \left(\frac{\text{Percentage change in earnings per share}}{\text{Percentage change in operating income}}\right)$$

$$DCL_{MLC} = \left(\frac{\text{Percentage change in earnings per share}}{\text{Percentage change in sales}}\right) = \frac{3.33}{13.96} = 0.24$$

$$DCL_{VMWare} = \frac{134.62}{88.35} = 1.52$$

For every 1 percent change in MLC's sales, earnings per share change by 0.34 percent; for every 1 percent change in VMWare's sales, earnings per share change by 1.52 percent.

With all other things being equal, when a company forecasts an increase in sales, then *earnings per share (EPS)* should increase by the multiple in the degree of combined leverage. So if VMware were to predict a 10 percent increase in sales, then earnings per share should increase by 15.2 percent, because their DCL is 1.52. In 2007, VMWare had basic earning per share of 62 cents, so if sales increase by 10 percent next year, earnings per share should increase from $0.62 to $0.71 ($0.62 \times 1.152 = 0.71$). Remember that a basis point is 1/100 of a percent (0.0001), just as a cent is 1/100 (0.01) of a dollar.

Financial leverage must be managed carefully, because too much leverage may place you in a noncompetitive position. Financial leverage is like a balloon being blown up—the air is the buildup of debt within the balloon. Because only a certain amount of surface area can withstand the increased air pressure, sooner or later, the balloon bursts from too much air. A business also can burst when the debt burden (the fixed costs of financing) becomes too much for the supporting structure of the business to handle. When the bubble bursts for a business, the business may be heading for bankruptcy.

BANKRUPTCY

Bankruptcy for a business often occurs when the liabilities of the firm exceed the assets, and the business lacks sufficient cash flow to make payments to creditors. This situation places the business in a negative equity situation, as shown in Table 5–3.

TABLE 5–3 Balance Sheet, The Tom Jones Company

The Tom Jones Company
Balance Sheet
As of December 31, 2008

Assets			
Current assets			
Checking account		$ 2,000	
Accounts receivable		10,000	
Inventory		35,000	
Total current assets			$ 47,000
Fixed assets			
Land		$ 50,000	
Buildings	$250,000		
Less: Accumulated depreciation	100,000	$150,000	
Equipment	50,000		
Less: Accumulated depreciation	30,000	$ 20,000	
Total fixed assets			$220,000
Total assets			$267,000
Liabilities and owner's equity			
Current liabilities			
Accounts payable trade		$ 20,000	
Notes payable bank		20,000	
Taxes payable		3,000	
Total current liabilities			$ 43,000
Long-term liabilities			
Building mortgage		$200,000	
Equipment loan		30,000	
Total long-term debt			$230,000
Total liabilities			$273,000
Owner's equity			(6,000)
Total liabilities and owner's equity			$267,000

The sequence of events typically runs along this path: If this business has only $2,000 in cash, it cannot pay the taxes that are due, the vendors, or the bank. The owner then starts missing payments to the vendors and the bank. The vendors then stop issuing credit to this company and begin to deliver on a *cash-on-delivery (COD)* basis. In order to have the cash to pay the vendor, the business misses another bank payment. The bank then calls the note and demands full payment. The owner does not have the cash to pay the bank, and the bank seeks to foreclose on the buildings and equipment. The owner applies for protection under Chapter 11 of the bankruptcy code. There are essentially three types of bankruptcy for a business: Chapter 11 for corporations and partnerships, Chapter 13 for individuals and sole proprietorships, and Chapter 7 for all businesses and individuals. Chapter 11 involves reorganization and restructuring debts. Chapter 13 is a wage–earner plan for an individual in business or on salary/commission and requires the establishment of a plan for repayment of debt. Chapter 7 is liquidating bankruptcy, where the assets are sold to repay the creditors in part or in full.

Chapter 11 Bankruptcy occurs when a business seeks court protection while it develops a reorganization plan to pay its creditors. While the business is in Chapter 11, it can continue operating and its creditors are effectively held at bay by the courts. Once the reorganization plan is submitted, more than half the creditors holding at least two-thirds of the dollar amount owed must approve the effectiveness of the plan. The plan often includes such provisions as paying creditors a portion of the money owed, restructuring loans, and possibly refinancing mortgages. The plan must include a method for paying all taxes owed. The tax creditors do not vote and must be repaid within 5 years. If the majority of the creditors reject the reorganization plan, then the company may be converted into Chapter 7 bankruptcy.

Chapter 13 Bankruptcy is reserved for individuals and sole proprietorships and is similar to, but much simpler than, Chapter 11. In Chapter 13, creditors do not vote for the reorganization plan, but can object to the terms of the plan. Chapter 13 is much less expensive to file and implement than Chapter 11, which is much more complicated and involves increased legal expenses. Chapter 13 has specific dollar limits and time limits specified by federal law for individuals.

Chapter 7 Bankruptcy requires liquidation of all assets of the business and payment to the creditors. As we see from the balance sheet in Table 5–3, even if all assets are sold for book value of $267,000, the claim holders do not receive all of the $273,000 that is owed to them by the Tom Jones Company. The owners have a negative equity position of ($6,000). Common stockholders must pay in new value to have any equity position in the reorganized company. They will receive nothing for their investment. In most cases, the assets of the company, especially the inventory and equipment, are sold for considerably less than book value. If this is the case, creditors will receive pennies on each dollar that is owed to them. For the individual, Chapter 7 requires liquidation of assets except for those exempt by federal or state law. These exemptions are discussed next.

On April 20, 2005, President Bush signed the Bankruptcy Abuse Prevention and Consumer Protection Act, which took effect October 17, 2005. It focuses primarily on consumers, but certain provisions involve commercial issues in cases involving Chapter 11 bankruptcy. These include, but are not limited to, an exclusive period for debtors to file a plan of reorganization, key employee retention and severance plans, unexpired leases of nonresidential real property, equipment and personal property leases, and utility deposits. The homestead exemption applies only in the cases of individuals. As you can see, the laws are so complex that any company contemplating bankruptcy should contact an attorney specializing in commercial bankruptcy.

Today, many businesses are organized as sole proprietorships. Businessowners would be negligent if they did not familiarize themselves with the new law, because it applies to them on both a personal and a business basis. The new law tends to steer people away from filing Chapter 7 (discharge of debt or liquidation bankruptcy) and directs them toward a Chapter 13 filing (repayment plan). As the ticket into bankruptcy, the new law imposes mandatory credit counseling for all individual debtors. During a 6-month period before filing Chapter 7 or Chapter 13, a debtor must complete a budget and credit counseling course. To receive a discharge, a debtor must complete a money management course. The burden is now on the debtor's attorney to make sure this occurs.

Bankruptcy petitions are filed in United States Federal Bankruptcy Court in the district where the debtor resides or the business has its principal place of business. Individual debtors file Chapter 7 bankruptcy, also known as *fresh start bankruptcy,* where assets of the debtor are sold and the proceeds are paid to the creditors. In other words, filing Chapter 7 discharges the individual's non-exempt debt, but the negative is that it remains on one's credit for 10 years. The advantage for those filing a Chapter 13 repayment plan is that debtors can keep their assets if they finish the repayment plan. Filing Chapter 13 affects one's credit rating for 7 years; filing Chapter 7 affects one's credit rating for 10 years. The following are exempt from bankruptcy: IRAs, 401k, 403B, 529 plans, and educational IRAs. Prepaid tuition plans are exempt if money was placed in the account at least 2 years or more before declaring bankruptcy. Some qualified pension plans are exempt from inclusion in bankruptcy. Luxury goods or services of $500 or more in purchases to a single creditor within 90 days of filing are not exempt and must be paid in full. Cash advances aggregating more than $750 made within 70 days or less in advance of filing are not dischargeable.

Debtors are given a certain dollars' worth of exemptions when they file a Chapter 7 petition. Examples are $1,225 in jewelry, $1,850 in tools, $18,450 in home equity, and $9,850 in household goods. All assets above these limits must be sold. For example, $18,450 is the amount the debtor has exempt or the amount protected from creditors. The previously mentioned exemptions are specific for the federal level; however, more than 30 states are known as *opt out states,* which means individual debtors must use state law exemptions rather than the federal exemptions.

The new law may affect the homestead exemption in an individual's bankruptcy. The homestead exemption is the amount of equity one has in his or her house. Some states such as Florida, Texas, Kansas, Iowa, South Dakota, and the District of Columbia permit an unlimited homestead exemption. This allows a sole proprietor to put his money in his house, declare bankruptcy, and sometimes shield millions of dollars from his creditors. Because bankruptcy is filed in U.S. courts, the new federal law changes the homestead exemption to a maximum $125,000 if the debtor has moved within certain time periods and purchased a home to shelter his non-exempt assets. One must become a resident of a state for at least 2 years to exempt a value greater than $125,000.

There is now a means test to determine if an individual filing a Chapter 7 petition is abusing the system. If the debtor's income is greater than the state's median income level, he or she must pass a means test in order to determine if he or she is able to proceed under Chapter 7. The means test is the debtor's ability to pay $100 per month over 5 years (60 months), or $6,000. If this cannot be accomplished, the debtor may file Chapter 7. For example, in Arizona, the state's median income is $35,648 for a single person and $45,818 for a family of four. However, if one's income exceeds the limit, then an individual is encouraged to file for Chapter 13 and develop a repayment plan. It is up to the bankruptcy attorney to determine if a client is qualified for Chapter 7 or Chapter 13. Chapter 13 is a repayment plan. The debtor is required to go on an approved monthly repayment plan that lasts 5 years. After completion, any debts remaining are discharged, and the debtor's assets are protected and not sold because they filed Chapter 13.[1]

 CONCLUSION

Now that we have some understanding of profit, profitability, break-even point, leverage, and bankruptcy, we must determine if our business will be profitable. Is it worth the entrepreneurial effort? Will we make a profit in our business? Can we obtain financing? To answer these questions, we must be able to predict the sales and expenses of our firm, and this is accomplished with financial planning, forecasting, and budgeting, which are the subjects of Chapter 6.

REVIEW AND DISCUSSION QUESTIONS

1. Compare *efficiency* and *effectiveness.*
2. What is the difference between *accounting profit* and *entrepreneurial profit?*
3. What financial ratio is predominantly used to determine profitability?
4. Describe the earning power of a company.
5. How is financial leverage related to bankruptcy?
6. Compare Chapter 11 bankruptcy with Chapter 7 bankruptcy.
7. What is the relationship among fixed costs, contribution margin, and the break-even point?
8. What are some factors that affect variable costs?
9. What are the basic steps that you must take to determine if you are able to make a profit?
10. The Handy Doll Manufacturing Company has the following information: The average doll sales price is $12, raw materials for a doll are $4, and it

---

[1]Complete text of the Bankruptcy Abuse Prevention and Consumer Protection Act of 2005 may be found at http://thomas.loc.gov/cgi-bin/query/D?c109:6:./temp/~c1096BEtWS:e67889.

takes 15 minutes to assemble a doll. Production labor is paid $8 per hour. Operating expenses are as follows: salaries, $2,500 per week; insurance, $1,200 per quarter; rent, $1,500 per month; and utilities, $800 per month. How many dolls must be sold per month to break even? How many dollars in sales does this represent? What is the contribution margin for each doll sold?

11. For the company in question 10, if the goal is to make a profit of $5,000 per month, how many dolls must be sold?

12. What is the effect of an increase in variable costs as a percentage of sales on the contribution margin and on the break-even dollar amount?

13. Discuss the changes in bankruptcy law and their impact on a personal and business basis.

EXERCISES AND PROBLEMS

1. John and Mary work for a direct marketing firm. They make calls to customers for a local carpet cleaning service. In a typical hour, John completes 50 calls and gets 2 sales; Mary completes 50 calls and gets 1 sale. Compare John and Mary from the viewpoint of effectiveness and efficiency.

2. Joan purchases a government bond for $10,000 that pays 7 percent annual interest. Jim purchases $20,000 worth of corporate bonds that pay 10 percent annual interest. Joan's goal is to earn $700 per year on her investment, and Jim's goal is to earn $2,000 per year on his investment.
   a. Is Joan or Jim more efficient? Why?
   b. Is Joan or Jim more effective? Why?

3. Sam quit a $30,000-a-year job with a local heating and air conditioning firm to go into business for himself. After his first year in business, his accountant showed him an income statement, which indicated Sam's firm had a profit of $40,000. During this year, Sam drew a salary of $20,000.
   a. What were Sam's accounting profit and entrepreneurial profit?
   b. Explain the difference between *accounting profit* and *entrepreneurial profit*.

4. Maury quit his job as an accountant with We Keep Books Accurately to open his own accounting firm. He earned $40,000 with the accounting firm We Keep Books Accurately. During the current year, Maury had revenues of $150,000 and total expenses of $110,000.
   a. What was Maury's accounting profit?
   b. What was Maury's entrepreneurial profit?

5. James builds brick walls for custom homes. His annual sales are approximately $300,000, and his net income is $18,000. He has assets of $100,000 invested in this business. Tom sells window shades. His annual sales are approximately $900,000, and his net income is $27,000. He has assets of $150,000 invested in his business.
   a. Compute the net profit margin for both James and Tom.
   b. Compute the asset turnover for both James and Tom.
   c. Compare the profitability of these two firms, and discuss the similarities and differences.

6. The Faster Modem Corporation was founded by two engineers who managed to capitalize their firm with $150,000. They were able to raise this money because their test model performed much faster than current modems on the market, and they received an initial commitment from a national firm to market their modem. However, a national modem manufacturer beat them to the market, and they found that they had invested $140,000 in obsolete technology. They now find that they have no sales, $500 in cash, and a $2,000 payment due to their creditor on the first of next month. What are the owners' options?

7. You are going to open a business making custom cabinets. You can sell each cabinet for $80. It takes a cabinetmaker approximately 45 minutes to make one cabinet. Each cabinetmaker works an 8-hour day earning $18 per hour. Each cabinet uses $25 in raw materials. You usually produce cabinets 20 days a month and can employ two cabinetmakers. You estimate that your fixed costs are $5,000 per month.
   a. What is your contribution margin?
   b. How many cabinets must you make each month to break even?
   c. What is your total monthly revenue if you want to earn a $2,000 profit?
   d. Construct a break-even chart for the custom cabinet firm.

8. Wanda wants to open a health-food store. She pays rent of $1,500 per month, utilities of $500, insurance of $100 per month, and payroll of $1,250. She estimates that her cost of goods is approximately 65 percent of sales. Wanda would like to make $2,000 a month for herself.
   a. What is Wanda's contribution margin?
   b. How much does she need in monthly sales to break even?
   c. How much does she need in monthly sales to make a profit of $2,000?
   d. Construct a break-even chart for Wanda's health-food store.

9. Woody's Widget Shop has the following information: The average widget has a sales price of $18; raw materials for the widget are $4; it takes 30 minutes to assemble one widget; and production labor is paid $8 per hour. Operating expenses are as follows: salaries, $2,500 per week; insurance, $1,200 per quarter; rent, $3,000 per month; and utilities, $1,000 per month.
   a. How many widgets must be sold each month in order to break even?
   b. How many dollars in sales does this represent?
   c. What is the contribution margin for each widget sold?
   d. If the goal is to make $100,000 profit per month, how many widgets must be sold?

10. You want to open up a custom skateboard shop. You can sell each skateboard for $160. It takes 3 hours to make each skateboard. Each skateboard maker earns $25 per hour. Each skateboard costs $15 in raw materials. You estimate that your fixed costs are $20,000 per month.
   a. What is the contribution margin?
   b. How many skateboards must be sold each month in order to break even?
   c. What is the break-even dollar amount?
   d. How many skateboards must be sold to earn a $10,000 profit each month?
   e. What is your total monthly revenue if you want to earn a profit of $8,000?

TABLE 5–4 Abreviated Income Statement The Van Accessible Corp

All figures in $thousands except Earnings per Share

	31–Dec–08	31–Dec–9
Total revenue	1,789,654	703,904
Cost of revenue	478,963	275,963
Gross profit	1,310,691	427,941
Operating expenses	65,987	57,896
Operating income	1,244,704	370,045
Interest and Taxes	544,444	289,635
Net income	700,260	80,410
Earnings Per Share 50,000,000 Shares outstanding	14.01	1.61

DOL = 1.5324
DFL = 3.2613
DCL = 5.00

11. Using the Van Accessible date from Table 5–4:
    a. Calculate the degree of operating leverage (DOL).
    b. Calculate the degree of financial leverage (DFL).
    c. Calculate the degree of combined leverage (DCL).
    d. Explain what DOL, DFL, and DCL mean.

RECOMMENDED TEAM ASSIGNMENT

1. Pick a large supermarket or discount retailer.
   a. Determine what the average store must sell on an annual and daily basis to maintain the corporation's profit margin.
   b. Using the corporation's income statement, determine the break-even point in dollars for each store.
2. Pick two companies in the same industry.
   a. Determine their DOL, DFL, and DCL.
   b. What affect does a change in sales have on their operating income?
   c. What affect does a change in sales have on earnings per share?

CASE STUDY: MARK WHEELER CRAFTSMAN, INC.

© 2008 Philip J. Adelman and Alan M. Marks

Mark Wheeler was born and raised in Brookfield, Connecticut, and graduated from Brookfield High School in 1979. As a teenager, he worked for his father's construction company and learned many skills associated with construction, such as electrical wiring, framing, and pouring concrete. Mark attended Rochester School of

Technology, where he obtained an associate of applied sciences degree. While in college, he continued working as a craftsman, building the sets for the college theater company. He got married to Laurie and joined the Marine Corps in 1982, and spent 4 years as a logistics specialist. After leaving the Marine Corps, he went to work for a construction company in Newtown, Connecticut, as a general craftsman, honing his construction skills. In 1988, with changes to the tax laws, the contractor had to lay off his full-time employees. At this point, Mark started a construction company with one of his co-workers. He borrowed $15,000 from his sister, talked the owner of a lot into allowing him to build a spec home on the property, and obtained a construction loan from Newtown Savings Bank. He built his first home, sold it prior to its completion, and paid his sister back with a 20 percent profit, paid the property owner for the lot, and paid the bank, all within 6 months. Mark and his partner then began building other homes and developed a relationship with the bank where his company would build homes on empty lots in subdivisions that the bank owned and then sell them for a fair profit. In the early 1990s, the housing market in Connecticut took a nosedive. Mark had purchased a lot for $110,000 and built a spec house that he thought was sold for more than $300,000. The purchaser could not obtain financing, the lot value dropped to less than $60,000, and Mark had to move into the home himself. Shortly thereafter, the business folded as he and his partner could not get along. Mark went out on his own and began working on historic restorations and smaller projects. For example, he moved a house that had been built in 1647. He took the house apart, rebuilt it in the new location, and restored the home to its original finishes. The hardest thing that Mark had to do was obtaining the building permits to put the house back together, because none of the original construction met current building codes. This project alone took Mark over a year.

In December 1996, Mark and Laurie went to Phoenix to visit friends and the Wheelers fell in love with the Valley of the Sun. They went home, put the house up for sale, and he and Laurie and their two children moved to Phoenix in July 1997. Mark took the general contractors license test and had his license by August. He went to work for a company building custom homes in September, and in January 1998, the Wheelers bought a home of their own. In June 1998, Mark quit the company and formed Mark Wheeler Craftsman, Incorporated, and he and Laurie have been partners in the corporation since its inception. The company is run from their home, where Laurie keeps the books and does the payroll, taxes, and general paperwork. Mark takes a tremendous amount of pride in his work. At one time, he took on too many projects at once and had as many as 10 full-time employees. He learned that the quality of work suffered and there was too much hassle managing several projects at one time. Mark is a full-service contractor who now has six full-time employees. Mark has one general foreman, an electrician, and four general laborers. He provides his foreman and electrician with a vehicle painted with the Mark Wheeler logo. He does no real advertising, because he finds that having his vehicle parked in front of areas where he is working and having satisfied customers who hand out his business cards provides him with as much work as he needs. During his 10 years in the Valley, he has located subcontractors who are extremely reliable and who perform their work on time and on budget. His contracts are all based on his cost of material and labor plus 20 percent. If someone wants a fixed price, it is usually higher, because Mark must include some contingencies. On average, Mark Wheeler Craftsman, Inc., handles about $1,500,000 worth of business a year. Based on a 20 percent profit margin, the business is quite successful.

QUESTIONS

1. In order to provide competitive bids in the construction industry, how important is it for a contractor like Mark Wheeler to know his labor costs and costs of materials? Why is this knowledge so important to a contractor who builds and modifies items for homes and businesses?

2. What effect do the business cycle and the general economy have on the construction industry? Explain how a change in home and property values has an impact on people in the construction industry.

CHAPTER 6

Forecasting and Pro Forma Financial Statements

Learning Objectives

When you have completed this chapter, you should be able to:

- Understand the importance of a sales forecast to a business.
- Understand the basic steps used in selecting a forecasting model.
- Know how to evaluate a forecasting model.
- Given a business situation, choose the proper forecasting model.
- Calculate a forecast using time series data.
- Explain the role that the mean absolute deviation (MAD) plays in selecting a forecasting model.
- Understand the relationships between a business's revenue base, sales forecast, assets, and need for financing.
- Construct pro forma financial statements from available data on a proposed or existing business.
- Apply the percentage of sales method in determining any required new financing needed for a business.

We now understand how to read and analyze financial statements. We also know that lending institutions, to comply with SBA guidelines, require *pro forma* (projected) financial statements for at least 3 years into the future. Because the first line on the income statement is total sales or total revenue, we cannot begin a financial statement without an estimate of sales. Our main objective in this chapter is to learn the procedure for obtaining an estimated sales figure. This procedure for estimating a future sales figure is called *forecasting*.

The sales forecast is what drives all other factors in our pro forma financial statements, which are used both by our firm and by any external users whom we want to have a stake in our firm. We need pro forma statements to develop internal budgets for the functional departments of our business. If we seek to convince investors to provide equity capital for our business, then we must also provide them with pro forma financial statements. Lenders want these financial statements because they must ensure that our business generates enough profit to pay back both the principal and the interest on a loan. Potential investors also want to ensure that the business is profitable enough to provide them with the desired return on their invested capital.

Because of the need for these pro forma financial statements, forecasts of future sales and revenues are required. The time horizon for these forecasts must meet or exceed that required by the lender or investor. Forecasting is a necessary beginning point for actually developing plans. In most cases, the forecast of the demand for our products and services determines the size of our physical plant. The forecasted demand for our products and services also helps us plan for the purchase of equipment (capital expenditures) and the hiring of personnel (wages, salaries, and benefits). Finally, the financial plan must be developed so all of the money required for the physical plant, equipment, and personnel is available, along with sufficient profit to meet the requirements of lenders and investors.

FORECASTING

A **forecast** is a quantifiable estimate of future demand. **Forecasting** in business is the process of estimating the future demand for our products and services. Forecasting for the financial manager also requires estimates of future interest rates. Because we are using an estimate, we know in advance that our forecast will not be completely accurate; however, firms that use forecasts have a much higher success rate than firms that do not. The process used involves several basic steps: (1) Determine the type of forecasting model to be used; (2) determine the forecast horizon; (3) select one or more forecasting models; (4) evaluate the models; (5) apply the chosen model; and (6) monitor and control the model. If the model is not appropriate, go back to step 1 and begin again.

1. Determine the Type of Forecasting Model to Be Used. The criteria for selecting a forecasting model require us to ask six basic questions: (1) Who will be using the forecast and what information do they require? (2) How relevant and available are historical data? (3) How accurate must the forecast be? (4) What is the time period of the forecast? (5) How much time do we have to develop the forecast? and (6) What is the cost or benefit (value) of this forecast to our company? Questions 3, 4, and 5 are tied together. The more accuracy you want, the higher the cost of gathering data. Long-term forecasts usually include more variables. Gathering information for more variables is more costly and time-consuming. The more time spent in gathering the information, the higher the cost.

2. Determine the Forecast Horizon. Several factors influence the length of the forecast horizon. The basic premise to remember is that there is an inverse relationship between forecast accuracy and time horizon. The longer the time horizon, the more inaccurate the forecast will be. The forecast horizon should be at least as long as the time period of your strategic plan. Utility companies may have to use forecast horizons of 10 to 15 years because of the time that it takes to construct new plants. Product life cycles also influence the length of forecasts. The demand for some products such as milk are very stable, and forecasts concerning these products can be made for years into the future. Other products such as digital video disks (DVDs) usually have very short life cycles, and forecasts of their sales and rentals are usually for less than 1 year.

3. Select One or More Forecasting Models. When selecting a forecasting model, it is important to consider the previous criteria (the six basic questions). In some instances you may want to use a combination of forecasting models.

4. Evaluate the Models. We can compare several similar forecasting models with evaluation criteria such as mean absolute deviation (MAD), a measure of how closely a forecasting model compares with actual sales data. We demonstrate the use of MAD after we develop our first time series model. We also can evaluate models based on our basic information requirements. A forecasting model is meant to assist us in managing our business—it is not supposed to make decisions for us. With modern computers, it is often too easy to allow the computer to generate a forecast and then blindly follow that forecast. The environment of business is constantly changing. Changing tastes of our customers, new competitors entering our area, and general economic changes that affect our business are not usually built into our forecasting models. As business owners and managers, we must be aware that changing market and economic conditions require us to constantly evaluate our forecasting models and change them when they no longer perform as desired.

5. Apply the Chosen Model. We apply the forecasting model in our business and use it to determine future requirements. Application of the model and the specific units of measurement it uses depends on the area of our business for which we are using the model. Long-range general business plans are typically expressed in terms of dollars. Production planning requires that these plans be expressed in units of production to determine future requirements for plant, equipment, and personnel. Personnel and production

planners also require that forecasts be broken down into human resource requirements. The financial planner must determine the cost of obtaining the
required financing to support all of the various plans. Many small businesses
have owners who perform all of the preceding functions. Using a forecasting
model often requires us to develop several functional business plans to support
the forecast.

6. Monitor and Control the Model. Forecasts should be adjusted by us
as managers any time they do not reflect reality; however, we must always
keep in mind that the forecast is not completely accurate. If it is good
enough to allow us to write business plans that accurately reflect our needs as
managers, then the forecast is adequate. When a forecasting model no longer
allows us to do this, then the model must be adjusted or a new model must
be developed.

TYPES OF FORECASTING MODELS

There are several forecasting models from which to choose. The three types of
methods used in these models are qualitative, quantitative, and cause and effect.
Qualitative methods use expert opinions to predict sales. *Quantitative methods* use
mathematical formulas and statistics to predict sales. *Cause-and-effect methods* use
statistical formulas based on models to predict sales. An example of cause and
effect is an increase in the sale of soda pop when the temperature increases. High
temperatures are the cause of increased sales; increased sales are the effect.

There are three basic categories of forecasting models, each of which is associated with a particular type of method: (1) **judgmental models,** which use
qualitative methods; (2) **time series models,** which use quantitative methods;
and (3) **causal models,** which use cause-and-effect methods. We begin by discussing the methodology used by each of these categories of models. We then
discuss specific models that are associated with each category. We also provide a
brief section on determining MAD.

Judgmental Models

Judgmental models are qualitative and essentially use estimates based on expert
opinion. People who are experienced in these specific areas develop both an in-
tuitive feel and a scientific method for determining what will sell and what the
customers want. Judgmental models forecast sales for both existing and new
products. Judgmental models that deal with existing products and services use
surveys of both sales forces and customers and various other types of market research. Judgmental models for forecasting sales for a new business or product use
historical analogies, market research, and the Delphi method.

Surveys of sales forces are conducted by managers to determine future
sales within the company's sales territories. Managers combine individual sales
estimates into a total company sales forecast. This method is the proper way to

determine sales if your company already has a sales force in place, if the sales force is stable and reliable, and if sales are made directly to major customers. Models based on these surveys are most appropriate for manufacturing and wholesale firms.

Surveys of customers are effective for virtually all firms, but particularly for the company that has a few large customers. Examples include firms that manufacture parts for a few large national chains, original equipment manufacturers, and unique specialty shops. Because the customers usually have sales forecasts of their own or know what their requirements are, they can provide fairly accurate requirements for future time periods. Surveys of customers also are appropriate for firms that want to know customer demographics. For a small firm with a limited advertising budget, a survey of customers allows the firm to target its advertising based on factors such as zip codes.

Historical analogy is useful in several areas. It can be used when a new product is introduced that has characteristics similar to those of previous products. For example, a bakery plans to introduce an oat-bran bread because of customers' concerns regarding fiber in their diets. If the bakery has previously introduced, for example, a seven-grain bread because of customer dietary concerns, then they can use this historical analogy (How did the previous product sell?) to determine demand for the new bread product. Historical analogy also can be used when a company is going to expand by opening a new store or sales outlet. Firms that have several outlets use historical analogy to determine where to place new outlets. If you shop in malls, you have probably noticed that jewelry stores usually locate at mall entrances, where they are visible to shoppers entering the mall and to shoppers who are walking through the mall from one large department store to another.

Historical analogy also can be used in planning for a new business or for the expansion of an existing business. It is rare to find a new business that is not similar to some other business in some given location. Many franchises and chain stores use historical analogy to determine what level of sales can be expected when a new facility is built. They use sales from previous locations with similar characteristics, such as population density, local population income, and traffic patterns, to determine the expected level of sales in the new location. For example, new convenience stores and gas stations are usually located at major intersections with high traffic flows.

Market research can include surveys, tests, and observation. Surveys can be conducted via telephone interviews, mail questionnaires, field interviews, and even interest groups on the Internet. Tests often involve marketing products in certain test areas. Results of surveys and tests are statistically extrapolated, and a forecast is developed based on those results. Market research is useful for introducing new products or for introducing existing products into new areas. It also can be used to start new businesses in specific areas where the products and services being offered are in short supply. Many firms use market research to build a customer profile in order to determine specific demographic characteristics about their customers. For example, if you have purchased a new appliance recently, you probably filled out a customer survey that you mailed in as part of the warranty card. Another example is being asked to give your zip code to the checkout clerk at your local appliance store. This information helps the store determine exactly where its customers live.

The **Delphi method** uses a panel of experts to obtain a consensus of opinion. Usually the Delphi method is used for unique new products or processes for which there are no previous data. It also has been used in areas in which market research might provide competitors with too much information about a new product or service; this holds true for high-tech products that can be copied easily by competitors. A committee of experts is selected by the Delphi model developer. Members of the committee are widely dispersed and typically do not even know the other committee members. A monitor is selected and a questionnaire is developed describing the proposed project. Committee members are asked for their best estimates of sales and other information that the monitor believes are significant. The monitor gathers and evaluates the information. A revised questionnaire is developed that includes relevant data from the first round. The revised questionnaire with new data is then sent out to the committee. The process is continued until committee members reach a consensus.

As discussed, judgmental models are considered to be qualitative because they use opinions and previous experience to determine the forecast. The forecast itself is quantitative, however, as it provides us with the number of units or dollar volume of expected sales during a specific time period. A new business entrepreneur should be somewhat of an expert or have a specific area of expertise in the type of business. Entrepreneurs usually know several other people who can provide them with expert opinions. They also subscribe to trade journals and professional magazines that provide them with essential data.

Time Series Models

Time series forecasting models usually use historical records that are readily available within a firm or industry to predict future sales. For this reason, they are often referred to as *internal* or *intrinsic models.* In marketing, they may be referred to as *primary data models.* Marketing texts usually refer to internal data as *primary data* and to information that is gathered from external sources as *secondary data.* The specific time series model chosen by a firm depends on the historical sales patterns of the firm and the use of evaluation criteria. The assumption in time series forecasting is that past sales are a fairly accurate predictor of future sales. We discuss four time series models in order of their simplicity, moving from the easiest models to the most complex: (1) the moving average model, (2) the weighted moving average model, (3) the exponential smoothing model, and (4) the linear regression model.

The following references are used in this chapter when discussing the variables associated with mathematics used in forecasting:

A = actual observation of the variable to be forecast.

F = forecast of the variable.

t = current time period. Time periods can be a measure of any time period (e.g., hour, day, month, year, decade). If time periods are being measured in months and the current month is April, then t = April.

$t - 1$ = one time period in the past. If time is being measured in months and t is April, then one time period in the past is March, or $t - 1$ = March.

$t - 2$ = two time periods in the past. If time is being measured in months and t is April, then two time periods in the past is February, or $t - 2$ = February.

$t + 1$ = one time period in the future. If time is being measured in months and t is April, then one time period in the future is May, or $t + 1$ = May.

$t + 2$ = two time periods in the future. If time is being measured in months and t is April, then two time periods in the future is June, or $t + 2$ = June.

Δ = the difference between two numbers. For example, $\Delta\,AF$ is actual observation of variable minus forecast.

Σ = sum of several numbers, usually in a column.

n = the number of observations used in a calculation. The n for months in a year equals 12, and the n for years in a decade is 10.

Moving Average Model.   The **moving average model** assumes that actual sales for some recent previous time periods are the best predictors of future sales. It also assumes that each time period taken in succession has an equal influence on the prediction of future sales. The procedure is to obtain the arithmetic average of actual sales for several past time periods. This average is then used as the forecast for the next time period. To obtain an arithmetic average, we sum actual sales for several time periods and divide this total by the number of time periods. Mathematically, we use the following formula:

$$F_{t+1} = \frac{A_{[t-(n-1)]} + \cdots + A_{t-1} + A_t}{n}$$

For our example, we use a 3-month moving average. Actual sales for two years (Year 1 and Year 2) are shown in Table 6–1. Let's assume that actual sales during the previous 3 months are a reasonable estimate of future sales in the following month. The procedure, therefore, is to add the previous 3 months' actual

TABLE 6–1 Moving Average Model

Formula for Moving Average: $F_{t+1} = \dfrac{A_{[t-(n-1)]} + \cdots + A_{t-1} + A_t}{n}$

Moving Average = Forecast

Year	Month	Time Period	Actual Sales	3-Month Moving Average	Actual Numeric Deviation = Actual − Forecast	Absolute Deviation $\Delta\,A - F$	4-Month Moving Average	Absolute Deviation $\Delta\,A - K$
		0						
Year 1	Jan	1	245					
	Feb	2	244					
	Mar	3	250					
	Apr	4	260	246.33	13.67	13.67		
	May	5	265	251.33	13.67	13.67	249.75	15.25
	Jun	6	260	258.33	1.67	1.67	254.75	5.25
	Jul	7	255	261.67	(6.67)	6.67	258.75	3.75
	Aug	8	245	260.00	(15.00)	15.00	260.00	15.00
	Sep	9	240	253.33	(13.33)	13.33	256.25	16.25
	Oct	10	255	246.67	8.33	8.33	250.00	5.00
	Nov	11	265	246.67	18.33	18.33	248.75	16.25
	Dec	12	270	253.33	16.67	16.67	251.25	18.75
Year 2	Jan	13	250	263.33	(13.33)	13.33	257.50	7.50
	Feb	14	250	261.67	(11.67)	11.67	260.00	10.00
	Mar	15	258	256.67	1.33	1.33	258.75	0.75
	Apr	16	267	252.67	14.33	14.33	257.00	10.00
	May	17	273	258.33	14.67	14.67	256.25	16.75
	Jun	18	278	266.00	12.00	12.00	262.00	16.00
	Jul	19	260	272.67	(12.67)	12.67	269.00	9.00
	Aug	20	256	270.33	(14.33)	14.33	269.50	13.50
	Sep	21	255	264.67	(9.67)	9.67	266.75	11.75
	Oct	22	270	257.00	13.00	13.00	262.25	7.75
	Nov	23	275	260.33	14.67	14.67	260.25	14.75
	Dec	24	283	266.67	16.33	16.33	264.00	19.00
Year 3	Jan	25		276.00			270.75	
	$\Sigma\,\Delta A$				62.00	255.33		232.25
	$-F =$							
	$n =$				21.00	21.00		20.00
	MAD =				2.95	12.16		11.61

sales and divide by 3 to obtain the arithmetic average. To obtain a forecast for Year 1 month 4 (Apr), we add known sales for months 1 (Jan), 2 (Feb), and 3 (Mar) and divide the total by 3, as shown here:

$$F_{t+1} = \frac{A_{t-2} + A_{t-1} + A_t}{3}$$

$$F_{April} = \frac{(245 + 244 + 250)}{3} = 246.33$$

We then use 246.33 as our forecast for month 4 (Apr). When actual sales for month 4 (Apr) are received, we drop month 1 (Jan) and use months 2, 3, and 4 to predict sales for month 5 (May).

$$F_{t+1} = \frac{A_{t-2} + A_{t-1} + A_t}{3}$$

$$F_{May} = \frac{(244 + 250 + 260)}{3} = 251.33$$

Our forecast for month 5 (May) is, therefore, 251.33. This procedure is repeated for every month, as shown in Table 6–1. We can use any number of previous time periods we believe to be relevant; however, most models use 3 months because of quarterly sales patterns and quarterly reporting requirements. Table 6–1 illustrates moving average forecasts using 3 and 4 months.

Mean Absolute Deviation

Three of the times series models discussed in this chapter—moving average, weighted moving average, and exponential smoothing—are for short-range forecasts. They are useful for determining the forecast for the next time period. As business owners and managers, when it may be necessary to use a short-term forecast, we must determine which of the three models to use for our particular situation. We also want to know what weights to use for the weighted moving average model and what value of alpha is most appropriate for the exponential smoothing model. We obviously want to select the model that comes closest to predicting our actual sales for our particular business. One method to accomplish these goals is to determine the error of a forecasting model by using *mean absolute deviation (MAD),* which is easy to calculate. For each time period for which we calculated a forecast, we subtract the absolute value of forecast sales from actual sales. The absolute value of any number is positive and is represented mathematically by vertical lines drawn on either side of the number or formula. The formula for absolute deviation in our forecasting models is

Absolute deviation $= |A - F|$

Referring to Table 6–1, we notice that the seventh column is absolute deviation $\Delta|A - F|$, where A equals actual sales and F equals forecast sales. If we go down the column to Aug of Year 1 we notice that the difference (deviation) between our actual sales of 245 and our forecast sales of 260 is −15; however, the absolute difference is 15, because the absolute value of any number is positive.

MAD is the measure of the overall forecast error and represents the average difference between our forecast and actual sales data. Figure 6–1 shows a plot of our actual sales and forecast sales using the data for a 3-month moving average taken from Table 6–1.

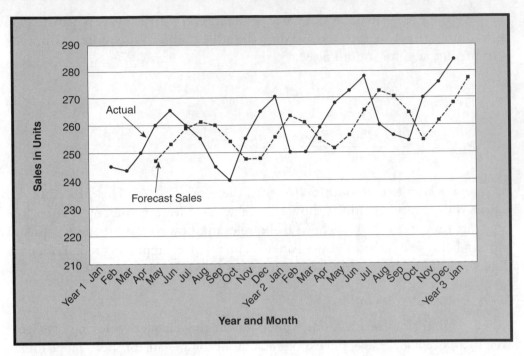

FIGURE 6–1
Plot of Actual Sales and Forecast Sales

Notice that our forecast is less than actual sales for Apr by 13.67 units, but more than actual sales in Sep by 13.33 units. If we try only to obtain the arithmetic average of this difference, then we would add the two numbers and divide by 2 to obtain 0.17 units as the average error of the forecast.

$$\text{Average arithmetic deviation} = \frac{13.67 + (-13.33)}{2} = \frac{0.34}{2} = 0.17$$

If, however, we use the average absolute deviation, then we have

$$\text{Average absolute deviation} = \frac{|13.67 + 13.33|}{2} = \frac{27}{2} = 13.5$$

Therefore, just taking the average difference does not give us an accurate overall forecast error; for this we must use the absolute difference.

To obtain the mean absolute deviation, we sum the absolute differences and then obtain the average difference as shown in column seven of Table 6–1. The mean absolute deviation is calculated by the formula

$$MAD = \frac{\sum |\text{Actual sales} - \text{Forecast sales}|}{n}$$

$$MAD = \frac{\sum |A - F|}{n}$$

Using the formula for MAD in column seven of Table 6–1, we have a sum of the absolute differences of 255.33; we then divide by the total number of differences, which is 21, and obtain a mean absolute deviation of 12.16 units. Table 6–1 also shows the calculation of MAD for our 4-month moving average forecast of 11.61 units. The inaccuracy of the actual numeric deviation is shown in the sixth column. We add the actual numeric deviations and obtain 62.00. We then divide by the total number of actual numeric differences, which is 21, and obtain 2.95. Notice how much smaller this deviation is than the 12.16 we obtained for the 3-month MAD.

Weighted Moving Average Model. What if we believe that previous-period actual sales are not equal in their influence on the next period's sales? We can then choose a **weighted moving average model,** which assumes that the closest time period is a more accurate predictor of future sales than previous time periods, although previous time periods have some influence on future sales. Using this model, we assign weights to the time periods based on personal judgment. The sum of the weights usually equals 1. When using 1 as the sum of the weights, we have a simple formula because the denominator in the following equation equals 1. If the forecaster does not want to use a sum of 1, then we sum the weights and use this sum as the denominator in our equation. The value of each weight is based on how much influence the forecaster believes the corresponding time period has on overall sales. The formula for this method, using months, is

$$F_{t+1} = \frac{(W_1)(A_{t-2}) + (W_2)(A_{t-1}) + (W_3)(A_t)}{\sum W}$$

Forecast for the next time period = (Weight assigned to time period 1 × Actual sales time period 1 + Weight assigned to time period 2 × Actual sales for time period 2 + Weight assigned to time period 3 × Actual sales for time period 3) ÷ the Sum of the weights. If the sum of the weights equals 1, then there is no need to divide, because any number divided by 1 is the number (e.g., $25 \div 1 = 25$).

For our example, we use the sales data in Table 6–2 and first assign weights of 0.1, 0.3, and 0.6. Because the sum of the weights equals 1 ($0.01 + 0.3 + 0.6 = 1$), we do not have to divide. We then plug values into our formula as follows:

Forecast for Apr of Year 1 $(0.1)(245) + (0.3)(244) + (0.6)(250) = 247.70$

$$F_{t+1} = (W_1)(A_{t-2}) + (W_2)(A_{t-1}) + (W_3)(A_t)$$

$$F_{Apr-01} = (0.1)(245) + (0.3)(244) + (0.6)(250)$$

$$F_{Apr-01} = 247.70$$

When actual sales are received for April (260), we drop the January sales figure and use actual sales for February, March, and April to obtain our forecast for May. Hence, the forecast for May = $(0.1)(244) + (0.3)(250) + (0.6)(260) = 255.40$.

TABLE 6–2 Weighted Moving Average Model

Formula for Weighted Moving Average: $F_{t+1} = \dfrac{(W_1)(A_{t-2}) + (W_2)(A_{t-1}) + (W_3)(A_t)}{\sum W}$

Year	Month	Time Period	Actual Sales	$W_1 = 0.1$ $W_2 = 0.3$ $W_3 = 0.6$	$\Delta\lvert A - F\rvert$	$W_1 = 0.25$ $W_2 = 0.35$ $W_3 = 0.40$	$\Delta\lvert A - F\rvert$	$W_1 = 4$ $W_2 = 5$ $W_3 = 8$	$\Delta\lvert A - F\rvert$
		0							
Year 1	Jan	1	245						
	Feb	2	244						
	Mar	3	250						
	Apr	4	260	247.70	12.30	246.65	13.35	247.06	12.94
	May	5	265	255.40	9.60	252.50	12.50	253.29	11.71
	Jun	6	260	262.00	2.00	259.50	0.50	260.00	0.00
	Jul	7	255	261.50	6.50	261.75	6.75	261.47	6.47
	Aug	8	245	257.50	12.50	259.25	14.25	258.82	13.82
	Sep	9	240	249.50	9.50	252.25	12.25	251.47	11.47
	Oct	10	255	243.00	12.00	245.50	9.50	245.00	10.00
	Nov	11	265	249.50	15.50	247.25	17.75	248.24	16.76
	Dec	12	270	259.50	10.50	255.25	14.75	256.18	13.82
Year 2	Jan	13	250	267.00	17.00	264.50	14.50	265.00	15.00
	Feb	14	250	257.50	7.50	260.75	10.75	259.41	9.41
	Mar	15	258	252.00	6.00	255.00	3.00	254.71	3.29
	Apr	16	267	254.80	12.20	253.20	13.80	253.76	13.24
	May	17	273	262.60	10.40	259.60	13.40	260.35	12.65
	Jun	18	278	269.70	8.30	267.15	10.85	267.71	10.29
	Jul	19	260	275.40	15.40	273.50	13.50	273.94	13.94
	Aug	20	256	266.70	10.70	269.55	13.55	268.35	12.35
	Sep	21	255	259.40	4.40	262.90	7.90	262.35	7.35
	Oct	22	270	255.80	14.20	256.60	13.40	256.47	13.53
	Nov	23	275	264.10	10.90	261.25	13.75	262.29	12.71
	Dec	24	283	271.50	11.50	268.25	14.75	268.82	14.18
Year 3	Jan	25		279.30		276.95		277.59	
	$\Sigma \Delta\lvert A-F\rvert = n =$				218.90		244.75		234.94
					21.00		21.00		21.00
	MAD $=$				10.42		11.65		11.19

We can assign weights of any values, provided that we use the sum of the weights in the denominator. In Table 6–2, we also illustrate use of the weighted moving average model using weights of 0.25, 0.35, and 0.40 and weights of 4, 5, and 8. As with the moving average model, we also can use any number of time periods. Let's work one more example and obtain the forecast for May of Year 2 using weights of 4, 5, and 8 and actual sales for February of 250, March of 258, and April of 267. Plugging these values into the following formula, we obtain a forecast of 260.35.

$$F_{t+1} = \frac{(W_1)(A_{t-2}) + (W_2)(A_{t-1}) + (W_3)(A_t)}{\sum W}$$

$$F_{May-02} = \frac{(4)(250) + (5)(258) + (8)(267)}{4 + 5 + 8}$$

$$F_{May-02} = \frac{(1,000) + (1,290) + (2,136)}{17} = \frac{4,426}{17}$$

$$F_{May-02} = 260.35$$

After calculating our forecasts, as shown in Table 6–2, we also calculate MAD to determine which series of weights are most appropriate for our company. If we chose a weighted moving average model for our forecast, we use weights of 0.1, 0.3, and 0.6 to do our forecasting because the MAD of 10.42 is the lowest. These weights—0.1, 0.3, and 0.6—provide us with the smallest overall forecasting error.

Exponential Smoothing Model. The **exponential smoothing model** uses a smoothing constant, alpha (α), as an adjustment in determining the forecast. A **smoothing constant** is a value assigned by the forecaster to adjust the forecast based on the forecaster's assumption of the relationship between sales in one time period and sales in the next time period. The α can have any value between 0 and 1; however, α is usually 0.1, 0.2, or 0.3. The higher the value of α, the greater the emphasis given to sales for the current time period. The lower the value of α, the greater the emphasis given to the smoothed forecast for the current time period. A higher value of α is assigned when the forecaster believes that current sales are more predictive of future sales. Conversely, a lower α is chosen when the forecaster believes that the smoothed forecast is more predictive of future sales. With exponential smoothing, we must begin with an assumed rather than an actual forecast. (Most models use actual sales in the first period of observation as the assumed forecast.)

Table 6–3 gives an example of the exponential smoothing model applied to our 2 years' worth of sales data. The formula used in Table 6–3 is either:

$$F_{t+1} = \alpha(A_t) + (1 - \alpha)(F_t)$$

or, simplified,

$$F_{t+1} = (F_t) + \alpha(A_t - F_t)$$

The authors have seen this formula presented both ways in various texts. You may use whichever formula you prefer.

The following symbols are used in the exponential smoothing formula:

F_{t+1} = the smoothed forecast for the next time period
α = the smoothing constant
A_t = actual sales for the current time period
F_t = the smoothed forecast for the current time period

We use actual sales for January of Year 1 as the assumed smoothed forecast for February to begin our calculations. Using an α of 0.1 (less weight

TABLE 6–3 Exponential Smoothing Model

Formulas for Exponential Smoothing Model: $F_{t+1} = \alpha(A_t) + (1 - \alpha)(F_t)$ $F_{t+1} = F_t + \alpha(A_t - F_t)$

Year	Month	Time Period	Actual Sales	With $\alpha = 0.1$ Forecast	$\Delta\|A - F\|$	With $\alpha = 0.2$ Forecast	$\Delta\|A - F\|$	With $\alpha = 0.25$ Forecast	$\Delta\|A - F\|$
		0							
Year 1	Jan	1	245						
	Feb	2	244	245.00		245.00		245.00	
	Mar	3	250	244.90	5.10	244.80	5.20	244.75	5.25
	Apr	4	260	245.41	14.59	245.84	14.16	246.06	13.94
	May	5	265	246.87	18.13	248.67	16.33	249.55	15.45
	Jun	6	260	248.68	11.32	251.94	8.06	253.41	6.59
	Jul	7	255	249.81	5.19	253.55	1.45	255.06	0.06
	Aug	8	245	250.33	5.33	253.84	8.84	255.04	10.04
	Sep	9	240	249.80	9.80	252.07	12.07	252.53	12.53
	Oct	10	255	248.82	6.18	249.66	5.34	249.40	5.60
	Nov	11	265	249.44	15.56	250.73	14.27	250.80	14.20
	Dec	12	270	250.99	19.01	253.58	16.42	254.35	15.65
Year 2	Jan	13	250	252.89	2.89	256.86	6.86	258.26	8.26
	Feb	14	250	252.60	2.60	255.49	5.49	256.20	6.20
	Mar	15	258	252.34	5.66	254.39	3.61	254.65	3.35
	Apr	16	267	252.91	14.09	255.11	11.89	255.49	11.51
	May	17	273	254.32	18.68	257.49	15.51	258.36	14.64
	Jun	18	278	256.19	21.81	260.59	17.41	262.02	15.98
	Jul	19	260	258.37	1.63	264.07	4.07	266.02	6.02
	Aug	20	256	258.53	2.53	263.26	7.26	264.51	8.51
	Sep	21	255	258.28	3.28	261.81	6.81	262.38	7.38
	Oct	22	270	257.95	12.05	260.45	9.55	260.54	9.46
	Nov	23	275	259.16	15.84	262.36	12.64	262.90	12.10
	Dec	24	283	260.74	22.26	264.89	18.11	265.93	17.07
Year 3	Jan	25		262.97		268.51		270.20	
	$\Sigma \Delta\|A - F\| =$				233.54		221.36		219.80
	$n =$				22.00		22.00		22.00
	MAD =				10.62		10.06		9.99

given to actual sales, more weight given to smoothed forecast), we plug the data into our formula to obtain the forecast for period 3, or Mar, as follows:

$$F_{t+1} = \alpha(A_t) + (1 - \alpha)(F_t)$$

$$F_{March} = (0.1)(244) + (1 - 0.1)(245) = 24.4 + (0.9)(245)$$

$$= 24.4 + 220.5$$

$$F_{March} = 244.90$$

Let's do one more example using the other formula. We want to obtain a forecast for January of Year 3. Using Table 6–3 and an α of 0.25, we obtain the actual sales for Dec of Year 2 of 283 and the forecast for Dec of 265.93.

Substituting in our formula, we obtain a forecast of 270.20 for Jan of Year 3. The procedure is as follows:

$$F_{t+1} = (F_t) + \alpha(A_t - F_t)$$

$$F_{Jan} = (265.93) + (0.25)(283 - 265.93) = (265.93) + (0.25)(17.07)$$

$$F_{Jan} = 270.20$$

We show the results of the exponential smoothing forecast for months 3 through 25 in Table 6–3 for α of 0.1, 0.2, and 0.25.

After calculating our exponential smoothing forecasts as shown in Table 6–3, we also calculate MAD to determine which value of α is most appropriate for our company. If we choose an exponential smoothing model for our forecast, we use an α of 0.25 because it produces a MAD of 9.99 units, which is the lowest.

Selecting the Model. If we are going to use one of the three models (moving average, weighted moving average, or exponential smoothing) for the business demonstrated in this chapter, we must compare the MAD figures in Tables 6–1, 6–2, and 6–3. We use an exponential smoothing model with an α of 0.25 for this business because a MAD of 9.99 is the smallest.

Linear Regression Model. MAD can be used for short-term forecasts such as those obtained with moving average, weighted moving average, and exponential smoothing models. In business, however, we must also forecast for the intermediate and long term. For intermediate and long-term forecasts, the model most often used is simple linear regression. **Linear regression** does not use MAD, but rather a statistical method known as *least squared regression*. The statistical formulas are beyond the scope of this text.

To develop a regression model, we analyze the actual sales data that we have used for Tables 6–1, 6–2, and 6–3. The sales data show certain variations. The four areas of variation present in data that are gathered over time are

1. Seasonal variation is caused by the predictable shopping habits of our customers or by annual climatic conditions. Seasonal variation for retail establishments may be expressed on a weekly basis. For a restaurant, Monday is usually the slowest day of the week; sales on Friday and Saturday are usually the best. For general retail sales, the fourth quarter of each calendar year shows the strongest sales because of the Christmas shopping season.

2. Trend variation is caused by growth or decline in demand for our product or service over time. The change in sales over time is represented by a *trend line*. This straight line is the regression line and is calculated by using linear regression. For industries that have relatively new products, this trend line may show annual growth of 20 to 50 percent. For mature products, the trend line may increase with population growth. For some products that are being replaced by newer ones, the trend line might be negative, or downward sloping.

3. Cyclical variation is caused by general economic factors that affect our industry. For most products and services, when the economy expands, sales also grow. When we enter a recession, sales usually decline.

4. Noise is random variation in our data that is not explained by the preceding factors. The value of noise is calculated in statistical models that are beyond the scope of this text. As an example of noise, let us say that a business experienced weekly sales of $50,000, $52,000, $54,000, $25,000, and $56,000 during a 5-week period. The economy has been good and sales, in general, have shown consistent growth. However, in week 4 of our example, sales were only $25,000. We check historical records, question others in the same business, and do everything else in our power to try to determine why sales were only $25,000 in this particular week. We conclude that there is no logical explanation. This variation, then, would be labeled *noise* or *random variation*. It is unexplained.

Linear regression is used to determine two factors: the slope and intercept of the regression line. As noted, the regression line is our trend line. The basic formula for the regression line as displayed in statistical texts is $y = a + bx$. This formula is similar to that for a straight line used in many math textbooks: $y = mx + b$. The definitions of the variables used in the regression formula are

- y is the **dependent variable,** which is a variable that relies on other variables for its value. The value of y is usually calculated, but the value depends on the other variables in our equation.
- x is the **independent variable**, which is the variable that does not depend on other variables for its value. In forecasting models, x is often a time period.
- b is the slope of the regression line. **Slope** is defined as rise over run. This is the change in y divided by the change in x, or the change in the dependent variable divided by the change in the independent variable. For our example problem, it is the change in sales over the change in time. Algebraically, it is expressed as

$$slope = \frac{\Delta y}{\Delta x} = \frac{y_2 - y_1}{x_2 - x_1}$$

   When slope is positive, the resulting regression line moves up and to the right. When slope is negative, the resulting regression line moves down and to the right.
- a is the y-intercept. The y-intercept is the value of y when x equals 0.

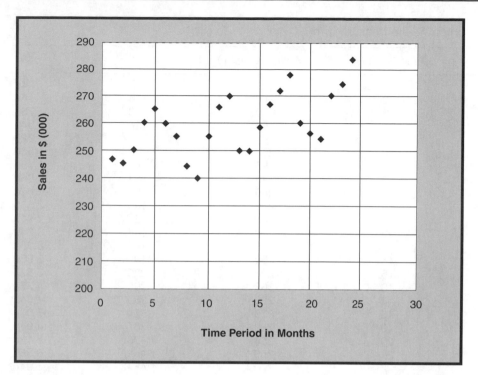

FIGURE 6–2
Scatter Diagram

The easiest method of introducing the regression function is to show a scatter diagram of basic sales data (Figure 6–2).

On a graph, the vertical y-axis represents sales and the horizontal x-axis represents time. A point has been plotted showing the sales value for each time period. In analyzing the diagram, we can see that sales appear to be seasonal. Sales in the first quarter of each year are low, then they increase in the second quarter, decline in the third quarter, and show a substantial increase in the fourth quarter. We also see that there is an increase in sales from one year to the next. If we could draw a straight line through the points in this diagram, we would have the trend line. Because we must produce a forecast predicting several years into the future, we must determine the value of the trend line, which is accomplished with the regression formula.

The mathematical steps for calculating regression are time-consuming, but the actual calculations are relatively easy. If you have a computer with a spreadsheet program such as Microsoft Excel, it takes very little time to calculate the values of the intercept and slope. Let's look at the mathematical calculation of the regression line as shown in Table 6–4, in which the formulas for the intercept (a) and slope (b) are given. You must first construct columns representing the variables in the formulas. We already have the time periods (x) and sales (y) from our basic data in Table 6–4: one column for x^2 and another column for the product of x and y. We then perform the required calculations. After

TABLE 6–4 Calculation of the Regression Line

Year	Month	Time Period (x)	Actual Sales (y)	x^2	xy
Year 1	Jan	1	245	1	245
	Feb	2	244	4	488
	Mar	3	250	9	750
	Apr	4	260	16	1,040
	May	5	265	25	1,325
	Jun	6	260	36	1,560
	Jul	7	255	49	1,785
	Aug	8	245	64	1,960
	Sep	9	240	81	2,160
	Oct	10	255	100	2,550
	Nov	11	265	121	2,915
	Dec	12	270	144	3,240
Year 2	Jan	13	250	169	3,250
	Feb	14	250	196	3,500
	Mar	15	258	225	3,870
	Apr	16	267	256	4,272
	May	17	273	289	4,641
	Jun	18	278	324	5,004
	Jul	19	260	361	4,940
	Aug	20	256	400	5,120
	Sep	21	255	441	5,355
	Oct	22	270	484	5,940
	Nov	23	275	529	6,325
	Dec	24	283	576	6,792
	SUMS (Σ)	300	6,229	4,900	79,027

Using the following formulas, we substitute from Table 6–3 and obtain an intercept (a) of 246.8841 and a slope (b) of 1.0126.

accomplishing this, we sum (Σ) each column to arrive at the total. We then plug the required numbers back into our formula, as shown in Table 6–4. The value of the y-intercept (a) is calculated as 246.8841, which is the value of y when x equals 0. The slope is calculated as 1.0126, which means that for every increase of 1 in the value of x, y increases in value by 1.0126. However, because y is sales in thousands of dollars, sales increase by an average of $1,012.60 each month. (Note: $1,012.60 is the change in the slope of the trend line).

$$a = \frac{\sum x^2 \sum y - \sum x \sum xy}{n \sum x^2 - (\sum x)^2} = \frac{(4,900)(6,229) - (300)(79,027)}{(24)(4,900) - (300)^2}$$

$$= \frac{(30,522,100) - (23,708,100)}{(117,600) - (90,000)} = \frac{6,814,000}{27,600} = 246.8841$$

$$b = \frac{n \sum xy - \sum x \sum y}{n \sum x^2 - (\sum x)^2} = \frac{(24)(79,027) - (300)(6,229)}{(24)(4,900) - (300)^2}$$

$$= \frac{1,896,648 - 1,868,700}{117,600 - 90,000} = \frac{27,948}{27,600} = 1.0126$$

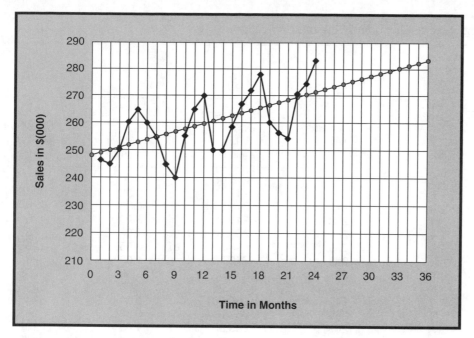

FIGURE 6–3
Sales Chart with Regression Line

If you have access to a computer with Microsoft Excel, you can simply use a *function wizard* to place the values of x and y into the function for slope. When you hit the Return key, the value of the slope is returned as 1.0126. Repeat this step for intercept, and the value of 246.8841 is returned. This process takes approximately 30 seconds with a spreadsheet program. Once the slope and intercept are derived, we can plot the regression line for any future time periods. The regression line eliminates the seasonal and noise variation in our data. It assumes a linear relationship between the value of y and x, as shown in Figure 6–3.

Using the data in Table 6–5, we have determined the value of the regression line for 36 time periods and plotted this data in Figure 6–3. Table 6–5 demonstrates how we take the data for slope and intercept and calculate the regression (trend) line for future time periods.

The regression forecast column in Table 6–5 provides the value of the regression line for time periods 1 through 36. This represents a regression forecast for y for these time periods. The actual calculation is performed mathematically by plugging the values of the slope and intercept into our regression formula as follows:

$$y = a + bx = 246.8841 + (1.0126)(x)$$

For $x = 0$,

$$y = 246.8841 + (1.0126)(0) = 246.8841$$

TABLE 6–5 Forecast of Sales, Including Seasonal Adjustment

$y = a + bx$
$a = 246.8841$
$b = 1.0126$

Year	Month	Time x	Actual Sales (A) Jan-01–Dec-02	Regression Forecast (F) $y = a + bx$	Seasonal Ratio (A)/(F)	Seasonal Forecast of Sales
		0		246.88		
Year 1	Jan	1	245	247.90	0.99	245
	Feb	2	244	248.91	0.98	244
	Mar	3	250	249.92	1.00	250
	Apr	4	260	250.93	1.04	260
	May	5	265	251.95	1.05	265
	Jun	6	260	252.96	1.03	260
	Jul	7	255	253.97	1.00	255
	Aug	8	245	254.98	0.96	245
	Sep	9	240	256.00	0.94	240
	Oct	10	255	257.01	0.99	255
	Nov	11	265	258.02	1.03	265
	Dec	12	270	259.04	1.04	270
Year 2	Jan	13	250	260.05	0.96	250
	Feb	14	250	261.06	0.96	250
	Mar	15	258	262.07	0.98	258
	Apr	16	267	263.09	1.01	267
	May	17	273	264.10	1.03	273
	Jun	18	278	265.11	1.05	278
	Jul	19	260	266.12	0.98	260
	Aug	20	256	267.14	0.96	256
	Sep	21	255	268.15	0.95	255
	Oct	22	270	269.16	1.00	270
	Nov	23	275	270.17	1.02	275
	Dec	24	283	271.19	1.04	283
Year 3	Jan	25		272.20	0.97	265
	Feb	26		273.21	0.97	265
	Mar	27		274.22	0.99	272
	Apr	28		275.24	1.03	282
	May	29		276.25	1.04	288
	Jun	30		277.26	1.04	288
	Jul	31		278.27	0.99	276
	Aug	32		279.29	0.96	268
	Sep	33		280.30	0.94	265
	Oct	34		281.31	1.00	281
	Nov	35		282.33	1.02	289
	Dec	36		283.34	1.04	296

For $x = 1$,

$y = 246.8841 + (1.0126)(1) = 247.8967$

For $x = 36$,

$y = 246.8841 + (1.0126)(36) = 283.3377$

Here, we substituted values of 0, 1, and 36 for *x*. We can, in the same way, obtain a value of *y* for any time frame we choose.

We can also use the regression line and our current data to obtain a forecast of future sales that includes seasonal data. To obtain the seasonal ratio, we divide actual sales by the regression forecast for the time period. The sixth column in Table 6–5 was calculated using this seasonal ratio formula. The seasonal ratio for Jan-01 equals 245/247.8967, which equals 0.9883, which we rounded to 0.99. We calculated the seasonal ratio for each period for which we have actual sales data.

Note: *All numbers in tables for the regression model are rounded to two decimal points, so 247.90 as shown in Table 6–5 is actually 247.8967. Therefore, if you use a calculator to check the numbers in the tables and you plug in 247.90, you will find that there is a slight variance in the answer.*

To obtain average seasonal ratios, we calculate the average seasonal ratio for each similar time period. For example, we add the seasonal ratio for Jan Year 1 and Jan Year 2 and divide by 2 [(0.9883 + 0.9614)/2]. We can then obtain an average seasonal ratio for Jan Year 3 of 0.9749. We multiply our average seasonal ratio for Jan of 0.9749 by the regression forecast for Jan Year 3 of 272.20 and obtain a seasonal sales forecast for Jan Year 3 of 265.35 (because we can't sell 0.35 units, we round to 265). The results of these calculations are shown in the seasonal forecast of sales column seven of Table 6–5 and graphically in Figure 6–4.

Often a trend can be computed using simple sales data and basic mathematics. The trend in business is usually expressed as a percentage increase or

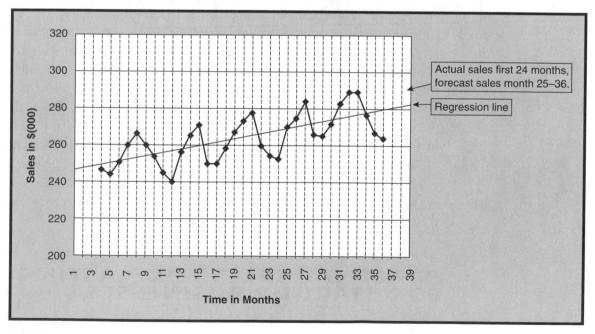

FIGURE 6–4
Three-Year Regression and Seasonal Forecast

decrease in sales during a time period, which is usually 1 year. Once we determine this trend, we can apply it to a sales forecast to estimate future sales. For example, if, for a given business, total sales in Year 1 were $320,000 and sales in Year 2 were $352,000, then the sales growth was 10 percent. To determine this, we use the same formula as in analyzing financial statements using horizontal analysis [i.e., (New − Old) ÷ Old]. For this example, it is $352,000 − $320,000 ÷ $320,000 (or $32,000/$320,000), which is 0.1, or 10 percent. If our assumption is that the business will continue to grow at a rate of 10 percent per year, then our forecast of sales for Year 3 is $387,200. This is computed by taking 10 percent of Year 2 sales and adding it to Year 2 sales. We can also compute this by multiplying current-year sales (Year 2 = $352,000) by 1.10. The formula is

$$F_{t+1} = F_t(1 + g)$$

where F_{t+1} is the sales forecast for time period t plus 1 unit of time, F_t is actual sales during time period t, and g is the growth rate expressed as a percentage.

Causal Models

Causal models also are known as *external* or *exogenous models,* and they take into account variables in the general economy that affect the revenue obtained by a company. Causal models can be simple or quite complex. Most require multiple regression analysis, which is usually beyond the scope of a small business manager, yet the manager should be aware of the effect these variables have on business. We can often include causal modeling as part of our forecasting technique. For example, if we sell home appliances to building contractors, then building permits allow us to predict sales growth or decline several months into the future. Also, consider that most businesses have their short- and long-term loans tied to the prime lending rate; therefore, a change in this interest rate has a direct impact on how much interest we pay on future and current loans.

The forecast drives our business planning. Good plans answer the questions of what, who, where, when, and how: What is to be done (mission and goals)? Who will do it? Where will they do it? When will they do it (specific time frame)? How will it be done (resource allocation and use of resources)? The basic sales forecast also provides us with one very important number—projected sales in dollars. This dollar figure is the necessary beginning point for developing pro forma financial statements.

 ## PRACTICAL SALES FORECASTING FOR START-UP BUSINESSES

The preceding forecasting methods primarily pertain to businesses that are established and have some history. However, the start-up business has very little history. Where then do we obtain a sales forecast for a start-up business? Fortunately, the vast majority of entrepreneurs desire to go into a business where they have some prior experience. For example, restaurant owners like to cook, invent new menu items, and have experience in the restaurant business. Plumbing, electrical, painting, and other trade contractors are people who are already licensed in their professions. Retail specialty shops are most often started by individuals who have prior experience in the field and have developed a unique idea to differentiate and position themselves in the marketplace. These attributes are of utmost importance to the entrepreneur. The small business administration, through its Service Core of Retired Executives (SCORE), conducts training classes and provides budding entrepreneurs with the opportunity to schedule meetings with other successful business owners who have experience and were successful entrepreneurs.

There are several businesses that do not require leased or purchased office space. For example, if you are starting a trade (plumber, electrician, painter, etc.) contracting business that can be conducted from your residence, you typically go to the client's job site to provide a bid. In addition, all work is done at the job site. An online service can also be provided from an in-home office. We recommend that you do this in order to keep your expenses at a minimum. If, however, you require a building or leased office space, then be prepared to increase your expenses significantly. In any event, it is essential to forecast all of your business expenses accurately.

Forecasting for the start-up business requires the budding entrepreneur to conduct a lot of legwork and use his or her prior business experience. There are several logical steps that one can take to obtain a sales forecast and create the initial pro forma financial statements. In developing a forecast, we must consider several factors. Some authorities recommend starting with a list of expenses; others recommend starting with a forecast. Because the first line of the pro forma income statement is revenue, we begin with a forecast. Forecasting for a start-up business is often a matter of listing what you know.

1. Most new businesses are formed by someone who has worked and managed that type of business before. They actually have access to a high degree of information.
   a. If you have experience and have worked in the trades (plumber, carpenter, painter, etc.) or a repair service company (automobile or heating and air conditioning repair), then you are familiar with both the pay scale and the hourly fee that a company like yours should charge. For example, if you are paid $30 per hour and the company bills $65 for a service call, then you can forecast a best (10 hours per day, 6 days per week) and worst (4 hours per day, 4 days per week) case scenario and subsequently place this information into a spreadsheet. Table 6–6 demonstrates this procedure and shows the gross revenue (profit) for a start-up business based on the these

TABLE 6–6 Forecast of Revenue for a Start-Up Service or Trade Business

	Hours per Day	Days per Week	Billed Hourly Rate	Hourly Wage	Overtime Wage	Number of Workers	Weeks Worked per Year
Best Case	10	6	65	30	45	1	50
Worst Case	4	4					

	Weekly		Annually	
	Best Case	Worst Case	Best Case	Worst Case
Gross Revenue	$3,900	$1,040	$195,000	$52,000
Labor Cost	2,100	480	105,000	24,000
Material Cost			—	—
Gross Profit	$1,800	$560	$90,000	$28,000

Note: All wages are based on a 40-hour workweek; any time worked beyond 40 hours per week are paid at an hourly wage of 1.5 times the hourly wage.

assumptions. Note that with one worker, the company can expect a gross annual profit of $28,000 in the worst case scenario and $90,000 in the best case scenario. With two workers, the company can expect gross annual profit of $56,000 in the worst case and $180,000 in the best case scenario.

b. If you have experience in the food–service business, you should have access to the following information: what employees are paid, what an average meal costs, and the number of meals served each day.

c. If you have experience in retail, you should know what the gross profit margin is. In other words, you should know what the cost of goods are and how much they are sold for.

2. If you don't have the specific cost and revenue information mentioned previously, you can often find financial statements of similar firms on the Internet. If the firms are publicly traded, go to the SEC home page at http://www.sec.gov and look up their financial statements via EDGAR. In order to have gross profit margins that match profitable firms in your industry, you must have a cost structure that is similar to those companies with regard to revenue and cost of goods. For example, with Starbucks, you can go to their annual reports and find the number of coffee shops, gross revenue, costs of goods, and gross profit. Dividing the number of shops into any of the previous categories provides you with average sales, cost of goods, and gross profit per shop.

In the previous scenarios, we covered only the basic forecast pertaining to the top three lines of a pro forma income statement—gross revenue, cost of goods, and gross profit. After obtaining the revenue and gross profit numbers, we must then estimate all our fixed costs (expenses) in order to determine if we can actually make a profit from the business. Another method of starting a new business is to begin with expense forecasting rather than with gross revenue forecasting. In either case, we must forecast all our fixed expenses to determine if the business will be profitable.

There are three types of expenses that must be considered—fixed, start-up, and variable.

1. Fixed expenses include, but are not limited to, leasing (equipment and property), utility bills, phone bills, insurance, licensing fees, postage, technology, advertising and marketing, and salaries. Most of this information can be obtained by determining initial location and actually finding out leasing costs, utility costs, and so on, for that area. Experienced people know what salaries or wages are being paid in the local community.

2. Start-up expenses are those expenses incurred by the business only once. They include, but are not limited to, first and last month's rent, utility deposits, security deposits, key deposits, and possibly architectural fees. You must determine if you are going to purchase or lease land, buildings, and equipment and if it will be paid out over time or purchased with a one-time payment. Any payment made at the onset of the business but not occurring again in the normal course of the business is a start-up expense.

3. Variable expenses are determined by the type of business. For a retailer, variable expenses include all costs of goods associated with sales, including purchase price of inventory, shipping charges, insurance while in transit, sales commissions, and so on. For a manufacturer, variable costs include manufactured parts and production labor. For a service business, variable costs include service parts and labor.

There are links to two Excel templates at http://www.prenhall.com/adelman help in organizing your expenses:"Start-Up Expenses" and "A 12-Month Profit and Loss Projection." Once all of the business expenses have been categorized, it is time to begin the preparation of our pro forma financial statements.

PRO FORMA FINANCIAL STATEMENTS

A **pro forma financial statement** is a projected statement based on the forecast. As our business increases its revenue base, increased sales create the need for additional assets. For example (see Hannah's Donut Shop case study at the end of this chapter), when Hannah's Donut Shop increased its number of wholesale customers, it had to purchase an additional delivery truck. Accounts receivable also increased, because new wholesale customers were, in fact, credit customers. Although Hannah extended credit to these customers, she experienced a direct buildup in fixed assets (delivery truck) and an indirect buildup in current assets in two areas: the increase in accounts receivable because of the increase in credit customers, and an increase in raw materials inventory because Hannah had to purchase additional doughnut mixes to make more doughnuts. Therefore, Hannah recognized the need for financial planning in her business.

To best address such concerns, a business should begin by preparing estimated financial statements for the future in a process called a **pro forma financial analysis.** Its goal is to predict individual financial variables and integrate each into the preparation of several pro forma financial statements. We, of course, realize that pro forma analysis is based on the sales forecast. Because total sales are the top line on an income statement, we begin our pro forma analysis by developing the pro forma income statement used to determine the expected profit of our firm.

PRO FORMA INCOME STATEMENT

Most businesses develop a pro forma income statement by using information from a current statement. For example, if we project an increase in sales, then cost of goods sold also will increase.

Table 6–7 shows a pro forma income statement for a hypothetical company whose forecast indicated that sales would increase by 25 percent from 2007 to 2008. Cost of goods sold (COGS) can be expected to be the same percentage of sales year after year. Because COGS was 50 percent of sales in 2007, COGS

TABLE 6–7 Pro Forma Income Statement

Income Statements for Time Periods Indicated

	Actual Sales for 2007	*Pro Forma Sales for 2008*
Sales	$200,000	$250,000
COG	100,000	$125,000
Gross Profit	$100,000	$125,000
Operating Expenses		
Rent	24,000	24,000
Utilities	3,000	3,600
Salaries	60,000	63,000
Insurance	2,400	3,000
Depreciation	5,000	7,000
Equipment	4,500	7,800
Total Operating Expenses	$ 98,900	$108,400
Operating Profit	$ 1,100	$ 16,600
Interest Expense	5,000	6,800
Net Profit	$ (3,900)	$ 9,800

for 2008 is expected to be 50 percent of $250,000, or $125,000. Therefore, gross profit will increase by 25 percent, to $125,000. One factor to remember is that operating expenses reflect some fixed costs that do not increase with increased sales; however, other operating expenses do increase with increased sales. Mortgage and lease payments do not usually increase with sales. In our case study, Hannah had to purchase a new truck to support the increase in sales; hence, her fixed bank payments increased. Operating expenses must be separated into two categories: those that we know will not increase with sales, and those that increase by some amount as sales increase. Because many operating expenses have a specific supplier or vendor, we can often check with them to forecast changes in these fixed expenses. For example, we can call our insurance agent to see if our insurance rates will increase and check with utility companies for any rate changes.

In our sample pro forma income statement (Table 6–7), we assumed that rent would remain the same at $24,000. Utilities increase by 20 percent from $3,000 to $3,600. In addition, we gave our employees a 5 percent pay raise, so salaries increased from $60,000 to $63,000. Our insurance agent stated that our annual premium would increase from $2,400 to $3,000, or 25 percent. We purchased a new piece of equipment, which increased depreciation by $2,000 per year, and financed the equipment with a long-term loan, so our equipment payment increased from $4,500 to $7,800 per year.

When sales increase, we must often increase our fixed assets by the purchase of additional equipment and machinery. This purchase of assets is frequently financed by long-term debt. Although the increase in monthly bank payments increases our operating expenses, the percentage increases in these expenses usually is not as great as the percentage increases in sales. The result is that our operating income often increases by a margin that is greater than our increase in sales. In our pro forma income statement example (Table 6–7), sales increased by 25 percent, but operating expenses increased only by 9.61 percent ($108,400 − $98,900) ÷ ($98,900). Hence, operating profit increases from $1,100 to $16,600, which reflects a 1,400 percent increase.

The pro forma income statement shown in Table 6–7 is for a business that has a historical record. For a start-up business, the pro forma income statement is more difficult to generate. (Start-up business costs are discussed in more detail at the end of this chapter.) For the start-up business, the owner must estimate sales using one or more of the methods previously discussed. Once the owner has an estimate of sales, then COGS should be a percentage based on industry standards. If the owner cannot obtain goods at or less than this industry standard, chances are that he or she will not be able to generate a profit. All operating expense figures must be inserted based on the owner's obtaining the necessary data. Once a location is determined, the owner has actual amounts for lease or mortgage payments and must then obtain an estimate of utility costs from the utility companies for the location selected. Insurance premiums, in most cases, are also based on the facility selected, and marketing expenses must be estimated. Each area of the income statement must be completed based on estimates of operating expenses because historical records do not exist. Once the pro forma income statement is developed, the owner should determine if the operating expenses are in line with industry averages. It is only then that the owner can determine if the new venture will be profitable.

PRO FORMA CASH BUDGET

Now that we have a pro forma income statement, we must look at how the categories on the income statement affect our pro forma balance sheet. When we discussed financial statements initially, we indicated that an income statement is not a cash flow statement. The next step, then, is to determine cash flow requirements by developing a pro forma cash budget. Once this budget is developed, we can construct a pro forma balance sheet.

A **pro forma cash budget** projects future receipts and expenditures and determines how much financing is needed on a monthly basis to correct any shortfalls in cash flow. It is important to note that a positive change (increase) in sales may have a negative impact on the business if financial planning does not occur. For example, when Hannah experienced increased doughnut sales, she was faced with a complicated chain of results. The increased sales of wholesale doughnuts required the purchase of an additional delivery truck. Where does one get the money to support such additional assets? The delivery truck could be paid for in cash or financed through a financial institution. In addition, we must note that an increase in sales often results in the granting of additional credit, and credit sales are not collected immediately. Hannah must make monthly payments to the bank for the delivery truck and to her vendors for the doughnut mixes. Many of the accounts receivable customers pay Hannah monthly; however, the doughnut vendor delivers weekly and wants to be paid within 2 weeks of delivery (net 15 days). Such a situation initially results in a negative cash flow, but the monthly income statement indicates a profit. This creates a discrepancy between the amount of sales stated on the income statement and the actual amount of cash available to pay bills. It is important to realize that sales are recognized on the income statement when the sale is made. If a business has $100,000 in sales but they are all on credit, then the business may have a serious cash flow problem if a large percentage of sales is in accounts receivable. It is for this reason that we must generate a pro forma cash budget on a monthly basis. A cash budget allows the business to monitor the actual cash on hand.

At this time, it is important for us to look at the meaning of the components of the pro forma cash budget (Table 6–8). Historical records show that 30 percent of sales are collected in the month of the sales. For January 2008, our forecast sales are $13,000, and we collect 30 percent, or $3,900, and have

TABLE 6-8 Pro Forma Cash Budget

Monthly Cash Receipts

	\<Actual Sales 2007\> Oct	Nov	Dec	\<Pro Forma Sales and Cash Receipts 2008\> Jan	Feb	Mar	Apr	May	Jun	Jul	Aug	Sep	Oct	Nov	Dec
Sales	$17,625	$20,250	$22,500	$13,000	$14,500	$14,000	$19,000	$23,000	$24,500	$21,000	$17,500	$23,000	$23,500	$27,000	$30,000
Current Month Collection at 30% of Sales	5,288	6,075	6,750	3,900	4,350	4,200	5,700	6,900	7,350	6,300	5,250	6,900	7,050	8,100	9,000
Outstanding Current Month Accounts Receivable (AR)	12,338	14,175	15,750	9,100	10,150	9,800	13,300	16,100	17,150	14,700	12,250	16,100	16,450	18,900	21,000
60% of AR Collected Month Following Sale		7,403	8,505	9,450	5,460	6,090	5,880	7,980	9,660	10,290	8,820	7,350	9,660	9,870	11,340
40% of AR Collected in 2nd Month Following Sale			4,935	5,670	6,300	3,640	4,060	3,920	5,320	6,440	6,860	5,880	4,900	6,440	6,580
Total Receipts			$20,190	$19,020	$16,110	$13,930	$15,640	$18,800	$22,330	$23,030	$20,930	$20,130	$21,610	$24,410	$26,920

Monthly Cash Payments

			Dec	Jan	Feb	Mar	Apr	May	Jun	Jul	Aug	Sep	Oct	Nov	Dec
Accounts Payable (AP) Previous Month			$10,125	$11,250	$6,500	$7,250	$7,000	$9,500	$11,500	$12,250	$10,500	$8,750	$11,500	$11,750	$13,500
Operating Expenses				8,450	8,450	8,450	8,450	8,450	8,450	8,450	8,450	8,450	8,450	8,450	8,450
Interest Payments				567	567	567	567	567	567	567	567	567	567	567	567
Total Payments			$20,267	$15,517	$16,267	$16,017	$18,517	$20,517	$21,267	$19,517	$17,767	$20,517	$20,767	$22,517	

Monthly Cash Budget

				Jan	Feb	Mar	Apr	May	Jun	Jul	Aug	Sep	Oct	Nov	Dec
Total Receipts				$19,020	$16,110	$13,930	$15,640	$18,800	$22,330	$23,030	$20,930	$20,130	$21,610	$24,410	$26,920
Total Payments				20,267	15,517	16,267	16,017	18,517	20,517	21,267	19,517	17,767	20,517	20,767	22,517
Net Cash Flow				$(1,247)	$593	$(2,337)	$(377)	$283	$1,813	$1,763	$1,413	$2,363	$1,093	$3,643	$4,403

Cash Budget With Borrowing and Repayment

				Jan	Feb	Mar	Apr	May	Jun	Jul	Aug	Sep	Oct	Nov	Dec
Net Cash Flow				$(1,247)	$593	$(2,337)	$(377)	$283	$1,813	$1,763	$1,413	$2,363	$1,093	$3,643	$4,403
Beginning Cash Balance				4000	$4,000	$4,000	4,000	4,000	4,000	4,000	4,000	4,000	4,000	4,000	4,003
Total Cash Balance				$2,753	$4,593	$1,663	3,623	4,283	5,813	5,763	5,413	6,363	5,093	7,643	8,406
Monthly Loan or (Repayment)				1,247	(593)	2,337	377	(283)	(1,813)	(1,763)	(1,413)	(2,363)	(1,093)	(3,640)	-
Cumulative Loan Balance			9000	10,247	9,654	11,991	12,368	12,085	10,272	8,509	7,096	4,733	3,640	-	-
Ending Cash Balance			$4,000	$4,000	$4,000	$4,000	$4,000	$4,000	$4,000	$4,000	$4,000	$4,000	$4,000	$4,003	$8,406

Note: Shaded rows, Sales and Outstanding Current Month Accounts Receivable and cumulative loan balance do not represent cash flow.

outstanding accounts receivable of $9,100. Historical records indicate that 60 percent of the outstanding amount will be collected in the month following the sale, and 40 percent of the outstanding accounts receivable will be collected in the second month following the sale. For January 2008, we collect 60 percent of $9,100, which is $5,460, in February; and we collect 40 percent of $9,100, which is $3,640, in March. To have accurate forecasted cash receipts for January, we must have the data for November and December 2007. For January, we collect 60 percent of December's outstanding receivables (0.6 × $15,750 = $9,450) and 40 percent of November's outstanding receivables (0.4 × $14,175 = $5,670). Note the shaded rows for Sales and Outstanding current month accounts receivable are not cash receipts. We need those numbers for our calculations. To determine actual cash receipts, we add cash collected in the current month and the amount of cash we collect in receivables for the previous 2 months. For January, we collect $3,900 + $9,450 + $5,670 for total receipts of $19,020. Moving down the January column, accounts payable for January are 50 percent of previous months sales (0.5 × $22,500 = $11,250). Operating expenses are one-twelfth of the pro forma operating expenses from the 2008 pro forma income statement minus depreciation (Table 6–7).

$$\text{Pro forma monthly operating expenses} = \frac{\text{Operating expenses} - \text{depreciation}}{12}$$

$$= \frac{\$108,400 - \$7,000}{12} = \frac{\$101,400}{12} = \$8,450$$

Interest payments is the pro forma income statement interest divided by 12 ($6,800 ÷ 12 = $567 rounded). Total payments are the sum of accounts payable, operating expenses, and interest payments ($11,250 + $8,450 + $567 = $20,267). We subtract total payments from total receipts to obtain net cash flow ($1,247). Note that in months of low sales, the company may have a negative cash flow and need to borrow additional funds in order to not fall below a level of cash that management must have on hand. In this case, the firm wants a minimum cash balance of $4,000. The negative cash balance of $1,247 eats into the $4,000 of required cash that the company must have on hand. This reduces the cash down to $2,753, which requires the company to borrow or use its line of credit to bring the cash balance back to $4,000. The company also had a cumulative loan balance of $9,000, which was taken from the balance sheet (Table 6–9) at the end of 2007. Note that the Cumulative loan balance line is shaded in gray because it does not represent a cash payment. In January, the company had to borrow its deficit of $1,247, which increased its cumulative loan balance to $10,247. The formulas that were discussed above are placed into our spreadsheet, and we generate a pro forma cash budget. Note that in those months where cash inflows exceed outflows, we repay the lender that amount which exceeds a minimum cash balance of $4,000. For example, in

TABLE 6–9 Pro Forma Balance Sheet

Balance Sheets for Year Ending December 31

	Actual for 2007	*Pro Forma for 2008*
Current Assets		
Cash	$ 4,000	$ 8,406
Accounts Receivabe	21,420	28,560
Inventory	15,000	18,750
Total Current Assets	$40,420	$55,716
Fixed Assets		
Net Machinery and Equipment	30,000	43,000
Total Assets	$70,420	$98,716
Liabilities and Owner's Equity		
Current Liabilities		
Accounts Payable	$11,250	$15,000
Salaries Payable	$ 2,500	$2,625
Notes Payable	9,000	
Total Current Liabilities	$22,750	$17,625
Long Term Liabilities		
Long Term Loan	$30,000	$50,000
Total Liabilities	$52,750	$67,625
Owner's Equity	17,670	31,091
Total Liabilities and Owner's Equity	$70,420	$98,716

February our inflow was a positive $4,593, which gave us an excess of $593. This $593 was then used to repay part of our cumulative loan balance. Notice that the business keeps score of its cumulative loan balance. The goal is to have no short-term debt and a positive cash flow. For our sample firm, we accomplish the payoff of our debt in November 2008 and end the year with a cash balance of $8,406. We then look at the maximum borrowing month for the year and arrange for our line of credit with our lender. For this firm, our accumulated borrowing went as high as $12,368 in April. Therefore, we must have a line of credit with our lender that exceeds this amount. We recommend $20,000 as our bank line of credit or as a home equity loan just in case sales fall short of our forecast and cash collections change.

We subtract sales paid in cash from total forecasted monthly sales to get outstanding current months accounts receivable. We use a seasonal forecast for the individual months to get the monthly sales figures for our cash budget. We next turn to our historical records. For our sample company, an analysis of the historical records indicates that 30 percent of current-month sales are collected in cash and the remaining 70 percent are outstanding accounts receivable. We also find that 60 percent of the accounts receivable will be collected in the month following the sale. The remaining 40 percent will be collected in the second month after the sale. We show this information in Table 6–8. We then use this information to determine total receipts for each month of our projected year.

Cash payments are arrived at for each month by taking into account inventory purchases, labor costs, operating expenses, and interest payments. Finally, a net cash flow figure for each month is derived, and subsequently a cash budget is constructed. We look at each month's net cash flow and determine those months for which we have a deficit. We should set up a line of credit with a bank or lender so that we have access to needed capital for those months. This access to capital also may include the entrepreneur's savings.

Under December on our pro forma cash budget are two figures that must be transferred to our pro forma balance sheet: outstanding accounts receivable and cash. Outstanding accounts receivable for December 2008 are $21,000, which will be collected in January and February of 2009 plus 40 percent of November's accounts receivable, which is scheduled to be collected in January 2009 (0.4 × $18,900 = $7,560). The total accounts receivable is $21,000 plus $7,560, which equals $28,560. Cash on hand is $8,406. Accounts payable that will be transferred to the 2008 pro forma are 50 percent of December's sales forecast, or ($30,000 × 0.50) = $15,000. We confirm this with December's accounts payable, which is November's forecast multiplied by 50 percent, or ($27,000 × 0.50) = $13,500. We are now ready to generate our pro forma balance sheet.

PRO FORMA BALANCE SHEET

The **pro forma balance sheet** is a projected balance sheet for a future time period. The increase in sales causes a buildup in assets and is reflected in the pro forma balance sheet. Looking at Table 6–9, we see that cash is projected to increase from $4,000 to $8,406 from 2007 to 2008. At the same time, we expect to experience an accounts receivable and inventory buildup as a result of increased sales. As of December 2008, accounts receivable is expected to be $28,560 and inventory is expected to be $18,750.

Equipment is expected to increase to $43,000 from $30,000. When sales increase substantially, we must determine if additional machinery and equipment are required to support this increase in sales. The purchase of this additional equipment is shown on our pro forma balance sheet as an increase in fixed assets. As we can see in Table 6–9, total assets increase from $70,420 in 2007 to a projected $98,716 for 2008. This additional $28,296 in assets must be financed by increasing liabilities, equity, or both.

With the increased sales, our company is expected to generate enough cash to completely pay off $9,000 of notes payable from the 2007 balance sheet. Accounts payable, however, increase from $11,250 to $15,000. This is a result of the additional inventory that we expect to purchase each month to support the additional sales. Overall, total assets increase by $28,296 ($98,716 pro forma for 2008 − $70,420 actual for 2007). This buildup in assets is to be financed by an additional $14,875 in total liabilities ($67,625 pro forma for 2008 − $52,750 actual for 2007) and $13,421 in additional owner's equity ($31,091 pro forma for 2008 − $17,670 actual for 2007). Going back to the pro forma income statement (Table 6–7), we see that net profit increases to $9,800. The difference between the $13,421 of increased owner's equity and the $9,800 profit from internal financing (retained earnings on a corporate balance sheet) is a $3,621 increase in owner's equity. This $3,621 must be obtained from the owner's personal financial sources. In a corporation, it may be the sale of additional stock.

A business owner has several choices in combinations of debt and equity financing. In this example, if net profit decreases, the owner is then forced to seek more debt financing. Depending on the economic situation, the owner must choose between short-term financing, long-term financing, or a combination of both. Long-term financing is less risky, but it costs more; short-term financing is more aggressive, but it costs less. Be aware that most lending institutions finance commercial buildings and equipment at only 70 percent of market value. Inventory and accounts receivable also can be used as collateral for financing; however, the lending institution bases its loan on the type of inventory that your firm carries. If you are in a business with perishable inventory, such as fresh vegetables, you cannot expect to be able to use inventory to obtain a loan. If your inventory is not perishable, such as automobiles, you can expect to receive higher value. You must check with your lending institution to determine the percentage of inventory value that can be financed. For the firm in our current example, we do not expect assets to be sufficient to support the increase in long-term debt from $30,000 to $50,000. The owner decreased short-term debt by $5,125 ($22,750 actual 2007 and $17,625 pro forma 2008), and increased long-term debt by $20,000, which is the $14,875 increase in liabilities. Because the balance sheet formula is Assets = Liabilities + Owner's equity, and assets increased by $28,296, then owner's equity must increase by $13,421 for our formula to balance.

The balance sheet in Table 6–9 was generated by using the pro forma income statement, capital budget (see Chapter 10), and cash budget to determine the pro forma balance sheet figures. Another manner of generating a pro forma balance sheet is by using a percentage of sales method.

Pro Forma Balance Sheet Using Percentage of Sales

The **percentage of sales method** is based on the fact that assets and liabilities historically vary with sales; thus, any increase in sales causes a subsequent buildup in both assets and liabilities. Both profit margins and dividend (owner) payout ratios determine the amount of internal financing that can be applied to support increased asset buildup. To use the percentage of sales method, take the previous year's balance sheet, as shown in Table 6–10.

TABLE 6–10 Pro Forma Balance Sheet Using Percentage of Sales Method

Balance Sheets for Year Ending December 31

Sales taken from Table 6–7	$200,000		$250,000
	Actual Sales for 2007	Percentage of 2007 Sales	Pro Forma Sales for 2008
Current Assets			
Cash	$ 4,000	2.00%	$ 5,000
Accounts Receivabe	21,420	10.71%	26,775
Inventory	15,000	7.50%	18,750
Total Current Assets	$40,420	20.21%	$50,525
Fixed Assets			
Net Machinery and Equipment	30,000	15.00%	37,500
Total Assets	$70,420	35.21%	$88,025
			$ -
Liabilities and Owner's Equity			$ -
Current Liabilities			$ -
Accounts Payable	$11,250	5.63%	$14,063
Salaries Payable	2,500	1.25%	3,125
Notes Payable	9,000	4.50%	11,250
Total Current Liabilities	$22,750	11.38%	$28,438
Long Term Liabilities			
Long Term Loan	$30,000	15.00%	$37,500
Total Liabilities	$52,750	26.38%	$65,938
Owner's Equity	17,670	8.84%	22,088
Total Liabilities and Owner's Equity	$70,420	35.21%	$88,025

Using the column *Actual Sales for 2007,* we divide each entry by the actual net sales for 2007 ($200,000 taken from Table 6–7) and display the result in a separate column labeled *Percentage of 2007 Sales.*

$$\text{Percentage of sales} = \left(\frac{\text{Balance sheet entry in \$}}{\text{Actual sales in \$}} \right) \times 100$$

$$= \left(\frac{\$4,000}{\$200,000} \right) \times 100 = 2\%$$

For example, cash of $4,000 divided by $200,000 equals 0.02, which when multiplied by 100 equals 2 percent of sales. We then take our pro forma sales of $250,000 of 2008 from Table 6–7 and multiply this figure by the percentage of sales to obtain our pro forma balance sheet cash figure for 2008 of $5,000, as shown in Table 6–10.

Pro forma balance sheet entry = (Pro forma sales)(Percentage of actual sales)

$$= (\$250,000)(0.02) = \$5,000$$

Our pro forma balance sheet entry for cash is $5,000. Pro forma accounts receivable are calculated as 10.71 percent of $250,000, or $26,775.

Using Percentage of Sales to Determine New Financing

When using the **percentage of sales method for determining new financing,** use the following formula:

$$\text{Required financing} = \Delta \text{Sales}\left(\frac{\text{Assets}}{\text{Sales}}\right) - \Delta \text{Sales}\left(\frac{\text{Liabilities}}{\text{Sales}}\right) - (S_2)(P)(1 - \text{Owner payout})$$

$$= (\$250,000 - \$200,000)\left(\frac{\$70,420}{\$200,000}\right) - (\$250,000 - \$200,000)\left(\frac{\$52,750}{\$200,000}\right) - (\$250,000)\left(\frac{-\$3,900}{\$200,000}\right)(1 - 0.66)$$

$$= (\$50,000)(0.3521) - (\$50,000)(0.2638) - (\$250,000)(-0.0195)(0.34)$$

$$= \$17,605 - \$13,190 + \$1,657.50$$

$$= \$6,072.50$$

In our formula, Δ Sales is the sales forecast minus current sales taken from the income statement (Table 6–7). Assets divided by sales is derived from our historical percentages taken from Table 6–10. Liabilities divided by sales is derived from our historical percentages taken from Table 6–10. S_2 is the sales forecast for 2008, and P is historical profit margin, which is net profit divided by sales (Table 6–7). In the previous example, we assume the owner takes 66 percent of the firm's profit as income.

We take the dollar amount of change in our sales as determined by our forecast and multiply it by the percentage that assets occupy with respect to sales. We subtract the dollar amount of change in our sales multiplied by the percentage that liabilities occupy with respect to sales. We then subtract the sales forecast times the profit margin times 1 minus the percentage of profit that the owner takes out of the business. If the number obtained is positive, we require new financing. If the number obtained is negative, owner's equity is sufficient, with the buildup in liabilities, to carry the increase in assets; therefore, additional financing is not required. In our example, because the company lost money in 2007, the owner must find additional financing of $6,072.50 in order to support a buildup in assets for 2008.

MONITORING AND CONTROLLING THE BUSINESS

We now have pro forma income statements, cash budgets, and balance sheets. These are required internally not only to project future needs, but also to monitor the actual performance of our company. The use of capital budgets as a monitoring and control tool is discussed in Chapter 10. We must realize, however, that all pro forma statements should be used as monitoring tools. When we monitor an activity, we essentially ask ourselves several questions: Are the actual sales meeting projections? Are the actual costs meeting projections? Are the profit margins meeting projections?

Most small businesses require only two budgets for monitoring and controlling purposes: the capital budget and the cash budget. Several other budgets also can be developed for a business; however, most of these budgets are developed as the business grows. Small businesses are not usually divided into departments; once they are, then separate budgets should be developed for each department. Once department budgets are developed, then the owner must determine if the department is one that generates revenue, or one that only spends money. Departments that generate revenue, such as production or marketing departments, are usually designated as profit centers for budgeting purposes. Departments that only spend money are designated as cost centers and include personnel and research and development.

The controlling process, as previously discussed, requires three steps: (1) establishing a standard, (2) comparing actual performance to the standard, and (3) taking corrective action if necessary. For our company, the standards are the budgets and pro forma financial statements that were developed. The monitoring process, as we discussed, compares actual performance (revenues and expenses) with the budget and pro forma statement. Ultimately, *controlling* consists of the corrective action that we take when actual performance deviates sufficiently to pose a problem.

Because these budgets are estimates of the future, we must realize that the actual numbers will vary from our forecast. The difference between an actual figure and a budgeted figure is known as a *variance*. As managers, we must establish an acceptable range of parameters for the variance. Corrective action is taken only when the variance exceeds the parameters that we established. Careful monitoring and taking necessary corrective action maximizes the usefulness of the budget as a tool in accomplishing the goals of financial management.

START-UP BUSINESS COSTS REVISITED

You must understand that when you begin a business, generating financial statements is difficult. The tendency is to underestimate both the costs and time that it takes to begin a business. How many times have you seen a storefront sign that stated something along the lines of "Coming soon, Joe's Deli"? When you passed the same location 3 months later, the sign and Joe's Deli were gone.

Start-up costs are associated with getting the enterprise up and running prior to generating any sales, which is a major project for any business owner. For example, when Hannah began her doughnut business, the utility companies required deposits equal to 2 months' total utility bills, based on the utility's estimates of the highest monthly payments for similar businesses. The electric company required a $1,400 deposit (estimates of bills for July and August), and the gas company required a $500 deposit (estimates of bills for December and January). Because of the high failure rates for small businesses, these utilities required that bills be paid on time for 2 years before the money was refunded. In the case of the gas company, Hannah was late by 10 days on one payment. The gas company began recounting the 2-year period after the late payment. As a result, it was 3 years before she received her deposit from the gas company. In addition, her equipment costs were $65,000, but the bank would only finance 75 percent ($48,750), so she had to come up with $16,250 in cash. It took 3 months to install the equipment, hire and train all employees, and actually open the business. Total start-up costs, including her $25,000 franchise fee, exceeded $75,000. These start-up costs were incurred before the first doughnut was sold.

GANTT CHART

Because of time and cost factors, we strongly recommend that the entrepreneur use a Gantt chart (Figure 6–5) to assist in writing a business plan when expanding or starting a business.

A **Gantt chart** shows all tasks that must be performed and the time that it takes to accomplish these tasks. The method suggested for using a Gantt chart is to develop a list of each task that must be performed to complete a project. A project is a unique, one-time activity with a definite goal and desired completion date. To perform this activity, several tasks must be accomplished. If you are going to open a new business by a specific date, then you must have a name, location, lease, utilities, licenses, and so forth. Each of these items is a task, and it may have several subtasks associated with it. Many of these tasks also have a cost. Some tasks can be accomplished in conjunction with others (such as making utility down payments and selecting equipment). Some tasks must be done in sequence; you must have a location before you can negotiate a lease.

After listing all tasks, review them and place them in sequential order. Then fill in your Gantt chart, listing the start and finish time for each task. Using a highlighter, draw a line from the beginning to the end of each task. When you begin a task, use a different color highlighter to show progress. Obtain the estimated cost of each task so you can estimate the cash required for starting up your business accurately and avoid the pitfall of underestimating both the time and

Project:		Manager:		Phone:		Page: ___
Plan Area:		Manager:		Phone:		of ___ Pages

Tsk No.	Task Description:	Task Time	Resource	Phone	Time Periods

FIGURE 6–5
Gantt Chart, Basic Entry Form

money it takes for start-up. There are several software programs that generate Gantt charts, including Microsoft Project.

Estimate critical tasks that must be accomplished in a specified time period. For example, if you plan to open your business in April, find out when the phone company requires a listing for its business section. If the listing must be in by December, obtain a phone number and get your listing in on time. If you open in April and have not done this, you may go an entire year without a phone number listing. This can kill a small business. For some businesses, especially service businesses such as plumbing and refrigeration repair, if you are not in the phone book, you do not exist. When the water heater starts leaking, how do you select a plumber? Make sure that critical tasks are accomplished on time.

 CONCLUSION

We now know how to obtain a forecast and generate those pro forma financial statements required for our internal use and by external parties interested in our business. We also understand the importance of analyzing cash flow to determine our financing requirements. The basic unique requirements of the start-up business have also been discussed. Our next task is to manage our current assets and liabilities to ensure that the business survives and that sufficient cash is generated to pay our bills and provide us with a steady source of income as business owners and managers. Current assets and liabilities make up the working capital of any business. The management of working capital is the subject of Chapter 7.

REVIEW AND DISCUSSION QUESTIONS

1. What is the purpose of pro forma financial statements (Tables 6–7 through 6–10)?
2. What are the basic criteria for selecting a forecasting model?
3. What role does MAD play in evaluating a forecasting model?
4. Compare judgmental, time series, and causal forecasting models.
5. List and describe at least three time series models.
6. In linear regression, compare independent and dependent variables.
7. Describe how to develop a pro forma income statement (Table 6–7).
8. What role does the pro forma cash budget play in financial forecasting (Table 6–8)?
9. What role does the pro forma balance sheet play in financial forecasting (Table 6–9)?
10. In generating a pro forma balance sheet, on what is the percentage of sales method based?
11. How are budgets used as monitoring and control tools?

EXERCISES AND PROBLEMS

1. Jane White has recorded the following sales figures for last year for her business: January, $35,645; February, $35,456; March, $31,270; April, $32,129; May, $34,456; June, $35,256; July, $36,218; August, $35,456; September, $34,250; October, $32,156; November, $30,125; December, $32,275. She wants to select from one of three models: a 3-month moving average, a weighted moving average (she believes that the weights should be 0.2, 0.3, and 0.5), and an exponential smoothing average in which she uses an α of 0.2 and an assumed forecast for January of Year 1 of $35,000.
   a. Construct a table that shows each of these forecasts for the current year and provide the forecast for January of Year 2.
   b. Using the available data and your forecasts, which model do you suggest that Jane use for her business?
2. Gary Fisher owns five successful health clubs. He believes that he can put a health club in a new community that currently has no such facility. His research indicates that communities such as this can support two health clubs.
   a. What type of information should Gary gather when selecting a specific site for his health club?
   b. What type of forecasting model should Gary use to determine the new location for a health club?
3. | Period | 1 | 2 | 3 | 4 |
   |--------|-----|-----|-----|-----|
   | Data | 32 | 14 | 41 | 30 |

   a. Make an exponential smoothing forecast for periods 2 through 5, with two values of α, 0.05 and 0.60, and an assumed forecast for period 1 of 30.
   b. Compute the MAD for each of the forecasts.
   c. Which value of α should you choose?
4. Develop a linear regression equation to predict future demand from the following data:

Demand	23	24	31	28	29
Year	2004	2005	2006	2007	2008

   a. Write the regression equation.
   b. Predict demand for 2009.
   c. Name the independent variable.
   d. Name the dependent variable.
5. Using the data in Table 6–11, calculate a 3-month moving average forecast for month 12.
6. Using the data in Table 6–11, calculate the following:
   a. A weighted moving average forecast for months 4 through 12, using weights of 3, 5, and 9.
   b. What is the MAD for this forecast?

TABLE 6–11 Actual Sales Data

Time Period	Actual Sales ($000)
1	$445
2	478
3	525
4	660
5	570
6	600
7	632
8	648
9	690
10	725
11	750
12	

7. Using the data in Table 6–11, calculate the following:
   a. What is the slope?
   b. What is the intercept?
   c. Write the regression equation.
   d. Calculate a regression forecast for month 25.

8. You have just completed the first year of operation for your business and have the following information: sales, $200,000; cost of goods, $140,000; rent, $18,000; utilities, $8,400; insurance, $2,000; equipment, $3,500; interest, $10,000. Your forecast indicates that your sales will increase by 20 percent. Your rental agreement provides for a 3 percent increase per year. You read an article indicating that utility costs in your area will increase by 10 percent next year. You just received a notice from your insurance company stating that your quarterly premium is increasing to $600 beginning the first quarter of next year. Your equipment expense will not change, but the amortization schedule on your current loan indicates that interest expense for next year should be $9,000.
   a. Using this data, construct an actual income statement for this year and a pro forma income statement for next year.
   b. By what percentage did your net income change?
   c. What are your current profit margin and your pro forma profit margin?
   d. In your business, assets and liabilities have historically varied with sales. Assets are usually 80 percent of sales, and liabilities are usually 55 percent of sales. You anticipate that you will have no owner payout of net profit. Using the percentage of sales method, determine if any additional financing is needed for your business next year.

9. Sam Jones has 2 years of historical sales data for his company. He is applying for a business loan and must supply his projections of sales by month for the next 2 years to the bank.
   a. Using the data from Table 6–12, provide a regression forecast for time periods 25 through 48.
   b. Does Sam's sales data show a seasonal pattern?

TABLE 6–12 Twenty-Four Months of Actual Data

Month	Actual Sales ($000)
1	$345
2	350
3	355
4	360
5	365
6	360
7	358
8	352
9	348
10	353
11	362
12	370
13	375
14	382
15	390
16	380
17	375
18	368
19	363
20	373
21	380
22	391
23	397
24	408

10. Your projected sales for the first 3 months of next year are as follows: January, $15,000; February, $20,000; and March, $25,000. Based on last year's data, cash sales are 20 percent of total sales for each month. Of the accounts receivable, 60 percent are collected in the month after the sale and 40 percent are collected in the second month following the sale. Sales for November of the current year are $15,000 and for December are $17,000. You have the following estimated payments: January, $4,500; February, $5,500; and March, $5,200.

    a. Using the format from the pro forma cash budget in Table 6–8, what is your monthly cash budget for January, February, and March?

    b. What will your accounts receivable be for the beginning of April?

    c. Will your company have any borrowing requirements for any month during this 3-month period?

11. Using Table 6–13, create a pro forma balance sheet using the percentage of sales method. If net income next year is $50,000, answer the following:

    a. How much did the owners take out of the business?

    b. What is the profit margin for next year?

12. Using Table 6–13, what is required in new financing if next year's sales forecast increases to $400,000, profit margin is 10 percent, and the payout ratio is 90 percent?

TABLE 6–13 Sample Balance Sheet

	Total Sales Current Year $275,000	Percentage of Sales (%)	Forecast Sales Next Year $350,000
Assets			
Current Assets			
Cash	$ 5,694		
Accounts Receivable	19,662		
Inventory	3,381		
Total Current Assets	$28,737		
Fixed Assets			
Furniture and Fixtures	5,595		
Transportation Equipment	25,456		
Total Fixed Assets	$31,051		
Total Assets	$59,788		
Liabilities and Owner's Equity			
Current Liabilities			
Notes Payable	$15,456		
Accrued Taxes Payable	3,598		
Total Current Liabilities	$19,054		
Long-Term Debt	18,654		
Total Liabilities	$37,708		
Owner's Equity	22,080		
Total Liabilities and Owner's Equity	$59,788		

References

Brase, C. H., & Brase, C. P. (1987). *Understandable Statistics* (3rd ed.) Lexington, MA: D.C. Heath and Co.

Gaither, N. (1994). *Production and Operations Management* (6th ed.) New York: Dryden Press.

Heizer, J., & Render, B. (1999). *Principles of Operations Management* (3rd ed.) Upper Saddle River, NJ: Prentice-Hall.

Neter, J., & Wasserman, W. (1974). *Applied Linear Statistical Models, Regression, Analysis of Variance, and Experimental Designs.* Homewood, IL: Richard D. Irwin.

Ruch, W. A., Fearon, H. E., & Wieters, D. C. (1992). *Fundamentals of Production: Operations Management* (5th ed.) New York: West Publishing Co.

RECOMMENDED TEAM ASSIGNMENT

1. Using a discount store or supermarket. What type of forecasting model would they use to plan for expansion into a particular city? What internal data and external data would they require to develop a 10-year expansion plan?

2. Using the financial statements for a public corporation, develop a pro forma income statement and balance sheet for this company.

CASE STUDY: HANNAH'S DONUT SHOP

An interview with Hannah follows:

I am an educator by trade, and I enjoyed the field very much. Everywhere we went, I was always able to find a job within religious school education as I am not a public school educator. In 1969, during our twelfth year as an Air Force family, Phil went to Vietnam, which brought about tremendous changes in my life and the lives of my family. In the days that followed, there were many lonely hours of the day, but it seemed that one in particular was morning coffee. We really enjoyed that time together to discuss the coming day, work schedule, children's programs, et cetera. When Phil left for Vietnam, mornings were intolerable. I'd drop my daughter off at preschool, but I couldn't stand the concept of coming home to an empty house. So I'd stop in at this doughnut shop as they are wonderful places to go for breakfast. Doughnut people are very special people, because there is a warmth, kindness, and acceptance that you find in doughnut shop patrons. When you break bread together and eat together, you've made a friend. First of all, you're sitting at a counter rather than a lonely table and you're with the lady at the right, or the gentleman on your left. You are sharing something that you can say, "Wow, doesn't this taste great?" or, "Isn't this good?" or, "Did you read this in the paper?" Somehow, it's fast and it's quick, but there is a very comfortable feeling. It's one of the very few places that a woman can walk in and sit down, talk to another adult, and not appear to be looking for anything else. You're just going to a doughnut shop for a nice cup of coffee and a doughnut, and then you are off and you feel that you can face the day.

So, every day for the rest of the year that my husband was in Vietnam, I would go to the doughnut shop. And after a while you get to know the names of the people. You know that it's just "Hi, Jim," "Hi, Mary." If you miss one day, they want to know who's sick or what's wrong. It's a very interesting extended family, but keep in mind that you don't know anyone's last name. There is no great depth to this friendship, but there is a certain amount of caring that goes on. Everyone knew my husband was in Vietnam, and they knew how many days were left until he was coming home. When he finally returned home, after a certain amount of time had passed, it was off to the doughnut shop to meet all of my new doughnut shop friends so they could personally welcome him home as well.

Then we were off, back to our Air Force tours and on to the next city and the next doughnut shop. I was still in education, but I was hooked on doughnuts. Now, however, every time I would go into a doughnut shop, the only difference was I began to say, "If it was my shop I would do it this way, or that way," or, "If I were the owner of this doughnut shop, I would do it a different way," and my husband patiently listened. As Phil approached retirement, I was offered a wonderful job in Phoenix. He felt that since I had travelled with him for 23 moves in 23 years, maybe it was his turn to follow me.

So we came to Phoenix and within the first several years of our Phoenix stay I was happy with my job. As the aggravation and frustration with the job grew, the doughnuts started to look better and happier. And my coming home day after day, saying, "You know, if I only had a doughnut shop." So finally he said one day, "Look, you know, either we're going to look into it and do it, or forget it as we're getting too old to keep talking about it." So we looked into it and found this franchise that I loved. I mean, they had this fabulous product, this wonderful doughnut.

HISTORICAL BACKGROUND

This is a case study of Hannah's Donut Shop (HDS), a small retail and wholesale doughnut shop in Phoenix, Arizona. HDS began operation in December 1985 as a member of a regional franchise. Hannah had considered purchasing a doughnut shop and decided to obtain experience in the industry prior to making a purchase decision. She worked for 6 months in a regional franchise doughnut shop. When she became convinced that this was what she wanted to do, she and her husband signed the franchise agreement and she opened her own shop. By December 1986, HDS was in trouble. The franchiser had a new chief executive officer (CEO) who attempted to expand the franchise from a regional chain to a national chain. Franchiser management concentrated on expansion, and franchiser service to HDS became nonexistent. At this point, HDS began to keep detailed records of conversations with the franchiser and cost differentials between franchiser product and independent purchase of similar products with comparable quality. HDS determined that operating with the franchiser's raw materials plus franchise fees resulted in a 13 percent increase in raw material cost as compared to purchasing the product as an independent shop. Also, the franchiser changed vendors three times during the first 18 months of operation. This resulted in changes in quality of product and eliminated standardization of product among shops, one of the primary advantages of franchising.

On February 20, 1987, the franchiser filed for Chapter 11 bankruptcy. HDS entered into suit, claiming breach of contract on the part of the franchiser, and ceased paying franchise and advertising fees to the franchiser. The court determined that the franchiser had in fact breached the contract and released HDS from all obligations to the franchiser in May 1988. Hannah changed the name of her shop and became an independent. The financial position of HDS at that time indicated that accumulated losses for the first 2 years of operation were $97,000.

Now HDS had to select its own vendors for product. The owners believed that quality and service were the two primary factors relating to success. They therefore tested products from the five primary vendors in the metropolitan area and selected two vendors who they believed provided the best quality. One vendor was selected for all doughnut products and another for muffin and paper products.

Until this point, the HDS owners could be described as following an "analyzer" strategy for their business (Miles and Snow, 1978). They attempted to conform to industry standards and kept their books in accordance with traditional cost accounting methodology. HDS had previously determined that the retail marketing area for their product was within 3 miles of the store on weekends and extended to 10 miles north of the shop on weekdays, when they sold primarily to commuters. The shop was located on the commuting side of the road for morning traffic, and 90 percent of all product was sold on a daily basis prior to 10 A.M.

ENVIRONMENTAL CHANGES

The environment had changed significantly between the time the shop opened in 1985 and 1991. In 1985, a freestanding retail doughnut shop could make a profit, because these locales were virtually the only place that doughnuts could be purchased. By 1991, four new supermarkets with in-store bakeries had been built within HDS's retail marketing area. These stores offered a convenience factor with which the freestanding shop could not compete. The shopper could purchase doughnut products at the supermarket and did not have to make another stop. However, shoppers were willing to make the extra stop if the doughnut shop had what was perceived by the customer to be a superior product.

In January 1991, the owners read *The Goal* and became interested in its applicability to the shop (Goldratt and Cox, 1992) . In June 1991, Hannah's husband attended a Jonah conference on the theory of constraints (TOC) held at the University of Georgia. When he returned, he and Hannah decided that TOC, if it was as powerful as indicated in the course, should be applicable to Hannah's Donut Shop.

CHANGES IN MEASUREMENT SYSTEMS

From the time that the shop became an independent enterprise until June 1991, the owners were using traditional cost accounting procedures. Cost of goods was determined by adding raw material costs and direct labor costs (salaries of production workers). The results of these bookkeeping procedures indicated that cost of sales was approximately 68 percent of sales, as seen in Table CS–1. The generation of selling prices for finished product using these procedures resulted in noncompetitive prices.

One of the first actions taken by the owners was to direct the bookkeeper to change the accounting system to one that conformed to the throughput principles of the TOC (Goldratt, 1990; Goldratt and Fox, 1990). All production wages were moved to the operating expense category, and the cost-of-goods section of the income statement now contained only raw material costs and the cost of paper goods that were sold as part of the product (e.g., packaging). Moving wages to operating expenses did not, of course, alter the bottom line (net profit) on the income statement, but it did allow the owners to determine a true and relevant cost of goods and to develop pricing strategies based on this actual variable cost (Table CS–1).

A break-even analysis using data from the first 6 months of 1991 indicates how powerful this concept is when using the standard break-even formula (Table CS–1).

$$\text{Break-even dollars} = \frac{\text{Fixed costs}}{1 - \text{Variable costs as a percentage of sales}}$$

There is a true break-even point, of no profit and no loss, for any business. Under a given set of conditions, this point is the same regardless of the categorization of expenses, labor, and so forth. A firm using traditional break-even point analysis could easily delude itself into thinking it could profitably compete at lower volumes than are actually possible. Such delusion could lead to losses that could only be found when after-the-fact variance reports brought reality to bear on the projected (fictitious) profits.

TABLE CS–1 Income Statement, January 1 through June 30, 1991

Hannah's Donut Shop Income Statement, January 1, 1991, through June 30, 1991

Cost Accounting Method			Theory of Constraints Method		
	$000	Percentage of Sales		$000	Pencentage of Sales
Sales			Sales		
Retail sales	46.2	49.1	Retail sales	46.2	49.1
Wholesale sales	47.9	50.9	Wholesale sales	47.9	50.9
Total sales	94.1	100.0	Total sales	94.1	100.0
Cost of sales			Cost of sales		
Raw materials	32.1	34.1	Raw materials	32.1	34.1
Production labor	31.8	33.8			
Total cost of sales	63.9	67.9	Total cost of sales	32.1	34.1
Gross profit	30.2	32.1	Gross profit = Sales – Raw materials = Throughput	62.0	65.9
Operating expenses	27.9	29.6	Operating expenses	59.7	63.4
Net profit	2.3	2.4	Net profit	2.3	2.4

In the same manner, a firm could easily misinterpret the true marginal cost of a product, which could lead to noncompetitive pricing of its product.

Using the break–even formula and the data from Table CS–1, the break–even point for standard cost accounting is $86,900; with TOC, it is $90,590. It appears that the use of TOC yields break–even points that are unreasonable. We contend that TOC presents a true picture because it considers production labor as a fixed cost, rather than as a variable cost that increases at a linear rate with production. In addition, when you consider the difference in contribution margin (cost accounting, 32.1 percent; TOC, 65.9 percent), you realize that if operating expenses can be held in check, then the firm can make a much higher profit with significantly fewer sales. For example, if the firm wanted to make $10,000 in profit, it would have to sell $118,000 or more using cost accounting, but only $105,000 or more using TOC. Realizing this, we see that the TOC firm is in a much better position to land contracts by using competitive bids that reflect actual costs rather than inflated accounting costs. Using the new figures, HDS was able to adjust prices to become more competitive in the wholesale arena. This resulted in large increases in throughput dollars and net profits, as indicated in the comparison of 1991 and 1992 data for the first year of operation under the throughput model (Table CS–2).

CHANGES IN STRATEGY

HDS had been selling some product at the wholesale level, as do most competitors in this industry. Baked goods are sold to retailing customers (e.g., convenience stores) who resell the product. The traditional practices of the industry require the bakery to repurchase

TABLE CS–2 Income Statement, First Six Months of 1991 and 1992

Hannah's Donut Shop Income Statements for Periods Indicated

Category	Jan. 1 through June 30, 1992	Percentage of Sales	Jan. 1 through June 30, 1991	Percentage of Sales
Revenues				
Retail sales	$72,335	45.5	$46,197	49.1
Wholesale sales	86,516	54.5	47,878	50.9
Total revenues	158,851	100.0	94,075	100.0
Cost of sales				
Raw materials	50,164	31.6	32,091	34.1
Total cost of sales	50,164	31.6	32,091	34.1
Gross profit (loss)	108,687	68.4	61,984	65.9
Operating expenses	90,056	56.7	59,337	63.1
Operating profit	18,631	11.7	2,647	2.8
Interest expense	(897)	−0.6	(388)	−0.4
Net profit (loss)	17,734	11.2	2,259	2.4

all unsold merchandise. For example, when $10 of product is delivered on a given day and $4 of product remains unsold, the vendor credits the reseller with $4 and bills only $6. This has a significant effect on *throughput* (defined as sales − raw material costs) (Goldratt, 1992). Because raw material costs are now correctly seen to represent approximately 30 percent of sales price, the gross profit on such a *sale with returns* nets $3 throughput ($10 revenue − $3 COGS − $4 returns = $3), not the original $7 ($10 − $3 = $7). Interesting to note is the fact that, prior to looking at the situation from a throughput viewpoint, the traditional analysis would have shown $0 as the result, because the cost of goods was previously considered to be about 60 percent of sales ($10 revenue − $6 COGS − $4 returns = $0). In any case, the throughput decreases because of the returns. Another significant factor relates to the fact that doughnut products (finished goods) have a very short shelf life (12 hours for raised products to 15 hours for cake products). Therefore, all returned products are scrapped because they have no residual value.

This *scrap factor,* per industry standards, does not apply in cases of wholesale sales to end users (e.g., hospitals, industrial cafeterias, restaurants). Purchases by these institutions are final, with no allowances for returns. HDS determined that throughput increases could best be achieved by concentrating on this second category of sales and by stopping all sales to convenience stores, unless the convenience store agreed to a no-buyback policy.

The shop had actually shown a pattern of declining wholesale sales between 1988 and 1990, during which time sales declined from $108,853 to $92,728, a decrease of 14.8 percent. This was because several wholesale accounts canceled because of product inconsistency, even though new accounts were being solicited. HDS realized there was a significant problem. Before the new market segmentation strategy of selling only to customers who would not require buyback could be implemented, significant improvements in quality had to be realized.

In addition, if significant production increases could not be accomplished by the night shift, no additional accounts could be established. The night shift, with current production methods, could only produce $500 to $550 worth of finished goods per shift. Because doughnuts are primarily served in the morning, wholesale accounts had to be delivered by 6 A.M. each day, or customers would refuse the product. An additional shift would not be added at an earlier time because the product would exceed the shelf life of finished goods. The night shift worked from 8 P.M. to 4 A.M.

As previously indicated, the owners had complete confidence in the quality of their raw materials and realized that the inconsistency in product must be in the internal production procedures. They set out to solve this problem through use of the five-step focusing process contained in TOC (Goldratt and Fox, 1990). To this point, HDS had been using the production methods established by the franchiser, including personal assignments and batch sizes. Most of the procedures given by the franchiser appeared to be standard for the industry, as evidenced by the comments of HDS's bakers, who had previously worked for other bakeries (e.g., Dunkin Donuts, Winchels). The standard procedure was to mix the minimum number of batches, based on the shelf life of the raised donut as it sat on the baker's table, or based on bowl capacity for cake doughnuts.

There are essentially two different processes used in the production of doughnuts: one for cake doughnuts and one for raised doughnuts (see Figure CS–1 and Descrip-

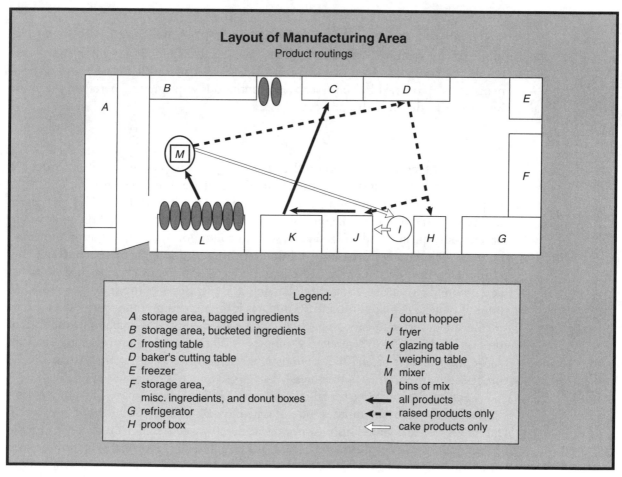

FIGURE CS–1
Layout of Manufacturing Area

tion of the Manufacturing Process at the end of this case study). There are three people who work the night shift at HDS. These people and their duties are described as follows:

- The **baker,** who traditionally is responsible for cutting raised product, serving as shift supervisor, and setting the pace for the night crew.
- The **fryer** who is responsible for frying all doughnut products.
- The **finisher,** who applies frosting and toppings (nuts, coconut, candy sprinkles, etc.), and fills doughnuts after they are processed by the fryer. The finisher assists the fryer with glazing product, waits on retail customers, and may assist the baker by operating the mixer and performing any other duties as required by the baker. The finisher usually comes to work 2 hours after the fryer and baker begin the bake so that there is sufficient product to process.

IMPLEMENTING THE FIVE-STEP PROCESS AND DRUM BUFFER ROPE

Step 1

Step 1 of the TOC focusing process (Goldratt, 1992; Goldratt and Fox, 1990) is to **identify the system's constraint(s).** The owners determined that the fryer was definitely the constraint. All processes prior to the fryer had excess capacity, and components to be processed by the fryer were continuously in queue. Therefore, the **fryer became the drum** in this process.

Step 2

The owners then concentrated on the second step of the process, which is to **decide how to exploit the system's constraint(s).** Several of the products were waiting to be processed by the fryer for a period well in excess of their shelf life. This resulted in the fryer's spending some time processing products of inferior quality. If the fryer was to process only quality products and process them continuously, several adjustments had to be made. The first, however, involved **determining the length of the buffer** (optimum batch sizes for both cake and raised products). Optimum cake batch size was set at 22 pounds 8 ounces using the following analysis: Because the fryer can process 3 pounds of cake in 4 minutes, and 30 minutes is the maximum time the product can sit in the queue prior to processing (without losing quality), the maximum number of process batches is 7.5 (30 minutes/4 minutes = 7.5 three-pound process batches). With a 3-pound process batch, 22.5 pounds is the maximum cake batch size that can be processed by the fryer in 30 minutes.

Setting the batch size for raised product is a little more complex. The product rises in the proof box for 20 minutes and can stay in queue (outside of the proof box) for 10 minutes prior to frying. This provides the same 30-minute buffer that is used for cake doughnuts. Frying time for raised product is 2 minutes. Thus 15 batches can be processed in 30 minutes. Average weight of product in queue is 2.5 pounds, because the mix of product includes about the same number of items with 3 pounds per screen as items with 2 pounds per screen. The batch size was thus set at 37 pounds 8 ounces. If these batches arrived at the fryer as soon as the previous batch was processed, the fryer could process product continuously. This required **tying the rope to the fryer** and redefining individual tasks to ensure that the fryer (machine) was never idle. These procedures exploit the constraint in an optimum way.

Step 3

The next obvious step, according to TOC, is to **subordinate everything else to the decision made in the previous step.** This was accomplished by reviewing all duties performed by the fryer (in this case the person doing the frying). The normal process was for the fryer to mix a batch of cake, fry the product, and mix the next batch of cake. While the fryer was frying the first batch, the baker (bakers typically concentrate on producing only raised product) put on the first batch of raised dough (usually a 50-pound batch). Using this process, the fryer was spending approximately 20 minutes out of each hour measuring and mixing product. In addition, the baker often had 50 pounds of raised product waiting to be fried, whereas the fryer was still concentrating on cake products.

The Change Process

One of the first steps was to provide the baker with a copy of *The Goal* (Goldratt and Cox, 1992) and let her read it at her own pace. Changes in duties were often suggested by her; other changes were directed by the owners only after the owners had worked the night shift with the crew to determine how actual flow conformed to theoretical flow (this was essentially a pilot production run). The resulting process involved the following changes:

1. The baker mixes all products for the fryer, rather than the fryer mixing the product.
2. When the fryer is down to 6 pounds of cake product in the hopper (approximately eight 8 minutes' worth of processing time), the baker mixes the next batch of cake product. This procedure ties the rope to the fryer.
3. To keep the fryer (machine) operating continuously, the baker or finisher continues to process product while the fryer (person) is on break.
4. The baker begins mixing raised dough when the fryer is halfway through processing the next-to-last batch of cake product.
5. Premixed raised products are placed in the proof box by the baker when the fryer starts processing the last batch of cake product.
6. The raised dough now mixes for 15 minutes, rests in the bowl for 20 minutes, rests on the table for 20 minutes, and is ready to be cut into various raised products 55 minutes after the mixing process begins.
7. As raised product is processed by the baker, it is placed in the proof box, and it is ready to fry 20 minutes later.

Note: Returning to step 3, the fryer has approximately 1 hour and 15 minutes of processing time when the baker begins mixing the raised dough—15 minutes for the next-to-last batch of cake product, 30 minutes for the last batch of cake product, and

30 minutes for the fritters. It also takes 1 hour and 15 minutes from the time the raised product begins mixing until the product is ready to fry.

8. The baker, while waiting for the dough to rise on the table, measures out the next batch of raised product and places it in the bowl at the mixer. When the batch is ready to cut, the baker turns on the mixer. It takes approximately 40 minutes for the baker to cut the batch of raised dough into product.

9. Before the cut is finished, the next batch of raised dough is placed on the table.

10. Steps 5 through 9 continue until all of the baking requirements are completed. These steps are required to tie the rope for the raised product.

Step 4

Step 4 (**elevate the system's constraint[s]**) of the five focusing steps was not used because the constraint was broken by the exploitation and subordination process.

Step 5

Step 5 of the TOC focusing process indicates the following: **If, in the previous steps, a constraint has been broken,** then one should **go back to step 1, but do not allow inertia** to take effect and **cause a system's constraint,** because TOC is a process of continuous improvement.

RESULTS

After we accomplished the first three steps of the TOC focusing process, the following results were noted. Potential production per shift increased from $500 to $1,000 with no additional operating expense. This allowed the owners to establish a goal of soliciting an additional $500 per day in wholesale accounts. If more than $500 per day in wholesale accounts was realized and these accounts could be serviced prior to 6 A.M., then additional sales could be accomplished by shifting some of the night bake, which included retail product, to the day shift. The night shift could generate just enough retail product to open the store and stock the shelves, and the day shift would bake fresh product for retail sales during the day.

Training the night crew and establishing a change in measurement systems were critical for success of the process; these efforts took the owners approximately 3 months. Changes in measurement included paying the baker a salary rather than an hourly wage, notifying employees that they would share in a bonus every 6 months that was equal to 10 percent of total profit, and paying the baker overtime if she worked in excess of 8 hours in a shift because of the volume of the bake. After implementation of these procedures, the night shift was actually finishing its work in 6 hours rather than 8, and the product quality was consistently high.

Improvement in quality could be measured accurately by the amount of shortening consumed in the process. As indicated in Description of the Manufacturing Process (at the end of this case study), when a raised doughnut is overproofed, it absorbs more shortening. The same is true when cake doughnut batter stays in queue too long and the temperature rises (which is the normal situation, because the hopper for cake doughnuts is physically located between the proof box and the fryer; see Figure CS–1). Shortening consumption decreased by 30 percent after the new process was instituted, resulting in a 2.5 percent decrease in cost of goods while simultaneously increasing the product quality. Thus in this case, the cost of improving quality was actually negative.

SHIFTING CONSTRAINTS

The TOC model is still being applied at HDS, and it has been used several times, because the constraint has been shifting between the shop and the market. In July 1991, one of Hannah's major accounts notified her that they were going to change vendors. Rather than accepting this, the situation that had existed prior to June 1991, Hannah asked what it would take to keep the account. The customer stated that the problem was with the muffins that were provided by the shop. They were too dry and did not have a long enough shelf life. Hannah's customer in this case was a major hotel that served breakfast to its patrons as part of the room cost. Hannah asked for 1 week, and stated that if she did not provide a superior product by that time, then she would understand being terminated as a vendor.

Hannah called her primary vendor and asked for the moistest muffin mix with the longest shelf life. The vendor introduced and demonstrated a superior product that had a 3-day, rather than 18-hour, shelf life. Hannah baked several dozen muffins and provided them to the customer for taste testing. Not only did the customer stay, but muffin production and throughput increased between July 1991 and December 1992 by 1,000 percent at the retail level (from 4 dozen per week to 42 dozen per week) and by 675 percent at the wholesale level (from 28 dozen per week to 217 dozen per week). As a result of this increase in muffin production, the oven became a constraint, and in August 1992, this constraint was elevated by the purchase of another oven.

Because of the 3-day shelf life and the fact that wholesale muffins are baked to order and retail muffins are maintained at a level where they are baked and sold daily, there is no waste in this product. All sales result in throughput, because HDS carries no more than 24 hours' worth of finished goods inventory for an item with a 72-hour shelf life.

The shop landed two large accounts in January 1992; the service and quality were such that these customers notified others, and by March 1992, Hannah had a waiting list of wholesale customers. The ability to deliver product to customers with current delivery vehicles became a constraint. The shop purchased another delivery vehicle and established two routes in the greater metropolitan area after determining that the increase in operating expense (monthly costs of operating the new vehicle) would be more than offset by the increase in throughput. During the past year, Hannah more than doubled the number of wholesale customers (from 15 to 35) without losing any accounts. All deliveries are being made between 1:30 A.M. and 6 A.M.

SUMMARY

The shop has been operating under TOC principles for just over 1 year. The results, using data from 1991 (prior to TOC) and 1992 (after implementation), are shown in Table CS–3, and indicate that TOC can be applied to the service industry (quasi-manufacturing sector) and result in significant improvements. The application of the focusing steps of the

TABLE CS–3 Results of TOC Implementation, First Year

Hannah's Donut Shop Income Statements for Periods Indicated

Category	Jan. 1 Through Dec. 31, 1992	Jan. 1 Through Dec. 31, 1991	Percentage Change
Sales			
Retail sales	149,618	96,183	55.55
Wholesale sales	177,878	106,441	67.11
Total sales	327,496	202,624	61.63
Cost of sales			
Raw materials	103,020	68,516	50.36
Total cost of sales	103,020	68,516	50.36
Gross profit (loss)	224,476	134,108	67.38
Operating expenses	187,549	127,264	47.37
Operating profit	40,038	6,844	485.01
Interest expense	3,111	993	213.29
Net profit (loss)	36,927	5,851	531.12
ROI	87.99%	30.94%	
Cash	15,670	3,112	403.53

theory can be easily seen and understood in this simple environment. The theory is thus seen in its simplicity, and the steps taken by the shop owners are illustrated for the benefit of those who would apply this new theory to their own industry. The three measures of TOC—net profit, ROI, and cash (a necessary condition, not a goal)—have increased significantly. Application of the theory resulted in the owners' shifting from being analyzers to being *prospectors* (Miles and Snow, 1978) and from a *cost world* to a *throughput world* thinking process (Goldratt, 1990).

References

Fearon, H. E., W. A. Ruch, & C. D. Wieters. *Fundamentals of Production: Operations Management.* (St. Paul: West Publishing Company, 1989).

Goldratt, E. M. *Theory of Constraints.* (Croton-on-Hudson, NY: North River Press, 1990).

Goldratt, E. M., & J. Cox. *The Goal* (rev. ed.). (Croton-on-Hudson, NY: North River Press, 1992).

Goldratt, E. M., & R. E. Fox. *The Race.* (Croton-on-Hudson, NY: North River Press, 1990).

Miles, R. E. & C. C. Snow. *Organization Strategy: Structure and Process.* (New York: McGraw-Hill, 1978).

CHAPTER 7

Working Capital Management

Learning Objectives

When you have completed this chapter, you should be able to:

- Understand the general concept of working capital management.
- Describe the asset categories that are included in working capital management.
- Determine the methods of managing disbursement and collection of cash to increase business profitability.
- Understand how a business balances extending credit and its ability to manage increased accounts receivable.
- Explain how accounts receivable are analyzed.
- Understand the role that proper inventory management plays in the profitability of a business enterprise.
- Understand how a business's current liabilities are managed.
- Understand the relationship between accrued liabilities management and obligations to federal and local government agencies.
- Understand the relationship of trade and cash discounts to the minimization of accounts payable.

Probably one of the most difficult tasks faced by the small business owner is the proper management of working capital. In the normal course of conducting business, we accumulate current liabilities that often must be paid in lump sums: rent, insurance, payroll taxes, sales taxes, and accounts payable are a few examples. Revenues, however, often flow in a sporadic but somewhat steady stream, and it can be difficult to equate the steady income stream to a lumpy payment schedule. The purpose of this chapter is to assist us in grappling with this problem.

WORKING CAPITAL

Working capital consists of the current assets and the current liabilities of a business. *Current assets,* as covered in Chapter 3, consist of those items that our business usually converts into cash within one year. Current assets also are referred to as **gross working capital,** and consist of cash, marketable securities, accounts receivable, and inventory. *Current liabilities* are those debts of our company that we usually expect to pay within 1 year, and are typically accounts payable, fixed payments (rent, utilities, insurance, and the current portion of our long-term debt), and accrued liabilities (payroll and taxes). **Net working capital** is the difference between a business's total current assets and its total current liabilities. If assets are what our business has a right to own and liabilities are what our company owes, then what is left (the difference between them) is net working capital. It is a measure of our company in terms of liquidity, which is the ability of our firm to turn its assets into cash. The formula for working capital is:

Net working capital = Gross working capital (current assets) − Current liabilities

For example, if our company has $5,000 in current assets, we have $5,000 in gross working capital. If our company has $3,000 in current liabilities, then we have $2,000 in net working capital. This $2,000 is a margin of safety for our business in its ability to pay short-term debt.

WORKING CAPITAL MANAGEMENT

Working capital management is our ability to effectively and efficiently control current assets and current liabilities in a manner that provides our firm with maximum return on its assets and minimizes payments for its liabilities. Proper working capital management promotes operational efficiency, but not necessarily long-term effectiveness. Creditors look at excess liquidity as a safety margin for paying short-term debt. As owners, however, we should look at excess liquidity as an opportunity to invest in items that will increase future productivity and profitability.

We discuss working capital management in general terms to see the relationship between these items. After covering the general relationships, we then recommend specific methods of dealing with current asset management and current liabilities management.

Current assets must be managed properly. In a retail business, cash is used to buy inventory, which we plan to sell at a markup to generate a return on our cash investment. Sales are typically made for cash or on credit. Credit sales become our accounts receivable, which are converted into cash that may be used to pay off liabilities and purchase more inventory for sale. We can enhance productivity by investing cash in fixed assets. For the retail establishment, this may involve new display cases or computerized cash registers that assist us in controlling inventory. For a manufacturer, this investment may be in new machinery that increases quality or speed of production. Regardless of the type of business, we should continually try to manage working capital so that there is an excess of current assets over current liabilities, one reason being that the possibility that some liabilities not currently listed as liabilities must be paid at the beginning of the next accounting period.

For example, let us assume that our company pays its employees twice monthly, on the fifth and the twentieth of each month. When we close our books on the last day of the month, the employees' time cards are still in the work area; therefore, the wages due from the twenty-first of the month until the end of the month do not appear on the books. Conversely, in managing working capital, we do not want excess cash. We can find some method of investing cash to increase the profitability of our firm. Increased profitability is obtained by increased productivity, which is obtained by investing in fixed (long-range) rather than current assets. Making long-range decisions involves capital budgeting, the topic of Chapter 10.

Note that excess working capital must be studied closely to determine how the excess cash aspect of the net working capital is being managed. Excess cash should not be left idle: We must determine if it should be invested in marketable securities [certificates of deposit (CDs) or treasury bills (T-bills)] or inventory. To accomplish this, we must determine inventory needs in terms of quantity and timing so that future cash requirements can be matched to inventory demand.

In addition, if we have credit accounts, then our business must be able to convert these accounts receivable into cash. If we cannot collect on accounts receivable in a timely manner, then we may not have enough cash to ensure timely payment to our own creditors. Therefore, if we are going to have credit accounts, we also must establish a plan for managing credit. A credit policy that is too strict could very well turn away potential customers, who then purchase from other firms. However, a credit policy that is too loose may cause cash flow problems because we may grant credit to people who do not pay their bills on time; in fact, we may grant credit to people who will never pay their bills.

A loose credit policy may cause two significant problems for our company: (1) a cash flow problem, because much of our cash is tied up in accounts receivable; and (2) we may be overstating the value of our current assets if we have accounts receivable on the books that are not collectable. This second situation tends to make our business look much healthier on the books than it actually is. For example, let us say that we have a business with $100,000 in current assets, which are broken down as follows: cash, $10,000; accounts receivable, $75,000; and inventory, $15,000. Our current liabilities total $38,460.

We usually determine the health of businesses in the same industry with ratio analysis. Recall from Chapter 4 that the current ratio provides us with a relative measure of liquidity.

$$\text{Current ratio} = \frac{\text{Current assets}}{\text{Current liabilities}}$$

In our example, the current ratio is determined by dividing $100,000 by $38,460, which is 2.60. This current ratio of 2.60 means that our firm has $2.60 in current assets for every $1.00 of current liabilities.

Let us now assume that of our $75,000 in accounts receivable, $25,000 is not collectable and is removed from the books. Therefore, our current assets are $75,000 (cash, $10,000; accounts receivable, $50,000; and inventory, $15,000). Consequently, our actual current ratio is $75,000 ÷ $38,460, or $1.95 for every $1.00 of current liabilities. As discussed in Chapter 4, a healthy firm usually has a current ratio in excess of 2. We looked quite healthy with a current ratio of 2.60, but the revised current ratio, because of our uncollectable accounts, is 1.95.

This discussion and the examples explain why it is important to understand the relationships between different items of working capital management. We next discuss specific strategies for managing each area of working capital.

CURRENT ASSET MANAGEMENT

Current asset management consists of managing cash, marketable securities, accounts receivable, and inventories.

CASH MANAGEMENT

The goal of cash management is to obtain the highest return possible on cash. This requires the firm to deposit cash and process checks as soon as possible and to disburse cash, by paying bills, as late as possible. At the same time, effective cash management involves investing idle cash in those short-term marketable securities that offer not only safety of principal but also a positive rate of return. Cash management is a part of effective working capital management that involves a trade-off between risk and return. On one hand, enough cash prevents the risk of insolvency caused by cash flowing in and out of our business at different rates, but on the other hand, too much cash results in less of a return. If we keep excess cash, we can pay our bills, but we lose interest on this money by not investing it for the short term.

For most businesses, cash consists of the following items:

1. Petty cash. A *petty cash* fund usually is used to pay for small daily items such as postage or minor supplies. We determine how much petty cash is required and store it in a cashbox or drawer that is reserved for this purpose only. Petty cash is exchanged for receipts, and every expenditure must have a matching receipt. When the petty cash fund must be replaced, a check is drawn for petty cash and all receipts are recorded in the books for the business.

2. Cash on hand. *Cash on hand* usually consists of daily sales and a change fund. The change fund is established when we determine how much cash is required for each cash register or cashier's station and stock a change depository with rolls of coins and small bills (typically $1 and $5 bills) required for daily transactions. Depending on the size of the business, the change fund may involve as little as $200 (for a small lunch counter with only one cash register and a check-cashing policy that limits checks to the exact amount of purchase), or as much as several thousand dollars (for a supermarket with several cash registers and a debit card policy that accepts the card and gives cash back in excess of the purchase amount). For a retail establishment, the change fund varies with the size of the business, the day of the week, and the season of the year. Wholesale businesses can often run with a small amount of cash on hand because the vast majority of sales are on credit and transactions are frequently by check. Because cash on hand does not provide interest and excess cash on hand increases business risk (possible robbery or theft), deposits should be made daily to minimize the amount. If the business deals with large cash deposits, a security firm is usually contracted to pick up deposits; but if the business is small, the bank provides drop bags and keys so that deposits can be made when the bank is closed.

3. Cash in bank, checking. Business checking accounts may draw interest, but usually they are charged for each check that is written against them. To minimize these charges, try to write the minimum number of checks. For example, it can usually be arranged to pay vendors weekly or monthly, rather than with each delivery (trade credit is a current liability, and management of this item is discussed later in this chapter).

4. Cash in bank, savings. Most businesses want to maintain a savings account in addition to a checking account for several reasons: (1) Savings accounts usually earn higher interest rates than checking accounts; (2) the small business must set aside employee taxes, sales taxes, and other payments due to governmental agencies; and (3) some funds should be reserved for emergency repairs and services (e.g., a broken window).

Thus, it makes sense to keep most of the business cash in the bank to earn interest and keep proper records. In addition, there are several advantages to maintaining as many records as possible using a checking account. The most obvious one is that the business has a record of all expenses, and if there is ever an audit by a government agency or other interested parties, canceled checks are considered to be absolute proof of payment. Another advantage of paying by check is that we can utilize the *float*.

The two types of float are *disbursement float* and *collections float*. The **disbursement float** is the time that elapses between payment by check and the check's actually clearing the bank, at which point funds are removed from the checking account. Most businesses write checks totaling several hundred thousands of dollars per year, and, of course, large businesses write checks totaling millions of dollars. Most government agencies and many vendors accept a U.S. post office postmark date as date of payment. We are all familiar with this concept because of our annual income tax payments, which are due on April 15 of each year. Obviously the Internal Revenue Service (IRS) does not actually receive payment on the fifteenth, but it accepts the postmark as proof of payment on that date. It takes time for a check to clear, especially if the creditor's bank is several thousand miles from the debtor. The longer the check takes to clear, the longer we collect interest on the funds that have not been removed from our account.

For example, let us say that our checking account earns interest of 5 percent per year. Then, interest earned on each $100,000 that we can keep for a 5-day period, because of float, amounts to approximately $68.50. This was computed as follows: Annual interest of 5 percent means daily interest of 0.000137, which is derived by dividing the annual interest (0.05) by 365, the number of days in the year.

$$\text{Daily interest} = \frac{\text{Annual interest}}{\text{Days in year}} = \frac{0.05}{365} = 0.000137$$

Next we multiply the amount by the interest rate, and then by the time period during which that interest is earned. Five days' worth of interest equals $100,000 × 0.000137 (daily interest) × 5 (number of days).

If you are the creditor rather than the debtor, then you try to counteract the use of float as much as possible by speeding collections time. **Collections float** is the amount of time that elapses between when you deposit a debtor's check in your account and the check clears, at which point the funds are actually placed in your account. Obviously the same principle applies here as in the preceding example: Cash in the bank earns interest; therefore, we want to speed collections time.

There are several methods of handling this collection with today's interstate banking. One method is to establish a lockbox system in conjunction with the bank. A **lockbox** is a post office box that is opened by an agent of the bank, and checks received there are deposited in our account immediately. Several collection points can be established throughout our marketing area, so debtors send payments to lockboxes at these collection points. Daily, a bank designated by us opens each payment and processes it. At the end of the business day, the bank wires the funds that have cleared to our bank. For the lockbox system to be profitable, your firm must be involved in high-volume transactions and realize a greater return on short-term investments than the cost incurred in bank charges for the lockbox system. An excellent method for making this determination is to calculate total cost. We calculate the total cost of the lockbox and total interest earned on invested short-term funds that clear the bank. If total interest earned is greater than the cost of the lockbox, we use a lockbox.

Another method used to speed cash receipt time is **electronic funds transfer (EFT),** which is accomplished when funds are transferred immediately from one bank account to another via computer. EFT currently makes use of high technology and can provide both our customer with a receipt and our account with immediate cash. The most familiar example of use of this method is at pay points in many service stations and grocery and convenience stores. At these pay points, you use your check guarantee card as a debit card. You insert the card in the machine, punch in your personal identification number (PIN), and enter the amount of the purchase or cash desired. The funds are immediately taken from your checking account and deposited in the business's account. For a business, using this system is much better than accepting a check because the funds, if the transaction goes through, are in the bank immediately, so the business does not have to worry about returned checks because of insufficient funds.

Using yet another method for speeding collections time, many large firms make arrangements for banks to accept payments to the firm when banking customers make deposits in the bank. Most utility companies make these arrangements. It is convenient for us to pay utility bills when making a deposit at the bank because it saves the cost of postage and lessens the possibility of lost payments. For the utility, it speeds collection of checks and increases the earnings on interest-bearing accounts. Many businesses and individuals are saying goodbye to stock of paper, envelopes, and stamps and going to online banking to pay monthly bills.

MARKETABLE SECURITIES MANAGEMENT

Marketable securities usually are those investment vehicles that include money market mutual funds, U.S. Treasury bills, certificates of deposit, government and corporate bonds, and stocks. For a larger business, they also include repurchase agreements, commercial paper, and banker's acceptances. Note that stocks and bonds are marketable securities, but they may not be as liquid as money market instruments. If our business has cash in excess of our requirements for paying monthly bills, then it makes sense to take the money out of our checking or savings account and invest it in some profit-making or interest-bearing instrument that usually pays more than we can obtain by keeping the funds in checking or savings accounts. We develop investment strategies for marketable securities in Chapter 11, dealing with individual investment. Because we are not primarily concerned with public corporations in this text; however, a corporation can use the same strategy as the individual in handling excess cash.

ACCOUNTS RECEIVABLE MANAGEMENT

Obviously, not all business transactions are handled in cash. Many of us, to stay competitive, must establish a credit accounting system. Accounts that are not paid in cash are referred to as *receivables* (debts owed to our firm). As with cash, our business must manage its accounts receivable properly to maximize profit.

The goal of accounts receivable management is to increase sales by offering credit to customers. However, we must weigh the costs incurred in having increased sales tied up in accounts receivable against the possible loss of business as a result of factors beyond the utility of a product or service. Many customers choose to deal with those businesses that offer instant credit rather than those that demand cash. As a business, we can use certain methods to provide credit to our customers without having to establish a credit department. The most common method is to use a credit factor.

Factoring is the process of selling our accounts receivable to another firm at a discount off of the original sales price. Factoring allows us to have credit sales and still obtain immediate cash for all sales. If you have ever bought a set of tires, charged them at the tire store, and then found that your payments were to be made to some financial management firm, then you have had an account factored. The tire store sold your bill to a third party at a discount.

Although banks do not like to consider themselves to be factors, they in fact perform the functions of a factor for many businesses. The factoring system most often used by a business involves making arrangements with a bank or financial institution to accept their credit card. For most businesses it is cheaper to allow customers to make use of credit cards such as MasterCard or Visa than to establish a credit system. The costs of billing, processing, and keeping records, in addition to the problem associated with having to wait 30 to 60 days for cash that has already been earned through a sale, can become a business nightmare.

The fact remains that the business owner, in making use of MasterCard, Visa, or some other card for credit sales, merely takes the day's credit transactions to the bank and receives a discounted amount of cash immediately. Although this discounted amount reduces the proceeds of the sale, we now have cash for working capital without the expense of determining if the customer is a good credit risk. The factor gives us immediate cash for sales receipts, provided that we abide by the rules of the factor. For example, say that we own a restaurant and a customer charges a $32 restaurant bill on a credit card. With the credit card, we are assured that we will be paid $32 minus a nominal discount of 4 to 5 percent of the bill. If the discount is 4 percent, then we receive $30.72 for the $32 charge and the bank charges us $1.28 for its processing. We receive $30.72 in cash immediately, rather than having to process a check, which could be uncollectable. Authorization by the credit card company is required and accomplished electronically. From a businessperson's point of view, the reduced proceeds of the sale may be made up by charging a higher price or just from the savings on the processing costs of credit.

If we choose not to use a factor and must establish a credit policy, then we must determine (1) to whom we will grant credit, (2) the terms of the credit granted, and (3) how we will monitor credit and deal with delinquent accounts. Often, the industry in which we establish our business dictates if we use a factor or establish our own credit department. For example, most retail firms accept bank cards, but wholesale and manufacturing firms establish their own credit departments.

Credit Evaluation

In determining which customers are allowed to use credit, we should adhere to established credit standards that serve as a yardstick in determining if a potential credit customer pays a bill successfully or defaults. Among the primary considerations used in deciding to grant credit to a customer are the three Cs of credit—character, capacity, and collateral. A customer's **character** is favorable if that customer has paid bills on time in the past and has good credit references from other creditors. This information usually is obtained from the customer application form, which lists other creditors and contains a signed statement that allows us to check these references. **Capacity** to pay refers to whether the customer has enough cash flow or disposable income to pay back a loan or pay off a bill. This information also is usually obtained from the credit application, which lists assets and bank references. Having a high capacity does not necessarily mean that applicants will pay their bills, because they may be saddled with other bills or debt to pay off. A business that grosses $100,000 may be paying off $90,000 in debt. **Collateral** is the ability to satisfy a debt or pay a creditor by selling assets for cash. When evaluating collateral, however, we also must determine if there is a market for the asset. The credit decision involves making sure that the customer is a good credit risk. If the applicant is a business, we often look for a specific rating from a credit rating service, such as Dun & Bradstreet. If the applicant is an individual, we often check credit references and obtain a credit rating from a commercial credit agency. The credit decision is based on all the facts that convey to the lender whether a customer is a good credit risk. Because the credit decision involves allowing a customer (individual or business) to borrow money from our firm, we usually set a limit on that amount when we make the credit decision.

Credit terms are the requirements that our business establishes for payment of a loan (the use of credit by a customer). The terms that are most familiar to us are those associated with bank cards such as Visa or MasterCard. If the account is paid in full within some specified period, usually 30 days or less, then there is no interest charged on the outstanding balance. If the account is not paid in full, then a monthly interest charge is made on the unpaid balance. In addition, a portion of the debt must be paid each month to guarantee the continuation of credit. The terms also establish a maximum amount of credit allowed the creditor. If we are in a business that requires the issuance of credit in order to stay competitive, then the terms we use are most often dictated by the standards of the industry. It is impossible to list all of the variances in this text; you must determine what the industry standards are and how you will apply them in your firm. We do provide, in later sections of this chapter, illustrations of cash and trade discounts that are usually used by business.

Analyzing Accounts Receivable

Analyzing accounts receivable is an important factor in determining how well our granting of credit matches our collection procedures. It is through this process that we are able to control credit. As stated previously, the control procedure involves establishing a standard, measuring actual performance against the standard, and taking corrective action if required. Let us say that we have established a credit policy of 60 days. In other words, people who have credit with our firm are supposed to pay their balances in full within 60 days of making a credit purchase. Recall from Chapter 4 that accounts receivable turnover is computed by taking credit sales and dividing them by accounts receivable.

$$\text{Accounts receivable turnover} = \frac{\text{Credit sales}}{\text{Average accounts receivable}}$$

If our firm has $300,000 in credit sales and $50,000 in average accounts receivable, then our accounts receivable turnover ratio is

$$\text{Accounts receivable turnover} = \frac{\$300,000}{\$50,000} = 6$$

Again from Chapter 4, the number of days in a year divided by our turnover ratio gives us the number of collection days.

$$\text{Collection days} = \frac{365}{6} = 60.8333 \text{ days} \approx 61 \text{ days}$$

Therefore, we have 60.8333 (or rounded to 61) days outstanding for our credit accounts. If this were our actual situation, then our credit terms and our granting of credit would be in line with our goals. Our customers would be paying their bills within the allocated time period. What if we find that we have $300,000 in credit sales, but our average accounts receivable are $100,000? Then, using the same mathematics, we find that our turnover ratio is 3 ($300,000 ÷ $100,000) and that our average collection days are 121.6667 (365 days ÷ 3), which rounds to 122 days. This indicates that corrective action must be taken with regard to our credit policy. We must reevaluate our three Cs of credit and tighten our procedures.

Aging of Accounts Receivable

Aging of accounts receivable is accomplished by determining the amounts of accounts receivable, the various lengths of time for which these accounts have been due, and the percentage of accounts that falls within each time frame. If there is a situation as in our second example, then aging of accounts receivable is necessary. The procedure can be described by following Table 7–1.

Table 7–1 consists of a listing of our customers, the outstanding balances of their accounts, and the number of days since the credit purchases were made. As

TABLE 7–1 Aging of Accounts Receivable

Customer	Outstanding Balance	Days Outstanding
1	$ 5,000	30
2	7,000	45
3	15,000	30
4	12,000	70
5	8,000	90
6	15,000	60
7	6,000	120
8	10,000	100
9	13,000	45
10	9,000	90
Total	$100,000	

Aging Schedule

	Days Outstanding			
Customer	0–30	31–60	61–90	90+
1	$ 5,000			
2		$ 7,000		
3	15,000			
4			$12,000	
5			8,000	
6		15,000		
7				$6,000
8				10,000
9		13,000		
10			9,000	
Totals	$20,000	$35,000	$29,000	$16,000
Percentage Outstanding	20	35	29	16

discussed, the outstanding balance for all accounts is $100,000. We take this information and create an aging schedule. If all of our accounts were in fact collected within the 60-day period established with our credit policy, then this procedure would not be necessary. However, because our accounts receivable turnover ratio is 3, rather than 6, it is necessary to analyze our outstanding credit accounts.

To construct the aging schedule, we take customer, balance, and number of days outstanding and arrange the information as shown in the bottom half of Table 7–1. We then obtain a total dollar figure for each time period and determine what percentage of our accounts receivable falls within each period. This amount is computed by dividing the total for each time period by the total credit accounts that are outstanding. For example, we have $20,000 in accounts that have been outstanding from 0 to 30 days. We divide this $20,000 by the $100,000 total outstanding balance from the top portion of the table and determine that 20 percent of our credit accounts fall within the 30-day time period. Thirty-five percent fall within 31 to 60 days, 29 percent fall within 61 to 90 days, and 16 percent have been outstanding for more than 90 days. Therefore, 45 percent of our accounts fall outside of the period that we established for our credit policy (60 days). Clearly we have a problem that calls for corrective action.

Our action involves several alternatives. The first is to notify these customers and try to obtain payment. Second, we can deny further credit to these customers if they do not bring their accounts within our criteria. Third, we can turn delinquent accounts over to a collection agency. Our last resort, if we determine that the account is not collectable, is to write off the account as a bad debt. The customer in this last situation may have filed for bankruptcy, gone out of business, or left the state without leaving a forwarding address.

Our decision depends on several factors. We should consider the following questions: How good a customer has this person been in the past? Can we afford to carry the customer during this temporary setback? Can we work with the customer on a cash-only basis until some payment is made on the outstanding debt? We cannot tell you how to handle each situation, because it depends on the specific relationship between your firm and the creditor. However, it should be clear that in addition to working with current accounts that are in arrears, we must reevaluate our credit terms. It appears that we have a policy that is too loose, as discussed in the first section of this chapter. We must tighten both our collection and credit granting procedures to bring our existing and potential creditors back in line.

INVENTORY MANAGEMENT

The final part of our current asset management involves managing inventory. For many businesses, inventory is where most of the current assets are located. Proper management of inventory is critical to operating efficiency. The goals of inventory management appear to be contradictory. We must have enough inventory on hand to satisfy customer demand, but we also must keep inventory at a minimum value to free up cash. If we maintain an inventory that is too large, we may be stuck with obsolete items or items that have short shelf lives (items that spoil or lose their effectiveness, such as milk products or vitamins) and must be disposed of with no sale. If our inventory is too small, we may lose sales and possibly customers to our competitors. The overall goal of inventory management, therefore, is to minimize total inventory costs while maximizing customer satisfaction. To accomplish this, we must decide how to establish the reorder quantity (the number of items to order) and the reorder point (that level of inventory at which a new order is placed).

Economic Order Quantity Formula

To minimize inventory costs, we must have some idea of the value of our inventory. This can be obtained by determining the total cost of inventory, which includes ordering costs, carrying costs, the price of the goods to be ordered, and the losses incurred by lost sales (opportunity costs). The most widely used formula for determining the reorder quantity is the *economic order quantity (EOQ)* formula, which takes into consideration all the factors mentioned, with the exception of the lost opportunity costs. The EOQ formula attempts to balance ordering costs against storage costs, and it provides us with the most economic quantity to order to minimize overall inventory costs.

The EOQ formula is

$$EOQ = \sqrt{\frac{2\,DS}{IP}}$$

where

    D = total annual demand for the item
    S = total ordering cost for the item
    I = carrying cost for the item, which is usually expressed as a percentage
    P = unit cost of the item

The total ordering cost (S) is an administrative expense and is usually determined by taking the cost of the purchasing department or activity and dividing it by the number of orders placed per year. Let's say that Markadel has two purchasing agents whose combined salaries are $80,000 and who have administrative expenses allocated of $20,000 per year. They process 10,000 orders per year. In this case, we would compute S by dividing $100,000 (the total cost of purchasing) by 10,000 (the number of orders placed per year); so we would use $10 in our EOQ formula for the value of S.

We determine inventory carrying costs (I) in a similar manner. The *carrying cost* is the cost of storing all inventory for a year, as a percentage of the average inventory value. For example, Markadel has a separate warehouse for inventory. The warehouse, on average, holds $3,000,000 in inventory. We total all costs of running the warehouse for 1 year, which includes salaries of warehouse workers, insurance, rent, and utilities, and arrive at a figure of $300,000. Therefore, for Markadel, the value of I is 10 percent of the average inventory value ($300,000 \div 3,000,000$).

Total annual demand (D) is simply the number of units ordered per year, and price (P) is the cost per unit.

Let us say that Markadel orders 16,000 units of a particular item each year, and the unit cost is $20. Using the values for S and I we just computed, we would arrive at an EOQ of 400 units.

$$EOQ = \sqrt{\frac{2DS}{IP}} = \sqrt{\frac{(2)(16,000)(\$10)}{(0.10)(\$20)}} = \sqrt{160,000} = 400$$

Although the preceding formula is the one most often used, there are several other factors that the businessowner must take into consideration. Most vendors require a minimum order for delivery. If the business is small or storage space is at a premium, orders that are smaller than the EOQ may have to be placed. If the business is large or uses items in quantity, then quantity discounts may override the EOQ formula.

Determining EOQ with quantity discounts requires the following procedures:

1. Compute EOQ for each discounted price.
2. If the computed EOQ falls within the discounted quantity area, then order the EOQ.
3. If the EOQ does not fall within the discounted quantity area, then compute total inventory costs.
4. Order the minimum quantity that provides the lowest overall inventory costs.

When quantity discounts are offered and the EOQ given by the formula does not fall within the quantity discount range, then you should compute total inventory costs at each of the discount points and determine if the benefits of ordering the larger quantity override the costs of storage. This requires that we compute total costs unless the EOQ formula provides us with results that fall within the quantity discount area.

In determining total costs, the following assumptions are used:

1. Inventory is used at a constant rate during the time period. Therefore, the average inventory in stock at any given time is half the order quantity, or $Q \div 2$, where Q is the order quantity.
2. The number of orders placed per year is equal to annual demand divided by the order quantity, or $D \div Q$.

Therefore, our total cost (TC) formula is

$$TC = DP + \frac{QIP}{2} + \frac{DS}{Q}$$

Table 7-2 EOQ with Quantity Discounts

Warehouse storage cost (I) = 0.40
Ordering cost (S) = $10.00
Annual demand (D) = 16,000

		Total Costs for Each Quantity		
Price	Discount Quantity	EOQ	Quantity to Order	Total Cost
$20.00	0–500	200.00	200	$321,600.00
$19.00	501–1,000	205.20	501	$306,223.16
$18.90	>1,000	205.74	1,001	$ 306,343.62

where

$$D \times P = \text{total cost of units}$$
$$Q \times I \times P \div 2 = \text{annual cost of carrying the inventory}$$
$$D \times S \div Q = \text{annual ordering cost}$$

Table 7–2 presents the following problem with relationship to quantity discounts and shows the solution to this type of problem.

We have a warehouse for which annual storage costs are 40 percent of inventory costs. It costs us $10 to place an order, and annual demand for the item is 16,000 units. The vendor provides us with a price list that indicates a price of $20 per unit for orders of 1 to 500 units, $19 per unit for orders of 501 to 1,000 units, and $18.90 per unit for orders in excess of 1,000 units. We first compute EOQ for each price, using the previous formula. The calculation of EOQ for a price of $20 is

$$EOQ = \sqrt{\frac{2DS}{IP}} = \sqrt{\frac{(2)(16,000)(\$10)}{(0.40)(\$20)}} = \sqrt{40,000} = 200$$

Calculation of EOQ for the $19 price yields an EOQ of 205.20, and for the price of $18.90 we obtain an EOQ of 205.74. Note that we cannot get the quantity discount price of $19 unless we order 501 units; therefore, we must calculate total cost at each discount quantity to determine which quantity provides us with the lowest total cost. Calculation for total cost with a price of $19 is

$$TC = DP + \frac{QIP}{2} + \frac{DS}{Q}$$

$$TC = (16,000)(\$19) + \frac{(501)(0.4)(\$19)}{2} + \frac{(16,000)(\$10)}{501}$$

$$= \$306,223.16$$

Notice that when we calculate total cost with a discount, P equals the discount price and Q is the minimum discount quantity that can be ordered to obtain the price. When we solve the equation for each price and quantity, note that our lowest total cost is with a price of $19. Therefore, we would order quantities of 501 if we had adequate storage space. Solving these equations gives us an idea about how much to order. Unfortunately, one of the assumptions made in the EOQ model is that the order is received instantaneously. Because we know this is not true, we must also determine when to place the order (our reorder point).

Reorder Point Calculations

The **reorder point (ROP)** has three factors that are used in determining the quantity of an item that exists when we actually place an order: lead time, daily demand, and safety stock. **Lead time (L)** is the time that lapses from order placement to order receipt. **Daily demand (d)** is the quantity of a product that is used per day. **Safety Stock (ss)** is the quantity of stock held for variations in demand. The formula for calculating the reorder point is

$$ROP = Ld + ss$$

In our previous example, if we use 16,000 units of an item per year and are open 250 days per year, then daily demand is 64 units (16,000 units/year ÷ 250 days/year = 64 units/day).

$$
\begin{aligned}
\text{Daily demand } (d) &= \frac{\text{Annual demand } (D)}{\text{Number of days open per year}} \\
&= \frac{16{,}000 \text{ units/year}}{250 \text{ days/year}} \\
&= 64 \text{ units/day}
\end{aligned}
$$

If it now takes 3 days from the time that we place an order until we receive the order, then our reorder point for lead time would be 3 days × 64 units = 192 units. Our safety stock is the number of units that we want on the shelf when the new order arrives. Safety stock accounts for daily variation in sales. The actual calculation of safety stock is based on statistical probability factors that are beyond the mathematics of this textbook. The following example can be used. Let's say that the item we are discussing is one that you definitely want to have in stock. In looking at your store records, the best day's sales of this item were 95 units. Therefore, you would have safety stock of 95, the best day's sales in addition to the safety lead time quantity of 192. We would then calculate our reorder point as:

$$ROP = Ld + ss = (3)(64) + 95 = 287$$

When in-store inventory reached 287 units, if we are not taking advantage of the quantity discount, we reorder our EOQ of 200 units; if we are taking advantage of the quantity discount, we order 501 units.

Just-in-Time (JIT)

Although EOQ, quantity discount, and reorder point calculations are the traditional method of calculating how much to order and when to order, many firms are moving to a *just-in-time (JIT)* model. If daily demand can be predicted accurately, vendor delivery reliability is outstanding, and vendors deliver on an hourly or daily basis, then JIT inventory can be used. The automobile industry is one example of JIT. Many automobile factories operate two or more shifts, with an automobile coming off of the assembly line every minute. This means in 16 hours the plant produces 960 automobiles (16 hours × 60 minutes × 1 car per minute). Each car requires four regular tires and one spare. The plant can schedule the delivery of 3,840 regular tires (960 automobiles × 4 regular tires) and 960 spare tires every day the plant produces. Because of the large quantity of tires, the plant may actually schedule several tire deliveries per day and eliminate the warehouse. Items are delivered directly to the assembly line.

If a company can operate on JIT, it does not have to calculate EOQ, quantity discounts, or reorder points. The requirement is to know how many of each part is required for each unit being assembled and to arrange with the vendor to deliver the exact quantity every day.

Many businesses operate with some combination of the methods described. For example, Hannah's Donut Shop (Chapter 6) received vendor delivery every Wednesday. She ordered from the vendor Monday afternoon, after the day's baking had been completed. Hannah knew her weekly and daily demand for each item. For example, she used 950 cubes of shortening per year (Table 7–3) and was open 365 days a year. Daily demand, therefore, was 2.6 cubes of shortening (950 cubes ÷ 365 operating days per year). She used a safety stock of 1 cube and ordered 2 days before delivery. When she took inventory on Monday, she would usually order 18 cubes of shortening (7 days × 2.6 cubes) if she had between 6 and 7 cubes in stock (2.6 cubes per day × 2 days lead time + 1 cube of safety stock). If she had fewer than 6 cubes, she would increase the order by 1 for each cube she was short. This is a simple application of our ROP formula.

Types of Inventories

Inventory falls into four basic classifications, or types:

1. Raw materials are the items that a company uses in producing its final product. These can be basic raw materials (iron ore, coal) for an industrial manufacturing firm, assembly parts (microchips, disk drives, power supplies) for a computer manufacturing firm, or ingredients (flour, yeast) for a bakery. Raw materials are transformed in some manner between their receipt by a business and their being offered for sale by that business as part of a final product.

TABLE 7–3 Hannah's Donut Shop Inventory List

Item Number	Item Description	Annual Demand	Unit Cost	Total Cost
1	Bavarian cream filling	100.0	$15.00	$ 1,500.00
2	Bleach	104.0	0.60	62.40
3	Blueberry filling	15.6	20.10	313.56
4	Bread flour for raised doughnuts	990.0	6.10	6,039.00
5	White frosting base	15.6	29.90	466.44
6	Buttermilk mix	35.0	23.30	815.50
7	Cake doughnut mix	625.0	30.50	19,062.50
8	Raised mix	990.0	21.50	21,285.00
9	Cherry fruit bits	26.0	13.80	358.80
10	Chocolate fudge base	26.0	37.60	977.60
11	Chocolate doughnut mix	52.0	25.10	1,305.20
12	Chunky apple	20.8	16.95	352.56
13	Comet	26.0	0.40	10.40
14	Degreaser	10.4	6.40	66.56
15	Dish washing lotion	52.0	3.99	207.48
16	H&R all-purpose flour	52.0	6.99	363.48
17	Lemon mist filling	10.4	13.20	137.28
18	Oat bran	26.0	25.95	674.70
19	Old-fashioned doughnuts	26.0	22.55	586.30
20	Raspberry filling	50.0	14.44	722.00
21	SAF instant yeast	45.0	33.15	1,491.75
22	Shortening	950.0	22.80	21,660.00
23	Stirrers, coffee	10.4	2.49	25.90
24	Straws, wrapped	5.2	4.00	20.80
25	Sugar packets	5.2	8.99	46.75
26	Sweet'N Low	2.6	8.39	21.81
27	Trash bags	10.4	8.70	90.48
28	Urn coffee	45.0	46.50	2,092.50
29	#1 doughnut trays	60.0	22.00	1,320.00
30	#2 doughnut trays	52.0	21.50	1,118.00
	Total inventory cost			$83,194.75

2. **Work-in-process** inventories consist of those items that are in the midst of the transformation process just mentioned; for example, the computer manufacturer takes microchips, disk drives, and other raw materials out of storage and puts them into the assembly process. These items are considered a work in process until the finished computer is ready for shipment.

3. **Finished goods** inventories consist of those items that are actually sold by the business—sheet steel for the steel company, computers for the computer manufacturer, or bread for the bakery. Finished goods also include spare parts and repair parts for the end item. For example, a computer manufacturing firm also has disk drives, motherboards, and other items that might fail in use that it sells to authorized computer repair facilities.

4. **Maintenance, repair, and operating (MRO)** inventories consist of those items that are used by the firm in usual operations but that are not manufactured or sold by the firm. These can range from lubricating oil and spare parts for machinery to business forms and paper clips.

ABC Inventory Analysis

In evaluating inventory for financial purposes, the cost of inventory items is an important consideration. It is difficult to determine which inventory items to emphasize unless we have some idea of the importance of these items with relationship to the overall operation of the business. One useful method of inventory analysis is **ABC analysis**. In most business operations, 5 to 10 percent of the inventory items (i.e., individual stock numbers or stock-keeping units) make up approximately 75 percent of total costs (A items); 10 to 15 percent of the inventory stock numbers make up 10 to 15 percent of the total costs (B items); and the remaining 75 to 80 percent of the stock numbers account for only 10 to 15 percent of total costs (C items). For manufacturing firms, A items are usually raw materials; for retail stores, the A items are the best-selling items and are finished goods. The B items are intermediate raw materials and next-best-selling items; whereas C items are usually MRO types of items. Table 7–3 gives a partial inventory for Hannah's Donut Shop, the company used in our case study in Chapter 6. Table 7–4 shows the ABC analysis for that partial inventory.

The method of determining A, B, and C items is to take the total quantity purchased and multiply it by the unit cost to determine total cost for the item, as shown in Table 7–3. Notice that the total cost is a function of both quantity and price. For example, Hannah uses 104 bottles of bleach per year, but bleach only costs 60 cents a gallon, so the total cost is only $62.40 a year. However, she uses only 45 cases of urn coffee a year, but each case costs $46.50; therefore the annual cost of coffee is $2,092.50. Once we determine the total cost of each inventory item, we are ready to perform an ABC analysis, as shown in Table 7–4. We take the inventory items and list them in descending order, based on total cost. We add the total cost of our inventory and then compute the percentage of total cost that each inventory item consumes by dividing each individual item's total cost by the total cost of the inventory. For example, to determine the percentage of total cost consumed by shortening, we take the annual cost of shortening, divide it by the total cost of inventory, and multiply the result by 100:

$$\text{Shortening percentage} = \frac{(\$21,660.00)(100)}{\$83,194.75} = 26.04\%$$

We continue this procedure with each inventory item, listing the percentage consumed in a separate column. We then determine ABC by adding the percentages in the next column. Shortening at 26.04 percent plus raised mix at 25.58 percent equals 51.62 percent of total inventory cost. When we reach approximately 75 percent of total cost, we have identified the A items. For Hannah's Donut Shop, the A items are shortening, raised mix, and cake doughnut mix. Notice that there are three A items out of the inventory list of 30 items. This represents 10 percent of the total inventory items by stock-keeping unit.

TABLE 7–4 Hannah's Donut Shop, ABC Analysis

Item Number	Item Description	Annual Demand	Unit Cost	Total Cost	Percentage	Cumulative Percentage
1	Shortening	950.0	$22.80	$21,660.00	26.04	26.04
2	Raised mix	990.0	21.50	21,285.00	25.58	51.62
3	Cake doughnut mix	625.0	30.50	19,062.50	22.91	74.53
4	Bread flour for raised doughnuts	990.0	6.10	6,039.00	7.26	81.79
5	Urn coffee	45.0	46.50	2,092.50	2.52	84.31
6	Bavarian cream filling	100.0	15.00	1,500.00	1.80	86.11
7	SAF instant yeast	45.0	33.15	1,491.75	1.79	87.90
8	#1 doughnut trays	60.0	22.00	1,320.00	1.59	89.49
9	Chocolate doughnut mix	52.0	25.10	1,305.20	1.57	91.06
10	#2 doughnut trays	52.0	21.50	1,118.00	1.34	92.40
11	Chocolate fudge base	26.0	37.60	977.60	1.18	93.58
12	Buttermilk mix	35.0	23.30	815.50	0.98	94.56
13	Raspberry filling	50.0	14.44	722.00	0.87	95.43
14	Oat bran	26.0	25.95	674.70	0.81	96.24
15	Old-fashioned doughnuts	26.0	22.55	586.30	0.70	96.94
16	White frosting base	15.6	29.90	466.44	0.56	97.50
17	H&R all-purpose flour	52.0	6.99	363.48	0.44	97.94
18	Cherry fruit bits	26.0	13.80	358.80	0.43	98.37
19	Chunky apple	20.8	16.95	352.56	0.42	98.79
20	Blueberry filling	15.6	20.10	313.56	0.38	99.17
21	Dishwashing lotion	52.0	3.99	207.48	0.25	99.42
22	Lemon mist filling	10.4	13.20	137.28	0.17	99.59
23	Trash bags	10.4	8.70	90.48	0.11	99.69
24	Degreaser	10.4	6.40	66.56	0.08	99.77
25	Bleach	104.0	0.60	62.40	0.08	99.85
26	Sugar packets	5.2	8.99	46.75	0.06	99.91
27	Stirrers, coffee	10.4	2.49	25.90	0.03	99.94
28	Sweet'N Low	2.6	8.39	21.81	0.03	99.96
29	Straws, wrapped	5.2	4.00	20.80	0.03	99.99
30	Comet	26.0	0.40	10.40	0.01	100.00
	Total inventory cost			$83,194.75	100.00	

We continue adding until we reach approximately 90 percent of total cost. The items between 75 percent and 90 percent are classified as B items. For the doughnut shop, items 4 through 8 are B items. Notice that out of the total items, five are B items, representing approximately 17 percent of the stock-keeping units. The remaining items are C items and make up more than 73 percent of total stock-keeping units.

Why would a business owner go through this procedure? The ABC analysis is based on the *20–80 rule,* which is a phenomenon observed in many aspects of business. Twenty percent of your customers usually account for 80 percent of your sales. Twenty percent of your customers file 80 percent of your complaints. Twenty percent of your employees pose 80 percent of your employee problems. Likewise, 20 percent of your inventory items consume approximately 80 percent of your inventory investment. In managing inventory, however, this rule provides us with a tremendous management advantage.

The 20–80 rule is also known as *Pareto's Law.* When A items are identified, because they consume approximately 75 percent of your costs, they should be managed carefully. Your concentration should be on these items. You must have time to negotiate contracts, obtain competitive bids, and establish control procedures in regard to these items. A small savings on the purchase of A items can increase profits and reduce inventory costs tremendously, whereas a large savings on a C item does little to boost your profit or reduce inventory cost. For example, in the case of Hannah's Donut Shop, Hannah managed to obtain bids from several vendors and reduce the cost of shortening from $22.80 a cube to $19.25. This is a savings of $3.55 a cube, or 15.57 percent. Because she uses 950 cubes of shortening a year, this is an annual savings of $3,372.50. Not only is it an annual savings, but it actually increases profit by the same amount. She has spent $3,372.50 less on cost of goods and has generated the same amount in sales. If you refer to an income statement, notice that a reduction in cost of goods, with no decrease in sales, results in an increase in profit of the amount saved in inventory expense.

For C items, however, you merely want a reliable vendor who delivers on time. We do not shop for C items but spend our time on A and B items. C items usually are purchased with open purchase orders from dependable vendors. Referring again to Table 7–3, notice that Hannah uses 52 bottles of dishwashing detergent a year. Detergent costs $3.99 per bottle. Let us assume that she finds detergent for $1.98 a bottle and can save more than 50 percent. Her annual cost for detergent is $207.48. If she buys all 52 bottles on sale, she saves $104.52 a year. But can she store 52 bottles of detergent? If not, then she probably buys a single case of only 6 bottles, which saves only $12.06. How much time will she spend in buying the detergent? In other words, is it worth shopping for C items? The answer, obviously, is no.

For C items, we usually do not go through the calculations of EOQ or establish elaborate control procedures. We establish some minimum quantity, and once that minimum is reached, we place an order with our vendor. We do not shop or negotiate for these items because we should spend most of our time on A items, an amount of time proportionate to their importance on B items, and as little time as possible on C items. You may find that many business owners who do not spend the time to develop an ABC analysis place their emphasis on the wrong items because the C items make up 75 percent of inventory items by stock number or item description. How many times have you seen people in your office shop for business cards, pencils, or paper clips? These are, for most businesses, C items. Could this time be better spent on A items?

CURRENT LIABILITIES MANAGEMENT

Current liabilities management consists of minimizing our obligations and payments for short-term debt, accrued liabilities, and accounts payable.

SHORT-TERM DEBT MANAGEMENT

Short-term debt consists of business obligations that will be paid within the current accounting period. These are usually (a) current payments on long-term debt (e.g., if we have a mortgage with a monthly payment of $2,000, then our current obligation is $24,000 per year) or (b) payments on short-term loans, such as bank lines of credit, or loans that will be paid during the current accounting year that appear on the balance sheet as notes payable. Long-term debt consists of obligations that usually are incurred as a result of capital budgeting, and it is covered more fully in Chapter 10. Our primary concern in current liabilities management is merely to pay these obligations when they are due. Because notes payable usually are used to defer the payment of cash and may indicate an inadequate cash flow, we should discuss this area in some detail.

The primary method of incurring notes payable for our business is through extending lines of credit or using promissory notes. A line of credit is similar to a credit card. With it, we obtain a credit limit, but we are not obligated to make payments unless we actually borrow the money. A line of credit usually is obtained from our primary bank. We determine the dollar requirement for this line based on our maximum estimated cash requirement that exceeds cash income. We apply for a line of credit for this amount through our bank. The bank grants this line of credit if we meet its standards, which are often based on the three Cs of credit discussed in the previous section.

The requirement for a line of credit is based on the fact that our cash flow may be insufficient to meet current monthly obligations as a result of seasonal sales and general economic factors. Recall from Chapter 3, when we discussed the statement of cash flow, that in some months cash flow exceeded our requirements and at other times was insufficient to meet our obligations. If we want to maintain a good credit rating, we must make payments on time even when our business does not generate sufficient cash. One way of making sure that we can make timely payments is to establish a line of credit that exceeds our estimate of any shortfall. Then when we run short of cash, we borrow against the line of credit and pay it off as rapidly as possible.

Assume that in our business we believe that our maximum shortfall during any single month will be $8,000 and that total borrowing will never exceed $10,000. If we establish a line of credit of $10,000, we are covered. The advantage of the line of credit is that no payments are required and no interest is accrued until the credit is actually used. For example, say that we have a $10,000 line of credit at 12 percent annual interest. In February, we run short of cash by $2,000 and borrow the money. Because we established the line of credit, we now have the use of this $2,000 to pay our creditors on time. If the cash flow in March is sufficient, we can then pay back the $2,000 plus interest for 1 month. We pay the bank $2,000 plus 1 percent interest on the money, or $2,020, because we actually borrowed the money for 1 month and a 12 percent annual interest rate is computed at 1 percent per month. This procedure saves us considerable interest because we pay interest only when we have a loan outstanding.

In some circumstances, however, we either cannot obtain a line of credit that is sufficient to meet our obligations or we want to borrow a large sum of money for less than one year. Such circumstances would call for obtaining a *short-term loan,* a loan taken for 1 year or less. The procedures are the same as those listed for the line of credit. We determine the amount and apply to the bank for the loan. The primary difference between a line of credit and a loan is with the loan, we borrow the entire sum at one time and are obligated to make monthly payments. Because we borrow for a longer period of time, we pay more interest and incur a fixed monthly payment that increases our current liabilities. In some cases, we can arrange for the loan to be paid in one lump sum, which involves a single payment plus accrued interest.

A short-term loan is typical if our business has a very short season that generates the majority of our sales. A toy business, in which 75 percent of annual sales are made during the 3 months from October through December, is a good example. Say that we are in the toy business and we must contract for a large increase in inventory during the summer months to ensure sufficient stock during our peak selling season. We might obtain a 6-month loan on the first of July, with a single balloon payment due on January 1. If we borrow $100,000 in July at 12 percent interest, we owe the bank $106,235 in January, because the bank usually computes interest owed on outstanding loans on a daily basis. Therefore, at the end of July, we owe $100,000 plus 31 days of interest, or a total of $101,024. The bank then computes the next month's interest on the $101,024. This process is known as *compounding interest,* and is discussed fully in Chapter 8.

ACCRUED LIABILITIES MANAGEMENT

In addition to paying short-term debt, we also are obligated to pay **accrued liabilities,** which are those obligations of the firm accumulated during the usual course of business; they are primarily payroll taxes and benefits, property taxes, and sales taxes. It is with accrued liabilities that the small business owner can get into the most trouble because of the severe penalties that government agencies can impose on a business. "For amounts not properly or timely deposited, the penalty rates are: 2%—Deposits made 1 to 5 days late; 5%—Deposits made 6 to 15 days late; 10%—Deposits made 16 or more days late."[1] Government agencies treat businesses as collection agencies for taxes. When you take payroll taxes out of an employee's pay, this tax money, which was earned by the employee, is not yours to keep. Therefore, you must pay this obligation to the IRS on the day that it is due or incur a severe penalty. Sales taxes are treated exactly the same by state and local

---

[1]Department of the Treasury, Internal Revenue Service, Publication 15 (rev. January 2002), Circular E, *Employer's Tax Guide,* p. 21.

municipalities. If you use a cash register to ring up sales, then sales taxes usually are added to the sale and collected by the business. Your closing daily report, a *Z report,* or *zero balance report,* lists the total sales tax collected that day.

It is our contention that the best way to avoid a problem with the government is to make sure that the money for these liabilities is set aside as they are accrued. The easiest method is to establish a separate savings account. Every time a payroll is met, determine how much has been withheld from your employees' paychecks, add the appropriate employer federal, state, and municipal taxes, and deposit this sum into the savings account. Then the money is then in the bank on the day that it must be paid. **Federal employment taxes** consist of income, Social Security, Medicare, and unemployment taxes. In addition, the employer is obligated to match the Social Security and Medicare tax that has been paid by the employee. **State employment taxes** usually consist of income, unemployment, and workmen's compensation taxes. Municipal employment taxes usually are only income tax.

On a daily or weekly basis, determine how much sales tax has been collected and deposit this amount in the savings account. This provides you with the funds to pay state and local agencies. In addition, if you own property or operate with a *triple-net lease* (lessee pays rent plus a share of property and rental taxes), then you receive an annual property tax bill that usually is paid in two installments (every 6 months). Determine the monthly obligation of this tax and set it aside in your savings account, otherwise you may use the money to pay other obligations and not have the cash to pay these taxes when they are due. Government agencies can impound your bank accounts and lock the doors of your business if these taxes are not paid in a timely manner. Therefore, accrued liabilities management must be of primary concern.

ACCOUNTS PAYABLE MANAGEMENT

The last item to be discussed in this section on current liabilities is accounts payable. The largest portion of accounts payable usually consists of the obligations of our firm that were obtained by purchasing inventory on credit. Of course, other items such as travel expenses, maintenance services, and entertainment expenses also may be charged. Our purpose in managing accounts payable is to minimize the cash paid for inventories and these other obligations. Because inventories make up the largest portion of accounts payable, we usually can minimize these cash payments by taking advantage of the discounts that are offered by vendors. The three primary types of discounts that vendors typically use are trade discounts, cash discounts, and quantity discounts.

Trade Discounts

Trade discounts are amounts deducted from list prices of items when specific services are performed by the trade customer. Trade discounts may be expressed as a single amount, such as 30 percent, or in a series, such as 30/20/10. If the discounts are expressed as a series or chain, the customer must accomplish specific tasks of the agreement to qualify for the entire chain discount. This may involve purchasing large quantities of an item or performing specific intermediary functions, such as providing point-of-sale displays or local advertising. When taking advantage of trade discounts, it is important to calculate them properly.

Calculation of trade discounts is accomplished by moving backward from the list price. In the previous example, the discount chain of 30/20/10 does not mean that the item may be purchased with a 60 percent discount (30 + 20 + 10 = 60). Rather, we calculate the total discount, in three steps or in one step, by using the net cost rate factor. We use the following example to illustrate both methods:

Tom's Appliance Store receives a washing machine that has a list price of $300 and for which the manufacturer shows discounts of 30/20/10. The manufacturer's wholesale catalog provides an explanation of each discount. For example, the manufacturer may specify that 30 percent is the normal markup from wholesale to retail, 20 percent is the allowance for free delivery and installation service, and 10 percent is an allowance for point-of-sale display and local advertising. Tom may take all three discounts if he is going to comply with all contractual obligations.

There are two methods of calculating discounts. One method is to work the long way, working backward from list with each discount. We determine what would be paid if we took each discount individually, as follows: List price minus the first discount is

$$\text{List price} - \text{Trade discount} = \text{Discounted price}$$
$$\$300 - (\$300 \times 0.3) = \$210$$

The discounted price minus the second discount is

$$\$210 - (210 \times 0.2) = \$210 - \$42 = \$168$$

The second discounted price minus the third discount is

$$\$168 - (168 \times 0.1) = \$168 - \$16.80 = \$151.20$$

The total invoice price paid, divided by the list price, provides us with the *net cost rate factor*, which is the actual percentage of the list price paid after taking all successive trade discounts—50.40 percent in this case. One minus the net cost rate factor is the single equivalent discount. Therefore, trade discounts of 30/20/10 amount to a single equivalent discount of 49.60 percent, not 60 percent.

A second, simpler way of determining the net cost rate factor is to multiply the complements of the trade discounts. For example, in the preceding problem the trade discounts were 30/20/10. The complement of a number is found by subtracting the number from 1. So for 30/20/10, the complements are 0.7 (1 − 0.3), 0.8 (1 − 0.2), and 0.9 (1 − 0.1), respectively. Then, multiplying these complements together results in a net cost rate factor of 0.5040, or 50.40 percent. Again, the mathematical calculations are as follows:

First complement = 1 − 0.3 = 0.7
Second complement = 1 − 0.2 = 0.8
Third complement = 1 − 0.1 = 0.9
Net cost rate factor = (0.7)(0.8)(0.9) = 0.504

The invoice price (the price that you actually pay the vendor) can be calculated simply by the following formula:

Invoice price = List price × net cost rate factor

Invoice price = ($300)(0.504) = $151.20

The invoice price of $151.20 is the amount that we pay the washing machine manufacturer if we take all discounts. A trade discount is very much involved in establishing the invoice price. Note, however, that the invoice price can be paid either in cash or on credit. If Tom does not pay for the merchandise when he receives it, then he is a credit customer.

Cash Discounts

Cash discounts are offered to credit customers to entice them to pay promptly. The seller views a cash discount as a sales discount; the customer views it as a purchase discount. The terms of a cash discount play an important role in determining how the invoice is paid. Cash discounts usually appear on an invoice in terms such as *2/10, n/30,* which means that customers may deduct 2 percent off of the invoice price if they pay within 10 days. If customers pay within 30 days, the net (*n*), or total amount of the invoice, is due. If they pay after 30 days, the credit agreement with the sellers usually stipulates that a monthly interest charge be added to the unpaid balance.

Suppose that Markadel sells goods to Tom's Appliance Store for $10,000 (the invoice price), terms 2/10, *n*/30, with an invoice date of November 1. Terms of 2/10, *n*/30 mean that Tom's Appliance Store can deduct 2 percent from the invoice price if payment is made within 10 days of the invoice date (up to November 11). If Tom's does not take advantage of the cash discount, then Tom must pay the entire invoice amount within 30 days of the invoice date. If payment is not made by day 30 (December 1), then interest charges of 1.5 percent monthly (18 percent annually) will be added to the unpaid balance. (The interest charged on the unpaid balance varies and is usually listed on the credit application that is signed by the business owner or agent of the business.)

In our example, Tom has several options. He can pay off the $10,000 with a payment of $9,800 within 10 days of the invoice date. This amount is computed by multiplying the invoice price by 1, minus the discount $(1 - 0.02 = 0.98$, and $\$10,000 \times 0.98 = \$9,800)$, or by taking the invoice price times the discount and subtracting it from the invoice price $(\$10,000 \times 0.02 = \$200$, and $\$10,000 - \$200 = \$9,800)$. He also can choose to pay the invoice price of $10,000 if payment is made any time between day 11 and day 30 after the invoice date. If this option is chosen, Tom pays the equivalent of 37.23 percent annual interest (if paid on day 30) and 744.60 percent (if paid on day 11) because he did not take advantage of the cash discount.

How do we determine that the effective rate of interest resulting from not taking the discount is 37.23 percent? The following procedures and assumptions are used to calculate the effective rate of interest. If Tom does not take the discount and chooses to pay on day 30, then this is the same as borrowing $9,800 for 20 days and paying $200 in interest on the loan, because after day 10, he must still pay the $9,800 by day 30 plus the additional $200, or the invoice amount of $10,000. In other words, it costs Tom 2 percent of the $10,000, or $200, for the use of $9,800 for the next 20 days. If this occurs every 20 days, then the effective rate of interest is calculated by multiplying the rate per period (dollar value of cash discount divided by amount of money used) by the number of 20-day periods in the year.

$$\text{Effective rate of interest} = \left(\frac{\text{Dollar value of cash discount}}{\text{Amount of money used}}\right) \times \left(\frac{\text{Days in the accounting year}}{\text{Net days} - \text{Discount days}}\right) \times 100$$

$$= \left(\frac{\$200}{\$9,800}\right) \times \left(\frac{365}{30 - 10}\right) \times 100$$

$$= (0.0204) \times 18.25 \times 100 = 37.23\%$$

Using the same formula, if payment is made on day 11, then the effective rate of interest is 744.60 percent.

$$\text{Effective rate of interest} = \left(\frac{\text{Dollar value of cash discount}}{\text{Amount of money used}}\right) \times \left(\frac{\text{Days in the accounting year}}{\text{Net days} - \text{Discount days}}\right) \times 100$$

$$= \left(\frac{\$200}{\$9,800}\right) \times \left(\frac{365}{11 - 10}\right) \times 100$$

$$= (0.0204) \times 365 \times 100 = 744.60\%$$

Annual interest is computed by going on the assumption that Tom chose to borrow $9,800 for 20 days and made an interest payment of $200 on this loan.

In other words, he chose to forfeit or pay $200 that could have been kept in order to keep the $9,800 debt for an additional 20 days (30 days − 10 days). Thus, Tom pays $200 on $9,800 for 20 days, or an interest rate of 2.04 percent [($200 ÷ $9,800) × 100]. The result is an effective annual interest rate of 37.23 percent [2.04 × (365 ÷ 20)]. The effective annual interest rate is obtained by multiplying the time period interest rate by the number of time periods. Most of us are familiar with this computation because of our use of credit cards, which may state, for example, that the unpaid balance will be charged at an interest rate of 1.5 percent per month, or 18 percent per annum (1.5 × 12 months).

Many times it may be more profitable for our business to borrow money to take advantage of a cash discount. This holds true if borrowing rates are lower than the rate or cost of money forfeited if the discount is not taken. Consider, for example, that the $9,800 can be borrowed by Tom's Appliance Store on day 10 from a bank to take advantage of the cash discount. Assume that a bank is charging a 12 percent annual interest rate. We use 20 days as the time period because $9,800 plus interest in both cases must be paid back after 20 days. Tom's, at the end of 20 days, must pay back the following amount:

$$S = \frac{P}{1 - dt}$$

where

S = amount to be paid back, or maturity value
P = proceeds borrowed from bank at a discount
d = discount rate
t = time period

When we substitute into this formula, we obtain:

$$S = \frac{P}{1 - dt} = \frac{\$9,800}{\left[1 - (0.12)\left(\dfrac{20}{365}\right)\right]} = \$9,864.86$$

So $9,864.86 is the amount due to the bank at the end of 20 days if Tom signs a bank note or uses his line of credit (10 days of discount period plus 20 days remaining until the entire amount is due). If he does not borrow the money, then he must pay the vendor $10,000 at the end of 30 days. Thus, he saves $135.14 ($200 − $64.86) by discounting a note and taking advantage of the cash discount, which adds to working capital. In other words, it costs the firm $64.86 in interest to borrow $9,800 and take advantage of the cash discount. Tom also saves the cost of $200 by paying his creditor $9,800 instead of $10,000. If economic conditions are such that bank lending rates were very high, then the amount saved decreases, because more money must be paid to the bank to use the $9,800 for 20 days.

TABLE 7–5 Quantity Discounts

Item Number	Quantity	Unit Cost
10010	1–99	$15.00
	100–499	14.50
	500–999	14.00

Quantity Discounts

Quantity discounts are offered by vendors to increase their own cash flow when they offer discounts to customers who purchase items in large quantities. Quantity discounts may be one-time discounts or cumulative discounts. A single-quantity discount is offered on a single large purchase order. For example, a manufacturing catalog may offer an item with the listing seen in Table 7–5.

If we choose to purchase any quantity up to 99 units, then we are billed $15 for each unit. An order of 100 to 499 units is billed at $14.50 per unit, and an order of 500 to 999 units is billed at $14 per unit. Often these discounts are not advantageous for our business because if the overall cost of inventory is not reduced by ordering in quantity, then we are just acting as a storage agency for our vendor and are decreasing our cash. In addition, inventory items are subject to becoming obsolete or spoiling if we hold them for too long. If we sell high quantities of the item in a short time, however, then single-quantity discounts provide us with several advantages. These include reducing our total inventory cost and providing us with more throughput and cash flow.

Cumulative Discounts

Cumulative discounts usually are offered on total purchases of an item during the vendor's fiscal year. When cumulative discounts are used, the vendor keeps track of the total quantity purchased during the year and provides the customer with a refund check based on this quantity at the year's end. These discounts are similar to frequent-flyer-club discounts offered by airline companies. If we assume that our company purchases 10 units of item 10010 each month, then each monthly invoice is for $150 (10 × $15). At the end of the year, we will have purchased 120 units (10 units per month × 12 months) of item 10010. Therefore, if the vending company is offering cumulative discounts, it will give us the cumulative discount price of $14.50 (Table 7–5) and provide us with a refund check for $60 (120 × $0.50). Cumulative discounts are given primarily to improve customer loyalty, especially if the majority of a firm's customers are small businesses that cannot take advantage of single-quantity discounts.

CONCLUSION

Proper management of working capital can improve the overall health of our business by increasing current assets and minimizing current liabilities. Several issues are important here. The only item that is definitely a current asset is cash. Accounts receivable can only be turned into cash if the customer pays the bill. Long-term accounts receivable, although carried as current assets, do nothing to increase our cash position and, therefore, should be analyzed carefully. Inventory is the single category of item contained within current assets that is subject to the most criticism by both business owners and the academic profession.

The basic problem is that an accountant and a business owner may look at inventories differently. Inventories are only an asset if they can be turned into cash. If not, they are actually a liability, even though generally accepted accounting principles (GAAP) require that they be listed as a current asset on the balance sheet. For the retail firm, if an item loses popularity, has a short shelf life, or becomes obsolete, then the cost of goods often cannot be recovered, even with a sale. We must therefore conclude that such an item is actually a liability. It often must be disposed of, rather than sold. For the manufacturing firm, the situation can be worse. Raw materials and work-in-process inventories cannot be sold until they are turned into finished goods. Finished goods have no value unless they can be sold. Ideally, the manufacturing firm should not even acquire the raw materials until there is a firm order for the finished goods. Then the raw materials should be turned into finished goods as rapidly as possible for cash. One primary goal of a for-profit firm is to make money now and to make more money in the future. This can only be accomplished when inventory is turned into cash.[2]

Current liabilities management is much more straightforward, because items that are listed as current liabilities are all liabilities. The primary problem for the business owner is in managing accrued liabilities. These items often do not appear on the books as they are accrued, but only afterward. The business owner, therefore, must establish some meaningful method for determining their value and ensuring that the cash is available when a payment is required.

Fixed assets and long-term liabilities are usually accumulated through the process of investing excess cash in items that provide us with more money in the future. The method of determining where to invest this money and how to evaluate the investment prior to making the commitment is the subject of Chapter 10.

---

[2]Eliyahu M. Goldratt and Jeff I. Cox, *The Goal: A Process of Ongoing Improvement,* rev. ed. (Croton-on-Hudson, NY: North River Press, 1986).

REVIEW AND DISCUSSION QUESTIONS

1. Compare *gross working capital* and *net working capital*.
2. For most businesses, what does cash consist of?
3. In current asset management, what is the *float*? How would paying by check allow a business to take advantage of the float?
4. List and describe at least three methods a business can use to speed cash receipt time from its debtors.
5. What role do marketable securities play in current asset management?
6. What methods can be used by small businesses to speed the collection of money that is owed to them?
7. What are the three Cs of credit? How do these serve as a yardstick for credit evaluation?
8. What corrective action can be taken for customers whose outstanding balances do not adhere to our credit terms?
9. What is an ABC analysis with regard to inventory?
10. List and describe three types of inventory.
11. How is a line of credit issued by a bank similar to a credit card?
12. What is the difference between a *line of credit* and a *short-term loan*?
13. If a firm does not provide for accrued liabilities, what problems may the firm face?
14. Compare standard quantity discounts to cumulative quantity discounts.

EXERCISES AND PROBLEMS

1. Joe Fellows is attempting to categorize several items from his company's financial statements so he can determine his working capital. Joe notices the following categories of accounts and amounts: cash, $3,500; accounts payable, $10,200; accounts receivable, $15,000; sales taxes due the city of Phoenix, $750; sales taxes due the Arizona Department of Revenue, $3,450; inventory, $17,500; wages payable, $5,350; taxes payable (federal), $2,570; money market fund, $12,300; and computer, $3,400.
   a. List accounts classified as current assets and as current liabilities.
   b. Determine the amount of gross working capital.
   c. Determine the amount of net working capital.
   d. What is Joe's current ratio?
2. If you have $50,000 in an interest-bearing savings account that pays 5 percent annual interest, how much interest will you earn during a 30-day month?
3. Jane James owns an appliance store. She usually receives $50,000 worth of appliances per month. She does not like to owe people money and always pays her bills on the day she receives the invoice. Someone told her that if she delayed payment, she could actually increase her profit because the

money would be earning interest in her account. She went through her bills and found that she actually had an additional 10 days, on average, to pay her invoices. She also found that she was earning 5 percent interest on the money she had in her money market savings account.

   a. If she delayed payment by the 10 days, how much additional interest would she earn for the year?

   b. Explain how this problem represents a disbursement float.

4. Jane Marks has a restaurant in which she accepts credit cards and checks. Several of the places that Jane shops now accept debit cards and do not accept checks. Jane's banker explained that a debit card would immediately transfer money into her account, but it would cost $50 per month for the equipment and bank charges. Although she requires proper identification, Jane loses approximately $590 a year as a result of bad checks. She also determined that on average, she loses 115 days of interest on all checks because the banks are closed on 11 holidays and weekends (52 weeks × 2 weekend days = 104 + 11 holidays). Jane currently earns 3 percent interest on her bank accounts and accepts an average of $2,000 a day in checks.

   a. What is the total annual cost to Jane for the debit card service?

   b. What is the benefit?

   c. Should Jane implement the system?

5. Larry's Lawn Equipment Company gives terms of 2/10, *n*/30. Larry has annual credit sales of $500,000 and average accounts receivable of $60,000.

   a. What is Larry's accounts receivable turnover?

   b. What is Larry's average daily collection?

   c. What is the relationship between the terms that Larry is giving and his average daily collection?

6. A firm has $400,000 in credit sales and $100,000 in accounts receivable. Compute accounts receivable turnover and average number of collection days. How do these numbers relate to the terms of 2/10, *n*/30?

7. If Larry in exercise 5 has accounts receivable of $100,000 rather than $60,000,

   a. What is Larry's accounts receivable turnover?

   b. What is Larry's average collection period?

   c. What should Larry do, if anything?

8. You are managing a company that stocks and distributes hardware. The company employs two purchasing agents who receive combined salaries of $90,000. They process 6,000 purchase requests per year. Average inventory in storage is $600,000, and the total cost of running the warehouse is $200,000. You are told that the company purchases 5,000 hammers per year at a cost of $5.34 per hammer.

   a. Using the economic order quantity (EOQ) formula, how many hammers should be ordered at one time?

   b. If the hammer vendor stated that it would charge $5.00 per hammer if you ordered 200 or more at a time, what should you do?

9. Calculate the EOQ for exercise 8 if annual demand is 10,000 units, inventory storage costs average 20 percent, unit price is $50, and ordering costs are $30.

10. Harriet has been told about an ABC inventory analysis. She has accumulated the following annual figures for her flower shop: roses, $10,000; ribbon, $100; bud vases, $1,000; pins, $15; glass bowls, $500; ceramic pots, $3,000; wrapping paper, $250; and carnations, $5,500.
    a. Using the percentage of total inventory costs, if these were her total inventory costs, what items should be classified as A items?
    b. What items are C items?

11. Your firm sells home appliances at retail. When ordering washing machines from the manufacturer, you notice the following terms listed in the catalog:

    ♦ List price, $400
    ♦ Trade discounts of 25/15/5

    If you take advantage of all trade discounts, find the net price you will pay for the washing machine.

12. Explain the following terms:
    a. 2/10, n/30
    b. 3/15, n/60
    c. n/40
    d. What is the effective rate of interest you will pay if you do not take advantage of the cash discounts described?

13. Bernie's Bike Shop receives the following trade discounts: 35/25/15. The vendor's price list indicates that 35 percent off list price is for purchasing bikes in quantities of 100 or more, 25 percent off list price is for assembling the bikes for customers, and 15 percent is for sales promotion and local advertising.
    a. If the manufacturer's list price is $470, what should Bernie pay for each bike if he orders 110 bikes at a time, assembles the bikes, and displays and advertises them?
    b. What is Bernie's single equivalent discount rate?
    c. How much will Bernie pay the manufacturer for each bike if he orders 10 bikes at a time and takes advantage of the other discounts?

14. In Exercise 13, Bernie is given terms of 4/15, n/30, and he pays by day 15.
    a. How much will he pay the manufacturer for the order of 110 bikes?
    b. For how much will the manufacturer credit Bernie's account?
    c. If Bernie has a cash flow problem and waits until day 30 to pay the manufacturer, what is his effective cost of financing for the year?

RECOMMENDED TEAM ASSIGNMENT

1. Interview several business owners or managers in the community in different industries. How important is proper inventory management to them with respect to its roll in the business enterprise?
2. Survey several businesses who receive large shipments from their vendors. Do they take advantage of discounts? What are the terms that they receive on their invoices?

CASE STUDY: ASSOCIATED STEEL TRADING, LLC

BACKGROUND

Ian Epstein was born and raised in Chicago and attended Southern Illinois University in Carbondale, Illinois. He graduated *cum laude* in 1973 with a double major in management and public relations and a minor in marketing. Following graduation, Ian went to work for a private scrap steel company that purchased and processed scrap steel from various manufacturing companies in the Hammond, Indiana, area. During his 2-year tenure, Ian learned the basics of the steel business, including purchasing, sales, and processing.

Ian was then hired by Signode Corporation of Glenview, Illinois, to handle all of their scrap. Signode is the world's largest manufacturer of metal and plastic strapping material. While working at Signode, Ian was in charge of getting scrap from all of their plant locations arranged, sorted, and sold at the highest profit margin. After 2 years, Ian was moved into the purchasing department as an assistant steel purchasing agent and within a year was promoted to chief purchasing agent. He purchased coil and sheet stock and various steel stock for the strapping division from major steel mills throughout the world.

In 1979, Ian became the second person in the United Stated to qualify as a certified purchasing manager, having passed all of the certification tests offered by the National Association of Purchasing Managers.

Based on this experience and his new certification, Ian believed he was worth more money and was hired by Quality Steel in Bensonville, Illinois, as the assistant to the Vice President for Purchasing. He worked with Quality Steel for 5 years until he had a major disagreement with one of the owners of the company. The company had committed to purchasing a machine that was designed strictly for American Motors Corporation (AMC). Ian believed this to be a terrible idea, because no contract had been provided nor was a market analysis done. He thought that this move could ultimately bankrupt the corporation. Because of this falling out, he was fired. Subsequently, AMC filed bankruptcy and ceased to produce automobiles; as a result, Quality Steel also went bankrupt.

Ian had constantly discussed the errors of the company with his wife Barbara, and most conversations started with, "If I owned this company, I would . . ." Ian had really spent several years developing a business plan and knew essentially what he wanted to do if he were to have his own business. When he was fired, although he had several job offers, his wife convinced him to start his own steel company. She said that she would get a job working evenings so she could stay with their son during the day and Ian could work out of the basement of their house. At this point, Ian had savings of about $15,000, a mortgage and a 1-year-old son. He formed Associated Steel Sales as a C corporation, purchased a business phone and a fax machine, and began the business out of his home. His original concept was that if he could purchase steel out of a steel mill at a low price and with no overhead or fixed expenses, he could sell the steel to small manufacturing companies in the Chicago area at a price below that of any competitor. Because of his experience in purchasing, Ian knew virtually all of the marketing people at the major steel mills, which typically did not take an order for less that 100 tons (200,000 lbs of steel). Because of this limit, most small manufacturing plants didn't have the volume of sales required to order directly from a steel mill. Sheet steel is used in everything from steel buildings to cars and trucks, appliances, and even that small bracket that is used to hold shelves. Most small manufacturers require only a few thousand pounds of steel and can't order from steel mills.

Knowing this, Ian purchased his first five coils of steel from Inland Steel on credit for $25,000 dollars with 30-day terms. A coil of sheet steel weighs up to 25 tons. Ian had the steel delivered to a public processing warehouse where he could have the coil slit into the widths required from his customers. It took him about a week to sell the five coils of steel to many small manufacturing plants. All of his steel is sold with a term of 2 percent net 10 days. This additional discount speeded his cash flow and he collected for his sales before the steel mill payment was due. This system provided him with sufficient cash flow to pay the steel mill and secure another load.

Ian took any excess profit and re-invested it into the company. He did not take any profit out of the company for more than 2 years. His family lived off savings and the salary that his wife Barbara earned. For the first year, Ian concentrated on this system of purchasing coils from the mills and selling it at a discount to small manufacturing plants. This allowed him to establish large lines of credit with the steel mills, which resulted in an excellent reputation and a big customer base. After 2 years, Ian hired two partners and the business really began to expand. One of the partners had different purchasing experience with other mills and the other partner had more marketing experience than Ian. After a couple of years, the marketing partner and Ian bought out the third partner.

The basic model never changed. Associated Steel Trading purchases from the mills directly at prices and in quantities that small manufacturing companies cannot afford. They bring the steel into a processing facility and process the steel for the customer or sell it on an as-is basis. The only thing that Associated Steel owns is steel; all processing, transportation, and storage is subcontracted. By 1996, with the use of computers and his basic customer base, Ian believed that he no longer had to be located in the Chicago area, and he and his family moved to Scottsdale, Arizona. In 1997, Ian bought out his partner and changed the name of the company from AST Corporation to Associated Steel Trading, LLC. He released all of his Chicago employees and hired an outside steel-marketing representative to market his products. As of 2008, Ian runs the company out of his home and he is his company's only employee. Sales for 2007 were approximately $5.5 million, and with no real fixed expenses, the company has net margins of about 11 percent.

1. How important was Ian's knowledge of the billing procedures used within the steel industry in his being able to establish his business? Given his cash position when he opened his business, could do you believe he would have been successful without this knowledge? How much risk did he take?
2. When providing a product like steel to a customer, how important is experience and knowledge of the industry to business success?

CHAPTER 8

Time Value of Money— Part I: Future and Present Value of Lump Sums

Learning Objectives

When you have completed this chapter, you should be able to:

- ◆ Explain the relationship between time value of money and inflation.
- ◆ Distinguish between *effective rate* and *stated rate.*
- ◆ Calculate the future value lump sum and present value lump sum factors that are used to solve time-value-of-money problems.
- ◆ Compare bank discount and simple interest.
- ◆ Calculate the internal rate of return with respect to present value of a lump sum and future value of a lump sum.
- ◆ Integrate the present value of a lump sum and the future of a lump sum to solve real-life financial problems.
- ◆ Present a spreadsheet of the mathematics of finance.
- ◆ Use financial tables to solve time-value-of-money problems.
- ◆ Use financial calculators to solve time-value-of-money problems.

All businesses must invest in plant and equipment to continue growing and to generate additional revenue now and in the future. The decision to invest is referred to as the *capital budgeting decision*. Chapter 10 is a detailed chapter on the various techniques that we can use in making capital budgeting decisions. Before going into detail about capital budgeting, it is important to understand some basic terms or tools that aid us in our evaluation of a capital budgeting proposal. We begin in this chapter by discussing the time value of money. Any time one has money, there is an opportunity cost that corresponds with the decision as to how one spends the money. The cost of that decision includes the cost of the best forgone opportunity. For example: Joe moviegoer spends $7.00 for a movie ticket. The time and the cost of what he might have enjoyed, had he not gone to the movies, is a foregone opportunity. There is always an opportunity cost involved in making a decision to spend money now or spend money later. This opportunity cost is one way of looking at the time value of money. Mathematically, the **time value of money** is the loss of purchasing power that occurs over time as a result of inflation. **Inflation** is an increase in average prices over time. It takes more future dollars than current dollars to buy the same items because the future dollar is inflated. In other words, a dollar received now can purchase more than a dollar received 5 years from now; and the dollar received 5 years from now is more valuable than the dollar received 40 years from now, ceteris paribus.

If you were a child in 1957, the cost of going to a movie was 25 cents; two hot dogs, French fries, and a beverage at a delicatessen cost 55 cents; and popcorn and a candy bar cost 20 cents. This appears to be a dollar well spent. In 2007, the movie alone costs $7.00. In 2007, we spend $23.75 to purchase the identical items we bought for $1.00 in 1957 (movie $7.00; two hot dogs $6.00; French fries $2.00; beverage $1.75; popcorn $4.00; candy bar $3.00). If the annual inflation rate averages 4 percent over 50 years, the purchasing power of a dollar 50 years from now will be approximately 14 cents. Therefore, the dollar will lose approximately 86 percent of its purchasing power over 50 years. However, if one were to invest that dollar, it would move through time, gain value, and create wealth to fund future goals such as retirement. This is especially true if the money can be invested at a rate that exceeds the inflation rate. For example, a dollar invested today at 6 percent interest over 50 years will have a value of $18.42 at the end of 50 years. In other words, money invested today can be spent for goods and services later. The methods used in the previous scenarios is discussed in this chapter so that we can fully understand the time value of money. Once the time value of money is understood, the entrepreneur can apply these tools in evaluating capital budgeting and several other personal and business financial planning decisions.

We first discuss the concepts of simple interest, bank discount, and compound interest and then distinguish between the three methods of calculation. However, prior to illustrating the mathematics of the time value of money, note that not all items can be measured by using these formulas. Some items, especially those that are produced by means of high technology, actually decrease in price over time as a result of increased productivity; some examples are color television sets, computers, digital watches, cell phones, and DVDs. Other factors that are not considered in mathematical calculations are opportunity costs, which are discussed in Chapter 1. This does not negate the fact that mathematical calculations are absolutely necessary when we are making business and personal plans. Therefore, we should use time-value-of-money calculations when making many business decisions.

SIMPLE INTEREST

Simple interest is the amount of interest earned on a principal amount stated. The **principal amount stated** is the base amount that we borrow or save. Simple interest is primarily used in short-term (less than 1 year) transactions and is computed initially based on original principal amount, interest rate, and time span. It is added to the principal to determine the total amount owed or due.

If \$1,000 is borrowed at 8 percent for 1 year, then simple interest is \$80. This is computed as follows:

$$I = Prt$$

where

I = interest
P = principal
r = rate
t = time
$I = (\$1,000)(0.08)(1) = \$80$

Because the interest is \$80, the amount owed at the end of 1 year is \$1,080. If \$1,000 is borrowed for one-half year at 8 percent, then simple interest (I) equals \$40. This is computed as follows:

$$I = (\$1,000)(0.08)(0.5) = \$40$$

Because the interest is \$40, then the amount owed at the end of 6 months is \$1,040.

Simple interest added to \$1,000 borrowed for 9 months at 8 percent is:

$$I = Prt$$
$$= (\$1,000)(0.08)\left(\frac{9}{12}\right) = \$60$$
$$S = P + I$$
$$= \$1,000 + \$60 = \$1,060$$

where S is the total amount due (*maturity amount*). Thus, $1,060 must be paid back at the end of 9 months. Or, if we place $1,000 in an account earning 8 percent, then we expect to have $1,060 in our account at the end of 9 months.

Notice that the formula for simple interest is a basic formula that can be manipulated to find any of the components. If we know any three of the four values in the formula, we should be able to calculate the missing factor. For example, consider the previous data. If we know that the interest amount is $60 and the rate and time are 8 percent and 9 months, respectively, then we can find the amount of the principal by the following method:

$$I = Prt$$

$$\$60 = P(0.08)\left(\frac{9}{12}\right)$$

$$P = \frac{\$60}{(0.08)(0.75)} = \$1,000$$

Another example occurs when your vendor is owed $1,000 and is scheduled to receive $1,060 on a promissory note that you signed at a simple interest rate of 8 percent. You wish to determine how long it will take to pay off your vendor. First, you must calculate the interest of $60 by subtracting $1,000 from the $1,060 you promised to pay the vendor. Thus, the following calculations can be applied:

$$I = Prt$$

$$\$60 = (\$1,000)(0.08)(t)$$

$$t = \frac{\$60}{(\$1,000)(0.08)} = \frac{\$60}{\$80} = 0.75, \text{ or } 9 \text{ months}$$

Therefore, it will take 0.75 years, or 9 months, to pay your vendor $1,060 at an 8 percent interest rate, based on a principal of $1,000. Note that simple interest is calculated up front and is immediately added to the principal to determine the amount owed.

Simple interest can also be used as a method of calculating monthly interest on a fixed principal, declining balance loan that is tied to the prime lending rate or some other lending rate or index. The *prime rate* is the rate the banks charge their very best customers.

FIXED PRINCIPAL COMMERCIAL LOANS

Many commercial loans are made using a fixed principal payment that remains constant for the life of the loan. The loan can be either a fixed interest loan or a variable interest loan tied to prime or some other federal rate (Table 8–1). Usually, commercial loans are quoted at prime plus some percentage based on the risk of the business enterprise, and these rates can vary from prime plus 1.75 percent

TABLE 8–1 Lending Rates

FOMC Release Date	Federal Funds	Discount Rate	Prime Rate
10/31/2007	4.50	5.00	7.50
12/11/2007	4.25	4.75	7.25
1/21/2008	3.50	4.00	6.50
1/30/2008	3.00	3.50	6.00
3/18/2008	2.25	2.50	5.50

Federal Open Market Committee Statements & Minutes. Retrieved February 27, 2008 from http://www.federalreserve.gov/monetarypolicy/fomc.htm.

to as much as prime plus 9.75 percent.[1] Remember that Small Business Administration (SBA) loans have limits of prime plus 2.25 percent to prime plus 4.75 percent, so it pays to shop for loans and interest rates. If the loan is a variable rate rather than a fixed rate loan, the interest amount of the loan is adjusted any time the prime lending rate changes. The Federal Open Market Committee meets on a regular basis and determines the Federal Funds Rate. Usually, the Federal Reserve Board of Governors also changes the Discount Rate in conjunction with changes in the Fed Funds rate. The changes in the federal rates affect the interest rates that banks pay for borrowing funds. When rates change for banks, then the prime lending rate (prime) changes, and this change in rate is transferred to the consumer. The prime lending rate tracks these changes as shown in Table 8–1. Let's look at each type of loan.

For example, if Andre Prenneur wants to open a French restaurant and needs $150,000 worth of equipment, he may get a fixed principal, fixed interest loan, which works like this: Andre will probably be required to put 20 percent down, or $30,000, which gives him a loan balance of $120,000. If the loan is for 5 years, then the principal balance (outstanding balance) is divided by 60 months, which results in a monthly principal payment of $2,000. The $2,000 part of the payment remains constant. Because this loan is for a fixed interest, the bank calculates an amortization table and gives Andre a payment book. We include the first 12 months of the amortization table to show how this loan works (Table 8–2). The amount paid the first month involves finding the dollar amount of interest and adding it onto the fixed payment. The monthly payment reduces the loan balance by $2,000 from $120,000 to $118,000. The bank calculates the monthly simple interest by multiplying the outstanding loan balance of $120,000 by the annual interest rate of 9.5 percent to obtain annual interest of $11,400. They then divide the total dollar amount of annual interest by 12 to

---

[1]Prime plus rates obtained from personal communication, Wells Fargo Bank Commercial Credit, on February 27, 2008.

TABLE 8–2 Andre's Loan Schedule

Principal Amount of loan = $120,000.00
Annual Interest Rate = 9.50%
Number of Years = 5
Number of Monthly Payments = 60
Monthly Principal Payment = $ 2,000.00
Total Interest Paid = $ 28,975.00

Payment Number	Amount Paid	Monthly Interest	Loan Balance
1	$2,950.00	$950.00	$118,000.00
2	2,934.17	934.17	116,000.00
3	2,918.33	918.33	114,000.00
4	2,902.50	902.50	112,000.00
5	2,886.67	886.67	110,000.00
6	2,870.83	870.83	108,000.00
7	2,855.00	855.00	106,000.00
8	2,839.17	839.17	104,000.00
9	2,823.33	823.33	102,000.00
10	2,807.50	807.50	100,000.00
11	2,791.67	791.67	98,000.00
12	2,775.83	775.83	96,000.00

get the monthly interest of $950.00. Month 1's loan payment is therefore $2,000 principal plus $950.00 interest for a total payment of $2,950.00.

For month 2, the bank uses a principal balance of $118,000 times 9.5 percent and obtains an annual interest of $11,210. This amount is divided by 12 for a monthly interest of $934.17. The loan payment for month 2 is therefore $2,000 principal plus interst of $934.17 for a total payment of $2,934.17. The primary advantage of this type of loan is that the borrower pays the least amount of interest over the life of the loan. The main reason for this is that the outstanding balance due is reduced by a $2,000 fixed payment each month. As a result, the monthly interest paid declines very rapidly. A disadvantage is that the initial monthly payments are quite high.

Rather than a fixed principal, fixed interest loan, the lender may also offer a fixed principal variable interest loan. If Andre takes this type of loan, then interest is calculated on a daily basis based on the outstanding balance at the time. Let's return to our example and use the prime lending rates shown in Table 8–1. Andre receives a loan in 2007 with the first payment due December 1, 2007, at an annual rate of prime plus 2 percent. Andre's initial interest rate of prime plus 2 percent is 9.5 percent when using Table 8–1. On December 1, 2007, he makes a principal payment of $2,000 plus interest of $583.33, which is based on an outstanding balance of $120,000 that he initially borrows. The interest part of the payment varies based on the interest rate in effect at the time. Overall, if interest rates increase as a result of changes in the prime, then Andre's monthly payment increases; conversely, if interest rates decrease as a result of changes in the prime, then the monthly payment decreases.

Now let's look at Andre's payment schedule based on the use of Table 8–1. Andre receives an invoice from the bank each month. On December 1, 2007, the invoice is for a principal payment of $2,000 and an interest payment of $936.99. The interest payment is calculated as $(0.095 \div 365) \times 30$ days for November $\times$ $120,000 = $936.99, for a total payment of $2,936.99. On January 1, 2008, the invoice is for a principal payment of $2,000 plus an interest payment of $935.11, which equals $2,935.11. This is calculated as follows: 10 days of interest on $118,000 at 9.5 percent and 21 days of interest on $118,000 at 9.25 percent because the prime lending rate dropped from 7.5 percent to 7.25 percent on December 11. Ten days of interest is calculated as $(0.095 \div 365) \times 10 \times $118,000 = 307.12, and 21 days of interest is calculated as $(0.0925 \div 365) \times 21 \times $118,000 = 627.99$. Total monthly interest is therefore $307.12 plus 627.99, which equals $935.11.

We realize, of course, that economic circumstances may dictate that the Fed raises the Federal Funds Rate and the Discount Rate in order to curtail inflation. If the Fed had raised the discount rate on December 11 to 5.5 percent rather than decrease it to 4.75 percent, then Prime would have increased to 8 percent and Andre's interest rate would have increased to 10 percent. Andre's payment then would have been $2,000 plus interest of $986.03. So, 10 days of interest is calculated as $(0.095 \div 365) \times 10 \times $118,000 = 307.12 and 21 days of interest is calculated as $(0.10 \div 365) \times 21 \times $118,000 = 678.90. Total monthly interest is therefore $307.12 plus $678.90, which equals $986.06. Notice that an increase of only three-quarters of 1 percent, or 75 basis points, results in an increased payment for 21 days of $49.95. As an entrepreneur, you should understand how interest rates on commercial loans work and how they may affect your business on a day-to-day basis. You don't want a lack of cash flow to eat up your profitability.

BRIDGE LOANS

Another example of a simple interest loan is a **bridge loan,** which is a loan that a homeowner or businessowner obtains when he or she wants to move up to a more expensive property, but has not sold the current home or business. There may be a gap in the time between the sale of the current property and the purchase of another property. The lender determines that the new owner will have sufficient cash for a down payment on the new property when the old property sells. The new owner simultaneously owns two properties until the old property is sold. In order to qualify for a bridge loan, the owner must have suffient income to make two mortgage payments.

Consider the following example: The Mayberry family currently owns a two-bedroom house that has been appraised for $200,000 and has a remaining mortgage of $125,000. They are expecting their third child and want to move into a four-bedroom house that is currently selling for $300,000. If they sell their current house, they will payoff their $125,000 dollar mortgage and walk away with equity of $75,000, less sales commissions and closing costs. Right now, they don't have the cash to make the down payment on the $300,000 home. They will have the cash once they sell their current residence. In order to fill this gap in time, they apply for a bridge loan to make the down payment on the new house.

The bridge loan uses simple interest and may be in existence for several months until the old property is sold. For example, the Mayberrys purchase the $300,000 property where the lender requires a 10 percent down payment plus closing costs. They must borrow a $30,000 down payment plus an additional $5,000 in order to cover the following items: Loan orgination fee, administration, escrow, title, recording, appaisal, notary and other fees that the lender may require. Hence, the bridge loan is $35,000. Let's assume the annual interest rate on the bridge loan is 9 percent and the closing date on the new house is April 1.

Interest on the bridge loan is calculated as follows. The lender takes $35,000 borrowed times annual interest of 9 percent to obtain annual interest of $3,150. We divide this by 12 to obtain a monthy interest of $252.50. We then divide the monthly interest by 30 to obtain a daily dollar amount of interest of $8.75. The Mayberry family finally sells their old house and reallocates their equity payment on July 15. The lender than calculates 106 days of interest due by adding the following: 30 days for April, 31 days for May, 30 days for June, and 15 days from July 1 through July 15. Then 106 days times the $8.75 of interest per day equals $927.50 total interest due on the loan. The Mayberrys are then required to pay $35,927.50, which is the $35,000 principal plus the $927.50 interest on the bridge loan. So, on July 15, the Mayberry family owns a single home with one mortgage payment.

 # BANK DISCOUNT

The *bank discount* is an amount of interest deducted from the amount you wish to borrow and is calculated by multiplying the amount you wish to borrow times the bank discount rate and the amount of time the loan is in effect. This is computed as follows:

$$D = Sdt$$

where

D = bank discount
S = maturity value of loan
d = discount rate
t = time

If we borrow $1,000 for 1 year at 8 percent, then bank discount (D) is equal to $80. This amount is deducted from the $1,000 that you wish to borrow. You receive proceeds of $920.

$$D = Sdt$$
$$= (\$1,000)(0.08)(1) = \$80$$
$$\text{Proceeds} = S - D$$
$$= \$1,000 - \$80 = \$920$$

The amount paid back to the bank 1 year later is $1,000 ($S$). This amount is the *maturity value* of the loan. The problem is that proceeds of $1,000—not $920—are what we need. The bank discount costs us $80 for the use of $920, not for the use of $1,000. Thus, the actual interest rate (effective rate) is based on the amount of proceeds we receive and the dollar cost for those proceeds. Therefore, the cost of the bank discount is higher than the cost of simple interest. We use the following formula, which allows us to calculate the amount that we must borrow:

$$\text{Amount borrowed} = \frac{\text{Proceeds}}{1 - dt} = \frac{\$1,000}{1 - (0.08)(1)}$$
$$= \frac{\$1,000}{0.92} = \$1,086.96$$

Notice that the stated rate of interest by the bank is 8 percent. However, if we must borrow $1,086.96 to have the use of $1,000 proceeds, interest of $86.96 is calculated on the $1,086.96 that we borrow, which is the cost of the $1,000 proceeds. The result is an effective annual interest rate of not 8 percent as stated by the bank, but 0.0870, or 8.70 percent. The **effective annual interest rate** is the actual interest rate paid, taking into account the cost of the money borrowed and the actual amount of the money used. The effective rate is

$$\text{Effective annual interst rate} = \left[\frac{\text{Interest rate}}{(\text{Proceeds})(t)}\right] \times 100$$
$$= \left[\frac{\$86.96}{(\$1,000)(1)}\right] \times 100 = 0.08696 \times 100 = 8.70\%$$

It is important to note that 0.0869 is 8 percent plus 69 (or 70, because of rounding) hundredths of a percent. Each hundredth of a percent is a *basis point;* 8.70 is 8 percent plus 70 basis points. Thus, for every $100 that we borrow using bank discount, we are not actually paying 8 percent, or $8 interest on every $100 used, but $8.70. As previously pointed out, the stated rate (8 percent) is the rate that the lender quotes (other names for stated rate are *nominal rate* or *quoted rate*). However, the actual rate paid (8.7 percent) is called the *effective rate.*

Entrepreneurs often need money for short periods of time, typically less than 1 year. Several bills must be paid on a quarterly or semiannual basis (e.g., taxes, insurance, vendor deliveries). When revenues are significantly less than expenditures, borrowing money for a short time may be required. For example, you need $2,000 of proceeds for a period of 90 days, and the going bank discount rate is 8 percent. The amount to be borrowed can be calculated as follows:

$$\text{Amount borrowed} = \frac{\text{Proceeds}}{1 - dt} = \frac{\$2,000}{1 - (0.08)\left(\dfrac{90}{365}\right)}$$

$$= \frac{\$2,000}{1 - 0.0197} = \frac{\$2,000}{0.9803} = \$2,040.25$$

Using our formula for effective annual interest rate, we see that the $40.25 paid on borrowed funds of $2,040.25 for the use of $2,000 for 90 days is an effective annual rate of 8.16 percent.

$$\text{Effective annual interest rate} = \left[\frac{\text{Interest paid}}{(\text{Proceeds})(t)}\right] \times 100$$

$$= \left[\frac{\$40.25}{(\$2,000)\left(\dfrac{90}{365}\right)}\right] \times 100 = 0.0816 \times 100 = 8.16\%$$

Notice that you can cross-multiply to check the math because the interest paid ($40.25) is the product of the amount of money you are using ($2,000), multiplied by the effective rate (8.16 percent), multiplied by the time (90 ÷ 365).

Federal Treasury Bills

In certain situations, the entrepreneur can actually perform the function of a bank. Businesses oftentimes have excess cash that they want to invest and collect interest on for a short period of time. The businesses need both safety of principal and ease of liquidity. What better source of investing than to lend the U.S. government money for a short time? The government is the borrower and the business is the lender. The government issues Treasury bills (T-bills) in denominations of $10,000 for 3 months, 6 months, and 1 year. Consider a 3-month (13 week) T-bill. As a business owner, you can send a check for $10,000 directly to the Federal Reserve Bank, which then calculates the bank discount to be paid on borrowing $10,000 for 3 months, or 91 days. They then send you a check for this amount of bank discount and borrow the remaining proceeds. For example, if the discount rate on 3-month T-bills is 1.905 percent, then a check for $47.49 of bank discount is sent to you. The government uses the remaining proceeds of $9,952.51. At the end of 3 months, they return your entire $10,000.

The Treasury auction of 91-day T-bills as of August, 14, 2008, used an interest rate of 1.905 percent.[2] This can be exemplified by the following:

$$D = Sdt = (\$10{,}000)(0.01905)\left(\frac{91}{365}\right) = \$47.49$$

$$\text{Proceeds} = S - D = \$10{,}000 - \$47.49 = \$9{,}952.51$$

Thus the government has the use of $9,952.51 (proceeds) for 91 days and pays interest of $47.49. This results in an effective rate of

$$\text{Effective annual interest rate} = \left[\frac{\text{Interest Paid}}{(\text{Proceeds}) \ (t)}\right] \times 100$$

$$= \left[\frac{\$47.49}{(\$9{,}952.51)\left(\dfrac{91}{365}\right)}\right] \times 100 = 1.91 \text{ percent}$$

Uses of Simple Interest and Bank Discount

As we have seen, entrepreneurs borrow and lend capital to others. For example, your friend needs $10,000 immediately as a down payment on a house. You decide to become a lender. Both of you agree that 6 percent would be a fair interest rate for 180 days. His current house is on the real estate market and he is sure it will sell within the 180 days, after which he will repay you. Your friend signs a note that is based on simple interest.

$$I = Prt = (\$10{,}000)(0.06)\left(\frac{180}{365}\right) = \$295.89$$

$$S = P + I = \$10{,}000 + \$295.89 = \$10{,}295.89$$

Your friend agrees to repay you $10,295.89 in 180 days for the use of $10,000 now. He is the payer and you are the payee. In 60 days, you find that you need cash to take advantage of a cash discount on equipment that you are buying for your business. You go to a bank and ask if it will buy the note from you. The bank says it will be happy to discount the note at 8.25 percent (prime rate of 4.75 percent plus 3.5 percent). The bank multiplies the maturity value of the note ($10,295.89) by 8.25 percent interest for the 120 days remaining (120 days remaining ÷ 365 days per year) and calculates the bank discount in dollars ($279.26). The bank subtracts the $279.26 from the maturity value ($10,295.89) of the note and gives you proceeds of $10,016.63, as shown:

$$D = Sdt = (\$10{,}295.89)(0.0825)\left(\frac{120}{365}\right) = \$279.26$$

$$\text{Proceeds} = S - D = \$10{,}295.89 - \$279.26 = \$10{,}016.63$$

---

[2]Treasury Direct, Recent Bill Auction Results. Retrieved August 15, 2008, from http://www.treasurydirect.gov/RI/OFBills.

Notice that the payee still made some money in discounting the note; however, he only made $16.63. If he did not need the money after 60 days and could wait until day 150, then the note would only have 30 days left until maturity. He would then receive $10,226.08 of proceeds and would have made $226.08 in interest while relinquishing $69.81 to the bank for discounting the note 30 days before the maturity date.

$$D = Sdt = (\$10,295.89)(0.0825)\left(\frac{30}{365}\right) = \$69.81$$

Proceeds $= S - D = \$10,295.89 - \$69.81 = \$10,226.08$

Of course, we realize that many loans are for long periods of time, and many of us have savings accounts, retirement accounts, and investments on which we expect to earn interest for several years. For these areas we typically use compound interest.

 COMPOUND INTEREST

Compound interest is the interest earned or charged on both the principal amount and the accrued interest that has been previously earned or charged. If $1,000 is saved for 3 years and is compounded yearly, or annually, at 4 percent, then the following interest amounts are computed for each of the individual years, using the formula $I = Prt$.

Interest for year 1 $= (\$1,000)(0.04)(1) = \$40$

Because our bank balance after the first year is equal to the principal of $1,000 plus the interest earned of $40, when computing our interest for the next year, we begin with a new principal amount of $1,040.

Interest for year 2 $= (\$1,040)(0.04)(1) = \$41.60$

Our bank balance at the end of year 2 is $1,040 plus the interest of $41.60 earned in year 2. We begin computing interest for year 3 with a new principal amount of $1,081.60 ($1,040 + $41.60).

Interest for year 3 $= (\$1,081.60)(0.04)(1) = \$43.26$

Over the course of 3 years, $124.86 of interest ($40 year 1 + $41.60 year 2 + $43.26 year 3) has been earned through compounding. This is a higher amount than the $120 earned through simple interest; or, stated another way, $4.86 more is earned if interest is earned on both principal and interest as a result of compounding, rather than on principal alone.

Although the simple interest formula can be used to determine compound interest, as we have shown, imagine the complexity of computing interest on a long-term investment in this way. For example, if you received an inheritance of $1 million and chose to take the cash and invest it in a money market account earning 4 percent interest compounded annually for 20 years, what would the value of your account be in 20 years? Using the following compound interest formula, we arrive at an answer of $2,191,123. As you can see, it would be quite tedious to run the simple interest formula 20 times.

We can bypass the multiple individual steps in computing compound interest by using the following compound interest formula to determine future value:

$$FV = PV(FVF)$$

where

$FV =$ future value
$PV =$ present value, or current principal amount
$i =$ interest rate earned per period of compounding
$n =$ number of compounding periods that the money will be invested
$FVF = (1 + i)^n$, future value factor

Once the future value factor is found, all that must be done is multiply the principal amount (PV) by the future value factor (FVF) to obtain the future value amount (FV). Thus, using the previous example of saving $1,000 for 3 years at 4 percent compounded yearly, we observe the following:

$$FV = PV(FVF) = \$1,000(1 + 0.04)^3 = \$1,000(1.1249) = \$1,124.86$$

ROUNDING ERRORS

Note that the future value of $1,124.86 is found by setting our calculator to display four decimal places in the future value factor. The calculator displayed 1.1249 after calculating the future value factor. However, there were other numbers not displayed that are being used by the calculator to calculate future value. The actual number in the calculator is 1.124864, but it is displayed as 1.1249 because we set the calculator to four decimal places. Appendix B of this textbook contains time-value-of-money tables that are also rounded to four decimal places. Using Table B–1 to find the future value of a lump sum at 4 percent interest compounded over 3 periods, we notice that the future value factor is 1.1249. If you use the table rather than a calculator or a computer spreadsheet, the answer varies by 4 cents ($1,124.86 vs. $1,124.90), which is immaterial when using a small amount of PV.

Note that this answer is exactly the same as that obtained using the simple interest formula. By using the compound interest formula, we eliminated the previous tedious steps of calculating interest for each year's principal amount and adding all resulting interest amounts. This formula allows us (especially now that many of us own home computers or calculators that include power functions) to easily calculate future values of virtually any investment.

Many of us buy lottery tickets. If you were to win a $1 million lottery, several states allow you to choose from two options: (1) Take the cash at a discounted rate of 50 percent and immediately pay taxes on this amount, or (2) take an annuity payable at $50,000 per year for 20 years. An annuity is a stream of equal payments made for *n* period of time at an *i* rate of return. If you take the cash, you receive a check for $300,000 ($500,000 minus taxes of about 40 percent, counting federal and local taxes). If you invest this money in a stock mutual fund that historically has averaged 10 percent return, how much money can you expect to have in your account at the end of 20 years? Using our formula, we find that you will have $2,018,250 in your account at the end of 20 years.

$$FV = PV(1 + i)^n = \$300,000(1 + 0.10)^{20}$$
$$= \$300,000(6.7275) = \$2,018,250$$

We can obtain the same information by using the tables in Appendix B. To use Appendix Table B–1, we must know two items: the interest rate per period of the investment and the number of periods. Going to Appendix Table B–1, "Future Value of a Lump Sum," we look for the *FVF* by going across to the 10 percent column and surfing down to the 20-period row. We find that the *FVF* is 6.7275. We then multiply the *FVF* by our present value of $300,000 to find that we will have $2,018,250 in 20 years. Notice that we obtain the same answer by either method.

 EFFECTIVE RATE

Interest rates take on two dimensions: (1) the rate that is stated or quoted by the lending institution and (2) the actual, or effective, rate that is earned or charged. The **stated** or **quoted rate** is the rate of interest that is listed, usually on an annual basis, and it disregards compounding. The **effective annual rate** is the actual rate paid by the borrower or earned by the investor when compounding is taken into consideration. For example, if you borrow money for a new car and the bank quotes a rate of 8 percent, then you may be under the impression that you will be paying back $8 a year in interest for every $100 you borrow. However, if the bank compounds the loan monthly, it will actually cost you more than 8 percent. Because the rate per period is 0.67 percent and there are 12 periods in a year, the effective rate can be calculated by using the following formula:

Effective annual rate $= (1 + i)^n - 1$

where

i = interest rate per period (found by dividing the quoted rate by the number of compounding periods)

n = number of compounding periods per year

Using our formula, 8 percent compounded monthly for 1 year gives an effective annual rate of 8.30 percent. The solution is calculated as follows:

$$\text{Effective annual rate} = (1 + i)^n - 1 = \left(1 + \frac{0.08}{12}\right)^{12} - 1$$

$$= (1 + 0.0067)^{12} - 1 = 1.0830 - 1$$

$$= 0.0830, \text{ or } 8.30\%$$

Therefore, if you borrow $10,000 to purchase a car and the stated rate is 8 percent, you might think that the annual interest would be $800, but because the effective rate is 8.30 percent, you would actually pay $8.30 for every $100 borrowed or $830 in annual interest on $10,000 borrowed.

In reality, however, banks now charge daily interest on many business loans and credit card balances; therefore, the effective rate of interest is actually higher than 8.30 percent. Because banks now use a 365-day year, the effective annual rate of interest on an 8 percent loan is 8.33 percent. The solution is calculated as follows:

$$\text{Effective annual rate} = (1 + i)^n - 1 = \left(1 + \frac{0.08}{365}\right)^{365} - 1$$

$$= (1.0002)^{365} - 1 = 1.0833 - 1 = 0.0833, \text{ or } 8.33\%$$

The interest rate is usually the stated, or quoted rate; the effective rate is the interest rate adjusted for compounding and is what should be used to determine the worth of funds that are to be received in the future or an actual payment that will be made.

TIME-VALUE-OF-MONEY METHODS

Now that we have a general understanding of the concept of the time value of money, we want to expand our knowledge to include the basic tools used by businesses in capital budgeting and financial planning. There are six time-value-of-money formulas that can be used in making capital budgeting and other business decisions. They can be used separately or in conjunction with one another. The actual formulas are discussed in this chapter and Chapter 9. Tables that can be used in lieu of the formulas are included in Appendix B at the end of the text. Each method is described here, as is with the basic question that it answers. All formulas have a basis of total *amount* equals *investment* (made or received) times the *factor*. To use any of the formulas, we must know two of these three items.

FUTURE VALUE OF A LUMP SUM

What is the future value of a lump sum amount for *n* periods at *i* rate of return? Some practical examples of using this formula occur as follows:

a. You receive a lump-sum inheritance and plan on investing the money at a specific interest rate for a set number of periods. You want to know what this investment will be worth in the future.

b. You sell a piece of business equipment or a piece of property and receive a lump sum of cash that you plan to invest at a specific interest rate for a set number of periods. You want to know what this investment will be worth in the future.

c. You wish to determine how much you would have to pay for a ticket to a Jonas Brothers concert 10 years from now if inflation averages 6 percent per year.

d. You have a 10-year-old daughter who may get married in 10 years. You just had a niece who was married and it cost your brother $20,000 for the wedding. How much must you set aside now to pay for your daugther's wedding in 10 years?

e. You have a newborn child who receives a cash gift that you want to invest for his or her future education. How much will the child have in 18 years?

The future value of a lump sum formula is

$$FV = PV(FVF)$$

where

FV = future value
PV = present value
$\quad i$ = interest rate per period
$\quad n$ = number of compounding periods per year times the number of years

FVF (future value factor) $= (1 + i)^n$

Your Uncle Louey gives you $10,000. You save the $10,000 at a 5 percent interest rate for 10 years compounded annually. What is the future value of this investment after 10 years? The answer is $16,289.00, calculated as follows:

$$FV = PV(FVF) = \$10,000(1 + i)^n$$
$$= \$10,000(1.05)^{10} = \$10,000(1.6289)$$
$$= \$16,289$$

Notice we can use a calculator or Appendix B, Table B–1 to confirm our answer. We go across to a 5 percent interest rate and then down to an n of 10 and obtain an *FVF* of 1.6289.

A company sells a piece of equipment for $10,000. It deposits the amount received for 5 years at 4 percent compounded quarterly. What dollar amount (future value) will the company have if it does not use the money for 5 years? The company will have approximately $12,201.90 in the bank at the end of 5 years. This is calculated as follows:

$$FV = PV(FVF) = \$10,000 \left(1 + \frac{0.04}{4}\right)^{(4 \times 5)} = \$10,000(1.01)^{20}$$
$$= \$10,000(1.2202) = \$12,202$$

Using our calculator, we take 1.01 [1 + (0.04 ÷ 4)] and raise it to the 20th power (5 years × 4 quarterly periods per year) and obtain a multiplier of 1.2202. We then multiply our present value of $10,000 by this factor to obtain $12,201.90. We also could use Appendix B, Table B–1. Going to the 1 percent column and down to 20 periods, we find a multiplier of 1.2202. When we multiply this factor, we get a dollar value of $12,202. The 10-cent difference between the calculator and the table is the result of rounding. Although the table is not as accurate as the calculator, it is easier for many people to use and provides approximately the same results. If we rely only on the use of tables, we limit our problem-solving ability because tables cannot represent all interest rates and time periods based on compounding. For example, the current certificate of deposit (CD) rate at one bank for a 1-year CD is 2.38 percent compounded monthly, and at another bank it is 2.38 percent compounded quarterly. Tables do not reflect these rates. We include tables in this text for the reader to reinforce the fact that they can solve the problems presented here with a calculator or the use of a spreadsheet. Most interest rates in the marketplace are not given in whole percentages.

A wedding costs $20,000 today; how much will the wedding cost 10 years from now if inflation averages 4 percent per year?

$$FV = PV(FVF) = \$20,000(1 + 0.04)^{(10)} = \$20,000(1.01)^{10}$$
$$= \$20,000(1.4802) = \$29,604$$

What is the cost of the same wedding if the inflation rate is 6.46 percent a year?

$$FV = PV(FVF) = \$20,000(1 + 0.0646)^{(10)} = \$20,000(1.0646)^{20}$$
$$= \$20,000(1.8701) = \$37,404$$

As you can see, the table can be used for the first wedding problem, but not for the second, because the interest rate cannot be looked up in the table.

Grandfather Joe deposits $100,000 in a bank account that starts compounding monthly at an annual rate of 6 percent when grandson Vinny is born. Joe wants to leave the money in a college account for 18 years so Vinny can go to an Ivy League university. How much money will Vinny have available for college at age 18?

$$FV = PV(FVF) = \$100,000 \left(1 + \frac{0.06}{12}\right)^{(12 \times 18)} = \$100,000(1.005)^{216}$$

$$= \$100,000(2.9368) = \$293,676.60$$

The $293,676.60 is the future value that you obtain with a calculator or spreadsheet, because these tools store numbers far beyond four decimal places. We can see that this investment provides interest of $193,676.60, because interest earned is nothing more than using the following formula to subtract what was invested from the future value amount:

$$\text{Interest earned} = FV - PV$$
$$= \$293,676.60 - \$100,000 = \$193,676.60$$

PRESENT VALUE OF A FUTURE LUMP SUM

What is the present value of a future lump-sum amount for n periods at i rate of return? This formula would be used in these situations:

a. You want to calculate the present value of a future balloon payment on a house so you know how much to deposit today to have the money available when the balloon payment is due.

b. You plan on selling a piece of equipment in the future and want to find out what it's worth now.

c. You want to find the present value of a future amount of a dollar, given a set inflation rate.

d. You want to calculate the present value of the maturity value of a bond. (The maturity value of all corporate bonds is $1,000.)

The present value of a lump-sum formula is

$$PV = FV(PVF)$$

where

PV = present value
FV = future value
i = interest rate per period
n = number of compounding periods per year × the number of years

$$PVF \text{ (present value factor)} = \left(\frac{1}{(1 + i)^n} \right)$$

An athlete signs a guaranteed contract with a local sports team that pays him a player's bonus of $10 million in 7 years. How much should the team deposit now if they want to have the $10 million available 7 years from now? They can earn 6 percent compounded annually.

$$PV = FV(PVF)$$

$$= \$10,000,000 \left[\frac{1}{(1 + 0.06)^7} \right] = \$10,000,000 \left(\frac{1}{1.5036} \right)$$

$$= \$10,000,000 \ (0.6651) = \$6,650,571.14$$

The sports team should deposit the $6,650,571.14 (present value) into an account now and make no deposits or withdrawls. The $6,650,571.14 accrues interest and results in $10,000,000 so they can pay the athlete in 7 years. In other words, $6,650,571.14 is the present value of the $10 million 7 years from now at 6 percent annual interest. The authors used a calculator to solve this problem. It can be solved by using Appendix B Table B–2, the Present Value of a Lump Sum. We go across the row to 6 percent and down to 7 years to find a PVF of 0.6651. When we multiply $10 million by 0.6651, the result is a present value of $6,651,000. The difference is the result of rounding, because the calculator displays four digits. The other digits in the calculator (57114), are hidden, but appear in the final calculation as $6,651,571.14. The table has four digits displayed, which is a rounding number (0.6651). Note that the PVF is simply 1 divided by FVF. Therefore, the FVF is always equal to or greater than 1, and the PVF is always equal to or less than 1.

This same sports team lures away Dutch Downe, a high-scoring running-back, and offers him a $20-million contract over 5 years with a $4-million signing bonus. The contract consists of $2 million for year 1, $3 million for year 2, $3 million for year 3, $3 million for year 4, and $5 million for year 5. What is the present value of this $20 million contract if money can earn 5 percent annual interest?

This is a present value problem that consists of finding the present value of a stream of uneven payments, not an annuity problem. Therefore, we must construct a present value table that allows us to determine the present value for each

TABLE 8–3 Present Value of a Contract

	Annual Interest = 6.00%		
Year	Present Value	PV Factor	Future Value
0	$ 4,000,000.00	1.0000	$ 4,000,000
1	1,886,792.45	0.9434	2,000,000
2	2,669,989.32	0.8900	3,000,000
3	2,518,857.85	0.8396	3,000,000
4	2,376,280.99	0.7921	3,000,000
5	3,736,290.86	0.7473	5,000,000
Totals	$17,188,211.48		$ 20,000,000
		Total interest earned =	$2,811,788.52

year of the contract. Subsequently, by adding up each year's present value, we obtain the total present value of the contract. Table 8–3 was constructed using Microsoft Excel.

The contract is spread over 5 years and each year has a time value of money. For example, the present value of the $4-million signing bonus is worth $4 million, because there is no time period—the money is being given or received now, which is the present. However, the present value of the $3 million received at the end of year 2 is worth more now than the present value of the $3 million received at the end of year 3. If the sports team deposits $17,188,211.48 into an account today, at 6 percent annual interest they will be able to make all payments on the $20-million contract to Dutch Downe because they will earn interest of $2,811,788.52 spread over 5 years.

The mechanism of this works out as follows: Dutch Downe receives a $4 million signing bonus in the beginning of year 1, which leaves the team with a $13,188,211.48 balance ($17,188,211.48 − $4,000,000) that earns interest during year 1 and increases to $13,979,504.17. The team pays out $2 million and is left with an ending year 1 balance of $11,979,504.17. During year 2, the $11,979,504.17 balance accrues 6 percent interest and becomes $12,698,274.42. The team pays out $3 million and is left with $9,698,274.42 as an ending year 2 balance. During year 3, the $9,698,274.42 becomes $10,280,170.89. The team pays out $3 million and is left with a balance of $7,280,170.89. During year 4, the $7,280,170.85 accrues interest and becomes $7,716,981.14. The team pays out $3 million and is left with $4,716,981.14. During year 5, the $4,716,981.14 accrues interest of $283,018.86 and becomes $5,000,000. The team pays Dutch $5 million at the end of year 5 and the account has a $0 balance.

A company plans to sell a piece of equipment in 5 years at a salvage value of $10,000, and current interest rates are 8 percent, compounded quarterly.

The present value of this future sale of assets is $6,729.71. This is calculated as follows:

$$PV = FV\left[\frac{1}{(1+i)^n}\right] = \$10,000\left[\frac{1}{\left(1 + \dfrac{0.08}{4}\right)^{(4 \times 5)}}\right]$$

$$= \$10,000\left[\frac{1}{(1.02)^{20}}\right] = \$10,000\left(\frac{1}{1.4859}\right)$$

$$= \$10,000(0.6730) = \$6,729.71$$

where the term in the square brackets is known as the *present value factor (PVF)*.

Using our calculator, we find the *FVF* of 1.485947 and divide 1 by this factor to obtain the *PVF* shown in the formula. We obtain a *PVF* of 0.672971. Multiplying this factor by our lump-sum amount of $10,000, we get a present value of $6,729.71. If we had set our calculator to four decimal places, 0.6730 would be displayed. If you don't clear your calculator and multiply the factor of 0.6730 by $10,000, you will still get $6,729.71, because the actual factor number stored in the calculator is 0.672971. If we go to Appendix B, Table B–2, "Present Value of a Future Lump Sum," go across to the 2 percent column and down to the 20-payment row, we also obtain a factor value of 0.6730. Multiplying 0.6730 by $10,000 gives us a present value of $6,730. The difference between the two answers ($6,729.71 and $6,730) is the result of rounding in the table (0.6730 versus 0.672971). We continue to use this method in determining subsequent factors for the remainder of this chapter.

Given the fact that inflation exists at some percentage, the value of a dollar can be determined by using the inflation rate and period of time. If the inflation rate is 4 percent for 4 years, we can calculate the present value of a future dollar 4 years from now.

$$PV = FV(PVF)$$

$$= \$1\left[\frac{1}{(1 + 0.04)^4}\right] = \$1\left(\frac{1}{1.1699}\right)$$

$$= \$1(0.8548) = \$0.85$$

So, if the inflation rate is 4 percent for 4 years, the present value of a future $1 bill is calculated to be 85 cents. In other words, 85 cents deposited at 4 percent for 4 years will equal $1. We can conclude that with 4 percent inflation for 4 years, $1 will buy 85 cents worth of goods. This can be interpreted as $1 losing 15 cents in purchasing power over 4 years. If the inflation rate is 12 percent for 4 years, the present value of a future $1 bill 4 years from now is calculated to be

64 cents. In other words, 64 cents deposited for 4 years at 12 percent equals $1. We can conclude that with 12 percent inflation for 4 years, $1 will lose 36 cents of purchasing power.

Americans are noted for having very low savings rates even though there are wonderful savings incentives provided by current law. These are discussed in detail in Chapter 11. However, the single thing to be aware of is that we must save now at a rate that exceeds inflation if we want to have sufficient funds to guarantee an effective retirement. You are currently 30 and plan on retiring at 70 and anticipate 4 percent inflation for the next 40 years. What is the present value of the future dollar when you are ready to retire?

$$PV = FV(PVF)$$

$$= \$1 \left[\frac{1}{(1 + 0.04)^{40}} \right] = \$1 \left(\frac{1}{1.8010} \right)$$

$$= \$1(0.2083) = \$0.21$$

The future dollar at retirement will purchase only 21 cents worth of goods and a $100,000 account at retirement will purchase only $21,000 worth of goods. In other words, $1 loses 79 cents in purchasing power over 40 years with an inflation rate of 4 percent. We can now see how important it is to fund retirement programs adequately. Many retirement programs are established that allow for a fixed annual contribution into a retirement account. These are a fixed stream of equal payments that are not future and present values of lump sums. An equal stream of payments is an annuity. Annuities are the subject of Chapter 9.

INTERNAL RATE OF RETURN

The items discussed so far in this chapter provide us with a method of determining which formula or table to use based on the type of financial terms and conditions that we face when obtaining a loan or making an investment. When we own a business or make an investment, however, we do not necessarily have neat little items that can be plugged into tables. For example, suppose that in January 2002 we bought 10,000 shares of stock in XYZ Company that were selling for $2 a share, or $20,000. We sold the shares in January 2006 for $3 a share, or $30,000. When we look at this initially, we believe that we made 50 percent on our investment, but we must take into consideration the time value of money because purchasing power was lost during the 4 years that the money was invested in the stock. Therefore, we want to find the actual rate of return, or internal rate of return, that equates a dollar invested now with a dollar received in the future. The **internal rate of return (IRR)** is the actual rate of return on an investment that takes into consideration the time value of money. It is the specific interest rate where the present value of the benefits equals the present value of the costs.

The primary formula for solving an internal rate of return problem when an amount invested culminates in a future lump sum is

$$IRR = \left(\sqrt[n]{\frac{FV}{PV}} - 1 \right) \times 100$$

Another way of depicting the same formula is

$$IRR = \left[\left(\frac{FV}{PV} \right)^{\left(\frac{1}{n}\right)} - 1 \right] \times 100$$

Using the previous problem with future value of $30,000 (amount received from our investment in 4 years) and present value of $20,000 (amount that we invested), we solve for IRR as follows:

$$IRR = \left(\sqrt[n]{\frac{FV}{PV}} - 1 \right) \times 100$$

$$= \left(\sqrt[4]{\frac{\$30,000}{\$20,000}} - 1 \right) \times 100$$

$$= (\sqrt[4]{1.5} - 1) \times 100 = (1.1067 - 1) \times 100$$

$$= (0.1067) \times 100 = 10.67\%$$

The number 10.67 percent means that for every $1 of cost of investment, the investment is generating 10.67 percent of interest, gain, or benefit. If we start out with $20,000 and let it grow at 10.67 percent for 4 years, we will have $30,000 in the account.

Another example of IRR is a real estate investment. Ned Worth buys a home in Phoenix in 2000 for $550,000 and sells this home in 2005 for $1,100,000. What is Ned Worth's internal rate of return for this investment?

$$IRR = \left(\sqrt[n]{\frac{FV}{PV}} - 1 \right) \times 100$$

$$IRR = \left[\left(\frac{FV}{PV} \right)^{\left(\frac{1}{n}\right)} - 1 \right] \times 100$$

$$= \left[\left(\frac{\$1,100,000}{\$550,000} \right)^{\left(\frac{1}{5}\right)} - 1 \right] \times 100$$

$$= [(2.0)^{(0.2)} - 1] \times 100$$

$$= (1.1487 - 1) \times 100$$
$$= (0.14870) \times 100 = 14.87\%$$

The preceding are examples of finding the IRR when we receive a lump-sum payment, are given the present and future values, and have the time element.

Rule of 72

We can also find an approximation of the amount of time that it takes a present value amount to double. We divide the number 72 by the interest rate earned on the investment. This procedure is known as the **rule of 72**. If we invest $10,000 at 12 percent annually, it should take approximately 6 years for the invested amount to double to $20,000.

$$\text{Time for investment to double} = \frac{72}{\text{Annual interest rate}}$$
$$= \frac{72}{12} = 6 \text{ years}$$

Using this formula, if we know the amount of time we want to wait for our money to double, we can find the annual interest rate that we must receive to reach our goal. We would be able to find the annual interest rate of 12 percent by dividing 72 by 6 years.

$$\text{Annual interest rate} = \frac{72}{\text{Time for investment to double}}$$
$$= \frac{72}{6} = 12 \text{ percent}$$

Going back to the Ned Worth example, we can use the rule of 72 to determine if we solved our IRR problems correctly as Ned's house doubled in value in 5 years ($550,000 to $1,100,000).

$$\text{Time for investment to double} = \frac{72}{\text{Annual interest rate}}$$
$$\text{Annual interest rate} = \frac{72}{\text{Time for investment to double}}$$
$$\text{Annual interest rate} = \frac{72}{5} = 14.40 \text{ percent}$$

Remember that the rule of 72 is an approximation, whereas IRR is exact.

 **CONCLUSION**

This chapter on the time value of money provides us with the tools that we require as financial managers and business entrepreneurs to solve many of the actual problems faced in decision making. We covered the following areas:

- ◆ Simple and compound interest
- ◆ Bank discount
- ◆ Interest rate variance and stated and effective rates of interest
- ◆ Present and future values of lump sums
- ◆ Findings rates by the use of tables and by the use of a calculator
- ◆ Internal rates of return and the rule of 72

Appendix A demonstrates how to place the formulas used in this chapter into spreadsheet programs and how to place the formulas into a programmable calculator.

This chapter concentrated on the time value of money with respect to finding both the future value and the present value of lump sums of money. However, there are many situations that involve annuities, which are streams of equal payments. Annuities are covered extensively in Chapter 9, in which we also demonstrate how we combine lump sums and annuities all in one problem.

REVIEW AND DISCUSSION QUESTIONS

1. What is the relationship between the time value of money and inflation?
2. Compare simple interest to compound interest.
3. What are the advantages and disadvantages of a fixed principal, fixed interest loan?
4. What is the purpose of a bridge loan?
5. Distinguish between *bank discount* and *simple interest*.
6. Differentiate between a *stated rate of interest* and *effective rate of interest*.
7. What is the significance of finding the internal rate of return?

EXERCISES AND PROBLEMS

1. Jill Kramer borrowed $25,000 to pay for her child's education. Jill must repay the loan at the end of 5 months in one payment with an 11.5 percent simple interest rate.
   a. What is the total amount that Jill must repay in 5 months?
   b. How much interest does Jill repay?
2. Joe Jones went to his bank to find out how long it will take for $1,000 to amount to $1,350 at 9 percent simple interest. Solve Joe's problem.

3. The Fed cuts the Federal Funds rate and the Discount rate and the Prime goes down to 6 percent. Al Truistyk owns an exercise center and needs to upgrade his equipment in order to meet his customers' needs. The equipment costs $275,000 and the lender requires a 10 percent down payment. Al must borrow $250,000 and the lender agrees to a 60-month fixed principal fixed interst rate loan with a rate of Prime plus 4 percent.
   a. Construct an amortization table for the first 3 months of this loan.
   b. Instead of a fixed interest loan, the lender gave Al a variable rate loan of prime plus 4 percent. Using Table 8–1, calculate Al's interest payments for the first 3 months of this loan if he borrowed the money on January 1, 2008.

4. The Smiths purchase a $600,000 house and must sell their old home in order to make a 20 percent down payment plus closing costs of $7,000 on the new house. Currently, they have a mortgage balance of $100,000 on their old home, which has been appraised at $300,000 They have been pre-approved by the lender to qualify for a $480,000 mortgage in the new home. The lender offers a bridge loan at 10 percent simple interest. The closing date on the new house is February 13, and the Smiths sell their old home on May 15.
   a. How much cash must the Smiths put down on their new house?
   b. How much equity do the Smiths have in their old house?
   c. How much must they borrow if they take a bridge loan?
   d. What is the dollar amount of interest paid on the bridge loan?

5. Hy Potenuse bought a $10,000 T-bill at a 1.55 percent discount for 13 weeks (91 days).
   a. How much does Hy pay for the bond?
   b. What is the effective rate of interest?
   c. Who is the borrower?

6. Alana Olsen borrowed $5,000 for 90 days from First Bank. The bank discounted the note at 10 percent.
   a. What proceeds did Olsen receive?
   b. What is the effective rate of the nearest basis point?

7. The face value of a simple interest note and simple discount note is $8,000 each. Assume both notes have 8.75 percent interest rates for 60 days. Calculate the following:
   a. The amount of interest charged for each.
   b. The maturity value of the simple interest note.
   c. The maturity value of the bank discount note.
   d. The amount the borrower receives for the simple interest note.
   e. The amount the borrower receives for the bank discount note.

8. You deposit $760 in an account one time that compounds monthly at 6 percent. How much will you have in your account at the end of 10 years?

9. A balloon payment of $21,000 on your house is due in 10 years. If you can earn an average of 5 percent per year for the 10-year period, how much must you place into an account today to have the $21,000 in 10 years?

10. A financial institution quotes a rate of 6.45 percent compounded monthly. What is the effective rate for the year?

11. If you want an effective rate of 5 percent, what is an acceptable quoted rate if money is compounded monthly?

12. If inflation averages 4 percent per year, how much purchasing power will $1.00 lose in 10 years?

13. How much will you pay for a $10,000 automobile in 20 years if the inflation rate averages 6 percent per year for 20 years?

14. At the beginning of each year, you deposit the following into a growth mutual fund that earns 6 percent per year:

Year	Deposit ($)
1	5,000
2	7,500
3	4,500
4	5,500
5	6,200

How much should the fund be worth at the end of 5 years?

15. Ican Tackel just signed an $11.5 million, 4-year contract with an NFL team. He received a signing bonus of $2 million; $1.5 million at the end of year 1; $3 million at the end of year 2; $3.5 million at the end of year 3; and $1.5 million at the end of year 4. What is the present value of his contract if money can earn 8 percent per year?

16. Bylo Selhi wants to know how many years it will take for his mutual investment fund of $50,000 to reach $500,000 if his mutual fund pays an average of 12 percent per year.

17. Ira Schwab wins the lottery and decides to take the one lump sum of $500,000 minus taxes. Ira receives a check for $300,000 after taxes. Using the rule of 72, determine the following:
   a. How long will it take him to get $600,000 if he can earn 8 percent?
   b. How long will it take him to get $600,000 if he can earn 18 percent?
   c. How long will it take him to get $1,200,000 if he can earn 12 percent?

18. Felice Navidad purchases 2,000 shares of NOW Technology stock at $4 in Christmas 2005. Four years later, in December 2009, she sell the stock for $28 a share. What is Felice's internal rate of return?

19. Carrie Haute buys a fast-food restaurant for $500,000. She is very successful and sells the business 6 years later for $1,375,000. What is Carrie's internal rate of return?

20. Rochelle Kotter wants to attend a university 5 years from now. She will need $88,000. Assume Rochelle's bank pays 6 percent interest compounded monthly. What must Rochelle deposit today to accumulate $88,000 in 5 years?

21. Compute the effective annual rates for the following:
   a. 6 percent compounded yearly.
   b. 6 percent compounded semi-annually.
   c. 6 percent compounded quarterly.
   d. 6 percent compounded monthly.
   e. 6 percent compounded daily (use 365 days per year).

22. Mr. N. invests $5,000 in a certificate of deposit (CD) at his local bank. He receives 8 percent compounded annually for 7 years. How much interest does his investment earn during this time period?

RECOMMENDED TEAM ASSIGNMENT

1. Contact at least three separate banks within your community. Interview the bank managers and determine how these banks provide a bridge loan to a business. What are the interest rates charged by these banks?

2. Pick two companies within the same industry that your group is interested in. Find the stock price of each company on January 1, 1990, and on January 1, 2008. If you had purchased this stock, what would have been your internal rate of return?

CASE STUDY: BLUE BONNET CAFÉ

© 2008 Philip J. Adelman and Alan M. Marks

Phil and Arlene Mobel were both born and raised in Denver, Colorado. Phil interrupted his high school education after Pearl Harbor and joined the United States Navy when he was 17 years old. He was at sea on a destroyer that was sunk, and he was stranded in the water for more than 4 hours before being picked up. He received survivor's leave and was then reassigned to Annapolis to take midshipmen out to sea. In 1945, after leaving the Navy, Phil moved back to Denver and married Arlene in 1947. Phil had many jobs after leaving the navy, including working in his father-in-law's liquor store.

Phil and Arlene wanted to own their own business. They saved their money and invested in a used furniture and piano store in 1962. In the early 1960s, students in the Denver public school system received free music lessons, and piano teachers would refer student families to the Mobel's piano store. However, by 1967, budget cutbacks in the schools resulted in the elimination of free music lessons, which resulted in fewer referrals for the piano store; this lack of referrals, coupled with a recession, led the Mobels to close the store. However, they still dreamed of owning their own business.

Arlene's father's accountant found a neighborhood bar for sale on Broadway in Denver, and they purchased the bar with financing from Arlene's father, who gave the owner a $10,000 down payment on a $37,000 total price. The Mobels leased the property from the building owner for $350 a month and agreed to pay the remaining $27,000 sales price within 5 years.

By this time, Phil and Arlene had three children and had to make arrangements for either Phil or Arlene to be home when the children were there. In order to generate enough cash to pay the business off in 5 years, they worked the following schedule: Phil opened the bar at 6 A.M. and the clean up man came in shortly afterward and cleaned up from the previous evening. The bar opened for business at 8 A.M. At 9, one additional employee came to work. Arlene came in at 10 after getting the three kids off to school or placed with the sitter. Phil left at 11 to purchase food for the kitchen and make a bank deposit, then went home and got some rest to come back to work at 5 P.M. where he stayed until the bar closed at 2 A.M. Arlene worked until 5 P.M., returned home, fixed supper, and took care of the kids. Phil got home at about 2:30 A.M. and went back to work at 6 A.M. The Mobels worked this schedule 7 days a week for 5 years, until they finished paying off the bar on May 1, 1972.

One evening, not long after Phil and Arlene bought the bar, several customers came in at about 11 A.M. and asked Phil if they could get some food, like green chili, because they had just gotten off work and were hungry. Phil knew nothing about Mexican food, but was receptive to the idea. He got a recipe for green chili from a Mexican woman who was a customer and was known in the neighborhood as a wonderful cook. He offered to give her a free pitcher of beer in exchange for the recipe. Phil had never eaten or made green chili, but figured that if he followed the recipe, he could cook an excellent pot of green chili. He went to Safeway, bought the ingredients, and cooked up a pot of green chili for the late crowd. The chili was a hit, and more customers ordered it when word got out. The restaurant continued to sell green chili and a variety of sandwiches, including a special menu for the late crowd. The Mobels really believed in customer service, and the green chili customers frequented the restaurant for more than 40 years.

On May 25, 1972, just 3 weeks after they paid off the restaurant, Phil's car was hit by a drunk driver and he was in intensive care for over a week and in a cast for several months. He was unable to work for more than 4 years. Arlene tried to run the bar by herself, but found that the employees had allegiance to Phil. The liquor and food salesmen knew that she had no experience with ordering and didn't know how to get specials and quantity discounts. Women really had a difficult time being in the bar business at that time. During the late 1960s, Arlene found that the employees, customers, and distributors did not respect women and tried to take advantage of them at every opportunity. Arlene and Phil discussed the business every day, and she was an excellent student who really learned how to run a bar and restaurant.

After 6 months Arlene fired all of the employees and contacted the liquor distributors and demanded new salesmen who would be honest with her or she would take her business elsewhere. She hired a new crew and explained that she was the boss and that they worked for her. She always believed in paying a fair wage and being honest with her employees. She also determined that there would be more profit in the business if they served a full menu rather than just a limited menu of green chili, pizza, and sandwiches. After doing considerable research, she determined that Mexican food coupled with the bar business would be the best combination. She found an excellent chef and offered him a good salary and benefits. Alex, the chef, determined the menu, worked with Arlene to establish prices, and developed recipes that could be cooked by other chefs. Arlene had hit on the perfect combination of food and drinks, and by 1973, the Blue Bonnet Café became a full-service Mexican restaurant and bar serving lunch and dinner.

Their liquor specialty is margaritas, and they developed a recipe that could be made in 60-gallon tanks, and the restaurant goes through three tanks of margaritas on a busy weekend. The restaurant is so successful that they receive three semi-truckloads of food each week. The restaurant uses more than 50,000 tortillas each week and more than 2 tons of cheese a month. On a slow day, they serve 300 meals; on their best day, they serve 2,000 meals. The woman who owned the property liked the Mobels and never raised their rent above $350 a month from 1973 to 1990, when she gave the Mobels a 20-year non-escalating lease, charging $1,500 per month.

In the early 1990s, Denver was installing light rail and declared the area around the restaurant an Urban Renewal zone, which was then purchased by a developer who also wanted to purchase the land at the restaurant. However, because of how successful the restaurant was, the developer wanted the Blue Bonnet Café to expand and stay where it was. The Mobels countered and stated that they would only stay if they could purchase the land where the restaurant was located. The building owner had promised Arlene that if she ever sold the land and the building, she would sell it to the Mobels. In 1992, they bought the building and the land and began to expand the restaurant.

Their son Gary went to work in the restaurant full time as soon as he was 21. He graduated college with a degree in accounting and a master's degree in tax accounting. Their daughter Marci graduated college and also began working in the restaurant. The area around the restaurant was expanding and a shopping center was being developed, which resulted in increased foot traffic and sales. In 2004, Phil and Arlene were approaching their 80s and decided to sell the restaurant to their children and retire. As of 2008, the Blue Bonnet Mexican Restaurant employed more than 90 people and is very successful. Many of the employees have been with the restaurant for more than 15 years. The liquor distributor recently told the Mobels that the Blue Bonnet is the single largest seller of tequila in the state of Colorado. It is now being run by the second generation of this amazing family.

QUESTIONS

1. The Blue Bonnet paid only $350 rent for 17 years between 1973 and 1990. Based on a 4 percent inflation rate, how much should their rent have been in by 1990? What advantage did this lease provide to the Mobel family?
2. Using the information in the case study and the current menu price of a burrito plate and a large soda on the Blue Bonnet Menu at http://www.bluebonnetrestaurant.com, how much revenue is derived on their worse day and on their best day?

CHAPTER 9

Time Value of Money— Part II: Annuities

Learning Objectives

When you have completed this chapter, you should be able to:

♦ Explain the differences between an *ordinary annuity* and an *annuity due*.
♦ Calculate the future value and present value annuity factors that are used to solve time value of money problems.
♦ Integrate several of the methods provided in time value of money to solve real–life financial problems.
♦ Use a financial calculator to solve time-value-of-money problems.
♦ Present spreadsheet applications of the mathematics of finance.
♦ Use financial tables to solve time-value-of-money problems.
♦ Calculate future and present value amounts by solving problems involving annuities and lump sums.

This chapter is devoted to a discussion of annuities and combining those lessons learned in Chapter 8 with annuities. An **annuity** is a stream of the same payments paid or received over time. An example of an *annuity paid* is a person having $25 deducted from each paycheck and putting the $25 into a savings account that accrues interest up to some future date. An example of an *annuity received* is a bank receiving a set amount of equal payments over the life of a mortgage loan on a house or automobile payments for a car.

In this chapter, we compare two types of annuities, an *ordinary annuity* and an *annuity due*. An **ordinary annuity** is an annuity where the same payments are made or received at the end of each time period, such as a payment made at the end of December each year, or a payment made at the end of each month. An **annuity due** is an annuity where the same payments are made or received in the beginning of the time period, such as a payment made at the beginning of January each year, or a payment that is made at the beginning of each month.

FUTURE VALUE OF AN ORDINARY ANNUITY

What is the future value of a stream of equal payments for *n* periods at *i* rate of return when the money is invested at the *end* of each compounding period? This formula is applied in these situations:

a. You want to determine how much you will have in a retirement account if you place a specific payment (the annuity) into an account at the end of each period of time (a month or a year).

b. A government agency wishes to determine how much it must pay at the end of each year (*sinking fund*) for *n* amount of years at a set rate of return in order to pay back bondholders for the amount of funds due them when the bonds mature.

c. If you know how much you want to have at some future date for a child's college education, you can determine the amount to pay (the annuity) into a college fund at the end of each period of time for *n* amount of periods at a set amount of interest.

The formula for the future value of an ordinary annuity is

$$FVOA = A(FVAF)$$

$$= A\left[\frac{(1 + i)^n - 1}{i}\right]$$

where

$FVOA$ = the future value of an ordinary annuity
A = the annuity

$FVAF$ (future value annuity factor) $= \left[\dfrac{(1 + i)^n - 1}{i}\right]$

i = the interest rate per time period
n = number of compounding periods per year times the number of years

Ira Saver qualifies for a Roth IRA and determines that he can invest $5,000 of after-tax money at the end of each year into a Roth IRA for the next 10 years. If his IRA can earn 6 percent compounded annually, how much will Ira Saver have in his account at the end of 10 years? The problem is solved as follows:

$$FVOA = A(FVAF)$$

$$= \$5,000\left[\frac{(1 + i)^n - 1}{i}\right] = \$5,000\left[\frac{(1 + 0.06)^{10} - 1}{0.06}\right]$$

$$= \$5,000\left(\frac{0.7908}{0.06}\right) = \$5,000(13.1808)$$

$$= \$65,903.97$$

Ira deposited a total of $50,000 in payments ($5,000 × 10 payments) and earned $15,903.97 in interest ($65,903.97 − $50,000 = $15,903.97). The previous problem was solved by using a financial calculator. If we use the "Future Value of an Ordinary Annuity" table (Appendix B, Table B–3), we go across the top row to 6 percent and down 10 periods and find an *FVAF* of 13.1808. Using this factor, we multiply it by our annuity of $5,000 and find an answer of $65,904.00. The difference between the two answers ($65,904.00 and $65,903.97) is rounding.

Unlike Ira Saver, who saves yearly, many of us find that we can only save $100 per month at the end of each month after all of our bills are paid. If this savings can be compounded monthly at an annual interest rate of 12 percent, what does the account contain after 3 years? This type of annuity is referred to as an **ordinary annuity**, because money is deposited at the end of each period and is calculated as follows:

$$FVOA = A(FVAF)$$

$$FVOA = A\left[\frac{(1 + i)^{(n)} - 1}{i}\right] = \$100\left[\frac{\left(1 + \frac{0.12}{12}\right)^{(12 \times 3)} - 1}{\frac{0.12}{12}}\right]$$

$$= \$100\left[\frac{(1 + 0.01)^{(36)} - 1}{0.01}\right] = \$100(43.0769) = \$4,307.69$$

The annuity (*A*) is the payment made during each period of compounding. Note that the mode of paying the annuity (paying monthly) must match the period of compounding (compounding monthly) for the formula to be used correctly. The number of periods, *n*, is the number of periods that the annuity is compounded; *FV* is the value of the annuity at the end of the compounding periods; and *i* is the interest rate per period of compounding, which is the stated rate (annual rate) divided by the number of compounding periods during the year. For example, if 12 percent is compounded monthly, then we would divide 0.12 by 12 to obtain a per-period rate of 0.01.

For this problem, using the annuity formula as shown, we obtain a future value factor of 43.076878 (rounded to 43.0769). We then multiply our annuity of $100 by this factor to obtain a future value of $4,307.69. We also can use Appendix B, Table B–3, "Future Value of an Ordinary Annuity." Using the 1 percent column and going to a value for *n* of 36, we obtain a future value factor of 43.0769. Multiplying this factor by our annuity of $100, we obtain $4,307.69. In this case, it is identical to the answer obtained with our calculator.

Another situation occurs when individuals make one deposit at the end of each year, but the money in the account is compounded monthly. Note that the mode of paying the annuity (paying yearly) must match the mode of compounding for the formula to be correct. In this scenario, $1,200 is deposited at the end of each year for 3 years, but money is compounded monthly. In order for the formula to work, we must find the effective rate, which becomes the rate that matches with the yearly mode of payment. First, we find the effective rate of 12 percent compounded monthly.

$$\text{Effective annual rate} = (1 + i)^n - 1$$

$$= \left(1 + \frac{0.12}{12}\right)^{12} - 1 = (1.01)^{12} - 1$$

$$= 1.1268 - 1 = 0.1268, \text{ which is } 12.68\%$$

The 12.68 percent is the interest rate that matches exactly with the mode of payment in order for the formula to work. We now substitute into our future value of an ordinary annuity problem by depositing $1,200 at the end of each year into an account that earns an annual effective rate of interest of 12.68 percent for 3 years.

$$FVOA = A(FVAF)$$

$$= A\left[\frac{(1 + i)^n - 1}{i}\right] = \$1,200\left[\frac{(1 + 0.1268)^3 - 1}{0.1268}\right]$$

$$= \$1,200\left[\frac{(1.4307) - 1}{0.1268}\right] = \$1,200\left(\frac{0.4307}{0.1268}\right)$$

$$= \$1,200(3.3965) = \$4,075.80$$

We deposited $1,200 per year, or $3,600, over 3 years, and earned interest of $475.80 ($4,075.80 – $3,600 = $475.80). Note that when we deposited the same $3,600 over 3 years but deposited it as $100 per month, we earned more interest because our account had a balance of $4,307.69, which resulted in interest earned of $707.69 ($4,307.69 – $3,600 = $707.69). Why is there more interest earned in the $100 per month deposit? The answer is that in the first problem, we deposited $100 every month, and it was compounded monthly. So, the $100 deposited in January earned compounded interest for 11 months (February through December), the $100 deposited in February earned compounded interest for 10 months (March through December), and so on. Although the effective rate was 12.68 percent when $1,200 was deposited yearly, there was actually no money in the account until the end of the first year, when a single $1,200 deposit was made.

FUTURE VALUE OF AN ANNUITY DUE

What is the future value of a stream of equal payments for n periods at i rate of return when the money is invested at the *beginning* of each compounding period? Some practical examples of using this formula include the following:

a. You want to determine how much you will have in a retirement account if you place a specific payment (the annuity) into an account in the beginning of each period of time (a month or a year).

b. A government agency wishes to determine how much it must pay in the beginning of each year (sinking fund) for n amount of years at a set rate of return in order to pay back bondholders for the amount of funds due them when the bonds mature.

c. If you know how much you want to have at some future date for a child's college education, you can determine the amount to pay (the annuity) into a college fund in the beginning of each period of time for n amount of periods at a set amount of interest.

The formula for the future value of an annuity due is

$$FVAD = A(FVAF)$$

$$= A\left\{ \left[\frac{(1 + i)^{(n+1)} - 1}{i} \right] - 1 \right\}$$

where

$FVAD$ = the future value of annuity due
A = the annuity

$$FVAF \text{ (future value annuity factor)} = \left\{ \left[\frac{(1 + i)^{(n+1)} - 1}{i} \right] - 1 \right\}$$

i = the interest rate per time period
n = number of compounding periods per year times the number of years

Here, we have the same problem solved initially when we used the future value of an ordinary annuity. We next show the difference between an ordinary annuity and an annuity due. Ira Saver qualifies for a Roth IRA and determines that he can invest $5,000 of after-tax money at the beginning of each year into a Roth IRA for the next 10 years. If his IRA can earn 6 percent compounded annually, how much will Ira Saver have in his account at the end of 10 years? The problem is solved as follows:

$$FVAD = A(FVAF)$$

$$= \$5,000\left\{\left[\frac{(1+i)^{(n+1)}-1}{i}\right]-1\right\} = \$5,000\left\{\left[\frac{(1+0.06)^{11}-1}{0.06}\right]-1\right\}$$

$$= \$5,000\left[\left(\frac{1.8983-1}{0.06}\right)-1\right] = \$5,000\left[\left(\frac{0.8983}{0.06}\right)-1\right]$$

$$= \$5,000(14.9716-1) = \$5,000(13.9716)$$

$$= \$69,858.21$$

Ira deposited a total of \$50,000 in payments (\$5,000 × 10 payments) and earns \$19,858.21 in interest (\$69,858.21 − \$50,000 = \$19,858.21). This problem is solved by using a financial calculator. If we use the "Future Value of an Annuity Due" table (Appendix B, Table B–4), we go across the top row to 6 percent and down 10 periods and find the *FVAF* (future value of an annuity due factor) of 13.9716. Using this factor, we multiply it by our annuity of \$5,000 and arrive at the following answer of \$69,858. The difference between the two answers is rounding. Note that Ira earned interest of \$15,903.97 when he deposited \$5,000 at the end of each year (ordinary annuity) and interest of \$19,858.21 when he deposited \$5,000 at the beginning of each year (annuity due). The almost \$6,000 difference in interest is because money deposited earned interest for a longer period of time in the annuity due problem. The initial deposit in the annuity due problem earned interest for the full 10 years, and even the last deposit earned interest for 1 year.

Unlike Ira, many of us find that we can only save \$100 per month at the beginning of each month. If this amount of savings can be compounded monthly at an annual interest rate of 12 percent, what will the account contain after 3 years? This type of annuity is referred to as an **annuity due**, because money is deposited in the beginning of each period and is calculated as follows:

$$FVAD = A(FVAF) = \$100\left\{\left[\frac{(1+i)^{(n+1)}-1}{i}\right]-1\right\}$$

$$FVAD = \$100\left\{\left[\frac{\left(1+\frac{0.12}{12}\right)^{(36+1)}-1}{\frac{0.12}{12}}\right]-1\right\}$$

$$= \$100\left\{\left[\frac{(1+0.01)^{(37)}-1}{0.01}\right]-1\right\}$$

$$FVAD = \$100\left[\left(\frac{1.4451-1}{0.01}\right)-1\right]$$

$$= \$100(44.5076-1) = \$100(43.5076)$$

$$FVAD = \$4,350.76$$

If we invest the money at the beginning of the month, rather than at the end, we find that our $100 grows to $4,350.76, rather than the $4,307.69 obtained by our previous investment. If we go to Appendix B, Table B–4, "Future Value of an Annuity Due," and look up the future value factor, we obtain 43.5076, which is the same factor that we obtained with the calculator. The difference between the future value of this annuity and the future value we obtained for the ordinary annuity is a result of the fact that our investment has one extra period of time to compound, because the payment is made at the beginning of the period. That is why we use 37 as the exponent (i.e., $n + 1$) rather than 36.

Another situation occurs when individuals make one deposit at the beginning of the year, but the money in the account is compounded monthly. Note that the mode of paying the annuity (paying yearly) must match the period of compounding for the formula to be correct. In this scenario, $1,200 is deposited at the beginning of each year, for 3 years, but money is being compounded monthly. In order for the formula to work, we must find the effective rate and that becomes the rate that matches with the mode of payment. The first thing that we do is find the effective rate of 12 percent compounded monthly.

$$\text{Effective annual rate} = (1 + i)^n - 1$$

$$= \left(1 + \frac{0.12}{12}\right)^{12} - 1 = (1.01)^{12} - 1$$

$$= 1.1268 - 1 = 0.1268, \text{ which is } 12.68\%$$

The 12.68 percent is the interest rate that exactly matches up with the mode of payment in order for the formula to work. We now substitute the numbers into our future value of an annuity due problem. We are depositing $1,200 at the beginning of each year into an account that earns an annual effective rate of interest of 12.68 percent for 3 years.

$$FVAD = A(FVAF)$$

$$= A\left\{\left[\frac{(1 + i)^{(n + 1)} - 1}{i}\right] - 1\right\} = \$1,200\left\{\left[\frac{(1 + 0.1268)^4 - 1}{0.1268}\right] - 1\right\}$$

$$= \$1,200\left\{\left[\frac{(1.6121) - 1}{0.1268}\right] - 1\right\} = \$1,200\left[\left(\frac{1.6121}{0.1268}\right) - 1\right]$$

$$= \$1,200(4.8273 - 1) = \$1,200(3.8273) = \$4,592.58$$

We deposited $1,200 per year, or $3,600, over 3 years and earned interest of $992.58 ($4,592.58 – $3,600 = $992.58). Note that we earned interest of $475.80 when we deposited $1,200 per year at the end of each year (ordinary annuity) and interest of $992.58 when we deposited the $1,200 per year at the beginning of the year. As mentioned previously, the primary factor is that interest was earned for a longer period of time in the annuity due than in the ordinary annuity.

We also would actually make one less payment during the three years. Table 9–1 demonstrates the difference between the payment schedule of an

TABLE 9–1 Payment Schedule for Future Value of an Ordinary Annuity and Annuity Due

Ordinary Annuity

| Payment Made | 100 | 100 | 100 | 100 | 100 | 100 | 100 | 100 | 100 |
| Time in Months | 1 | 2 | 3 | 4 | 5 | 6 | 7 | 8 | 9 |

Annuity Due

| Payment Made | 100 | 100 | 100 | 100 | 100 | 100 | 100 | 100 | 100 |
| Time in Months | 1 | 2 | 3 | 4 | 5 | 6 | 7 | 8 | 9 |

ordinary annuity and that of an annuity due. Table 9–1 shows our investment during the first 9 months of our 3-year term. In the case of the ordinary annuity, we make nine payments during the nine periods, numbered from 1 to 9. Because the payments are made at the end of the period (month), the ninth payment does not compound (receive any interest). Therefore, the ordinary annuity uses an exponential factor of n. For the annuity due, we make the same number of payments, but each payment receives interest for the entire compounding period (month). Therefore, the first payment, because it is put in at the beginning of the period, receives interest, resulting in one more period of interest than in the ordinary annuity. Hence, our exponent in the formula for an annuity due is $n + 1$, rather than n.

PRESENT VALUE OF AN ORDINARY ANNUITY

What is the present value of a stream of equal payments for n periods at i rate of return when the payment is received at the end of each period? Some practical examples of using this formula are

a. You want to determine how much you need in a retirement account at retirement if you want a specific dollar amount of income (the annuity) paid at the end of each period of time (a month or a year) for n periods of time (expected lifespan).

b. All consumer bank loans use the present value (dollar amount of the loan) of an ordinary annuity to determine the monthly payment (annuity) based on a rate of interest (i) and a set number of periods (n).

c. For capital budgeting situations in which a purchased piece of equipment produces an equal amount of cash flow for n periods at a fixed interest rate i per period, we determine the present value of the benefits of each period's cash flow (the annuity).

The formula for the present value of an ordinary annuity is

$$PVOA = A(PVAF)$$

$$= A\left[\frac{(1 + i)^{(n)} - 1}{i(1 + i)^n}\right]$$

where

$PVOA$ = the present value of ordinary annuity
A = the annuity

$PVAF$ (present value annuity factor) = $\left[\dfrac{(1 + i)^{(n)} - 1}{i(1 + i)^n}\right]$

i = the interest rate per time period
n = number of compounding periods per year times the number of years

In order to have enough breathing room at retirement, Al Veoli, a medical technician, determines that he must receive \$60,000 per year at the end of each year for 30 years. If Al can earn 8 percent compounded annually on his money during retirement, find the present value, or the amount that Al needs in his account at retirement.

$$PVOA = A(PVAF)$$
$$= A\left[\frac{(1 + i)^{(n)} - 1}{i(1 + i)^n}\right]$$
$$= \$60,000\left[\frac{(1 + 0.08)^{(30)} - 1}{0.08\,(1 + 0.08)^{30}}\right] = \$60,000\left[\frac{10.0627 - 1}{0.08\,(10.0627)}\right]$$
$$= \$60,000\left(\frac{9.0627}{0.8050}\right) = \$60,000\,(11.2578)$$
$$= \$675,467$$

So if Al accumulates \$675,467 in his retirement account, he will be able to withdraw \$60,000 at the end of each year for the next 30 years provided he can earn 8 percent on his money.

How much do we have to place in an account today to receive a stream of \$100 payments at the end of each month for 36 months, or 3 years? In other words, what is the present value of such a stream of payments? We know that we will receive a total of \$3,600 during the 3-year period. Let's say that we are retiring and will receive a retirement payment of \$100 per month at the end of each month for 3 years. We assume the same interest rate of 12 percent as was used for calculating future values of annuities. Let's also assume that the money is received at the end of each month (an ordinary annuity). The present value in this case is

$$PVOA = A\left[\frac{(1 + i)^n - 1}{i(1 + i)^n}\right] = \$100\left[\frac{\left(1 + \dfrac{0.12}{12}\right)^{(12 \times 3)} - 1}{\dfrac{0.12}{12}\left(1 + \dfrac{0.12}{12}\right)^{(12 \times 3)}}\right]$$
$$= \$100\left[\frac{(1 + 0.01)^{36} - 1}{0.01(1 + 0.01)^{36}}\right] = \$100\,(30.1075) = \$3,010.75$$

Using the preceding formula, we obtain a present value factor of 30.1075. In this example, the present value of the retirement payments, which we receive at the end of the month, is $3,010.75. If we use Appendix B, Table B–5, "Present Value of an Ordinary Annuity," we obtain a present value factor of 30.1075, which is identical to our calculator result. Multiplying the annuity of $100 by the present value factor, we get an identical answer of $3,010.75. Therefore, if we place $3,010.75 in an account today at 12 percent interest, compounded monthly, we can receive monthly payments of $100 for the next 3 years.

PRESENT VALUE OF AN ANNUITY DUE

What is the present value of a stream of payments for n periods at i rate of return when the payment is received in the beginning of each period? This formula is needed in the following situations:

a. You want to determine how much you need in a retirement account at retirement if you want a specific dollar amount of income (the annuity) paid in the beginning of each period of time (the first of each month, or January 1 of each year) for n periods of time (expected lifespan).

b. Most lotteries pay an insurance company the present value of an annuity due. The annuity amount is then paid to the lottery winner at the beginning of each year. Given the lottery time period and rate of interest, we can determine the present value of the winnings that is paid to the insurance company.

The formula for the present value of an annuity due is

$$PVAD = A(PVAF)$$

$$= A\left\{\left[\frac{(1 + i)^{(n-1)} - 1}{i(1 + i)^{(n-1)}}\right] + 1\right\}$$

where

$PVAD$ = the present value of an annuity due
A = the annuity

$$PVAF \text{ (present value annuity factor)} = \left\{\left[\frac{(1 + i)^{(n-1)} - 1}{i(1 + i)^{(n-1)}}\right] + 1\right\}$$

i = the interest rate per time period
n = number of compounding periods per year times the number of years

Lotta Dough just won the million-dollar state lottery and has elected to receive the $50,000 per year at the beginning of each year for 20 years. What is the present value of this equal stream of payments if money can earn 7 percent annual interest?

$$PVAD = A(PVAF)$$

$$= A\left\{\left[\frac{(1 + i)^{(n-1)} - 1}{i(1 + i)^{(n-1)}}\right] + 1\right\} = \$50,000\left\{\left[\frac{(1 + 0.07)^{(19)} - 1}{0.07(1 + 0.07)^{(19)}}\right] + 1\right\}$$

$$= \$50,000\left\{\left[\frac{3.6165 - 1}{0.07(3.6165)}\right] + 1\right\} = \$50,000\left[\left(\frac{2.6165}{0.2532}\right) + 1\right]$$

$$= \$50,000[(10.3356) + 1] = \$50,000(11.3356)$$

$$= \$566,779.76$$

So Lotta receives $1,000,000 over 20 years in the form of an annuity due (beginning of the year) payment of $50,000 a year for 20 years. More importantly, the state lottery can now buy an annuity policy from an insurance company by placing $566,779.76 into an account that earns 7 percent annual interest. The policy pays Lotta $50,000 per year for 20 years in the beginning of each year.

How much do we have to place in an account today to receive a $100 payment in the beginning of each month for 36 months if the money earns an annual interest rate of 12 percent compounded monthly? This is a present value of an annuity due problem, and is solved as follows:

$$PVAD = A(PVAF)$$

$$= A\left\{\left[\frac{(1 + i)^{(n-1)} - 1}{i(1 + i)^{(n-1)}}\right] + 1\right\}$$

$$= \$100\left\{\left[\frac{\left(1 + \frac{0.12}{12}\right)^{(36-1)} - 1}{\frac{0.12}{12}\left(1 + \frac{0.12}{12}\right)^{(36-1)}}\right] + 1\right\}$$

$$= \$50,000\left\{\left[\frac{1.4166 - 1}{0.01(1.4166)}\right] + 1\right\} = \$100\left[\left(\frac{0.4166}{0.0142}\right) + 1\right]$$

$$= \$100[(29.4086) + 1] = \$100(30.4086)$$

$$= \$3,040.86$$

TABLE 9–2 Payment Schedule for Present Value of an Ordinary Annuity and Annuity Due

Ordinary Annuity

Payment Received	100	100	100	100	100	100	100	100	100
Time in Months	1	2	3	4	5	6	7	8	9

Annuity Due

Payment Received	100	100	100	100	100	100	100	100	100
Time in Months	1	2	3	4	5	6	7	8	9

Using the formula, we obtain a present value factor of 30.4086. In this example, the present value of the retirement payments, if we receive them at the beginning of the month, is $3,040.86. If we use Appendix B, Table B–6, "Present Value of an Annuity Due," we find a present value factor of 30.4086. Notice the difference in the present value of these two annuities ($3,010.75 ordinary annuity and $3,040.86 annuity due). If we receive the payment at the beginning of the month, we must place $3,040.86 in our account.

The reasons for this difference are shown in Table 9–2, which shows the payments received during the first 9 months of our 3-year term. In the case of an ordinary annuity, we receive nine payments during the nine periods, numbered from 1 to 9. Because the payments are received at the end of the period (month), the last payment we receive has nine periods to compound (earn interest). Therefore, the ordinary annuity uses an exponential factor of n.

In the case of an annuity due, however, we receive the same number of payments, but the ninth payment does not earn interest for the ninth period (month). The present value of the last payment compounds for one less period because the last payment is received immediately at the beginning of the last time period; hence, our exponent in the formula is $n - 1$, rather than n. In addition, the formula for the present value of an annuity due has a "+1" at the end because you receive your first payment immediately at beginning the annuity.

This is the reason why we must start with more money in the case of an annuity due to receive the same payment as we would with an ordinary annuity. Our example showed that we must invest $3,010.75 to receive $100 a month with an ordinary annuity, but $3,040.86 with an annuity due to receive the same payment. In addition, because we begin withdrawal of money immediately with an annuity due, the money received in the first period has not accumulated any interest.

The previous problems show how to solve present value of both an ordinary annuity and an annuity due using both the calculator and tables. The tables are included only so that the reader can verify answers obtained with a calculator or spreadsheet. In reality, banks and many other financial institutions now compound interest on a daily basis. For example, what is the present value of an account where you receive \$1,200 a year at the beginning of each year for 3 years, at 12 percent annual interest compounded daily? The first thing we must calculate is the annual effective rate of interest, because the mode of payment must match the mode of compounding.

$$\text{Effective annual rate} = (1 + i)^n - 1$$

$$= \left(1 + \frac{0.12}{365}\right)^{365} - 1 = (1.0003)^{365} - 1$$

$$= 1.1275 - 1 = 0.1275, \text{ which is } 12.75\%$$

Therefore, the effective annual rate is 12.75 percent, which is used to calculate the present value of our account as follows:

$$PVAD = A(PVAF)$$

$$= A\left\{\left[\frac{(1 + i)^{(n-1)} - 1}{i(1 + i)^{(n-1)}}\right] + 1\right\}$$

$$= \$1,200\left\{\left[\frac{(1 + 0.1275)^{(2)} - 1}{0.1275(1 + 0.1275)^{(2)}}\right] + 1\right\} = \$1,200\left\{\left[\frac{1.2713 - 1}{0.1275(1.2713)}\right] + 1\right\}$$

$$= \$1,200\left[\left(\frac{0.2713}{0.1621}\right) + 1\right] = \$1,200[(1.6735) + 1] = \$1.200(2.6735)$$

$$= \$3,208.24$$

If we placed \$3,208.24 into an account today earning 12 percent annual interest compounded daily, we could withdraw \$1,200 at the beginning of each year for 3 years. Although we used small numbers in this example, many people are familiar with multimillion dollar construction projects such as the new Cardinals' stadium in Glendale, Arizona. Construction may take up to 5 years, but these contracts are performance contracts, and the stadium authority must make payments to the contractors as portions of the stadium are completed. Typically, money is deposited today into interest earning accounts that guarantee those payments. The money deposited becomes the present value of a stream of payments that will be paid to the contractors for performance. In addition, \$450 million worth of bonds must be paid back to the bondholders by the time the bonds mature in July 2036.[1]

In order to have the amount to pay the bondholders, a sinking fund can be set up. If \$450 million becomes the future value and the going rate of interest is 6 percent, we can substitute the numbers in the following future value of an ordinary annuity formula and determine that \$5,692,010.17 should be deposited each year. Making 30 annual payments gives us a total of \$170,760,305.10. The \$279,239,694.90 difference (\$450,000,000 − \$170,760,305.10) is interest.

---

[1]Jim Watts, "Arizona Sports Authority Plans Final Bonds for Stadium," *The Financial Times*, August 2, 2005.

$$FVOA = A(FVAF)$$

$$\$450{,}000{,}000 = A\left[\frac{(1+i)^n - 1}{i}\right] = A\left[\frac{(1+0.06)^{30} - 1}{0.06}\right]$$

$$\$450{,}000{,}000 = A\left[\frac{(5.7435) - 1}{0.06}\right] = A\left(\frac{4.7435}{0.06}\right)$$

$$\$450{,}000{,}000 = A(79.0583)$$

$$A = \frac{\$450{,}000{,}000}{79.0583} = \$5{,}692{,}010.17$$

PRESENT VALUE AND AMORTIZATION

You are probably thinking at this point that all of this is nice to know, but what value does it have for you in real life? Most likely, you have a mortgage or know someone who does. All of us, at one time or another, finance items such as automobiles, furniture, and houses. As business owners, we finance equipment, facilities, and inventory; so, let's look at a real-life example.

The present value of a stream of monthly payments (an ordinary annuity) is actually the mortgage amount that you agree on when you finance your home. It is the amount that is agreed on by the borrower and the lender. For example, if you borrow $100,000 for 30 years at 8 percent interest, then the $100,000 is the present value of the stream of payments (monthly mortgage payments) paid at the beginning of each month, but it is calculated as an ordinary annuity, which would make payment due at the end of the month. Why? The bank wants to collect your mortgage payment one month in advance because they will not let you live in the house for free. For example, the bank requires you to make the mortgage payment for the month of January on January 1, but the payment is calculated as if you made the payment on January 31. You always pay the bank one month in advance for the privilege of living in your house for the month. Thus, if you borrow $100,000, the mortgage payment for the agreed-on fixed interest rate of 8 percent compounded monthly for 30 years is $733.76. Because you are obligated to make monthly payments for 30 years, you will make 360 payments (30 years × 12 months). We plug this into our equation for an ordinary annuity, which is

$$PVOA = A\left[\frac{(1+i)^n - 1}{i(1+i)^n}\right]$$

$$\$100{,}000 = A\left[\frac{\left(1 + \dfrac{0.08}{12}\right)^{(12 \times 30)} - 1}{\dfrac{0.08}{12}\left(1 + \dfrac{0.08}{12}\right)^{(12 \times 30)}}\right]$$

$$\$100{,}000 = A(136.2835)$$

$$A = \frac{\$100{,}000}{136.2835} = \$733.76$$

Therefore, $733.76 is the monthly mortgage payment, or ordinary annuity. This payment is made for 30 years, or 360 months, times $733.76, for a total of $264,153.60. Note that your mortgage is only $100,000; therefore, you pay $164,153.60 in interest over the life of the loan. Total interest on a loan equals total payments minus loan amount ($264,153.60 − $100,000 = $164,153.60).

Now if you borrow the same $100,000 but decide to pay it off in 15 years, what is the difference in mortgage payments and total amount of interest paid? You now borrow $100,000 for 15 years at 8 percent interest. The $100,000 is the present value of the stream of payments (monthly mortgage payments) paid 1 month in advance at the beginning of each month at the agreed-on fixed interest rate of 8 percent compounded monthly but calculated by the bank as an ordinary annuity. We now plug the new values into the same formula:

$$PVOA = A\left[\frac{(1 + i)^{(n)} - 1}{i(1 + i)^{(n)}}\right]$$

$$\$100,000 = A\left[\frac{\left(1 + \dfrac{0.08}{12}\right)^{(12 \times 15)} - 1}{\dfrac{0.18}{12}\left(1 + \dfrac{0.08}{12}\right)^{(12 \times 15)}}\right]$$

$$\$100,000 = A(104.6406)$$

$$A = \frac{\$100,000}{104.6406} = \$955.65$$

With a 15-year mortgage at the same 8 percent interest rate, $955.65 is the monthly mortgage payment, or ordinary annuity. This payment is made for 15 years, or 180 months, times $955.65, for a total of $172,017. Note that your mortgage is still $100,000; therefore, you now pay $72,017 in interest over the life of the loan. As we can see from comparing the two mortgages, $164,153.60 of interest on the 30-year mortgage minus $72,017 of interest on the 15-year mortgage equals $92,136.60. So $92,136.60 is saved in interest if you finance for 15 years versus 30 years. The key question is whether you can afford the additional $221.89-a-month payment for the 15-year mortgage. If you are not sure, you can take the 30-year mortgage and make additional principal payments when possible. You can be sure that additional payments made toward reducing the outstanding principal amount result in your paying off the mortgage sooner, and subsequently, you pay less in interest over the life of the loan.

Banks are in business to make as much profit as possible; therefore, they use the ordinary annuity rather than the annuity due method of calculating payments for all loans, because the lender collects a larger monthly payment over the life of the loan. If we take the same $100,000 mortgage over a 15-year payment schedule but calculate the payment using the annuity due, then you have a smaller monthly payment and, over the 180 months, you pay the bank less interest. These calculations are as follows:

$$PVAD = A\left\{\frac{(1 + i)^{(n-1)} - 1}{i(1 + i)^{(n-1)}} + 1\right\}$$

$$\$100{,}000 = A\left\{\left[\frac{\left(1 + \dfrac{0.08}{12}\right)^{[(12 \times 15)-1]} - 1}{\dfrac{0.08}{12}\left(1 + \dfrac{0.08}{12}\right)^{[(12 \times 15)-1]}}\right] + 1\right\}$$

$$\$100{,}000 = A(105.3382)$$

$$A = \frac{\$100{,}000}{105.3382} = \$949.32$$

We see that with a 15-year mortgage at the same 8 percent interest rate, $949.32 is the monthly mortgage payment, or annuity due. This payment is made for 15 years, or 180 months, times $949.32 (versus the $955.65 ordinary annuity payment), for a total of $170,877.60 rather than the $172,017. Note that the bank collects an additional $1,139.40 in interest over the life of the loan by calculating the mortgage using the ordinary annuity formula. Considering the thousands of loans that banks finance each year, this difference in profit is huge.

AMORTIZATION

At this point, it is important for us to understand that the monthly payment made to the lender consists of an interest amount calculated on the previous loan balance and a principal amount that reduces that loan balance. The reduction of the loan balance by applying each month's principal payment is known as **amortization**. To further clarify amortization, Table 9–3 addresses several components, including payment number, date of payment, payment amount, interest paid, principal payment, and loan balance. We used the sample $100,000 mortgage for 30 years at 8 percent compounded monthly to show an amortization schedule for the first 2 years of the loan.

Table 9–3 was constructed in Microsoft Excel using the following logic. We insert the years of the loan and the compounding interval in two cells. We then place the loan amount and the annual interest rate into two separate cells. The number of payments is determined by multiplying the years times the months. The monthly payment is calculated by solving for the annuity using the present value of an ordinary annuity formula. This monthly payment cell is placed at the top of the spreadsheet using the data for the loan. All this information is then placed at the top of the spreadsheet as shown in Table 9-3. We now construct the spreadsheet columns. The Payment Number column represents the total number of payments due on the loan. The Date of Payment is a chronological listing of all monthly due dates over the entire length of the loan. Because this is an annuity, the

TABLE 9–3 Loan Amortization for Mortgage

		Years = 30		Compounds 12	
	Loan Date of Origin	Loan Amount	Annual Interest Rate	No. of Payments	Monthly Payment
	1/1/2007	$100,000.00	8.00%	360	$733.76
Payment Number	Date of Payment	Monthly Payment	Monthly Interest	Principal Payment	Remaining Loan Balance
					$100,000.00
1	1/1/2007	$ 733.76	$ 666.67	$ 67.10	99,932.90
2	2/1/2007	733.76	666.22	67.55	99,865.36
3	3/1/2007	733.76	665.77	68.00	99,797.36
4	4/1/2007	733.76	665.32	68.45	99,728.91
5	5/1/2007	733.76	664.86	68.91	99,660.01
6	6/1/2007	733.76	664.40	69.36	99,590.64
7	7/1/2007	733.76	663.94	69.83	99,520.82
8	8/1/2007	733.76	663.47	70.29	99,450.52
9	9/1/2007	733.76	663.00	70.76	99,379.76
10	10/1/2007	733.76	662.53	71.23	99,308.53
11	11/1/2007	733.76	662.06	71.71	99,236.82
12	12/1/2007	733.76	661.58	72.19	99,164.64
Annual Totals		$8,805.17	$7,969.81	$835.36	
13	1/1/2008	733.76	661.10	72.67	99,091.97
14	2/1/2008	733.76	660.61	73.15	99,018.82
15	3/1/2008	733.76	660.13	73.64	98,945.18
16	4/1/2008	733.76	659.63	74.13	98,871.05
17	5/1/2008	733.76	659.14	74.62	98,796.42
18	6/1/2008	733.76	658.64	75.12	98,721.30
19	7/1/2008	733.76	658.14	75.62	98,645.68
20	8/1/2008	733.76	657.64	76.13	98,569.55
21	9/1/2008	733.76	657.13	76.63	98,492.92
22	10/1/2008	733.76	656.62	77.15	98,415.77
23	11/1/2008	733.76	656.11	77.66	98,338.11
24	12/1/2008	733.76	655.59	78.18	98,259.94
Annual Totals		$8,805.17	$7,900.48	$904.70	

amounts of the payments in the Monthly Payment column are all the same. This is the initial mortgage amount divided by the present value annuity factor for an ordinary annuity. The Monthly Interest column is calculated by multiplying the previous month's remaining loan balance times the monthly interest rate, as follows:

Monthly interest month 1 = Previous month's loan balance times monthly interest

$$= \$100,000\left(\frac{0.08}{12}\right) = \$100,000(0.00667) = \$666.67$$

Monthly interest month 2 = Previous month's loan balance times monthly interest

$$= \$99,932.90\left(\frac{0.08}{12}\right) = \$99,932.90(0.00667)$$

$$= \$666.22$$

The Principal Payment column is calculated by subtracting the monthly interest from the monthly annuity payment. For month 1, $733.76 monthly payment –$666.67 monthly interest = $67.10 (rounded) monthly principle payment, which reduces the Remaining Loan Balance, as calculated by subtracting the Principal Payment from the previous month's Remaining Loan Balance. For month 1, $100,000 remaining loan balance – $67.10 principle payment = $99,932.90 remaining loan balance. Once these formulas are placed into the proper cells, they can just be copied down the spreadsheet for the term of the loan. There is an amortization table contained with the spreadsheet applications that accompany this textbook.

There are several methods that one can use to reduce the number of payments made on a loan and thus the total interest paid on a mortgage. We cannot calculate all of the variations, but we can explain the underlying logic. If you increase the principle payment each month by any amount, you reduce the remaining balance on the loan. For example, if you have the $100,000 mortgage mentioned previously and make a payment of $833.76, rather than the mortgage payment of $733.76, you will pay $167.10 on the principle balance rather than $67.10. This reduces the principle balance to $99,832.90, which is then used to calculate the following month's interest payment. A reduced balance means you pay less interest on the loan, and hence pay the loan off at a faster rate.

There are essentially three types of mortgage loans granted by lenders. They are Prime Mortgages, Near Prime Mortgages (Alt A Mortgages) and Subprime Mortgages. The borrower qualifies for one of these categories based on the credit information received from credit rating agencies like Trans Union, Equifax, and Experian. The credit information is turned into a credit score by the Fair Isaac Corporation and is referred to as the *FICO Score*. These scores range from 500 for extremely poor credit to 850 for outstanding credit. Mortgage interest rates are adjusted by lenders based on these scores and can vary from less than 6 percent to more than 10 percent.[2]

Prime mortgages are granted to borrowers with outstanding credit scores and at the same time have sufficient capital to make substantial down payments. These people and businesses qualify for the lowest lending rates. **Near Prime Mortgages (Alt A)** are loans that fall between the prime and subprime. They are higher-risk mortgages aimed primarily at individuals with lower credit scores than the prime mortgage group. These Alt A loans are offered to people who are improving their credit now, but in the past had something on their credit score that decreased their credit rating, such as missed or late payments.

Subprime loans are provided to a borrower who has a poor credit rating and is considered to be a high risk. The applicant has probably been told that he or she does not qualify for a prime or near prime mortgage, but owning his or her own home or business is their dream, so they seek out a subprime lender

---

[2]Data obtained from MyFICO, a division of Fair Isaac Corporation. Retrieved March 14, 2008, from http://www.myfico.com.

and obtain a subprime mortgage. The Subprime Mortgage gives the high-risk borrower an opportunity to achieve the goal of owning a home or business. However, the lender's perceived risk increases the interest rate as well as closing costs for the subprime borrower. The lender is selling money at a high interest rate and the borrower pays that rate in order to purchase a home. Both lenders and borrowers are aggressive in finding each other. As we will see, some unscrupulous lenders quote very low rates in order to hook the borrower.

Caveat emptor is Latin for "Let the buyer beware." Many of the subprime loans that were issued several years ago were based on the false assumption that housing values would continue to increase as they had during the late 1990s and early part of the 21st century. Often these loans were provided with no money down and had an adjustable rate mortgage (ARM) teaser rates of 1 to 5 percent. These ARMs were either not fully explained or not understood by the borrowers. An ARM typically is issued for 1 to 5 years, with the rate increasing substantially at the end of the ARM. Let's say that Heywood U. Ripmeeoff and family qualified for a subprime 3-year arm on a $300,000 home at a teaser rate of 2 percent. The loan was for 30 years, but will be adjusted in 3 years. The monthly payment on a 2 percent loan for 30 years on a $300,000 mortgage is $1,108.86. If we use 30 percent of monthly income for the mortgage payment, the family qualifies for this loan if their income is only $3,696 a month, or $44,354 a year. At the end of the first 3 years the mortgage rate adjusts upward, but the family still owes $277,428.51 on the home.[3]

The new mortgage adjusts by using prime (6 percent) plus 2 percent, so the new mortgage rate based on Table 8–1 is 8 percent for 27 years, because the Ripmeeoffs already paid for 3 years. His new monthly mortgage payments are $2,092.59 which is more than half of his monthly income. The family was initially told by the lender that they could refinance their home at the end of 3 years but find themselves with a problem. They decide to refinance the home, but find that home prices have actually decreased, and that similar homes in their area are now selling for less than $250,000. This price is less than the existing mortgage of $277,428.51, so in order to qualify for refinancing, the family must pay the difference, plus closing costs, which amount to more than $27,428.51. The family is upside down on the home, because they actually owe more on the home that the home is worth. Because they have poor credit and obtained the home with no money down and cannot afford the new mortgage payments, they will probably lose the home and end up with even worse credit that they began with.

This could all have been avoided if the lender was upfront with the borrower and explained that the Ripmeeoffs could have a problem if interest rates increased or home prices decreased. Mr. Ripmeeoff should have been made to understand that if he didn't increase his income considerably over the next 3 years, his current income would fall well short of the adjusted required

---

[3]Mortgage payment data for this section were obtained by using the Home Loan Amortization table that accompanies this textbook.

mortgage payment. If the industry had been totally honest, Mr. Ripmeeoff and others like him should have never been permitted to purchase these homes. The minimum down payment of 10 percent would have required him to put $30,000 down, which would have left him with a $270,000 mortgage. At 6 percent interest for 30 years, his monthly payments would have been $1,618.79. With this payment, where the industry standard is 30 percent of income for the mortgage payment, he would have had to have monthly income of approximately $5,396, or an annual income of $64,750 per year. With an annual income of $44,354, there was no way he should have been able to purchase this home. Currently, Congress and the banking community are attempting to determine what, if anything, should be done about the mortgage crisis in America as thousands of homeowners in Mr. Ripmeeoff's situation are losing their homes due to foreclosure.

COMBINING LUMP SUM AND ANNUITIES INTO THE SAME PROBLEM

Although Chapter 8 concentrates on time value of money involving lump sums and Chapter 9 concentrates on time value of money involving annuities, there are several situations in which both the stream of unequal payments (lump sums) and a stream of equal payments (annuities) are combined into the same problem. Many of these problems involve capital budgeting, which is the topic of Chapter 10. However, for people who work and contribute to a 401k retirement account, we provide two practical examples of combining lump sums and annuities into the same problem.

For example: Fortuna Teller graduates college at 26. She qualifies for a 401k retirement account and knows that she can contribute up to $15,000 per year. However, with her current debt and salary she feels she can only contribute $300 each month during the first year and will be able to increase her contribution by $200 per month each subsequent year, based on annual pay raises, until she reaches the $15,000 annual maximum, which is $1,250 per month. She will then continue contributing $15,000 per year until she reaches her retirement age of 67. Many employers take a 401k contribution out of each paycheck and remit the money to a financial institution at the end of each month. Let's assume that Fortuna invests in a series of mutual funds that pay an average of 11 percent annually compounded monthly. For each year until the maximum contribution is reached, this problem starts out as the future value of a stream of equal payments, which is treated as finding the future value of an ordinary annuity (the employer deposits each month's contribution at the end of the month). Once the year ends, then the problem becomes the future value of a lump sum, because the amount deposited in the previous year remains in the

TABLE 9–4 Fortune Teller's 401k Retirement Account

Current Age = 26
Retirement Age = 67
Annual Interest Rate = 11.00%
Compounds per Year = 12

Year of Contribution	Years to Retirement	Annual Contribution	Monthly Contribution	FVOA Factor	End of Year Value	FVF	Future Value
1	41	$ 3,600.00	$ 300.00	12.6239	$ 3,787.16	79.8345	$ 302,346.17
2	40	6,000.00	500.00	12.6239	$ 6,311.94	71.5543	$ 451,646.31
3	39	8,400.00	700.00	12.6239	$ 8,836.71	64.1329	$ 566,724.17
4	38	10,800.00	900.00	12.6239	$ 11,361.49	57.4813	$ 653,072.56
5	37	13,200.00	1,100.00	12.6239	$ 13,886.26	51.5195	$ 715,413.03
6–36	36	15,000.00	1,250.00	5511.2170			$ 6,889,021.20

Total 401k Value $ 9,578,223.45

Future Value of a Lump Sum = PV(FVF)   FVF (future value factor) = $(1 + i)^n$

Future Value of an Ordinary Annuity Formula   FVOA = A(FVAF)

$$= A \left[\frac{(1 + i)^n - 1}{i} \right]$$

account and accrues interest until retirement. Table 9–4 shows this situation for the first 5 years. Fortuna reaches the maximum contribution of $1,250 per month ($15,000 per year) in the sixth year. Once the $15,000 maximum contribution is reached, she then contributes $1,250 every month, which is the future value of an ordinary annuity. We recommend that you solve this type of problem by constructing a table representing both the future value of the lump sum aspect and future value of an ordinary annuity aspect. Table 9–4 depicts Fortuna Teller's 401k retirement account. If her mutual funds perform to their historical averages, she can expect to retire with $9,578,223.45 in her account.

Note: The mechanism used to solve Fortuna's problem is to first find the future value of the equal payments for a single year; this sum becomes a lump sum. We then calculate the future value of a lump sum to find the value at retirement. This involves finding the future value of the monthly payments of $300, $500, $700, $900, and $1,100, respectively. For example, using the $300 monthly payment as an ordinary annuity for 12 months, we find that Fortuna has $3,787.16 in her account at the end of 1 year. The $3,787.16 is then left in the account as a lump sum until retirement 40 years later, when it is worth $302,346.17. At the end of the first year, she increases her annuity from $300 to $500 for the second year. As shown in Table 9–4, we perform the same calculations until she reaches her maximum annual contribution.

Second, we find the future value of the $1,250 monthly payment ($15,000 for the year) compounded monthly at 11 percent interest for the next 36 years. This problem is a future value of an ordinary annuity. Using the formula for the future value of an ordinary annuity, we find the factor to be 5,511.2170. The annuity is given at $1,250 per month. Multiplying the $1,250 by the *FVAF* of 5,511.2170, we determine that the annuity will be worth $6,889,021.20 at retirement. We add the lump sums from the first 5 years of contributions to the $6,889,021.20 and find her 401k retirement account at age 67 to be $9,578,223.45. The odd penny in the table is to the result of rounding in Microsoft Excel.

Fortuna's coworker, Krystal Bahl, who is the same age, desires to do exactly as her friend with a slight variation. Krystal noticed that the 401k law allows people who are 50 years of age or older to contribute $20,000 per year. In both cases, each starts off by funding the 401k modestly with monthly payment of $300, $500, $700, $900, and $1,100, respectively for the first 5 years. Beginning with the 6th year, Krystal contributes $1,250 per month ($15,000 per year) for 18 years until she reaches age 49. At age 50 and until she retires at age 67, Krystal contributes $1,666.67 per month ($20,000 per year) for 18 years. Table 9–5 depicts Krystal's retirement strategy using a spreadsheet.

At retirement, Krystal will have $2,689,202.24, which is the sum of the lump sum payments from the first 5 years. Her annuity of $1,250 for 18 years accumulates a total of $842,414.70, which then becomes a lump sum invested at 11 percent compounded monthly for 18 years, resulting in a total of $6,046,606.51. For the final 18 years she is contributing $1,666.67 per

TABLE 9-5 Krystal Bahl's 401k Retirement Account

Current Age = 26
Retirement Age = 67
Annual Interest Rate = 11.00%
Compounds per Year = 12

Age at Contribution	Years to Retirement	Annual Contribution	Monthly Contribution	FVOA Factor	End of Year Value	FVF	Future Value
26	41	$ 3,600.00	$ 300.00	12.6239	$ 3,787.16	79.8345	$ 302,346.17
27	40	6,000.00	500.00	12.6239	6,311.94	71.5543	$ 451,646.31
28	39	8,400.00	700.00	12.6239	8,836.71	64.1329	$ 566,724.17
29	38	10,800.00	900.00	12.6239	11,361.49	57.4813	$ 653,072.56
30	37	13,200.00	1,100.00	12.6239	13,886.26	51.5195	$ 715,413.03
31–49	18	15,000.00	1,250.00	673.9318			$6,046,606.51
50–67	18	20,000.00	1,666.67	673.9318	842,414.70	7.1777	$1,123,219.59

Total 401k Value $ 9,859,028.35

Future Value of a Lump Sum = $PV(FVF)$ FVF (future value factor) $= (1 + i)^n$

Future Value of an Ordinary Annuity Formula $FVOA = A(FVAF)$

$$= A\left[\frac{(1 + i)^n - 1}{i}\right]$$

month, which accumulates to a total of $1,123,219.59. This all adds up to $9,859,028.35, as shown in Table 9–5. Notice that by using this strategy, Krystal will have more than $280,000 additional on reaching retirement.

CONCLUSION

These chapters on the time value of money provide us with the tools that we require as financial managers and small-business entrepreneurs to solve many of the actual problems faced in decision making. We covered the following areas:

- Ordinary annuities and annuities due
- Future value and present value of annuities
- Sinking funds
- Loans and amortization
- Combination of lump sum and annuity problems

These time value of money tools, which are covered extensively in Chapters 8 and 9, are vital for making capital budgeting decisions as described in Chapter 10.

Appendix A demonstrates how to place the formulas used in this chapter into spreadsheet programs and how to place the formulas into a programmable calculator.

We use most of these formulas when making decisions on the purchase of equipment and the investment of money in personal or business ventures that have a life of 1 year or longer. The process for making these decisions is capital budgeting, which is the topic of Chapter 10.

REVIEW AND DISCUSSION QUESTIONS

1. What is the difference between the *present value of an annuity* and the *future value of an annuity*?
2. What is the difference between an *ordinary annuity* and an *annuity due*?
3. How do banks calculate the monthly payment on a loan?
4. Describe situations in which you have an integration of future lump sums and streams of equal and unequal payments.

EXERCISES AND PROBLEMS

1. Ira Schwab opens up a Schwab IRA and places $2,000 in his retirement account at the beginning of each year for 10 years. He believes the account will earn 5 percent interest per year, compounded quarterly. How much will he have in his retirement account in 10 years?

2. The city of Glendale borrows $48 million by issuing municipal bonds to help build the Arizona Cardinals football stadium. It plans to set up a sinking fund that will repay the loan at the end of 10 years. Assume a 4 percent interest rate per year. What should the city place into the fund at the end of each year to have $48 million in the account to pay back their bondholders?

3. Congratulations! You have just won the lottery and have elected to receive $50,000 per year for 20 years. Assume that a 4 percent interest rate is used to evaluate the annuity and that you receive each payment at the beginning of the year.
   a. What is the present value of the lottery?
   b. How much interest is earned on the present value to make the $50,000-per-year payment?

4. Calculate the monthly mortgage payment made at the beginning of each month on a $100,000 mortgage. The mortgage is for 15 years and the interest rate is 5.5 percent.

5. Easy Leifer plans to retire at the age of 65 and believes he will live to be 90. Easy wants to receive an annual retirement payment of $50,000 at the beginning of each year. He set up a retirement account that is estimated to earn 6 percent annually.
   a. How much money must Easy have in the account when he reaches 65 years old?
   b. Easy is currently 29 years of age. How much must he invest in this account at the end of each year for the next 36 years to have this amount in his account at age 65?

6. Tom and Mary James just had a baby. They heard that the cost of providing a college education for this baby will be $100,000 in 18 years. Tom normally receives a Christmas bonus of $4,000 every year in the paycheck prior to Christmas. He read that a good stock mutual fund should pay him an average of 10 percent per year. Tom and Mary want to make sure their son has $100,000 for college. Consider each of the following questions:
   a. How much must Tom invest in this mutual fund at the end of each year to have $100,000 in 18 years?
   b. If the bonus is not paid until the first of the year, how much must Tom invest at the beginning of each year to have $100,000 in 18 years?
   c. Tom's father said he would provide for his grandson's education. He puts $10,000 in a government bond that pays 7 percent interest. His dad said this should be enough. Do you agree?
   d. If Mary has a savings account worth $50,000, how much must she withdraw from savings and set aside in this mutual fund to have the $100,000 for her son's education in 18 years?
   e. If Mary has been advised to keep the $50,000 in her savings account earning 4 percent compounded monthly, how much additional money would she have to set aside in the stock mutual fund to have the $100,000 for her son's education in 18 years?

7. Sam is currently 30 years of age. He owns his own business and wants to retire at the age of 60. He has little confidence in the current Social Security system. He wants to retire with an annual income of $72,000 a year.
   a. If Sam believes he will live to age 90, how much does he have to accumulate by the time he reaches age 60 to receive $72,000 at the end of each year for the rest of his life? Sam believes he can earn 8 percent on his money in a stock mutual fund.
   b. How much does he have to accumulate if he wants the payment of $72,000 at the beginning of each year?
   c. What dollar amount of interest will Sam have earned during retirement if he receives his $72,000 at the beginning of each year?

8. Regarding question 7b, if Sam believes he will earn 10 percent on his investment for retirement, how much does he have to contribute to his retirement account at the beginning of each year to accumulate his retirement nest egg?

9. You have been shopping for a new home. You have a choice of financing. You can choose either a $200,000 mortgage at 5.75 percent for 30 years, or a $200,000 mortgage at 5.5 percent for 15 years.
   a. Calculate the monthly payment for both the 30-year and 15-year mortgages.
   b. Calculate the amount of interest paid over the life of the loan for both mortgages.
   c. Choose the best mortgage for you and explain your answer.

10. You like to buy lottery tickets every week. The lottery pays an insurance company that pays the winner an annuity. If you win a $1,000,000 lottery and elect to take an annuity, you get $50,000 per year at the beginning of each year for the next 20 years.
    a. How much must the state pay the insurance company if money can earn 6 percent?
    b. How much interest is earned on this lump-sum payment over the 20 years?
    c. If you take the cash rather than the annuity, the state pays you $500,000 in one lump sum today. You must pay 40 percent of this in taxes. If you are currently working and invest this money at 6 percent, how much money will you have in a mutual fund at the end of 20 years?
    d. Are you better off with the annuity, or should you take the cash? Explain.

11. Mr. Bates is creating a college investment fund for his daughter. He will put in $850 at the end of each year for the next 15 years. He expects to earn 6.35 percent annually. How much money will his daughter have in her college fund?

12. Blushing Rose invests $1,000 into her Roth IRA. She can increase this investment annually by $1,000 until she reaches the $5,000 annual contribution limit. She will then invest $5,000 per year at the beginning of each year for 30 years. How much will Blushing have in her IRA at the end of 34 years if her IRA earns 8 percent?

RECOMMENDED TEAM ASSIGNMENT

1. As a team, investigate how credit information is used to produce a credit score. How is credit information used to produce a credit score that determines what type of mortgage loan would be granted by a lender? Include FICO scores.
2. Devise a methodology for educating the public about mortgage lending.

CASE STUDY: ENTREPRENEURIAL SPIRIT

© 2008 Philip J. Adelman and Alan M. Marks

Albert Smith was born and raised in New York City. After graduating from high school, Albert enrolled in Brooklyn College of the City University of New York, majoring in Biology and Chemistry with a minor in theater. After graduating from college, he took a job as a biology teacher in an inner-city high school. Albert decided to get an MBA, because he knew he would end up in the business world, and found a program that was right for him. He had a long way to go, because he had not taken any business courses as an undergraduate. He knew about business from a practical standpoint, and this prior knowledge seamed to lessen the amount of time Albert needed to put in on his studies.

In March 1969, Albert met his wife Carol, a fourth-grade teacher, at a special teaching event, and they were married 9 months later. The two educators traveled together during their summer break and then settled down and raised a family.

In 1973, Albert received his MBA from Baruch College of the City University of New York, yet at the same time he enjoyed teaching high school biology to inner-city kids, because he found it very rewarding. Time passed, and Albert continued to think about business. He always enjoyed finance and was fascinated with how insurance worked. He answered an ad in the newspaper that turned out to be an insurance agency looking to expand their sales staff. The insurance agency was impressed with Albert, and hired him as an agent with the provision that Albert pass all of the licensing examinations.

Albert prepared to take the state insurance agents' exam and passed it the first time. He was now licensed in life and health insurance. Albert found that his teaching skills could be applied in explaining the more difficult concepts of insurance. He wanted to learn more about insurance, so he enrolled in a Chartered Life Underwriter (CLU) program in order to have additional knowledge that in time would make him an expert in the insurance field. The CLU is a designation that indicates proficiency and having the latest information in order to best serve the customer.

Although Albert was extremely successful in the insurance business (life and heath), his clients wanted him to serve all their insurance needs. Because he was not licensed in casualty insurance, the only way he could serve his clientele with one-stop shopping was for him to pass the casualty brokers' examination. He enrolled in an all-day preparation class, passed the test, and now was licensed in all areas of insurance.

Albert continued teaching during the day and marketed insurance during the evening hours. He would leave his house at 6 A.M., return at 6:30 P.M., eat dinner, and then go on two appointments each evening, often coming home at 11:00 P.M. Albert did very well, amassing about 75 clients in the 2 years that he worked for the agency. Albert's success made the agency's owner uneasy. One day, the owner approached Albert and asked him to sign a document that stated if he ever left the agency; the owners of the agency would keep his renewals. Renewals are the future dollars paid to agents for sales they make now. Albert asked his boss what would happen if he refused to sign. The boss said he would no longer be provided with office space—in short, fired. Albert refused to sign and set up his own business from his home. He contacted the insurance company that the agency did most of its business with and asked if he could be a general agent. Initially, they said yes, but later reneged after receiving a call from his former employer, who stated if they granted Albert his own agency, the former employer would pull all their clients and direct them to another insurance company. In effect, Albert was blackballed and couldn't function as a general agent.

Meanwhile Carol developed Raynaud's disease and needed to live in a warm climate, so they chose Arizona. The Smiths put their house up for sale in New York and managed to recoup their $10,000 down payment. After paying the moving company in Arizona, they now had $5,000 in their pocket. With a great deal of determination, the Smiths purchased a house on Aster Dr. in northeast Phoenix in less than a year. After 4 years, they decided they needed a larger house and put their house up for sale, but couldn't sell it. They had their eye on a new house that was being built and decided to rent out their former home to a couple relocating to Phoenix. What the Smiths did not know was that the renters' furniture and moving boxes would arrive ahead of the renters, and now the Smiths had cardboard boxes everywhere. The Smiths charged the couple $650, which did not cover their $900 monthly expense. What the Smiths experienced was negative cash flow. However, when the Smiths paid their taxes, they were able to declare a $3,000 business loss. This calculation is ($650 rent × 12 months) = $7,800 − ($900 mortgage payment × 12) = $10,800, leaving them with $3,000 out of pocket. Because they were in a 25 percent tax bracket, the $3,000 loss saved the Smiths about $750 in taxes. In 1983, the Smiths had one rental on Aster with a $55,000 mortgage debt.

The Smiths enjoyed being landlords and determined that if they could come up with a down payment and closing costs, they could purchase a house and rent it out. What made this especially attractive was that the builder bought down the interest rate for 3 years, so in 1984, they bought a new house on 34th Way. The Smiths purchased the house for $78,000 with a $3,000 down payment, which left a $75,000 mortgage. In 1985, they bought an $85,000 new house on Grandview with an $8,000 down payment. Therefore, the house on Grandview had a $77,000 mortgage. The house that the Smiths resided in cost $99,000 with a $90,000 mortgage. As a result of these purchases, the Smiths have about $300,000 in mortgage debt. They took a risk, and based on this risk they wanted to be rewarded heavily. As interest rates dropped during the 1990s and demand for housing in the Scottsdale–Phoenix market increased, the Smiths began thinking about selling the three rentals and investing in more lucrative newer real estate.

The 34th Way house now had a positive cash flow and the renter asked if he could purchase the house. The $140,000 selling price offered was accepted by the Smiths for a gain of $71,500 ($140,000 selling price − $68,500 mortgage debt = $71,500). Taxes must be paid on this gain, and the depreciation deducted each year must be recaptured.

The Smiths decided they would treat this as Section 1031 Exchange Property, allowing them to defer the taxes they would have to pay if they rolled over the $71,500 gain into like kind property. The Smiths wanted to invest in the Scottsdale area and found a condominium in the Grayhawk Community of North Scottsdale, Arizona. The price was $243,500 and the $71,500 rollover gain plus $24,500 was the down payment. The mortgage was a 30-year fixed at 6.00 percent on $147,500. In 2008, the condo was worth about $450,000; with $138,000 mortgage debt, they have $312,000 in equity.

The Smiths have since decided to sell both the Aster and Grandview houses and have been successful in both areas. Grandview was sold for $159,000, for a gain of $95,000, and Aster was sold for $120,000, for a gain of $70,000. Aster's proceeds of $70,000 and Grandview's proceeds of $95,000, totaling $165,000, were applied as a down payment on another Grayhawk condominium. The $278,000 mortgage was a 30-year fixed at 6.5 percent. Today, it is worth $450,000, and $113,000 remains on the mortgage to give the Smiths $337,000 of equity. Just for the record, the Smiths have $649,000 of equity in their two rentals. If they add on their own personal residence, they have an additional $800,000 in equity for a grand total of $1,449,000 in real estate.

A strategy employed by the Smiths is to make additional payments to reduce the principal balance of the mortgage, which cuts the time it takes to finish paying the mortgage. Not bad for two teachers.

QUESTIONS

1. Evaluate the equity that the Smiths have in their properties. What advice would you give the Smiths with regard to their tolerance for risk?
2. Using current market interest rates for 15- and 30-year mortgages, construct an amortization schedule for each of the Smith's properties. What is the difference in monthly payments if market interest rates jump to 12 percent for the 30-year mortgage?
3. If Albert's insurance premium renewals amounted to $10,000 a year for 10 years and the going interest rate at the time was 14 percent, find the present value of Albert's renewals.

CHAPTER 10

Capital Budgeting

Learning Objectives

When you have completed this chapter, you should be able to:

♦ Understand the purpose and need for capital budgeting.

♦ Explain the impact that government regulations may have on a company's capital budgeting decision.

♦ List and explain the steps required in making a capital budgeting decision.

♦ Distinguish among start-up costs, working capital commitment costs, and tax factor costs as well as the role each plays in the capital budgeting decision.

♦ Compare the relationship between increased efficiency benefits and tax factor benefits and understand their effect on a company's cash flow.

♦ Understand payback, net present value, profitability index, internal rate of return, and accounting rate of return as techniques of capital budgeting.

♦ Compute the payback of a capital budgeting project.

♦ Using time value of money, compute the net present value of a capital budgeting project.

♦ Given a company's investment costs, calculate the weighted average cost of capital.

♦ Calculate and compare a company's internal rate of return with its accounting rate of return.

♦ Determine how a company's capital budgeting decision makes a project mutually exclusive.

♦ Determine how a company's capital budgeting decision is influenced by capital rationing.

♦ Understand the importance of following up, controlling, and taking corrective action after a capital budgeting decision has been made.

As businessowners, we constantly strive to ensure the profitability of our company by working hard to generate a high rate of return on both short- and long-term investments. In Chapter 7 we discussed how we manage working capital to maintain liquidity and to meet our short-term obligations. We pointed out that excess cash could be invested temporarily in short-term marketable securities to generate a more positive return on investment without too much risk. We also mentioned that we invest in assets that are expected to result in cash returns for a period of 1 year or more. These investments in capital expenditures (assets having a useful life of 1 year or more) are expected to help generate increased revenues that make our firm more profitable in the future. Our business must constantly make decisions about whether to purchase new equipment or expand operations with the addition of new buildings. The method we use to make these determinations is referred to as *capital budgeting.*

CAPITAL BUDGETING

Capital budgeting is the method we use to justify the acquisition of capital goods (those items that have a useful life in excess of 1 year). These long-term assets may be used by our business to generate increased cash flow by improving the efficiency or the effectiveness of our business. We purchase these assets only when we determine that the benefits we will receive over the life of each asset exceed the costs of acquiring and maintaining it over its useful life. Capital budgeting investments are based on the assumption that rates of return on investments, as well as the current inflation rate, remain the same throughout the useful lives of the investments.

A company should make the decision to enter into a specific project, acquire another company, or purchase a computer only if, after capital budgeting analysis, it is determined that the present value of the benefits received outweighs the present value of the costs incurred. It is important to note that future cash flow resulting from increased efficiency is a future benefit. These future benefits must be brought back, or *translated,* into the present and quantified for a profitable decision to be made. The value of future monies over time must be translated into a value now and matched with the costs incurred. These future monies or benefits should be measured in after-tax dollars or cash flows. The benefits received vary from one investment to the next.

The risk involved in making an investment and the investment's ability to generate enough cash flow force companies to categorize capital budgeting decisions according to different standards. These standards are applied to determine whether specific projects or investments should be accepted or rejected. We find that some investments are a necessity for the well-being of a business. For example, a business must replace its worn-out equipment to continue operating. Hannah's Donut Shop delivery vans require replacement after several years because of the mileage put on the vehicles in distributing the product. Capital budgeting is used to make the most profitable decisions regarding the purchase of delivery vehicles.

FACTORS AFFECTING CAPITAL BUDGETING

CHANGES IN GOVERNMENT REGULATIONS

Government regulations placed on certain businesses often cost a company money in complying with the regulations. For example, the environment has been found to be damaged by chlorofluorocarbon (CFC) emissions when automobile air conditioners are serviced. All automobile repair facilities that wish to continue to service air conditioners have been forced to buy expensive recovery equipment. This mandatory requirement left a company that did not want to comply with only one choice—to quit servicing air-conditioning equipment. If we owned an auto repair facility, we would have to use capital budgeting to determine if we wanted to comply with the new law or stop repairing and servicing air-conditioning equipment. First, we must determine how much revenue would be lost if we stopped repairs. Second, we must determine the present value of the cost of compliance, which involves purchasing the CFC equipment and training our employees to use it. If the lost revenue (present value of the benefits we expect to receive) is greater than the cost of purchasing the equipment and training our employees, then we should buy the equipment. Conversely, if the lost revenue is less than the cost of the equipment and training, then we should cease to service air conditioners that use CFCs. Thus, the owners of a business need some method of determining if the cost of purchasing the recovery equipment is exceeded by the future revenues obtained by servicing air-conditioning equipment. The process of making the capital budgeting decision is the subject of this chapter.

We know from previous discussions that our goal in running a business is to make a profit, both now and in the future; hence, our business is always looking for ways to generate additional revenue and cash flow. *Cash flow* is the actual cash in our pockets that can be used to pay bills. We often find that we incur additional expenses to increase revenue, but we also can generate additional cash by reducing costs. Numerous methods of cost reduction can be used to add to our cash flow. If we save $1 in expenses during the process of generating $2 in cash, then we have an additional $3. In other words, whatever amount we save through cost reduction can also be viewed as money earned. The benefits of increased cash flow and cost reduction are computed on an after-tax basis.

RESEARCH AND DEVELOPMENT

Another example of capital budgeting can be found in a company's new-product development program. Companies must seek new products to remain competitive. The additional costs associated with new-product development can be justified if the expected benefits to be received from the new product exceed the costs incurred. It is important to note the significant risk associated with new-product development because more than half of all new products fail. When a product fails, it means that the expected benefits from the new product do not materialize; therefore, the benefits do not exceed the costs of developing the new product. Obviously, developing new products is a risky proposition. Risk can be overcome by acquiring companies that already have a proven product. Risk can also be minimized when companies make decisions that correspond to their existing company strategy.

CHANGES IN BUSINESS STRATEGY

In the 1980s, financial service businesses increased risk by changing strategies. With deregulation and changes in tax laws, many of them entered into businesses with little or no experience. When the economy changed, the risk associated with these changes in strategies increased. Financial managers did not change their strategies when the economy changed, and several businesses failed. Many of these failures could have been avoided if conservative strategies had been maintained or adopted through proper decision making. For example, savings and loan institutions had traditionally financed home mortgages. In the 1970s, when market interest rates were low, these institutions loaned money (financed 30-year home mortgages) at rates ranging from 7 percent to 9 percent while paying their depositors rates of less than 5 percent. When interest rates soared in the late 1970s and early 1980s, to attract depositors, they had to offer interest rates of 12 percent or more. Hence the present value of their costs (interest rates given to depositors) exceeded the value of the benefits (interest rates collected on mortgages), and the result was a heavy loss for savings and loan institutions.

With changes in banking regulation, savings and loan institutions were allowed to enter new markets involving commercial real estate development. Financial managers saw the entry into these new markets as a way to reduce their losses from current interest rates and home mortgage collections. Thus, savings and loans changed their strategy and entered into markets (commercial real estate) where they had little or no experience. Many of them incurred risk that exceeded any benefits anticipated. The results were massive failure, bankruptcies, and corruption. Thousands of stockholders and bondholders lost most of their savings when these institutions failed. It is apparent that proper decision making was not used in the savings and loan industry.

In early 2008, interest rates dropped to extremely low values, with home mortgage rates for 30-year mortgages at 5.62 percent and and 15-year mortgages at 5.08 percent.[1] Banks were paying less than 2 percent interest on savings

---

[1]Quotes on home mortgages and CD rates. Retrieved March 21, 2008, from http://www. Bankrate.com.

accounts, with 1-year certificate of deposit (CD) rates at an all-time low of 2.13 percent. If interest rates were to rise because of inflation or war, then we expect that banks, in order to lure depositors, must offer higher interest rates on saving accounts. For example, if banks offer 10 percent on a 5-year CD, they are spending $10 for every $100 of depositor's money. However, they are still collecting $5.08 for every $100 of 15-year mortgage money loaned out in 2008. Thus, the cycle that we saw in the late 1970s and early 1980s could repeat itself. We believe that this could lead to some banks failing in the future.

The early 21st century is one where we see tremendous job shifts occurring in the global business sector because of the decreased price of communication and transportation. Many U.S. businesses are exporting call centers to countries like India. Hyundai, a Korean manufacturing company, completed a $1.1 billion manufacturing plant in Montgomery, Alabama, where they build Sonata and Santa Fe automobiles.[2] All of these job shifts require capital budgeting decisions on the part of the company.

To ensure proper decision making, a business should take the necessary steps carefully in making a capital budgeting decision. The five steps involved in capital budgeting are as follows:

1. **Formulate a proposal,** which identifies the various costs incurred and benefits received in after-tax cash flows.
2. **Evaluate the data** generated with respect to the benefits and costs to see whether the investment will be profitable.
3. **Make a decision** about the data. Choose the course of action that provides the greatest future benefit while minimizing future costs.
4. **Follow up** on the capital budgeting decision through a post-audit to see if the benefits received in reality exceed the additional costs incurred.
5. **Take corrective action** if the post-audit indicates that the benefits received are not meeting our expectations.

FORMULATING A PROPOSAL

To formulate a proposal, we must first identify all costs and benefits associated with our project.

COSTS IN CAPITAL BUDGETING

Several costs must be determined when evaluating a capital budgeting decision. Those most often considered by businessowners and managers are *start-up costs, working capital commitment costs,* and *tax factor costs.*

---

[2]Hyundai. Retrieved August 19, 2008, from http://www.hmmausa.com.

Start-up costs are the total dollars spent to get a project under way. These costs include acquisition costs for a new piece of equipment, training costs of employees, and any maintenance costs, as well as the costs of service agreements, hiring new personnel, changes in inventory, additional storage space, and so forth. Include all money that must be committed to the proposal. The acquisition costs of a new piece of equipment must include installation. The cost of hiring new personnel includes the costs associated with recruiting, interviewing, selecting, and training. Cash flow and revenue are not generated by a new project until after start-up costs are incurred.

Therefore, we must have sufficient financing to pay for all start-up costs without obtaining any additional cash flow. We strongly recommend using Gantt charts, as previously discussed, to chart all start-up costs over time. For a new business or a business expansion, start-up costs also would include utility deposits, security deposits on rented property, and possibly costs associated with construction of new facilities.

Working capital commitment costs involve maintaining specific levels of working capital that are required by lending institutions. Working capital, aside from cash, also consists of investments in inventory and accounts receivable. Banks and other lending institutions do not normally lend money to finance a capital budgeting investment unless the borrower shows possession of the working capital to make monthly payments. This money is legally tied up and is committed to the lender in such a manner that it cannot be used by the borrower for investment or other purposes. Funds tied up in inventory and accounts receivable cannot be used. Therefore, the working capital commitment is an opportunity cost that must be considered in formulating the proposal, because this money cannot be invested in any other area.

Tax factor costs result from additional taxes that have to be paid. For example, your city, county, or state may have an annual property tax and a personal property tax assessment. When you buy new equipment or increase the value of your building, the assessor includes these additions when determining your tax liability.

BENEFITS IN CAPITAL BUDGETING

In identifying the benefits from a capital investment, we should note that most businesses derive their benefits from the increased amount of cash flow that the investment brings and the increased amount of efficiency that the investment causes in day-to-day operations. Another factor is the ability of an organization to write off an investment, which in turn reduces its tax liability. We discussed the use of depreciation as a means of writing off an investment in Chapter 3; however, tax laws change so frequently that benefits from such information are unreliable. What must be stressed is the enhanced cash flow and increased efficiency that an asset investment—whether it be a piece of equipment, a new facility, or an acquisition—brings. This ensures the success of a business by increasing its productivity through proper managerial decision making. It is important to note that decreasing the tax liability of a business is subject to modification as tax laws change. What appears to be a benefit today can very well change to a cost in the future as new legislation is enacted.

In dealing with increased efficiency, the benefit derived must have taxes paid on it before it can be deemed to be a true benefit. A company that increases efficiency from the purchase of an asset to increase profit by $10,000 each year pays taxes on $10,000. The tax rate may be as high as approximately 39 percent, or $3,900, in which case the company can actually count on only $6,100 of benefit from $10,000 in profit. Thus $6,100 is the increased future cash flow resulting from the purchase of the asset. In making the capital budgeting decision, we see how the present value of this future cash flow benefit can be matched up against the present value of the costs incurred in generating this benefit. Note that after taxes are paid on increased profit, a cash flow benefit results. So $3,900 of taxes are paid on $10,000 worth of increased profit, resulting in $6,100 worth of benefit.

However, a benefit resulting from reducing taxable income is equal to the amount saved in paying those taxes. Recall that we used $3,900 as the amount of tax paid on $10,000 worth of taxable income. If we can reduce the amount of taxable income by $10,000, then we save $3,900 in taxes, which is an increased cash flow benefit to the business. What we try to show here is how to determine the present value of this future constant benefit of $3,900 saved in taxes per year. However, once again, because tax laws change constantly, uncertainty is always present. Thus, cash flows from tax savings are merely estimates and have a large degree of uncertainty that adds to the risk of the investment. This can be further exemplified by what transpired in the real estate industry. Tax savings decreased noticeably with the Tax Reform Act of 1986.

Some companies use different depreciation methods for tax purposes and financial accounting purposes. The straight-line method takes a conservative approach to depreciation. Accelerated methods are often used for tax purposes and write off more income to save taxes and generate increased cash flow for a business. This is done, for the most part, because high depreciation in the early years of an asset's useful life results in a greater write-off, which further reduces taxes paid on income. Thus, benefits include all additional cash flows that accrue to our business as a result of making the capital budgeting decision. Those benefits that are most often considered are the tax factor benefits.

Tax factor benefits include those items that current tax law allow you to deduct or write off once the new investment is made. These items include annual depreciation, interest on loans, or investment tax credits. For example, say that you want to start a computer consulting business. You need computers and peripheral equipment, office machinery (faxes, copy machines), and a good automobile to be used in visiting clients. The total cost of this equipment is $110,000, and this equipment is subject to a 5-year straight-line depreciation method according to the Modified Accelerated Cost Recovery System (MACRS).[3] You estimate that the equipment will be worth $10,000 (salvage value) at the end of the 5 years. Furthermore, you put $20,000 down and get a bank to finance the remaining $90,000 at an annual rate of prime plus 4 percent. You estimate that you will be in a 28-percent tax bracket.

Calculating depreciation is accomplished by using the following procedure:

1. Subtract the salvage value of $10,000 from the cost of $110,000, leaving $100,000 of wearing value to be depreciated over 5 years, straight-line.
2. Determine annual depreciation. Divide the $100,000 by 5 (the number of years) to determine the annual depreciation of $20,000.
3. Calculate the annual tax savings, which is a benefit and is derived by multiplying those items that can be deducted from income by the expected tax rate. Items that can be excluded from taxes, under current tax law, are annual depreciation and interest expenses. Therefore, annual depreciation of $20,000 can be deducted from taxable income prior to calculating annual taxes. If you are in a 28-percent tax bracket, you save 28 cents for every dollar of depreciation deducted, or 28 percent of $20,000, which is equal to $5,600 each year for 5 years.

Additional tax savings are obtained because the annual interest that you pay on the loan is a business expense. For example, say the prime lending rate was 7.25 percent in January 2008.[4] The bank financed the equipment loan at prime plus 3.75 percent, so your annual interest is 11.00 percent compounded monthly. If you believe that interest rates will not change during the period of this loan, then each yearly payment of $26,090.88 can be calculated by finding the monthly loan payment of $2,174.24 and multiplying by 12. We recommend that you obtain an amortization schedule from the bank, an Internet search engine such as Google, or generate one from a spreadsheet program such as Microsoft Excel or Lotus 123. (*Note:* A link to an amortization table can be found at www.prenhall.com/adelman.)

Table 10–1 is based on the following assumptions: We bought the $110,000 in assets and financed $100,000 for 5 years at a stated rate of 11.00 percent. We also assumed that our tax bracket was 28 percent. Using these figures, we generated a 5-year monthly amortization table and came up with the following results: annual interest for year 1 is $10,215.43; for year 2, $8,378.34; for year 3, $6,328.67; for year 4, $4,041.80; and for year 5, $1,490.30. Annual tax savings are calculated the same way as we calculated tax savings for depreciation. Tax sav-

---

[3]IRS Publication 946, "How to Depreciate Property" for use in preparing 2007 returns. Retrieved August 19, 2008, from http://www.irs.gov/pub/irs-pdf/p946.pdf.

[4]Federal Reserve Statistical Release, H.15. Retrieved March 24, 2008, from http://www.federalreserve.gov/releases/h15.

TABLE 10–1 Annual Interest Payments and Tax Savings for a Five-Year Loan

Amount Borrowed	Annual Interest Rate	Number of Months	Monthly Payment	Income Tax Rate
$100,000.00	11.00%	60	$2,174.24	28.00%

Year	Annual Loan Payment	Principal Payment	Interest Payment	Tax Savings
1	$26,090.91	$15,875.48	$10,215.43	$2,860.32
2	26,090.91	17,712.57	8,378.34	2,345.94
3	26,090.91	19,762.24	6,328.67	1,772.03
4	26,090.91	22,049.11	4,041.80	1,131.70
5	26,090.91	24,600.61	1,490.30	417.28
Totals	$130,454.54	$100,000.00	$30,454.54	$8,527.27

ings in year 1 equals 0.28 times $10,215.43, or $2,860.32. As shown in Table 10–1, the total tax savings expected over the life of the loan is $8,527.27. What is interesting to note with tax factor benefits is that the $130,454.54 that was paid over five years actually resulted in a cost to the business of $121,927.27 ($130,454.54 total loan payments − $8,527.27 total tax savings) due to tax savings from interest expense. (*Note:* Rounding may cause what appears to be an error of a penny in some columns.)

Total tax factor benefits for the 5-year purchase of our office equipment equal $28,000 ($5,600 annual tax savings × 5 years) of reduced taxes because of depreciation as well as $8,527.27 of reduced taxes because of an annual interest deduction. Our company saved a total of $36,527.27 in taxes by purchasing $110,000 in equipment and subtracting both depreciation and interest from our business income prior to calculating taxes.

EVALUATING THE DATA (TECHNIQUES OF CAPITAL BUDGETING)

Now that we understand the costs and benefits in a capital budgeting decision, it is time to discuss methods of evaluating the data contained in our capital budgeting proposal.

Businesses allocating capital properly use several techniques to make a profitable decision through a logical evaluation process. Six techniques used to assure profitable capital budgeting decisions are those that use the calculations of (1) payback, (2) net present value (NPV), (3) profitability index (PI), (4) internal rate of return (IRR), (5) accounting rate of return (ARR, also known as *average rate of return*), and (6) lowest total cost (LTC).

As we discussed earlier, capital budgeting determines whether the business should make an investment now that will eventually result in after-tax benefits. These techniques require us to forecast future cash flows resulting from increased revenue, increased operational efficiency or effectiveness, or tax benefits that allow our business to hold on to more of our income.

PAYBACK

Payback deals with the number of years that it takes a business to get back the money that it invested in a project or asset. In determining payback, a business looks at how long an asset's cost is tied up in the investment as well as the project's profitability. To calculate payback, we determine the investment cost and divide this by the annual after tax benefits that the investment generates. The formula for calculating payback is

$$\text{Payback} = \frac{C}{ATB}$$

where

C = cost of the project
ATB = annual after-tax benefit of the project

If a company invests \$25,000 in a project and generates \$3,000 a year in after-tax benefits, then payback occurs in approximately 8.33 years (25,000/3,000 = 8.33). The advantages of payback are that it is easy to compute and simple to explain. It readily compares investments that have unequal initial costs. Its main disadvantages are that it does not consider the time value of money and it tends to lead to concentration on investments that satisfy immediate goals or those with a fast payback. How many businesspeople are willing to wait more than 8 years to recoup their investment, even though in the long run they can earn a substantial return on it?

NET PRESENT VALUE

The **net present value (NPV)** method of capital budgeting uses the time value of money by discounting future benefits and costs back to the present. It applies the techniques of the present value of a stream of payments for even cash flows and the present value of a future lump sum for unequal yearly cash flows. The calculations are made using an interest rate that matches our cost of capital for the investment. This rate is used because the company must pay that cost on an annual basis to obtain the financial capital necessary to make the investment.

When making a capital budgeting decision, we must arrive at a forecast of future interest rates. The two interest rates we must consider are (1) the interest rate charged by the supplier of funds, or the lender; and (2) the interest rate that the borrower could receive by investing in some other enterprise. The latter is the borrower's opportunity cost.

The interest rate charged by the lender is a comfortable interest rate—one that the bank or lending institution finds acceptable and believes is realistic with regard to the future. Lenders use the following three components to determine this interest rate: (1) the *real rate of return* (the return received after factoring out inflation), (2) the *inflation premium* (the expected average inflation rate for the term of the investment), and (3) the *risk premium* (the rate added to the interest rate to take into account the risk of the investment). For example, when a company goes into a new area of business, it assumes more risk (potential for failure) than if it had stayed in its original area. When the savings and loans went into commercial real estate, they did not include a sufficient risk premium, and therefore entered into a market in which they experienced losses that were much greater than anticipated. If the real rate of return is 2 percent and the inflation premium is 2.75 percent, then a risk-free investment uses an interest rate of 4.75 percent. For practical purposes, this interest rate is the *prime lending rate,* the interest rate charged by lenders to companies that pose very little risk to the lender. Conversely, if the lender believes there is risk of default on the loan, then a risk premium is added to this prime lending rate. If the risk premium is 4 percent, then 8.75 percent will be used as the loan rate charged by the lender (4.75 percent prime lending rate + 4 percent risk premium = 8.75 percent).

The cost of capital to the borrower consists of the opportunity cost on the amount of equity invested in the business. It is the interest that is forgone because the businessowner decided to invest in his or her own business rather than put the money in some other investment vehicle. For example, if you normally invest in government bonds that on average have paid you a 4 percent annual return over time, then 4 percent is your opportunity cost when you decide to invest your money in your own business. It is the amount you could have earned had you not invested in your own business. Therefore, we use both the lender's interest rate and the borrower's opportunity cost to determine the interest rate for the *NPV* method of capital budgeting. We combine these two rates into a weighted average cost of capital (WACC).

The **weighted average cost of capital (WACC)** is obtained by multiplying the cost of debt (rate that the lender charges) by its proportion of total funds raised, and then multiplying the cost of equity (opportunity cost to the owner) by its proportion of total funds raised. For example, say you are going to buy a piece of equipment for $100,000. You put $30,000 down and finance the remaining $70,000. Using the interest rates discussed earlier, your opportunity cost is 4 percent for the $30,000 and 8.75 percent for the $70,000 loan. We obtain the proportions by dividing the total investment by the amount of the investment financed by each resource. Therefore, 30 percent of the investment is financed by the owner and 70 percent is financed by the lender.

$$\text{Owner's equity} + \text{Amount financed} = \text{Total amount paid}$$
$$\$30,000 + \$70,000 = \$100,000$$

$$\text{Equity proportion} = \frac{\text{Owners equity}}{\text{Total amount paid}} = \frac{\$30,000}{\$100,000} = 0.30$$

$$\text{Debt proportion} = \frac{\text{Amount financed}}{\text{Total amount paid}} = \frac{\$70,000}{\$100,000} = 0.70$$

We then calculate the weighted average cost of capital as follows:

$$
\begin{aligned}
WACC &= (\text{Equity cost})(\text{Equity proportion}) + (\text{Debt cost})(\text{Debt proportion}) \\
&= (0.04)(0.30) + (0.0875)(0.70) \\
&= 0.0120 + 0.0613 \\
&= 0.0733, \text{ or } 7.33\%
\end{aligned}
$$

This weighted average cost of capital is the interest rate used in calculating the NPV for capital budgeting in a business. Most corporate financial textbooks would include common stock, preferred stock, bonds, and possibly loan financing in determining the WACC. However, for most businessowners, the two factors we use are sufficient because bond financing is not available and there are no multiple classes of stock.

NPV considers all of the future cash flows over an asset's entire economic life, including benefits and costs. Once the present value of the benefits is determined, we then subtract the present value of the costs to determine if there is a positive NPV. The formula used in the NPV method of capital budgeting is

$$NPV = PVB - PVC$$

where

NPV = net present value of the investment
PVB = present value of the benefit (as calculated in the following example)
PVC = present value of the cost of the investment (as calculated in the following example)

If NPV is positive using the WACC, the investment should be made. If NPV is negative using the WACC, the investment should not be made, because it is matched against the present value of the costs of the investment. For example, it costs our company $100,000 to add a sales office to its current production facility. We estimate that we will increase our after-tax cash flow by $35,000 a year, each year, for 7 years. For this problem, we assume our WACC and our required rate of return, or discount rate, are 10 percent. Referring to Appendix B, Table B–5, we find that at 10 percent, the present value of the ordinary annuity factor is 4.8684. Picture a money machine that earns interest on whatever amount of money is present in the machine at a specified time. If you started with $4.8684, which is also the present value of an annuity factor, in a machine that was earning compound interest of 10 percent, you could pull out $1 each year for 7 years. At the end of 7 years you pull out your last dollar and nothing is left in the machine. To get the present value associated with pulling out $35,000 per year for 7 years, we use the following formula:

$$PVB = Annuity(PVAF)$$

where

PVB = present value of the benefits
$Annuity$ = annual cash flow from the investment
$PVAF$ = present value annuity factor (from Appendix B, Table B–5

From our example, PVB = $35,000 (4.8684) = $170,394. Thus $170,394 is the present value of $35,000 a year for 7 years at a required rate of return, or discount rate, of 10 percent. Although $35,000 a year for 7 years amounts to $245,000 (7 years × $35,000), the actual present value is $170,394, because the $35,000 received at the end of the seventh year is worth less now than the $35,000 received at the end of the first year. As explained in Chapter 8, money has a time value and an opportunity cost.

$$
\begin{aligned}
NPV &= PVB - PVC \\
&= (\$35,000)(4.8684) - \$100,000 \\
&= \$170,394 - \$100,000 \\
&= \$70,394
\end{aligned}
$$

If we subtract the present value of the cost of $100,000 from the present value of the benefit of $170,394, we get $70,394, which is the NPV. The addition of a sales office has a positive NPV, meaning that the office is expected to generate a return higher than 10 percent. A business should accept an investment if the NPV is greater than 0, and should reject the investment if the NPV is less than 0. For example, if our estimated cash flow were $19,000 per year for each of the next 7 years, we would receive $133,000 in total benefits. However, the present value of this cash flow is only $92,500 ($19,000 × 4.8684). Using the earlier procedure, we see that the NPV equals the $92,500 PVB minus the $100,000 PVC, which equals a negative amount of –$7,500. Because NPV is negative at a weighted cost of capital of 10 percent, we should reject this investment.

$$
\begin{aligned}
NPV &= PVB - PVC \\
&= (\$19,000)(4.8684) - \$100,000 \\
&= \$92,500 - \$100,000 \\
&= (\$7,500)
\end{aligned}
$$

NPV has two primary advantages: (1) Future cash flows that will be paid and received can be discounted back to the present so that a decision on the investment can be made now. (2) Interest rates are determined by and based on the weighted average cost of capital that takes risk into consideration. Note that a high-risk investment includes higher interest rates, which tends to lower the present value of the benefits. A low-risk investment includes lower interest rates, which tends to increase the present value of the benefits. The major disadvantage of NPV is that it requires estimates of future interest rates. These rates may change in the future. In addition, NPV uses estimates of cash flow costs and benefits, which also may change in the future.

Because of the complexity of the NPV calculation, let us consider another example. You want to buy an automobile that is selling for $20,000. You believe that you can use the car in your business to increase your cash flow by $10,000 each year over the next 5 years. You also believe that you can sell the car at the end of 5 years for $4,000. Table 10–2 shows the NPV calculations for this problem.

Recall that the salvage, or residual, value of an asset is what you might receive on selling the asset when its useful life is completed. To help us with this decision, we must estimate the current value of selling an asset at a future date. In other words, we wish to determine the present amount of an estimated future residual value of an asset. You estimate that you can sell the automobile in 5 years for $4,000. What is the present value of this $4,000 lump-sum payment that you will receive in 5 years? To determine this value, you must use an interest rate that you believe is comparable to your weighted average cost of capital or required rate of return. It is important to note that the interest rate chosen is based on an assumption that rates do not change over the next 5 years; if rates change, the present value of the future $4,000 lump sum also changes. In

TABLE 10–2 NPV of an Automobile Purchase

Benefits

Item	Cash Flow per Time Period	PVAF at 10.00%	Present Value at 10%	PVAF at 14.00%	Present Value at 14%
Cash flow	$10,000.00 per year	3.7908	$37,908.00	3.4331	$34,331.00
Salvage value	$4,000.00 end of 5 years	0.6209	2,483.60	0.5194	2,077.60
PVB			$40,391.60		$36,408.60

Costs

Item	Cash Flow per Time Period	PVAF at 10.00%	Present Value at 10%	PVAF at 14.00%	Present Value at 14%
Purchase price	($20,000.00) Present Value		($20,000.00)		($20,000.00)
Insurance	($100.00) per month	47.4576	(4,745.76)	43.4784	(4,347.84)
Gas and maintenance	($300.00) per month	47.4576	(14,237.28)	43.4784	(13,043.52)
PVC			($38,983.04)		($37,391.36)
NPV = PVB − PVC			$1,408.56		($982.76)

addition, the $4,000 lump sum itself is only an estimate. The car could, and most probably will, be worth some amount other than $4,000 in 5 years.

Because we are using two estimated variables (cash flow and interest rate), we believe that you should take risk into consideration: Either underestimate the future residual value or add a risk premium to your required rate of return. For this problem, we added a risk premium of 4 percent to our required rate of return (WACC) of 10 percent that was used in the previous problem. Justification of the numbers in Table 10–2 is described as follows.

First, you must calculate the present value of the benefits. The $10,000-per-year cash flow has a present value of $37,908 using the 10 percent WACC and $34,331 using the 14 percent WACC that takes risk into consideration. These figures were obtained by using the present value of an ordinary annuity factor because the cash flow is not realized until the end of the year (ordinary annuity). You estimate that you can sell the car in 5 years for $4,000. This estimated figure can be obtained from any bank via the *Kelley Blue Book,*[5] which provides the value of a 5-year-old car of the same model and equipment that you are buying. To avoid overestimating the future benefit, we recommend using the low book value. Using the formula for present value of a future lump sum, or Appendix B, Table B–2, we arrive at a present value of $2,483.60 ($4,000 × 0.6209). Now let's add the risk premium of 4 percent because you are unsure if you actually can get $4,000 for the car, or if interest rates in the future will stay at or below 10 percent. The present value of $4,000, using a 14 percent interest rate, is now only $2,077.60 ($4,000 × 0.5194). Therefore, the sum of the present value of the benefits (PVB) for a 10 percent assumption is $40,391.60; for a 14 percent assumption, it is $36,408.60. Did you actually lose more than $3,983? No, but the anticipated benefit as determined now in our capital budgeting decision is less than it was using the basic interest rate of 10 percent.

Your next step is to put in the present value of the car and the costs associated with using the vehicle over time. For an automobile, typical costs include insurance, gas, and maintenance. Your records indicate that the insurance premium is $100 per month. Gas and maintenance for this car should be about $300 per month. These payments should be *allocated* (set aside) at the beginning of each month, so we use the present value of an annuity due in our calculations. Calculating the present value of these costs and adding them to the present value of the automobile ($20,000 is paid for the automobile now) gives us a total present value of the costs of $38,983.04 at 10 percent and $37,391.36 at 14 percent. Using the formula NPV = PVB – PVC, we see that the car should be purchased at a risk level (WACC) of 10 percent, because our NPV is positive at this rate ($1,408.56). If the risk level increases the rate to 14 percent, the car should not be purchased, because the NPV is now negative ($982.76). In other words, at

---

[5]The *Kelly Blue Book* is used by most banks and lending institutions to provide book value on used automobiles. You can also find the book on the Internet at http://www.kbb.com.

10 percent, the present value of the benefits exceeds the present value of the costs, as shown by the result of a positive NPV. When we increase the discount rate to 14 percent because of greater risk, the present value of the benefits is less than the present value of the costs, as shown by a negative net present value.

Most business loans are tied to the prime interest rate and are adjusted when the prime rate changes. It would be imprudent for a businessowner to use a lower rate in decision making and not take into consideration that interest rates tend to fluctuate during the period of a loan. Because of the availability of personal computers, the small business owner now has the capability of analyzing an investment decision based on **sensitivity analysis**—the process of analyzing an investment using what-if situations. In this particular case, the interest rate variable can be modified and the resulting present value of benefits and costs can be analyzed to determine if specific situations meet the criteria of the investment decision. Therefore, we recommend that the businessowner or manager use the NPV technique in conjunction with sensitivity analysis to determine the value of an investment.

PROFITABILITY INDEX

The **profitability index (PI)** is the ratio of the present value of the benefits to the present value of the costs. The formula for PI is

$$PI = \frac{PVB}{PVC}$$

Using the previous sales-office example, our investment has a present value of $170,394 and a cost of $100,000. The PI is 1.70, which means that at a discounted or required rate of return of 10 percent, a project returns approximately $1.70 in benefit for every $1.00 invested. This project is profitable because the PI is greater than 1. We can see the relationship between NPV and profitability index as follows: A positive NPV results in a PI greater than 1, and a negative NPV results in a PI that is less than 1. For example, if our project had a *PI* of 0.85, this indicates that for every $1.00 invested, the project was returning only $0.85 as benefit over time. The advantages of the profitability index are that it is easy to calculate once you determine both PVB and PVC, it is easy to explain, and it provides a clear picture of cost–benefit analysis. The disadvantage is that it may give a false sense of security for a project if interest rate estimates are too low or cash flow estimates are too high.

INTERNAL RATE OF RETURN

The **internal rate of return (IRR)** is the actual rate of return of an investment, and it uses the time value of money in its calculation. The IRR is the interest rate that matches the present value of the cost of our investment directly against the present value of the future benefits received. The future benefits can be seen in the form of a stream of payments over a period of time or a lump sum (salvage value) received. The IRR is the interest rate that occurs when the NPV is 0. If the NPV is 0, then by definition, the present value of the costs must equal the present value of the benefits. The IRR is an interest rate that corresponds to a present value annuity factor that is found by dividing the present value of the cost by the period's cash flow.

For example, if Kerry O'Key invests $40,000 in a lounge and is able to generate $7,000 in cash flow each year for 7 years, we can find the rate that allows this to happen. This problem is the present value of an ordinary annuity—in other words, money has a time value. Using a calculator that has the time value of money formulas, we plug in three variables in our calculator. These include the present value of the costs—$40,000; the present value of the benefits—$7,000; and the amount of time—7 years. We then solve for the fourth variable, which is the IRR. The IRR is 5.35 percent. Other examples include a $100,000 investment generating $35,000 each year for 7 years. Notice that we are given the cost, the benefit, and the time element and are asked to find the IRR, which is 29.16 percent. We can also find the IRR in solving future value of ordinary and annuity due problems. If you do not have a business or programmable calculator, we can still find the IRR through the process of interpolation, using the following formula:

$$IRR \text{ factor} = \frac{\text{Present value of the cost of the investment}}{\text{Periods cash flow}}$$

An investment costs $25,000, and has a $3,000 annual benefit each year for 20 years. At the IRR, the present value of the $25,000 investment is equal to the present value of the $3,000 annual benefit and the NPV equals 0. The IRR factor is identical to the present value annuity factor (PVAF) and is found by using the previous formula. Calculate $x\%$ PVAF by dividing $25,000 by $3,000, and arrive at a value of 8.3333. We look in Appendix B, Table B–5, and go across the 20-year row to find the interest rate that corresponds to a factor of 8.3333. Note that 8.3333 falls between 8.5136, which corresponds to 10 percent, and 7.9633, which corresponds to 11 percent. We now know that the IRR lies somewhere between 10 and 11 percent.

To find the actual IRR, if we don't have a business calculator, we must use **interpolation**, which is the process of using mathematics to find an unknown value between two known values. We know that 7.9633 corresponds to an 11 percent interest rate and 8.5136 corresponds to a 10 percent interest rate. Because 8.3333 lies between these two known values, we interpolate by setting up the following proportion:

$$1 \left[\, ? \! \left(\begin{matrix} 10 ----8.5136 \\ x ----8.3333 \end{matrix} \right) 0.1803 \atop 11 ----7.9633 \right] 0.5503$$

In our proportion, we take the difference between the lower-interest 10 percent PVAF of 8.5136 and the x% PVAF of 8.3333 and divide this difference of 0.1803 by the difference between the higher-interest-rate 11 percent PVAF of 7.9633 and the lower-interest-rate 10 percent PVAF of 8.5136 to get 0.5503. We now have the numerator of 0.1803 and the denominator of 0.5503, which is a proportion that we will set equal to ? divided by the difference in interest rates. Thus, ? divided by 1 equals 0.1803 divided by 0.5503. Solving for ?, we obtain 0.3276, which we add to the lower interest rate and get an internal rate of return of 10.33 percent. Mathematically, the proportion described here yields the following formula:

$$\left| \frac{?}{i_1 - i_2} \right| = \left| \frac{\text{Partial distance } (10\%PVAF - x\% \, PVAF)}{\text{Total distance } (10\%PVAF - 11\% \, PVAF)} \right|$$

$$\left| \frac{?}{10 - 11} \right| = \left| \frac{(8.5136 - 8.3333)}{(8.5136 - 7.9633)} \right|$$

$$\frac{?}{1} = \frac{0.1803}{0.5503}$$

$$? = \frac{(1)(0.1803)}{0.5503} = 0.3276$$

$$IRR = i_1 + ? = 10\% + 0.3276\% \approx 10.33\%$$

It is important to realize that not all investments produce consistently equal cash flows year after year—most investments produce unequal cash flows. Finding the IRR of an investment with unequal cash flows can be illustrated in the following example.

A company is considering the purchase of a new machine that would increase the speed of manufacturing electronic equipment. The annual cash flow projections are shown in Table 10–3.

The cost of the machine is $66,000. To find the actual IRR, we must interpolate. However, we interpolate using present-value dollars rather than

TABLE 10–3 Five-Year Projected Cash Flow
(Initial Investment: $66,000)

Year	Projected Cash Flow
1	$21,000
2	29,000
3	36,000
4	16,000
5	8,000

TABLE 10–4 Present Value of an Unequal Stream of Projected Cash Benefits

Year	Projected Cash Flow	PVF for Interest of 20.00%	Present Value in Dollars	PVF for Interest of 25.00%	Present Value in Dollars
1	$21,000.00	0.8333	$17,499.30	0.8000	$16,800.00
2	29,000.00	0.6944	20,137.60	0.6400	18,560.00
3	36,000.00	0.5787	20,833.20	0.5120	18,432.00
4	16,000.00	0.4823	7,716.80	0.4096	6,553.60
5	8,000.00	0.4019	3,215.20	0.3277	2,621.60
Total *PV*			$69,402.10		$62,967.20

factors, as in the equal cash flow example. First we must find interest rates that provide us with projected present values of more than $66,000 and less than $166,000. Using trial and error or what-if analysis, we determine that rates of 20 percent and 25 percent, as shown in Table 10–4, meet these criteria.

In our example, first we find the present value of the cash flows at 20 percent by using the formula for the present value of a future lump sum for all individual cash flows. Next we find the present value in dollars of the cash flows at 25 percent.

We also wish to find the IRR, which is the interest rate that corresponds to a present value of $66,000. This is the present value of the investment cost. We know that $69,402.10 corresponds to a 20-percent interest rate and that $62,967.20 corresponds to a 25 percent interest rate. Because $66,000 lies between these two values, we interpolate by setting up the following proportion:

$$5 \left[? \left(\begin{array}{l} 20 \text{ – – – – } \$69,402.10 \\ x \text{ – – – – } \$66,000.00 \end{array} \right) \$3,402.10 \right) \$6,434.90 \\ 25 \text{ – – – – } \$62,967.20 \right]$$

We set up a proportion in which we take the difference between the lower-interest-rate (20 percent) present value in dollars and the IRR present value in dollars, which is $3,402.10. We divide by the difference between the lower interest rate's present value amount in dollars and the higher interest rate's present value amount in dollars, which is $6,434.90. We now have the numerator of $3,402.10 and the denominator of $6,434.90, a proportion that we set equal to ? divided by the difference in interest rates. Thus, ? divided by 5 equals $3,402.10 divided by $6,434.90. Solving for ?, we find that it equals 2.6435. We then add this number to the lower interest rate and get an internal rate of return of 22.64 percent. Mathematically, the proportion described here yields the following formula:

$$\left| \frac{?}{i_1 - i_2} \right| = \left| \frac{\text{Partial distance } (20\% \ PFV\$ \ - \ x\% \ PV\$)}{\text{Total distance } (20\% \ PV\$ \ - \ 25\% \ PV\$)} \right|$$

$$\left| \frac{?}{20 - 25} \right| = \left| \frac{(\$69,402.10 \ - \ \$66,000.00)}{(\$69,402.10 \ - \ \$62,967.20)} \right|$$

$$\frac{?}{5} = \frac{\$3,402.10}{\$6,434.90}$$

$$? = \frac{(5)(\$3,402.10)}{(\$6,434.90)} = \frac{\$17,010.50}{\$6,434.90} = 2.6435$$

$$IRR = i_1 + ? = 20\% + 2.6435\% \approx 22.64\%$$

As shown by the previous examples, the IRR follows the time value of money by discounting future benefits and costs back to the present. It is most appropriate for comparing investments that have unequal initial cash outlays and unequal lives. A disadvantage of the IRR is that it requires complex interest calculations and may be difficult to explain in some cases. However, keep in mind that a business usually has a cutoff rate, or *hurdle rate* (a minimum rate of return for investments), that is used with the NPV method. If the present value of the benefits exceeds the present value of the costs using this hurdle rate, then the internal rate of return must be higher than the hurdle rate. Therefore, the IRR is only required by a businessowner or manager who wants to know the actual return on investment. We recommend the NPV method because cash flows are assumed to be reinvested at the hurdle (WACC) rate. In using IRR, cash flows are assumed to be reinvested at the IRR. If a project shows an IRR of 38 percent, it is unrealistic to assume that cash flows could be reinvested at this rate. Because the NPV method uses an interest rate that is actually expected by both the investor and the lender, it is a more realistic approach.

ACCOUNTING RATE OF RETURN

The **accounting rate of return (ARR)** is the average annual income from a project divided by the average cost of the project. This method bases its rate of return on income and does not incorporate the time value of money or the present value of future cash flows. For example, an individual spent $10,000 to develop a software program that generated $3,000 a year for 4 years. The ARR is equal to the average amount of yearly income ($3,000) generated over the life of the project divided by the cost of the project ($10,000). The formula for ARR is

$$ARR = \left(\frac{\text{Average annual income}}{\text{Average cost of investment over its life}} \right)$$

Using this ARR example, $3,000 divided by $10,000 is a 30 percent ARR. This measure is not as accurate as the IRR because the IRR tells us the actual rate of return, or how $10,000 generates $3,000 each year. Our $10,000 is the cost of the investment and is the present value of the discounted amount of a future stream of payments; from it we get our actual return. The ARR is an average return from income generated over an investment's life. The advantage of the ARR is that it is easy to calculate; however, there are several disadvantages. The ARR does not consider the time value of money. It also provides rates of return that are not realistic, because it is based on the average value of the investment over its life rather than the original cost. It uses average income without discounting each year's cash flow back to the present. We know that $3,000 received in the fourth year has less value currently than $3,000 received in the first year. The ARR assumes that each $3,000 cash flow provides the same benefit, resulting in an ARR of 30 percent. The IRR is only 7.72 percent. Because of the large differences between ARR and IRR, we do never recommend using the ARR; we include *it* in this discussion because some advisors may use this method to convince people to invest in a project; in this way, you understand what is happening and can evaluate the project with a keener insight of what you are getting into. According to our example, use of the ARR often shows returns that are far in excess of reality. For example, a $100,000 investment that gives off an annual return of $20,000 for 10 years provides an IRR of 15.10 percent. As a result, the accounting rate of return is inflated to 20 percent.

LOWEST TOTAL COST

The **lowest total cost (LTC)** method of capital budgeting is similar to the NPV method because it uses the time value of money by discounting future costs and benefits back to the present. It applies the technique of present value of a stream of payments for even cash flows as well as the technique of present value of a future lump sum for unequal yearly cash flows. The calculations are made using an interest rate that matches our weighted average cost of capital for the investment, because the company must pay this cost on an annual basis to obtain the financial capital necessary to make the investment.

Businesses must replace equipment as it wears out. If a business is already in operation, then the capital budgeting decision often involves choosing the investment that provides the lowest total cost (LTC) for the replacement of existing equipment that has worn out or has become obsolete—for example, a delivery company that must replace its trucks, a bakery that replaces its ovens, or an office complex that replaces its air-conditioning system.

The method used to determine the lowest present value of total cost is as follows:

1. Include all costs associated with two or more competing investments.
2. Calculate the present value of these costs.

TABLE 10–5 Lowest Total Cost (LTC) of a Truck Purchase

Category	Quantity
Fuel cost per gallon	$3.97
Annual mileage	25,000
WACC	12.00%
Ownership in years	6
PVAF Table B–5 or Formula	4.1114
PVF Table B–2 or Formula	0.5066

	Truck Model A		Truck Model B		Truck Model C	
Category	(Costs) and Benefits	PV	(Costs) and Benefits	PV	(Costs) and Benefits	PV
Mileage per gallon	16		13		15	
Purchase price	$(26,955.00)	$(26,955.00)	$(25,695.00)	$(25,695.00)	$(30,556.00)	$(30,556.00)
Annual fuel costs	(6,203.13)	(25,503.57)	(7,634.62)	(31,389.01)	(6,616.67)	(27,203.81)
Annual insurance cost	(1,347.40)	(5,539.71)	(1,532.44)	(6,300.49)	(1,358.52)	(5,585.43)
Salvage value	10,800.00	5,471.62	10,800.00	5,471.62	12,250.00	6,206.23
Total cost for 6 years		$(52,526.66)		$(57,912.88)		$(57,139.01)

3. Add the present value of any residual benefits (salvage value) that may be obtained on the investment.
4. Select the investment with the lowest overall total cost.

Jonathan Lury is a contractor who must replace a long-bed pickup truck. Jonathan has the following constraints for his truck: It must have a towing capacity of 4,000 pounds and a cargo capacity of at least 3,000 pounds. It must have an extended cab, because he often takes three or four workers to the construction site. Jonathan developed Table 10–5 using information that he obtained for three models of different competing trucks. Jonathan estimated that fuel costs $3.97 per gallon. He drives an average of 25,000 miles a year and expects to use the truck for 6 years. His weighted average cost of capital (WACC) is 12 percent. The purchase price of each truck is its present value and is listed in Table 10–5. Jonathan obtained the EPA mileage estimates for city driving on each vehicle and computed the annual cost of fuel. He then calculated the present value of his fuel cost by using the present value of an ordinary annuity. Maintenance costs on the three vehicles were the same, so he did not include maintenance costs in the table. Jonathan called his insurance company and obtained an annual premium for each vehicle. He then calculated the present value of the costs of his insurance premiums. Using the Internet, he obtained salvage values for 6-year-old trucks. He determined the present value of the salvage value by using the present value of a future lump sum. (Note that the present value of the salvage value reduces the cost of each vehicle.) Using this methodology, Jonathan then computes the total cost of each vehicle. Using the LTC criteria, he should purchase Truck Model A with a PV total cost of $52,526.66, because it has the lowest total cost of the three trucks. It is not the least expensive truck to purchase. Truck Model A has a purchase price of $26,955, compared with Truck Model B, which has a purchase price of $25,695. His decision, however, is based on the present value of the lowest total cost, not lowest initial cost.

The LTC procedure actually is used many times by the businessowner because he or she must replace equipment on a regular basis. NPV is not used to calculate this type of investment. The emphasis here is placed on minimizing total expenses and on expenses being somewhat offset by residual benefits. When this is the case, the LTC method of capital budgeting should be used.

MAKING THE DECISION

If a firm has limited funds and a multitude of investments from which to choose, then it finds itself having to choose some alternatives and sacrifice others. Some investments are **mutually exclusive**, because one is chosen and others are automatically sacrificed or excluded. For example, a businessowner evaluates several locations before opening a new business or expanding an existing one. If the owner decides to open in a single location, then the decision precludes all other sites and is a mutually exclusive decision, even though most sites may have positive NPVs. Referring to Table 10–6, if a businessowner had less than $96,000 to invest, then location 1 is the only choice—it is mutually exclusive. If he had $96,000 exactly, he could invest in two locations.

Investments that are not mutually exclusive are chosen because they have positive NPVs. Using Table 10–6, if the firm had sufficient capital, the owner could open up nine new sites, because the first nine sites all have positive net present values, so the selection of one site would not preclude the selection of others.

TABLE 10–6 Capital Budgeting Choices

Business Location	Capital Investment Cost	Cumulative Investment Cost	Net Present Value
1	$50,000	$50,000	$125,000
2	46,000	96,000	121,000
3	52,000	148,000	119,000
4	47,500	195,500	116,000
5	67,300	262,800	115,000
6	48,000	310,800	113,000
7	63,000	373,800	112,500
8	48,700	422,500	111,000
9	54,200	476,700	110,250
10	62,500	539,200	(15,000)
11	48,500	587,700	(17,000)
12	65,000	652,700	(25,000)

These investments are *non-mutually exclusive.* However, most businesses have limited access to capital, which often requires making capital rationing decisions.

Capital rationing is a constraint placed on the amount of funds that can be invested in a given time period. For a large corporation, this constraint is often artificial because the corporation has a choice of issuing new bonds or stock. For most businesses, this constraint results from limited funds. In our example for Table 10–6, if the owner could invest no more than $373,800, then he would choose to open seven new sites, even though nine have positive net present values (sites 10 through 12 would not be chosen by any businessowner because they have negative net present values).

FOLLOWING UP

Following up consists of monitoring and controlling our cash flows. *Monitoring* is determining if the actual benefits received exceed the additional costs incurred on an ongoing basis. This is the equivalent of a **post-audit**, which requires the owner or manager to establish procedures that determine how well the outcome of a decision correlates with the proposal. Cash inflows and outflows should be monitored by setting up a budget to determine if proposed costs and benefits are realized. *Controlling,* as stated previously, is a three-step process: (1) establish standards for measuring a project, (2) measure actual performance against the standards established, and (3) take corrective action if required. *Establishing standards* is the process of creating annual budgets based on our capital budgeting decision. This provides us with expected costs and benefits on an annual basis. Measuring actual performance is accomplished by comparing actual costs and benefits with our annual budget. Because of the seasonal nature of most businesses, the annual budget should be broken down into monthly budgets. Both cash inflow and cash outflow should operate within a range of acceptable variance. In reality, cash flows are based on a forecast, which we know are not accurate. Taking corrective action is required only when actual cash flows are outside the parameters of the variances that we have established.

TAKING CORRECTIVE ACTION

Once we determine that our cash flows are outside of acceptable parameters, we must take corrective action, which, from the viewpoint of the financial manager, consists of cutting costs, increasing cash flows, or developing some method of doing both. For example, when Hannah's Donut Shop opened (see Chapter 6 Case Study), it was the only doughnut shop within a 5-mile radius. Sales and cash flow exceeded projections, and Hannah operated the doughnut shop using night bakers and finishers while she worked the day shift. One year after the shop opened, a national doughnut chain built a shop within 1 mile of Hannah's shop. Her sales declined by 30 percent. Specific fixed expenses such as rent and equipment payments to the bank could not be cut, because Hannah and her husband Phil had signed long-term contracts. The shop had been staying open 24 hours a day. An audit of sales indicated that afternoon sales did not exceed the labor costs of the afternoon shift, so Hannah decided to cut operating hours and lay off the afternoon shift. This resulted in reduced labor costs and lower utility bills, but the cuts were still not sufficient to offset the 30 percent reduction in sales as a result of the competition from the national chain.

Hannah and Phil decided that they would have to work the night shift themselves and lay off the night baker and finisher. This procedure resulted in additional cost savings and a positive cash flow. They were then working 12 to 14 hours a day, 7 days a week, which resulted in the business turning a positive cash flow. They determined that the only way to increase sales consistently was to go after the industrial market, and realized that this market required consistency of product, competitive pricing, and prompt delivery. Phil developed baking and finishing procedures that resulted in meeting the required standards. Phoenix had several large factories with cafeterias for their employees. After developing the product standards, Hannah hired a delivery driver who was paid based on his obtaining industrial accounts. Within 1 year, the cash flow from the industrial accounts was sufficient for Hannah to purchase an additional delivery vehicle, hire a baker and finisher to work nights, and go back to working the day shift only.

From this scenario, it should be obvious that taking corrective action is not an instantaneous process. It requires carefully thought out methods for cutting costs and increasing cash flows. It takes time, patience, and the commitment of the businessowner.

CONCLUSION

Capital budgeting is the method we use to justify the acquisition of capital goods. It is a process of making a decision based on ensuring that the businessowner or manager is entering into a project for which benefits exceed costs over time. Capital budgeting requires a five-step process:

1. Formulate a proposal, which serves the purpose of identifying the various costs incurred and benefits received in after-tax cash flows.
2. Evaluate the data generated with respect to the benefits and costs to see whether the investment will be profitable.
3. Make a decision by choosing the course of action that provides the greatest future benefit while minimizing future costs.
4. Follow up on the capital budgeting decision through a post-audit to see if the actual benefits received exceed the additional costs incurred.
5. Take corrective action if the post-audit indicates that the benefits received are not meeting our expectations.

Evaluation of the data uses one or more of these six methods: (1) payback, (2) net present value (NPV), (3) profitability index (PI), (4) internal rate of return (IRR), (5) accounting rate of return (ARR), and (6) lowest total cost (LTC). We recommend using NPV and IRR, although the actual choice is up to the owner or manager. For existing operations (replacing equipment and service contracts), we recommend LTC.

POSTSCRIPT

In the case of Hannah's Donut Shop, the owners' perseverance paid off in the long run. The national chain closed its doughnut shop, and Hannah's again became the only doughnut shop within a 5-mile radius. After 10 years, Hannah and Phil sold the shop. It is currently being operated by the new owners at a profit. Small businesses are the essence of the American enterprise system. We hope that this text helps more people in opening and operating small businesses successfully.

Given the fact that we anticipate business success, we must address one additional issue that has an impact on many businessowners and managers. Most businessowners concentrate heavily on day-to-day operational tactics to accomplish their immediate goal of making a profit, yet fail to form an adequate strategy that revolves around their own personal finances. It is our intent to cover those areas of personal finance that are of utmost concern to the small business owner. Chapter 11 is devoted to personal finance and areas of concern to the small-business entrepreneur.

REVIEW AND DISCUSSION QUESTIONS

1. What distinguishes a capital investment from other investments?
2. List and briefly explain the five-step capital budgeting process.
3. What are the various costs that must be evaluated in a capital budgeting decision?
4. What are some of the tax-factor benefits of capital budgeting?
5. List the advantages and disadvantages of the payback method.
6. How does a company determine the interest rate it uses in making an net present value (NPV) decision?
7. What are three components used by a lender in determining the interest rate charged for a loan?
8. What is the actual cost of capital to the borrower?
9. Describe the process of calculating NPV.
10. List two advantages of using NPV.
11. What is the relationship between NPV and profitability index (PI)?
12. What are the advantages of the PI method of capital budgeting?

13. How does accounting rate of return (ARR) differ from the internal rate of return (IRR)?

14. Discuss the method of capital budgeting that you would use in your own business. Justify your decision.

15. What are the differences between mutually exclusive, non–mutually exclusive, and capital rationing decisions?

16. What is the three-step process of controlling?

EXERCISES AND PROBLEMS

1. What is the payback if investment cost is $45,000 and the after-tax benefit is $2,000?

2. An interest payment of $650 in a 20 percent tax bracket would result in a tax savings of _____.

3. Joe Morton buys a piece of equipment for $200,000. He puts down $40,000 and finances $160,000. Joe's opportunity cost is 4 percent, and the lender's interest rate is 8 percent. Find the weighted average cost of capital (WACC).

4. Lisa Camry bought a $15,000 car with a $3,000 down payment. The balance is financed by a manufacturer's sale offering 0–percent annual interest. If Lisa's opportunity cost is 5 percent, what is her WACC?

5. If the 10 percent present value ordinary annuity factor (PVAF) is 8.5136 and the 11 percent PVAF is 7.9633, a PVAF of 8.1234 correlates to an internal rate of return of _____.

6. The Ohm Depot Co. is currently considering the purchase of a new machine that would increase the speed of manufacturing electronic equipment and save money. He net cost of the new machine is $66,000. The annual cash flows have the following projections:

Year	Amount
1	$21,000
2	29,000
3	36,000
4	16,000
5	8,000

If the cost of capital is 10 percent, find the following:
   a. The PVB
   b. The NPV
   c. The IRR (*Hint:* Use interpolation. IRR is between 20 percent and 25 percent)
   d. Payback
   e. PI

7. Kay Sadilla is considering investing in a franchise that requires an initial outlay of $75,000. She conducted market research and found that after-tax cash flows on the investment should be about $15,000 per year for the next

7 years. The franchiser stated that Kay would generate a 20 percent return. Her cost of capital is 10 percent. Find the following:
   a. The PVB
   b. The PVC
   c. The NPV
   d. The IRR (*Hint:* Use interpolation. IRR is between 8 percent and 10 percent)

8. Meg O'Byte wants to buy a new computer for her business for Internet access on a cable modem. The computer system cost is $5,100. The cable company charges $200 (including the cable modem) for installation and has a $50 a month usage fee for businesses, paid at the end of the month. Meg expects to buy the system with a $100 down payment, financing the balance at 8 percent over the next 4 years. She will sell the computer for $1,000 when she upgrades. She expects a $500 a month increase in cash flow and is in the 25 percent tax bracket.
   a. The start-up costs are _____.
   b. The PVC is _____.
   c. The PVB is _____.
   d. The monthly payment for the computer is _____.

9. The LJB Company must replace a freezer and is trying to decide between the following two alternatives:

	Freezer A	Freezer B
Investment required	$29,000	$25,000
Annual electrical bill	$3,000	$4,000
Salvage value	$6,000	$5,000
Project life	11 years	11 years

The LJB Company's cost of capital is 8 percent.
Which investment provides LJB with the lowest total cost?

10. Manny Kurr is considering the purchase of a beauty salon. The initial cost of this purchase is $16,000. The after-tax cash flows from this investment should be $4,000 per year for the next 5 years. His opportunity cost of capital is 10 percent. Calculate the following:
   a. Payback—Should Manny buy the beauty salon based on payback if his required payback is less than 3 years?
   b. The present value of the benefits (*PVB*),
   c. The present value of the costs (*PVC*),
   d. The net present value (*NPV*)—Should Manny buy the beauty salon based on NPV rules?
   e. Profitability index (*PI*)—What does the profitability index mean in terms of buying the beauty salon?
   f. Internal rate of return (*IRR*), (*Hint:* Use interpolation)—Should Manny buy the beauty salon based on *IRR* rules?
   g. Accounting rate of return (*ARR*)—Should Manny buy the beauty salon based on the *ARR*?

11. I. M. Aruban has a sandwich shop in a downtown business district. Several of his customers have said that they would purchase from his shop more often if he offered a delivery service. I.M. is considering establishing a delivery service to meet the needs of his market. He believes that he will have to purchase a fax machine, install a new phone line for the fax machine, purchase a delivery van, and hire at least one delivery person. I.M. asks your advice in determining whether he should take on the delivery service venture.

    a. What steps would you recommend that I.M. use in reaching a profitable decision?

    b. Explain to I.M. what each step involves.

12. You decide to help I.M. with his analysis. A good fax machine costs $500 and functions properly for 5 years. The phone company charges $300 for installing a new line and $60 a month for the line. A new delivery van costs $20,000 and can be financed for 60 months with a $4,000 down payment. I.M.'s bank will finance the van at 5.5 percent compounded monthly, and you calculated his weighted average cost of capital at 8 percent. You found that a 5-year-old van of this model sells for $5,000. After discussing the business venture with several retired restaurant owners at the local SCORE office, you believe that I.M., after paying his food costs, will increase his breakfast and lunch trade by $2,000 a month. I.M. can hire a part-time driver for $600 a month. The vehicle depreciates straight line for 5 years, or $3,000 per year. I.M. is a sole proprietor and is in a 20-percent tax bracket. You estimate that it will cost I.M. $300 a month to pay for maintenance, upkeep, and insurance on the van.

    a. If I.M. decides to establish a delivery service and pays for the fax machine in cash, how much cash does he need now?

    b. What is the monthly payment for the delivery van?

    c. Using the time value of money and a 5-year life for this project, what is the present value of all of I.M.'s costs?

    d. Using the time value of money and a 5-year life for this project, what is the present value of all of I.M.'s benefits?

    e. What is the NPV of the delivery service?

    f. What is the PI of the delivery service?

    g. What is the payback?

    h. What recommendation would you give to I.M. with regard to this project?

13. Herb E. Vore is considering investing in a Salad Stop franchise that requires an initial outlay of $100,000. He conducted market research and found that after-tax cash flows on this investment should be about $20,000 a year for the next 7 years. The franchiser states that Herb will generate a 20 percent rate of return. Herb currently has his money in a mutual fund, which has grown at an average annual rate of 10 percent. He tells the franchiser that money has a time value, and the actual rate of return according to his calculations is much less than 20 percent.

    a. Do you agree with the franchiser or with Herb?

    b. What rate of return is the franchiser using, and what method did Salad Stop use to calculate it?

     c. What rate of return is Herb using, and what method did he use?

     d. Should Herb make the investment? Explain your answer.

14. Buster Block represents a video chain store that is expanding into a new, large metropolitan area. He currently has $2 million to invest and wants to open several video stores. He found that each site will require a cash outlay of $230,000 for leasing, equipment, and initial inventory. Buster is currently looking at 20 sites. The first 15 sites have positive net present values; sites 16 through 20 have negative net present values.

     a. What is the maximum number of video stores in which Buster can invest for his company? Explain.

     b. How many stores can Buster open if his employer increases his budget to $5 million? Explain.

15. Buster's boss stated that after reviewing first-quarter earnings, the company decided to invest in only one store in the city. After evaluating the performance of the store, the company will determine if it wants to increase its presence in the area.

     a. If you were Buster, what method of evaluation would you use to recommend a site for a new video store?

     b. Explain how you would determine which site to invest in.

RECOMMENDED GROUP ACTIVITY

1. You have a business that requires the replacement of two 50,000-BTU heating units. Compare the total costs of these units from three manufacturers. Assume that the heaters will be placed in use and will last 10 years. Which company provides heaters with the lowest total cost?

2. Your group receives a phone proposal to invest in a new business. The caller informs you that it will take a $70,000 down payment and the investment will return $10,000 a year for the next 10 years. He tells you that the investment will return 14 percent. If current interest rates are 8 percent, what is the present value of this investment? How did the caller get 14 percent?

CASE STUDY: SWAN REHABILITATION COMPANY: A GREAT SUCCESS STORY

© 2008 Philip J. Adelman and Alan M. Marks

Kay Wing never knew how successful she was going to be in 1998 when she was working in a rehab facility. In early 2003, Kay decided to start her own business, and it appears that she has done everything right—she's become a very successful entrepreneur, including finding her niche with a clinical practice for stroke survivors based on current research while using an intensive treatment approach.

In the mid-1990s, an increased amount of research was being done on the importance of intensive therapy for neurological diseases. Kay tried to start a program in her facility but did not have management support. The Balanced Budget Act (BBA) of 1997 hit the health-care industry and in the space of a few months her facility had decreased their staff by 50 percent and doubled their productivity requirement. She was so unhappy about the quality of patient care that her group was being forced to administer that Kay decided to quit. She wrote a program and presented it to a large Phoenix health-care system, but they were not interested. Although she was reluctant to open her own program, she believed it was her only option.

After she quit her job, she worked as a fill-in therapist for several months while she was deciding what to do. A few months later, Kay started South West Advanced Neurological Rehabilitation (SWAN Rehab) in a warehouse in Tempe, Arizona. A vendor who was developing a piece of equipment for stroke rehab had space in the warehouse district and offered it to her at no cost. Kay used their equipment on her patients, so it was a win–win situation. She didn't borrow any money; instead, she used her own seed money and bought equipment when she could afford to pay for it. She took a leap of faith and started her dream practice. Kay soon outgrew the free space and subsequently rented space in a another warehouse, where she and a part-time physical therapist treated patients using a radical, non-traditional, intensive, research-based therapy. As her reputation grew, she began to see patients who came to Phoenix from all over the United States. Her website, http://www.swanrehab.com, recommends housing, and schedules patients daily during their time in Phoenix. As proof that there was a market for this niche, in just 5½ years the practice has grown to 10 employees, and they are moving from a rented 2,000-square foot facility to a new 6,000-square foot clinic.

Kay is filling a very small niche because there are more than 700,000 new stroke victims every year, most of whom do not get proper therapy. Her business is a clinical practice for stroke survivors based on current research using an intensive treatment approach. From her own experience and after doing much research, Kay planned a unique practice using intensity and repetition. *Intensive training* is defined in her practice as 4–5 days per week, 3–6 hours per day, and one-on-one with a skilled neurotherapist. The repetitions are necessary to cause neuroplastic changes that are not possible in a more traditional setting, where patients are seen 2–3 times a week for only an hour at a time.

SWAN maintains a friendly, feel-good atmosphere. Her patients believe that SWAN cares about them. When a new piece of equipment or therapeutic technique is available, Kay makes sure that it is based on solid research and her staff gets educated on its use. They were one of the first clinics to be qualified to use several pieces of technology (SaeboFlex, Bioness H-200 and L-300, ReoGo, and the technique of BIG). Because of her relationships with companies that develop and sell equipment, she is often asked to Beta test new equipment. Companies know that if SWAN uses the product, they can use SWAN's name in marketing their products. SWAN has formalized caregiver support; contacts patients and family members after discharge to see how things are going; and sends get-well cards if someone goes into the hospital or is sick and sympathy cards or flowers if there is a death in the family. SWAN helps more needy patients who do not have a support group with finding rides to their facility.

Several years ago, Kay realized that every other disease process in the United States had a camp that was just for fun, but stroke, with the largest population of disabled people in the United States, did not. She started a stroke camp in 2003. The first year, they had 25 stroke survivors, caregivers, and family members; this year (2008), it will probably be about 150 people. They go to a camp in northern Arizona for 5 days every fall. Occupational therapy (OT) and physical therapy (PT) schools as well as therapists in the community volunteer. They provide a full camping experience. One of their patients told SWAN that his few days at camp were the most fun he had experienced since his stroke. This camp is not just for their patients, but for stroke support groups throughout the Phoenix metropolitan area as well.

Several years ago, the neurological instructor in the PT department at Northern Arizona University and Kay started a class for PT students called the *neuro clinic.* It is an intense course where the students complete the class with more than 30 hours of real patient care. When they graduate and go into their clinical rotations, their clinical instructors are very enthusiastic because their students have had this experience. Kay requires all new employees to take this class so they come to SWAN already trained.

SWAN has no patient van, and patients must find their own way to the clinic. Kay's philosophy right now is that they will have one quality clinic that is growing. Even though they have an excellent staff, the clinic revolves around Kay, who is the face behind the business. Like many small businesses, Kay is not able to offer good health insurance, but gives each employee a monthly insurance allotment.

Several other clinics that claim to be "just like SWAN Rehab" have opened, increasing Kay's competition, and insurance companies have reduced the benefits patients get for long-term therapy. Business expertise was needed to help the clinic grow. Kay had been department head of physical therapy, occupational therapy, and speech therapy in several large hospital systems, and therefore had experience with budgeting, purchasing of equipment, designing and implementing new programming, and supervising of employees. This experience prepared her for many aspects of a private practice. However, she got to the point where her business knowledge was inadequate and needed immediate expert advice. She researched and retained the services of a competent group of consultants where she could get ongoing help with effective billing and reimbursement practices, marketing, setting short- and long-term goals, handling payroll and taxes, building a web page, and setting and reaching financial goals.

In an interview with Kay, I asked her to classify her business with respect to its degree of contact with the public. She is a woman who is truly an expert in her field. She has taught courses to physical and occupational therapists on therapeutic intervention, speaks at the Arizona Physical Therapy association, and has submitted and had proposals accepted at national conventions. She is active in the professional associations and will be a speaker at the national convention in June 2009. She is the president of the Arizona Physical Therapy Association. The Bio-Engineering Department and the Industrial Design section of the Architectural School at Arizona State University use her clinic for their students when they have projects that involve stroke survivors.

SWAN administers therapy to people who suffered a stroke or head injury, have Parkinson's disease, have multiple sclerosis, as well as offering occupational and physical therapy. Each patient is seen by a PT or OT every minute they are in her clinic. SWAN does free trials on certain pieces of equipment so patients know if it is beneficial before they start therapy or buy the equipment. They do free re-fittings on equipment if necessary, even years after the equipment was purchased. Family members and caregivers are encouraged to ask questions and receive information. They perform patient and family education, both formally in the structure of evening seminars (free) and informally during therapy. Kay believes it is critical for patients to understand why hard work is important, how it reorganizes the brain, how therapy must be supported at home to be most successful, and what types of equipment and supplies are beneficial. She maintains a lending library of books about stroke, brain injuries, and other neurological diseases for patients and patient families.

Quality patient care and work output is expected of all staff and employees, who are expected to be experts in the use of all equipment. SWAN provides the continuing education needed by employees, and there is ample continuing education funding.

SWAN positions their service in the mind of the consumer as a leader in state-of-the-art neurological rehab. In addition, they are experts who are creative and work hard on behalf of the customer to get them services. Pricing strategies used by SWAN include a survey of the community to keep their pricing structure within community standards and working with their accountant to make sure they are being fiscally prudent.

Because SWAN is moving into a new facility, Kay's start-up costs will be a phone system, $4,000; building upgrades, $5,000; network computer, $4,000; capital equipment, $40,000; new network computer, $4,000; office equipment, $50,000; and a lease increase from $4,500 to $12,500 per month. SWAN's gross revenues from inception were: 2003, $7,000; 2004, $370,000; 2005, $426,800; 2006, $670,000 and 2007, 887,500. The company has a positive cash flow and earns a profit.

Kay's personal goals are to continue growing over the next 5 years and obtain grants for clinical research. She hopes to get her work week down to 40–50 hours and to be able to take a long vacation and a couple of short vacations every year. Her 10-year goals include selling the business while continuing to teach and consult. She expects that when she sells the business, she will stay on for a couple of years to ensure a smooth transition.

SWAN Rehab is a success. Many entrepreneurs are smart, but not successful. Kay Wing knows that the one thing that made a difference between being smart enough and being successful is her drive. It is obvious that her level of aspiration has also increased as a result of her many successes. SWAN gives the people what they want, and most definitely can serve as a positive model to the rest of the business community.

QUESTIONS

1. What steps should a business take in making a capital budgeting decision? What steps did Kay take in making a capital budgeting decision? Compare your answers.
2. Which method of making capital budgeting decisions do you believe would work best for Kay in purchasing new equipment for SWAN?
3. What barriers to entry did Kay face when she went into business for herself?
4. Do a SWOT analysis on SWAN Rehabilitation.

CHAPTER 11

Personal Finance

Learning Objectives

When you have completed this chapter, you should be able to:

- ◆ Understand the overall nature of risk as it pertains to both individuals and businesses.
- ◆ Distinguish between *speculative risk* and *pure risk*.
- ◆ Identify the programs used by individuals and businesses in managing risk.
- ◆ Understand the role that insurance plays in the transfer of risk.
- ◆ Understand the role of capital accumulation in achieving financial success.
- ◆ Analyze and determine which investment vehicles to select in order to accumulate and preserve capital efficiently.
- ◆ Understand the importance of retirement planning.
- ◆ Distinguish between the various retirement programs and strategies available to the business owner and the individual.
- ◆ Understand the importance that estate planning plays for the individual and business owner in the transfer of wealth.

Personal finance is difficult to separate from business finance for the business owner. First, the funds used to start and maintain the business are either your own or are borrowed financial capital used to acquire assets that will generate revenue for the business. In either case, as a business owner, you may be liable personally for all debts of the business. Conversely, all assets acquired by the business not only strengthen the business, but also have a positive impact on your personal wealth. As your individual business assets increase, your ability to borrow funds, your individual credit rating, and the complexity of determining how to invest and protect these assets also increase. For example, excess cash should be invested in a manner that guarantees your financial future and meets the liquidity needs of the business. Inventory, key personnel, and physical and real property must be safeguarded against loss. In financial terms, the methods of investing excess cash and guarding assets against loss are referred to as *risk management.*

RISK

Risk is a term that is based on the uncertainty of future outcomes. It involves both the probability that an expected outcome will occur and the variability in that expected outcome. If there is no variability in future outcome, there is no risk. For example, when you buy a U.S. government bond that pays 5 percent annual interest, it is considered to be a risk-free investment, because the probability that the government will pay the interest is virtually 100 percent. If you buy a corporate bond, however, there is a probability that the corporation may lose money and may not be able to pay the interest on your bond. If the corporation goes into bankruptcy, you may lose both the interest payment and the principal amount of your investment. Therefore, your risk in purchasing a corporate bond is higher than the risk of purchasing a U.S. government bond, and you want to be compensated for the additional risk by having a risk premium added to the investment. The risk premium for a bond is reflected both in the interest (coupon) rate that the corporation must pay to the bondholder and in the discount from par that the bond sells for. For the reader who is not familiar with the terms *coupon rate, discount rate,* and *par,* refer to "Bonds" later in this chapter. Both factors (coupon rate and discount amount) result in a higher rate of return because of the variability and uncertainty of getting back your principal and interest.

For the businessperson, risk occurs when there is a possibility that a venture will fail or incur a loss instead of succeeding. In other words, *risk* is the uncertainty that a loss may occur to a business and prevent it from generating a specific amount of revenue that allows it to stay afloat.

The two types of risk are speculative risk and pure risk. **Speculative risk** involves a possible gain or loss, such as the risk of investing in the stock market or gambling in Las Vegas. This type of risk is uninsurable. **Pure risk** involves only a chance of loss, such as experiencing a theft, fire, or automobile accident. This type of risk is insurable. An example of speculative business risk involves new-product introduction. If a business markets a new product and it fails, then the business has risked a great deal of time and capital only to find itself with excess unplanned inventory. This type of risk is uninsurable because just as the business experienced a loss, it also could have experienced a gain if the product had sold. An example of pure risk occurs if a business experiences a theft. If you have an insurance policy that includes theft, then your insurance will pay for the loss resulting from the theft, because a loss has actually occurred. If there had been no theft, there would have been no loss.

To have an insurable loss, the following criteria must apply:

1. Potential losses must be reasonably predictable for an insurance company to estimate the probability of a loss so that it can set the price of the insurance policy. If your business buys a liability policy and the number of your liability claims exceeds the probability predicted by the insurance company, then the price of liability premiums as charged by the insurance company will increase. If you have too many claims, your insurance premiums may increase to the point at which your business can no longer support the payments and continue to make a profit. In addition, the insurance company may cancel your coverage because it is no longer making a profit. We have seen this happen in the medical field. Some communities no longer have obstetricians because the cost of liability insurance has increased so much that they have chosen to quit the business of delivering babies.

2. The loss must be accidental. If the loss was incurred on purpose, then it is not covered by insurance.

3. The loss should be beyond the control of the insured. For example, the business does not want to promote theft. When theft occurs, it is beyond the control of the business owners.

4. The loss should not be catastrophic to the insurance company. For example, it is difficult, if not impossible, to buy hurricane, earthquake, or flood insurance in certain areas.

IDENTIFICATION OF RISK EXPOSURE

As business owners, we have risk exposure when we place ourselves or our businesses in a situation in which there is uncertainty of outcomes. Marketing risk offers an example of a risk exposure. As indicated, a business suffers a loss if it brings the wrong product or products to market. A business, in its quest to increase sales, may extend credit to its customers. It may have a credit risk if these customers do not pay on time, and it definitely has a credit risk if they do not pay at all. The business is exposed to a loss because the owner thinks that revenue has been earned, but no money is ever received from the customers to increase cash on hand. These risks are not insurable. However, the loss of one's service to a business as a result of death or disability is insurable, as is the interruption of a business's activities as a result of fire or theft.

RISK MANAGEMENT

Risk management involves performing the management planning function in a manner that reduces uncertainty. When uncertainty cannot be reduced, risk management should be used to control the risk at an acceptable level. Risk management applies to insurable business risks and involves a total approach to insuring against these risks, including programs to reduce, avoid, and transfer risk. One example of **risk reduction** is a business that installs sprinkler systems to curtail any damage if a fire should break out.

A company financially unable to sustain or experience any risk can follow a program of **risk avoidance**. A company can avoid any physical hazard that exposes it to risk. To avoid credit risk, a business can use a cash-only policy with no issuance of credit, thus eliminating the late payments and lack of payments associated with issuing credit. This policy, however, might trigger a risk of losing potential sales and becoming noncompetitive if an industry's standard is to issue credit.

For the majority of firms, it is common and most feasible to engage in **risk transfer**. With this practice, risk is transferred to another party, usually a factor or an insurance company. A *factor* is some third party who, for a percentage of the accounts receivable, provides you with immediate payment. The factor is responsible for collecting the payment, and the factor bears the risk of payment not being made. Therefore, when you use a factor, you can issue credit, but you do not have the risk associated with nonpayment as long as you comply with the requirements of the factor. The best example of this is companies that accept MasterCard, Visa, or American Express in payment for products or services. Each company actually provides credit to its customers, but it immediately transfers the risk to the factor (the credit card company). Of course, nothing is free. The factor charges the company a percentage of the accounts receivable as a collection fee. In other words, the risk associated with a particular event is transferred to someone else for a fee. Most firms recognize the fact that potential losses such as a fire might put them totally out of business because they do not have the capabilities to absorb large losses by themselves. Transfer of risk is accomplished by the purchase of an insurance policy. Risk transfer to an insurance company is explained later in the chapter.

Risk assumption occurs when a company believes that the loss it might incur is less than the cost of risk avoidance or risk transfer. Most of us are familiar with this concept as it applies to carrying comprehensive insurance on an automobile. When the value of the car decreases to a certain point, we cancel our collision and comprehensive coverage because the premiums exceed the value of the car. Another example occurs when firms grow. At some point, a firm is large enough to become a self-insurer. If you own one pizza parlor and rely on it for your total income, then you had better use risk transfer and insure your building against fire, theft, and other potential losses in income. If you have 1,000 pizza parlors and 1 burns down, you have enough income generated by the others to rebuild, and you do not have to carry fire insurance. (*Note:* Some large firms may buy a blanket insurance policy that covers all of their outlets at a much lower premium than the cost of individual policies.) In addition, risk assumption may be the only alternative for a company because it cannot find an insurance company willing to insure it against losses—for example, insuring a building against earth-quake damage in certain areas of California.

LIFE, HEALTH, DISABILITY, PROPERTY, AND LIABILITY INSURANCE

Life insurance is discussed in terms of its basics, with permanent and term insurance being the most basic types. The business use of life insurance is discussed in terms of key-man insurance, group insurance, and health and retirement programs. Property and casualty insurance include fire, auto, theft, and liability insurance.

Life insurance is a method of transferring risk from the insured to the insurance company. This allows the insured to create an estate for his or her beneficiaries to receive on the insured's death. The actual amount of life insurance should be based on the financial planning goals of the individual, as discussed in this section. Usually, the amount of insurance that a person requires depends on several factors, including the number and ages of dependent children, the value of a business, the value of a home, and all other outstanding debts. The value also should include the earning potential of the insured and of a surviving spouse. Typically, the amount of insurance required decreases as you get older, because you have more equity in your home and business with time, and your children reach an age at which they are no longer dependents and do not rely on you for their education and sustenance. Group insurance for life and health can be provided at lower premiums because of the reduced risks to the insurance company. Many businesses offer group insurance as a benefit for their employees.

There are essentially two basic schools of thought with regard to life insurance, and there are several variations and combinations within these schools. The first school supports **term insurance,** which assumes that you pay the premium for pure life insurance. A term life insurance premium is based on the mortality rate of the insured's age group. Therefore, as your age increases, the *premium* (the payment you make to the insurance company) also increases. Most term policies are issued with a level premium for a term of 5 to 10 years and then must be renewed at a higher rate. The second school supports **permanent** or **whole-life insurance,** which allocates part of the premium to building equity, or cash value, that can be used on retirement or borrowed against in case of an emergency. If you die without a loan against the policy, however, the insurance company pays only the face value of the policy. Any cash value that you have accumulated is retained by the insurance company. If you cancel a whole-life policy, you receive a *cash surrender value (CSV).* If you cancel a term policy, there is no cash value returned. Under whole-life policies, premiums are set by the insurance companies based on long-term interest rates and actuarial tables.

In the late 1970s and early 1980s when interest rates skyrocketed, individuals took a hard look at their whole-life policy rates of return. They compared these returns with what they could be earning if their money were invested in stocks, bonds, or money market funds. To compete with investment products, the insurance industry developed **universal life insurance**, a policy in which purchasers set the premiums and the death benefits themselves. Premiums are set lower than whole-life policies because at high interest rates a lower initial amount can generate the same investment return. However, if rates fall after the universal life policy is purchased, the premium may be inadequate to cover the death benefit. This creates a risk to the insurance company, which must increase the premium in order to maintain the policy in force.

Another variation of insurance is **variable life insurance,** which allows the individual to buy insurance and at the same time make choices among investment options; thus, all investment risk is placed on the policyholder. Investment choices may include a money market fund, bond fund, equity fund, or any combination of mutual funds.

In the 1990s, those who purchased cash-value life insurance policies that were universal or variable intended to build up cash over the years that paid the premiums in their later years. Interest was credited as cash at a 7 percent rate for universal policies. The minimum guaranteed rate was set at 4 percent. The recent decrease in both interest rates and stock prices have caused these insurance policies to grow more slowly than the rates anticipated when the policies were purchased. Variable life policies were expected to have a 10 percent rate of return; however, some of these policies generated a negative rate of return. Thus, current policyholders have two options: reduce the amount of insurance coverage or, in order to maintain the original death benefit, increase their premiums.

Health insurance is purchased to transfer risk to an insurance company to alleviate the cost of an illness or other health problem. There are several types of health insurance programs, but the two primary types are the *Health Maintenance Organization (HMO)* and *Preferred Provider Organization (PPO)*. The primary difference is that when you join an HMO, you must use their doctors, specialists, and hospitals, except in an emergency. With a PPO, you have a choice of doctors, hospitals, laboratories, and medical facilities that are within the PPO network. You can use doctors, hospitals, and providers outside of the network for an additional cost. Many employers who offer health-care benefits offer employees a choice of these programs. Usually, the HMO premiums are less than those of the PPO. In both situations there are usually copayments and coinsurance.

Medicare is a federal health insurance program offered by the federal government to all citizens 65 or older, or those persons who have been on disability for at least 24 months. There are essentially four parts to Medicare insurance:

1. Medicare Part A covers most expenses and the hospital if they are medically necessary. Part A has no cost because most people paid medicare taxes while working. Hospital stays, home health care services, blood, hospice care, and skilled nursing facility care are covered under Part A.

2. Medicare Part B helps cover doctor services, outpatient care and other items that Part A does not cover, such as ambulance services, blood, bone mass measurement, cardiovascular screenings, chiropractic services (limited), clincal lab services and clinical trials. These items must be medically necessary. Part B primarily covers needed medical services from doctors and outpatient hospital care as well as occupational and physical therapy. The *beneficiary* (the one who receives this service) paid a monthly base premium of $96.40 per month in 2008. This premium is adjusted for inflation and income on an annual basis and is deducted from a person's Social Security benefit payment.

It is important to understand that the coverage discussed here along with drug coverage are a part of the original Medicare fee-for-service plan managed by the federal government. Particiants can go to any doctor, supplier, hospital, or other facility that accepts Medicare and is accepting new Medicare patients. You are in the Original Medicare Plan unless you choose to join a Medicare Advantage Plan like a Health Maintenance Organization (HMO) or a Preferred Provider Organization (PPO). Medicare Advantage plans also include Medicare Private Fee-for-Service (PFFS) plans, Medicare special needs plans, and Medicare Medical Savings Account (MSA) Plans.

3. Medicare Part C consists of Medicare Supplemental insurance plans or Medicare Advantage Plans that provide for the coverage that Part A and B do not cover. These private insurance plans fill in the gaps in the original Medicare Plan. They may pay for coinsurance or copayments for covered services and supplies.

4. Medicare Part D is the federal government's drug program that began in 2006. It was set up for senior citizens to have access to covered prescription drugs. Many find this drug plan very difficult to understand.

There are two ways to get Medicare prescription drug coverage:

1. You can join a Medicare Prescription Drug Plan that adds drug coverage to the Original Medicare Plan, or you can join a private Medicare plan like an HMO or a PPO. In oher words, coverage is available as a stand-alone Medicare Prescription Drug Plan or as part of a Medicare Advantage Plan.

2. You can participate in Medicare's Part D plan.

We now describe the Medicare Part D drug plan. You select a drug plan. Some plans have no premium and some have no deductible, whereas some plans have both. You pay a deductible up front and then you pay a copay. If the deductible is $275, you pay the full price of your prescription(s) out of your own pocket unil you have met your deductible of $275. At that time, your Medicare Part D coverage kicks in. Under Part D, the beneficiary pays 25 percent and Medicare pays 75 percent of all prescription drug costs until the total amount of prescription drugs equals $2,510 for 2008. Essentially, the beneficiary paid $558.75 in copayments plus the initial $275 out of pocket. This $2,510 is the threshold amount that must be reached before the next phase applies. The $275 deductible has already been paid by the beneficiary. When both plan and beneficiary have paid a total of $2,510 (for 2008), the beneficiary can now enter the *coverage gap,* where the beneficiary (you) pays it all. Note that premiums paid by the beneficiary are not included in reaching the $2,510.

Between $2,510 and $5,726.25, the beneficiary pays for all prescription costs. You pay everything until you have spent $4,050 out-of-pocket. This is the "donut hole," and you remain in it until you have paid the $4,050. At this point, the beneficiary has spent a total of $275 deductible plus the $558.75 initial benefit period plus the $3,216.25 donut hole, all of which total $4,050. This indicates the point where catastrophic coverage begins, and you pay a small coinsurance (5 percent) or a small copayment (e.g., $2.25 for generic drugs; $5.60 for brandname drugs). There is no upper limit to this amount.[1]

Health insurance includes disability insurance, which lessens the cost of being disabled and losing the ability to earn an income. *Disability insurance* replaces lost income when an employee is unable to do the job as the result of a physical or mental handicap. Businesses should have a plan that addresses a cost-effective benefits solution for disability that is easy to administer and implement. Many small businesses with 500 or fewer employees have customized disability insurance policies designed for them based on their needs and goals. Benefits are employee focused and provide protection and security if loss of income occurs.

Disability policies replace income. Under Social Security, disability is based on an employee's inability to work, and Social Security rules consider an employee disabled if the employee cannot do the work that he or she did before and cannot adjust to other work because of his or her medical condition(s). The disability must also last or be expected to last for at least 1 year or to result in death.[2] Many insurance plans do not include this strict definition and must be consulted to determine when one qualifies to receive disability insurance payments. Health-care costs have exceeded the inflation rate in the United States for several years, and these costs are a major concern of individuals, government, and business. If you receive disability insurance payments, you are not being paid by your company, but are receiving your payments from an insurance company who has assumed the risk that was transferred in exchange for your payment of premium.

---

[1] All references explaining health care were obtained from *Medicare and You, 2008.* Retrieved August 20, 2008, from http://www.medicare.gov/Publications/Pubs/pdf/10050.pdf.

[2] Social Security's "Disability Planner." Retrieved August 20, 2008, from http://www.ssa.gov/dibplan/dqualify4.htm.

Another type of disability insurance is a Retirement Contribution Policy (RCP) that pays the employees contribuions to a 401k plan in the event the employee beomes disabled and cannot work for a period of time or the rest of his or her career. Without an RCP, the interuption of one's contributions to a 401k retirement or some other retirement program at work decrease the future value of your retirement plan. You can buy this protection as an additional rider to a disabilty insurance policy, or you can buy a stand-alone policy to provide funds for retirement.

For example, Sherry Jones is temporarily disabled as the result of an illness and can't work for a period of 2 years. If she has disability insurance, she will continue to collect an income, but would not be receiving pay from her employer. Sherry was used to contributing the maximum amount to her 401k retirement plan. If she had purchased an RCP, these payments would continue to be made to her 401k retirement plan during her illness.

Many of today's business owners were born between 1946 and 1964. These individuals belong to the baby-boomer generation. Baby boomers, because of their age, are concerned with retirement, risk, and death issues. In addition, these business owners should also understand long-term care insurance.

Long-term care insurance provides assistance for people who have chronic illnesses or who are disabled for an extended period of time. Although most long-term care is needed by older individuals, young or middle-age individuals may require such care if they have been in an accident or experience a debilitating disease. In summation, a business owner pays an affordable premium that provides benefits that lessen out-of-pocket expenses in the event that a mishap occurs. Today's policies cover care in a nursing home and home care. When considering long-term care insurance, we advise shopping around to several companies, because they vary considerably with regard to waiting period, time and type of care, and premium.

Liability insurance is used to transfer the risk of property damage and personal injury that might result from your business operation or individual actions. In our litigious society, it is essential that individuals and businesses carry liability insurance. For example, if you are a plumber and are installing a water heater in a home, there is a possibility that the installation may be faulty and damage to both the property and the occupants of the home may occur. In that case, because you did the installation, you are personally liable for any damages that result from the installation. In the worst-case scenario, if you or one of your employees fail to tighten a natural gas fixture adequately when the heater is installed, the house could burn down and any or all of the occupants could be seriously injured. Without liability insurance, you would probably lose your business and most of your personal assets. Liability insurance premiums vary with the degree of risk associated with your business and the amount of damages paid in a typical lawsuit; therefore, the premiums for a plumber are much lower than the premiums for a physician.

FINANCIAL PLANNING GOALS

The first step in the financial planning process, as in establishing a business, is to establish goals that are realistic and attainable. Every business owner desires to achieve financial success in life. We all have this general goal, but we must become precise in terms of specific dollar amounts desired and the time frame for these financial goals. We must note that financial goals usually begin with the acquisition stage of capital accumulation involving savings and investments. Once acquired, our financial capital must be maintained and preserved. To actually preserve capital, we must invest in vehicles that provide us with a return that is greater than the inflation rate and that take into consideration our individual tolerance for risk. Ultimately, our capital will be distributed through retirement income or estate transfer.

Tolerance for risk typically decreases with age because we realize that we no longer have time to correct mistakes, and we become more dependent on our financial capital to sustain us because our ability to work decreases. For example, a young person who is just starting out can afford to take risks with regard to business and investments in order to accumulate wealth. If the young entrepreneur makes a mistake, he or she has the time to regroup and start again. An older person, however, usually wants a safer investment, because if a mistake is made, that person may not have the time to recover lost capital and may have to live in poverty. Therefore, once financial capital is accumulated, we must preserve and maintain it in an environment that is subject to both systematic and unsystematic risk, as discussed in Chapter 1.

INVESTMENTS

Investment vehicles are the specific financial instruments that we use to generate growth and income. We discuss each investment vehicle in this section.

CASH EQUIVALENTS

Cash equivalents are liquid assets that are invested in savings accounts or brokerage money market accounts. The money market consists of highly liquid current assets, such as Treasury bills (T-bills), banker's acceptances, certificates of deposits (CDs), and repurchase agreements. A **money market account** is a mutual fund that invests in these assets. These accounts earn interest and allow you to have liquidity for running your business. The interest earned on brokerage money market accounts is usually higher than the interest paid by banks on passbook savings accounts. However, most bank passbook savings accounts are federally insured through the Federal Deposit Insurance Corporation (FDIC), whereas brokerage accounts are insured by the brokerage house through the Securities Investment Protection Corporation (SIPC). There is a perception of increased risk in having funds held by a financial institution that is not federally insured. Therefore, having funds in a brokerage house rather than in a bank is considered a higher risk, and we do find higher interest rates in brokerage accounts because of the increased risk.

Although most bank savings accounts are of the passbook variety and usually require you to be present to withdraw funds, a money market brokerage account can usually be accessed with a check. However, these are not your usual bank checking accounts, because you are usually limited in some accounts to a minimum value for check writing ($500 to $1,000) and to the number of checks that can be written in a month. These accounts are useful for accumulating money for payment of items that are short-term in nature, but not monthly—for example, payment of quarterly or semiannual taxes, insurance premiums, and in some cases, retirement or profit-sharing payments.

CERTIFICATES OF DEPOSIT

Certificates of deposit (**CDs**) are promissory notes whereby a bank promises to pay the purchaser the principal amount plus interest after a stipulated period of time. Interest may be simple or compounded daily, monthly, or quarterly. CDs are issued for time periods as short as 30 days or as long as 5 years. As with most investments, the longer you tie up your money, the higher the interest rate, so you can expect to earn a higher return on a 5-year CD than on a 30-day CD. It is important to note that if you purchase a 5-year CD and need the money before it matures, you pay a significant penalty that has the effect of decreasing the interest that you thought you would earn on the CD. Thus you lose the liquidity available in savings and money market accounts for the additional interest that is earned on a CD. For this reason, we do not recommend using these investment vehicles unless you are extremely confident that the money you invest will not be needed until the CD matures.

You can time CD maturities in order to meet short- and long-term obligations. For example, 6-month CD rates are usually one-half percent higher than passbook savings account rates. If you have a $10,000 property-tax payment due in July and you have $10,000 in excess cash in December of the previous year, purchasing a 6-month CD that is compounded daily provides you with a little less than $25 in additional interest on the $10,000 during the 6 months.

BONDS

Bonds (government and corporate) are contractual agreements made between a borrower (government or corporation) and a lender of financial capital, such as an individual, business, pension fund, mutual fund, or insurance company. There are several types of bonds and several degrees of risk associated with them. We discuss each type in ascending order of risk.

U.S. Treasury Bonds

U.S. Treasury bonds are issued by the United States to finance the government when its spending exceeds its tax revenue, which is referred to, on an annual basis, as the government having a *deficit budget*. The total amount of bonds issued by the government that are outstanding at any given time is the *national debt*. Federal bonds are considered to be risk-free or to have the least amount of risk because they are backed by the full faith and credit of the federal government. Although short-term federal bills (T-bills) are risk free, long-term federal bonds are subject to interest rate swings and could be risky if you need the principal prior to maturity. In addition, the federal government is the only agency in the United States that can absolutely guarantee payment of interest, because it can print money. U.S. Treasury bonds come in three varieties, which are based on the maturity dates of the bonds. **T-bills** (or Treasury bills) are risk-free investments that mature in less than 1 year, typically in 3 or 6 months. **T-notes** are bonds that mature in 10 years or less, typically 10, 5, and 2 years. **Federal bonds** mature in periods that are greater than 10 years and range up to 30 years.

Municipal Bonds

Municipal bonds are issued by state and local governments, not the federal government, to finance projects. Municipal bonds are issued as either general revenue or general obligation bonds. **General revenue bonds** are issued to build specific projects for the municipality that will use the income from the project to pay the bondholder. For example, the city of Phoenix must expand its sewer system to provide sewer service for new homes. The city borrows the money, installs the sewer lines, and charges a sewer fee to homeowners. This money is then used to pay the bondholders. **General obligation bonds** are used to build projects that do not usually generate revenue, such as public schools and roads, so these bonds are based on the taxing ability of the municipality. For example, Phoenix must widen the roads because of increased traffic flow. Because the city does not collect a road tax, it issues a general obligation bond and pays bondholders by collecting taxes in other areas (such as a sales tax). Interest payments on municipal bonds are free of federal income tax liability and are usually free of state and local taxes in the state in which they are issued. Therefore, they usually pay a lower interest rate than corporate bonds, but a higher rate than federal bonds. This lower tax-free interest rate equates to a higher before-tax interest rate. For example, a 30-year tax-free municipal bond paying 5 percent issued to a taxpayer in the 30-percent bracket (federal and state combined) is equivalent to a taxable rate of 7.14 percent.

$$\text{Before-tax rate} = \frac{\text{Tax-free rate}}{1 - \text{Tax rate}}$$

$$= \frac{0.05}{1 - 0.30} = \frac{0.05}{0.70}$$

$$= 0.0714, \text{ or } 7.14\%$$

Corporate Bonds

Corporate bonds are issued by a public corporation that wants to borrow money to invest in assets that will help it earn revenue. These assets can be used as collateral and are pledged to the buyer of the bond in the event that the corporation cannot pay back the money due to the bondholder. When a corporation guarantees the bond in this manner, it is referred to as *secured debt*. The term **secured debt** refers to the fact that the corporation pledges specific assets to guarantee the bonds. For example, Yantze Corporation wants to build a new office building that costs $75 million. The corporation has only $25 million in cash for this project, so it issues $50 million in bonds and pledges the office building as collateral to the bondholders. When a bond is not backed by secured debt, it is referred to as a **debenture**. Debenture bondholders have a claim on the remaining assets of the company (those that are not secured).

Mechanics of Bond Financing

A brief explanation of several terms may help you understand how bonds relate to your own personal goals. First, bonds are issued in denominations of $1,000. This is the **par value** of the bond—also referred to as the **face value** or **principal value** of the bond. This value never changes and is the amount of money that is paid to the bondholder at *maturity* (the due date of the bond). The **coupon rate** is the rate of interest that the issuer (government or corporation) agrees to pay to the lender (bondholder) on an annual basis. This value also is referred to as the **stated** or **quoted rate,** and it never changes. For example, the Yantze Corporation issued a 10-year bond in January 2003 that pays 6 percent interest. If you bought this bond, you would receive $60 in interest payments each year until 2013. The $60 interest payment is calculated by multiplying the contractual 6 percent coupon rate by the par value of $1,000. The payments are usually made semiannually, or every 6 months. Therefore, you receive a check for $30 twice a year from June 2003 until January 2013, when you return the bond to the Yantze Corporation and receive a check for $1,000 (the maturity value of the bond). Note that even if you do not return the bond, the corporation will no longer pay you interest, because their contract with you or whoever holds the bond is only for the life of the bond.

Corporate bonds are purchased through *intermediaries* (brokerage firms) and not directly from a corporation. We can buy bonds either when they are issued (as in purchasing the bond mentioned earlier in January 2003) or in the aftermarket. Let us say that we bought 10 Yantze bonds for $10,000 (at par $1,000 each) in January 2003, when the bonds were issued at 6 percent. We now decide that we have another investment to make and no longer want to be a creditor of Yantze Corporation. We can contact a broker and offer the bonds for sale. The price received for these bonds depends on two primary factors: current market interest rates and risk.

The **current market interest rate** is the prevailing interest rate in the market on the day we decide to sell the bond. For example, if the current bond-market rate is 8 percent, then a currently issued bond at par ($1,000) has a coupon rate of 8 percent, or pays $80 interest per annum. Therefore, any purchaser of a bond wants to earn 8 percent as the minimum rate on his or her investment. Consequently, when we sell our Yantze bonds in the current market, we cannot get the $1,000 par value for the bonds because Yantze pays the new bondholder $60, or a 6 percent coupon rate, on the face value. We must reduce the price (sell the bond at a discount) until the price of our bond gives the purchaser a market interest rate of 8 percent or more in annual interest on the amount that he pays for the bond. Bonds that are sold at a value above par are sold at a **premium**; bonds that are sold at a value below par are sold at a **discount**. The procedures for determining the current value of a bond are covered in Chapters 8 and 9, when we discuss the present value (PV) of an ordinary annuity and the present value (PV) of a lump sum. The method requires us to use the following factors:

1. Using current interest rates, find the present value of the bond's interest payments, paid over the remaining life of the bond. Our Yantze bond has 5 more years to maturity, with current market interest rates of 8 percent. Because the bond is paying 6 percent, or $60 per year, we want to determine how much money we must invest now at 8 percent to provide us with $60 per year for 5 years. Because Yantze sends us $30 checks semiannually, this is the same as receiving 10 payments of $30 at 4 percent interest. We therefore want to find the present value of a $30 annuity for 10 periods at 4 percent interest. We use the formula PVOA = A (present value annuity factor), where PVOA is the present value of an ordinary annuity, *A* is the value of the annuity, and the annuity factor is obtained from Appendix B, Table B–5. Using the table, we find a factor of 8.1109 for 10 periods at 4 percent. We then multiply this factor by the $30 annuity payment and determine that the PV is $243.33.
2. Using current interest rates, find the PV of the $1,000 maturity value of the bond after 10 periods at 4 percent interest per period. First, we go to Appendix B, Table B–2 and find a factor of 0.6756. Using the formula *PVLS = FV* times the present value factor, we multiply the $1,000 future value payment by the 0.6756 factor from the table to obtain $675.60. Thus, if $675.60 were deposited in a bank today at 8 percent interest compouded semiannually, it would grow to $1,000 in 5 years.
3. Therefore, as a bond purchaser, the maximum price that you would be willing to pay for this bond is $243.33 plus $675.60, or $918.93.

Sometimes it may be necessary to sell our bond at a further discount that would give the purchaser an interest rate of more than 8 percent because of increased risk. For example, let us say that during the period of time from our January 2003 purchase of the bond until now, the Yantze Corporation has fallen on financial difficulties and its bond rating has gone from Aa (double a) to B. Note that, by definition, a B bond (Table 11–1) is considerably less attractive than an Aa bond. Because the investor perceives the purchase of this bond as being more risky, he or she wants an interest rate higher than 8 percent. These bonds are **junk bonds** (termed *high-income-yielding bonds* by the brokerage industry) because they have a rating of B or less. Therefore, the price that we have computed, $918.93, is the maximum price that a buyer is willing to pay for this bond. Notice that 8 percent is the market rate that is based on systematic risk. However, Yantze has increased risk because of its B bond rating, so we must increase the discount and lower the price to less than $918.93 to give the new bondholder an interest rate of more than 8 percent.

Some bonds sell at very deep discounts when firms have poor bond ratings. When the Circle K Corporation was in Chapter 11 bankruptcy in 1992, you could have purchased a $1,000 bond for $70. This is somewhat akin to playing the lottery. The market perceived that this company would not recover from bankruptcy, so it valued the bonds at 7 cents on the dollar. While in bankruptcy, a corporation usually ceases all payments to bondholders. The only hope is that if the company is sold or emerges from bankruptcy, some payment will be made to the company's creditors—and bondholders are creditors.

STOCK

Common Stock

Common stock is issued by public or private corporations to raise financial capital. The *stockholders* (owners of shares of common stock) are the owners of the corporation, and each share of stock is usually worth one vote. Every public corporation must hold an annual meeting. The usual agenda for these meetings includes election of the members of the board of directors, selection of an independent auditor to perform the annual audit of the corporate books, and any other business deemed necessary by the owners. The board of directors is responsible for selecting the professional management of the corporation: the chief executive officer, the chairman of the board, and the president. The stockholders determine who sits on the board of directors, and the number of shares of common stock to be issued by the corporation is determined by the board of directors, who assign a par value to the stock. The **par value** is an arbitrary dollar amount that is used for accounting purposes to determine the number of shares of stock that have been sold by the corporation.

The par value has no relationship to the actual market price of the stock. For example, the Yantze Corporation decides to issue 1 million shares of common stock at a par value of $1 per share, and the market is willing to buy this stock at an average price of $10 per share. We say that the market has paid in $9 per share of additional capital. Recall from our previous discussion that

---

TABLE 11–1 Corporate Bond Ratings

Key to Moody's Corporate Bond Ratings

Aaa

Bonds which are rated **Aaa** are judged to be of the best quality. They carry the smallest degree of investment risk and are generally referred to as "gilt edge." Interest payments are protected by a large or by an exceptionally stable margin and principal is secure. While the various, protective elements are likely to change, such changes as can be visualized are most unlikely to impair the fundamentally strong position of such issues.

Aa

Bonds which are rated **Aa** are judged to be of high quality by all standards. Together with the **Aaa** group they comprise what are generally known as high-grade bonds. They are rated lower than the best bonds because margins of protection may not be as large as in **Aaa** securities, or fluctuation of protective elements may be of greater amplitude, or there may be other elements present which make the long-term risks appear somewhat larger than in **Aaa** securities.

A

Bonds which are rated **A** possess many favorable investment attributes and are to be considered as upper medium-grade obligations. Factors giving security to principal and interest are considered adequate, but elements may be present which suggest a susceptibility to impairment some time in the future.

Baa

Bonds which are rated **Baa** are considered as medium-grade obligations, i.e., they are neither highly protected nor poorly secured. Interest payment and principal security appear adequate for the present but certain protective elements may be lacking or may be characteristically unreliable over any great length of time. Such bonds lack outstanding investment Characteristics and in fact have speculative Characteristics as well.

Ba

Bonds which are rated **Ba** are judged to have speculative elements; their future cannot be considered as well assured. Often the protection of interest and principal payments may be very moderate and thereby not well safeguarded during both good and bad times over the future. Uncertainty of position characterizes bonds in this class.

B

Bonds which are rated **B** generally lack characteristics of the desirable investment. Assurance of interest and principal payments or of maintenance of other terms of the contract over any long period of time may be small.

Caa

Bonds which are rated **Caa** are of poor standing. Such issues may be in default or there may be present elements of danger with respect to principal or interest.

Ca

Bonds which are rated **Ca** represent obligations which are speculative in a high degree. Such issues are often in default or have other marked shortcomings.

C

Bonds which are rated **C** are the lowest rated class of bonds and issues so rated can be regarded as having extremely poor prospects of ever attaining any real investment standing.

Source: Copyright Moody's Investors Service, Inc., 1996. All rights reserved. Reprinted by permission.

Assets = Liabilities + Stockholders' equity. Because the common stock is the stockholders' (owner's) equity, the sale of these shares of stock is listed on the balance sheet as follows: stock at par, $1 million ($1 × 1 million shares = $1 million); additional paid-in capital, $9 million ($9 × 1 million shares = $9 million). Notice that the stockholders' equity is $10 million—the total amount raised by Yantze Corporation for the sale of this stock. In reality, the stock has sold at a price slightly higher than $10 per share, because there are charges to the corporation by the investment banking firms and brokerage firms who act as intermediaries between the corporation and potential investors. The initial sale of stock by corporations to the public is the **primary securities market** and is referred to as an *Initial Public Offering (IPO)*.

Once a stock is sold by a corporation, all resales of this stock are usually carried out by the owners of individual shares (not by the corporation) in the **secondary securities market**. Common stocks usually have two values: book value and market value. The **book value** of the corporation's stock is the total stockholders' equity that is carried on the corporate balance sheet. It includes three factors: stock at par, additional paid-in capital, and retained earnings. Only one of these figures—retained earnings—changes, unless the corporation buys back stock or issues additional shares of stock. The total value of the owners' equity (Stock at par + Additional paid-in capital + Retained earnings) divided by the number of shares outstanding is the book value of a share of common stock. The formula is

$$\begin{array}{l}\text{Book value per share}\\ \text{of common stock}\end{array} = \frac{\text{Total common stockholders' equity}}{\text{Number of shares of common stock outstanding}}$$

The **market value** of a share of stock is the price at which the owners of current shares are buying and selling the stock at the time that a share is actually traded. Several factors affect the market value of a share of stock.

1. Supply and demand for shares of the company stock. As discussed in Chapter 1, if there are more people who want to buy available shares in a specific corporation than there are people who are willing to offer shares for sale, then the share price is bid up by competition. Conversely, when there are more shares available for sale than there are purchasers of the stock, then the price falls. For example, when Enron filed for Chapter 11 bankruptcy, shareholders panicked and offered thousands of shares for sale. Because of the company's financial position, there were very few takers, and the price of the stock fell from a high of $27.30 in October 2001 to a low of 2 cents by August 2002.

2. Actual earnings and anticipation of changes in earnings by the corporation. For example, if the Yantze Corporation announces that it just received a patent for a new product that the market perceives as a best-seller, then the stock price will probably rise. However, if stockholders read an article that states that the Yantze Corporation lost money, had a plant burn down, or is involved in a product liability lawsuit, then the price of the stock will probably fall. An additional factor is analysts' earnings expectations and the company's abilities to meet these expectations with actual earnings. For example, in March 2008, Big Lots reported annual earnings of $1.55 cents per diluted share, which was 72 cents better than analysts' estimates. Within 1 week, Big Lots stock increased $4.28 per share, from $16.85 on February 29, 2008, to $21.23 per share on March 5, 2008.[3]

---

[3]Big Lots Inc., Headlines and Historical Prices. Retrieved April 2, 2008, from http://finance.yahoo.com/q?s=Big.

3. The book value of the stock and the number of shares of stock outstanding. For example, if the Yantze Corporation currently has 1 million shares of stock outstanding and the board of directors decides to issue an additional 1 million shares, then the book value of each share is reduced by 50 percent and any earnings per share of the corporation is also diluted because of the additional number of shares. This reduction is reflected in a reduced market value of each share of stock.

4. General economic conditions. Economic conditions in general also affect the price of a stock, even if a corporation does everything correctly. If the economy is in a recession with a high unemployment rate, then corporate sales in general will be lower. Low sales decrease corporate earnings; therefore, the stock investor is not willing to pay as high a price for the corporation's stock, because as a corporation's earnings decline, the price of its stock usually follows. With broad-based indications of a pending recession in early 2008 and crude oil prices exceeding $100 a barrel, the Dow Jones Industrial average fell from 13,043.96 on January 2, 2008, to 12,644.36 on April 1, 2008, and the NASDAQ fell from 2,609.63 to 2,362.75 during the same time period—a drop of 246.88, or 9.46 percent. Other factors in the economy can affect specific industries. For example, with oil prices of more than $100, we expect the costs of energy-dependent items such as food, electricity, paint, and plastic goods to increase. Another economic factor is market interest rates. If interest rates are rising, then money becomes more expensive to borrow, and it becomes more expensive for corporations to raise money through bond sales or bank borrowing. If corporations must pay more interest on their debt, they will not be able to make as much profit, and stock prices in general will fall as a result of anticipated decreased earnings. The reverse of these situations usually leads to increasing stock prices.

Preferred Stock

Preferred stock (cumulative preferred, convertible preferred, and callable preferred) is also issued by a corporation to raise financial capital; however, it occupies an intermediate position between common stock and bonds. Preferred stock is a hybrid vehicle because it has features of both bonds and common stock. Preferred stockholders are quasi-owners of the corporation—they do not have voting rights, but they are guaranteed a specific percentage return on their investments if the corporation pays a dividend. The original selling price and par value of preferred stock are the same, and preferred stock is usually sold at values of $25, $50, or $100 per share, with a stated dividend that is a percentage of the par value. For example, if the Yantze Corporation issues $1 million (10,000 shares) of preferred stock at $100 par value, paying $7, or 7 percent per share, then the purchaser knows in advance that he or she should receive a $7 dividend per share in each year that the corporation declares a dividend. Preferred stock has an important feature of the long-term bond (fixed annual payments), and owners relinquish their voting rights for this feature. However, like the common stockholders, they still have a residual claim on income; and in fact, their claim is senior to that of common stockholders.

Recall that Yantze Corporation issued 1 million shares of common stock and 10,000 shares of preferred stock. The corporation makes an annual profit of $4 million, and the board of directors determines that it pays a dividend of $1 million and have retained earnings of $3 million. When a dividend is declared, the preferred stockholders receive their payment first (in this case, $7 × 10,000 shares). Dividend distributions are calculated as follows:

$$\text{Total dividend} = \text{Total preferred dividend} + \text{Total common stock dividend}$$

$$\begin{aligned}\frac{\text{Total common}}{\text{stock dividend}} &= \text{Total dividend} - \text{Total preferred dividend}\\[6pt] &= \$1,000,000 - (\$7)(10,000 \text{ preferred shares})\\ &= \$1,000,000 - \$70,000\\ &= \$930,000\end{aligned}$$

$$\begin{aligned}\frac{\text{Common stock}}{\text{dividend per share}} &= \frac{\text{Total common stock dividend}}{\text{Total number of shares of common stock outstanding}}\\[6pt] &= \frac{\$930,000}{1,000,000 \text{ shares of common stock}}\\ &= 0.93 \text{ per share of common stock}\end{aligned}$$

Because each of the 10,000 shares of preferred stock receives a dividend payment of $7, Yantze preferred stockholders receive $70,000 in total dividends. This leaves $930,000 to be paid to common stockholders. Because there are 1 million shares of common stock outstanding, each share of common stock receives a dividend of 93 cents. Therefore, if you owned 1,000 shares of preferred stock, you would receive a dividend check for $7,000. If you owned 1,000 shares of common stock, you would receive a dividend check for $930.

Cumulative Preferred Stock.   Cumulative preferred stock has an important feature. There may be a year or two in which a dividend is not paid (the corporation may have lost money or retained earnings to finance some project) because of financial circumstances of a corporation. When the corporation decides to pay a dividend, the preferred stockholder receives back dividends, or dividends in arrears. This feature is not available to common stockholders. Let's say that the Yantze Corporation has not paid any dividends during the previous 2 years, and then it decides to pay a $1 million dividend in the current year. The payout of preferred dividends is calculated as follows: $70,000 for year 1, plus $70,000 for year 2, plus $70,000 for the current year, or $210,000; therefore, the preferred stockholder receives $21 per share in preferred dividends. The common stock dividend is calculated as $1,000,000 − $210,000 = $790,000, or 79 cents a share. Most preferred stock is cumulative.

Convertible Preferred Stock.

Convertible preferred stock may be exchanged for shares of common stock. If the preferred stock is convertible, this feature is stated when the stock is issued, with minimal time frames within which the option may be exercised. This feature is used to add value to a preferred stock issue because the stock has the advantage of fixed earnings in the near term and it appreciates in value in the long term if the corporation's common stock does well in the market. In addition, the preferred stockholders have the senior position on whatever funds are available to stockholders should the corporation be liquidated.

Callable Preferred Stock.

Callable preferred stock can be called back by the company at some specified price. It is not attractive to investors, so the company usually must provide investors with a *call premium* (an amount of money above the stock's current selling price). Companies usually call back preferred stock when interest rates are low because they believe they can raise capital and pay less interest to a lender than they would pay in dividends to the preferred stockholder. For example, if the prime lending rate falls to 5 percent when the company has 7 percent preferred stock, then Yantze can borrow $1 million and can use these funds to buy back its preferred stock and make interest payments of $50,000 per year when it would have had to pay the preferred stockholders a dividend of $70,000. Another method that a company can use to raise capital when market interest rates are low is to issue common stock. Because stock prices are usually high when interest rates are low, the company could issue common stock and use the capital to call back the preferred stock. This has the advantage of eliminating the entire $70,000 preferred dividend.

Strategies of Stock Investment

Strategies of stock investment are varied. Stocks are considered to be high-risk investments because when you supply equity capital to a company, you position yourself as a claimant on any income that the company may generate. As a small investor, however, you have such a small share of the company that you, in reality, have no voice in how your investment is used. Owning 100 shares of a corporation that has 30 million shares of common stock provides you with no real authority in regard to the corporation. In addition, any corporation, regardless of size, may lose vast amounts of money (as General Motors did in 2007) or may declare bankruptcy (as Limited, ATA, and Aloha Airlines did in 2008). When companies lose money, the market value of their stock goes down (Bear Sterns Companies stock price fell from $76.62 on March 3, 2008, to $2.84 on March 17, 2008). If a company goes into bankruptcy, you may very well lose all of your money because the value of the stock can go to zero. On average, however, stockholders earn 9 percent on their investment each year. The problem is that, to earn this average, you must have stock in all publicly traded companies. Some go bankrupt, and you lose your investment; others generate income and gain in stock price far in excess of 9 percent. Thus, you must diversify your portfolio by owning stock in several corporations at the same time. To equal or beat this 9 percent average return, you must either spend substantial amounts of time studying individual corporations, hire a broker in whom you have absolute confidence, or set up a pool of funds with other investors who share your goals and risk-tolerance levels. We believe that the best method of pooling your investment, based on goals and risk-tolerance level, is to invest in mutual funds.

MUTUAL FUNDS

Mutual funds are companies that are involved in collecting the funds of investors and using these funds to purchase large blocks of stocks, bonds, or other investment vehicles. Each fund is established with a specific goal and risk objective. When you invest in a mutual fund, you are essentially hiring a professional manager to research and purchase those investment vehicles that match your own individual goals. Mutual funds are priced at the end of each trading day using **net asset value (NAV),** obtained after the market closes each day. It is the total value of the holdings of the fund minus any liabilities divided by the number of shares that the fund issued. Unlike stocks, which are traded throughout the day, mutual funds orders are filled only after the NAV has been calculated at the end of the trading day. The investment objectives of most mutual funds fall into one or more of the following general categories.

Growth Funds

Growth funds are the most popular of mutual funds. They invest primarily in common stock of publicly held corporations and their objective is capital appreciation. Growth funds vary from aggressive growth (investing in small high-tech companies that also provide high risk) to long-term growth (investing primarily in stable, well-established blue-chip companies with low risk) to sector funds that specialize in the stocks of specific industries (pharmaceuticals, chemicals, metals, etc.).

Income Funds

Income funds are attractive to people who are retired. These funds specialize in corporate and government bonds. Their objective is to provide the investor with a relatively high level of stable income. As with growth funds, the level of risk varies based on the specialized area of fund investment. Some funds invest only in U.S. government bonds; others may invest only in high-quality corporate bonds or home mortgages (Ginnie Mae bond funds); and others may invest only in low-quality corporate bonds (junk bonds), which are usually listed as high-income or high-income-yielding bond funds.

Growth and Income Funds, or Balanced Funds

Growth and income funds, or **balanced funds,** invest in both stocks and bonds. These funds provide both capital growth through stock and bond acquisition, and fixed income through bond coupon payments. The balance is achieved because if there is a shift by investors out of the stock market, bond prices usually increase because of increased demand for bonds. There is also an inverse relationship: If investors shift from bonds to stock, then stock prices are bid up by increased demand. These funds usually appeal to the investor who has a moderate tolerance for risk.

Global and International Funds

Global and international funds have the same basic objectives as the balanced funds, but they invest in stocks and bonds of companies primarily outside of the United States. These funds may be global (i.e., investing in opportunities in any area of the world), regional (e.g., European, Asian), or specialized (e.g., Japan, Israel, France).

Money Market Funds

Money market funds invest primarily in short-term, highly liquid investments such as CDs, short-term government Treasuries, commercial paper, repurchase agreements, and banker's acceptances. These funds are the mutual fund equivalent of a checking account. If you hold money in a money market fund, you may request check-writing privileges; however, these are not the usual checkbooks in that the number of checks you can write per month is limited and the minimum amount of the check may be set by the fund. These funds usually generate income greater than what is being paid by commercial banks because they have a portfolio of investments. When you purchase a CD or Treasury instrument through a commercial bank, you get only the interest rate of the specific vehicle. We (the authors) each have money market accounts so that we have some liquidity, but we use the accounts to shift assets to and from mutual funds, purchase stock, and make other investments.

Other Funds

Other funds include a whole category of specialized funds that are very high risk and operate in such areas as options, futures contracts, commodity markets, and currency exchanges. Because this book is written primarily for the nonfinancial entrepreneur and small businesses; therefore, these high-risk operations are beyond its focus.

Mutual Fund Families

A **mutual fund family,** such as Fidelity, Janus, and Vanguard, is an investment group that may have mutual fund portfolios in all of the preceding categories. Each has several categories of mutual funds and may sell no-load or load funds.

♦ **No-load funds** do not charge commissions on the amount invested. If you invest $100 and the fund share price is $10, you purchase 10 shares. However, these funds may involve assessed charges when you sell the mutual fund shares.

♦ **Load funds** charge a commission on the initial investment, but they have no sales charges when you sell the shares. If you invest $100 in a front-loaded fund that charges a commission of 5 percent, then you purchase $95 worth of shares and pay $5 in commission.

There are advantages to both of these types of funds. No-load funds are used primarily by people who do their own research and determine in which fund and which fund family to invest. Load funds, because they involve a commission, are preferred by most brokers. However, it is in their best financial interest to provide you with advice that makes you a long-term client. One should choose funds and families that meet individual investment needs. The choice of which type of fund to invest in is based on your own perceptions. The authors of this text invest primarily in no-load funds.

When you are in a family of funds, you can switch your investments from one fund to another without paying a transaction fee based on the amount transferred. This usually saves you time and paperwork.

Mutual fund families are based on the assumption that individuals consider certain investment vehicles more appropriate than others over time as a result of both individual and economic changes. For example, if you start investing when you are young and single, what type of investments should you make? Because you have no family and no responsibility to others, you probably have a higher tolerance for risk and will consider placing most of your investments in growth funds. Later, you marry and have children, who need a college education. Your goals become more focused as you take on the additional responsibility of providing for your offspring's education. You might invest in growth mutual funds when your children are young, but as college age approaches, you may want to lock in a principal amount and be in a position to write checks for tuition, books, and other incidental expenses. At this point, you may want to switch some of your investments into money market funds, which guarantee principal but still provide some growth in the form of interest. As you approach retirement, you may want to begin accumulating wealth for retirement; but after you retire, you probably want a specified level of income. This may be accomplished by investing in low-risk income funds rather than aggressive growth funds. As discussed earlier, if all your investments are in a single family of funds (no-load, load), then you can switch from one investment vehicle to another without paying a transaction fee based on a percentage of the reallocated investment.

In addition to changes that occur because of your family circumstances, other factors in the economy may have an impact on your investments. If you invested in a growth fund that has been growing by 12 percent per year on average and market interest rates go to 18 percent (as they did during the 1980s), you may want to shift some of your investment from stock to bonds. As mentioned, bond prices decrease as interest rates increase, so you can buy more bonds with a given amount of investment principal. You can increase your wealth by this shift in investments. You were getting 12 percent in your growth fund, but now you can get 18 percent interest on bonds. When interest rates drop, the income generated from the bond fund decreases, but the value of the bond fund shares increases. With declining interest rates, there is a point at which you may decide to sell the bond fund and reinvest in stock funds. For the small investor, mutual fund families are probably the best investment vehicle.

REAL ESTATE

Real estate is an investment in land and buildings. In general, these investments fall into three separate categories: owner-occupied residential, non-owner-occupied residential, and commercial. Each category is treated differently for tax purposes and is discussed separately.

Owner-Occupied Residential Real Estate

Owner-occupied residential real estate is any kind of building in which people live. It is limited by law to your primary residence and one additional vacation home. This property may or may not appreciate (increase in market value) in the future. The factors that affect market value are based on the laws of supply and demand, as discussed in Chapter 1. However, real estate can be used as a form of savings, and it historically has kept pace with inflation. The house in which you live and have a right to own because you are paying off a mortgage is your investment in real estate. As you pay down your mortgage, you are building equity in the home, and this equity is a form of investment that you actually own. The equity comes in two forms: the paying down of the mortgage and the appreciation of home values in the market. Historically, housing has increased in value by about 10 percent a year, although in any given area and for any time period, this may not be true. Therefore, an investment in a home is considered to be one that beats inflation over time. The tax advantage of home ownership is that you may subtract the interest paid on your mortgage from your personal income before determining your tax liability. Because of this, it usually pays the homeowner to itemize deductions for income tax purposes.

Non-Owner-Occupied Residential Real Estate

Non-owner-occupied residential real estate is property that can be leased by the owner to the tenant for the purpose of generating income. This property may be in the form of houses, apartments, motels, or hotels. You can convert a residential property to non-owner-occupied residential property by renting out your house. Variations on this include living in one part of the house and renting out the other part (the portion of the house that you rent out is depreciable) or buying a rental house for investment. The property is subject to depreciation because it is an asset that generates income. Under tax law, the depreciation rate is not the same as that for commercial real estate. The advantages of owning non-owner-occupied residential real estate are primarily in tax benefits. The owner of the property may deduct mortgage interest, depreciation, and all other usual business expenses, which include employee salaries and expenses needed to help generate income (e.g., maintenance and repair of the property).

Commercial Real Estate

Commercial real estate includes both land and improved property that are used by the owner to generate income. Examples are commercial office buildings, shopping centers, factories, and warehouses. Commercial property is subject to different depreciation rates than non-owner-occupied residential property. Commercial property and non-owner-occupied residential property differ from owner-occupied residential property for tax purposes because they can be depreciated and the interest payments on commercial mortgages are considered business expenses. There may be a large shift in commercial real estate value as a result of the impact of technology and online shopping via the Internet. If this mode of shopping has a severe adverse effect on retail stores, then there may be a large shift from retail stores and malls to centralized warehouses that store and ship products purchased on the Internet, such as Amazon.com.

Real Estate Investment Trusts

A **real estate investment trust (REIT)** provides an investor with the opportunity to participate in the commercial and non-residential real estate market. A REIT is a pooling of individual investor funds, much like a mutual fund. You buy shares in the trust, then the trust invests in real estate. If the investment value goes up, the shares appreciate. When you sell the shares, you realize a gain, as with any other investment. The shares usually pay dividends, which can be taken as income or can be reinvested. Like all real estate investments, however, the property held by the trust may actually go down in value. When this happens, you lose money on your investment if you sell your shares. These investments are considered by some to be highly speculative and risky.

In 2000 and 2001, stock prices and interest rates decreased and REITs became very popular. By the summer of 2002, REITs became less popular because the commercial real estate market was weakening and many owners of REITs thought that dividends would be cut. REITs usually pay healthy dividends because they own and operate income-producing property, such as office buildings, apartment buildings, shopping centers, hotels, and warehouses. In order to qualify as a REIT, a company must distribute at least 90 percent of its taxable income to its shareholders each year. The REIT is allowed to deduct dividends from its corporate tax bill.

PRECIOUS METALS

Precious metals fall into the area of commodity trading. They are primarily gold, silver, and platinum. Precious metals, especially gold, are considered hedges against inflation. With an increase in the inflation rate, the value of currency (in terms of its purchasing power) decreases. In some countries, this happens at such a fast rate that the currency of the country becomes worthless. Gold, however, is in universal demand and can maintain its value when transported across international boundaries. Investments in precious metals can be in the commodity itself (bars or bullion) or in mining stocks. Mutual funds that deal in precious metals actually deal in mining stocks rather than a commodity itself. Over time, however, precious metals are not as good an investment as equity, bonds, and real estate. These investments do not earn interest and depend primarily on their marketability at the time of sale. Most investment advisors recommend that no more than 5 percent of the average portfolio be invested in precious metals. If you do not want to invest in bullion but would rather collect coins, then you are no longer investing in the commodity but are investing in collectibles.

COLLECTIBLES

Collectibles are items that become valuable or appreciate with time because of their scarcity. Some examples are coins, paintings, sculptures, antiques, stamps, and even baseball cards and comic books. The reason these items increase in value is there are more people who want a specific item than there are items available for sale. The primary reason is that a particular item is no longer being produced. An artist such as Picasso can produce only a certain number of paintings during his lifetime. Because Picasso is dead, there can never be another original Picasso. Therefore, the original Picasso painting becomes a collectible and continues to increase in value because there are not enough paintings to allow everyone who wants one to have one.

Investing in collectibles is highly speculative because much of its success depends on the marketability of an item when the owner wants to sell. There also are problems associated with insurance and security of collectibles. If you place an item somewhere where you do not have high protection costs and insurance premiums (such as a bank vault or safety deposit box), your access to the item is limited because you must go to the storage facility to view the collectible. If you place it where you have constant access to it (such as on the wall in your home), then the insurance premiums and security issues can become quite expensive because everyone has access. Therefore, collectibles have a tendency to lead to additional risk that is not associated with the purchase price of the item, and this risk cuts into the profitability of the collectible. Many collectibles look much more attractive on paper than they are in reality.

INVESTMENT STRATEGIES

SHORT-TERM INVESTMENT STRATEGIES

Short-term investment strategies are specifically developed to get a return on an investment in time periods that are usually less than 1 year. These investments include buying stock on margin, selling short, and option trading. These strategies are very speculative and incorporate very high risk. We do not recommend short-term strategies for small businesses or novice investors. Let's look at a margin-requirement example to demonstrate the risk. If you have a brokerage account, you may be able to buy on *margin,* which means borrowing from the brokerage house. Current margin requirements are 50 percent. Let us say that you have $5,000 in a brokerage account. You can purchase $10,000 in stock from the broker, who uses your $5,000 and lends you $5,000. You do this because you have read an article that says that the ABC Pharmaceutical Company has developed a cure for acquired immunodeficiency syndrome (AIDS). The article states that Food and Drug Administration (FDA) approval should be received next month. You, therefore, believe that the stock's price will increase. You purchase 1,000 shares of stock in the ABC Company for $10 a share on Monday. You use your $5,000 plus the broker's $5,000. You notice that the stock increases to $15 a share on Tuesday, and you sell the stock at $15. The shares are now worth $15,000. You pay your broker the $5,000 that was used on margin, and you have a profit of $5,000, or a total of $10,000 in cash.

This is the ideal short-term investment. However, let us say that on Monday afternoon, the FDA finds that the potential AIDS cure causes prostate cancer and requires additional long-term studies. On Tuesday, the stock price falls to $5 a share. The broker calls the margin account and wants repayment of the $5,000 loan. You sell the stock at $5 a share and pay the broker. Now you have lost $5,000 and have no cash. This is an example of the speculative nature of short-term investing, and why we recommend long-term strategies only.

LONG-TERM INVESTMENT STRATEGIES

Long-term investment strategies are developed to provide future income and growth. Long-term strategies include selecting investments based on individual goals that are established for some time in the future. These strategies include basic stock and bond investment strategies, retirement planning, and tax planning. Two basic techniques in stock investment are buy and hold and dollar cost averaging.

Buy and hold can be realized by purchasing common and preferred stocks and holding on to them for a number of years. Because the basic objective of corporations is growth and profit over time, purchasing stock in these corporations should provide you with growth and profit over time as well.

Dollar cost averaging involves regular systematic investments. Markets fluctuate over time. Prices of stocks increase and decrease. Most of us cannot predict the future and have limited funds for investment. Dollar cost averaging allows us to purchase an equal dollar amount of the same stock at equal time intervals (e.g., every month). For example, you buy or purchase $500 worth of XYZ mutual fund every month. In January, you pay $50 per share and buy 10 shares. In February, the price drops to $25 and you buy 20 shares. In March, the price increases to $50 per share and you buy 10 shares. You now own 40 shares of this fund and paid an average price of $37.50 per share ($1,500 ÷ 40 shares = $37.50/share). The average price per share purchased is based on the total number of dollars invested divided by the number of shares purchased. This technique eliminates the problem of trying to guess what the market will do. Your dollar cost averaging provides you with normal growth and income over time.

PENSION PLANNING

Pension planning consists of making plans to guarantee a system of conserving future income for the time when you choose to retire or are forced into retirement because of circumstances beyond your control. The three main sources of retirement income are Social Security, employer-sponsored retirement plans, and individual retirement plans and personal savings. We currently have no control over Social Security, but we do have significant control over employer-sponsored retirement plans and total control over individual retirement plans and personal savings. Our contention that we have significant control over employer-sponsored retirement plans is explained in detail as we define the different types of retirement plans in the following section.

RETIREMENT PLANS

Retirement plans are broken down into contribution–oriented plans, benefit-oriented plans, and combined plans that allow one portion of an investment to be classified as a contribution and the other portion as a benefit. **Contribution-oriented plans** provide benefits to the retiree based on the account balance that has been accumulated during the working life of the pensioner. **Benefit-oriented plans** provide a defined benefit to the retiree at retirement, which is generally a percentage of the compensation paid to the employee during the last several years of employment and the total term of employment—for example, military retirement pay. **Combined retirement plans** are designed by individuals or employers. They are based on factors that allow one to take maximum advantage of current tax law. Examples are plans that provide for both tax deferment of salaries and employer contributions into a retirement plan.

Tax consequences of all retirement accounts are as follows: If the money that is contributed is pretax dollars, then the tax on these dollars is deferred until they are withdrawn. If the money contributed is after-tax dollars, then only the return on the money invested is taxed when it is withdrawn [except in the case of the **Roth Individual Retirement Account (IRA)**]. For example, if your adjusted gross income is $20,000 and you contribute $4,000 in pretax dollars to a retirement account because you are under age 50 in 2008, then you pay income tax on a recomputed adjusted gross income of $16,000 that year. If you retire in 20 years and use funds from your retirement account, all the money you withdraw is considered to be income and is taxed at the rate that exists at the time of withdrawal. If, however, you contribute after-tax dollars, your adjusted gross income remains $20,000 and you pay current taxes on the entire $20,000. When you retire, if 20 percent of your retirement account consists of after-tax contributions that were made during your working years and 80 percent consists of the return on your investment, then you pay taxes on 80 percent of your retirement income, except in the case of the Roth IRA.

Note: The retirement plans discussed in this section were current in accordance with IRS Publication 560, IRS Publication 3998, and other IRS publications at the time the textbook was written. Because Congress continually updates tax laws and the IRS responds, it is our belief that the reader must check current tax laws pertaining to small business. Particular attention should be given to IRS Publication 560, Retirement Plans for Small Business, and to IRS Publication 3998, Choosing a Retirement Solution for Your Small Business.[4]

Specific types of retirement plans are as follows:

♦ Individual retirement accounts (IRAs) are plans that allow us to contribute current annual income into retirement accounts. The specific investment vehicle can be chosen by us, but the investments must be maintained by a trustee. There are several types of IRAs.

    1. *Deductible IRAs* are those in which you can contribute pretax dollars up to an amount specified by current law. In 2007, you could contribute earned income up to $4,000 ($8,000 for married couples filing jointly) or $5,000 if you were age 50 or older of pretax income, provided you or

---

[4]*IRS Publication 560, Retirement Plans for Small Business,* and *IRS Publication 3998, Choosing* a *Retirement Solution for Your Small Business* (Catalog Number 340665) (rev. 2004).

    Choosing a *Retirement Solution for Your Small Business* is a joint project of the U.S. Department of Labor's Pension and Welfare Benefits Administration, the Internal Revenue Service, the U.S. Small Business Administration, and the U.S. Chamber of Commerce. Its publication does constitute legal, accounting or other professional advice.

your spouse was not covered by an employer-sponsored pension plan and your adjusted gross income did not exceed certain limitations. Your modified adjusted gross income in a traditional IRA cannot exceed $63,000 if you are single and $105,000 if you are married and file jointly. Your contribution is reduced gradually above $53,000 for singles and above $85,000 for married people filing jointly and then completely eliminated at $63,000 (single) and $105,000 (married filing jointly).

2. Nondeductible IRAs allow you to contribute the same amounts as deductible IRAs, but the contribution is after-tax dollars. For both of these plans, the returns on investment accumulate tax free until they are withdrawn. You can begin taking funds from these accounts at age $59\frac{1}{2}$ and must begin withdrawing at age $70\frac{1}{2}$.

3. Roth IRAs allow you to contribute up to $4,000 for 2006 through 2007 ($5,000 if you are 50 or older by the end of the year) of after-tax dollars. (Contribution limits are shown in Table 11–2.) For 2008, there is a $5,000 contribution limit ($6,000 if you are 50 or older) and a $10,000 limit for couples. If the funds are held in the account for at least 5 years and you are $59\frac{1}{2}$, there are no taxes due if you withdraw. Your original contributions can be withdrawn tax-free at any time. You may roll a traditional IRA into a Roth IRA, provided that you pay all taxes due on the distribution at your current tax rate and your modified adjusted gross income is $100,000 or less. For years prior to 2010, you cannot convert a traditional IRA into a Roth IRA if your modified adjusted gross income is greater than $100,000. In a Roth IRA, you can withdraw $10,000 penalty-free and income tax–free, provided the money is used to purchase a first home and the IRA is more than 5 years old. To qualify for a Roth IRA first-home contribution, you must not have owned a home for the previous 2 years. You also can use the money to buy or build a first home for yourself, your children, or your grandchildren. As with other IRAs, you can begin to take withdrawals at age $59\frac{1}{2}$, but the Roth IRA does not have an age limit with regard to mandatory withdrawals. You may continue to contribute to your Roth IRA beyond age $70\frac{1}{2}$.

TABLE 11–2 IRA Contribution Limits

Years	Maximum Annual Contribution	Maximum Annual Contribution Age 50 or older
2002–2004	$3,000	$3,500
2005–2007	$4,000	$5,000
2008	$5,000	$6,000
2009–2010	$5,000 indexed	$6,000 indexed

Source: IRS Publication 3998 (*rev. 2004*). Retrieved August 21, 2008, from http://www.irs.gov/pub/irs-pdf/p3998.pdf.

The Roth IRA can be established even if you contribute to an employee-sponsored retirement plan. However, in order to make the maximum contribution, there are limits. Your modified adjusted gross income cannot exceed $101,000 if you are single and $159,000 if you are married and file jointly. Your contribution is reduced gradually above $101,000 for singles and above $159,000 for married people filing jointly, and then completely eliminated at $116,000 (single) and $169,000 (married filing jointly). The Roth IRA is also tax-free to your heirs. Before 2008, you could roll over or convert amounts from either a traditional, a simplified employee pension (SEP), or a simple IRA into a Roth IRA. As of 2008, you can roll over amounts from a qualified pension, profit sharing, or stock bonus plan [including a 401k plan, an annuity plan, a tax-sheltered annuity plan, section 403b plan, a deferred compensation plan of a state or local government (section 457 plan)].

4. Coverdell Education Savings accounts or educational IRAs allow non-deductible contributions up to $2,000 per child per year under the age of 18. These contributions are subject to certain phaseout and other limitations. The income from an educational IRA accumulates tax-free and remains tax-free as long as it is used for the child's higher educational expenses. Educational expenses now cover elementary school and high school expenses, including tuition, fees, academic tutoring, books, supplies, special need services, and transportation. Funds withdrawn are tax-free if used before the child is age 30. The account can be transferred between family members. Current law must be consulted prior to any distribution because of the complexity of the requirements.

5. Section 529 plans include prepaid tuition and savings plans. Funds in both accounts grow tax-free. These plans are offered by states with the help of financial services companies. The contribution limitation on prepaid tuition depends on the plan and the age of the student. The contribution limitation for savings plans depends on the plan and may vary from $100,000 to $305,000. In both cases, withdrawals are tax-free if used for qualified expenses. Qualified expenses are tuition, fees, and room and board at qualified higher education institutions. Unless Congress extends the current law, distributions will count as income to the student in 2011. Some states allow contributions to be partially or completely deductible. In most states, control of the account remains with the contributor. Accounts can be assigned to immediate family, including cousins, step-relatives, and in-laws. The penalty for non-qualified withdrawal is that the withdrawal is taxed as ordinary income plus a 10 percent penalty.[5]

---

[5]IRS publication 970: Tax Benefits for Education and 529 Miscellaneous Deductions (2007). Retrieved August 21, 2008 from http://www.irs.gov.

♦ **Simplified employee pension (SEP) plans** are IRAs that are funded by employers or business owners who have a handful of employees. The employer contributes to a retirement account that covers the eligible employee. Employee contributions are not allowed. For an employer to establish a SEP, all eligible employees must agree to the account. If any eligible employee does not choose to have an IRA, then the company cannot establish a SEP. An eligible employee must be 21 years old, have worked for the employer for 3 of the previous 5 years, and have earned at least $500 the previous year. These plans are common for the self-employed and the business owner. Contributions are deductible to the business owner. Contributions and deduction limits in 2008 cannot exceed the lesser of $46,000 or 25 percent of the participants' compensation, provided that the employer was contributing to a defined contribution plan.[6] The maximum annual compensation limit as of 2008 is $230,000. The advantages of the SEP are that it can be opened as late as the extended due date of your income tax return, it is as easy to open as a deductible IRA but it allows much larger contributions, it is not subject to annual government reports, and the administrative expenses are quite low.

♦ In 1997, many firms considered switching from a SEP IRA to a Savings Incentive Match Plan for Employees (SIMPLE) plan. SIMPLE IRA plans may be established by an employer who has fewer than 100 employees if each employee received at least $5,000 in employee compensation during any two preceding years and earned at least $5,000 in the current year. The company must match employee contributions dollar-for-dollar up to 3 percent of salary or make a non-elective contribution by putting in 2 percent of salary for all eligible employees. The maximum contribution was $10,500 in 2007 and 2008; if you are 50 or older, the contribution limit is $12,500. Participants are completely vested immediately. This is a great plan for employees. It allows for employee contributions through salary reduction and an employer match. What better way is there for employees to earn 100 percent on their 3 percent contribution? However, it does not allow the employer to put away as much for the employer's retirement as with the SEP IRA.

♦ **Tax-sheltered annuities (TSAs 403b plans)** are plans that allow employees of not-for-profit organizations (churches, public schools, charitable organizations, etc.) to establish a retirement fund that is purchased and approved by the employer. You can contribute a part of your annual salary on a pretax basis. Maximum contributions are imposed by current tax law. Maximum contributions for 2005 were $14,000 and for 2006 were $15,000; for individuals age 50 and older, maximum contributions were $15,000 in 2005 and $20,000 in 2006. For 2008, the basic salary deferral limit is $15,500. If you are 50 or older, there is a possibility of contributing an additional $5,000. Each pay

---

[6]IRS publication 560: Retirement Plans for Small Business (2007). Retrieved August 21, 2008, from http://www.irs.gov.

period, the employer deducts the contribution from the paycheck and sends it to the contract administrator. The deduction is not subject to income taxes. The employees can begin drawing retirement pay when they retire, and they pay taxes on both the contributions and the earnings.

♦ **Keogh plans** are for self-employed individuals in sole proprietorships, partnerships, and limited liability companies (LLC). If you are self-employed, you can set up a self-directed retirement plan and contribute up to the lesser of 100 percent of earned income or $46,000 for 2008. The maximum deductible contribution is 25 percent of compensation. With a Keogh plan, you can define both the contribution amounts and the benefits derived from the account. If you choose to have a defined-contribution plan based on a percentage of earned income, contributions can vary from year to year because they are based on profit. They may be skipped if there were no profits one year. If you choose to have a defined-benefit plan, annual contributions must be calculated by an actuary and you must make this contribution yearly. It is set up to produce an annual pension payment of the lesser of $185,000 or 100 percent of average compensation for the three highest years ($180,000 in 2007; $175,000 in 2006). For example, if you determine that you want to retire with an annual income as high as a $185,000 limit, then the amount that you must contribute each year is determined by an actuary based on your income, target benefit, and years until retirement. The actuary also looks at expected investment returns.

♦ **Profit sharing plans** are established by employers who have determined that a portion of each dollar in profit will be allocated to the employees of the company. The method of allocation can vary, but it usually is based on employee compensation and length of service. Annual contributions to these plans vary drastically, because profits fluctuate as a result of total-economy, industry, and specific-company reasons. These plans almost never stand alone; they are incorporated into other types of retirement plans, such as 401k retirement plans.

♦ **401k retirement plans** are established to accept employee contributions. The primary 401k plan is based on salary reduction. Employees may contribute a specified percentage of their pretax salary, which is collected by the employer as a payroll deduction. The employer may match a portion of the contribution on some basis, such as 25 cents of employer contribution for every dollar of employee contribution. The employer also may choose the 401k as the vehicle for distributing profit sharing contributions. For 2006 to 2010, the deferral limit for individuals under 50 is $15,000, and $20,000 for individuals age 50 and above. The IRS states that 401k plans cannot favor highly compensated employees over lower-paid workers. A modification of the 401k plan currently used today is the SIMPLE 401k. This plan allows employees to shelter up to $15,000 per year. It is for businesses with fewer than 100 employees.

Employers can contribute 3 percent of worker's compensation. This plan must be the only plan that the business offers, and employers are spared the discrimination testing for highly compensated employees of the regular 401k plan.

◆ **Roth 401k plans** were offered by businesses beginning in January 2006. A Roth 401k plan is an after-tax elective contribution to a 401k plan. It is funded with after-tax dollars. The contributions have been taxed and are not taxed on distribution to the plan participants if a 5-year holding period has been met. The contributions are not deductible. The contribution grows tax-free and any earnings created by the contribution are tax-free. The major issue in choosing a Roth 401k is whether you want to be taxed now or later. For those who will be in a high tax bracket at retirement, the Roth 401k is the way to go. With a traditional 401k, you benefit if you end up in a lower tax bracket at retirement. The annual contribution limit is higher for a Roth 401k than it is for a Roth IRA—$15,000 in 2006 ($20,000 if age 50 or older). In addition, with a traditional 401k, you must start taking minimum distribution at age 70 and 1/2; with a Roth 401k, no such rule exists. All funds can be passed on tax-free to one's beneficiaries. Beginning January 1, 2008, a distribution from a qualified retirement plan can be rolled over to a Roth IRA subject to the restrictions that currently apply to a rollover from a traditional IRA to a Roth IRA.

◆ **Money purchase plans** are defined-contribution plans established by the employer to contribute a fixed percentage of payroll into a retirement fund for employees. The maximum contribution is 25 percent of payroll. The employee does not contribute to this plan, but all contributions are considered pretax income. The employer must contribute each year even if the company makes no profit.

◆ **Stock bonus plans** are similar to profit sharing plans except that the employer contributes shares of stock rather than money into the retirement account. The employee, therefore, is investing primarily in the common stock of the employing firm. The employer gets a 25 percent deduction for the value of the stock contributed to the plan, so the contribution is pretax dollars.

◆ Creative money managers have come up with ways for self-employed entrepreneurs to put away more funds for retirement than has been allowed. The plans are sometimes named 401k Keogh plans and are combinations of a Keogh profit-sharing plan and a conventional 401k plan. They are aimed primarily at self-employed people who do not have employees working for them. The self-employed entrepreneur may contribute as much as 25 percent of earnings to an individual 401k plan, plus a maximum elective deferral of $15,000, as long as he or she does not exceed $42,000. For example, an individual earning $50,000 in self-employment income can contribute 25 percent of income, or $12,500. In addition, a self-employed person can contribute $15,000 as an elective deferral, which results in a total contribution of $27,500, or 55 percent of self-employment earnings. If you are an unincorporated business, then self-employment payroll taxes must be factored in, which reduces the percentage of income contributed.

RETIREMENT STRATEGIES

Retirement strategies are the plans that individuals make to take care of themselves and their families when they can no longer work or no longer wish to work. As business owners, each of us must determine which of the preceding plans or combination of plans should be used to establish future income for us and our employees. Certain basics, however, benefit all individuals.

- ◆ Establish a goal or minimum income level that you desire when you retire. This should be at least 70 percent of your annual income at the time of retirement.
- ◆ Do not wait until you believe you can afford to start a retirement account, because if you wait, there will always be emergencies that require current income, and you will probably never start the account.
- ◆ Plan for capital preservation and continued growth. The principal amount of your retirement account should provide a return that gives you the desired income, and it should continue to grow by at least the inflation rate that exists at the time of your retirement. Because none of us know how long we will live after retirement, it is absolutely essential that the principal amount of our retirement account remain intact during our retirement years.
- ◆ Invest in instruments that provide you with a degree of risk that is comfortable to you (i.e., based on your tolerance for risk).
- ◆ If you work for an employer who provides you with a 401k or similar plan in which the money in the account is maintained by a trustee who is not the employer, then try to invest the maximum amount, but never less than the amount that the employer uses to calculate profit sharing or matching contributions. If your 401k plan accepts a $1,000 maximum monthly contribution ($12,000 per year) and the employer matches the first 3 percent ($360), then you should invest at least $360. Where else can you invest and earn 100 percent on your investment?
- ◆ Consider opening a Roth IRA even if you have an employer-sponsored plan.

RETIREMENT STRATEGY EXAMPLES

Table 11–3 provides a visual representation of two example retirement strategies; they use a worst-case scenario and a best-case scenario from the retirement programs described here. We assume that you begin investing in a retirement account at age 25. Your income at age 25 is $20,000, and you never receive a promotion, but you do get annual pay raises equal to the rate of

TABLE 11–3 Retirement Strategies

$4,000 Annual IRA Contribution

| Age | Annual Income (3% Inflation Rate) | Total Value at Year End | |
		Low-Risk Strategy (5%)	High-Risk Strategy (10%)
25	$20,000		
26	20,600	$ 4,000	$ 4,000
27	21,218	8,200	8,400
28	21,855	12,610	13,240
29	22,510	17,241	18,564
30	23,185	22,103	24,420
31	23,881	27,208	30,862
32	24,597	32,568	37,949
33	25,335	38,196	45,744
34	26,095	44,106	54,318
35	26,878	50,312	63,750
36	27,685	56,827	74,125
37	28,515	63,669	85,537
38	29,371	70,852	98,091
39	30,252	78,395	111,900
40	31,159	86,314	127,090
41	32,094	94,630	143,799
42	33,057	103,361	162,179
43	34,049	112,530	182,397
44	35,070	122,156	204,636
45	36,122	132,264	229,100
46	37,206	142,877	256,010
47	38,322	154,021	285,611
48	39,472	165,722	318,172
49	40,656	178,008	353,989
50	41,876	190,908	393,388
51	43,132	204,454	436,727
52	44,426	218,677	484,400
53	45,759	233,610	536,840
54	47,131	249,291	594,524
55	48,545	265,755	657,976
56	50,002	283,043	727,774
57	51,502	301,195	804,551
58	53,047	320,255	889,006
59	54,638	340,268	981,907
60	56,277	361,281	1,084,097
61	57,966	383,345	1,196,507
62	59,705	406,513	1,320,158
63	61,496	430,838	1,456,174
64	63,341	456,380	1,605,790
65	65,241	483,199	1,770,370
Retirement income at age 66 =		$ 28,992	$ 106,222

inflation. We assume that the rate of inflation averages 3 percent until you retire; therefore, your salary at retirement at age 65 is $65,241. We know that this sounds unreasonable, but ask your father or grandfather how much they were making 40 years ago. We believe you will find that the figures match your parents' experiences.

The worst retirement program, from the viewpoint of annual contributions, is the IRA, which is limited to $4,000 for 2005 through 2007. If you invest $4,000 a year and invest at the end of each year (worst case, because the money does not earn anything during the year) in safe securities (U.S. government bonds or government-bond mutual funds), you earn an average yield of 5 percent. Your retirement nest egg has a value of $483,199 when you retire. If you decide to retire on an income equal to 6 percent of your retirement account, your income is $28,992 per year—hardly a comfortable retirement when your income before retirement was $65,241. This obviously does not meet the goal of 70 percent of income.

If you have a high tolerance for risk and place the $4,000 in a stock mutual fund that averages 10 percent annual return, your retirement account has $1,770,370. If you take 6 percent as income and let the remainder grow, your annual income is $106,222 and grows by an average of 4 percent each year (10 percent growth − 6 percent income).

These are the two extremes. Most financial advisors recommend a combined strategy in which all of your retirement dollars are diversified in various investment vehicles. There are other factors that you should also consider. In our example, we assume that all contributions are pretax dollars, so the entire amount of your retirement income is subject to taxation at the rate that exists in the year you withdraw the income. If you made the contribution in after-tax dollars to a Roth IRA, then the entire amount that you accumulate at age 65 is not subject to taxes. Several advisors recommend that a portion of contributions to retirement accounts be made in after-tax dollars because none of us know what the tax rates will be at the time of retirement, whereas we do know current tax rates.

A third example is based on making everyday life choices. An 18-year-old male, Heywood U. Quitnow, works part time and earns about $10,000 each year. He decides to give up smoking for the next 4 years while he attends college. Heywood estimates that he spends $3.50 per day on cigarettes, or $1,277.50 per year (365 days × $3.50 per day). On a 1-month basis, he spends $106.46 ($1,277.50 ÷ 12 months per year). If he opens a Roth IRA and invests the $106.46 each month in a stock mutual fund earning an average of 12 percent, Heywood will have $6,434.82 at the end of 4 years. To solve this problem, we must first find the monthly effective rate and then solve for the future value of an ordinary annuity.

$$\text{Monthly rate} = \sqrt[n]{1 + i} - 1$$
$$= \sqrt[n]{1.12} - 1$$
$$= 0.0095 = 0.95\,\% \text{ per month}$$
$$FVOA = A\left[\frac{(1 + i)^n - 1}{i}\right]$$
$$= \$106.46\left[\frac{(1.0095)^{48} - 1}{0.0095}\right] = \$106.46(60.4436)$$
$$= \$6,434.82$$

Heywood invested $5,110.08 ($106.46 × 48 months) and earned $1,324.74 on his investment ($6,434.82 − $5,110.08 = $1,324.74). He now has several options:

1. Close his Roth IRA and pay a 10 percent penalty ($132.47) for early withdrawal on his earnings of $1,324.74. Because his income is only $10,000 per year, he pays no income tax. He can now take the $6,302.35 ($6,434.82 − $132.47 = $6,302.35) and go on a vacation.
2. Put a down payment of $6,302.35 on a new car.
3. Leave the money without making any additional contributions in the stock mutual fund set up as a Roth IRA until age 65.
4. Leave the money in the stock mutual fund set up as a Roth IRA until age 70.

If he spends the money on a vacation, he has nothing of lasting value except a few pictures and a suntan. If he spends the money on a car, he has a depreciating asset worth a small percentage of the original purchase price. If he chooses the Roth IRA route and does not touch the money but keeps it in the stock mutual fund earning an average annual rate of 12 percent, then he has $841,223.46 at age 65. If he keeps it another 5 years to age 70, he has $1,482,523.18. This is a future value of a lump-sum problem, and the solution appears next. Because it is in a Roth IRA, all the values in the accounts are tax-free to Heywood and his heirs.

$$FV_{age\ 65} = PV(1 + i)^n$$
$$= \$6,434.82(1.12)^{(65-22)} = \$6,434.82(1.12)^{43}$$
$$= \$6,433.82(130.7299) = \$841,223.46$$

$$FV_{age70} = \$6,434.82(1.12)^{(70-22)} = \$6,434.82(1.12)^{48}$$
$$= \$6,433.82(230.3908) = \$1,482,523.18$$

ESTATE PLANNING

As a business owner, you should plan for the use, conservation, and, in estate planning, the transfer of your wealth as efficiently as possible. Basically, you are doing financial planning with the anticipation of eventual death. It is in your best interest to create documents with proper professional advice to accomplish these goals. A business succession plan, as discussed in Chapter 2, must address the issue of the eventual death of the business owner. An estate plan serves as a tool that allows the business to continue as a separate entity. These plans must have a will, a living will, a living trust, and several advanced directives.

Property transfer at death is an inevitable fact. As a business owner, it is imperative that you plan for this transfer to be made in a manner that allows the business to remain intact, rather than being dissolved. If you are a sole proprietor, your business is transferred to your spouse or whomever you designate in your will. If you are in a partnership, the business is transferred to the surviving partners and possibly your spouse in accordance with the partnership agreement.

In each of these instances, there are large financial costs incurred by the business. For example, if you have very specific skills that are required by the business, your spouse or surviving partners must hire others with these skills to take your place. The best method of handling this circumstance is through the use of a life insurance policy on each of the key personnel in the firm. The policy is purchased by the business so that adequate financial capital is available to continue the business when one of the key individuals dies.

In other words, proper estate planning allows for the creation of capital (via life insurance) on the death of one of the owners. In some partnership agreements, it is specified that the policy is of sufficient value to allow the surviving partners to purchase the deceased's share of the business from the surviving spouse or family members. **Wills** are written documents that provide direction to others about how you want your wishes carried out after death. Everyone should have a will, but it is absolutely essential that married couples with children have wills to ensure that their children are raised by people who carry out their wishes. If you and your spouse both die, whom do you want to take care of your children? Do you want separate funds set aside for your children? Are there certain keepsakes and mementos that you want to go to a particular friend or relative? In other words, you are actually giving directions to others about how you want your assets distributed on your death. Without a will, the government makes those decisions for you. Dying without a will is known as dying *intestate.* If you die intestate, the court appoints an administrator to distribute your estate in accordance with the probate laws in your state.

Wills also describe how you want your probate property disposed of at death. **Probate** is a legal court process that addresses and focuses on the will and the probate estate. Probate adds cost to estate distribution, increases the time to settle the estate, and in addition, private family information is not protected, because probate is a matter of public record. The probate property value is the value of the gross assets owned by the deceased, other than life insurance. For example, if you own a house that is valued at $300,000 and you owe $100,000, then the net estate is $200,000, but the gross estate for probate is $300,000. Because probate costs are a percentage of the gross estate, then good estate planning should remove as much of the gross assets as possible from the portion of the estate that is subject to probate. There are essentially three methods of accomplishing this: joint ownership with right of survivorship (temporary removal), trusts (permanent removal), and gifting.

In the first method, you purchase as many assets as possible with joint property ownership with right of survivorship. In other words, if the house is purchased in your name only and you die, then the entire value is subject to probate. If you purchase it in joint tenancy with your spouse, then there is no probate on the property on your death; however, when your spouse dies, then all property is subject to probate. There is one caveat to this process. If your spouse later wants to sell the house, your spouse must get the property into his or her name prior to sale. At that point, the deceased spouse's half of the property is subject to probate. To totally remove the home from probate, you could place the home in a trust.

There is one caveat that we must mention here. It is usually not a good idea to make a child a joint tenant, because life changes, people get divorced, go bankrupt, and get sued. For example, if Seymore Dough, son of Lotta Dough, became a joint tenant and subsequently files for bankruptcy, Lotta's 50 percent joint tenancy in the house may be exposed to creditors' claims. As a result, she may lose her house because of her son's bankruptcy. In addition, the matter can become even more complicated, because if Lotta needs money out of the equity in her house for living expenses and wants to use a home equity line of credit, Seymore is vital because he must sign off on the transaction.

Trusts are legal arrangements that actually divide legal and beneficial interests among two or more people. The trust is created by a trustor or grantor, and beneficiaries or trustees are named by the trustor. The trustor also can be the trustee. The trust is a separate entity, similar to a corporation, that has a legal persona of its own. Property placed in a trust is separate from that of its owner, but it can be managed by the owner because the owner can be the trustee. When a trust is set up during the life of the trustor, it is referred to as a **living trust**. When a trust is established at death, it is referred to as a **testamentary trust**. Trusts also may be revocable or irrevocable. A **revocable trust** is one in which the trustor has the right to cancel the trust during his or her lifetime. An **irrevocable trust** is unalterable during a person's lifetime. There are several legal and tax issues with relationship to revocable and irrevocable trusts that are too complex to handle in this text. In addition, laws pertaining to trusts and taxes are constantly changing. Therefore, if you want to set up a will or a trust or some combination, we recommend that you seek professional legal advice.

A third method is to use gift giving as a way to reduce your taxable estate. You can gift $12,000 a year to each one of your children, grandchildren, son-in-law, and daughter-in law. You can also speed up the process by gifting 5 years in advance ($60,000) for your beneficiary in a 529 plan.

Irrevocable Grantor Trusts (Rabbi trusts) are established by employers for executives and key employees. With this form of trust, annual bonuses and other items of deferred income are placed into the trust. The items in the trust are not considered income to the employee until they are paid to the employee under the terms of the trust.[7]

---

[7]IRS Bulletin 2000–43, October 23, 2000.

CONCLUSION

Risk management for a business owner is a must. We identify risk exposure and use the methods that guarantee both the continuation of the business and personal financial security. This requires that we establish financial goals that are viable and obtainable. Each owner must base individual goals on a combination of factors that include personal tolerance for risk. A plan should include a mix of several financial vehicles, including insurance for pure risk and financial-investment vehicles for speculative risk. We should select investment vehicles based on where we wish to be at some future date, such as at retirement. The planning should include both business and individual pension planning to provide us with the lifestyle we desire in retirement. We also want to include estate planning to ensure that our business continues after our death and that our families are provided for. Only through advance planning and the proper implementation of these plans can we guarantee the future viability of our business and the ability to provide for our own and our families' well-being.

REVIEW AND DISCUSSION QUESTIONS

1. Compare the risk of buying a U.S. government bond to that of buying a corporate bond.
2. Compare *speculative risk* and *pure risk*.
3. How can a business owner identify risk exposure?
4. What are some programs that an entrepreneur can use to reduce risk?
5. Compare whole-life and term insurance.
6. List and describe some investment vehicles that a small business owner might select.
7. What is the difference between the *coupon rate* and the *current market interest rate* of a bond?
8. If the coupon rate on a bond is 8 percent and current market interest rates are 6 percent, should this bond be selling at a premium or a discount?
9. How do we determine the book value of a stock?
10. Compare *cumulative, convertible,* and *callable preferred stock.*
11. What is the difference between a *mutual fund* and a *mutual fund family*?
12. List and briefly describe three types of mutual funds.
13. Compare *no-load* and *load* mutual funds.
14. Compare short-term and long-term investment strategies.
15. What is the difference between a contribution- and a benefit-oriented retirement plan?
16. What are the basic factors that should be considered when establishing an individual retirement plan?
17. How may a small business owner plan for the use, conservation, and transfer of wealth as efficiently as possible?
18. What is the role of trusts in estate planning?

EXERCISES AND PROBLEMS

1. You have a friend, Icahn Betitall, who just started a small business. He is paying a hefty premium for insurance. Icahn's insurance agent told him that he is insuring against the risk of loss on fire, theft, liability, and business interruption. Icahn also has policies for life, health, and automobiles. Icahn is planning a trip to Las Vegas. He plans to contact his agent and obtain a policy on the risk of losing his money at the blackjack table.

   a. What should you tell Icahn about being able to purchase such a policy?

   b. What are several methods that Icahn can choose to manage his risk exposure in Las Vegas?

2. Your city is expanding. There have been several problems with street flooding, which is affecting your business. You decide to attend a city council meeting, during which there is a discussion on building storm and sewer lines in advance of home construction. At the meeting, Tom Frank, the city manager, states that the city is prohibited by law from financing these projects through a sales or property tax. He says that after the new homes are built, the city will be able to charge a monthly sewer fee to each homeowner and business. He asks for suggestions on financing the new sewer system.

   a. What would you propose the city do to raise this money?

   b. Why is this investment vehicle attractive to investors?

3. Grandpa Russ thinks he needs a fixed income for the next 10 years. He currently has $10,000 in CDs, which are maturing at the end of this month. The CDs can be renewed for one year at $4\frac{1}{2}$ percent. Russ calls his broker, Ben Seller, and learns that his $10,000 can be put to better use by purchasing debentures issued by Grab-n–Run, Inc. These bonds are 10-year bonds with a coupon rate of 8 percent, which is paid semiannually. The current market interest rate is 6 percent for bonds of a similar nature. The broker tells Grandpa Russ that he may buy each bond for $1,400. Grandpa knows that he must pay a premium, but he believes that a $400 premium is too high.

   a. What is the maximum price you should tell Grandpa to pay for each bond?

   b. Compare the risk of the CD with the risk of the bond.

   c. What else would you advise Grandpa with regard to this type of investment?

4. Sarah Mix is a single 30-year-old business owner who has $500 a month to invest. This money is in excess of the contribution to her company pension plan. Sarah hears that many of her friends are investing in mutual funds. Her grandfather, Grandpa Russ, invested in the stock market and lost everything. He advises her to invest only in bonds. Her uncle, Sam, thinks that she should invest in stock mutual funds, but only in conservatively managed funds that invest in U.S. blue-chip stocks. Sarah notes that her Grandpa is 70 years old and her uncle is 55 years old. Her friend Jane, who is also 30 years old, said she only invests in small capital growth funds.

   a. What should you advise Sarah to invest in?

   b. Why do you think these people have different investment strategies?

TABLE 11–4 Price per Share in Dollars

Month	Large Cap Fund	Small Cap Fund	International Fund
1	$35.45	$27.00	$29.00
2	32.35	27.25	28.50
3	28.36	26.55	28.00
4	32.15	28.00	28.25
5	33.12	28.50	28.75
6	35.00	27.60	29.00

5. Sarah Mix decides to invest $500 per month in three funds, with $200 going into a small capital growth fund, $150 going into a large capital growth fund, and $150 into an international fund. She tracked the price she paid for stock in these funds over a 6-month period, as shown in Table 11–4.
   a. What was the average price paid per share in each mutual fund?
   b. How much has Sarah invested in mutual funds?
   c. What is the current value of her investment?
   d. Which fund is currently performing best for Sarah?

6. Larry Kraft owns a restaurant that is open 7 days a week. He has 25 full-time employees, but he has fairly high employee turnover. He believes that he can stabilize his workforce if he has a pension plan for his employees. Larry hears about a new small business retirement plan called the SIMPLE IRA. What are the qualifications and limitations for him to establish this plan?

7. Larry Kraft plans to open six more restaurants during the next 5 years. He believes that he will then have 125 employees.
   a. What recommendations would you make for Larry at this time?
   b. Could Larry set up a tax-sheltered annuity pension plan for his company?

8. Larry has expanded his business. When he met with his accountant at the end of the year, he learned that his total assets are in excess of $1 million. His accountant asked Larry if he had a will, and Larry said he had been too busy to develop one. His accountant strongly recommended that Larry contact an estate planning attorney.
   a. What advice do you think the estate planner will give Larry with respect to establishing a will?
   b. What do you advise?

9. You purchase a tax-free municipal bond paying an annual rate of 6 percent. Find the before-tax rate if you are in the
   a. 15-percent tax bracket.
   b. 28-percent tax bracket.
   c. 36-percent tax bracket.

10. A 10-year bond with a $1,000 face value has a coupon rate of 8 percent paid semiannually. If current interest rates are 7 percent for bonds of a similar nature, calculate the price of the bond.

11. A corporation has total assets of $85 million and total liabilities of $5 million. If the corporation has 4 million shares of common stock outstanding, what is the book value per share of common stock?

12. The book value of a company is $15 per share and the total common stock-holders' equity is $45 million. How many shares of common stock has this corporation issued?

13. ABC Corporation issues 10 million shares of common stock and 20,000 shares of 8 percent preferred stock at $50 par. The corporation makes an annual profit of $10 million, and the board of directors declares a $5-million-dollar stock dividend.
    a. What is the preferred stock dividend per share?
    b. What is the common stock dividend per share?

14. Best-Cost Corporation issues 5 million shares of common stock and 100,000 shares of 6 percent cumulative preferred stock at $100 par. The corporation has not paid any dividend during the previous 3 years. The board of directors decides to pay $5 million in dividends for the current year.
    a. How much in dividends is paid for each share of preferred stock?
    b. What is the total amount of dividends paid to preferred stockholders?
    c. How much is the dividend payment for each share of common stock?
    d. What is the total amount of dividends paid to common stockholders?

15. David Nash has $100,000 to invest in a mutual fund.
    a. How many shares can he purchase in a no-load mutual fund whose net asset value (NAV) is $50 per share?
    b. How many shares can he purchase in a loaded mutual fund whose NAV is $50 per share and that has a front-loaded sales charge of 5 percent?

16. Shakee Venture wants to purchase 1,000 shares of an Internet technology stock for $15 a share. She figures that she needs $15,000 plus $90 brokerage commission to purchase the stock. She currently has $8,000 of liquidity in her money market account.
    a. What can Shakee borrow on margin in order to make the transaction?
    b. If the stock jumps to $50 per share within a week, how much will Shakee realize in profit after paying her broker?
    c. If the stock dropped to $5 per share, rather than increasing to $50, and the broker put in the margin call, how much must Shakee pay the broker?
    d. Based on beginning account balance of $8,000, what is Shakee's loss?

17. You deposit the following at the end of each year into a growth mutual fund that earns 11 percent per year:

Year	Deposit
1	$ 4,000
2	3,500
3	2,500
4	2,000
5	1,700
	$13,700

    a. How much should the fund be worth at the end of 5 years?
    b. How much interest have you earned in total?

18. Starting in 2005, Ira Roth places $4,000 in a Roth IRA at the beginning of each year for the next 40 years. Ira believes the account will earn 10 percent

a year compounded yearly. How much will he have in his account in 40 years?

19. N. Ebriate, a college student at a party university, decides to forego beer drinking and invest the $100 he saves at the end of each month in a mutual fund that is currently earning 18 percent annually. He has a job where he earns income and invests this money in a Roth IRA.

    a. How much will he have in his fund in 4 years on graduation?

    b. If he graduates at 22 and leaves this investment in the mutual fund without adding any additional funds, how much will he have at age 60?

    c. If he really enjoys his work and decides to leave the money in the fund until age 75, how much will he have?

    d. If he never touches this mutual fund and dies at the age of 90, how much will he leave in his estate from only this investment?

RECOMMENDED GROUP ACTIVITIES

1. Given three entrepreneurs: one is in her early 20s, two is in his mid-40s, and the third is just approaching 65. Each one is married with two children. What type of health and casualty insurance would you recommend to these individuals?

2. In pension planning, some people rely on the Social Security system for their entire retirement program. Using two groups, have one argue for Social Security and have one argue against the system.

3. The current Social Security System takes a 6.2 percent payment from the employee and a 6.2 percent payment from the employer for a total of 12.4 percent of income. Assume the groups average current age and average income. If you have the option of investing 12.4 percent of your income in a self-directed IRA, how much will you have in your individual retirement program at the retirement age of 67 if you invest your money in the DOW? Would you rather have the current system or one which is self-directed?

CASE STUDY: THE GILBERTS: AN ENTREPRENEURIAL FAMILY

© 2008 Philip J. Adelman and Alan M. Marks

Harvey and Deanne Gilbert were both born and raised in Kansas City, Missouri. Harvey attended the University of Missouri in Kansas City, majoring in pre-med, and then completed medical school at the University of Missouri in Columbia. Deanne graduated from the University of Missouri with a degree in Elementary Education and began her teaching career in Raytown, Missouri, a suburb of Kansas City. During Harvey's junior year in college, Harvey and Deanne were married. While Harvey attended medical school, Deanne taught fifth grade in Centralia, Missouri. Following graduation from medical school, Harvey was commissioned as a lieutenant in the United States Navy and completed his internship at the Oakland Naval Hospital. He spent 1 year in Vietnam as a physician on a troop transport ship. On returning from Vietnam, he was stationed in Stockton and San Diego, California. While stationed in Stockton, Deanne taught sixth grade at Colonial Heights Elementary School.

Harvey had spent 4 years as a physician in the Navy. After leaving the Navy, he became a resident in radiation oncology at Mt. Zion Hospital in San Francisco. After Deanne and Harvey had their first child, Jill, Deanne gave up teaching to be a full-time stay-at-home mom to Jill and her younger brother, Jason. Harvey continued his studies, doing research at Stanford, and completed his training in radiation oncology at UCLA in 1973.

Harvey began practice at the Kaiser Hospital in Los Angeles and worked for them for about 9 years. The Gilberts firmly believed in the time value of money and the power of investing. They saved a percentage of their income from the time they were married. They always paid themselves first and invested their money, primarily in stock and mutual funds, which they selected carefully. They always invested the maximum in retirement accounts and fully funded their 401k and self-directed IRA.

Then Harvey entered private practice in a community hospital in Los Angeles for anther 10 years as director of a regional cancer center. When Jill entered college at USC, Deanne determined that student housing in the area was rundown and not very safe, so she decided to buy a piece of property that Jill could live in while attending the university. She worked with several brokers until she found a piece of property that she really liked. When her friend Diane Futterman, another physician's wife, found out what she was doing, she wanted to work with Deanne and they formed a Subchapter S corporation to purchase affordable rental housing for students in the USC area. They bought houses and remodeled them to meet their own high standards; furnished them; installed security systems, including bars on the windows and security doors; and rented to students. In the first year, they bought one house; the next year, they bought three more houses. Deanne and Diane invested primarily in student housing and then gradually expanded into apartments and rental real estate. The work in the corporation was divided very carefully, with both partners doing what they were most interested in and did best. Diane specialized in contracts and the legal aspects of the business, whereas Deanne specialized in the physical maintenance, decorating, and security of the units. They prided themselves in offering safe, affordable, and secure housing for students and tenants in the Southern California area.

By 1992, both of the Gilberts' children had settled in the San Francisco area. Deanne and Harvey moved to northern California in 1993 to take advantage of an opportunity for Harvey to practice in the Modesto area. In 1997, Harvey and Deanne decided to go out on their own and build a cancer center in Lodi, California, where Deanne became the office manager and Harvey was the primary physician and medical director. The decision was made early on to stay in the specialty of radiation oncology with their services being used by several health plans, HMOs, and other physician groups. Between 1997 and 2004, the center grew from 4 employees to 12. In 2004, the radiation facility was sold to a national radiation oncology organization with Harvey continuing as the practicing physician and Deanne as the manager. When the center was sold, all the original investors were paid off.

Harvey and Deanne were retained by the purchasing entity to continue their roles as medical director and office manager. The acquisition agreement also provided them with the opportunity to participate in profit sharing, and as such, they have continued to participate in the revenues of the practice.

Over his years in practice, Harvey was continually asked for recommendations regarding long-term care and assisted living; thus the idea of the *Gilbert Guide* was developed and founded by the entire family. By this time, their daughter Jill, a graduate of USC with more than 10 years of experience in the film industry, and their son Jason, a graduate of UCLA with many years of experience in the area of strategic planning, operations, finance, and product management, were looking for a new venture. Gilbert Guide, Inc. was developed to address the dire need for comprehensive and practical consumer guides for long-term care planning in every major metropolitan area in the United States. Founded by the Gilbert family—Jill, Jason, Deanne, and Harvey—the *Gilbert Guide* has grown from its inception in 2003 as a groundbreaking guidebook setting new standards and criteria for assessing the quality of the many types of long-term care available to become the biggest senior care site on the web, offering an even wider range of resources to help families and caregivers in their time of senior care need. This is truly an entrepreneurial family venture, with their daughter Jill as president and CEO, their son Jason as COO and CFO, and Harvey as medical and policies director. The *Gilbert Guide* can be found on the Internet at http://www.gilbertguide.com.

1. How much of the Gilbert's success do you attribute to their persistence?
2. How important do you believe the Gilbert's investments and understanding of time value of money contributed to their overall success?

Working with Spreadsheets and Calculators

Many businesses and individuals have a personal computer that can be used to automate the functions shown in this appendix. The following formulas are in Microsoft Excel format. Each of the formulas used in this appendix is presented with a problem. We then show how the problem is entered into Excel so that we have the basic procedures and uses of these formulas.

SPREADSHEET BASICS

Most spreadsheets look like the following:

	A	B	C	D	E	F	G
1							
2							
3							
4							
5					cell E5		

Most spreadsheet programs accept the following standards:

1. *Cells.* All data are entered in cells. Cells are identified by columns and rows.
   - Columns run vertical and are lettered across the top and are alphabetic, beginning with the letter *A*. The first column is A; the second column, B; the third column, C; and so forth. When the

alphabet is exhausted, we then begin over with AA, AB, AC, and so forth; then BA, BB, BC, and so forth.

- Rows run across the worksheet horizontally and are numbered, beginning with the number 1.
- Cells are referred to by their column and row designation. For example, the cell for the fifth column and fifth row is cell E5.

2. *Functions.* All functions must begin with an = (equal sign), a + (plus), a − (minus) sign, or a parenthesis. Spreadsheet programs may accept other characters, but if you begin with any other keyboard symbol, the program assumes you are entering a title rather than a mathematical function. Basic numbers can be entered as numbers (e.g., 5, 5000, 50). Note that numbers can contain commas; thus the number 5,000 is entered as 5000.

3. *Formatting.* Cells are formatted to display the entry or the result of calculation as you wish. Cells can be formatted as follows:

   a. **Text.** The entry is not used in calculations, even if it is a number. This is important when you enter items that you do not want to change accidentally. For example, if you have customer addresses and zip codes in a spreadsheet and you enter a zip code, you do not want to add 5 accidentally to every zip code. Format this column as text, rather than as a number.

   b. **Numeric formats.** There are several numeric formats that you can use. For business, we usually are concerned with using the following formats:

      - **Number.** Number formats allow us to assign decimal places and basic styles. For example, suppose we enter the number 5000.0124. If the specified cell is formatted as #,##0.00, then when we hit the ENTER key, it shows us 5,000.01. If we enter 5000.0156, we see 5,000.02 when we hit the ENTER key, because the program automatically rounds our entry to the number of decimal places we selected when we formatted the cell.

      - **Currency.** Currency formats usually display numbers as previously described, but give the formatter the option of selecting the symbol for currency display, such as the dollar ($), pound (£), yen (¥), and so on. It also allows you to choose the method that a negative number appears—with a minus sign or in parentheses. When displayed, the symbol shows up immediately left of the first number in the cell (e.g., $1,000.29, $1.29).

      - **Accounting.** Accounting formats usually display numbers as previously described with regard to currency formatting but have the symbol left column justified and the number right column justified. If we use accounting format and the column width is 10, then 1,000.29 displays as $ 1,000.29, and 1.29 displays as $ 1.29. We can also choose to have negative numbers display with parentheses or with the minus sign; –50 displays as (50) or –50, depending on the format we choose. In most cases, we recommend using accounting rather than currency formatting, because all financial statements are displayed using accounting format.

- **Date.** When we choose date formatting, we obtain a list of displays from which we can choose—for example, D/M/Y or D-MMM-YY. When we enter a date in the cell, it appears in the format we have chosen. Therefore, having chosen the first format, if we enter 3/29/09 it displays as 3/29/09; however, if we chose the second format, it displays as 29-Mar-09.
- **Percentage.** When we choose a percentage format, the number we enter displays as a percentage and displays the percent sign (%). For example, if we choose 0% and enter .08, we see 8% displayed. However, if we choose 0.00% and enter .08, we see 8.00%. A word of warning: If you enter 8, you will see either 800.00% or 8.00%, depending on which version of the software you own.
- **Fraction.** If we choose fraction formatting, we can enter fractions and have them display as such. For example, if we choose fraction formatting and enter 3/4, our display is 3/4.

Note: The display you receive is based on how the cell is formatted. If we enter 3/4 and have percentage cell formatting, we will see 75% displayed. However, if we have fraction formatting, we will see 3/4. If we did not choose any formatting, we will see 4–Mar, because Excel assumes that a 3/4 entry should display as a date.

4. *Entering formulas and numbers.* Spreadsheet programs use the following keyboard characters for entering formulas:
   - + for addition, − for subtraction, ∗ for multiplication, / for division. *Note:* Make sure you use the usual slash and not the backslash (\) for division.
   - = for equal to, >= for greater than or equal to, <= for less than or equal to.
   - ^ to raise a number to a power. For example, 2^3 is entered as 2^3.
   - $ preceding cell identifiers locks the position of the cell so that other cells can refer to this location for a formula or number. $B$5 locks cell B5 so that it can be used in further calculations in other cells. Usually, when a cell is copied, the value of the subsequent cell increases; but if the cell is locked, it does not. For example: Cell A2 has the number 1, and cell A3 has the formula =A2+1; when we hit the return key, we see the number 2. When we copy the formula in cell A3 to cell A4, we see the formula as A3+1 and we see the number 3. If, however, cell B5 had the number 10, and we entered the formula in cell A3 as =A2+$B$5, we see the number 11. If we then copy this to cell A4,

we get the number 12, and we see the formula as =A3+$B$5. Notice that the A2 increases to A3, but the locked cell value does not change. *Note:* This capability of spreadsheets allows us to ask "what if" questions. With the present or future value factor formula located in cell B5, we could change the interest rates in cells A3 through some range of cells and obtain factors for several interest rates. This is the method that we use to construct the tables in this appendix and Appendix B.

* ( ) for calculations that are to be completed prior to the remainder of the formula.
* : to indicate a range of cells; for example, all cells from A2 through A15 are entered as (A2:A15).
* **Functions.** Most spreadsheets have formulas already built in. These spreadsheets have either a function key f_x *(which stands for function of x)* that can be clicked on with the mouse to see various functions or a HELP key that allows you to type in the function you want and obtain the formula that the spreadsheet program uses. These also provide you with the formula for the function. For example, in Excel, if you click on the function SUM, you see SUM(number 1, number 2, —), beneath which a brief explanation of what the SUM function does appears—in this case, "adds its arguments."

An example of a spreadsheet and the use of the preceding formatting and mathematical standards follows. Row 1 is a title row, row 2 displays the entry that we type on the keyboard, row 3 shows the result of the entry with no formatting, and rows 4 and 5 show the results of the entry with formatting.

	A	B	C	D	E	F	G
1	Date	Principal	Interest	Formula	Formula	Formula	Formula
2	1/4/08	1000.00	.0725	=2*(3/4)	=2^3	=2*(3+5)	=B2*C2
3	1/4/2008	1000	0.0725	1.5	8	16	72.5
4	4-Jan-08	1,000.00	7.25%	1.50	8.00	16.00	72.50
5	4-Jan	$ 1,000.00	$ 0.07	$ 1.50	$ 8.00	$ 16.00	$ 72.50

In row 1, we typed in the title of each column. In row 2, we show what number or formula was typed on the keyboard. In row 3, we see the result of pressing the enter key after our entry with no formatting. For row 4, we formatted cell A4 as date D-MMM-YY, cell B4 and cells D4 through G4 as a number with two decimal places, and cell C4 as a percentage with two decimal places. For row 5, we formatted cell A5 as date D-MMM, and cells B5 through G5 as accounting with two decimal places. As we discussed previously, formatting provides us with the result of our calculation in the form in which we want to view it.

FORMULA ENTRY
Simple Interest

The simple interest formula is $I = Prt$, where I = interest, P = principal amount stated, r = rate, and t = time. What is the annual interest paid on a loan of $5,000 at 8 percent? To enter this formula into Excel, we type the following:

$$= 5000\star(.08)\star(1)$$

The standard used in Excel for formula entry is to begin with the = (equal sign); you can also begin entering a formula with the + or −.

When we press the ENTER key, we receive an answer of 400. How this result of our calculation appears on the screen is based on formatting.

COMPOUND INTEREST OR FUTURE VALUE OF A LUMP SUM

The formula for future value of a lump sum amount is

$$FV = PV(FVF), \text{ where } FVF = (1 + i)^n$$

What is the future value of $5,000 that earns interest of 12 percent, compounded monthly, for 3 years? We enter this formula as =5000$\star$(1+(.12/12))^(3$\star$12) and obtain an answer of $7,153.84. We could also enter the amount in one cell, the formula for the factor in another cell, and the formula for the future value in a third cell. This way we can use any of the values to conduct a *what-if analysis*, also known as a *sensitivity analysis*, which allows you to create hypothetical situations that change the variables of the formula. This then allows you to compare several proposals at varying interest rates, or with varying terms. For example, you could compare a 3-year note that compounds monthly at 8 percent to a 3-year note compounding annually at 9 percent to determine which of two offers from two different banks is the best.

	A	B	C	D	E
1	FV	PV	Annual *i*	*n* in Years	Factor
2	=B2*E2	5000	.12	3	=(1+(C2/12))^(D2*12)
3	$7,153.84	$5,000.00	12%	3	1.430769
4					
5					

Again, we used the same convention, with row 1 containing titles, row 2 containing the formula we enter into a cell, and row 3 showing the formatted result of the formula after we hit the return key. If we check Appendix B, Table B–1, we note that the future value factor for 1 percent interest for 36 months is 1.4308. (Note that this is not the same factor we would get if the loan were not compounded monthly.) We then go to the 12 percent column for 3 time periods and obtain a factor of 1.4049.

PRESENT VALUE OF A FUTURE LUMP SUM

The formula for the present value of a future lump-sum amount is given as

$$PV = FS(PVF), \text{ where } PVF = \left[\frac{1}{(1 + i)^n}\right]$$

If we have a trust that pays us $50,000 in 10 years and we assume that the inflation rate will be 5 percent for this 10-year period, what purchasing power does this $50,000 payment have? To obtain the present value factor for this problem directly, we enter $=(1/(1+.05)^{10})$ and obtain 0.613913. Using Appendix B, Table B–2 to verify our answer, we obtain a value of 0.6139. The difference is to the result of rounding. To obtain the present value, we multiply this factor by our lump-sum amount of $50,000 and obtain $30,695.66. The spreadsheet entries appear as follows:

	A	B	C	D	E
1	PV	FVOA	Annual *i*	*n* in Years	Factor
2	=B2*E2	50000	.05	10	=(1/(1+C2)^D2)
3	$30.695.66	$50,000.00	5%	10	0.613913
4					
5					

FUTURE VALUE OF AN ORDINARY ANNUITY

The formula for the future value of an ordinary annuity is given as

$$FVOA = A\left[\frac{(1 + i)^n - 1}{i}\right]$$

If you deposit $2,000 a year, at the end of each year, in an individual retirement account (IRA) for 20 years and assume you get an average return of 8 percent compounded annually, how much will your account contain at the end of 20 years? The spreadsheet entries are as follows:

	A	B	C	D	E
1	FV	A	Annual *i*	*n* in Years	Factor
2	=B2*E2	2000	.08	20	=((1+C2)^(D2)−1)/C2
3	$91,523.93	$2,000.00	8%	20	45.76196
4					
5					

We can again cross-check our calculations with Appendix B, Table B–2 and notice a factor of 45.7620, with the difference because of rounding. Our conclusion is that you will have approximately $91,524 in your retirement account in 20 years. This problem is realistic for many of us because we have to wait until the last minute to fund our IRA. However, what if you knew that you would definitely be funding the IRA every year and decided to invest at the beginning of the year, rather than at the end of the year? In that case, we are dealing with an annuity due.

FUTURE VALUE OF AN ANNUITY DUE

The formula for the future value of an annuity due is given as

$$FVAD = A\left\{\left[\frac{(1 + i)^{n+1} - 1}{i}\right] - 1\right\}$$

We use the same problem as in our previous example, with the only difference being that you place the $2,000 in your account at the beginning of each year instead of at the end. The spreadsheet entries are as follows:

	A	B	C	D	E
1	FVAD	A	Annual *i*	*n* in Years	Factor
2	=B2*E2	2000	.08	20	=((((1+C2)^(D2+1))−1)/(C2))−1
3	$98,845.84	$2,000.00	8%	20	49.42292
4					
5					

Therefore, if we knew that we will definitely invest each year in an IRA, we absolutely want to invest at the beginning of the year and at the end, because we would have an extra $7,321.91 in our account as a result of early investing.

PRESENT VALUE OF AN ORDINARY ANNUITY

The formula for the present value of an ordinary annuity is given as

$$PVOA = A\left[\frac{(1 + i)^n - 1}{i(1 + i)^n}\right]$$

You want to retire at the age of 60 and plan to live to be 90. You want a retirement income of no less than $60,000 per year. How much do you need in your account when you are 60, if you plan to receive the money at the end of each year for the next 30 years and assume the account will continue to earn an annual rate of 8 percent? The spreadsheet entries are as follows:

	A	B	C	D	E
1	PVOA	A	*Annual i*	*n* in Years	Factor
2	=B2*E2	60000	.08	30	=(((1+C2)^(D2))−1)/((C2*(1+C2)^(D2)))
3	$675,467.00	$60,000.00	8%	30	11.25778
4					
5					

So if you had $675,467 in this account, you would have a 30-year income of $60,000. At the end of 30 years, you would have nothing left in the account. What if you wanted the income at the beginning of the year instead of at the end of the year? Again, this takes us into the realm of an annuity due.

PRESENT VALUE OF AN ANNUITY DUE

Let's use the same problem as in previous examples, except that you get your retirement check at the beginning of the year (January 1) rather than the end of the year (December 31). The formula for this (the present value of an annuity due) is given as

$$PVAD = A\left\{\left[\frac{(1+i)^{n-1} - 1}{i(1 + i)^{n-1}}\right] + 1\right\}$$

The spreadsheet entries are as follows:

	A	B	C	D	E
1	PVAD	A	Annual *i*	*n* in Years	Factor
2	=B2*E2	60000	.08	30	=((((1+C2)^(D2−1))−1)/((C2*(1+C2)^(D2−1)))+1)
3	$729,504.36	$60,000.00	8%	30	12.15841
4					
5					

Notice that if you take the payment out at the beginning of each year, you must have significantly more money in your account. With the ordinary annuity, you only have to have $675,467; but with the annuity due, you must have $729,504. This means that you must generate an additional $54,037 in your account before you reach 60.

WORKING WITH CALCULATORS

Many of us have programmable calculators. If you have a business calculator, then many of the formulas for time value of money and other items discussed in this book are already entered in your calculator; it is just a matter of experimenting to find the formula that matches the textbook examples. If you don't have a business calculator, but have a programmable calculator, we show how to match the formula used in the textbook with the formula that should be entered into your calculator. We do not use a keystroke entry program, because many calculators differ on how to get into the formula mode.

Get the instruction book that came with your calculator and determine the keystrokes to enter a new formula. Once you accomplish this, the formulas that follow work in virtually all programmable calculators. Formulas are listed by chapter, as they are shown in the textbook, and then how they should be entered into a calculator. Once the formulas are entered, the problems can be solved easily by recalling the formula and entering the data.

Chapter 5 Formulas: Break-Even Quantity Formula

$$BEQ = \frac{FC}{P - VC}$$

where

FC = fixed costs
P = price charged per unit
VC = variable cost per unit
Calculator formula: $BEQ = (FC) \div (P - VC)$

Break-Even Dollars Formula for Most Retail and Service Establishments

$$BE\$ = \frac{FC}{1 - \left(\dfrac{COG}{S}\right)}$$

where

FC = fixed costs
COG = cost of goods sold from the income statement
S = net sales from the income statement
Calculator formula: $BEQ = (FC) \div (1 - (COG \div S))$

Chapter 7 Formulas Economic Order Quantity Formula

$$EO\$ = \sqrt{\frac{2DS}{IP}}$$

where

> D = total annual demand for the item
> S = total ordering cost for the item
> I = carrying cost for the item, which is usually expressed as a percentage
> P = unit cost of the item
> Calculator formula: $\underline{EOQ = (((2 \times D \times S) \div (I \times P)) \times (0.5))}$

Total Annual Cost of a Product Formula

$$TC = DP + \frac{QIP}{2} + \frac{DS}{Q}$$

where

> DP = total cost of units
> $QIP \div 2$ = annual cost of carrying the inventory
> $DS \div Q$ = annual ordering cost
> Calculator total cost formula: $TC = (D \times P) + ((Q \times I \times P) \div 2)$
> $+ ((D \times S) \div Q)$

Chapter 8 Formulas: Future Value of a Lump Sum Formula

$$FVLS = PV(FVF)$$

where

> $FVLS$ = future value of a lump sum
> PV = present value
> i = interest rate per period
> n = number of compounding periods per year times the number of years

FVF (future value factor) $= (1 + i)^n$

> Calculator formula: $FVLS = PV \times (1 + I) \wedge (N)$

Present Value of a Lump Sum Formula

$$PVLS = FV(PVF)$$

where

> $PVLS$ = present value of a lump sum
> FV = future value
> i = interest rate per period
> n = number of compounding periods per year times the number of years

$$PVF\text{(present value factor)} = \left[\frac{1}{(1 + i)^n}\right]$$

Calculator formula: $PVLS = FV \times ((1) \div (1 + I)\,^\wedge\,(N))$

Internal Rate of Return Formula

$$IRR = \left(\sqrt[n]{\frac{FV}{PV}} - 1\right) \times 100$$

Another way of depicting the same formula is

$$IRR = \left[\left(\frac{FV}{PV}\right)^{\left(\frac{1}{n}\right)} - 1\right] \times 100$$

Calculator formula: $IRR = (((FV \div PV)\,^\wedge\,(1 \div N)) - 1) \times 100$

Chapter 9 Formulas: Future Value of an Ordinary Annuity Formula

$$FVOA = A(FVAF)$$
$$= A\left[\frac{(1 + i)^n - 1}{i}\right]$$

where

$FVOA$ = the future value
A = the annuity

$$FVAF\text{(future value annuity factor)} = \left[\frac{(1 + i)^n - 1}{i}\right]$$

i = the interest rate per time period
n = number of compounding periods per year times the number of years
Calculator formula: $FVOA = A \times (((1 + I)\,^\wedge\,(N) - 1) \div I)$

Future Value of an Annuity Due Formula

$$FVAD = A(FVAF)$$
$$= A\left\{\left[\frac{(1 + i)^{(n+1)} - 1}{i}\right] - 1\right\}$$

where

$FVAD$ = the future value
A = the annuity

$$FVAF\text{(future value annuity factor)} = \left\{\left[\frac{(1 + i)^{(n+1)} - 1}{i}\right] - 1\right\}$$

i = the interest rate per time period
n = number of compounding periods per year times the number of years
Calculator formula: $FVAD = A \times ((((1 + I) \char`\^ (N + 1) - 1) \div I) - 1)$

Present Value of an Ordinary Annuity Formula

$$PVOA = A(PVAF)$$

$$= A\left[\frac{(1 + i)^{(n)} - 1}{i(1 + i)^n}\right]$$

where

$PVOA$ = the present value
A = the annuity

$$PVAF\text{(present value annuity factor)} = \left[\frac{(1 + i)^{(n)} - 1}{i(1 + i)^n}\right]$$

i = the interest rate per time period
n = number of compounding periods per year times the number of years
Calculator formula: $PVOA = A \times (((1 + I) \char`\^ (N) - 1) \div (I \times (1 + I) \char`\^(N)))$

Present Value of an Annuity Due Formula

$$PVAD = A(PVAF)$$

$$= A\left\{\left[\frac{(1+i)^{(n-1)} - 1}{i(1 + i)^{(n-1)}}\right] + 1\right\}$$

where

$PVAD$ = the present value
A = the annuity

$$PVAF \text{ (present value annuity factor)} = \left\{\left[\frac{(1 + i)^{(n-1)} - 1}{i(1 + i)^{(n-1)}}\right] + 1\right\}$$

i = the interest rate per time period
n = number of compounding periods per year times the number of years
Calculator formula: $PVAD = A \times ((((1 + I) \char`\^ (N - 1) - 1) \div ((I) \times (1 + I) \char`\^ (N - 1)) + 1)$

Time-Value-of-Money Tables

The time-value-of-money tables in this appendix assist the reader by providing

- A cross-reference for confirming values returned with calculators.
- A cross-reference for confirming values returned with spreadsheets and other computer programs.
- Reference tables for solving time-value-of-money problems when calculators or computers are not readily available.

TABLE B–1 Future Value of a Lump Sum

Formula: $FVLS = PV(1+i)^n$

Interest Rate (i)

Periods (n)	1%	2%	3%	4%	5%	6%	7%	8%	9%	10%	11%	12%	13%	14%	15%	16%	17%	18%	19%	20%
1	1.0100	1.0200	1.0300	1.0400	1.0500	1.0600	1.0700	1.0800	1.0900	1.1000	1.1100	1.1200	1.1300	1.1400	1.1500	1.1600	1.1700	1.1800	1.1900	1.2000
2	1.0201	1.0404	1.0609	1.0816	1.1025	1.1236	1.1449	1.1664	1.1881	1.2100	1.2321	1.2544	1.2769	1.2996	1.3225	1.3456	1.3689	1.3924	1.4161	1.4400
3	1.0303	1.0612	1.0927	1.1249	1.1576	1.1910	1.2250	1.2597	1.2950	1.3310	1.3676	1.4049	1.4429	1.4815	1.5209	1.5609	1.6016	1.6430	1.6852	1.7280
4	1.0406	1.0824	1.1255	1.1699	1.2155	1.2625	1.3108	1.3605	1.4116	1.4641	1.5181	1.5735	1.6305	1.6890	1.7490	1.8106	1.8739	1.9388	2.0053	2.0736
5	1.0510	1.1041	1.1593	1.2167	1.2763	1.3382	1.4026	1.4693	1.5386	1.6105	1.6851	1.7623	1.8424	1.9254	2.0114	2.1003	2.1924	2.2878	2.3864	2.4883
6	1.0615	1.1262	1.1941	1.2653	1.3401	1.4185	1.5007	1.5869	1.6771	1.7716	1.8704	1.9738	2.0820	2.1950	2.3131	2.4364	2.5652	2.6996	2.8398	2.9860
7	1.0721	1.1487	1.2299	1.3159	1.4071	1.5036	1.6058	1.7138	1.8280	1.9487	2.0762	2.2107	2.3526	2.5023	2.6600	2.8262	3.0012	3.1855	3.3793	3.5832
8	1.0829	1.1717	1.2668	1.3686	1.4775	1.5938	1.7182	1.8509	1.9926	2.1436	2.3045	2.4760	2.6584	2.8526	3.0590	3.2784	3.5115	3.7589	4.0214	4.2998
9	1.0937	1.1951	1.3048	1.4233	1.5513	1.6895	1.8385	1.9990	2.1719	2.3579	2.5580	2.7731	3.0040	3.2519	3.5179	3.8030	4.1084	4.4355	4.7854	5.1598
10	1.1046	1.2190	1.3439	1.4802	1.6289	1.7908	1.9672	2.1589	2.3674	2.5937	2.8394	3.1058	3.3946	3.7072	4.0456	4.4114	4.8068	5.2338	5.6947	6.1917
11	1.1157	1.2434	1.3842	1.5395	1.7103	1.8983	2.1049	2.3316	2.5804	2.8531	3.1518	3.4785	3.8359	4.2262	4.6524	5.1173	5.6240	6.1759	6.7767	7.4301
12	1.1268	1.2682	1.4258	1.6010	1.7959	2.0122	2.2522	2.5182	2.8127	3.1384	3.4985	3.8960	4.3345	4.8179	5.3503	5.9360	6.5801	7.2876	8.0642	8.9161
13	1.1381	1.2936	1.4685	1.6651	1.8856	2.1329	2.4098	2.7196	3.0658	3.4523	3.8833	4.3635	4.8980	5.4924	6.1528	6.8858	7.6987	8.5994	9.5964	10.6993
14	1.1495	1.3195	1.5126	1.7317	1.9799	2.2609	2.5785	2.9372	3.3417	3.7975	4.3104	4.8871	5.5348	6.2613	7.0757	7.9875	9.0075	10.1472	11.4198	12.8392
15	1.1610	1.3459	1.5580	1.8009	2.0789	2.3966	2.7590	3.1722	3.6425	4.1772	4.7846	5.4736	6.2543	7.1379	8.1371	9.2655	10.5387	11.9737	13.5895	15.4070
16	1.1726	1.3728	1.6047	1.8730	2.1829	2.5404	2.9522	3.4259	3.9703	4.5950	5.3109	6.1304	7.0673	8.1372	9.3576	10.7480	12.3303	14.1290	16.1715	18.4884
17	1.1843	1.4002	1.6528	1.9479	2.2920	2.6928	3.1588	3.7000	4.3276	5.0545	5.8951	6.8660	7.9861	9.2765	10.7613	12.4677	14.4265	16.6722	19.2441	22.1861
18	1.1961	1.4282	1.7024	2.0258	2.4066	2.8543	3.3799	3.9960	4.7171	5.5599	6.5436	7.6900	9.0243	10.5752	12.3755	14.4625	16.8790	19.6733	22.9005	26.6233
19	1.2081	1.4568	1.7535	2.1068	2.5270	3.0256	3.6165	4.3157	5.1417	6.1159	7.2633	8.6128	10.1974	12.0557	14.2318	16.7765	19.7484	23.2144	27.2516	31.9480
20	1.2202	1.4859	1.8061	2.1911	2.6533	3.2071	3.8697	4.6610	5.6044	6.7275	8.0623	9.6463	11.5231	13.7435	16.3665	19.4608	23.1056	27.3930	32.4294	38.3376
21	1.2324	1.5157	1.8603	2.2788	2.7860	3.3996	4.1406	5.0338	6.1088	7.4002	8.9492	10.8038	13.0211	15.6676	18.8215	22.5745	27.0336	32.3238	38.5910	46.0051
22	1.2447	1.5460	1.9161	2.3699	2.9253	3.6035	4.4304	5.4365	6.6586	8.1403	9.9336	12.1003	14.7138	17.8610	21.6447	26.1864	31.6293	38.1421	45.9233	55.2061
23	1.2572	1.5769	1.9736	2.4647	3.0715	3.8197	4.7405	5.8715	7.2579	8.9543	11.0263	13.5523	16.6266	20.3616	24.8915	30.3762	37.0062	45.0076	54.6487	66.2474
24	1.2697	1.6084	2.0328	2.5633	3.2251	4.0489	5.0724	6.3412	7.9111	9.8497	12.2392	15.1786	18.7881	23.2122	28.6252	35.2364	43.2973	53.1090	65.0320	79.4968
25	1.2824	1.6406	2.0938	2.6658	3.3864	4.2919	5.4274	6.8485	8.6231	10.8347	13.5855	17.0001	21.2305	26.4619	32.9190	40.8742	50.6578	62.6686	77.3881	95.3962
26	1.2953	1.6734	2.1566	2.7725	3.5557	4.5494	5.8074	7.3964	9.3992	11.9182	15.0799	19.0401	23.9905	30.1666	37.8568	47.4141	59.2697	73.9490	92.0918	114.4755
27	1.3082	1.7069	2.2213	2.8834	3.7335	4.8223	6.2139	7.9881	10.2451	13.1100	16.7386	21.3249	27.1093	34.3899	43.5353	55.0004	69.3455	87.2598	109.5893	137.3706
28	1.3213	1.7410	2.2879	2.9987	3.9201	5.1117	6.6488	8.6271	11.1671	14.4210	18.5799	23.8839	30.6335	39.2045	50.0656	63.8004	81.1342	102.9666	130.4112	164.8447
29	1.3345	1.7758	2.3566	3.1187	4.1161	5.4184	7.1143	9.3173	12.1722	15.8631	20.6237	26.7499	34.6158	44.6931	57.5755	74.0085	94.9271	121.5005	155.1893	197.8136
30	1.3478	1.8114	2.4273	3.2434	4.3219	5.7435	7.6123	10.0627	13.2677	17.4494	22.8923	29.9599	39.1159	50.9502	66.2118	85.8499	111.0647	143.3706	184.6753	237.3763
31	1.3613	1.8476	2.5001	3.3731	4.5380	6.0881	8.1451	10.8677	14.4618	19.1943	25.4104	33.5551	44.2010	58.0832	76.1435	99.5859	129.9456	169.1774	219.7636	284.8516
32	1.3749	1.8845	2.5751	3.5081	4.7649	6.4534	8.7153	11.7371	15.7633	21.1138	28.2056	37.5817	49.9471	66.2148	87.5651	115.5196	152.0364	199.6293	261.5187	341.8219
33	1.3887	1.9222	2.6523	3.6484	5.0032	6.8406	9.3253	12.6760	17.1820	23.2252	31.3082	42.0915	56.4402	75.4849	100.6998	134.0027	177.8826	235.5625	311.2073	410.1863
34	1.4026	1.9607	2.7319	3.7943	5.2533	7.2510	9.9781	13.6901	18.7284	25.5477	34.7521	47.1425	63.7774	86.0528	115.8048	155.4432	208.1226	277.9638	370.3366	492.2235
35	1.4166	1.9999	2.8139	3.9461	5.5160	7.6861	10.6766	14.7853	20.4140	28.1024	38.5749	52.7996	72.0685	98.1002	133.1755	180.3141	243.5035	327.9973	440.7006	590.6682
36	1.4308	2.0399	2.8983	4.1039	5.7918	8.1473	11.4239	15.9682	22.2512	30.9127	42.8181	59.1356	81.4374	111.8342	153.1519	209.1643	284.8991	387.0368	524.4337	708.8019

TABLE B–2 Present Value of a Future Lump Sum

Formula $PVLs = FV\left[\dfrac{1}{(1+i)^n}\right]$

Interest Rate (i)

Periods (n)	1%	2%	3%	4%	5%	6%	7%	8%	9%	10%	11%	12%	13%	14%	15%	16%	17%	18%	19%	20%
1	0.9901	0.9804	0.9709	0.9615	0.9524	0.9434	0.9346	0.9259	0.9174	0.9091	0.9009	0.8929	0.8850	0.8772	0.8696	0.8621	0.8547	0.8475	0.8403	0.8333
2	0.9803	0.9612	0.9426	0.9246	0.9070	0.8900	0.8734	0.8573	0.8417	0.8264	0.8116	0.7972	0.7831	0.7695	0.7561	0.7432	0.7305	0.7182	0.7062	0.6944
3	0.9706	0.9423	0.9151	0.8890	0.8638	0.8396	0.8163	0.7938	0.7722	0.7513	0.7312	0.7118	0.6931	0.6750	0.6575	0.6407	0.6244	0.6086	0.5934	0.5787
4	0.9610	0.9238	0.8885	0.8548	0.8227	0.7921	0.7629	0.7350	0.7084	0.6830	0.6587	0.6355	0.6133	0.5921	0.5718	0.5523	0.5337	0.5158	0.4987	0.4823
5	0.9515	0.9057	0.8626	0.8219	0.7835	0.7473	0.7130	0.6806	0.6499	0.6209	0.5935	0.5674	0.5428	0.5194	0.4972	0.4761	0.4561	0.4371	0.4190	0.4019
6	0.9420	0.8880	0.8375	0.7903	0.7462	0.7050	0.6663	0.6302	0.5963	0.5645	0.5346	0.5066	0.4803	0.4556	0.4323	0.4104	0.3898	0.3704	0.3521	0.3349
7	0.9327	0.8706	0.8131	0.7599	0.7107	0.6651	0.6227	0.5835	0.5470	0.5132	0.4817	0.4523	0.4251	0.3996	0.3759	0.3538	0.3332	0.3139	0.2959	0.2791
8	0.9235	0.8535	0.7894	0.7307	0.6768	0.6274	0.5820	0.5403	0.5019	0.4665	0.4339	0.4039	0.3762	0.3506	0.3269	0.3050	0.2848	0.2660	0.2487	0.2326
9	0.9143	0.8368	0.7664	0.7026	0.6446	0.5919	0.5439	0.5002	0.4604	0.4241	0.3909	0.3606	0.3329	0.3075	0.2843	0.2630	0.2434	0.2255	0.2090	0.1938
10	0.9053	0.8203	0.7441	0.6756	0.6139	0.5584	0.5083	0.4632	0.4224	0.3855	0.3522	0.3220	0.2946	0.2697	0.2472	0.2267	0.2080	0.1911	0.1756	0.1615
11	0.8963	0.8043	0.7224	0.6496	0.5847	0.5268	0.4751	0.4289	0.3875	0.3505	0.3173	0.2875	0.2607	0.2366	0.2149	0.1954	0.1778	0.1619	0.1476	0.1346
12	0.8874	0.7885	0.7014	0.6246	0.5568	0.4970	0.4440	0.3971	0.3555	0.3186	0.2858	0.2567	0.2307	0.2076	0.1869	0.1685	0.1520	0.1372	0.1240	0.1122
13	0.8787	0.7730	0.6810	0.6006	0.5303	0.4688	0.4150	0.3677	0.3262	0.2897	0.2575	0.2292	0.2042	0.1821	0.1625	0.1452	0.1299	0.1163	0.1042	0.0935
14	0.8700	0.7579	0.6611	0.5775	0.5051	0.4423	0.3878	0.3405	0.2992	0.2633	0.2320	0.2046	0.1807	0.1597	0.1413	0.1252	0.1110	0.0985	0.0876	0.0779
15	0.8613	0.7430	0.6419	0.5553	0.4810	0.4173	0.3624	0.3152	0.2745	0.2394	0.2090	0.1827	0.1599	0.1401	0.1229	0.1079	0.0949	0.0835	0.0736	0.0649
16	0.8528	0.7284	0.6232	0.5339	0.4581	0.3936	0.3387	0.2919	0.2519	0.2176	0.1883	0.1631	0.1415	0.1229	0.1069	0.0930	0.0811	0.0708	0.0618	0.0541
17	0.8444	0.7142	0.6050	0.5134	0.4363	0.3714	0.3166	0.2703	0.2311	0.1978	0.1696	0.1456	0.1252	0.1078	0.0929	0.0802	0.0693	0.0600	0.0520	0.0451
18	0.8360	0.7002	0.5874	0.4936	0.4155	0.3503	0.2959	0.2502	0.2120	0.1799	0.1528	0.1300	0.1108	0.0946	0.0808	0.0691	0.0592	0.0508	0.0437	0.0376
19	0.8277	0.6864	0.5703	0.4746	0.3957	0.3305	0.2765	0.2317	0.1945	0.1635	0.1377	0.1161	0.0981	0.0829	0.0703	0.0596	0.0506	0.0431	0.0367	0.0313
20	0.8195	0.6730	0.5537	0.4564	0.3769	0.3118	0.2584	0.2145	0.1784	0.1486	0.1240	0.1037	0.0868	0.0728	0.0611	0.0514	0.0433	0.0365	0.0308	0.0261
21	0.8114	0.6598	0.5375	0.4388	0.3589	0.2942	0.2415	0.1987	0.1637	0.1351	0.1117	0.0926	0.0768	0.0638	0.0531	0.0443	0.0370	0.0309	0.0259	0.0217
22	0.8034	0.6468	0.5219	0.4220	0.3418	0.2775	0.2257	0.1839	0.1502	0.1228	0.1007	0.0826	0.0680	0.0560	0.0462	0.0382	0.0316	0.0262	0.0218	0.0181
23	0.7954	0.6342	0.5067	0.4057	0.3256	0.2618	0.2109	0.1703	0.1378	0.1117	0.0907	0.0738	0.0601	0.0491	0.0402	0.0329	0.0270	0.0222	0.0183	0.0151
24	0.7876	0.6217	0.4919	0.3901	0.3101	0.2470	0.1971	0.1577	0.1264	0.1015	0.0817	0.0659	0.0532	0.0431	0.0349	0.0284	0.0231	0.0188	0.0154	0.0126
25	0.7798	0.6095	0.4776	0.3751	0.2953	0.2330	0.1842	0.1460	0.1160	0.0923	0.0736	0.0588	0.0471	0.0378	0.0304	0.0245	0.0197	0.0160	0.0129	0.0105
26	0.7720	0.5976	0.4637	0.3607	0.2812	0.2198	0.1722	0.1352	0.1064	0.0839	0.0663	0.0525	0.0417	0.0331	0.0264	0.0211	0.0169	0.0135	0.0109	0.0087
27	0.7644	0.5859	0.4502	0.3468	0.2678	0.2074	0.1609	0.1252	0.0976	0.0763	0.0597	0.0469	0.0369	0.0291	0.0230	0.0182	0.0144	0.0115	0.0091	0.0073
28	0.7568	0.5744	0.4371	0.3335	0.2551	0.1956	0.1504	0.1159	0.0895	0.0693	0.0538	0.0419	0.0326	0.0255	0.0200	0.0157	0.0123	0.0097	0.0077	0.0061
29	0.7493	0.5631	0.4243	0.3207	0.2429	0.1846	0.1406	0.1073	0.0822	0.0630	0.0485	0.0374	0.0289	0.0224	0.0174	0.0135	0.0105	0.0082	0.0064	0.0051
30	0.7419	0.5521	0.4120	0.3083	0.2314	0.1741	0.1314	0.0994	0.0754	0.0573	0.0437	0.0334	0.0256	0.0196	0.0151	0.0116	0.0090	0.0070	0.0054	0.0042
31	0.7346	0.5412	0.4000	0.2965	0.2204	0.1643	0.1228	0.0920	0.0691	0.0521	0.0394	0.0298	0.0226	0.0172	0.0131	0.0100	0.0077	0.0059	0.0046	0.0035
32	0.7273	0.5306	0.3883	0.2851	0.2099	0.1550	0.1147	0.0852	0.0634	0.0474	0.0355	0.0266	0.0200	0.0151	0.0114	0.0087	0.0066	0.0050	0.0038	0.0029
33	0.7201	0.5202	0.3770	0.2741	0.1999	0.1462	0.1072	0.0789	0.0582	0.0431	0.0319	0.0238	0.0177	0.0132	0.0099	0.0075	0.0056	0.0042	0.0032	0.0024
34	0.7130	0.5100	0.3660	0.2636	0.1904	0.1379	0.1002	0.0730	0.0534	0.0391	0.0288	0.0212	0.0157	0.0116	0.0086	0.0064	0.0048	0.0036	0.0027	0.0020
35	0.7059	0.5000	0.3554	0.2534	0.1813	0.1301	0.0937	0.0676	0.0490	0.0356	0.0259	0.0189	0.0139	0.0102	0.0075	0.0055	0.0041	0.0030	0.0023	0.0017
36	0.6989	0.4902	0.3450	0.2437	0.1727	0.1227	0.0875	0.0626	0.0449	0.0323	0.0234	0.0169	0.0123	0.0089	0.0065	0.0048	0.0035	0.0026	0.0019	0.0014

TABLE B-3 Future Value of an Ordinary Annuity

Formula $FVOA = A\left[\dfrac{(1+i)^n - 1}{i}\right]$

Interest Rate (i)

Periods (n)	1%	2%	3%	4%	5%	6%	7%	8%	9%	10%	11%	12%	13%	14%	15%	16%	17%	18%	19%	20%
1	1.000	1.000	1.000	1.000	1.000	1.000	1.000	1.000	1.000	1.000	1.000	1.000	1.000	1.000	1.000	1.000	1.000	1.000	1.000	1.000
2	2.0100	2.0200	2.0300	2.0400	2.0500	2.0600	2.0700	2.0800	2.0900	2.1000	2.1100	2.1200	2.1300	2.1400	2.1500	2.1600	2.1700	2.1800	2.1900	2.2000
3	3.0301	3.0604	3.0909	3.1216	3.1525	3.1836	3.2149	3.2464	3.2781	3.3100	3.3421	3.3744	3.4069	3.4396	3.4725	3.5056	3.5389	3.5724	3.6061	3.6400
4	4.0604	4.1216	4.1836	4.2465	4.3101	4.3746	4.4399	4.5061	4.5731	4.6410	4.7097	4.7793	4.8498	4.9211	4.9934	5.0665	5.1405	5.2154	5.2913	5.3680
5	5.1010	5.2040	5.3091	5.4163	5.5256	5.6371	5.7507	5.8666	5.9847	6.1051	6.2278	6.3528	6.4803	6.6101	6.7424	6.8771	7.0144	7.1542	7.2966	7.4416
6	6.1520	6.3081	6.4684	6.6330	6.8019	6.9753	7.1533	7.3359	7.5233	7.7156	7.9129	8.1152	8.3227	8.5355	8.7537	8.9775	9.2068	9.4420	9.6830	9.9299
7	7.2135	7.4343	7.6625	7.8983	8.1420	8.3938	8.6540	8.9228	9.2004	9.4872	9.7833	10.0890	10.4047	10.7305	11.0668	11.4139	11.7720	12.1415	12.5227	12.9159
8	8.2857	8.5830	8.8923	9.2142	9.5491	9.8975	10.2598	10.6366	11.0285	11.4359	11.8594	12.2997	12.7573	13.2328	13.7268	14.2401	14.7733	15.3270	15.9020	16.4991
9	9.3685	9.7546	10.1591	10.5828	11.0266	11.4913	11.9780	12.4876	13.0210	13.5795	14.1640	14.7757	15.4157	16.0853	16.7858	17.5185	18.2847	19.0859	19.9234	20.7989
10	10.4622	10.9497	11.4639	12.0061	12.5779	13.1808	13.8164	14.4866	15.1929	15.9374	16.7220	17.5487	18.4197	19.3373	20.3037	21.3215	22.3931	23.5213	24.7089	25.9587
11	11.5668	12.1687	12.8078	13.4864	14.2068	14.9716	15.7836	16.6455	17.5603	18.5312	19.5614	20.6546	21.8143	23.0445	24.3493	25.7329	27.1999	28.7551	30.4035	32.1504
12	12.6825	13.4121	14.1920	15.0258	15.9171	16.8699	17.8885	18.9771	20.1407	21.3843	22.7132	24.1331	25.6502	27.2707	29.0017	30.8502	32.8239	34.9311	37.1802	39.5805
13	13.8093	14.6803	15.6178	16.6268	17.7130	18.8821	20.1406	21.4953	22.9534	24.5227	26.2116	28.0291	29.9847	32.0887	34.3519	36.7862	39.4040	42.2187	45.2445	48.4966
14	14.9474	15.9739	17.0863	18.2919	19.5986	21.0151	22.5505	24.2149	26.0192	27.9750	30.0949	32.3926	34.8827	37.5811	40.5047	43.6720	47.1027	50.8180	54.8409	59.1959
15	16.0969	17.2934	18.5989	20.0236	21.5786	23.2760	25.1290	27.1521	29.3609	31.7725	34.4054	37.2797	40.4175	43.8424	47.5804	51.6595	56.1101	60.9653	66.2607	72.0351
16	17.2579	18.6393	20.1569	21.8245	23.6575	25.6725	27.8881	30.3243	33.0034	35.9497	39.1899	42.7533	46.6717	50.9804	55.7175	60.9250	66.6488	72.9390	79.8502	87.4421
17	18.4304	20.0121	21.7616	23.6975	25.8404	28.2129	30.8402	33.7502	36.9737	40.5447	44.5008	48.8837	53.7391	59.1176	65.0751	71.6730	78.9792	87.0680	96.0218	105.9306
18	19.6147	21.4123	23.4144	25.6454	28.1324	30.9057	33.9990	37.4502	41.3013	45.5992	50.3959	55.7497	61.7251	68.3941	75.8364	84.1407	93.4056	103.7403	115.2659	128.1167
19	20.8109	22.8406	25.1169	27.6712	30.5390	33.7600	37.3790	41.4463	46.0185	51.1591	56.9395	63.4397	70.7494	78.9692	88.2118	98.6032	110.2846	123.4135	138.1664	154.7400
20	22.0190	24.2974	26.8704	29.7781	33.0660	36.7856	40.9955	45.7620	51.1601	57.2750	64.2028	72.0524	80.9468	91.0249	102.4436	115.3797	130.0329	146.6280	165.4180	186.6880
21	23.2392	25.7833	28.6765	31.9692	35.7193	39.9927	44.8652	50.4229	56.7645	64.0025	72.2651	81.6987	92.4699	104.7684	118.3101	134.8405	153.1385	174.0210	197.8474	225.0256
22	24.4716	27.2990	30.5368	34.2480	38.5052	43.3923	49.0057	55.4568	62.8733	71.4027	81.2143	92.5026	105.4910	120.4360	137.6316	157.4150	180.1721	206.3448	236.4385	271.0307
23	25.7163	28.8450	32.4529	36.6179	41.4305	46.9958	53.4361	60.8933	69.5319	79.5430	91.1479	104.6029	120.2048	138.2970	159.2764	183.6014	211.8013	244.4868	282.3618	326.2369
24	26.9735	30.4219	34.4265	39.0826	44.5020	50.8156	58.1767	66.7648	76.7898	88.4973	102.1742	118.1552	136.8315	158.6586	184.1678	213.9776	248.8076	289.4945	337.0105	392.4842
25	28.2432	32.0303	36.4593	41.6459	47.7271	54.8645	63.2490	73.1059	84.7009	98.3471	114.4133	133.3339	155.6196	181.8708	212.7930	249.2140	292.1049	342.6035	402.0425	471.9811
26	29.5256	33.6709	38.5530	44.3117	51.1135	59.1564	68.6765	79.9544	93.3240	109.1818	127.9988	150.3339	176.8501	208.3327	245.7120	290.0883	342.7627	405.2721	479.4306	567.3773
27	30.8209	35.3443	40.7096	47.0842	54.6691	63.7058	74.4838	87.3508	102.7231	121.0999	143.0786	169.3740	200.8406	238.4993	283.5688	337.5024	402.0323	479.2211	571.5224	681.8528
28	32.1291	37.0512	42.9309	49.9676	58.4026	68.5281	80.6977	95.3388	112.9682	134.2099	159.8173	190.6989	227.9499	272.8892	327.1041	392.5028	471.3778	566.4809	681.1116	819.2233
29	33.4504	38.7922	45.2189	52.9663	62.3227	73.6398	87.3465	103.9659	124.1354	148.6309	178.3972	214.5828	258.5834	312.0937	377.1697	456.3032	552.5121	669.4475	811.5228	984.0680
30	34.7849	40.5681	47.5754	56.0849	66.4388	79.0582	94.4608	113.2832	136.3075	164.4940	199.0209	241.3327	293.1992	356.7868	434.7451	530.3117	647.4391	790.9480	966.7122	1,181.8816
31	36.1327	42.3794	50.0027	59.3283	70.7608	84.8017	102.0730	123.3459	149.5752	181.9434	221.9132	271.2926	332.3151	407.7370	500.9569	616.1616	758.5038	934.3186	1,151.3875	1,419.2579
32	37.4941	44.2270	52.5028	62.7015	75.2988	90.8898	110.2182	134.2135	164.0370	201.1378	247.3236	304.8477	376.5161	465.8202	577.1005	715.7475	888.4494	1,103.4960	1,371.1511	1,704.1095
33	38.8690	46.1116	55.0778	66.2095	80.0638	97.3432	118.9334	145.9506	179.8003	222.2515	275.5292	342.4294	426.4632	532.0350	664.6655	831.2671	1,040.4858	1,303.1253	1,632.6698	2,045.9314
34	40.2577	48.0338	57.7302	69.8579	85.0670	104.1838	128.2588	158.6267	196.9823	245.4767	306.8374	384.5210	482.9034	607.5199	765.3654	965.2698	1,218.3684	1,538.6878	1,943.8771	2,456.1176
35	41.6603	49.9945	60.4621	73.6522	90.3203	111.4348	138.2369	172.3168	215.7108	271.0244	341.5896	431.6635	546.6808	693.5727	881.1702	1,120.7130	1,426.4910	1,816.6516	2,314.2137	2,948.3411
36	43.0769	51.9944	63.2759	77.5983	95.8363	119.1209	148.9135	187.1021	236.1247	299.1268	380.1644	484.4631	618.7493	791.6729	1,014.3457	1,301.0270	1,669.9945	2,144.6489	2,754.9143	3,539.0094

TABLE B-4 Future Value of an Annuity Due

Formula $FVAD = A \left\{ \left[\dfrac{(1 + i)^{(n+1)} - 1}{i} \right] - 1 \right\}$

Interest Rate (i)

Periods (n)	1%	2%	3%	4%	5%	6%	7%	8%	9%	10%	11%	12%	13%	14%	15%	16%	17%	18%	19%	20%
1	1.0100	1.0200	1.0300	1.0400	1.0500	1.0600	1.0700	1.0800	1.0900	1.1000	1.1100	1.1200	1.1300	1.1400	1.1500	1.1600	1.1700	1.1800	1.1900	1.2000
2	2.0301	2.0604	2.0909	2.1216	2.1525	2.1836	2.2149	2.2484	2.2781	2.3100	2.3421	2.3744	2.4069	2.4396	2.4725	2.5056	2.5389	2.5724	2.6061	2.6400
3	3.0604	3.1216	3.1836	3.2465	3.3101	3.3746	3.4399	3.5061	3.5731	3.6410	3.7097	3.7793	3.8498	3.9211	3.9934	4.0665	4.1405	4.2154	4.2913	4.3680
4	4.1010	4.2040	4.3091	4.4163	4.5256	4.6371	4.7507	4.8666	4.9847	5.1051	5.2278	5.3528	5.4803	5.6101	5.7424	5.8771	6.0144	6.1542	6.2966	6.4416
5	5.1520	5.3081	5.4684	5.6330	5.8019	5.9753	6.1533	6.3359	6.5233	6.7156	6.9129	7.1152	7.3227	7.5355	7.7537	7.9775	8.2068	8.4420	8.6830	8.9299
6	6.2135	6.4343	6.6625	6.8983	7.1420	7.3938	7.6540	7.9228	8.2004	8.4872	8.7833	9.0890	9.4047	9.7305	10.0668	10.4139	10.7720	11.1415	11.5227	11.9159
7	7.2857	7.5830	7.8923	8.2142	8.5491	8.8975	9.2598	9.6366	10.0285	10.4359	10.8594	11.2997	11.7573	12.2328	12.7268	13.2401	13.7733	14.3270	14.9020	15.4991
8	8.3685	8.7546	9.1591	9.5828	10.0266	10.4913	10.9780	11.4876	12.0210	12.5795	13.1640	13.7757	14.4157	15.0853	15.7858	16.5185	17.2847	18.0859	18.9234	19.7989
9	9.4622	9.9497	10.4639	11.0061	11.5779	12.1808	12.8164	13.4866	14.1929	14.9374	15.7220	16.5487	17.4197	18.3373	19.3037	20.3215	21.3931	22.5213	23.7089	24.9587
10	10.5668	11.1687	11.8078	12.4864	13.2068	13.9716	14.7836	15.6455	16.5603	17.5312	18.5614	19.6546	20.8143	22.0445	23.3493	24.7329	26.1999	27.7551	29.4035	31.1504
11	11.6825	12.4121	13.1920	14.0253	14.9171	15.8699	16.8885	17.9771	19.1407	20.3843	21.7132	23.1331	24.6502	26.2707	28.0017	29.8502	31.8239	33.9311	36.1802	38.5805
12	12.8093	13.6803	14.6178	15.6263	16.7130	17.8821	19.1406	20.4953	21.9534	23.5227	25.2116	27.0291	28.9647	31.0887	33.3519	35.7862	38.4040	41.2187	44.2445	47.4966
13	13.9474	14.9739	16.0863	17.2919	18.5986	20.0151	21.5505	23.2149	25.0192	26.9750	29.0949	31.3926	33.8827	36.5811	39.5047	42.6720	46.1027	49.8180	53.8409	58.1959
14	15.0969	16.2934	17.5989	19.0236	20.5786	22.2760	24.1290	26.1521	28.3609	30.7725	33.4054	36.2797	39.4175	42.8424	46.5804	50.6595	55.1101	59.9653	65.2607	71.0351
15	16.2579	17.6393	19.1569	20.8245	22.6575	24.6725	26.8881	29.3243	32.0034	34.9497	38.1899	41.7533	45.6717	49.9604	54.7175	59.9250	65.6488	71.9390	78.8502	86.4421
16	17.4304	19.0121	20.7616	22.6975	24.8404	27.2129	29.6402	32.7502	35.9737	39.5447	43.5008	47.8837	52.7391	58.1176	64.0751	70.6730	77.9792	86.0680	95.0218	104.9306
17	18.6147	20.4123	22.4144	24.6454	27.1324	29.9057	32.9990	36.4502	40.3013	44.5992	49.3959	54.7497	60.7251	67.3941	74.8364	83.1407	92.4056	102.7403	114.2659	127.1167
18	19.8109	21.8406	24.1169	26.6712	29.5390	32.7600	36.3790	40.4463	45.0185	50.1591	55.9395	62.4397	69.7494	77.9692	87.2118	97.6032	109.2846	122.4135	137.1664	153.7400
19	21.0190	23.2974	25.8704	28.7781	32.0660	35.7856	39.9955	44.7620	50.1601	56.2750	63.2028	71.0524	79.9468	90.0249	101.4436	114.3797	129.0329	145.5280	164.4180	185.6880
20	22.2392	24.7833	27.6765	30.9692	34.7193	38.9927	43.8652	49.4229	55.7645	63.0025	71.2651	80.6987	91.4699	103.7684	117.8101	133.8405	152.1385	173.0210	196.8474	224.0256
21	23.4716	26.2990	29.5368	33.2480	37.5052	42.3923	48.0057	54.4568	61.8733	70.4027	80.2143	91.5026	104.4910	119.4360	136.6316	156.4150	179.1721	205.3448	235.4385	270.0307
22	24.7163	27.8450	31.4529	35.6179	40.4305	45.9958	52.4361	59.8933	68.5319	78.5430	90.1479	103.6029	119.2048	137.2970	158.2764	182.6014	210.8013	243.4868	281.3618	325.2369
23	25.9735	29.4219	33.4265	38.0826	43.5020	49.8156	57.1767	65.7648	75.7898	87.4973	101.1742	117.1552	135.8315	157.6586	183.1678	212.9776	247.8076	288.4945	336.0105	391.4842
24	27.2432	31.0303	35.4593	40.6459	46.7271	53.8645	62.2490	72.1059	83.7009	97.3471	113.4133	132.3339	154.6196	180.8708	211.7930	248.2140	291.1049	341.6035	401.0425	470.9811
25	28.5256	32.6709	37.5530	43.3117	50.1135	58.1564	67.6765	78.9544	92.3240	108.1818	126.9988	149.3339	175.8501	207.3327	244.7120	289.0883	341.7627	404.2721	478.4306	566.3773
26	29.8209	34.3443	39.7096	46.0842	53.6691	62.7058	73.4838	86.3508	101.7231	120.0999	142.0786	168.3740	199.8406	237.4993	282.5688	336.5024	401.0323	478.2211	570.5224	680.8528
27	31.1291	36.0512	41.9309	48.9676	57.4026	67.5281	79.6977	94.3388	111.9682	133.2099	158.8173	189.6989	226.9499	271.8892	326.1041	391.5028	470.3778	565.4809	680.1116	818.2233
28	32.4504	37.7922	44.2189	51.9663	61.3227	72.6398	86.3465	102.9659	123.1354	147.6309	177.3972	213.5828	257.5834	311.0937	376.1697	455.3032	551.5121	668.4475	810.5228	983.0680
29	33.7849	39.5681	46.5754	55.0849	65.4388	78.0582	93.4608	112.2832	135.3075	163.4940	198.0209	240.3327	292.1992	355.7868	433.7451	529.3117	646.4391	789.9480	965.7122	1,180.8816
30	35.1327	41.3794	49.0027	58.3283	69.7608	83.8017	101.0730	122.3459	148.5752	180.9434	220.9130	270.2926	331.3151	406.7370	499.9569	615.1616	757.5038	933.3186	1,150.3875	1,418.2579
31	36.4941	43.2270	51.5028	61.7015	74.2988	89.8898	109.2182	133.2135	163.0370	200.1378	246.3236	303.8477	375.5161	464.8202	576.1005	714.7475	887.4494	1,102.4960	1,370.1511	1,703.1095
32	37.8690	45.1116	54.0778	65.2095	79.0638	96.3432	117.9334	144.9506	178.8003	221.2515	274.5292	341.4294	425.4632	531.0350	663.6655	830.2671	1,039.4858	1,302.1253	1,631.6698	2,044.9314
33	39.2577	47.0338	56.7302	68.8579	84.0670	103.1838	127.2588	157.6267	195.9823	244.4767	305.8374	383.5210	481.9034	606.5199	764.3654	964.2698	1,217.3684	1,537.6878	1,942.8771	2,445.1176
34	40.6603	48.9944	59.4621	72.6522	89.3203	110.4348	137.2369	171.3168	214.7108	270.0244	340.5896	430.6635	545.6808	692.5727	880.1702	1,119.7130	1,425.4910	1,815.6516	2,313.2137	2,947.3411
35	42.0769	50.9944	62.2759	76.5983	94.8363	118.1209	147.9135	186.1021	235.1247	298.1268	379.1644	483.4631	617.7493	790.6729	1,013.3457	1,300.0270	1,668.9945	2,143.6489	2,753.9143	3,538.0094
36	43.5076	53.0343	65.1742	80.7022	100.6281	126.2681	159.3374	202.0703	257.3759	329.0395	421.9825	542.5987	699.1867	902.5071	1,166.4975	1,509.1914	1,953.8936	2,530.6857	3,278.3481	4,246.8112

TABLE B-5 Present Value of an Ordinary Annuity

Formula $PVOA = A\left[\dfrac{(1+i)^n - 1}{i(1+i)^n}\right]$

Interest Rate (i)

Periods (n)	1%	2%	3%	4%	5%	6%	7%	8%	9%	10%	11%	12%	13%	14%	15%	16%	17%	18%	19%	20%
1	0.9901	0.9804	0.9709	0.9615	0.9524	0.9434	0.9346	0.9259	0.9174	0.9091	0.9009	0.8929	0.8850	0.8772	0.8696	0.8621	0.8547	0.8475	0.8403	0.8333
2	1.9704	1.9416	1.9135	1.8861	1.8594	1.8334	1.8080	1.7833	1.7591	1.7355	1.7125	1.6901	1.6681	1.6467	1.6257	1.6052	1.5852	1.5656	1.5465	1.5278
3	2.9410	2.8839	2.8286	2.7751	2.7232	2.6730	2.6243	2.5771	2.5313	2.4869	2.4437	2.4018	2.3612	2.3216	2.2832	2.2459	2.2096	2.1743	2.1399	2.1065
4	3.9020	3.8077	3.7171	3.6299	3.5460	3.4651	3.3872	3.3121	3.2397	3.1699	3.1024	3.0373	2.9745	2.9137	2.8550	2.7982	2.7432	2.6901	2.6386	2.5887
5	4.8534	4.7135	4.5797	4.4518	4.3295	4.2124	4.1002	3.9927	3.8897	3.7908	3.6959	3.6048	3.5172	3.4331	3.3522	3.2743	3.1993	3.1272	3.0576	2.9906
6	5.7955	5.6014	5.4172	5.2421	5.0757	4.9173	4.7665	4.6229	4.4859	4.3553	4.2305	4.1114	3.9975	3.8887	3.7845	3.6847	3.5892	3.4976	3.4098	3.3255
7	6.7282	6.4720	6.2303	6.0021	5.7864	5.5824	5.3893	5.2064	5.0330	4.8684	4.7122	4.5638	4.4226	4.2883	4.1604	4.0386	3.9224	3.8115	3.7057	3.6046
8	7.6517	7.3255	7.0197	6.7327	6.4632	6.2098	5.9713	5.7466	5.5348	5.3349	5.1461	4.9676	4.7988	4.6389	4.4873	4.3436	4.2072	4.0776	3.9544	3.8372
9	8.5660	8.1622	7.7861	7.4353	7.1078	6.8017	6.5152	6.2469	5.9952	5.7590	5.5370	5.3282	5.1317	4.9464	4.7716	4.6065	4.4506	4.3030	4.1633	4.0310
10	9.4713	8.9826	8.5302	8.1109	7.7217	7.3601	7.0236	6.7101	6.4177	6.1446	5.8892	5.6502	5.4262	5.2161	5.0188	4.8332	4.6586	4.4941	4.3389	4.1925
11	10.3676	9.7868	9.2526	8.7605	8.3064	7.8869	7.4987	7.1390	6.8052	6.4951	6.2065	5.9377	5.6869	5.4527	5.2337	5.0286	4.8364	4.6560	4.4865	4.3271
12	11.2551	10.5753	9.9540	9.3851	8.8633	8.3838	7.9427	7.5361	7.1607	6.8137	6.4924	6.1944	5.9176	5.6603	5.4206	5.1971	4.9884	4.7932	4.6105	4.4392
13	12.1337	11.3484	10.6350	9.9856	9.3936	8.8527	8.3577	7.9038	7.4869	7.1034	6.7499	6.4235	6.1218	5.8424	5.5831	5.3423	5.1183	4.9095	4.7147	4.5327
14	13.0037	12.1062	11.2961	10.5631	9.8986	9.2950	8.7455	8.2442	7.7862	7.3667	6.9819	6.6282	6.3025	6.0021	5.7245	5.4675	5.2293	5.0081	4.8023	4.6106
15	13.8651	12.8493	11.9379	11.1184	10.3797	9.7122	9.1079	8.5595	8.0607	7.6061	7.1909	6.8109	6.4624	6.1422	5.8474	5.5755	5.3242	5.0916	4.8759	4.6755
16	14.7179	13.5777	12.5611	11.6523	10.8378	10.1059	9.4466	8.8514	8.3126	7.8237	7.3792	6.9740	6.6039	6.2651	5.9542	5.6685	5.4053	5.1624	4.9377	4.7296
17	15.5623	14.2919	13.1661	12.1657	11.2741	10.4773	9.7632	9.1216	8.5436	8.0216	7.5488	7.1196	6.7291	6.3729	6.0472	5.7487	5.4746	5.2223	4.9897	4.7746
18	16.3983	14.9920	13.7535	12.6593	11.6896	10.8276	10.0591	9.3719	8.7556	8.2014	7.7016	7.2497	6.8399	6.4674	6.1280	5.8178	5.5339	5.2732	5.0333	4.8122
19	17.2260	15.6785	14.3238	13.1339	12.0853	11.1581	10.3356	9.6036	8.9501	8.3649	7.8393	7.3658	6.9380	6.5504	6.1982	5.8775	5.5845	5.3162	5.0700	4.8435
20	18.0456	16.3514	14.8775	13.5903	12.4622	11.4699	10.5940	9.8181	9.1285	8.5136	7.9633	7.4694	7.0248	6.6231	6.2593	5.9288	5.6278	5.3527	5.1009	4.8696
21	18.8570	17.0112	15.4150	14.0292	12.8212	11.7641	10.8355	10.0168	9.2922	8.6487	8.0751	7.5620	7.1016	6.6870	6.3125	5.9731	5.6648	5.3837	5.1268	4.8913
22	19.6604	17.6580	15.9369	14.4511	13.1630	12.0416	11.0612	10.2007	9.4424	8.7715	8.1757	7.6446	7.1695	6.7429	6.3587	6.0113	5.6964	5.4099	5.1486	4.9094
23	20.4558	18.2922	16.4436	14.8568	13.4886	12.3034	11.2722	10.3711	9.5802	8.8832	8.2664	7.7184	7.2297	6.7921	6.3988	6.0442	5.7234	5.4321	5.1668	4.9245
24	21.2434	18.9139	16.9355	15.2470	13.7986	12.5504	11.4693	10.5288	9.7066	8.9847	8.3481	7.7843	7.2829	6.8351	6.4338	6.0726	5.7465	5.4509	5.1822	4.9371
25	22.0232	19.5235	17.4131	15.6221	14.0939	12.7834	11.6536	10.6748	9.8226	9.0770	8.4217	7.8431	7.3300	6.8729	6.4641	6.0971	5.7662	5.4669	5.1951	4.9476
26	22.7952	20.1210	17.8768	15.9828	14.3752	13.0032	11.8258	10.8100	9.9290	9.1609	8.4881	7.8957	7.3717	6.9061	6.4906	6.1182	5.7831	5.4804	5.2060	4.9563
27	23.5596	20.7069	18.3270	16.3296	14.6430	13.2105	11.9867	10.9352	10.0266	9.2372	8.5478	7.9426	7.4086	6.9352	6.5135	6.1364	5.7975	5.4919	5.2151	4.9636
28	24.3164	21.2813	18.7641	16.6631	14.8981	13.4062	12.1371	11.0511	10.1161	9.3066	8.6016	7.9844	7.4412	6.9607	6.5335	6.1520	5.8099	5.5016	5.2228	4.9697
29	25.0658	21.8444	19.1885	16.9837	15.1411	13.5907	12.2777	11.1584	10.1983	9.3696	8.6501	8.0218	7.4701	6.9830	6.5509	6.1656	5.8204	5.5098	5.2292	4.9747
30	25.8077	22.3965	19.6004	17.2920	15.3725	13.7648	12.4090	11.2578	10.2737	9.4269	8.6938	8.0552	7.4957	7.0027	6.5660	6.1772	5.8294	5.5168	5.2347	4.9789
31	26.5423	22.9377	20.0004	17.5885	15.5928	13.9291	12.5318	11.3498	10.3428	9.4790	8.7331	8.0850	7.5183	7.0199	6.5791	6.1872	5.8371	5.5227	5.2392	4.9824
32	27.2696	23.4683	20.3888	17.8736	15.8027	14.0840	12.6466	11.4350	10.4062	9.5264	8.7686	8.1116	7.5383	7.0350	6.5905	6.1959	5.8437	5.5277	5.2430	4.9854
33	27.9897	23.9886	20.7658	18.1476	16.0025	14.2302	12.7538	11.5139	10.4644	9.5694	8.8005	8.1354	7.5560	7.0482	6.6005	6.2034	5.8493	5.5320	5.2462	4.9878
34	28.7027	24.4986	21.1318	18.4112	16.1929	14.3681	12.8540	11.5869	10.5178	9.6086	8.8293	8.1566	7.5717	7.0599	6.6091	6.2098	5.8541	5.5356	5.2489	4.9898
35	29.4086	24.9986	21.4872	18.6646	16.3742	14.4982	12.9477	11.6546	10.5668	9.6442	8.8552	8.1755	7.5856	7.0700	6.6166	6.2153	5.8582	5.5386	5.2512	4.9915
36	30.1075	25.4888	21.8323	18.9083	16.5469	14.6210	13.0352	11.7172	10.6118	9.6765	8.8786	8.1924	7.5979	7.0790	6.6231	6.2201	5.8617	5.5412	5.2531	4.9929

TABLE B-6 Present Value of an Annuity Due

Formula $PVAD = A\left\{\left[\dfrac{(1+i)^{(n-1)}-1}{i(1+i)^{(n-1)}}\right]+1\right\}$

Interest Rate (i)

Periods (n)	1%	2%	3%	4%	5%	6%	7%	8%	9%	10%	11%	12%	13%	14%	15%	16%	17%	18%	19%	20%
1	1.0000	1.0000	1.0000	1.0000	1.0000	1.0000	1.0000	1.0000	1.0000	1.0000	1.0000	1.0000	1.0000	1.0000	1.0000	1.0000	1.0000	1.0000	1.0000	1.0000
2	1.9901	1.9804	1.9709	1.9615	1.9524	1.9434	1.9346	1.9259	1.9174	1.9091	1.9009	1.8929	1.8850	1.8772	1.8696	1.8621	1.8547	1.8475	1.8403	1.8333
3	2.9704	2.9416	2.9135	2.8861	2.8594	2.8334	2.8080	2.7833	2.7591	2.7355	2.7125	2.6901	2.6681	2.6467	2.6257	2.6052	2.5852	2.5656	2.5465	2.5278
4	3.9410	3.8839	3.8286	3.7751	3.7232	3.6730	3.6243	3.5771	3.5313	3.4869	3.4437	3.4018	3.3612	3.3216	3.2832	3.2459	3.2096	3.1743	3.1399	3.1065
5	4.9020	4.8077	4.7171	4.6299	4.5460	4.4651	4.3872	4.3121	4.2397	4.1699	4.1024	4.0373	3.9745	3.9137	3.8550	3.7982	3.7432	3.6901	3.6386	3.5887
6	5.8534	5.7135	5.5797	5.4518	5.3295	5.2124	5.1002	4.9927	4.8897	4.7908	4.6959	4.6048	4.5172	4.4331	4.3522	4.2743	4.1993	4.1272	4.0576	3.9906
7	6.7955	6.6014	6.4172	6.2421	6.0757	5.9173	5.7665	5.6229	5.4859	5.3553	5.2305	5.1114	4.9975	4.8887	4.7845	4.6847	4.5892	4.4976	4.4098	4.3255
8	7.7282	7.4720	7.2303	7.0021	6.7864	6.5824	6.3893	6.2064	6.0330	5.8684	5.7122	5.5638	5.4226	5.2883	5.1604	5.0386	4.9224	4.8115	4.7057	4.6046
9	8.6517	8.3255	8.0197	7.7327	7.4632	7.2098	6.9713	6.7466	6.5348	6.3349	6.1461	5.9676	5.7988	5.6389	5.4873	5.3436	5.2072	5.0776	4.9544	4.8372
10	9.5660	9.1622	8.7861	8.4353	8.1078	7.8017	7.5152	7.2469	6.9952	6.7590	6.5370	6.3282	6.1317	5.9464	5.7716	5.6065	5.4506	5.3030	5.1633	5.0310
11	10.4713	9.9826	9.5302	9.1109	8.7217	8.3601	8.0236	7.7101	7.4177	7.1446	6.8892	6.6502	6.4262	6.2161	6.0188	5.8332	5.6586	5.4941	5.3389	5.1925
12	11.3676	10.7868	10.2526	9.7605	9.3064	8.8869	8.4987	8.1390	7.8052	7.4951	7.2065	6.9377	6.6869	6.4527	6.2337	6.0286	5.8364	5.6560	5.4865	5.3271
13	12.2551	11.5753	10.9540	10.3851	9.8633	9.3838	8.9427	8.5361	8.1607	7.8137	7.4924	7.1944	6.9176	6.6603	6.4206	6.1971	5.9984	5.7932	5.6105	5.4392
14	13.1337	12.3484	11.6350	10.9856	10.3936	9.8527	9.3577	8.9038	8.4869	8.1034	7.7499	7.4235	7.1218	6.8424	6.5831	6.3423	6.1183	5.9095	5.7147	5.5327
15	14.0037	13.1062	12.2961	11.5631	10.8986	10.2950	9.7455	9.2442	8.7862	8.3667	7.9819	7.6282	7.3025	7.0021	6.7245	6.4675	6.2293	6.0081	5.8023	5.6106
16	14.8651	13.8493	12.9379	12.1184	11.3797	10.7122	10.1079	9.5595	9.0607	8.6061	8.1909	7.8109	7.4624	7.1422	6.8474	6.5755	6.3242	6.0916	5.8759	5.6755
17	15.7179	14.5777	13.5611	12.6523	11.8378	11.1059	10.4466	9.8514	9.3126	8.8237	8.3792	7.9740	7.6039	7.2651	6.9542	6.6685	6.4053	6.1624	5.9377	5.7296
18	16.5623	15.2919	14.1661	13.1657	12.2741	11.4773	10.7632	10.1216	9.5436	9.0216	8.5488	8.1196	7.7291	7.3729	7.0472	6.7487	6.4746	6.2223	5.9897	5.7746
19	17.3983	15.9920	14.7535	13.6593	12.6896	11.8276	11.0591	10.3719	9.7556	9.2014	8.7016	8.2497	7.8399	7.4674	7.1280	6.8178	6.5339	6.2732	6.0333	5.8122
20	18.2260	16.6785	15.3238	14.1339	13.0853	12.1581	11.3356	10.6036	9.9501	9.3649	8.8393	8.3658	7.9380	7.5504	7.1982	6.8775	6.5845	6.3162	6.0700	5.8435
21	19.0456	17.3514	15.8775	14.5903	13.4622	12.4699	11.5940	10.8181	10.1285	9.5136	8.9633	8.4694	8.0248	7.6231	7.2593	6.9288	6.6278	6.3527	6.1009	5.8696
22	19.8570	18.0112	16.4150	15.0292	13.8212	12.7641	11.8355	11.0168	10.2922	9.6487	9.0751	8.5620	8.1016	7.6870	7.3125	6.9731	6.6648	6.3837	6.1268	5.8913
23	20.6604	18.6580	16.9369	15.4568	14.1630	13.0416	12.0612	11.2007	10.4424	9.7715	9.1757	8.6446	8.1695	7.7429	7.3587	7.0113	6.6964	6.4099	6.1486	5.9094
24	21.4558	19.2922	17.4436	15.8568	14.4886	13.3034	12.2722	11.3711	10.5802	9.8832	9.2664	8.7184	8.2297	7.7921	7.3988	7.0442	6.7234	6.4321	6.1668	5.9245
25	22.2434	19.9139	17.9355	16.2470	14.7986	13.5504	12.4693	11.5288	10.7066	9.9847	9.3481	8.7843	8.2829	7.8351	7.4338	7.0726	6.7465	6.4509	6.1822	5.9371
26	23.0232	20.5235	18.4131	16.6221	15.0939	13.7834	12.6536	11.6748	10.8226	10.0770	9.4217	8.8431	8.3300	7.8729	7.4641	7.0971	6.7662	6.4669	6.1951	5.9476
27	23.7952	21.1210	18.8768	16.9828	15.3752	14.0032	12.8258	11.8100	10.9290	10.1609	9.4881	8.8957	8.3717	7.9061	7.4906	7.1182	6.7831	6.4804	6.2060	5.9563
28	24.5596	21.7069	19.3270	17.3296	15.6430	14.2105	12.9867	11.9352	11.0266	10.2372	9.5478	8.9426	8.4086	7.9352	7.5135	7.1364	6.7975	6.4919	6.2151	5.9636
29	25.3164	22.2813	19.7641	17.6631	15.8981	14.4062	13.1371	12.0511	11.1161	10.3066	9.6016	8.9844	8.4412	7.9607	7.5335	7.1520	6.8099	6.5016	6.2228	5.9697
30	26.0658	22.8444	20.1885	17.9837	16.1411	14.5907	13.2777	12.1584	11.1983	10.3696	9.6501	9.0218	8.4701	7.9830	7.5509	7.1656	6.8204	6.5098	6.2292	5.9747
31	26.8077	23.3965	20.6004	18.2920	16.3725	14.7648	13.4090	12.2578	11.2737	10.4269	9.6938	9.0552	8.4957	8.0027	7.5660	7.1772	6.8294	6.5168	6.2347	5.9789
32	27.5423	23.9377	21.0004	18.5885	16.5928	14.9291	13.5318	12.3498	11.3426	10.4790	9.7331	9.0850	8.5183	8.0199	7.5791	7.1872	6.8371	6.5227	6.2392	5.9824
33	28.2696	24.4683	21.3888	18.8736	16.8027	15.0840	13.6466	12.4350	11.4062	10.5264	9.7686	9.1116	8.5383	8.0350	7.5905	7.1959	6.8437	6.5277	6.2430	5.9854
34	28.9897	24.9886	21.7658	19.1476	17.0025	15.2302	13.7538	12.5139	11.4644	10.5694	9.8005	9.1354	8.5560	8.0482	7.6005	7.2034	6.8493	6.5320	6.2462	5.9878
35	29.7027	25.4986	22.1318	19.4112	17.1929	15.3681	13.8540	12.5869	11.5178	10.6086	9.8293	9.1566	8.5717	8.0599	7.6091	7.2098	6.8541	6.5356	6.2489	5.9898
36	30.4086	25.9986	22.4872	19.6646	17.3742	15.4982	13.9477	12.6546	11.5668	10.6442	9.8552	9.1755	8.5856	8.0700	7.6166	7.2153	6.8582	6.5386	6.2512	5.9915

Answers to Even-Numbered Exercises and Problems

CHAPTER 1

2. 3 appliance repairs per hour × $30 = $90 marginal revenue product. Maximum hourly wage equals marginal revenue product, or $90.
4. Sara Lee's opportunity cost was Bean Counters CPA at $35,000.
6. They most likely would raise the discount rate, the federal funds rate, or both. They could also sell more government securities to decrease the money supply.

CHAPTER 2

2. The memo that Jerry received relates to the strategic overall plan for his company. When Jerry develops a personnel plan, he is working on a functional plan (personnel) designed to support the strategic plan.
4. $6,000, which is your cost. Common stockholders cannot lose more than their initial investment when a company is sued or goes bankrupt.
6. **Strengths:** Barry has 5 years of experience; the dry cleaning business is already established; assumable lease; fixed rent for the next 5 years; commercial accounts are 20 percent of business.
   Weakness: None listed.
   Opportunities: Business is located in a busy shopping center; population is growing at 6 percent a year; residential area with residents being professionals who wear suits to work; no new competition because of favorable zoning.
   Threats: Competition from price-cutting business across the street.

8. Joe's first step should be to complete a business plan and contact the local Small Business Association (SBA) and SCORE office to determine what financing is available. He should also check with local and state agencies for small business assistance. Depending on his credit rating and bank standing he can also contact local banks and financial institutions and shop for the best loan and interest rates. Chances of obtaining a grant for this type of business are very slim.

CHAPTER 3

2. Answer is individualized. No single correct answer.
4. Income statement Humperdinck Family.

Income			
Salaries	$42,000		
Interest income	150		
Dividend income	190		
Total income			$42,340
Fixed expenses			
Mortgage payment	7,980		
Automobile payment	3,060		
Student loan payment	1,700		
Property taxes	1,100		
Insurance	2,100		
Income taxes	9,700		
Total fixed expenses		$25,640	
Variable expenses			
Food	2,400		
Transportation	1,200		
Utilities	3,000		
Clothes and personal	2,000		
Recreation and vacation	2,000		
Total variable expenses		10,600	
Total expenses			36,240
Disposable income			
(Cash balance at end of the year)			$6,100

6.

Net sales	$500,000
Cost of goods sold	**250,000**
Gross profit	**$250,000**
Operating expenses	
Salaries	100,000
Rent	24,000
Utilities	25,000
Payroll taxes	25,000
Insurance	12,000
Total operating expenses	186,000
Operating income	64,000
Interest expenses	5,450
Net income	**$ 58,550**

8. $1,500,000 + $3,675,000 = $5,175,000 Total retained earnings
   $1,000,000 + $12,500,000 + $5,175,000 = $18,675,000

CHAPTER 4

2. **You receive the following partial balance sheet (Table 4–5) for 2008 and 2007 for a company that you are considering making an investment in. Perform a vertical analysis for each year on these accounts. Compare the two years, and describe those changes that were beneficial or detrimental to this company in one sentence.** The beneficial items include the fact that fixed assets decreased by the same amount that current assets increased and current liabilities decreased and owner's equity increased. The detrimental item may be that fixed assets decreased, which may have an impact on the ability of the firm to earn money in the long run.

4. Public library sources include *Dun's Review, Value Line Investment Survey, Moody's, Standard & Poors, New York Times* archives, *Wall Street Journal* archives, *Investor's Business Daily, Barrons, Zack's Financial,* and several others that the instructor of the course may have access to. Internet resources include EDGAR; http://finance.yahoo.com, which gives immediate news stories on companies; stocksmart; the websites of business sections of large national newspapers; and many search engines such as Google, CNET, Yahoo!, Alta Vista, and several others that the instructor may suggest. We also include businesswire, prwire, Dow Jones news retrieval, Associated Press, and EDGAR online. The most important source is often the company's own home page (e.g., http://www.starbucks.com).

TABLE 4–5 Balance Sheet, Sample Company

Category	2007	Vertical Analysis 2007	2008	Vertical Analysis 2008
Current assets	$ 7,000,000	46.67%	$ 9,000,000	60.00%
Total fixed assets	8,000,000	56.33%	6,000,000	40.00%
Total assets	15,000,000	100.00%	15,000,000	100.00%
Current liabilities	$ 3,000,000	20.00%	$ 1,000,000	6.67%
Long term debt	4,000,000	26.67%	4,000,000	26.67%
Owner's equity	8,000,000	53.33%	10,000,000	66.67%
Total liabilities & owner's equity	$15,000,000	100.00%	$15,000,000	100.00%

TABLE 4–4 Moderately Large Corporation Consolidated Balance Sheet

Moderately Large Corporation Consolidated Balance Sheet
(in thousands, except share data)

Fiscal Year Ended	Dec. 31, 2008	Dec. 31, 2007	Horizontal Analysis
ASSETS			
Current assets			
Cash and cash equivalents	$1,369	$1,427	−4.04%
Accounts receivable, net	1,008	876	15.03%
Inventories	1,489	481	209.60%
Prepaid expenses and other current assets	157	126	24.54%
Deferred income taxes, net	44	40	9.11%
Total current assets	4,066	2,950	37.86%
Property, plant, and equipment, net	3,137	2,287	37.17%
Other assets	168	161	4.35%
TOTAL ASSETS	$7,371	$5,398	36.57%
LIABILITIES AND SHAREHOLDERS' EQUITY			
Current liabilities			
Accounts payable	$ 429	$ 242	77.22%
Accrued compensation and related costs	104	98	6.34%
Accrued taxes	132	141	−6.21%
Current portion of long-term debt	89	82	8.54%
Total current liabilities	754	563	34.01%
Long-term debt	2,630	1,830	43.75%
Total liabilities	3,384	2,392	41.46%
Shareholders' equity			
Common stock ($0.1 par value)—authorized, 4,000,000 shares; issued and outstanding, 3,500,000	350	350	0.00%
Paid-in capital in excess of par	2,415	2,415	0.00%
Retained earnings	1,222	241	407.05%
Total shareholders' equity	3,987	3,006	32.63%
TOTAL LIABILITIES AND SHAREHOLDERS' EQUITY	$7,371	$5,398	36.54%

6. Perform a horizontal analysis of the MLC balance sheet (Table 4–4).
   a. **Compare assets, liabilities, and owner's equity from one year to the next.** Assets increased by 36.57 percent, liabilities increased by 41.46 percent and owner's equity increased by 32.63 percent between December 31, 2007 and December 31, 2008.
   b. **Is the corporation better off in 2008 or in 2007?** Although assets and owner's equity have increased, there is a disturbing trend in current assets because cash decreased by 4.04 percent, and accounts receivable increased by 15.03 percent, inventories increased by 209.60 percent, and property, plant and equipment increased by 37.17 percent. If the economy is actually in a recession, they may

have problems disposing of inventory and collecting accounts receivable.

8. **Given the income statement for MLC, Table 4–7 and balance sheet (Table 4–4), answer the following:**
   a. **Calculate the following ratios for 2008: operating profit margin, net profit margin, operating return on assets, net return on assets, and return on equity.**

Ratio	*2008*
Operating profit margin	($1,522 ÷ $8,935) × 100 = 17.03%
Net profit margin	($983 ÷ $8,935) × 100 = 11.00%

$$\text{Operating return on assets} \qquad \left[\frac{\$1,522}{\left(\dfrac{\$7,371 + \$5,398}{2}\right)} \right] \times 100 = \left(\frac{\$1,522}{\$6,384.5}\right) \times 100 = 23.84\%$$

$$\text{Net return on assets} \qquad \left[\frac{\$983}{\left(\dfrac{\$7,371 + \$5,398}{2}\right)} \right] \times 100 = \left(\frac{\$983}{\$6,384.5}\right) \times 100 = 15.40\%$$

$$\text{Return on equity} \qquad \left[\frac{\$983}{\left(\dfrac{\$3,987 + \$3,006}{2}\right)} \right] \times 100 = \left(\frac{\$983}{\$3,496.5}\right) \times 100 = 28.11\%$$

   b. **In a written explanation, describe what each of these ratios means.** *Operating profit margin* means that for every dollar in net sales, the company earns a percentage of net sales as a result of operations. The MLC earned 17 cents on every dollar of operating income. *Net profit margin* means that for every dollar in net sales, the company earns a percentage of net sales as a result of operations, paying interest, and taxes. The MLC earned 11 cents on every dollar of net income. *Operating return on assets* is the percentage of operating income that each dollar of assets generates. The MLC generated 23.84 cents on every dollar of assets. *Net return on assets* is the percentage of net income that each dollar of assets generates. The MLC generated 15.4 cents on every dollar of assets. *Return on equity* is the percentage of net income generated by each dollar of owner's equity. The MLC generated 28.11 cents on every dollar of shareholder's equity.
   c. **In a brief paragraph, describe the overall profitability of MLC.** Moderately Large Corporation's operating profit margin and net profit margin both increased. They still have very good return on equity for the stockholders.

10. **Using both the balance sheet (Table 4–4) and the income statement (Table 4–7) for the MLC, answer the following:**
    a. **Calculate the following ratios for 2008: inventory turnover, total asset turnover, and fixed asset turnover.**

Ratio	*2008*

    Inventory turnover $\quad \dfrac{\$5,361}{\left(\dfrac{\$1,489 + \$481}{2}\right)} = \dfrac{\$5,361}{\$985} = 5.44$

    Total asset turnover $\quad \dfrac{\$8,935}{\left(\dfrac{\$7,371 + \$5,398}{2}\right)} = \dfrac{\$8,935}{\$6,384.5} = 1.399$

    Fixed asset turnover $\quad \dfrac{\$8,935}{\left(\dfrac{\$3,137 + \$2,287}{2}\right)} = \dfrac{\$8,935}{\$2,712} = 3.2946$

    b. **In a written explanation, describe what each of these ratios means.** The *inventory turnover ratio* means that inventory is used up on the average of 5.44 times per year in 2008 or every 67 days. *Total asset turnover* indicates that for each dollar of assets committed, they generated $1.399 in sales in 2008. *Fixed asset turnover* indicates that for each dollar of fixed assets, Moderately Large Corporation generated $3.29 in sales in 2008. This indicates that for the assets committed, both total and fixed, a sufficient amount of sales is being generated.
    c. **In a brief paragraph, describe how well you believe the MLC is managing its assets.** The student paragraph should incorporate the data from both a and b.

12. Library assignment, no definitive answer.

14. **The Namleda Corporation has an income statement that indicates that operating income is $2,375,486 and pays interest of $100,000 and taxes of $900,000. The corporation currently has an average of 3 million shares of common stock outstanding and 1 million shares of preferred stock, which pays a dividend of $1.00 per share. What is the corporation's approximate earnings per share?**

$$\text{EPS} = \dfrac{\$1,375,486 - \$1,000,000 \text{ preferred stock dividend}}{3,000,000 \text{ shares of common stock}}$$

$$= \dfrac{\$375,486}{3,000,000 \text{ shares}}$$

$$\text{EPS} = \$0.1252 \text{ per share}$$

CHAPTER 5

2. a. Jim is more efficient because he gets a higher return on his money.

   b. They are both effective because each one got the desired return.

4. a.

Revenues	$150,000
Expenses	110,000
Profit	$ 40,000

   b. Maury was earning $40,000 with the accounting firm, so entrepreneurial profit is zero.

6. They can try to declare Chapter 11 bankruptcy, but chances are that they will be denied because they have nothing of value to sell. In this instance, they will probably be forced into Chapter 7 bankruptcy and will have to sell any assets of the corporation in order to satisfy their debt. The good news is that they incorporated, so they do not face personal bankruptcy because only the assets of the corporation will be sold to pay off creditors' claims. (*Note:* With a small corporation, often the owners must personally guarantee notes and loans. If this is the case, then the two engineers are personally liable for the $150,000 loan.)

8. a. CM = 1 − 0.65 = 0.35, or 35 percent.

   b. Total fixed costs are $3,350, which is $1,500 + $500 + $100 + $1,250.

   $BE = FC \div$ Contribution margin $= \$3,350 \div 0.35 = \$9,571.43.$

   c. $BE +$ Profit $= (\$3,350 + \$2,000) \div 0.35 = \$15,285.71.$

   d. Break-Even Chart

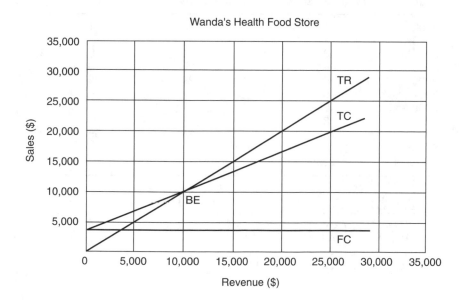

10. a. CM = $70

   b. BEQ = 286 skateboards

c. BE\$ = 286 skateboards × \$160 = \$45,760, or with the formula,

$$BE\$ = \frac{FC}{1 - VC} = \frac{\$20,000}{1 - \left(\dfrac{\$90}{\$160}\right)} = \frac{\$20,000}{0.4375} = \$45,714.29$$

d. BEQ = 429 skateboards

e. Monthly revenue = \$64,000

CHAPTER 6

2. a. He should use demographic information on the new community and compare it to the information for his existing health-club members. He needs information on traffic patterns, rent, utilities, and other factors that affect general operating expenses. He should then compare those numbers to his current successful clubs. He wants sites that compare favorably with his current sites.

b. He should use a judgmental model, but specifically a historical analogy to determine the specific site. Market research should also be used to determine if the new community's residents have the same general demographic characteristics as his current customers.

4. a.

Table for Problem 4

Year	Time Period (x)	Actual Demand (y)	x^2	xy
2002	1	23	1	23
2003	2	24	4	48
2004	3	31	9	93
2005	4	28	16	112
2006	5	29	25	145
2007	6			
2008	7			
2009	8			
Σ =	15	135	55	421
Slope =	1.6			
Intercept =	22.2			

$$a = \frac{\sum x^2 \sum y - \sum x \sum xy}{n\sum x^2 - \left(\sum x\right)^2} = \frac{(55)(135) - (15)(421)}{5(55) - (15)^2} = \frac{1,110}{50} = 22.2$$

$$b = \frac{n\sum xy - \sum x \sum y}{n\sum x^2 - \left(\sum x\right)^2} = \frac{5(421) - (15)(135)}{5(55) - (15)^2} = \frac{80}{50} = 1.6$$

$$y = 22.2 + 1.6x$$

b. $y = a + bx = 22.2 + 1.6(8) = 35$

c. year expressed as a time period

d. demand

6.

Time Period	Actual Sales ($000)	Weighted Moving Average Forecast	Absolute Deviation
1	$445		
2	478		
3	525		
4	660	$497.06	$162.94
5	570	588.18	18.18
6	600	588.53	11.47
7	632	601.76	30.24
8	648	611.65	36.35
9	690	634.82	55.18
10	725	667.41	57.59
11	750	701.12	48.88
12		732.06	
Sum			$420.82
n			$ 8.00
MAD			$ 52.60

a. $732.06

b. $52.60

8. a. Income Statement

Income Statement for Current and Next Year		
	Actual (This Year)	*Pro Forma (Next Year)*
Sales	$200,000	$240,000
COG	140,000	168,000
Gross Profit	$ 60,000	$ 72,000
Operating Expenses		
Rent	18,000	18,540
Utilities	8,400	9,240
Insurance	2,000	2,400
Equipment	3,500	3,500
Total Operating Expenses	$ 31,900	$ 33,680
Operating Profit	$ 28,100	$ 38,320
Interest Expense	10,000	9,000
Net Profit (income)	$ 18,100	$ 29,320

b. Percentage change $= \dfrac{N - O}{O} \times 100 = \dfrac{29{,}320 - 18{,}100}{18{,}100} \times 100$

$= 61.99\%$

c. Profit margin $= \dfrac{\text{Net income}}{\text{Sales}}$

Profit margin (current year) $= \dfrac{\$18{,}000}{\$200{,}000} = 0.0900$, or 9.00%

Profit margin (next year) $= \dfrac{\$29{,}320}{\$240{,}000} = 0.1222$, or 12.22%

d.
$$\Delta \text{Sales}\left(\frac{\text{Assets}}{\text{Sales}}\right) - \Delta \text{Sales}\left(\frac{\text{Liabilities}}{\text{Sales}}\right) - (S2)(P)(1 - \text{Owner payment})$$
$$= \text{Required financing} = \$40{,}000(0.80) - \$40{,}000(0.55)$$
$$- (\$240{,}000)(0.1222)(1) = -\$19{,}328 \text{ Required financing}$$

Because this figure is negative, the business does not require any external financing; it has financed any buildup in assets internally. (*Note:* If the owner drew $20,000, he would need some external financing, because there would not be enough money from internal financing to cover the shortfall.)

10. a.

Pro Forma Cash Budget

Monthly Cash Receipts (in $)

	November	December	January	February	March
Sales	$15,000	$17,000	$15,000	$20,000	$25,000
Current month collection at 20% of sales	3,000	3,400	3,000	4,000	5,000
Outstanding current month accounts receivable	$12,000	$13,600	$12,000	$16,000	$20,000
60% of AR collected month following sale		7,200	8,160	7,200	9,600
40% of AR collected second month following sale			$4,800	$5,440	$4,800
Total receipts			$15,960	$16,640	$19,400

Monthly Cash Payments

	November	December	January	February	March
Estimated cash payments			$4,500	$5,500	$5,200
Total payments			4,500	5,500	5,200

Monthly Cash Budget

	November	December	January	February	March
Total receipts			$15,960	$16,640	$19,400
Total payments			4,500	5,500	5,200
Net cash flow			$11,460	$11,140	$14,200

b. We have 40 percent of February accounts receivable of $16,000, or $6,400, plus 100 percent of March accounts receivable of $20,000, for a total accounts receivable of $26,400.

c. No, because all of the cash budgets have a positive balance.

12. (*Note:* If you use a calculator or Excel and do not round, you will obtain $6,036.36 rather than $6,037.50. In any event, new financing is required because the solution is positive.)

$$\Delta \text{Sales}\left(\frac{\text{Assets}}{\text{Sales}}\right) - \Delta \text{Sales}\left(\frac{\text{Liabilities}}{\text{Sales}}\right) - (S2)(P)(1 - \text{Owner payout}) = \text{Required financing}$$

$$(\$400,000 - \$275,000)\left(\frac{\$59,788}{\$275,000}\right) - (\$400,000 - \$275,000)\left(\frac{\$37,708}{\$275,000}\right) - (\$400,000)$$

$$(0.10)(1 - .90) = \text{Required financing}$$

$$(\$125,000)(0.2174) - (\$125,000)(0.1371) - (\$4,000) = \text{Required financing}$$

$$\$27,175 - \$17,137.50 - \$4,000 = \$6,037.50 \text{ Required financing}$$

CHAPTER 7

2. $i = \text{PRT} = (\$50,000)(.05)\left(\dfrac{30}{365}\right) = \$205.48$

4. **a.** The total annual cost to Jane is $50 per month times 12 months for equipment and bank charges, or $600.

 b. She would save $590 in bad-check losses. She would also earn (0.03) (1/365) = 0.0001 daily interest times 115 days' worth of interest times $2,000 average checking deposit; and she makes an additional $18.90 in interest. Therefore, the benefits are $608.90 and the costs are $600.

 c. With this problem, it is a toss-up. Would she lose some customers by not accepting checks and accepting only debit cards? If she lost just one customer whose checks were good as a result of this new policy, her costs of $600 would definitely outweigh her benefits. However, she gets paid immediately and has the use of the money.

6. Accounts receivable turnover = 4; collection days = 91.25, or 92. With net 30, he is collecting in 92 days. He should age accounts receivable and determine if some accounts are uncollectable or must be turned over to a collection agency.

8. **a.** 290.3069, or, rounded up, 291.

 b. Because the EOQ is greater than 200 hammers, we would order the EOQ and take advantage of the quantity discount.

10. **a.** Roses and carnations make up approximately 75 percent of our total cost of inventory. They are the A items.

 b. C items that make up approximately 10 percent of our total cost are bud vases, glass bowls, wrapping paper, ribbons, and pins.

12. **a.** 2 percent discount if paid within 10 days; otherwise, the entire amount is due within 30 days.

 b. 3 percent discount if paid within 15 days; otherwise, the entire amount is due within 60 days.

    c. The entire amount is due by the fortieth day.

    d. For 2/10 *n* 30, 36.72 percent; for 3/15 *n* 60, 24.72 percent, and no effective rate for *c*.

14. a. $20,566.66

    b. $21,423.60

    c. 100 percent

CHAPTER 8

2. **Joe Jones went to his bank to find out how long it will take for $1,000 to amount to $1,350 at 9 percent simple interest. Solve Joe's problem.**

$$t = \frac{i}{pr} = \frac{\$350}{(\$1,000)(0.09)} = 3.89 \text{ years}$$

4. **The Smiths purchase a $600,000 house and must sell their old home in order to make a 20 percent down payment plus closing costs of $7,000 on the new house. The Smiths have only $50,000 in savings, which they use as part of the down payment on the new house. Currently, they have a mortgage balance of $100,000 on their old home, which has been appraised at $300,000. They have been pre-approved by the lender to qualify for a $480,000 mortgage in the new home. The lender offers a bridge loan at 10 percent simple interest. The closing date on the new house is February 13, and the Smiths sell their old home on May 15.**

    a. **How much cash must the Smiths put down on their new house?** They must put down 20 percent of $600,000, which is $120,000, plus $7,000 closing costs, for a total of $127,000.

    b. **How much equity do the Smiths have in their old house?** They have $200,000 in equity, which is $300,000 appraisal minus the $100,000 mortgage.

    c. **How much must they borrow if they take a bridge loan?** They must borrow $77,000, which is the $127,000 cash that they need minus the $50,000 that they have in savings.

    d. **What is the dollar amount of interest paid on the bridge loan?** Daily interest is calculated at $77,000 times 10 percent, which is $7,700 ÷ 12 months equals monthy interest of $641.67. Divide $641.67 by 30 days to get daily interest of $21.39. There are 15 days left in February (28 − 13), 31 days in March, 30 days in April, and 15 days in May, for a total of 91 days interest multiplied by the daily rate of $21.39 equals $1,946.49 total interest due on the bridge loan. The total payment is $78,946.49.

6. **Alana Olsen borrowed $5,000 for 90 days from First Bank. The bank discounted the note at 10 percent.**
   a. **What proceeds did Olsen receive?**

   $$D = Sdt = (\$5,000)(0.10)\left(\frac{90}{365}\right) = \$123.29$$

   Proceeds $= \$5,000 - \$123.29 = \$4,876.71$

   b. **What is the effective rate, to the nearest basis point?**

   $$ER = \left[\frac{\$123.29}{\$4,876.71\left(\frac{90}{365}\right)}\right] = 0.1025 = 10.25\%$$

8. **You deposit $760 in an account that compounds monthly at 6 percent. How much do you have in your account at the end of 10 years?** This is a future value of a lump-sum question, which is solved as follows: There are 120 months in 10 years, so the future value of a lump-sum formula is: $FV = PV(1 + i)^n$. Therefore,

   $$FV = 760\left(1 + \frac{.06}{12}\right)^{120} = 760(1.8194) = 1,382.74$$

   Or we could use Appendix B, Table B–1.

10. **A financial institution quotes a rate of 6.45 percent compounded monthly. What is the effective rate for the year?**
    This is an effective rate problem and uses the formula

    $$ER = (1 + i)^n - 1 = \left(1 + \frac{0.0645}{12}\right)^{12} - 1 = (1.0054)^{12} - 1$$

    $$= 1.0664 - 1 = 0.0664 = 6.64\%$$

12. **Inflation averages 4 percent per year. How much purchasing power will $1.00 lose in 10 years?** In this problem, you are finding the present value of a dollar 4 years from now; the formula is

    $$PV = FV\left[\frac{1}{(1 + i)^n}\right]$$

    $PV = \$1(0.6756) = 68$ cents is the approximate value of the dollar; therefore, the dollar lost 32 cents in purchasing power.

14. **You deposit the following, at the beginning of each year, into a growth mutual fund that earns 6 percent per year. How much should the fund be worth at the end of 5 years?**

Annual Interest = 6.00%			
Year	Deposit	FV Factor	Future Value
1	$5,000,00	1.3382	$6,691.13
2	7,500.00	1.2625	9,468.58
3	4,500.00	1.1910	5,359.57
4	5,500.00	1.1236	6,179.80
5	6,200.00	1.0600	6,572.00
	$28,700.00		$34,271.08

16. **Bylo Selhi wants to know how many years it will take for his mutual investment fund of $50,000 to reach $500,000 if his mutual fund pays an average of 12 percent per year.** This is a future value of a lump-sum problem, with $500,000 as the future value, $50,000 as the lump sum, and 12 percent as the annual interest rate. A programmable calculator produces the answer: 20.317 years.

18. **Felice Navidad purchases 2,000 shares of a stock in NOW Technology at $4 in Christmas 2005. Four years later, Christmas 2009, she sells the stock for $28 a share. What is Felice's internal rate of return?**

$$IRR = \left(\sqrt{\frac{FV}{PV}} - 1 \right) \times 100 = \left[\sqrt{\frac{(2,000)(\$28)}{(2,000)(\$4)}} - 1 \right] \times 100$$

$$= \left(\sqrt[4]{\frac{\$56,000}{\$8,000}} - 1 \right) \times 100 = \left(\sqrt[4]{7} - 1 \right) \times 100$$

$$= (1.6266 - 1) \times 100 = 0.6266 \times 100 = 62.66\%$$

20. **Rochelle Kotter wants to attend a university 5 years from now. She will need $88,000. Assume Rochelle's bank pays 6 percent interest compounded monthly. What must Rochelle deposit today to get $88,000 in 5 years?**

$$PV = FV(PVF)$$

$$= \$88,000 \left[\frac{1}{\left(1 + \frac{0.06}{12} \right)^{(5 \times 12)}} \right] = \$88,000 \left(\frac{1}{1.3489} \right)$$

$$= \$88,000(0.7414) = \$65,240.75$$

22. **Mr. N. invests $5,000 in a cetificate of deposit (CD) at his local bank. He receives 8 percent compounded annually for 7 years. How much interest does his investment earn during this time period?**

$$FVLS = PV(FVF) = PV(1 + i)^n = \$5,000(1.08)^7$$

$$= \$5,000(1.7138) = \$8,569.12$$

$$\text{Interest earned} = FV - PV = \$8,569.12 - \$5,000.00$$
$$= \$3.569.12$$

CHAPTER 9

2. **The city of Glendale borrows $48 million by issuing municipal bonds to help build the Arizona Cardinals football stadium. It plans to set up a sinking fund that will repay the loan at the end of 10 years. Assume a 4 percent interest rate per year. What should the city place into the fund at the end of each year to have $48 million in the account to pay back their bondholders?**

This is a future value of an ordinary annuity problem. The formula is

$$FVOA = A\left[\frac{(1 + i)^n - 1}{i}\right]$$

$$\$48,000,000 = A\left[\frac{(1 + 0.04)^{10} - 1}{0.04}\right]$$

$$\$48,000,000 = A(12.0061)$$

$$A = \frac{\$48,000,000}{12.0061} = \$3,997,965.33$$

Therefore, the city should place $3,997,965.33 into the sinking fund at the end of each year. With interest compounded yearly, it will accrue to $48 million at the end of 10 years.

4. **Calculate the monthly mortgage payment made at the beginning of each month on a $100,000 mortgage. The mortgage is for 15 years and the interest rate is 5.5 percent.**

This is also a present value of an ordinary annuity because a mortgage is a bank loan. However, we are solving for the annuity and the mortgage is the present value.

$$PVOA = A\left[\frac{(1 + i)^n - 1}{i(1 + i)^n}\right]$$

$$\$100,000 = A\left[\frac{\left(1 + \dfrac{0.055}{12}\right)^{(12 \times 15)} - 1}{\dfrac{0.055}{12}\left(1 + \dfrac{0.055}{12}\right)^{(12 \times 15)}}\right]$$

$$A = \frac{\$100,000}{122.3865} = \$817.08$$

Therefore, your monthly mortgage payment is $817.08, not counting taxes and insurance.

6. **Tom and Mary James just had a baby. They heard that the cost of providing a college education for this baby will be $100,000 in 18 years. Tom normally receives a Christmas bonus of $4,000 every year in the paycheck prior to Christmas. He read that a good stock mutual fund should pay him an average of 10 percent per year. Tom and Mary want to make sure their son has $100,000 for college. Consider each of the following questions.**

a. **How much must Tom invest in this mutual fund at the end of each year to have $100,000 in 18 years?** This is a sinking fund problem, which uses Appendix B, Table B–3, which is an ordinary annuity. The formula is

$$FVOA = A\left[\frac{(1 + i)^n - 1}{i}\right] = A(\text{future value annuity factor})$$

$$A = \frac{FV}{\left[\dfrac{(1.10)^{18} - 1}{0.10}\right]} = \frac{\$100,000}{45.5992} = \$2,193.02$$

b. **If the bonus is not paid until the first of the year, how much must Tom invest at the beginning of each year to have $100,000 in 18 years?** Because the bonus is not paid until the first of the year, the problem becomes a future value of an annuity due for 18 years. The problem is that we actually have one less payment, but the number of periods is 18. The eighteenth payment is paid in the beginning of the eighteenth year.

$$FVAD = A\left\{\left[\frac{(1 + i)^{(n+1)} - 1}{i}\right] - 1\right\}$$

$$\$100,000 = A\left\{\left[\frac{(1 + 0.10)^{(18+1)} - 1}{0.10}\right] - 1\right\}$$

$$\$100,000 = A(50.1591)$$

$$A = \frac{\$100,000}{50.1591} = \$1,993.66$$

c. **Tom's father said he would provide for his grandson's education. He will put $10,000 in a government bond that pays 7 percent interest. His dad said this should be enough. Do you agree?** No, because he will only have $33,799 instead of $100,000. This is a future value of a lump sum, Appendix B, Table B–1. The formula is

$$FV = PV(1 + i)^n = \$10,000(1.07)^{18} = \$10,000(3.3799) = \$33,799$$

d. **If Mary has a savings account worth $50,000, how much must she withdraw from savings and set aside in this mutual fund to have the $100,000 for her son's education in 18 years?** Mary is going to take money out of her savings account and set it aside in the mutual fund that will grow to $100,000. This is the present value of a lump-sum problem as shown in Appendix B, Table B–2. The formula is

$$PV = FV\left[\frac{1}{(1 + i)^n}\right] = 100{,}000\left[\frac{1}{(1.10)^{18}}\right] = \$100{,}000(0.1799) = \$17{,}985.88$$

If the table is used, the answer is $17,990, but if a calculator is used, the answer is as shown. This problem was inserted to show the student that there are several options that a family has with regard to saving for a child's education. We used a family situation and provided several separate scenarios.

e. **If Mary has been advised to keep the $50,000 in her savings account earning 4 percent compounded monthly, how much additional money must she set aside in the stock mutual fund to have the $100,000 for her son's education in 18 years?**

$$FV = PV(1 + i)^n = \$50{,}000\left(1 + \frac{0.04}{12}\right)^{(12\times 18)}$$

$$= \$50{,}000(1.0033)^{216} = \$50{,}000(2.0520) = \$102{,}598.73$$

Mary doesn't have to set aside any money out of her savings for her mutual fund. Her savings account, which is a conservative investment, will generate more than the $100,000 ($102,598.73) needed for her son's college education.

8. **Regarding question 7b, if Sam believes he will earn 10 percent on his investment for retirement, how much does he have to contribute to his retirement account at the beginning of each year to accumulate his retirement nest egg?** Sam needs $875,405.23 in his account when he retires 30 years from now (he is now 30 and plans to retire at 60). We want to determine the amount of payment made in the beginning of each year for the next 30 years that will allow Sam to reach $875,405.23. This is a future value of an annuity due problem, as shown in Appendix B, Table B–4. The formula is

$$FV = A\left\{\left[\frac{(1 + i)^{(n+1)} - 1}{i}\right] - 1\right\}$$

$$\$875{,}405.23 = A\left\{\left[\frac{(1.10)^{(31)} - 1}{0.10}\right] - 1\right\}$$

$$A = \frac{\$875{,}405.23}{180.9434} = \$4{,}838.00$$

In this case, the formula and calculator provide the same answer.

10. **You like to buy lottery tickets every week. The lottery pays an insurance company that pays the winner an annuity. If you win a $1 million lottery and elect to take an annuity, you get $50,000 per year at the beginning of each year for the next 20 years.**

a. **How much must the state pay the insurance company if money can earn 6 percent?** For this problem, the state pays the insurance company the present value of $50,000 per year to be received in the beginning of each year for the next 20 years. Therefore, we are using the present value of an annuity due, as shown in Appendix B, Table B–6. The formula is

$$PVAD = A\left\{\left[\frac{(1+i)^{(n-1)} - 1}{i(1+1)^{n-1}}\right] + 1\right\}$$

$$= \$50,000\left\{\left[\frac{(1.06)^{19} - 1}{0.06(1.06)^{19}}\right] + 1\right\}$$

$$PVAD = \$50,000(12.1581) = \$607,905.82$$

The answer was calculated as $607,905.82. If you use the table, the answer is $607,905.

b. **How much interest is earned on this lump-sum payment over the 20 years?** The total of the payments is $1 million and the present value is $607,905.82. The difference is interest earned, which is $392,094.18.

c. **If you take the cash, rather than the annuity, the state pays you $500,000 in one lump sum today. You must pay 40 percent of this in taxes. If you are currently working and invest this money at 6 percent, how much money will you have in a mutual fund at the end of 20 years?** You will have $300,000 to invest, because you pay taxes of $200,000, which is the 40 percent of $500,000. We now have a future value of a lump-sum problem, as shown in Appendix B, Table B–1, with $300,000 being the lump sum. The formula is

$$FV = PV(1 + i)^n = \$300,000(1.06)^{20} = \$300,000(3.2071)$$

$$= \$962,140.64$$

d. **Are you better off with the annuity or should you take the cash? Explain.** We (the authors) advise taking the annual annuity of $50,000, as you will receive $1 million over 20 years versus having to wait 20 years to receive $962,140.64.

12. **Blushing Rose invests $1,000 into her Roth IRA. She can increase this investment annually by $1,000 until she reaches the $5,000 annual contribution limit. She can then invest $5,000 per year at the beginning of each year for 30 years. How much will**

Blushing have in her IRA at the end of 34 years if her IRA earns 8 percent?

	Annual Interest Rate = 8.00%			
	Compounds per Year = 1			
Contribution Year	Years to Retirement	Annual Contribution	Future Value Factor	Future Value
1	34	$1,000.00	13.6901	$ 13,690.13
2	33	2,000.00	12.6760	25,352.10
3	32	3,000.00	11.7371	35,211.25
4	31	4,000.00	10.8677	43,470.68
Years 5–34	30	5,000.00	113.2832	566,416.06
Total Lump-Sum Value				$684,140.22

Future Value of a
Lump Sum = $PV(FVF)$ FVF (future value factor) $= (1 + i)^n$

Future Value of an Ordinary Annuity Formula $FV = A(FVAF) = A\left[\dfrac{(1 + i)^n - 1}{i}\right]$

CHAPTER 10

2. $130.00

4. $WACC = (0.05)\left(\dfrac{\$3,000}{\$15,000}\right) + (0.00)\left(\dfrac{\$12,000}{\$15,000}\right)$

$= (0.05)(0.20) + 0 = 0.0100 = 1\%$

6.

Year	Amount	PVF	PV
1	$21,000	0.9091	$19,090.91
2	29,000	0.8264	23,966.94
3	36,000	0.7513	27,047.33
4	16,000	0.6830	10,928.22
5	8,000	0.6209	4,967.37
			$ 86,000.77

a. $86,000.77

b. $20,000.77

c. $\left|\dfrac{?}{i_1 - i_2}\right| = \left|\dfrac{\text{Partial distance } (20\% \ PV\$ - xPV\$)}{\text{Total distance } (20\% \ PV\$ - 25\%PV\$)}\right|$

$\left|\dfrac{?}{20 - 25}\right| = \left|\dfrac{\$69,403.29 - \$66,000.00}{\$69,403.29 - \$66,967.04}\right|$

$\dfrac{?}{5} = \dfrac{\$3,403.29}{\$6,436.25}$

$$? = \frac{(5)(\$3,403.29)}{\$6,436.25} = \frac{\$17,016.45}{\$6,436.25} = 2.6438\%$$

$$IRR = 20\%; + ? = 20\%; + 2.6438\% \approx 22.64\%$$

d. Payback = Time for annual cash flows to equal the cost of investment ($66,000)

Payback = 1st year ($21,000) + 2nd year ($29,000)

$$+ \left(\frac{16,000}{36,000}\right) \text{of 3rd year} = 2.44 \text{ years}$$

e. $PI = \dfrac{\text{Present value of benefits}}{\text{Present value of costs}} = \dfrac{\$86,000.77}{\$66,000} = 1.30$

8. a. $300

b.

Cost of Capital = 8.00%			
Item	Cost	PV Factor	Present Value
Install cable	$ 200.00	1	$ 200.00
Computer	5,100.00	1	5,100.00
Cable usage fee	50.00	40.9619	2,048.10
			$7,348.10

c. $PVOA + PVLS$

$$PVOA = (75)(500)(PVF)$$

$$= (375)(56.3499)$$

$$= 15,360.78$$

$$PVLS = FV(PVF) = 1,000(0.7350) = 735$$

$$= 15,360.78 + 735 = \$16,095.78$$

d. $PVOA = A (PVF)$

$$5,000 = A (40.9619)$$

$$A = 122.06$$

10. a. No. Payback is 4 years.

b. $PV = A\left[\dfrac{(1 + i)^n - 1}{i(1 + i)^n}\right] = \$4,000\left[\dfrac{(1 + 0.10)^5 - 1}{0.10(1 + 0.10)^5}\right]$

$$PV = \$4,000(3.7908) = \$15,163.15$$

c. $16,000

d. No, because it's negative.

$$NPV = PVB = PVC = \$15,163.15 - \$16,000 = -\$836.85$$

e. Don't buy, because it is less than 1.

$$PI = \frac{PVB}{PVC} = \frac{\$15,163.15}{\$16,000} = 0.9477$$

f. No. Cost of capital is 10 percent.

$$IRR \text{ factor} = \frac{\$16,000}{\$4,000} = 4.00$$

$$\left| \frac{?}{i_1 - i_2} \right| = \left| \frac{\text{Partial distance (7\% } PVAF - x\% \, PVAF)}{\text{Total distance (7\% } PVAF - 8)\% \, PVAF} \right|$$

$$\left| \frac{?}{7 - 8} \right| = \left| \frac{(4.1002 - 4.000)}{(4.1002 - 3.9927)} \right|$$

$$\frac{?}{1} = \frac{0.1002}{0.1075}$$

$$? = \frac{(1)(0.1002)}{0.1075} = 0.9321$$

$$IRR = i_1 + ? = 7\% + 0.9321\% \approx 7.93\%$$

g. Yes.

$$ARR = \frac{\text{Period cash flow}}{\text{Total cost}} = \frac{\$4,000}{\$16,000} = .25, \text{ or } 25\%$$

12. a. $4,800

b.
$$PVOA = A\left[\frac{(1 + i)^n - 1}{i(1 + i)^n} \right]$$

$$\$16,000 = A\left[\frac{\left(1 + \dfrac{0.055}{12}\right)^{60} - 1}{\left(\dfrac{0.055}{12}\right)\left(1 + \dfrac{0.055}{12}\right)^{60}} \right]$$

$$\$16,000 = A(52.3528)$$

$$A = \frac{\$16,000}{52.3528} = \$305.62$$

c. $67,218.40
d. $104.435.42
e. $67,218.40
f. 1.55
g. 2.2098 years
h. Recommend, because it is profitable.

14. **a.** 8 stores

    b. 21 stores, but only 15 have positive NPVs.

CHAPTER 11

2. **a.** The proposal would be for the city to issue general revenue municipal bonds.

    b. Interest payments made on municipal bonds are exempt from federal income tax. Because the bonds are being issued by the city, the interest is also free from state and local income taxes.

4. **a.** Because Sarah is young, she should definitely invest in mutual funds. She must evaluate her own tolerance for risk. However, at her age, she may have a relatively high tolerance for risk. We advise a diversified mutual fund portfolio, with a percentage of her money going into an aggressive growth (small-cap stock) fund, some in a long-term growth (blue-chip stock) fund, and some in a global fund. She may also consider a balanced fund as well as sector funds.

    b. Grandpa Russ is 70 years old, and typically individuals at that time in their lives have a very low risk tolerance. He is primarily interested in protecting his principal and minimizing his risk, a strategy best served by government bonds, government bond mutual funds, and CDs. Uncle Sam is 55, and probably still has 7 to 10 years to invest before retirement. He is looking toward a conservative growth strategy by investing in U.S. blue-chip stocks. Jane is 30 years old and has many years remaining before she retires. She obviously has a high tolerance for risk and invests in small-cap (aggressive) growth mutual funds.

6. In order to invest in the Savings Incentive Match Plan for Employees (SIMPLE), he must have fewer than 100 employees, and each employee must have received at least $5,000 in employee compensation in each of the previous 2 years. The company must match, dollar for dollar, the employee's contribution up to 3 percent of salary, or put in 2 percent of salary for all eligible employees, even if they do not contribute. Each employee's contribution limit is $10,500 for 2007 through 2008. If the employee is 50 or older, the limit is $12,500.

8. **a.** He tells Larry to establish the will because he doesn't want him to die intestate. The estate planner wants Larry to have a written document to indicate Larry's wishes with regard to the disposition of his assets on his death.

    b. We recommend that Larry put his assets into a revocable living trust. Because assets in a trust do not have to go through probate, money is saved for his heirs—probate costs are a percentage of the gross estate.

10. $PVOA = A\left[\dfrac{(1 + i)^{(n)} - 1}{i(1 + i)^n}\right] = \$40\left[\dfrac{\left(1 + \dfrac{0.07}{2}\right)^{(20)} - 1}{\left(1 + \dfrac{0.07}{2}\right)^{(20)}}\right]$

$PVOA = \$40(14.2124) = \$568.50$

$PVLS = FV\left[\dfrac{1}{(1 + i)^n}\right] = \$1,000\left[\dfrac{1}{(1.035)^{20}}\right] = \$502.57$

Price $= \$568.50 + \$502.57 = \$1,071.07$

12. 3 million shares

14. **a.** $24
   b. $2,400,000
   c. 52 cents
   d. $2,600,000

16. **a.** She could borrow $8,000, but she would borrow only $7,000 plus the $90 commission.
   b. $35 per share profit, or $35,000. After paying the broker $180 ($90 to buy and $90 to sell), her net profit is $34,820.
   c. She must pay the broker back the $7,000 plus the $90 commission.
   d. She lost her $8,000 investment plus $2,000, plus the commission to the broker, a total of $10,090.

18. $FVAD = \left\{A\left[\dfrac{(1 + i)^{(n+1)} - 1}{i}\right] - 1\right\}$

$= \$4,000\left\{\left[\dfrac{(1 + 10)^{41} - 1}{0.10}\right] - 1\right\}$

$= \$4,000(486.8518) = \$1,947,407.25$

Glossary

10-K *See* Form 10-K.

401k plans Retirement plans established to accept employee contributions through salary reductions. Employers may match a portion of the employee's contribution. The 401k is also a vehicle for distributing profit-sharing contributions.

503b *See* Tax-sheltered annuities.

Absolute deviation The difference between the actual amount and the forecasted amount is always expressed as a positive number. Represented mathematically by a vertical line on either side of the numbers (e.g., $|8 - 10| = 2$).

Absolute value The absolute value of any number is positive and is represented mathematically by two vertical lines drawn on either side of a number or equation. The absolute value of $|5 - 8|$ is 3.

Accelerated cost recovery system (ACRS) A U.S. depreciation schedule that covered items placed in use prior to January 1, 1987.

Accounting profit Is what a business has left from its revenues after paying all of its expenses. Is typically shown on the bottom of a business income statement.

Accounting rate of return (ARR) In capital budgeting, it is the rate of return on an investment that is found by dividing the average annual income by the average cost.

Accounts payable Are those debts of a business that are owed to vendors.

Accounts receivable A current asset carried on the balance sheet, which indicates the amount owed to our firm as a result of credit sales. The value of credit sales for which the money has not yet been collected.

Accounts receivable turnover A ratio that allows a business to determine how fast a company is turning its credit sales into cash. It states the number of times per year a company collects its accounts receivable. The formula is credit sales divided by average net accounts receivable.

Accrual method of accounting A method of accounting that recognizes revenue when earned and expenses when incurred.

Accrued liabilities The obligations of a firm that are accumulated during the usual course of business and are paid after the books are closed.

Accumulated depreciation The total depreciation (wearing allowance) that an asset has on a balance sheet, from the asset's acquisition until the asset is disposed of by the business.

Acid test ratio *See* Quick ratio.

Activity ratios Those ratios that indicate how efficiently a business is using its assets.

Additional paid in capital The equity contributions to a corporation in excess of the par value of common stock as shown on a corporate balance sheet.

Amortization The reduction of the loan balance by applying each month's principal payment.

Angel investors Investors who provide the seed money for the start-up and early stages of a company's growth.

Annuity A stream of the same payments paid or received over time.

Annuity due Payments made or received at the beginning of each time period.

Asset An item used or owned by an individual, business or corporation. For business assets normally generate revenue.

Average collection period A ratio that divides the number of days in a year by accounts receivable turnover and determines how many days, on average, it takes a company to collect its accounts receivable.

Balance sheet A financial statement that lists all assets, liabilities, and equity of a company or individual at a given point in time. The balance sheet uses the basic accounting equation: Assets = Liabilities + Owner's Equity.

Balanced mutual funds   Mutual funds that invest in both stocks and bonds. They provide both capital growth and fixed income.

Bank discount   An amount of interest deducted from the amount you wish to borrow. It is calculated by multiplying what you wish to borrow by the bank discount rate and the amount of time that the loan is in effect.

Bankruptcy   A state of insolvency in which the liabilities of a firm or individual exceed the assets and the firm or individual does not have sufficient cash flow to make payment to creditors.

Bankruptcy Abuse Prevention and Consumer Protection Act   A law that took effect October 17, 2005. It mainly focuses on consumers and Chapter 13 bankruptcy, but certain provisions involve commercial issues in cases involving Chapter 11 bankruptcy.

Bankruptcy, Chapter 7   *See* Chapter 7 bankruptcy.

Bankruptcy, Chapter 11   *See* Chapter 11 bankruptcy.

Bankruptcy, Chapter 13   *See* Chapter 13 bankruptcy.

Bond   A contractual agreement made between a borrower (government or corporation) and a lender (individual, pension fund, mutual fund, insurance company)

Bond, federal   *See* Federal bond.

Bond, municipal   *See* Municipal bond.

Book value   The value of a fixed asset on a company's books after depreciation has been accounted for. In addition, the value of a share of common stock based on the amount of common stockholder's equity divided by the number of outstanding shares of common stock.

Break-even analysis   A process of determining how many units of production must be sold or how much revenue must be obtained before a business begins to earn a profit.

Break-even chart   A graph used to visually depict total revenue, total cost, break even, and profit and loss in terms of sales volume.

Break-even dollars (BE$)   The dollar amount of revenue that equals the total cost. The formula is Fixed Costs ÷ 1 – Variable Costs (expressed as a percentage of net sales).

Break-even quantity   The number of units that must be produced in order to cover the total costs of production. The formula is Fixed Costs ÷ Sales Price – Variable Costs.

Bridge loan   A loan that a homeowner or business owner obtains when he or she wants to move up to a more expensive property, but has not yet sold the current home or business.

Buy and hold   A method of investing in which once purchased, the investment is held for a number of years.

Callable preferred stock   The preferred stock of a corporation that may be redeemed by the corporation at a specified price plus a premium.

Capacity   A term used in credit evaluation to determine whether a customer has enough cash flow or disposable income to pay back a loan or pay off a bill.

Capital asset   A plant, facility, equipment, machinery, or factory used in business to increase revenue or sales.

Capital budgeting   A method used by a business to justify the acquisition of those items that have a useful life of one year or more. Capital budgeting aids the decision maker by comparing the costs and benefits of a project.

Capital expenditure   The money spent to acquire or upgrade physical assets that include equipment, property, or industrial buildings.

Capital intensive   A business concern that has heavy investment in machinery and equipment and low labor costs as a percentage of its production costs.

Capital rationing   When a constraint is placed on the amount of funds that can be invested in a given time period.

Capital resources   Capital resources consist of economic capital and financial capital.

Cash discounts   A discount offered to credit customers as an incentive to get them to pay promptly. For example 2/10, *net* 30.

Cash equivalents   Are liquid assets that are invested in savings accounts or money market brokerage accounts.

Cash flow from financing activities   The section of a statement of cash flows that includes cash received from stocks or bonds, the actual cash paid to owners in the form of dividends, and the repayment of long-term debt.

Cash flow from investing activities   The section of a statement of cash flows that identifies all long-term investments made by a firm. It includes cash paid for the acquisitions and cash received from sales of investments.

Cash flow from operating activities   The first section of a statement of cash flows that identifies all operating sources and uses of cash.

Cash flow statement   *See* Statement of cash flows.

Causal models   Also known as *exogenous* or *external models,* they take into account variables in the general economy that affect the sales of a firm or industry. For example, housing starts would be the cause for increased sales of plumbing fixtures.

Certificate of deposit (CD)   Promissory notes issued primarily by banks in which the promisor (bank) agrees to pay the promisee (purchaser) the principal amount plus interest after a stipulated period of time.

Certified public accountant (CPA)   A public accountant who passed a rigorous examination administered by the American Institute of Certified Public Accountants and completed a work experience requirement (usually 2 years) prescribed by the state.

Ceteris paribus   A Latin phrase meaning "all else remains the same."

Chapter 7 bankruptcy   A form of bankruptcy that requires the company or individual to liquidate all of its assets and make payment to its creditors.

Chapter 11 bankruptcy   A form of bankruptcy in which a business seeks court protection while it develops a plan to pay off its creditors.

Chapter 13 bankruptcy   Reserved for individuals and sole proprietorships. It is similar to, but much simpler than, Chapter 11 bankruptcy. It also requires a plan to pay creditors. In Chapter 13 bankruptcy, creditors do not vote for a reorganization plan, but can object to the terms of the plan.

Character   Used in credit evaluation to determine if a customer has paid his or her bills on time in the past and has favorable credit references.

Collateral   Used in credit evaluation to determine the ability of a customer to satisfy a debt or pay a creditor by selling assets for cash. In finance and banking, collateral is the asset actually used to secure a loan.

Collectables   Items that have a tendency to appreciate in value over time because of their scarcity, such as coins, paintings, and sculptures.

Collections float   The amount of time that elapses between your depositing a debtor's check in your account and the check clearing the bank.

Commercial real estate   Land and improved property that is used by the owner to generate income.

Common stock   Stock issued by public or private corporations to raise financial capital. Stock is issued in shares, and each share represents ownership of the corporation.

Company goals   Where a business should be at some future date.

Company objectives   The milestones of progress markers used to see if a business is on track for reaching its goals.

Compound interest   The interest earned or charged on both the principal amount and on the accrued interest that has been previously earned. The formula is $FV = PV (1 + I)^n$.

Consumer price index (CPI)   A measure of inflation that represents a market basket of goods and services that the average American purchases each month.

Contribution margin   The amount of profit or loss realized by a company on each unit sold. Its formula is Price per Unit − Variable Cost per Unit.

Controlling   A three-step process that involves establishing standards, measuring performance against standards, and taking corrective action when necessary.

Convertible preferred stock   The preferred stock of a corporation that may be exchanged for shares of common stock.

Corporate bond   A bond issued by a public corporation that wants to borrow money to invest in assets that help it earn revenue.

Corporation (C corporation)   A form of business that is incorporated in one of the 50 states. Ownership is based on shares of stock or percentage of ownership. A corporation is a legal entity that may accomplish all of the tasks that can be accomplished by an individual.

Cost of goods sold (COGS)   Usually includes the cost of materials, direct labor, and overhead allocated specifically to the product.

Coupon rate   The stated rate or nominal rate of interest that is contractual and attached to a bond. The coupon payment is calculated by multiplying the coupon rate by the face amount of the bond.

Credit evaluation   A method of determining which customers are allowed to use credit based on established credit standards, such as character, capacity, and collateral.

Credit terms   The requirements that a business establishes for the payment of a loan (the use of credit by a customer).

Creditor   An individual, business firm, institution, or government that has money due presently or in the future.

Cumulative discounts   A discount offered by a vendor to a customer based on the total quantity purchased during the vendor's fiscal year.

Cumulative preferred stock   Preferred stock in which the owners receive back dividends for those years when a dividend was not paid by a corporation.

Current assets   Assets with a useful life of 1 year or less, such as cash, accounts receivable, and inventories.

Current liabilities   All obligations that a firm expects to pay off during the accounting year, such as accounts payable, notes payable, and taxes payable.

Current market interest rate   The prevailing rate in the market on the day we decide to sell a bond.

Current ratio   A liquidity ratio in which total current assets are divided by total current liabilities.

Cyclical variation   The variation in company sales as a result of economic cycles such as recessions and growth.

Debenture   A corporate bond that is not backed by the collateral of the company.

Debt ratios   *See* Leverage (debt) ratios.

Debt-to-equity ratio   A ratio that indicates what percentage of the owner's equity is debt. The formula is Total Liabilities ÷ Owner's Equity.

Debt-to-total-assets ratio   A ratio that indicates what percentage of a business' assets is owned by creditors. The formula is Total Liabilities ÷ Total Assets.

Degree of combined leverage (DCL)   The percentage change in sales that has a multiplier effect on the change in earnings per share.

Degree of financial leverage (DCL)   The percentage change in earnings per share as a result of the percentage change in operating income.

Degree of operating leverage (DCL)   The percentage change in operating income that occurs as a result of the percentage change in sales.

Delphi method   A qualitative forecasting method that uses a panel of experts to obtain a consensus of opinion.

Demand curve   A curve obtained by horizontally summing the quantity demanded at various prices in the marketplace.

Demand table   A table generated by determining how much of an item people are willing to purchase at various prices in the marketplace.

Dependent variable   A variable that relies on other variables for its value. In the formula $y = a + bx$, y is the dependent variable.

Depreciation   A dollar value assigned to the wearing out of a business asset during its useful life.

Directing (leading)   Leading and motivating employees to accomplish the goals of the business.

Disbursement float   The time that elapses between payment by check and the check actually clearing the bank.

Discount rate   The rate of interest that the Federal Reserve charges banks to borrow money from the Fed.

Discretionary income   The income remaining after paying taxes and fixed expenses such as rent and insurance.

Disposable income   The income remaining after paying federal, state, and city taxes. This income can either be spent (consumed) or saved.

Dividend   An after-tax payment that may be made by a corporation to a stockholder, usually declared by the board of directors of the company.

Dollar cost averaging   A method of investing by making regular systematic payments over time in order to take advantage of market fluctuations. It allows us to purchase an equal dollar amount of an investment at equal time intervals.

Earning power   The product of a company's ability to generate income on the amount of revenue it receives (net profit margin) and its ability to maximize sales revenue from proper asset employment (total asset turnover). The formula is Net Profit Margin ÷ Total Asset Turnover.

Earnings before taxes   A corporation's income before paying corporate taxes to the government; shown on corporate income statements.

Earnings per share   A corporation's earnings for each share of common stock outstanding. The formula is (Net Income − Preferred Dividends) ÷ The Weighted Average Number of Common Shares Outstanding.

Economic capital   Those items that humans manufacture by combining natural and human resources, and includes buildings, machinery, and equipment used by business and government. *Economic capital, physical capital,* and *fixed assets* are often used synonymously.

Economic order quantity (EOQ)   The quantity of items for a business to order that balances the ordering costs against the storage costs of inventory. The most economic quantity to order to minimize overall inventory costs.

EDGAR   *See* Electronic Data Gathering and Retrieval System (EDGAR).

Effective rate (Effective annual interest rate)   The rate of interest actually earned or charged when compounding is taken into consideration.

Effectiveness   Accomplishing a specific task or reaching a goal.

Efficiency   Obtaining the highest possible return with the minimum use of resources.

Electronic Data Gathering and Retrieval System (EDGAR)   A Securities and Exchange (SEC) computer filing system used by public corporations to file reports required by the SEC. The SEC provides the public with access to these corporate reports.

Electronic funds transfer (EFT)   A process used to transfer funds from one bank account to another immediately via computer.

Entrepreneur (Entrepreneurial resources)   An individual who assumes risk and begins business enterprises. The entrepreneur combines land, labor, and capital resources to produce a good or service that society values more highly than the sum of the individual parts.

Entrepreneurial profit   An amount earned above and beyond what the entrepreneur would have earned if he or she had chosen to invest time and money in some other enterprise. It is most closely related to the economic concept of opportunity cost.

Equilibrium   The point at which a supply curve and a demand curve for a market intersect.

Estate planning   A method of planning for use, conservation, and transfer of wealth as efficiently as possible. It is financial planning with the anticipation of eventual death.

Executive summary   The part of the business plan that investors review before they determine whether they want to read further.

Exponential smoothing forecasting model   A forecasting model that uses a smoothing constant α as an adjustment in determining the forecast. The assumption is that both the forecast of current period sales and actual sales can be used to predict future sales. The higher the value of α, the more emphasis that is placed on current period sales.

Face value   *See* Par value.

Factoring   The process of a business selling its accounts receivable to another firm at a discount off of the original sales price.

Federal bond   A bond issued by the Fed with maturities greater than 10 years and up to 30 years.

Federal funds rate   The interest rate that banks charge each other for overnight loans. The minimum amount of these loans is $1 million.

Federal Insurance Contribution Act (FICA) Taxes paid by a wage earner and a business to the federal government for Social Security and Medicare. Social Security tax is 6.20 percent for the wage earner and the business for a total of 12.4 percent on the first $102,000 of earned income in 2008. Medicare is 1.45 percent for the wage earner and 1.45 percent for the business, or a total of 2.90 percent on all earned income. The total FICA contribution can be as high as 15.30 percent.

Federal Reserve The central bank of the United States, often called the Fed. It is the banker's bank. The United States is divided into 12 districts, with each district having a Federal Reserve Bank.

Federal Treasury bills U.S. government bonds of 3-months, 6-months, and 1-year duration that are issued at a discount.

Finance Any transaction in which money or a money-like instrument is exchanged for money or a money-like instrument.

Financial Accounting Standards Board (FASB) An independent board responsible for establishing and interpreting Generally Accepted Accounting Principles (GAAP). Founded in 1973, it succeeded and continued the activities of the Accounting Principles Board (APB). It works in conjunction with the Securities and Exchange Commission (SEC).

Financial asset Assets such as stocks, bonds, or savings that may be used to increase revenue and acquire capital assets.

Financial capital A dollar value claim on economic capital. Financial capital may include cash, accounts receivable, stocks, or bonds.

Financial leverage Financing a company with other people's money.

Financial planning Financial planning consists of establishing monetary goals and developing methods and processes for achieving these goals.

Financial statement (personal form) A form required by a bank when one applies for a loan. Consists of two segments, a statement of financial position and a personal cash flow statement.

Finished goods The inventories that a company has that are actually sold by the business; also includes spare parts and repair parts.

Fixed asset turnover A ratio indicating how efficiently fixed assets are being used to generate revenue for the firm. The formula is Net Sales ÷ Average Fixed Assets.

Fixed assets (use assets) Assets that have a useful life of 1 year or more. *See* also Capital asset.

Fixed costs *See* Operating expenses (fixed costs).

Fixed expenses Expenses over which we have little or no control, such as mortgage payments, automobile loan or lease payments, property taxes, insurance, and income taxes.

Forecast A quantifiable estimate of the future.

Forecasting The process and procedures used to develop a forecast. In business, it is usually the process of estimating future demand for a business' products and services.

Form 10-K An annual report that most public corporations must file with the Securities and Exchange Commission (SEC). Form 10-K provides a comprehensive overview of the corporation's business. The report must be filed within 90 days after the end of the company's fiscal year and is filed electronically through EDGAR.

Franchise A business in which the buyer, who is the franchisee, purchases the rights to sell the goods and services of the seller, who is the franchiser.

Free cash flow per share Cash flow from operations minus capital expenditures divided by average common shares of stocks outstanding.

Functional planning Planning for a business driven by strategic planning and related to specific functional areas of our business such as personnel, finance, operations, and marketing.

Gantt chart A chart that uses time on its horizontal axis and tasks to be performed on its vertical axis. Developed by Henry Gantt and used extensively in business planning. Gantt charts are often generated by project management software programs.

General obligation bond A municipal bond used to build projects that do not usually generate revenue. The bondholder is paid on the taxing ability of the municipality.

General partner Is in charge of day-to-day operations and is personally liable for the partnership.

General revenue bond A municipal bond issued to build specific projects that use the income from the project to pay the bondholder.

Generally accepted accounting principles (GAAP) Rules, procedures, and guidelines that accounting follows as acceptable accounting practices.

Global and international mutual funds Invest in stocks and bonds of companies primarily outside of the United States.

Goal A measurable objective that can be reached in a specific time frame. All goals must be measurable, achievable, and have a time frame.

Gross income All money received from all sources during a year, including wages, tips, interest earned on savings and bonds, income from rental property, and profits to entrepreneurs.

Gross profit Determined by subtracting Cost of Goods Sold (COGS) from Net Sales.

Gross profit margin A ratio used to determine how much gross profit is generated by each dollar of net sales. The formula is Gross Profit ÷ Net Sales.

Gross working capital   The current assets of a business; consisting of cash, marketable securities, accounts receivable, and inventory.

Growth mutual funds   Mutual funds that invest primarily in corporate common stock with an investment goal of capital appreciation.

Historical analogy   A qualitative forecast that uses historic similarities to project the possible success or failure of new products or services.

Horizontal analysis   A process of determining the percentage increase or decrease in an account on a financial statement from a base time period to successive time periods.

Human resources (labor)   The mental and physical talents of humans.

Income mutual funds   Mutual funds that invest primarily in government and corporate bonds to provide the investor with stable income.

Income statement   A financial statement that shows what has happened to a business during a specific accounting period with regard to revenues and expenditures.

Independent variable   A variable that does not depend on other variables for its value. It is the actual observation of data. In the formula $y = a + bx$, x is the independent variable.

Individual retirement accounts (IRAs)   Retirement plans that allow one to contribute current annual income that have favorable tax treatment. They allow accumulation of tax-deferred benefits until withdrawal.

Inflation   An increase in the average price of goods. Most often measured by the Consumer Price Index (CPI).

Insurance   The transfer of risk to a third party for a premium.

Insurance, disability   The transfer of risk to an insurance company to provide income in the event an employee becomes disabled and is no longer able to work.

Insurance, health   The transfer of risk to an insurance company to alleviate the cost of an illness or a disability.

Insurance, liability   The transfer of risk to an insurance company to alleviate the cost of property damage and personal injury to others as a result of your action.

Insurance, life (whole life, universal life, term, variable)   The transfer of risk to an insurance company for a premium by one who has an insurable interest in the life of an individual. Life insurance can be purchased by a company, spouse, child, and so on.

Insurance, long-term care   An insurance policy that provides assistance for people who have a chronic illness or are disabled for an extended period of time.

Insurance, property   The transfer of risk to an insurance company for a premium by one who has an insurable interest in the property.

Interest   The rent charged for money borrowed or loaned. The premium paid to the supplier of funds by the user (demander) of funds.

Interest expense   Interest accrued during an accounting period on money borrowed by a company. Found on an income statement.

Internal rate of return (IRR)   The actual rate of return on an investment that takes into consideration the time value of money. It is that specific interest rate in which the present value of the benefits equals the present value of the cost. At the IRR, net present value (NPV) is equal to 0 and the profitability index (PI) is equal to 1.

Interpolation   The process of using mathematics to find an unknown value that lies between two known values.

Inventory   The items that a business has in stock that have not been sold.

Inventory turnover   A ratio used to indicate how efficiently a firm is moving its inventory, stated as how many times per year a firm moves its average inventory.

Invested assets   Those assets found on a statement of financial position that are marketable securities, such as stocks, bonds, and life insurance cash values. These items are usually listed on a business balance sheet under current assets.

Investment vehicle   Any item that allows one to attain an investment goal. Examples are stocks, bonds, savings accounts, real estate, and so on.

Irrevocable grantor trust (Rabbi Trust)   Established by employers for executives and key employees. With this form of trust, annual bonuses and other items of deferred income are placed into the trust.

Irrevocable trusts   A trust that cannot be changed by the grantor or trustees once it is established.

Judgmental models   Forecasting models that are qualitative and essentially use estimates based on expert opinion.

Junk bonds   A bond issued by a corporation or municipal government that is rated B or less and sold at a deep discount from the face amount ($1,000).

Keogh plan   A retirement plan for self-employed individuals in sole proprietorships and partnerships. Under the laws governing Keogh, a retirement plan can be established based on profit sharing, money purchase, or paired. The percentage and total contribution may differ depending on the type of Keogh plan selected.

Labor intensive   A business concern that has relatively low investment in machinery and equipment and relatively high labor costs as a percentage of its production costs.

Land   *See* Natural resources (land).

Law of demand   As the price of an item decreases, people will demand a larger quantity of that item, ceteris paribus.

Law of supply   As the payment for or price of an item increases, the quantity of the item supplied to the market will also increase, *ceteris paribus.*

Lead time   Time lapse from order placement to order receipt.

Leverage   The magnification of a return to a company by using fixed costs of operations and financing efficiently.

Leverage (debt) ratios   Ratios that indicate what percentage of the assets of a business actually belong to the owners and what percentage is subject to creditors' claims.

Leverage, degree of combined (DCL)   The percentage change in sales that has a multiplier effect on the change in earnings per share.

Leverage, degree of financial (DCL)   *See* Degree of financial leverage.

Leverage, degree of operating (DCL)   *See* Degree of operating leverage.

Leverage, financial   The percentage change in earnings per share that occurs as a result of the percentage change in operating income.

Leverage, operating   The percentage change in operating income that occurs as a result of the percentage change in sales.

Liabilities   That part of assets owed to others. Liabilities and debts are synonymous.

Limited liability company (LLC)   A hybrid business entity having features of both a partnership and a corporation. It is taxed as a partnership and its members enjoy limited liability like corporate shareholders.

Limited liability partnership (LLP)   A business entity in which all of the partners have limited liability and can participate in the day-to-day management of the company. It is not legal in all states.

Limited partner   An investor in a partnership who is not involved in day-to-day operations and whose liability is limited to the amount of his or her investment in the partnership.

Limited partnership   A partnership having one or more general partners and several limited partners.

Linear regression model   A time series forecasting model that uses a statistical method known as least squared regression. Regression models are typically used for intermediate and long-term forecasts.

Line of credit   A credit limit extended to a business that may be drawn on when required by the business. There are no payments due on the line of credit unless the business actually borrows the money.

Liquidity   A measure of how fast an asset can be converted into cash.

Liquidity ratios   A ratio that determines how much of a firm's current assets are available to meet short-term creditors' claims.

Living trust   A trust that is set up during the life of the trustor.

Load mutual funds   Mutual funds that charge a commission on the initial investment.

Lockbox   A post office box opened by an agent of the bank; checks received there are immediately deposited in a company account.

Long-term debt   The debt a company owes that it does not expect to pay during the current accounting year. Used synonymously with *long-term liabilities*. Found on the company's balance sheet.

Lowest total cost   A method of using time value of money by discounting future costs and benefits to determine the lowest total cost of a capital budgeting decision.

M1   *See* Money supply (M1).

M2   *See* Money supply (M2).

Maintenance, repair, and operating (MRO) supplies   The inventories of a firm used in normal operations and are not manufactured or sold by the firm.

Management   The process of working with or through others to achieve an individual or business goal by using resources efficiently and effectively.

Marginal   The last additional unit that one measures. The addition of one more unit of measurement.

Marginal cost   The cost of hiring one more unit of labor or the cost of producing one more unit of output.

Marginal physical product   The additional product that results from hiring one more unit of labor.

Marginal revenue product   The additional revenue a business obtains when it adds one more unit of labor. Can also be the additional revenue a business obtains when it adds one more machine or other fixed asset.

Market   Any organized effort through which buyers and sellers freely exchange goods and services.

Market ratios   Ratios used by investors to determine if they should invest capital in a company in exchange for ownership.

Market research   A qualitative method of forecasting that uses surveys, tests, and observations to project sales.

Market value   The value of a share of common stock that the investor is willing to pay in the marketplace. Also the value of any asset that an investor is willing to pay in the marketplace.

Marketable securities   Those investment vehicles that include U.S. Treasury bills, government and corporate bonds, and stock.

Marketing plan   The part of a business plan that describes how a business will move products or services from the producer to the consumer.

Master limited partnership   A variation of the limited partnership. Ownership interests are sold as ownership percentages that trade as shares on a stock exchange.

Maturity value   *See* Par value.

Mean absolute deviation (MAD)   A measure of how closely a forecasting model compares to actual data.

Medicare   *See* Federal Insurance Contribution Act (FICA).

Mission statement   A brief statement explaining the purpose of the company and its guiding principles.

Modified accelerated cost recovery system (MACRS)   A U.S. depreciation schedule that became effective for assets placed in use on or after January 1, 1987.

Monetary policy   Governmental action to change the supply of money to expand or contract economic activity.

Money market mutual funds   Mutual funds that invest primarily in short-term, highly liquid investments such as CDs, short-term government treasuries, commercial paper, repurchase agreements, and banker's acceptances. These funds are the mutual fund equivalent of a checking account.

Money purchase plans   A retirement plan that is a defined contribution plan established by an employer who contributes a fixed percentage of payroll into a retirement fund for employees. The employer must contribute each year even if the company does not make a profit.

Money supply (M1)   Money in circulation plus the money in checking accounts.

Money supply (M2)   M1 plus the money in passbook savings accounts plus money market accounts plus small-time deposits (CDs).

Mortgage   A debt instrument on real property which is secured by the property (CDs).

Mortgage, near prime   *See* Near prime mortgage.

Mortgage, prime   *See* Prime mortgage.

Mortgage, subprime   *See* Subprime loans.

Moving average forecasting model   A forecasting model that assumes some recent time periods are the best predictor of future sales.

Municipal bond   A bond issued by a government agency other than the federal government. State and local governments usually issue these bonds to finance projects.

Mutual fund   A pool of money invested by a manager in specific investment vehicles with a defined goal and risk objective.

Mutual fund family   An investment group with a portfolio of mutual funds with different goals and objectives.

Mutually exclusive   When several choices are available, but selection criteria obligates the decision maker to select only one and exclude all other choices.

Natural resources (land)   Consist of natural products such as minerals, land, and wildlife.

Near prime mortgage   Offered to people who are improving their credit now, but in the past had something on their credit score that decreased their credit rating, such as missed or late payments.

Net asset value (NAV)   Obtained after the market closes each day. It is the total value of the holdings of the mutual fund minus any liabilities divided by the number of shares that the fund has issued.

Net cost rate factor   The actual percentage of the list price paid after taking all successive trade discounts.

Net income   The profit after provision for income taxes and interest expenses for the corporation, and the profit after interest expense for the sole proprietorship, partnership, LLC, or Subchapter S corporation. This is the bottom line of a business income statement.

Net present value (NPV)   In capital budgeting, a technique that uses the time value of money by discounting future benefits and costs back to the present. The NPV is the difference between the present value of the benefits and the present value of the costs.

Net profit margin   A ratio used to determine how much a firm earned on each dollar of net sales after paying its obligations of tax and interest. The formula is Net Profit ÷ Net Sales.

Net return on assets (ROA)   Also known as return on investment (ROI); a ratio that determines how much a firm earns on each dollar in assets after paying both interest and taxes. The formula is Net Profit ÷ Average Total Assets.

Net sales   The revenue that a business has after accounting for returns and allowances. The formula is Net sales = Gross Sales − Returns and Allowances.

Net working capital   The difference between a business' total current assets and its total current liabilities. It is a measure of a company in terms of liquidity.

Net worth   The assets of an individual or firm minus its liabilities.

Noise (random variation)   The changes in company sales that cannot be explained by trend, cyclical, or seasonal variation.

No-load mutual funds   Mutual funds that do not charge a commission on an initial investment.

Non-owner-occupied residential real estate   Real estate rented by the owner to the tenant with the purpose of generating income.

Notes payable   A business promises to pay a creditor or lender an amount owed plus interest for a specified period of time, usually 1 year or less.

Open market operations   The purchase and sale of U.S. securities by the Federal Reserve.

Operating cash flow per share ratio   A comparison of the operating cash flows on the statement of cash flows to the average number of shares of common stock outstanding.

Operating expenses (fixed costs)   Those payments for expenses of a business that are not directly related to revenues or cost of goods sold.

Operating income   The result of subtracting Operating Expenses from Gross Profit on an income statement.

Operating leverage   *See* Leverage, operating.

Operating profit margin   A ratio used to determine how much each dollar of sales generates in operating income. The formula is Operating Income ÷ Net Sales.

Operating return on assets   A ratio that determines how much a company earns on each dollar of assets prior to paying interest and taxes. The formula is Operating Income ÷ Average Total Assets.

Opportunities   Those factors that exist in the business environment that if utilized help the business prosper and grow.

Opportunity cost   The highest value surrendered when a decision is made. If you give up a $30,000-a-year job to attend school full time, the opportunity cost was $30,000.

Ordinary annuity   Payments that are made or received at the end of each time period.

Organizing   A structure developed by managers that allows them to carry out a plan.

Owner-occupied residential real estate   Real estate purchased as your primary residence or your one additional vacation home.

Owner's equity   The net worth of a company or individual. It is found by subtracting Total Liabilities from Total Assets.

Par value (bonds)   The value of a bond that is printed on the bond and is the value at which the bond is redeemed for by the issuer at maturity. Also referred to as the *face value, maturity value,* or *principal value of a bond.* For corporate bonds, the face value is $1,000.

Par value (stock)   An arbitrary value placed on each share of stock when a corporation issues stock. This is the face value of one share of stock and does not usually change during the life of the corporation.

Partnership (general partnership)   An association of two or more persons who carry out a business as co-owners for a profit.

Payback   In capital budgeting, a technique of determining the number of years it will take a business to get back the money it has invested in a project or an asset.

Pension planning   *See* Retirement plans.

Percentage change   Percentage Change = (New Time Period Amount – Old Time Period Amount ÷ Old Time Period Amount) × 100.

Percentage of sales method for calculating a pro forma balance sheet   A method of calculating a pro forma balance sheet based on the fact that assets and liabilities historically vary with sales.

Percentage of sales method for determining new financing   A method of determining how much new financing a company will need in the future based on the fact that assets and liabilities historically vary with sales.

Personal cash flow statement   A personal income statement consisting of all annual income before taxes and outflows of fixed expenses and variable expenses.

Petty cash   A cash fund usually used to pay for small daily items such as postage or minor supplies.

Planning   A systematic process that takes us from some current state to some future desired state.

Post audit   Procedures that determine how well the outcome of a decision correlates with the proposal.

Precious metals   Fall into the area of commodity trading. They are primarily gold, silver, and platinum. Precious metals, especially gold, are considered hedges against inflation.

Preferred stock   A hybrid vehicle with features of both bonds and common stock. Owners of preferred stock are guaranteed a percentage return on their investment, but are stockholders with no voting rights.

Price   The amount of money a company charges for a product or service.

Price earnings ratio   A ratio indicating what multiple of earnings per share investors are willing to pay for stock. The formula is Market Price of Stock ÷ Earnings per Share.

Price earnings to growth ratio (PEG ratio)   A ratio comparing the price earnings ratio to the earning-per-share growth rate.

Primary securities market   The initial sale of stock by a corporation to the public.

Prime mortgage   Granted to borrowers with outstanding credit ratings and who have sufficient capital to make substantial down payments.

Prime rate   The rate of interest that a bank charges to its very best customers.

Principal value   *See* Par value.

Private corporation   A corporation formed under state law, but that does not sell its shares of stock to the public.

Pro forma balance sheet   A projected balance sheet for a future time period. It is required by lenders when evaluating a company to determine if the company is a good financial risk.

Pro forma cash budget   Projects future receipts and expenditures and determines how much financing is needed on a monthly basis to correct any shortfalls in cash flow.

Pro forma financial statement   A financial statement that is developed to project the future condition of a business based on a forecast.

Pro forma income statement   Projected income statement that is used in budgeting and to determine the amount of expected profit or loss.

Probate   A legal court process that addresses and focuses in on an individual's estate at the time of death.

Proceeds   The amount you receive after the bank discount is deducted from the maturity value of the loan.

Profit   An absolute number (actual dollar value) earned on an investment.

Profit sharing plans   A retirement plan established by employers who have determined that a portion of each dollar in profit will be allocated to employees of the company. Allocation is usually based on employee compensation and length of service.

Profitability   The return on investment (ROI), and is measured by dividing Net Profit by Average total assets.

Profitability index (PI)   In capital budgeting, a ratio that consists of the present value of the benefits divided by the present value of the costs. If the PI is greater than 1, the investment also has a positive net present value.

Profitability ratios   Ratios that determine how much of an investment will be returned from either earnings on revenues or appreciation of assets.

Progressive taxes   A tax that takes a larger percentage of your income as your income increases.

Proportional taxes   A tax in which the percentage paid stays the same regardless of income.

Provision for income taxes   The total of corporate tax owed to federal, state, and possibly municipal governments.

Public corporation   A corporation whose stock is traded on the open market.

Pure risk   *See* Risk, pure.

Quantity discount   A discount offered by vendors to customers who order items in large quantities. The vendor specifies the minimum quantity that qualifies for the discount.

Quick ratio (Acid test ratio)   A liquidity ratio that divides current assets minus a company's inventory and minus prepaids by current liabilities. It measures the liquidity of a company without liquidating its inventory in meeting current obligations.

Quoted rate   The rate of interest listed, usually on an annual basis, and it disregards compounding. This also may be referred to as the *stated rate*.

Random variation   *See* Noise (random variation).

Ratio   A relationship between two variables expressed as a fraction.

Ratio analysis   A process used to determine the health of a business as it compares to other firms in the same industry or similar industries. The process makes use of mathematical ratios to express numbers.

Raw materials   The inventories that a production company uses in producing its final product.

Real estate   An investment in land and buildings, also referred to as *real property*.

Real estate, commercial   *See* Commercial real estate.

Real estate, non-owner-occupied residential   *See* Non-owner-occupied residential real estate.

Real estate, owner-occupied residential   *See* Owner-occupied residential real estate.

Real estate investment trust (REIT)   A pool of investors that participate in buying shares in the trust. The trust buys real estate.

Regression   *See* Linear regression model.

Regressive taxes   A tax that takes a higher percentage of your income as your income decreases.

Reserve requirement   A percentage of deposits that are placed in banks to conduct daily operations and that cannot be used for loans. Reserve requirements are established by the Fed. These reserves must be kept in the bank's vault or kept on deposit with the Fed.

Retained earnings   The amount of a corporation's profit not distributed to the owners but is retained by a corporation for future investment.

Retirement plans (pension)   The establishment of an investment structure to accumulate wealth for use upon retirement. Under current law, most plans require that money may be withdrawn after age $59\frac{1}{2}$, and money must be withdrawn after age $70\frac{1}{2}$.

Retirement plans, benefit-oriented   A defined benefit plan to the retiree based on employment longevity and compensation.

Retirement plans, combined   A plan designed by individuals and the employer based on tax-deferred salary contributions and employer contributions.

Retirement plans, contribution-oriented   A plan in which benefits to the retiree are based on an account balance that has been accumulated during the employee's tenure.

Returns and allowances   A method of accounting that provides the customer with an avenue to return unwanted items as well as providing discounts to the customer for taking advantage of special promotions.

Return on equity (ROE)   A ratio that indicates to the stockholder or individual owner what each dollar of his or her investment is generating in net income. The formula is Net Income (Profit) ÷ Average Owner's Equity.

Return on investment (ROI)   *See* Net return on assets (ROA).

Revenues   The money generated as a result of sales of a product and services for a company.

Revocable trusts   A trust in which the trustor has the right to cancel the trust during his or her lifetime.

Risk   The probability that an expected outcome will occur, and the variability in that expected outcome. In financial terms, the probability that the actual return on an investment will be different from the desired return.

Risk assumption   When you believe that the loss you might incur is less than the cost of risk avoidance or risk transfer.

Risk avoidance   A method of managing a business by distancing yourself from a hazard that may cause a loss. *Example:* Dealing in only cash to avoid credit risk.

Risk exposure   The placement of a business in a situation in which there is uncertainty of outcome. Smoking cigarettes for an individual is risk exposure, some but not all smokers get cancer. Introducing a new product for a business is risk exposure, some but not all products succeed.

Risk premium   An interest rate added onto the real rate of return that takes into consideration the risk of a project.

Risk, pure   Pure risk involves only the chance of loss, and it is therefore insurable. *Example:* Having your house catch on fire is pure risk.

Risk reduction   A program used by a business or individual to lessen the severity of an outcome as the result of risk. Fastening your seat belt or having air bags in a car are methods of risk reduction.

Risk, speculative   The risk in which there may be a possible gain or loss that is uninsurable. *Example:* Buying a lottery ticket is speculative risk. You can either gain a dollar or more or lose a dollar.

Risk transfer   Having another party assume the risk and agreeing to pay you for your loss as long as you pay the fee (or premium) charged by the agency assuming the risk. *Example:* A fire insurance policy on your house.

Roth 401k   An after-tax elective contribution to a 401k plan funded with after-tax dollars and not taxed on distribution.

Roth IRA   An individual retirement account that allows you to contribute up to $5,000 of after-tax dollars ($6,000 if age 50 or older as of 2008). The earnings on this account are tax-free and will be indexed beginning in 2009.

Rule of 72   An approximation of the amount of time that it takes for a present sum of money to double by dividing 72 by the annual interest rate.

Safety stock   The quantity of stock held to satisfy variations in demand.

Salvage (residual) value   The value of an asset after it has been depreciated over its useful life.

Savings Incentive Match Plan for Employees (SIMPLE)   An IRA established after 1996 by an employer with fewer than 100 employees. The company must match dollar for dollar the employees' contribution up to 3 percent of salary.

Scarcity   A condition that exists because human beings want more than they currently have.

Seasonal variation   The variation that exists in company sales based on predictable differences in climate, holidays, and buyer behavior.

Secondary securities market   A market in which stock is bought and sold by the existing owners of individual shares.

Secured debt   Debt of a company or individual backed by specific assets, which are pledged to guarantee the debt.

Securities and Exchange Commission (SEC)   An agency that regulates the sale and exchange of publicly traded securities. The SEC is an independent, nonpartisan, quasi-judicial regulatory agency with responsibility for administering the federal securities laws.

Sensitivity analysis   Also known as *what-if analysis.* It uses a mathematical spreadsheet program or other computer program that allows us to change some variable to determine what would happen with a decision when the variable is changed. *Example:* What is the result of loan payments on a loan at various interest rates?

Service Corporation of Retired Executives (SCORE)   A consulting service provided by the Small Business Administration (SBA) that consists of a group of retired business owners and managers who have years of experience in various businesses.

Short-term debt   The obligations of a business that will be paid during the current accounting period, usually 1 year or less.

Simple interest   The amount of money earned on the principal amount stated.

Simplified Employee Pension plans (SEPs)   IRAs funded by employers. SEPs are common for the self-employed; the participating employee makes no contribution.

Single equivalent discount   A discount equal to 100 percent of the list price minus the actual percentage of the list price paid (net cost rate factor).

Slope   Rise of a line (change in y) divided by the run of a line (change in x). In the formula $y = a + bx$, b is the slope of the line.

Smoothing constant   A value (alpha α) assigned by the forecaster to adjust the forecast based on the forecaster's assumption of the relationship of sales in one time period and sales in the next time period. Used in the exponential smoothing forecasting model.

Social Security   *See* Federal Insurance Contribution Act.

Sole proprietorship   A business operated by an individual for his or her own profit.

Speculative risk   *See* Risk, speculative.

Staffing   Obtaining the most capable personnel in order to implement business plans.

Start-up costs   All the money a business spends to get a project under way. Start-up costs usually include acquisition costs, training costs, and maintenance costs.

Stated (quoted) rate   The rate of interest that is listed, usually on an annual basis, and it disregards compounding.

Statement of cash flows   A financial statement that determines what has happened to the working capital account (the amount of cash available) of a company between the beginning and end of an accounting period.

Statement of financial position   On a personal balance sheet, it indicates all items owned and all items owed by an individual or family at a specific point in time.

Stock   Ownership in a corporation divided into shares. The individual shares are referred to as *stock*.

Stock bonus plans　A retirement plan in which the employer contributes shares of stock rather than money into a retirement account.

Strategic planning　Establishing an overall long-range plan for a business.

Strategic plans　The long-range overall plans for a business.

Strengths　The core competencies of a business.

Subchapter S corporation　One that is privately held, has more than 1 owner but not more than 100, and is granted Subchapter S status by the Internal Revenue Service. Subchapter S corporations have favorable tax status.

Subprime loan (mortgage)　Offered to people who have poor credit ratings and are considered to be high risk.

Supply curve　A curve generated from a supply table by horizontally summing the total product or service provided at various prices in the marketplace.

Supply table　A table generated by determining how much of a product or service people and business are willing and able to provide to the market at various prices.

SWOT　An acronym that stands for Strengths, Weaknesses, Opportunities, and Threats that pertain to both the internal workings (strengths, weaknesses) and external factors (opportunities, threats) of a company. *See also* Individual entries.

Systematic risk　Risk that is associated with economic, political, and sociological changes that affect all participants on an equal basis.

Tax-factor benefits　In capital budgeting, the benefits that current tax law allows a business to deduct or write off once a new investment is made.

Tax-factor costs　In capital budgeting, the calculation of the costs that result in additional taxes that must be paid by a firm.

Tax-sheltered annuities (TSAs)　Retirement plans that allow employees of not-for-profit organizations to establish a retirement fund purchased and approved by the employer.

Taxes　Payments to government for goods and services provided by government.

Taxes payable　The accrued taxes owed by a business, but not actually paid as of the date of the business balance sheet. *Example:* Sales taxes collected in December that are not paid to the state until January of the following year.

T-bill　U.S. Treasury bond that matures in less than 1 year, typically 3 and 6 months.

T-bond　U.S. Treasury bond that has a maturity greater than 10 years.

Testamentary trust　A trust established at the death of the trustor.

Theory of constraints (TOC)　A theory developed by Eliyahu M. Goldratt used to find business's primary problem(s)/(constraints), generate a simple solution to the problem, and provide an implementation strategy.

Threats　Factors in the environment that may impede the growth of a business, directly or indirectly.

Time series forecasting models　Forecasting models that use historical records that are readily available within a firm or industry to predict future sales.

Times-interest-earned　A ratio that shows the relationship between operating income and the amount of interest in dollars the company must pay to its creditors on an annual basis. The formula is Operating Income ÷ Interest.

Time value of money　The loss of purchasing power that occurs over time as a result of inflation.

T-note　U.S. Treasury bonds that mature in 10 years or less.

Total asset turnover　A ratio that indicates how efficiently total assets are being used to generate revenue for the firm. The formula is Net Sales ÷ Average Total Assets.

Total assets　The sum of current and fixed assets.

Total liabilities　The sum of current liabilities and long-term debt.

Trade discount　These are amounts deducted from the list price of items when specific services are performed by the customer. Usually given by manufacturers to wholesalers or retailers.

Treasury bonds　Bonds issued by the government of the United States.

Trend variation　The change in sales over time, represented by a straight line that depicts changes in sales over time. The trend line uses least square regression to eliminate seasonal variation, cyclical variation, and noise.

Trusts　A legal entity similar to a corporation that has a legal persona of its own. Property placed in a trust is separate from that of its owner. A trust is created by a trustor or grantor and beneficiaries or trustees are named by the trustor.

Unsecured debt　A debt not backed by collateral.

Unsystematic risk　Risk that is unique to an individual, firm, or industry.

Use assets　*See* Fixed assets.

Variable costs　Costs driven directly by the volume of product flow.

Variable expenses　Pertains to a personal cash flow statement. Expenses over which we have some control, such as food, clothing, and automobile expenses.

Variance　A deviation from the norm. If a company establishes a personnel budget of $250,000, and actual spending is $260,000, then the variance is a negative $10,000.

Venture capitalists　Investors who provide financing at the expansion and later stages of business development.

Vertical analysis　A process of using a single variable on a financial statement as a constant and determining how all of the other variables relate as a percentage of the single variable.

Warranty The guarantee that a product or service will perform under certain terms and conditions. Usually lists the remedy the purchaser may pursue if the warranty is not carried out.

Weaknesses The areas in which a company definitely needs improvement.

Weighted average cost of capital (WACC) The method of determining a company's cost of capital when it takes into consideration the rate charged by the lender(s) and the opportunity cost foregone by the borrower(s). Using these rates and the proportion of total financing funded by the lender and borrower, the WACC is calculated.

Weighted moving average forecasting model A model that assumes that some recent time periods are a more accurate predictor of sales than previous time periods, but that the predictive ability of the time periods used is not equal.

Will A document that directs others as to how you want your wishes carried out after death with regard to disposition of property.

Work-in-process The inventories that a firm uses while in the assembly or transformation process.

Working capital The current assets and current liabilities of a business.

Working capital commitment costs In capital budgeting, the costs of maintaining a specific level of working capital that are required by lending institutions. *Example:* Inventory and accounts receivable costs committed to back up a loan.

Working capital management The ability to effectively and efficiently control current assets and current liabilities in a manner that provides the firm with maximum return on its assets and minimizes payments for its liabilities.

Index